KHALISTAN STRUGGLE

A Non-movement

KHALISTAN STRUGGLE
A Non-movement

JAGTAR SINGH

AAKAR

KHALISTAN STRUGGLE – A Non-movement
Jagtar Singh

First Published, 2011
Reprinted 2021

ISBN 978-93-5002-124-8 (Hb)

Published by
AAKAR BOOKS
28 E Pocket IV, Mayur Vihar Phase I, Delhi 110 091
Phone: 011 2279 5505 Telefax : 011 2279 5641
aakarbooks@gmail.com; www.aakarbooks.com

Printed at
Sapra Brothers, Noida.

Contents

Introduction

From revenge psyche to more than a decade long violent political struggle for the creation of Khalistan that claimed thousands of lives but failed to shape up as a cohesive movement, to be forgotten as a bitter dream even by the majority of the Sikh community whose liberation was its agenda, sums up the turbulence that rocked the strategically located Indian Punjab with its tremors felt all over the country in the eighties. Hundreds of others just disappeared without any trace, many of them cremated by the security forces as unclaimed bodies. Prime Minister Indira Gandhi who was one of the key players in the brutal politics played during that period, herself became a victim, assassinated by her own Sikh security guards. Apart from the then Prime Minister, this movement also claimed the life of Punjab Chief Minister Beant Singh and retired chief of the Indian Army General A.S. Vaidya. At one time it used to be said that Punjab had entered the long dark tunnel without an end in sight but then this struggle that was in the first phase for the "restoration of the dignity of the Sikhs" in the words of Sant Jarnail Singh Bhindranwale, remained a non-movement in the absence of any unified command structure, lack of mass support and effective political front. It is Sant Bhindranwale who symbolizes this struggle and attained iconic status after his death during the army attack on the Darbar Sahib (Golden Temple) complex. An action which was code named Operation Bluestar.

The Shiromani Akali Dal, the second oldest political party in the country whose President Harchand Singh Longowal also fell to the politics of violence, provided legitimacy to the revenge psyche in the first stage though at the political level, he never subscribed to the use of violence as instrument of conflict resolution and it was the Congress, the oldest political party that encouraged the radical tendencies. It is the Shiromani Akali Dal that used to articulate the ambitions and aspirations of the Sikhs who ruled this region at one time in history. The Sikh agenda of the Akali Dal over the years, both during and after Independence, created the much needed political space for these radical tendencies to proliferate. All these years, the Akali Dal had repeatedly hammered the issue of the creation of the geo-political environment for the Sikhs in one form or the other and the struggle for Khalistan thrived on the psyche nurtured by this ambition of the Sikhs, articulated by this party and the all powerful Shiromani Gurdwara Parbandhak Committee which plays a vital role in the religio-political affairs of this minority community, which is in majority in this border state.

Initially, Sant Bhindranwale had the tacit support from Akali Dal stalwart and Shiromani Gurdwara Parbandhak Committee President Gurcharan Singh Tohra. Once this man with the death wish set his foot on the path of confrontation with the Indian state, the machinations of the Indira Gandhi government closed all options for Sant Bhindranwale except martyrdom for which he was fully prepared from the day one. From the party created to articulate the ambitions and aspirations of the Sikhs which had once demanded Sikhstan and then supported the demand for Khalistan, the Shiromani Akali Dal, after the turbulence was contained, moved to the other extreme, dissociated itself from this struggle completely and finally got transformed into just another political party and this metamorphosis of this Sikh party under the leadership of Parkash Singh Badal is equally significant.

Punjab's tryst with political violence was not a new phenomenon as the state had earlier witnessed the Left radical Naxalite movement which had attracted the educated youth but lacked the much needed support and was contained without much effort. There can be no comparison between the two movements, as apart from other factors, the violence during the Sikh militant movement was unprecedented. However, the interesting aspect is that the Naxalite movement left its lasting imprints on the literary, cultural and art scene of the state while contrary to it, the Khalistan struggle failed to produce even a single good poem, a short story, a play or a painting. The Left radical movement was rooted in ideology whereas what provided the fertile ground for the Sikh militancy were the politics of grievances and the perception of being discriminated against right from the Independence of the country in 1947. Immediately after the partition of the country, the Lal Communist Party in Punjab also resorted to the militant tactics for the rights of the tenant cultivators. Militancy is a cyclical phenomenon in this region and perhaps rooted in the psyche of the people, shaped by history, as this region was subjected to repeated invasions from Central Asia.

The Sikh militant movement in Punjab coincided with the Soviet intervention in Afghanistan and it was the KGB of the Soviet Union which was the first to publicly accuse its US counterpart the Central Intelligence Agency and the Inter-Services Intelligence of Pakistan of fomenting trouble in the border state of Punjab to destabilise India. The question arises as to why Indira Gandhi also played the same politics which encouraged the secessionist tendencies and suited the designs of the CIA, the ISI and Sant Bhindranwale. The government did not disturb the supply chain of weapons to Sant Bhindranwale and the Babbar Khalsa, the other main militant organisation, in the Darbar Sahib complex. The demand for Khalistan as a buffer state between "Hindu India" and Muslim Pakistan" could also be part of the international power play in this region.

The Anandpur Sahib resolution, though passed by the Akali Dal working committee way back in 1973, came to be projected by the Congress as a threat to the unity and integrity of the country years later. This happened as the party had launched its agitation known as the Dharamyudh Morcha in 1982 after negotiations with Indira Gandhi on its demands ended in a deadlock. The Prime Minister and the Akali Dal leadership never shared the negotiating table once the agitation was launched. The implementation of this resolution of the Akali Dal was adopted as the agenda by Sant Bhindranwale who never formally raised the demand for Khalistan. The political objective defined in the Anandpur Sahib resolution came to be enshrined in the constitution of the Akali Dal in 1974 with slight change in its wording. And the Akali Dal had earlier contested the 1967 Assembly elections on the issue of Sikhstan based on the resolution adopted by the party in 1966 of which the Anandpur Sahib resolution is a modified version. As such, the Anandpur Sahib resolution was not something new, nor the demand for Khalistan which used to be raised by some fringe elements. The Congress contested the December, 1984 election raising the bogey of this resolution as secessionist while the Akali Dal had already gone to the people to seek their mandate on its earlier version in 1967. This is not all. The Akali Dal had diluted the 1973 version of the Anandpur Sahib resolution when in power in 1978 at its Ludhiana convention omitting even the word Sikh. However, when out of power, the party again hammered the contents of the 1973 resolution at its working committee meeting in 1980 in which the resolution hailing the killing of the Nirankari chief Gurbachan Singh had also been adopted.

The demand for Khalistan was formally raised by the militants only in 1986. Ironically, it was the raising of this demand from the precincts of the Darbar Sahib complex which provided ipso facto legitimacy to

Operation Bluestar and this design was put into operation when Punjab was ruled by the Akali Dal government headed by Surjit Singh Barnala who wasted no time in sending security forces into the shrine despite the intelligence reports that the militants had escaped from its precincts immediately after raising the demand.

By the time militancy was contained, more members of the Sikh community than the Hindus had become its victim for whose liberation this struggle had been launched. Increasing incidents of rape and extortions along with these killings resulted in the isolation of the so called militants whose ranks had been infiltrated by the instruments of the security forces. It was perhaps for this reason that there were few mass protests against blatant violations of human rights by the security forces as the record of the militants was also not clean. Moreover, the militants lacked mass political front. The use of the Darbar Sahib complex by the militants for launching this agitation despite the location of the Akal Takht, the supreme Sikh institution for prayer and politics symbolizing Sikh sovereignty just opposite the holiest of the holy shrine, could never be justified. While this shrine complex was desecrated by the armed forces during Operation Bluestar, the Darbar Sahib was defiled by the militants themselves subsequently during Operation Blackthunder. This struggle perhaps carried the terminator seed.

What appeared to be the only serious effort at conflict resolution through negotiations was the signing of what has come to be known as the Punjab Accord between Prime Minister Rajiv Gandhi and Longowal. However, this negotiated settlement had deeper design. By the time this accord was signed, the Akali Dal had ceased to be of any relevance. The secret correspondence exchanged between Rajiv Gandhi and Longowal reveals for the first time significant aspects of the way the negotiations were conducted culminating in what till then was the first ever accord signed by an Indian Prime Minister with the president of a political party in the country which was also later ratified by the Parliament. This Accord failed to take off as it had ignored the militants who were the main party in this confrontation with the Indian state and not the Akali Dal. This Accord was part of the design to get legitimacy for Operation Bluestar from the Akali Dal itself which was facilitated into power in the state as part of the covert understanding of this agreement and this design succeeded.

The role of Pakistan became more pronounced during the post Bluestar period when young Sikhs, both militants and non-militants, crossed over to the other side in large numbers. Sant Bhindranwale somehow believed that Pakistan would directly intervene in case the Indian army attacked the Darbar Sahib complex. However, Pakistan avoided any such direct involvement and opted for the proxy war by supplying sophisticated arms and ammunition to the militants and providing them sanctuaries.

The Shiromani Akali Dal and some opposition parties had blamed the Congress for encouraging militancy and the party in its manifesto for the 1997 Assembly elections promised to order judicial inquiry but that was never done. Perhaps the findings would not have been convenient even for the Akali Dal. The truth must come out.

This is the first analysis of the militant struggle in Punjab by a journalist who has been covering the state since 1978 (for about a quarter of a century with The Indian Express) and as such, contains off the record conversations and observations starting from the period when Sant Bhindranwale was still to hit the headlines along with details of political events. The book refers to all major political developments in Punjab till Tohra's death along with his last comments on Badal, the other Akali stalwart with whom he enjoyed love hate relationship which provides an insight into the power struggle in the Akali stream. Tohra, the Akali leader with a clean personal life who dictated the Akali political discourse at crucial movements and lorded over the SGPC for more than a quarter of a century died with a feeling of having been betrayed by Badal during his last days, the feeling he shared at his last meeting with this author a few days before his death. Tohra incidentally was the one senior Akali leader who never removed the photograph of Sant Bhindranwale from his drawing room.

1

Under Army Occupation

The morning of June 15, 1984, felt hotter than usual. The even hotter Indian Air Force twin engine Dakota of the World War II vintage with aluminum bucket seats added to the gloomy, apprehensive and tense atmosphere. Soon, it took off for the war zone with about a dozen journalists, the first group from Chandigarh. The war zone was none other than the Darbar Sahib complex[1], the holiest of the holy shrines of the Sikhs, in Amritsar. The sizzling temperature inside the non-pressurised aircraft came down after it gained some height.

As the aircraft landed in the Air Force area of Amritsar's Raja Sansi Airport, it was 'greeted' by armoured combat vehicles of the Army, guns pointing towards it as if an enemy plane had intruded. The Air Force was expecting the district administration to arrange transportation for taking journalists to the scene of action. However, it turned out to be a long wait for the Punjab Roadways bus to arrive. The temperature hovered above 40 degrees Celsius and the Air Force officials tried to make the scribes comfortable in the small briefing room within the limited resources available with them. One of the two women journalists almost fainted. The rickety bus arrived only two hours later. Initially, it appeared a lack of coordination. However, the delay was part of some design as the journalists were not to be taken around the entire shrine complex, as we came to know later.

The bus headed for the command headquarters. We entered the operations room where a large map of the 'battlefield' that was Darbar Sahib complex was displayed on the wall. After briefing by the commander of the operation Major General Kuldip Singh Brar, the press party proceeded towards the war zone.

From the main entrance towards the Ghanta Ghar (Clock Tower demolished years ago) side, the shrine complex which had been subjected to very heavy firing reminded of the ravages of World War II.

The big clock above this entrance had stopped ticking, somewhere around the time the action had begun early in the morning on June 4. And there it hung, frozen in time. Inside, the stink of the fetid human flesh was palpable. The silence was deafening.

On the historic, intricately carved silver doors of the Darshani Deodi leading to the sanctum sanctorum, a notice had been pasted: UNDER ARMY OCCUPATION, rightly proclaimed in capital letters.

The Army authorities went an extra mile to explain how the damage to the central shrine had been averted. But what about the irreparable damage inflicted upon the collective Sikh psyche? It was not for the first time that the complex had been attacked. It had been ruined earlier also. The Sikhs haven't yet forgotten the invasion by Afghan king Ahmad Shah Abdali, who wrecked Punjab during his eighth incursion on India in 1762. He had blown up this centre of inspiration for Sikhs with explosives and had filled the sarovar, the holy tank around the shrine, with earth and animal bones. But, those were foreign invaders from the Central Asian region. Here, the forces of occupation were our very own people. Haversacks of the soldiers lay piled up in the two staircases leading to the first floor of Darbar Sahib.

The historic Bir of Guru Granth Sahib (holy scriptures bestowed upon the high status of the Guru) on the first floor was partially covered in a white bloodstained sheet. Putting the Bir in order was a traumatic experience, which continued to haunt me for many years despite my Leftist background.

In the war zone, the only order was disorder. This was a place where even a person in uniform would not be allowed inside with belt on. The House of God recognizes no worldly power. But then the shrine had already been desecrated by the gun-wielding militants, who had taken control of it much before the June action. The situation had deteriorated to such an extent that young women preferred to stay away from Darbar Sahib. This author is witness to a situation when in January, 1984, a young married woman who had gone to pay obeisance from Chandigarh was aghast at what was happening there, bowed her head from outside and came back.

It was perhaps for the first time in history that the shrine had become the centre of the armed Sikh struggle for an independent state. This had, however, not been proclaimed as the aim of the confrontation with the Indian state till then. Even the location of Akal Takht[2] just opposite Darbar Sahib would never justify such fortification of the shrine by the militants. The complex has a fortress known as Bunga Ramgarhia overlooking Darbar Sahib but it had been built for its protection. The Shiromani Akali Dal had been launching all its peaceful agitations after offering prayers at Akal Takht. However, converting it into the centre of Sikh armed struggle never stood justified.

At the same time, all these actions of the militants too can never provide legitimacy to Operation Bluestar.

While coming out of the sanctum sanctorum, a senior officer pointed at the exact place where Sant Jarnail Singh Bhindranwale[3] had been shot dead. This differed from the briefing by higher authorities in the operations room earlier. Predictably, as he realized the mistake, he quickly 'corrected' it. Contrary to the then official claim that the body of Sant Bhindranwale was recovered from the basement of the Akal Takht along with that of his associates Major General Shabeg Singh (retd.) and All India Sikh Students Federation President Amrik Singh, he was shot in front of Jhanda Bunga[4] as he came out from the basement. The ashes of Sant Bhindranwale, Amrik Singh and Major General Shabeg Singh were immersed along with 200 other persons at Kiratpur Sahib on June 14[5]. Heaps of stinking unidentified bodies were loaded onto the municipal corporation's garbage trucks and carried to the cremation ground near Gurdwara Shaheedan.

For years, the myth of Sant Bhindranwale having escaped was perpetuated both by the Damdami Taksal and indirectly by the government agencies, though for different reasons. Sant Bhindranwale was denied martyrdom by the very organisation he headed and was formally accorded the exalted status by the Damdami Taksal years later on May 28, 2005. This, despite the fact that the bodies of the trio had been identified by Deputy Superintendent of Police (City) Apar Singh Bajwa, the eye witness from Punjab Police, and Subedar Harcharan Singh, brother of Sant Bhindranwale. Their bodies were consigned to flames as per the Sikh rites in the presence of Amritsar Deputy Commissioner Ramesh Inder Singh.

It was Baba Joginder Singh, father of Sant Bhindranwale, who had pleaded the then Shiromani Gurdwara Parbandhak Committee President Gurcharan Singh Tohra not to use the expression martyr for him. He held that Sant Bhindrawale had not been killed during the Army action, but had escaped. However, he had already been accorded this status as per the Sikh tradition, indirectly in a joint statement by Akali leaders Parkash Singh Badal and Surjit Singh Barnala, both of whom were moderates.

Most of the bodies – of men, women and children — were cremated without identifying them. It was years later that Dal Khalsa came out with a list of militants, majority of them from the Damdami Taksal, who died during the action. The youngest to have been shot in the Army action was the two-week-old son of Rachhpal Singh, the soft-spoken personal assistant to Bhindranwale. He died in the lap of his mother who survived the bullet injury. Many of those killed were devotees and Akali Dal workers who were camping to court arrest as part of the agitation launched by the party. The SGPC also has an incomplete list, based upon the applications it received from the families seeking compensation for the next of kin who died in the Army action, mostly the Akali workers. "A large majority of those who died inside the Golden Temple during Operation Bluestar were common devotees who had come to the shrine on June 3 on the occasion of the fifth Sikh Guru Arjan Dev's Martyrdom Day. Apart from Bhindranwale's armed followers, I counted a little over 800 dead bodies inside the temple complex," DSP Apar Singh Bajwa told BBC News in an interview on June 3, 2004.

Akal Takht[6], which over the years had come to acquire the distinction of being the unique supreme Sikh institution for prayer and politics, was still smoldering. During the Army attack, Sant Bhindranwale and most of his men had holed up in the heavily fortified basement of this building, which had been subjected to intense tank firing. As the team of journalists reached Akal Takht, Abinashi Singh, personal assistant to Tohra, and Akal Takht Jathedar Giani Kirpal Singh, were seen trying to salvage whatever they could from the debris. The stink in the Akal Takht area was nauseating; it appeared as if some bodies were still buried in there. Abinashi Singh greeted us with an uneasy grin amid that shocking and horrific atmosphere and the face of Giani Kirpal Singh looked glum.

Though Operation Bluestar was pre-meditated and planned months in advance, the calculations had gone awry in the face of stiff and unanticipated resistance put up by the militants. The militants' dedication and conviction to the cause and their fighting spirit was conceded even by Lt. General K. Sundarji, General Officer Commanding, Western Command, at the first press conference held at Chandigarh on the operation.

Entry was still forbidden into the serai[7] area. Escorting Army officers prevented journalists from going there and the media convoy was taken back to Raja Sansi. The water tank in the serai area with gaping holes caused by artillery firing and the two watch towers of the fortress Bunga Ramgarhia spoke of the gravity of the battle that had been fought here. It was later known that armed tanks had been taken inside the complex to attack the Akal Takht, the last point of resistance. The complex stood mute witness to the three-day battle. Every inch of every wall, except the sanctum sanctorum, bore bullet marks. The Akal Takht lay in ruins.

It was perhaps for the first time after it was rebuilt (after its destruction in 1762) that the doors of Darbar Sahib had been closed to devotees for such a long time. And this is the shrine that symbolizes openness of this faith, a faith devoted to Sarbat Da Bhala[8]. The holy city of Amritsar where no one sleeps hungry had been developed around the shrine.

The operation ended with the death of Sant Bhindranwale, Amrik Singh, Major General Shabeg Singh and hundreds of others, and arrest of the Shiromani Akali Dal chief and Dharamyudh Morcha (the political agitation launched by the Akali Dal) dictator (The leader commanding the agitation is known as morcha dictator) Harchand Singh Longowal and Tohra, besides others. Expectedly, the attack triggered revolt in the Army and the Sikh soldiers in many cantonments deserted their barracks. Several of these were killed in encounters with the security forces while heading towards Amritsar.

The Army also targeted 42 other gurdwaras across the state as part of this operation. These attacks raised questions at the intention of the government as these shrines were not being used by the militants to take shelter. Tanks had also entered the historic Gurdwara Dukhniwaran at Patiala. Lieutenant General Sundarji, at his press conference in Chandigarh on June 6 evening as reported in The Indian Express the next day, had said, "We went in with prayers on our lips and humility and reverence in our hearts". Operation Bluestar, the code name for perhaps the biggest ever Army action of its kind in post-independence India, was carried out by imposing three days of curfew across Punjab and Chandigarh, during which even the movement of bullock carts was banned on rural dirt tracks. Punjab, which had been turned into garrison, was cut-off from rest of the world.

Entire Punjab had come to a standstill to thwart the movement of protestors marching towards the holy shrine to resist the action. Several of them were killed at different places in the open fire by the security personnel. But the news wasn't going out; everything was censored in the media. The Sikh protesters were not even spared in Delhi and Srinagar.

Tohra's last meeting with Sant Bhindranwale took place in the Darbar Sahib complex in the presence of General Shabeg Singh late in the night on June 3 after the imposition of curfew in the state. Sant Bhindranwale offered Tohra a safe passage to escape from the complex and leave the country to organise the Sikh struggle from abroad. Tohra, in turn, said that Sant Bhindranwale should himself take this responsibility as he was best suited for the job. Tohra held that his fate would be no different from that of Dr Jagjit Singh Chohan, the rootless Khalistani leader who had returned to England before the launch of the Akali agitation. Tohra had disclosed this years later to me. He had even offered that if need be, in accordance with the Sikh traditions, he could get a directive issued to him from the Panj Piaras[9] on the spot to leave the shrine and go abroad. He cited the example of Panj Piaras directing Guru Gobind Singh to quit the fortress at Chamkaur Sahib after it was surrounded by the Mughal forces. Sant Bhindranwale told Tohra that he would have to repent later. The meeting ended on that note. There was no communication between the two after that. Tohra left for Teja Singh Samundari Hall, which houses the offices of the SGPC, while Sant Bhindranwale went back to Akal Takht.

As some close associates of Sant Bhindranwale say, he somehow believed that Pakistan will come to their rescue once the Army attacks Darbar Sahib. However, he never shared with them the basis of this belief. As the events unfolded, this hope turned out to be baseless. Later Tohra also confirmed this in a recorded interview.

There might have been some basis of this hope of support from across the border. This also indicates the level of involvement of Pakistan's Inter-Services Intelligence, which was working in league with the Central Intelligence Agency, especially after the intervention of the Soviet Union in Afghanistan. But then, how come Indira Gandhi played that destructive politics in this region, which also suited the design of these powers, despite having been alerted by the KGB?

However, more important was the situation in Punjab, which fueled this deadly politics. The role of the catalyst, though important, was secondary.

Tohra was perhaps the senior most Akali leader who provided the much-needed legitimacy to Sant Bhindranwale in the initial stages while advising him against jumping into the political space, which is evident from some of his statements and actions. At the same time, as he later stated in his recorded interview, he felt that the Central government had used him to sabotage the Akali struggle as part of a sinister conspiracy. At one stage, he had come to believe due to his increasing popularity that he could achieve where the Akalis had failed. Some people around him were government agents who would shower praise on him all the time to strengthen this perception of his about himself. The Akali leaders never expected the government to stoop so low. They were trapped in a situation where they could not avoid confrontation with the government. At the same time, in his perception, no other Sikh leader had proved more sincere and committed to the cause of the Panth[10] during the last more than half a century. Tohra never removed the photograph of Sant Bhindranwale from his living room. And this, perhaps, was the best tribute he paid to him.

Tohra was of the view that their agitation, the Dharamyudh Morcha, had taken a path, which the Akalis never thought of treading. The militant movement, which was not under the control of the Akalis, had changed the scenario. Militancy had begun to raise its head in Punjab by the time the Akali Dal launched the agitation.

The maverick lived upto his determination of making the supreme sacrifice for the cause. Many years back, in the presence of this author, he had expressed this in a meeting at Gurdwara Gurdarshan Parkash, the headquarters of Damdami Taksal at Mehta Chowk. He could have also escaped from the Darbar Sahib complex and that too, honourably, as suggested by Tohra. But he had chosen his destiny much earlier, though he might not have visualised the future course of events then. He would often tell his associates that he will never fall in the hands of the security forces alive. (Indication available from the speech of Sant Bhindranwale on May 18, 1983 in the Manji Sahib Diwan Hall in the Darbar Sahib complex). And he did not. The escape would have been interpreted as his defeat.

As per the post-mortem report, his body bore 14 wounds, including half a dozen in the head. The other lacerated wounds were in the heart and left lung, causing shock and haemorrhage, which led to his death. The six wounds in the head were caused by explosives. These wounds were in the left eye, forehead and between the nose and the eye. There was one wound each in the left side of the chest, the left arm, the back of the arm and the back portion below the heart and four in the feet. As per the post mortem report, death was instantaneous. The body was brought to the mortuary at 7.30 pm on June 7.

Tohra never accused Sant Bhindranwale of being an agent of the Congress government in Delhi. However, that he was used by some forces at a later stage is a different issue. Sant Bhindranwale was conscious of this allegation. Once when it was pointed out to him that somebody around him who projects himself as an advocate of Khalistan was close to some people in the ruling Congress in Delhi, his quick reaction was that as long as that person served his politics, it did not matter to him. This person was a senior journalist from Jalandhar who had also been hobnobbing with the Akali politics.

Being the head of the SGPC, religio-political compulsions at that time dictated his actions. That could be one reason behind the legitimacy Tohra provided to Sant Bhindranwale so early. Yet, another reason cited is to use him in the power struggle within the Akali Dal vis-à-vis Badal. He nurtured political ambition, but Tohra never ventured into legislative politics by way of contesting Assembly elections where he could pose a challenge to Badal, though he remained member of both Houses of Parliament. He realised this blunder when it was too late.

At one of the party working committee meetings in 1981, senior party leader Atma Singh had raised the issue of Sant Bhindranwale being critical of some Akali leaders at times. This criticism mainly centered on the lifestyle of some of them, including members of the SGPC. Tohra had pointed out that there must be some truth in the issues being raised by Sant Bhindranwale. Later, he had advised Sant Bhindranwale to not venture into politics and confine himself to the religious domain. This despite the fact that Sikhism advocates the synergy of religion and politics symbolized by Akal Takht[11].

According to senior officials at that time, one of the central intelligence agencies in its assessment report sent to the Centre before the Army operation had made it clear that any such action in the shrine would have adverse reactions and would result in the alienation of the Sikhs. The advice was to avoid such a confrontation. It was proposed that in case Sant Bhindranwale was to be arrested, some other strategy and tactics should be adopted rather than sending the Army to invade the shrine. After he shifted to the Akal Takht, Sant Bhindranwale used to meet people on the roof of the langar[12] hall. A senior officer, having access to the strategic plans, later revealed on the condition of anonymity that one of the proposals envisaged lightening commando action to pick up Bhindranwale from that building. The advice was, however, ignored by those at the helm of affairs. Even the Army had initially planned that rather than entering the fortified shrine from the main gates, some other strategy should be adopted, including use of gas to paralyze those inside.

The Army action aimed at putting an end to the militant violence. However, the situation became uncontrollable in the aftermath. Punjab continued to burn for years, putting a question mark on the strategy and tactics adopted by the then rulers to deal with the situation and the ulterior designs. Prime Minister Indira Gandhi paid the price at the personal level as she was gunned down within months of Operation Bluestar.

Sikh soldiers revolted in several cantonments. As per the official records, 48 Non-Commissioned Officers and 1058 other ranks deserted their barracks. Ramgarh in Bihar, Lalgarh in Ganganagar district of Rajasthan and Pune in Mahrashtra were the main centers of revolt. Many were killed in the exchange of fire with the security forces as they tried to head towards the Darbar Sahib in Army trucks.

The Sikhs felt insulted, alienated and humiliated in their own homeland. What followed was a long period of turmoil. The traditional Akali leadership got marginalized over the years as the radicals took over the political scene as evident from the 1989 Lok Sabha elections in which the Akali Dal was wiped out. From the demand for the implementation of the Anandpur Sahib Resolution advocating state autonomy in the pre-Bluestar period, the militant struggle shifted to the establishment of a sovereign Sikh state in 1986. At that time, the Akali Dal was not a party to this, though later, the Akali leaders including Badal supported the demand for Khalistan, more as a form of protest against the government or political compulsions.

Punjab was pushed into a long dark tunnel. However, to some extent Congress was successful in achieving its political goals by making a clean sweep in the general elections held in December 1984. The price paid for this success, however, was too colossal. Both Sant Bhindranwale and Indira Gandhi adopted the confrontationist mode and both of them became victims of their own politics of the gun.

Tohra had gone to Amritsar to attend a meeting of the senior party leaders on June 1, which was later cancelled[13]. Longowal had also convened a meeting of the party MPs, MLAs, executive committee members and the district jathedar on June 4 to discuss the situation arising out of the Army deployment in the state. Earlier, on June 2, both Longowal and Tohra had strongly reacted to the Centre's move describing it as a "terrible blow to the peaceful and democratic agitation of the Akali Dal". However, the statement was silent on the build up of the militants holed up in the shrine complex. The bunkers had first appeared in the complex in October 1983.

The Army action evoked reactions on expected and, by and large, diametrically opposite lines from different sections. A section of the Hindus in Amritsar distributed sweets. For them, it was an end of the atmosphere of fear and terror created by the gun-wielding supporters of Sant Bhindranwale while the other section was equally shocked. The collective Sikh psyche was bleeding. However, there was no organized violent reaction against Hindu symbols in the state. At the cultural level, the society in this part of Punjab (the other Punjab is in Pakistan) is characterized by cohesiveness. Significantly, more Sikhs than Hindus became target of militant violence during the more than a decade long period of turbulence and according to the available data, more than 6000 thousand Sikhs were gunned down as compared to around 3800 Hindus. The militants had resorted to mass killing of Hindus in buses and trains.

The anger against the Army action was not just confined to Sikhs in India alone. Members of the Sikh community staged an angry demonstration in England too. Petrol bombs were thrown into an Indian bank and a travel agency office in Brimingham while two Hindu temples were attacked in London. Demonstrations were also staged in front of the Indian High Commission. The Sikh community also protested in Kathmandu in Nepal[14].

At the political level too, the reaction was as expected. Former Prime Minister Morarji Desai described the operation as "a long delayed action", while Janata Party President Chandra Shekhar termed it as "unfortunate". He was critical of the deployment of the Army for the resolution of such conflicts. He also proposed a white paper by the Centre to identity on who was responsible for the formation of the radical Dal Khalsa and issuing of arm licences to the associates of Sant Bhindranwale in the initial stage.

The Central Secretariat of the Communist Party of India said that if instead of drifting the Prime Minister had seriously worked for a solution on the lines of the formula earlier evolved by the Opposition, many of the painful events could have been avoided. Expressing concern, the CPI (M) appealed to the people in the state to use utmost restraint and defend their unity against all provocations. The party said that the tragic happenings could have been avoided if the Prime Minister and the Congress (I) had accepted the proposals of the Opposition parties for the solution[15].

Bharatiya Janata Party President Atal Behari Vajpayee squarely blamed Indira Gandhi for the creation of Sant Bhindranwale who provided religious respectability to the politics of terrorism and violence in the state. In Delhi on June 26, he said that the government's Punjab policy had been conditioned all along by considerations of political advantage. Instead of trying to isolate the extremists, it concentrated on isolating the Akalis and pursued a policy of deliberate drift and brought Punjab to the brink of disaster. He also referred to the statement of Rajiv Gandhi describing Sant Bhindranwale as a religious person with no political ambition[16].

However, what the Congress didn't expect was the resignation by Amarinder Singh, the scion of the former royal family of Patiala, from the party and the Parliament to register his strong protest. He was close to the Gandhi family and had been active during the parleys between the government and the Akali leaders. He was lambasted by the state party leaders for this action. On the other extreme was the support extended by the Congress MLAs from Punjab to the Army action as about 30 of them met Rajiv Gandhi on June 12 to justify the action. These MLAs disapproved of Amarinder Singh's action describing it as "direct encouragement to anti-national and communal forces". They called the step as nothing short of betrayal towards the people who had reposed confidence in him and the Congress[17]. At that time, they would have never anticipated that after spending a few years with the

Akali Dal, this very man would lead them, first as the state Congress chief, and then as the Chief Minister in the coming years. However, the Sikh Congressmen also supported the Army action for the record, though the situation was diametrically opposite and this author is witness to heated discussions between the Hindu and the Sikh Congressmen on this issue. However, only Amarinder Singh was bold enough to resign to register his protest.

The Prime Minister, in her radio broadcast on the evening of June 2, said that the unity and integrity of the country faced a serious challenge from those holed up in the Darbar Sahib complex. Ironically, it was Operation Bluestar that provided sustainability to the secessionist movement. Spearheading the militant movement before Operation Bluestar were Sant Bhindranwale and the Babbar Khalsa. But Sant Bhindranwale had never formally raised the demand for Khalistan. It had not even become such a movement till Operation Bluestar. Radical organizations like the Dal Khalsa and the National Council of Khalistan lacked popular support. Of course, the Army action acted as a big damper on the activities of the radicals and the militants for some time. In an effort to further put pressure on the radicals, the Congress government at the Centre lured the traditional Akalis into an accord in 1985, which further pushed them to the margins as they were not a party to the fight between the Indian state and the secessionist forces. The so-called Khalistan movement might have withered away on its own had there not been the Army action in the absence of popular support to sustain such a struggle.

SIKH NATION IN CHAINS: BADAL

Senior Akali leaders Parkash Singh Badal and Surjit Singh Barnala before their detention issued a historic statement at a press conference at Chandigarh on June 11 the political content of which did not appear in the media at that time.

They said, "This is the voice of anguish of the Sikh people who today stand mortally wounded, for the repository of their faith to uphold the principles of justice, equality and dignity of man and love of God stands destroyed by the might of the Indian Army. After nearly two centuries of Abadali's invasion, Sri Akal Takht stands blasted. The Golden Temple complex is drenched with the blood of the Sikh martyrs. Delhi once again has embarked upon a pogrom of systematic and well-planned genocide of the Sikh people. The whole of Punjab is under the jackboots of the Indian Army and no one can get on the roads or even drive a bicycle in the whole state. Punjab is a prison house. Sikh nation is in chains".

It was in this statement that these leaders glorified Sant Bhindranwale describing the fight put up by him and his associates as "glorious" and described them as "martyrs"[18].

They called upon the Sikhs all over the world to observe June 17, 1984, as Ardas Divas (Prayer Day) and organise prayers for the martyrs who laid down their lives while defending Darbar Sahib and Sri Akal Takht Sahib. Sikh men and women were told to wear black turbans and veils on that day. They said, "No Sikh household should light fire in their hearths. Every Sikh should sleep on the floor on the 17th night. By that day Sikhs should return every medal or award received from government of India as has already been done by some respectable Sikhs, the President, Sikh ministers, MPs, MLAs, Sikhs holding nominative or elective positions in corporations, boards etc should resign and show unity of mind and spirit with the martyrs and prepare themselves for the ensuing struggle."

These moderate Akali leaders were the first to pay glowing tributes to Sant Bhindranwale and accord the status of martyr to those who had died fighting the Indian Army. Ironically, neither Badal nor Barnala later participated in the functions in the memory of those whom they themselves had described as the martyrs and subsequently disowned him. These traditional Akali leaders did not subscribe to the radical thought but political compulsions during those times brought them closer to the radicals.

While praising the Army action, Punjab Bharatiya Janata Party General Secretary Hit Abhilashi said the people who were living under constant fear for about two years had heaved a sigh of relief.

A senior Sikh IAS officer Chiranjeev Singh, then Director of Mines and Geology in Karnataka, was in the forefront of a procession, which marched to the Raj Bhavan in Bangalore while protesting against the Army action in Punjab. The processionists, in a memorandum submitted to the Governor on June 10, sought resignation of Giani Zail Singh for having backtracked from his earlier statement against sending Army into the Darbar Sahib. Chief Minister Ramakrishna Hegde viewed Singh's conduct as an emotional outburst. The Karnataka government turned down the directive from the Centre to take action against the IAS officer.

In Punjab, four senior IAS officers reacted against the Army action in a different way. They applied for leave to participate in the Kar Sewa of the shrine. These included Rajinder Singh, G.P.S. Sahi, Hardyal Singh and Swaran Singh Boparai.

Jathedar Giani Kirpal Singh went on the air saying the Darbar Sahib and Kotha Sahib[19] were undamaged. He appealed to the Hindus and the Sikhs to maintain amity. Later, it came to be known that he issued the appeal in consultation with Abinashi Singh and Balwant Singh Ramoowalia. His statement evoked strong reaction from the community.

The state government, on June 11, imposed pre-censorship on publication of material relating to the Akali agitation and operations of the security forces.

It was around this time that Longowal, then under detention, is said to have written a secret letter to the government saying that what had happened had happened and that the Kar Sewa, which included repair or construction through voluntary labour, of Akal Takht should be handed over to the Sikh community. Both sides maintained total secrecy about this communication. Badal, at his press conference on June 11, had also said the repair of the complex should be executed by the SGPC.

Isolated violent reactions followed Operation Bluestar in some areas of the state. In nine reported cases of violence in the districts of Gurdaspur, Faridkot, Jalandhar and Bathinda in the month of June, 15 Hindus, besides Goraya Congress chief Hardial Singh, were killed as per the official records. In July, posters were put up in villages falling under Sudhar police station in Ludhiana asking the Sikhs to boycott Hindus and forbidding them from supplying them milk or fodder or making any purchases from the shopkeepers from that community. Angry Sikh protesters at Sudhar also approached the police to lodge first information report against the Army action. A poster pasted on the wall of Gurdwara Shaheedan at Amritsar threatened liquidation of the Prime Minister, blowing up of Durgiana Mandir and Shivala Bhaiyan and killing the Hindus. Similarly, on August 15, handwritten posters calling upon the Sikhs to target Nirankaris, those who disobeyed the Akal Takht and the prominent Congressmen were seen in Patiala, Gurdaspur and Ludhiana districts.

Despite the fact that the Punjabi society in the state was sharply polarised at the time of the Army action, barring some sporadic incidents, there was no immediate organized communal backlash, especially in the countryside. The liberal Punjabi tradition dominated communal tendencies.

As per the police reports, four militants arrested by the Amritsar police on October 26 provided details of Pakistani support to the militancy by way of arms, weapons and money.

Even years after this unprecedented event, questions continue to be raised on the necessity of the Army operation. The attack on other gurdwaras which were not being used as hide outs itself counters the argument that it was undertaken to flush out the militants. It was a strange convergence of the bloody politics being pursued by Indira Gandhi, Sant Bhindranwale, Sikh radical groups and the machinations of the CIA and the ISI. Punjab had already become highly fertile at the time these forces were unleashed and that is all the more important.

Though Sant Bhindranwale did not formally raise the slogan of Khalistan, discussions had already started in about the sustainability of the proposed geo-political entity due to its location being land locked. However, Harminder Singh Sandhu, general secretary of the All India Sikh Students Federation used to argue that what the Sikhs needed was a foothold and the rest would follow. The issue was the domination of Sikh identity, even if it was limited to a few districts of Punjab being made part of Khalistan. This is the region where the Sikh and the Hindu identity are part of the broader and dominant Punjabi identity, the secular identity.

However, there were contradictions and clash of interest within the matrix of Sikh identity. As such, the demand for Sikh homeland as a sovereign state lacked the much-needed support to sustain the movement. Romanticism of militancy is just one part of the movement. There was little support from the urban Sikhs who controlled commerce and trade along with their Hindu counterparts. The militant movement had its recruits mainly from the countryside. The lack of broad based support was one of the major factors behind the movement withering away years later. The issue of Sikh identity had been there all these years. It used to be raised repeatedly by the Shiromani Akali Dal and the SGPC and this was forcefully hammered in the radical politics. Punjab happened to be the homeland of the Sikhs, a minority at the national level but majority in Punjab. It is a minority that once ruled this region and even captured Delhi with the Sikh flag flying from the ramparts of the historic Red Fort. Hence the ambition to rule continued to be nurtured. The Akali Dal had repeatedly raised the demand for autonomous Sikhstan, the homeland for the Sikhs, and contested Assembly elections on this issue much before the adoption of the Anandpur Sahib resolution. However, the Akali Dal had always raised such issues within the democratic framework. It is the idea that matters. It was the trauma that was Operation Bluestar which broadened the space for the radical politics.

NOTES

1. Darbar Sahib, the Sikh shrine better known as the Golden Temple across the world, the name it acquired after it was gold plated by Maharaja Ranjit Singh.

2. The supreme institution symbolising the sovereignty of the Sikh doctrine in the Darbar Sahib complex.
3. Projected as the symbol of militancy and given out to be the main target of attack.
4. The Jhanda Bunga is the flag post where the twin flags of Darbar Sahib and Akal Takht are installed, the flag of Darbar Sahib being higher by two and a half feet, symbolising the supremacy of the temporal over the spiritual.
5. The details about the immersion of their assets are available in the register at Patalpuri Sahib, Entry No. 8239 on page 12 dated June 14, 1984. However, the government for some reasons, did not come out with the exact information at that time.
6. The unique of Sikh sovereignty and struggle in front of Darbar Sahib conceptualised by the Sixth Guru, Guru Hargobind and constructed by Bhai Gurdas and Baba Buddha alone.
7. Residential area in the complex.
8. Panth.
9. The institution of five beloved ones who were the first to be baptised by Guru Gobind Singh to create the Khalsa.
10. Panth.
11. Quoted from the transcript of Gurcharan Singh Tohra's interview.
12. Community kitchen.
13. The headquarters of the Shiromani Akali Dal ever since its creation had been located in the Darbar Sahib complex and most of the meetings used to be held there. Moreover, the tradition is that the Morcha chief designated as dictator is not supposed to leave the complex till the agitation is over, except to court arrest.
14. The Indian Express, June 9, 1984.
15. The Indian Express, June 8, 1984.
16. The Indian Express, June 27, 1984.
17. The Times of India, June 13, 1984.
18. Full statement at annexure.
19. Kotha Sahib is the portion in the Akal Takht where Guru Granth Sahib is taken at night from Darbar Sahib.

2

Quest for Martyrdom

On a cold, sunny afternoon of December 1983, Sant Jarnail Singh Bhindranwale, as usual, was holding his court on the sprawling roof of the red-bricked langar hall in the Darbar Sahib complex. His sten-gun wielding associates were closely guarding the stairs that led to the roof. Himself Sant Bhindranwale always used to carry a 9 MM mouser from which he had perhaps never fired a shot till then. He would also carry about 2-feet long metallic arrow, which christened him as 'Tir wala baba'[1]. People would flock to him everyday and he would also address the volunteers from Shiromani Akali Dal in the Manji Sahib Diwan Hall of the complex before they would give court arrest as part of the party agitation known as the Dharamyudh Morcha. This was when after spat with Babbar Khalsa, the other main militant organization, he shifted from Guru Nanak Niwas – from where both were operating – to Akal Takht.

He sat on the floor in the verandah, half covered by a quilt and his back to the wall. He invited me to sit with him, sharing his quilt. I had hardly exchanged greetings when a group of around 10 boys dropped in. They were students from the countryside college at Sathiala, about 40 km from Amritsar. Activists of Punjab Students Union, a radical Left organization, these youth didn't seem much conscious about maintaining the Sikh symbols.

The Bhindranwale charisma was soon at work. "You assign us duties; we will carry out your command," they said almost in unison after interacting with him for about an hour. Sant Bhindranwale smiled at me, "You say that I misguide and incite young minds. Now, have I said anything which you might find objectionable or provocative?" Well, he hadn't. By then, militancy was less than three year old.

Sant Bhindranwale would talk of defending the Sikh Panth and restoring dignity and honour of the community and repeatedly reiterate his commitment to that end. Perhaps he desired to be part of the Sikh lore. Those who would keep him company included not just gun totting young men but also retired army generals and intellectuals. They were overawed by the charismatic personality of this otherwise an ordinary looking semi-literate person from the hinterland of Malwa. By now, he had become a cult figure and his mythification had started. At the same time, he came under attack from a section within the Akali Dal on the allegation of his being an agent of the then ruling Congress party, a charge he would stoutly deny publicly from the Manji Sahib Diwan Hall stage. Of course, he openly used to announce that he would take care of the person who had killed those indulging in anti-Panthic activities and resorting to repression against the Sikhs. And in case of the loss suffered in the process by a Sikh, he promised to pay a compensation of Rs 10 lakh, provided he went out of the Darbar Sahib complex alive after achieving the aim of the ongoing struggle. He had not gone out of the complex since July, 1982, ever since he launched the agitation to secure the release of two of his associates which was later taken over by the Akali Dal.

He had perhaps unconsciously opted for the ultimate collision course within days of the Sikh-Nirankari clash on April 13, 1978 in Amritsar when he was a non-entity. Within days on April 22, at the bhog ceremony of the thirteen Sikhs who had been killed in that Baisakhi clash, he had, from Manji Sahib Diwan Hall, announced his resolve to 'wage war' against the Nirankaris in case the Akali Dal government fails to dispense justice while demanding ban on the Sant Nirankari Mandal in the state. He made it clear he would wait for the action programme to be announced by the Akali Dal and the Shiromani Gurdwara Parbandhak Committee and the government action and nothing would be done in haste. He was 30 year old lonely avenger till then. Apprehensions had been raised by the way the situation had been handled by the state administration in the aftermath of the shocking incident, which pushed Punjab into more than a decade long era of unprecedented politics of violence. Not that political violence in this state was a new phenomenon. It was the scale of violence that was unprecedented. Apart from the Damdami Taksal, the other organization which spearheaded militancy was the Babbar Khalsa with global links.

It was the Damdami Taksal which had been leading other Sikh organizations for more than a year against some anti-Sikh practices and writings of the Nirankari Mandal. The Amritsar clash was the culmination of the tension which had been brewing up for some time on the issue. The Damdami Taksal he headed traces its lineage to the legendary Sikh warrior Baba Deep Singh who had given his life defending the Panth. Sant Bhindranwale had also donned the role of the defender of the Panth. The action programme to avenge the killing of the Sikhs came into operation after the judicial system failed to impart justice and this is a very significant aspect of the situation.

The goal of the militant struggle till Operation Bluestar happened to be the implementation of the Anandpur Sahib Resolution which had earlier been envisaged and adopted by the Shiromani Akali Dal and its political objective incorporated in its constitution in 1974. Interestingly in one of his speeches in 1983, Bhindranwale also spoke of referring the river water dispute with the adjoining states of Haryana and Rajasthan to the Supreme Court and transfer of Chandigarh to Punjab. These were, in fact, the demands of the Akali Dal, though during the post-Bluestar period, the issue of apportionment of river waters became very dear to the militants also, especially the Babbar Khalsa. Sant Bhindranwale had only taken up the issues which had been repeatedly raised by the Akali Dal and he had no explicit different agenda. The Akali Dal had put these issues on the backburner when in power. However, he differed with the Akali Dal on tactics but that was at a later stage. In support of the armed struggle, he would repeatedly quote from the Sikh history saying that no two generations have ever followed peaceful methods as the second generation had always revenged through armed struggle. He had his logic for resorting to violence as an instrument for the achievement of political demands. The Akali agitations have been example of the most peaceful agitations in pre as well as post-independence India. He was instrumental in unleashing the revenge psyche which turned into political violence.

For him, the Sikhs were slaves in India and in this context, while referring to Khalistan, he would say, "This is not our demand, but, in case the government opts to give us Khalistan, we will not decline the offer. It is for the Centre to decide whether to live with the Sikhs or not". He would also refer to the contribution of the Sikhs to India's freedom struggle and vaguely demand proportionate share in power. In one of his video recorded interview, he made it very clear that he was prepared to die for the attainment of Anandpur Sahib Resolution and nothing less would be acceptable to the Sikhs. He had asserted that he would not allow the Akali leadership to wriggle out from this demand. Significantly, in the same interview, he had denied advocating killing of the Hindus and the innocents. He had also condemned the first such incident of the killing of bus passengers in October, 1983. Starting with the punishment to the Nirankaris for the killing of the Sikhs, he moved on to appropriate the agenda of the Akali Dal. He never formally and unequivocally raised the demand for Khalistan. The implementation of the Anandpur sahib resolution came on his agenda only after Shiromani Akali Dal launched its struggle in August, 1982. The disillusionment of the Sikh masses, mainly in the rural areas, with the discredited Akali leadership, provided the necessary religio-political space for Sant Bhindranwale to emerge as a hero as the party when in power had swept under the carpet all those issues which it had been articulating earlier. He also came to the rescue of the Akali Dal at the time when it appeared that the Dharmyudh morcha was failing. In that sense, at times, he combined in himself both the streams in the Sikh politics at that time.

Going by their names like Jarnail Singh, Karnail Singh, Major Singh and the like, the Sikhs seem to have a certain fixation for the Army ranks. Jarnail is derived from the rank of a General. Major from Major and Karnail from Colonel. At one time, Punjab was the most fertile ground for recruitment in the British Indian Army. It is a strange coincidence. The person who came to symbolize the Sikh militancy in the eighties was named by his parents as Jarnail Singh. Bhindranwale was added after he took over as chief of the Sikh seminary Damdami Taksal at a comparatively young age. The enigmatic but phenomenal rise of this rustic young man lacking formal education is an insight into one of the most fierce liberation struggles.

I met him last on May 25, 1984. The Army had been given the green signal for the decisive action by then. It continued for more than an hour, one-to-one, off the record meeting. He was aware of what was going to happen and was candid about the situation. His associates were oiling their guns in the adjoining room at Akal Takht. He was not averse to a settlement provided it was honourable. And the solution proposed was to be within the framework of the Indian constitution. Broadly, in that framework, the political demands were to be 'honourably' settled with the Akali Dal, apart from general amnesty for his men.

However, an individual always has a limited though important role to play. What is more important is that Sant Bhindranwale emerged at a critical time when the Green revolution had ushered into this agrarian state and pressure was building up under the Punjab fault line.

Sant Bhindranwale had made the implementation of the 1973 version of the Anandpur Sahib resolution as his one point agenda. The Congress contested the 1984 Lok Sabha elections on the plank of this resolution slamming it as anti-national. The Akali Dal never contested any Lok Sabha or the Assembly election on the agenda of this resolution. However, it was not first such document adopted by the Shiromani Akali Dal. The Akali Dal, at its Ludhiana conference in 1966, had adopted a resolution of which the Anandpur Sahib resolution is a modified version. It was on the basis of the 1966 resolution that the Akali Dal had raised the demand for Sikhstan which was to be an autonomous state on the pattern of Jammu and Kashmir. Not only that. The demand for Sikhstan was part of the manifesto on which the Akali Dal contested the Assembly elections in 1967. That was the only time that the party raised this demand in any of its election manifestoes. However, there was no such controversy at that time. Given this background, the storm that was kicked up on the Anandpur Sahib Resolution could be part of some grand design.

Punjab is a border state in which a national minority is in majority and this demographic feature to a large extent dictates the political discourse. Historically, Punjab, one of the most fertile and prosperous regions of the Indian sub-continent, has been witness to periodic political turbulences and turmoil. This historical situation had also contributed in shaping the psyche of the people. In the recent history, however, the 1980s saw Indian Punjab in the throes of unprecedented political confrontation, which ultimately pitted the Sikh community at large against the Indian state.

However, this violence as instrument of conflict resolution was initially rooted elsewhere in the revenge psyche, which is part of the Sikh folklore and was not anti-Indian state in character as such. This confrontation has some astounding aspects. It would perhaps be difficult to find another parallel in the recent world history where thousands of people died in more than a decade long bloody confrontation and at one stage, it appeared that Khalistan could be reality. This, which has come to be known as the liberation struggle waged by a section of the Sikh community, ended abruptly and dramatically and is regarded as a dark chapter even by the majority of the community itself for whose liberation the armed struggle was waged. A chronicler of contemporary history is left amazed at this enigmatic phenomenon, characterized by mavericks, martyrs and monsters.

The militancy witnessed in Punjab in the Eighties, though not a new phenomenon in recent history in this region was comparatively distinct in many aspects. It was for the first time that it had been linked to ethnicity with the ultimate political aim being the establishment of a sovereign Sikh state. Even the intensity of violence was unparallel compared to earlier movements witnessed here. However, this militant struggle in the first phase had the unique distinction of having been launched without a distinct political goal of Khalistan. The first phase ended with Operation Bluestar. The goal of an independent state for the Sikhs was formally adopted only during the second phase and it was Operation Bluestar, which acted as the catalyst and sustained the movement in the second phase. What triggered the political struggle was the revenge psyche that finally shaped up into a movement, which, however, was far from being cohesive and lacked a unified command structure from the very beginning. The armed struggle for Khalistan was virtually a non-movement. Independent groups of armed people moved about in the state with all of them claiming to be fighting for the establishment of a Sikh state but these groups were not the "fighting vanguard of the people". Of course, the victory of the candidates supported by the militants in the 1989 Lok Sabha elections and the boycott of the Assembly elections in 1992 are cited by the radical leaders as examples of mass support to the radicals. However, these two are isolated examples and not the trend. Thousands died or just disappeared and many were cremated as unclaimed bodies by the police. The phenomenal appeal of Sant Bhindranwale to the Sikh masses is a different dimension. While Operation Bluestar was one extreme, the assassination of Prime Minister Indira Gandhi was the other. This assassination was not planned by the groups and organisations directly involved in the militant movement but part of the revenge psyche. The price paid by the country for this brutal politics was too heavy.

At the political level, it was the Shiromani Akali Dal which was hit hard, totally marginalized but resurrected and managed to stage a come back after the armed struggle was contained. The Shiromani Akali Dal, in the process, distanced itself from the concerns it used to articulate over the years, to end up as any other ordinary political party and this journey of this once Sikh party is yet another aspect in the backdrop of the militant struggle for Khalistan. It was the Akali Dal which was responsible for the Congress recapturing the political space again after having been identified with the brutal politics. This transformation of the Akali Dal betrays its opportunistic face. Thus when the Akali Dal while in power revisited some issues associated with this struggle, it was mainly with an eye on the electoral politics.

The revenge psyche was initially targeted against the members of the Nirankari sect. All along, the traditional Akali leaders have blamed the Congress for aiding and abetting militancy for vested political interests. However, no investigation was ever held into this aspect despite the Akali Dal having captured power in the state in 1997 after the restoration of normalcy. Who used whom at the later stage is a matter of debate and thorough investigation, including the role of the intelligence agencies. At one stage, Punjab seemed to have entered into one long dark tunnel with the end nowhere in sight. Even the moderate traditional Akalis finally recognized the primary role of the radicals in any likely negotiations with the Centre. The situation triggered migration of people from the rural areas to the urban centers and from Punjab to the neighbouring states. Fear of the unknown came to haunt Punjab.

Punjab witnessed Left radical Naxalite movement a couple of years before the Sikh militancy surfaced. The Naxalite movement, which had its epicenter at a faraway Naxalbari village in West Bengal, lacked mass base in Punjab and it was contained within a few years with brutal police methods, mainly fake encounters, without creating much tremors in the socio-political climate of the region. The victims of the fake encounters included committed leftists as Baba Bujha Singh and Baba Hari Singh Margind, both above 70 years of age. Many of these encounters relate to the period when the Shiromani Akali Dal government headed by Parkash Singh Badal ruled Punjab from March 27, 1970 to June 14, 1971. However, though confined to certain pockets in the state, this movement left a distinct mark on the cultural, literary and artistic scene of Punjab.

This was not the case with the Sikh militant struggle that failed to inspire a single good poem, novel, short story, a play or a painting. The Sikh armed struggle lacked ideological content and as it did not question the system, it was not aimed at changing it. It carried the terminator seed. The state once again resorted to police methods, though more brutal this time, to crush it. At the initial stage, it was this very state repression, which fuelled the militant movement apart from other factors. This had earlier happened during the Naxalite movement also. I myself was witness to the case of Beant Singh, a student of History at Punjabi University, Patiala, who went underground from the hostel fearing arrest and police repression after his house in the village was raided as his name came to be linked with some Naxalite activist though he was not involved in any case till then. He was arrested along with two others within a few days of having gone underground, tortured and killed in a fake encounter near Barnala in January 1972. Most of the people drawn to the Naxalite movement in Punjab were educated but frustrated with the insensitive and brutal system which failed to address the concerns of the ordinary people. The police eliminated most of the Naxalite leaders and activists but the influence of the Left radical thought widened in some mass organizations including the students. The Punjab Students Union dominated the scene for years before the Sikh radical movement took over.

None could have anticipated the phenomenal rise of Sant Bhindranwale when this non-descript 1947-born lanky young man from an obscure Rode village near Moga in the Malwa hinterland, lacking in formal education, took over as head of the Damdami Taksal in August 1977. He joined the organization, till then a little known Sikh seminary, to study scriptures at an early age in 1964. No Sikh leader in the recent times has come to command such a massive following and that too, in such a short span, and has also been target of such abhorrence and love in equal measures.

His rise was meteoric and he left behind a legacy, which is considered contentious by many. However, more important was the conviction and credibility of the man who had come up from a peasant family at a time when the feudal stranglehold was tightening its grip on the Akali Dal. More than any other factor, this phenomenon of his dramatic ascendancy is rooted in the socio-economic forces at play at that time. That was also a period when religion was losing its appeal in this region. His refrain would be to live and die for the Sikh Panth.

By the time militancy appeared on the scene, Punjab had faced many a political agitations launched mainly by the Akali Dal, the political party which claimed to articulate the aspirations and ambitions of the Sikhs at large, against the government at the Centre and for years, it was the Congress which ruled the country. The confrontation of the Sikhs with the government at the Centre started within no time after the partition of the country in 1947 in which this region had suffered the most. Several Akali leaders had repeatedly been to jails for political causes. The change in the attitude of the ruling Congress immediately after partition of the country strengthened the feeling of being discriminated against and this perception continued to persist, against which the Akali Dal frequently launched agitations. Sant Bhindranwale used to touch this very chord saying the Sikhs were slaves in India.

Historically, Shiromani Akali Dal shared an interesting relationship with the Congress both before and after the partition of the country. The Akali leaders, including Parkash Singh Badal, had contested the 1957 Assembly elections on the Congress tickets as part of the political settlement. However, subsequently as this arrangement did not work, the Congress and the Akali Dal had been pitted against each other, which defined their confrontationist attitude. However, a major section of the Akali leadership also stood discredited over the years and was considered to be a bunch of power-hungry and corrupt politicians exploiting sentiments of the Sikh community just to come to power and then forgetting the concerns they had been claiming were dear to them when out of power. Sant Bhindranwale, on the other hand, enjoyed the image of being committed to the Panth and not just one of those hankering after political power.

The immediate genesis of militancy is traced to certain events relating to the period when Punjab was being ruled by the Shiromani Akali Dal-Janata Party coalition with Badal as the Chief Minister during his second term. The party was also partner in the Janata Party led coalition government at the Centre which had replaced the Congress in 1977. Sant Bhindranwale made his dramatic entry on the Punjab stage during this period. The Akali Dal came to power in the June 1977 Assembly elections after the withdrawal of Emergency against which the party had launched a sustained agitation from Akal Takht. This was one Akali agitation which had nothing to do with the identity assertion or such related issues and the main concern was the human rights, a role which was appreciated by the non-Congress political parties at the national level. The Akali Dal earned the distinction of being the only regional political party to do so. By the time the Akali Dal-Janata Party coalition government was made to exit from the state in 1980, the Akali Dal was in a badly fractured state. Sant Bhindranwale had little active role in the Akali politics during that period. Of course, at one stage, Sant Bhindranwale got the much needed legitimacy from some of the senior Akali leaders like Gurcharan Singh Tohra who was targeting Badal in the power struggle within the party. Initially, he used to visit the Darbar Sahib complex in a rickety jeep to pay obeisance and would stay in Guru Ram Das Niwas in the room earmarked for the Damdami Taksal.

'Maverick in quest of martyrdom' was the caption of the interview — perhaps his first formal interview that appeared in any English daily – he gave to me for The Indian Express. Stories on his informal interaction with a section of the media had been occasionally appearing. Initially reluctant to give interview for the fear that he was often misquoted, misinterpreted or quoted out of context, he sought assurance. "Go ahead. Paint me as the villain. That's what you [the media] have been doing all the time. You have called me even an agent of Darbara Singh [the then Chief Minister of Punjab]", he burst out in the very beginning of the interaction[2]. His apprehension was not unfounded. That was the last time he expressed such apprehension with me during the long association till his death. He had referred to Darbara Singh while his name used to be linked to his rival Giani Zail Singh, who rose to be the President of India.

Months before this prognostic headline appeared in The Indian Express, three Amritsar based journalists, including me, had called upon him at Gurdwara Gurdarshan Parkash, the headquarters of Damdami Taksal at Mehta Chowk. The informal discussion revolved around the Panthic affairs. An hour into the interaction, he bowed his head with folded hands, his face a grim picture, came out with his resolve to make the supreme sacrifice for the Panth. Though the discussion revolved around the religio-political issues, there was no talk of the political goal, despite the slogan of Khalistan having already been raised by fringe organizations like the Dal Khalsa and individuals like London-based Dr. Jagjit Singh Chohan. His resolve mirrored his exceptional commitment to the Panth. This was much before militancy had been triggered. However, by then, he had already come into the focus during the bloody Sikh-Nirankari confrontation in April 1978, within less than a year this father of two boys had taken over as the head of the Damdami Taksal, the seminary mainly engaged in the propagation of religion and training of priests. The discussion focused on the Panthic affairs — the contemporary traditional Akali leadership and the ongoing tension with the Nirankaris. Some important developments of late had invited his attention.

It came to the light years later in 1992 that the aforesaid meeting was not that innocuous as former Chief Minister Giani Zail Singh got in touch with one of the three journalists later in the evening. The idea was to assess the man. A similar exercise was undertaken when Sant Bhindranwale had been lodged in Ferozepur Jail during his only detention for a few days in a case relating to the assassination of newspaper proprietor-editor Lala Jagat Narain. However, this was not the only aspect. The meteoric rise of the man had more to it than such machinations of the people who were trying to exploit the situation that had begun to develop in the aftermath of the Sikh-Nirankari clash.

This period was marked by intriguing convergence of forces that shaped certain developments, triggering militancy in the state. It was around this time that the Khalistani leader and former Punjab Finance Minister Chohan, returned from London and Congress returned to power at the Centre in the January 1980 parliamentary elections. He had raised the slogan of Khalistan way back in September 1971 in England and on October 13, 1971, he placed an advertisement in The New York Times on October 13 proclaiming Independent Sikh state. He had been frequently visiting United States of America and Pakistan. Now, he was back with a mission and that was to make his own assessment of Sant Bhindranwale. Chohan managed his first meeting with him with the help of a retired police officer who had worked in the intelligence unit at Amritsar for years. The first couple of meetings were simply exploratory in nature since the mission was to assess the man. At a later stage, as he claimed, he came up with the offer to arrange arms and ammunition for him from Pakistan. The role of Pakistan thus figured, though indirectly, from the very beginning.

US-based Sikh leader Ganga Singh Dhillon who had set up Nankana

Sahib Foundation was another prominent leader active abroad at that time with strong links in Pakistan. At a personal level, he was close to then Pakistan President Zia-ul-Haq. In an informal interaction with journalists in Chandigarh in 1981, he had circulated his picture with the Pakistan President, which was not used at that time. Ironically, the same picture much later appeared in newspapers as the evidence of his complicity with the Pakistani regime.

The fault line in Punjab did not erupt suddenly. In the first stage, the Sikh militancy fed on revenge psyche triggered by the Sikh - Nirankari clash. The first leader to publicly give a call to avenge the killing of the Sikhs in this confrontation was none other than Sant Bhindranwale who announced that he would weigh the assassin of Nirankari chief Gurbachan Singh in gold. It was the Damdami Taksal, which had been spearheading the crusade against the Nirankaris for some years and Sant Bhindranwale had only inherited the situation. There is a gap of more than two years between the Baisakhi clash and the first militant action on record. The radical stream in the Sikh political matrix got activated during this period. Significantly, the legitimacy to this revenge psyche was provided by the Shiromani Akali Dal, then out of power. It was the Congress which had returned to power both at the Centre and in Punjab by then. Here is the first detailed account as to what happened on the day, which laid the foundation for the Sikh armed struggle.

The Sikh-Nirankari Clash

The tension between the Sikh organizations and the Sant Nirankari Mandal, a religious sect headed by a Sikh with multi-religious following, mainly from the lower middle classes, had been simmering for sometime and the decision of the Nirankaris to organize its annual meet on April 13, 1978, the Baisakhi day, at Amritsar became the flashpoint. Baisakhi in Punjab is associated with the birth of the Khalsa by Guru Gobind Singh in 1699. It was the Damdami Taksal and some other Sikh organizations, which had been spearheading the campaign against this sect that had come under attack for distorting and denigrating the Sikh theology. Both the time and place of organizing the Nirankari meet are significant. Thousands of Sikhs throng to Darbar Sahib on Baisakhi to pay their obeisance. This sect was also well-entrenched in a section of the bureaucracy in Punjab.

Tension in the city mounted as the Nirankaris took out a procession on the morning of April 13, which converged at the venue of the conclave. The situation remained under control and the security forces went into the relaxation mode. As the procession was winding through the roads of the holy city, the Sikh groups were holding deliberations on the issue at two different places. The Taksal men led by Sant Bhindranwale were at Manji Sahib Diwan Hall in the Darbar Sahib complex where Revenue Minister Jiwan Singh Umranangal was also present at the function organised to celebrate Baisakhi. The followers of the Akhand Kirtani Jatha, another religious organization of the dyed-in-the-wool Sikhs, had gathered at nearby Ajit Nagar where a function had been organized in the memory of Bhai Randhir Singh, the founder of the organization. The roots of the militant outfit Babbar Khalsa are traced to this organization.

Sant Bhindranwale took up the issue with Umranangal and pleaded him to take action against the Nirankaris for their anti-Sikh activities. As the minister expressed his helplessness, they exchanged some hot words too. Sant Bhindranwale announced that he would lead the protesters to the venue of the Nirankari congregation to demonstrate against their anti-Sikh activities. Simultaneously, an announcement was made by the Akhand Kirtani Jatha leaders about the decision taken by Sant Bhindranwale to stage protest near the venue of the Nirankari meet and immediately, about 200 members left for Manji Sahib Hall. About 150 Sikhs from the Akhand Kirtani Jatha and the Damdami Taksal led by Fauja Singh later left for the venue of Nirankari congregation to mark their protest, unarmed. Sant Bhindranwale had been convinced to stay back. Fauja Singh was also closely associated with US based Harbhajan Singh Yogi and the Americans converted to Sikhism under his influence. The interaction between members of the Akhand Kirtani jatha and the American Sikhs was frequent.

Two ministers from Punjab, Hit Abhilashi and Balramji Dass Tandon, both from the Janata Party (and hailing from the Hindu fundamentalist Sangh Parivar background), and Lala Jagat Narain, proprietor-editor of the Hind Samachar group of newspapers and a Congressman, were to attend the Nirankari congregation at Amritsar as per the information with the district administration. Lala Jagat Narain was to be the state guest as per instructions from the state headquarters. The tour programme of the two ministers had been circulated from the state capital.

Going by the tour programme of the ministers and the instructions to treat Lala Jagat Narain as the state guest, the Badal government did not apprehend breach of peace despite the palpable tension in the air. Had there been any assessment of trouble, the ministers and Lala Jagat Narain would have been advised against the visit. Something was wrong somewhere. It was perhaps for this reason that the district administration had not taken the adequate precautionary measures. The

Nirankari procession had passed off peacefully and the district administration was taking it easy, treating the congregation as a normal exercise.

Only a small posse of police was posted at the venue of the meet outside the walled city near the Gobindgarh fort under the command of City Inspector Anoop Singh. Fauja Singh from the Akhand Kirtani Jatha, who was leading the Sikh protesters, conveyed the Sikh sentiments to the police while pressing that the congregation be dispersed immediately. However, suddenly, the protesters came under attack from the Nirankaris about 100 meters away from the venue without any provocation. The Nirankaris appeared fully prepared as several of them carried firearms. In the attack, which lasted only a few minutes, 13 Sikh protesters lay dead. Strangely, the function continued undisturbed as if nothing had happened. Some Sikhs protesters were carrying only traditional swords but no fire arms.

Amritsar Deputy Commissioner Kuldip Singh Janjua got the information about the incident at his residence. He tried to contact Senior Superintendent of Police Gurbachan Jagat who had joined at Amritsar only a few days earlier and was told that he had already left for the spot. As he was stepping into his car, Janjua was handed over a report from the local intelligence wing about the likely trouble. It was too late. Gurdaspur Deputy Commissioner Naranjan Singh had also reached the residence of the Amritsar Deputy Commissioner and wanted to accompany Janjua in his car, who refused to take him along. Niranjan Singh was himself part of the top hierarchy of the Nirankari Mandal. By the time Janjua reached the site, dead bodies had reportedly been removed. It is intriguing as to why the police removed the dead bodies from the scene within minutes, even before the District Magistrate reached there.

The DC then rushed to the Nirankari chief and told him not to proceed to the venue and leave the city immediately to which he agreed, at first. He was also told to call off the function. However, he went on to address the congregation as if nothing had happened. When Janjua came to know that the Nirankari Baba had gone to address the congregation, he rushed to the venue and virtually forced him to leave immediately after snatching the mike from him. Naranjan Singh was also present on the stage. Hit Abhilashi was at the circuit house at that time while Tandon had not reached Amritsar. Lala Jagat Narain left Amritsar without attending the Nirankari congregation.

By the time Badal reached Amritsar, Army authorities had been alerted. The DC advised the Chief Minister against attending the cremation of those killed by the Nirankaris the next day. No concerted effort seems to have been made to arrest the culprits. This police inaction is intriguing. Some of the protesters had died due to injuries from the blunt edged weapons while others had received bullet injuries. Some of them had been attacked with swords. A group of armed Nirankaris was seen sitting in a tent at the venue when the first journalist reached there.

It is also questionable as to why the Nirankari congregation was allowed to be held on Baisakhi and that too at Amritsar when thousands of Sikh devotees visit Darbar Sahib as the confrontation between the Sikh organizations and the Nirankaris had already been escalating. This should have been realized by the Akali Dal-Janata Party government in the state. Both the inaction by the police in arresting the culprits and the selection of Baisakhi day and Amritsar as the venue for the annual congregation by the Nirankaris remain a mystery till date. Some people were arrested hours later when the real culprits had already escaped.

The reaction among the Sikh organizations was expectedly at the religio-political level. The Akal Takht issued the Hukamnama (edict) on June 10, 1978, directing the community to boycott the Nirankaris at every level. Earlier, the SGPC had convened a representative Sikh meet to discuss the situation on May 17, which recommended to the Akal Takht chief to issue the edict. That directive, issued under the signature of then Akal Takht chief Jathedar Sadhu Singh Bhaura, is still in force though at one stage, the initiative had been taken to end this confrontation.

The Sikh Nirankari-clash was snowballing outside Punjab also. In yet another similar incident at Kanpur in Uttar Pradesh on September 26, scores of Sikhs were killed when they were attacked while protesting against the Nirankaris. The Sikhs in Delhi organized a protest march and presented a memorandum to the government at the Centre on September 30 demanding complete ban on Nirankari functions. However, the Nirankaris continued with their activities and took out a procession in Delhi on November 4 on the occasion of their annual conference. The Sikhs retaliated with a counter protest march. The confrontation did not remain confined to Punjab. Meanwhile, Sant Bhindranwale gave the call on August 16 to get the Niranrakri Bhawan at Amritsar closed by August 20. This call was opposed by Umranangal.

In far away USA, Sikh Dharma Brotherhood of Yogi Harbhajan passed a resolution on May 2 giving a call to the global Sikhs to organize protests from May 27 demanding the arrest of culprits and their prosecution. The Indian Embassy was notified of the resolution which got back on May 19 with the request to avoid world wide protests. The same day, the SGPC also got in touch with the Brotherhood with a similar request. The revenge psyche had the support from Sikhs settled abroad at this very stage itself.

The general house of the SGPC, at its meeting on October 7, 1978, at Amritsar, while demanding ban on the religious books of the Nirankaris, gave a call to the Sikhs to organise meetings to pay homage to those killed at Kanpur. This mini-Parliament of the Sikhs was headed by Tohra at that time. The first resolution adopted at the two-day 18th All India convention of the Akali Dal beginning October 28 at Ludhiana also referred to the Nirankari issue and demanded a complete ban on the movement of the Nirankari chief and the proposed Delhi convention of the sect. The resolution also demanded a ban on the controversial Nirankari books Yug Purush and Avtar Bani. The Working Committee of the Akali Dal, then headed by Jagdev Singh Talwandi, at a meeting on November 6, decided to recall Surjit Singh Barnala and Dhanna Singh Gulshan from the Union Cabinet in protest against the excesses on the agitating Sikhs in Delhi on the Nirankari issue a day earlier. Radical Sikh organizations like Dal Khalsa were already trying to dictate agenda on this issue while accusing the Badal government of soft-pedaling it.

The elections to the general house of the SGPC were held on March 31, 1979, at the time when such developments were taking place. These elections further polarized the political scene in the state. The Dal Khalsa and the All India Sikh Students Federation headed by Sant Bhindranwale's associate Amrik Singh decided to jointly work for the achievement of Khalistan and contest the SGPC elections. Significantly, the Punjab Congress, on March 16, opted for indirect intervention in these elections by extending support to the candidates opposing the ruling Akali Dal candidates. On March 29, Finance Minister Balwant Singh attacked the Congress for supporting the candidates put up by Sant Bhindranwale and Dal Khalsa. The mandate of the Sikh masses went in favour of the Akali Dal, which swept the polls by winning 132 out of the total of 140 seats. The candidates opposed to the Akali Dal had support from Sant Bhindranwale. The Congress party has never entered the arena of SGPC general house elections directly. It was this support to radical candidates extended by the state Congress that invited the charge against the party of aiding and abettimng the Sikh radicals. The charge was not unfounded.

Among those who lost the elections included Amrik Singh who had contested against Umranangal. Sant Bhindranwale had proposed that only those candidates be given tickets by the Akali Dal who were baptised and committed to the edict (Hukamnama) against the Nirankaris and, in turn, offered to support them. For him, Umranangal was one of those responsible for the killing of the Sikhs on Baisakhi. He made the offer to withdraw Amrik Singh, son of his predecessor Kartar Singh, on the condition that the Akali Dal does not field Umranangal. This was not acceptable to Badal. The issue of the victory of Umranangal raises the question about the nature of this democratic mandate. The Sikhs at large were in favour of action against the Nirankaris. However, the mandate in the general election to this statutory Sikh body in general and the victory of Umranangal in particular could be interpreted against the policy of confrontation against the Nirankaris as a section of the Akali Dal in general and Badal in particular had been under attack for soft pedaling the issue under pressure from the alliance partner despite the edict from Akal Takht which had been issued on the recommendations of the Akali Dal dominated SGPC. However, the electoral politics has its own logic. Of course, the challenge to the Akali Dal was not formidable as there was no mass based Sikh political party to confront the ruling dispensation in the SGPC. A few months later, Badal was to come under sharp attack from both Tohra and Akali Dal President Jagdev Singh Talwandi on this very issue of being soft towards the Nirankaris.

Within weeks of the SGPC general house elections Chohan intensified his activities and announced the setting up of a new Akali Dal at a convention at Jalandhar on May 5, 1979 to be known as Akali Dal (Revolutionary). This group installed a symbolic transmitter to relay Gurbani in the Darbar Sahib complex on November 4, 1979. Its small antenna on a bamboo pole atop one of the observation towers of the fortress Bunga Ramgarhian in the Darbar Sahib complex fell down only during Operation Bluestar. Having a range of about 200 meters, the low powered transmitter went on the air on November 12 at 2.30 pm with the opening announcement, "This is Radio Golden Temple, Amritsar. We greet the listeners from all over the world. Waheguru Ji Ka Khalsa, Waheguru Ji Ki Fateh. This day would be a historic one in the history of the Sikhs as from now on, it would enable the people to listen to live broadcast of kirtan from the Golden Temple. We would continue to struggle for a high-powered transmitter at the Golden Temple." Its control room was set up in room number 7 in the parkarma of the shrine where the symbolic transmitter had been kept. The control room could not be set up in that room without tacit support from the SGPC. This radical faction without any support base was already in competitive mode.

Earlier, five leaders from this Akali faction including Chohan, party General Secretary Arjan Singh Budhiraja, Sulakhan Singh, Ram Singh and Jodh Singh had started their march from Anandpur Sahib on October 30 for the installation of transmitter at Darbar Sahib on

November 4 but could not be commissioned that day. It was Budhiraja who carried the small transmitter disguised as a radio into the shrine complex. Private radio stations were not allowed in the country at that time. The Sikh organisations in general and the Akali Dal in particular had been demanding transmission of Gurbani live from Darbar Sahib and installation of this symbolic transmitter was to protest the stubborn attitude of the government on this issue.

While Sant Bhindranwale emerged as a symbol of resistance against the Nirankaris in Punjab, the other epicenter of the militant movement was in Canada where the revenge psyche had taken roots among the members of the Akhand Kirtani Jatha. And this fight against the Nirankaris was not led by the Akali Dal then in power in the state. Rather, the resignation letter submitted jointly by Tohra and Talwandi on September 27, 1979, to the Akal Takht Jathedar had severely reprimanded the Akali Dal government in general and Badal in particular on this issue. These leaders had alleged that the escape of the Nirankari chief from Amritsar to Delhi was facilitated at the level of Badal and the then state Chief Secretary S.S. Puri. The two leaders further stated that numerous resolutions adopted by the Akali Dal working committee from time-to-time demanding ban on Nirankari books continued to be ignored by the Badal government. Battle lines were already being drawn in the Sikh political matrix.

The forces which were to dictate the situation in this volatile region for more than a decade were finally unleashed with the assassination of Nirankari chief Gurbachan Singh in Delhi on April 24, 1980, the first victim of this revenge psyche, to avenge the killing of the Sikhs by the Nirankaris. The plan was put into operation by an unknown Ranjit Singh, a young carpenter who worked for sometime in the Nirankari Bhavan, the headquarters of the Nirankari Mandal in Delhi. The man had no political background but was deeply religious. He was subsequently elevated to the exalted office of the Jathedar of Akal Takht while in jail. Ranjit Singh contacted Sant Bhindranwale for the weapon through one Gian Singh Gatka Master of Delhi to carry out his plan. He had met the Sant for the first time. He was handed over a licensed Carbine belonging to one of Sant Bhindranwale's brothers. The revenge psyche was in operation. The weapon used in the assassination was never recovered. Kabal Singh, an accomplice of Ranjit Singh associated with the Damdami Taksal, mysteriously disappeared later. The trial proceedings in the case relating to the killing of the Sikhs by the Nirankaris had been held at Karnal in Haryana, but the accused were acquitted on January 4, 1980, just two days before the Lok Sabha elections in which the Congress recaptured power with Indira Gandhi staging a come back as the Prime Minister. The revenge psyche had come into operation only after the judicial system had failed to deliver justice.

Immediately after the murder of the Nirankari chief, Sant Bhindranwale shifted to the safe haven on the top floor of the Guru Nanak Niwas (one of the guest houses) in the Darbar Sahib complex for sometime where the entry of the visitors was restricted with the sign: 'No admission without permission'. His hand was suspected behind this assassination. The investigation of this case was assigned to the Central Bureau of Investigation. Sant Bhindranwale was questioned by a CBI team in this case on May 5 in the office of the SGPC. It was a convention that the police would not raid the Darbar Sahib complex. Amrik Singh objected to The Indian Express report which detailed the scene on that floor where strict watch was maintained by the associates of Sant Bhindranwale.

Dal Khalsa, another radical Sikh organization with international links but lacking in support base in the native soil, on June 22, 1980, threatened to create an Assam-like situation in case Sant Bhindranwale was arrested in the assassination conspiracy case. This North-Eastern state was the potential area of turmoil at that time. The militancy in this part also coincides with the uprising in the North-East. The outfit also decided to mobilise legal aid to the Sikhs arrested by the CBI in this case.

However, what was all the more important was the stand taken by senior Akali Dal leader Harchand Singh Longowal, considered to be a moderate, who, on July 7, threatened to launch an agitation in case Sant Bhindranwale was arrested. Sant Bhindranwale was on the rise.

The Sikhs took out a procession in Delhi on July 20 against the harassment of the members of the community in the Nirankari chief assassination case. The investigating agency had been rounding up people during investigation.

Akali Dal's Legitimacy to Revenge Psyche

Institutionalised legitimacy to this revenge psyche for the first time was provided by the Shiromani Akali Dal and that too in a resolution. This party resolution No. 3 circulated at its two-day general body meeting, which began on August 19, 1980, eulogized the killing of the Nirankari chief saying, "The brave act of killing the Narakdhari[3] by a gutsy person is a matter of pride". The resolution expressed sympathy with those arrested in the case and stated that the entire Sikh community was with them. It also condemned the harassment of the Sikhs by the CBI and the efforts to frame Sant Bhindranwale in this case. The revenge psyche could not have received greater legitimacy than this resolution, that too from one of the oldest mainstream political party in the country with its base among the Sikhs. The Akali Dal was out of power at the time the party adopted this resolution. This positioning of the Akali Dal in the very first case of the use of the gun is very significant in the context of providing legitimacy to militancy.

This resolution should also be seen in the context that the politics in the state was getting highly polarized on the Nirankari issue as clear from the post-June 1978 developments at various levels. The Akal Takht's edict to the Sikhs to socially and economically boycott the Nirankaris had been disapproved of by the Congress, the Communist Party of India and a section of the media, mainly the Jalandhar based non-English press. Like always, the Jalandhar based media was getting divided on communal lines on the Sikh-Nirankari confrontation, thus vitiating the atmosphere in the state.

Organizations like Dal Khalsa were further heating up the atmosphere in the state. The Dal Khalsa had been set up on August 6, 1978, after a meeting at the Sector 22 gurudwara at Chandigarh, a few months after the Baisakhi clash. Interestingly, Giani Zail Singh happened to hold his press conference at the same hotel in Sector 22, which was the venue of the Dal Khalsa press meet too and virtually at the same time. Giani Zail Singh offered to clear the bill of the Dal Khalsa press conference amounting to Rs 98, which was politely declined by the organizers. It was this incident — to which I was also a witness — which had linked the creation of Dal Khalsa to the Congress. The members of the apex committee of Dal Khalsa included Mohinder Singh Dilli, Harsimran Singh, Satnam Singh Paonta Sahib, Surjan Singh Thekedar and H. S. Dilgeer. Gajinder Singh later replaced Dilgeer in the presidium.

The AISSF under Sant Bhindranwale's patronage, the Dal Khalsa and the National Council of Khalistan were emerging as the main players in the Sikh radical stream. Some of the splinter Akali factions were also taking comparatively the hard line. These organizations had blamed the ruling Akali Dal for having failed to come up to the expectations of the community in the aftermath of the Sikh-Nirankari clash.

The assassination of Gurbachan Singh took place in this backdrop. The radical streak, though not much distinct, was already discernible in the Sikh political matrix.

Significantly, the rise of the militant movement in Punjab also coincided with the Soviet military intervention in Afghanistan in 1979, which was against the interests of United States and Pakistan. India was an ally of the Soviet Union. In view of the developments taking place in the Sikh religio-political matrix, the situation was becoming fertile in Punjab for the CIA and the ISI, which had joined hands to launch counter operations in Afghanistan against the Russian occupation. With the Sikhs feeling persecuted and discriminated against over the years, Punjab was the potential fault line. Punjab could be another buffer state in this strategic game to check the expansionist designs of the Soviet Union in case Pakistan became its next target. The logic extended by the Sikh radicals subsequently was different as the argument was that Khalistan would be a buffer state between Hindu India and Muslim Pakistan. The creation of Pakistan, apart from other factors, is also considered to be part of the strategic designs of the British to check the Soviet expansion. It was not without reason that during the pre-Bluestar period, the communists were listed as enemies by the AISSF. The activities of the Sikh secessionist organizations intensified after 1980.

The supply of weapons to Sant Bhindranwale was initially arranged by Chohan from Pakistan, as claimed by him. These were mainly small weapons like pistols and revolvers. It was an open border with virtually free movement on both the sides. The farmers on the two the sides would even share lunch as fields touched the borderline and in some areas in Amritsar district, even the demarcation pillars were missing. Border villages thrived on smuggling. One of the conduits was Balbir Singh Sandhu, general secretary of the National Council of Khalistan headed by Chohan. Sandhu escaped to Pakistan during Operation Bluestar and died there years later. However, sophisticated weapons like the rapid fire Kalashnikovs appeared on the Punjab scene during the second phase, though some weapons of this category were spotted during the pre-Bluestar period also. Parts of consignments arranged through Sandhu also went to the Babbars. Chohan would later claim that Sant Bhindranwale would have been a sitting duck for the Indian army but for these weapons. He used to make much bigger claims. Sant Bhindranwale's associates had earlier been provided licensed weapons by the government and it was these weapons that they would flaunt.

Dismissal of Akali Government

Soon after reclaiming Delhi in the January 1980 general elections with Indira Gandhi as Prime Minister, the Akali government was unceremoniously dismissed on February 15 along with other non-Congress state governments, adding another chapter to the long list of Akali grievances against the Congress and the persecution syndrome. The faction ridden Akali Dal had been washed out in the state in these elections retaining just one out of the 13 seats. The party stood rejected by the people within less than three years of coming into power. The Congress was also voted to power in the Assembly elections held on May 31, 1980 in Punjab. It won 63 seats in the house of 117. The Akali Dal had 37 seats. The Akali Dal was once again heading for confrontation with the ruling Congress after a gap of three years, having strongly opposed the Emergency earlier.

At the same time, spurt was witnessed in the activities of the radical groups and the radical tinge was getting more and more distinct. Going ahead with his radical agenda, Chohan hoisted the Khalistan flag at Anandpur Sahib on March 2. Following closely, the Dal Khalsa, at a seminar at Chandigarh on April 6, hammered the demand for Khalistan and called for political and financial support from the Sikhs. A section of the Sikhs disillusioned with the mainstream Akali Dal for ignoring the Sikh agenda while in power, particularly with reference to the confrontation with the Nirankaris, provided fertile ground for the radicals to function.

The National Council of Khalistan was set up on June 16, 1980, with Chohan as the President. The announcement was made by Balbir Singh Sandhu in the Darbar Sahib complex. Chohan had gone back to England by that time and Sandhu stayed in Guru Nanak Niwas in the shrine complex. For all practical purposes, it was nothing more than a two-man organization on the surface. The Dal Khalsa organized a seminar at Chandigarh on July 13, 1980, where Khalistan was described as the birthright of the Sikhs. The National Council of Khalistan, on July 8, issued a 'circular' calling upon the government servants to function in the framework of the concept of Khalistan and threatened severe punishment to corrupt officials. The effort was to mobilise public support. The organization's call to the people to set up Khalsa panchayats and Khalistan brigades at the village level, however, failed to elicit any response from the public.

As the activities of the radicals intensified in Punjab, a procession was taken out by the Sikh organizations against the harassment of Sikhs in the Nirankari chief murder case in Delhi on July 20, 1980. It was this harassment that brought the state repression on the agenda of the Shiromani Akali Dal. Though state repression had been witnessed in the state earlier also during the first tenure of the Badal government to curb the Naxalites, now it was being perceived as repression against the Sikhs which further strengthened the persecution complex and strengthened the radicals.

Queering the pitch of the radical politics in the Sikh political matrix, the Dal Khalsa, at a meeting in Chandigarh on August 3, 1980, reiterated the demand for Khalistan and gave a call to the Sikhs to boycott

Independence Day functions. Posters started appearing in the state demanding Khalistan while seminars on this issue were already being organized. The National Council of Khalistan and the Dal Khalsa organized a convention in the Darbar Sahib complex on August 15 on the Khalistan issue. The Council flagged-off a five-member team from Amritsar on October 23 to tour the rural areas of Amritsar district for the propagation of Khalistan.

The Hindu leaders opposed the demand for Khalistan and set up Punjab Public Front on August 10 at a meeting at Ludhiana, which, among others, was attended by Congress MLA Yash, Lala Jagat Narain and Kali Charan. The Hindu leaders had earlier opposed the Akali Dal demand for re-organization of Punjab on linguistic basis.

The radical organizations took out a procession in Amritsar on August 15. Khalistan slogans appeared on the walls of the office of the Lala Jagat Narain's Hind Samachar group of newspapers at Jalandhar on December 7, 1980.

The Dal Khalsa gave a call to the Sikhs on January 2, 1981, to boycott the Republic Day celebrations to press for the 'Sikhs are a separate nation' doctrine. The exclusive and independent Sikh identity was not a new issue, the only difference being that it was being hammered by a radical outfit and at a time when tension in the Punjabi society was palpable and the faction-ridden Akali Dal was in search of a new agenda under the changing political situation. At the time when the Akali Dal was in power in the state, Badal was constantly attacked for subjugating this issue under pressure from the Hindu fundamentalist RSS, which considers Sikhs to be part of the greater Hindu family. The National Council of Khalistan observed the Republic Day on June 26 as Black Day at Amritsar. Even the radical organizations were in a competitive mode. Khalistan posters were distributed by Khalsa Mukti Dal in Patiala on January 15, an organization which was comparatively unknown.

To mobilize the support of other minorities, especially Muslims, for the demand for Khalistan, the Shahi Imam of Jama Masjid in Delhi, Syed Abdullah Bukhari, was roped in. He attended a seminar at Chandigarh organized on February 1 by the Dal Khalsa and the Sikh Sophisticates Forum headed by Dr Sohan Singh who had retired as the Director, Health Services. Dr. Sohan Singh crossed over to Pakistan after Operation Bluestar and his name came to be associated with the Panthic Committee, one of the umbrella organizations of the militant outfits. The Imam obliged the organizers by supporting the demand. It was Dal Khalsa leader Gajinder Singh who had personally invited the Shahi Imam and accompanied him from Delhi to Chandigarh. The rallying point for radicals like Gajinder Singh and Dr. Sohan Singh was former

ICS officer Sirdar Kapur Singh, considered a Sikh ideologue credited for drafting the Anandpur Sahib resolution of 1973 adopted by the Akali Dal.

As the radicals intensified their propaganda, Hindu organizations represented by the Arya Pratinidhi Sabha, Vishwa Hindu Parishad and the Dharam Parchar Samiti issued an appeal to the Hindus to register Hindi as the mother tongue during the ensuing census operations in February 1981. The Hindu organizations were using the same tactics adopted earlier to oppose the Punjabi Suba demand of the Akali Dal. The activities of the Sikh radical organizations received the much-needed response at the communal level from the Hindu fundamentalist organizations. The designs of the Khalistanis to polarize the Punjabi society were succeeding despite the fact that the radicals did not have much support base in the Sikh masses. The protagonists of Khalistan took out a march at Anandpur Sahib on March 20, 1981.

SGPC and Akali Dal on Sikh Identity

At a time when communal tension was intensifying in the state mainly due to the activities of the radicals, which were being reciprocated by the communal Hindu organizations at one level, the SGPC, at its general house meeting at Amritsar on March 29, adopted the resolution hammering a separate and exclusive identity of the Sikhs. The resolution was moved by moderate leader Harchand Singh Longowal, then senior vice-president of the SGPC. Though it was not for the first time that the SGPC had taken up the issue, the agenda was now being dictated by the radical organizations in competitive politics. This religio-political body entrusted mainly with the management of the Sikh shrines, under the presidency of Gurcharan Singh Tohra, was all set to reinforce this doctrine, which was already being drummed by the radicals. The SGPC, from the very beginning, has been performing a pro-active political role, and, as such, its resolution hammering the exclusive and separate Sikh identity was not unusual. Thus, an atmosphere, which was to provide the necessary space to the radical ideology, was already building up in the state. Earlier, it was the resolution adopted by the Akali Dal, which had provided legitimacy to the revenge psyche.

The state unit of the Bharatiya Janata Party denounced this resolution of the SGPC on April 8. The All India Janata Yuva Morcha, an affiliate of the Sangh Parivar, also opposed the demand for Khalistan and the SGPC resolution. This resolution was being seen by the Hindu organizations in the context of the demand for an independent Sikh state. The Sikh organizations were now trying to out-compete each other on issues like Sikh identity and a separate nation.

Longowal was re-elected as President of the Akali Dal at the general house meeting on May 17 at Amritsar. Significantly, the meeting adopted resolutions demanding the acceptance of the 'Sikhs are a separate nation' doctrine, implementation of the Anandpur Sahib Resolution and the holy city status for Amritsar. It was the Shiromani Akali Dal, known to be a moderate organization, which was now pressing for a separate nation. While in power, the party had distanced itself from the Sikh agenda.

During that period, communal polarization in Amritsar was also discernible on the demand raised by the AISSF to declare Amritsar a holy city by banning the sale of meat, tobacco and liquor within the walled city. Other bodies, including the Shiromani Akali Dal, had already raised this demand at one stage or the other.

The situation took a qualitative turn as the AISSF decided to take out a procession on July 31, 1981, to press for the acceptance of this demand. Longowal would later trace the genesis of the agitation (Dharamyudh Morcha) launched by his party to the developments associated with this demand. In reaction to announcement by the AISSF, the diehards among the Hindus organized a pro-tobacco procession on July 29 in the city with cigarette cases hanging on the poles in their hands. Some of those leading the procession were from the Sangh Parivar. Highly provocative anti-Sikh slogans were raised. This was enough to offend the Sikhs. One of the persons who got highly outraged by the action of these elements was octogenarian Baba Kharak Singh from the border area of Jhabal. He was a religious leader engaged mainly in the construction of gurudwaras and educational institutions. It was he who persuaded Sant Bhindranwale to give a befitting reply to the organizers of the procession. He provided funds and vehicles to mobilize Sikh volunteers. The march no longer remained an AISSF affair. Provoked by the pro-tobacco march, thousands of Sikhs participated in a peaceful march led by Sant Bhindranwale on July 31. Later, in the pamphlet circulated among the Members of Parliament, Longowal alleged that some ministers in the state Congress government headed by Darbara Singh encouraged the people who took out the pro-tobacco procession. In the coming years, the holy city was not to remain the same. Photographs of Sant Bhindranwale leading the procession hit front pages of the newspapers in the region. He had come to occupy the centre stage and was all set to dictate the future political discourse.

A section of the Jalandhar based print media was fueling the tension. The media in Jalandhar had always been sharply divided on communal lines. The AISSF, at a meeting at Chandigarh on July 12, 1981, took strong exception to the anti-Sikh articles being published by the Hind Samachar group and demanded apology from the proprietor-editor, Lala Jagat Narain, by August 22. A demonstration was also staged against the newspaper group. The AISSF warned of dire consequences in case of failure to extend apology.

The Council of Khalistan observed the first anniversary of the announcement of Khalistan on June 14, 1981, at the Akal Takht. This radical outfit organized another convention in the Darbar Sahib complex on August 30 on the Khalistan issue and took out a procession in Batala on September 5. A small section of the Sikhs was responding to such fringe organizations.

A case was registered against Sant Bhindranwale for the possession of illegal arms under Sections 25, 54 and 59 of the Arms Act at Amritsar in June 1981. The Punjab Police also made a futile attempt to arrest him in Bombay (Mumbai) where he was camping then. However, he managed to escape and safely reached Mehta Chowk by a car, completing the journey non-stop in about 28 hours. This was the first case registered against him. Gurbachan Singh Manochahal acted as his decoy in Bombay during his escape as he was also of the same built.

Militant groups in the state were already getting organised. The people who constituted the first two groups of militants were mainly the associates of Fauja Singh, who led the protesters against the Nirankaris on April 13, 1978, and was killed. The diehard but emotionally disturbed youth were mainly organized by Canada-based Talwinder Singh Parmar from the Akhand Kirtani Jatha. One group headed by him included Wadhawa Singh, Gurnam Singh, Amarjit Singh Daheru, Sewa Singh and Tarsem Singh, while the second group headed by Surinder Singh Nagoke included Anokh Singh, Sukhdev Singh, Sulakhan Singh and Amolak Singh. Almost all of them owed their allegiance to the Akhand Kirtani Jatha engaged in propagating Sikh religion. There was no political agenda at that time. The Akhand Kirtani Jatha and the Damdami Taksal were the two main epicenters of this militancy, which had been triggered by the revenge psyche. Babbar Khalsa was later created as the militant wing from the Akhand Kirtani Jatha.

These first two motley groups of militants initially faced the problem of money and weapons. Talwinder Singh went back to Canada to arrange for both. He managed to smuggle in small arms. That was before the other channels became active. He gifted one of these weapons, a Mouser, to Sant Bhindranwale who always carried it on his person. Sant Bhindranwale once offered that Mouser to me standing on the top of Guru Nanak Niwas. Of course, the offer was politely declined.

After a long lull, the second person to become the target of the revenge psyche was Shadi Lal Angra, President, Municipal Committee and Nirankari Pramukh of Anandpur Sahib, who was shot dead on August 5, 1981. This killing was executed by Sukhdev Singh, who later headed the Babbar Khalsa.

However, it was the killing of Lala Jagat Narain on September 9, 1981, near Ludhiana, which marked a qualitative shift in the situation. Though he had already hit the headlines, the phenomenal rise of Sant Bhindranwale started with this killing. The Hind Samachar group had been supporting the Nirankaris. What was stated to be the immediate provocation for the assassination of Lala Jagat Narain was an editorial highly critical of the foreign visit of then Akal Takht chief Jathedar Gurdial Singh Ajnoha and Tohra. The outburst had its effect on his associates. Lala Jagat Narain was perceived by the Sant as representative of the communal Hindus who was not only supporting the Nirankaris but also openly hostile towards the Sikhs.

Arrest warrants were issued against Sant Bhindranwale who was on tour in Lala Jagat Narain murder case and the police raided village Chando Kalan in Sirsa district of Haryana. He escaped but the police burnt two buses of the Taksal carrying religious books. The Sant managed to reach Mehta Chowk early in the morning. The police officials manning the picket near Gurdwara Gurdarshan Parkash, the Taksal headquarters, sought orders to arrest him but were denied. Later, Sant Bhindranwale used to hammer his point of Sikhs being slaves quoting the Chando Kalan incident.

On September 20, Sant Bhindranwale offered arrest on his own terms after addressing a massive gathering. It was Delhi Sikh Gurdwara Management Committee President and Akali leader Santokh Singh whose provocative speech triggered the trouble as the Sant offered arrest. He was also considered to be close to then Union Home Minister Giani Zail Singh. The police fired on the agitated crowd in which 15 persons including those near Nath Di Khui village, a few kilometers away, were killed. Jathedar Ajnoha, who was also present at the function, warned the state government against any ill-treatment to Sant Bhindranwale during custody. The arrest had been negotiated by a senior police officer. In the early morning on the day of his arrest, Sant Bhindranwale visited the Darbar Sahib complex to pay obeisance and take a holy dip in the sarovar.

The issue of arrest warrants against Sant Bhindranwale came up at a meeting of the Akali Dal Working Committee at Anandpur Sahib on September 16 where Tohra took the stand in his favour. According to Tohra, he received a telephone call from Amrik Singh during the meeting and pleaded him to reach Mehta Chowk immediately. The police had encircled Gurdwara Gurdarshan Parkash by that time. Tohra said that some working committee members were of the view that the party should not extend any help to Sant Bhindranwale as he was neither a member of the Akali Dal nor subscribed to its policies. These leaders included Badal, Atma Singh, Ujagar Singh Sekhwan, Sucha Singh Chhotepur and Talab Singh Sandhu. While the meeting was still on, Amrik Singh telephoned Tohra again. Disagreeing with these leaders, Tohra said that as the SGPC chief he was bound to support Sant Bhindranwale. He left for Mehta Chowk immediately along with Sheshpal Singh, an Akali leader from Amritsar. Jathedar Ajnoha, Baba Kharak Singh and some other religious leaders were already there. It was Tohra who counseled Sant Bhindranwale to offer himself for arrest to which all others agreed. It was Tohra who finalized the modalities of his arrest with the district administration. Badal, as the Chief Minister, had participated in the installation ceremony of Sant Bhindranwale as the Damdami Taksal chief.

His arrest provoked violent protests. Some youth fired at the Hindus at Tarn Taran on September 21 killing one person and injuring 13. Four persons were shot by three motorcyclists in Jalandhar. Militancy had been unleashed in an organized form. Babbar Khalsa was already in action. The 3.5 horse power Enfield motorcycle (popularly called Bullet) became the standard mode of transport among the militants and the state government subsequently banned its use among civilians.

Badal blamed Santokh Singh for inciting trouble at Mehta Chowk. Badal and Barnala conveyed this to Prime Minister Indira Gandhi during their meeting in Chandigarh on September 22.

The First Hijacking

In protest against the arrest of Sant Bhindranwale, the first major militant action came in the form of hijacking an Indian Airlines plane to Lahore on September 29. The hijacking of the Delhi-Amritsar-Srinagar flight was executed by members of the Dal Khalsa including Gajinder Singh, Satnam Singh Paonta Sahib, Tejinderpal Singh, Jasbir Singh and Karan Singh. They were arrested and sentenced in Pakistan. The hijackers had purchased tickets in Mumbai and boarded the flight from Delhi.

This hijacking has many dimensions in the context of ISI's support to the secessionist movement in the first stage. The hijackers were kept in solitary confinement in a military jail for three years. They met each other only once during that period on Gurpurab, the birth anniversary of Guru Nanak Dev. Initially, they were suspects. As the creation of Dal Khalsa had been linked to Giani Zail Singh, Pakistan tried to read some ulterior designs of Indira Gandhi in that hijacking to start a war with Pakistan. It was Sant Bhindranwale who later provided the hijackers the much-needed legitimacy when he started praising them publicly. And then it was Tohra who came to their rescue. These 'boys' should be looked after properly as they were dear to the Sikh nation (Sikh qaum di amanat) — his message was conveyed to Pakistan President General Zia by the Akali leader heading the pilgrims to Nankana Sahib. Those days, it was customary for the contingent chief to call on the Pakistan President. Following these interventions, they were shifted to the civil jail three years later. According to the militants who stayed across the border, Pakistan started taking more interest in the affairs of Indian Punjab towards the middle of 1983.

The protest against the arrest of Sant Bhindranwale was not just confined to Punjab. Sikh students staged a protest demonstration in Delhi University and 51 of them taken into custody by the police to be let off later.

Continuing the offensive against the Nirankaris, the militants targeted Kapurthala Nirankari Mandal Pramukh Parhlad Chand on November 16, 1981, within weeks of gunning down Lala Jagat Narain.

Meanwhile, Tohra was busy building up the image of Sant Bhindranwale. A few weeks after the killing of Lala Jagat Narain, Tohra said at Amritsar that Sant Bhindranwale would never enter politics as he was a missionary pursuing the religious goals of Akali Dal. He asserted the Akali Dal was duty bond to protect him in case the Sant faced trouble[4].

Sant Bhindranwale was released from Ferozepur jail on October 15. His incarceration was marked by bomb explosions, indiscriminate firings at public places and sabotage of railway tracks. Immediately after his release, he started touring the state extensively – the ostensible mission being the propagation of religion and de-addiction campaign, which he started from his own area of Moga. However, he aimed at assessing the mood of the people and his support base. People would flock to him in thousands. His communication was direct and the mission religious. This was an area where the radical Left influenced Punjab Students Union was strong. The Left fortress was to crumble making way for the All India Sikh Students Federation within a few months. This was something the Left radicals failed to visualize despite it having appeared in print. It was the then non-existent AISSF that was organizing conferences of Sant Bhindranwale in educational institutions. His rustic logic was convincing. He was mobilizing the Sikhs for a bigger cause and the response was not only tremendous but unprecedented in the recent years.

It was during this period that a meeting of the Akali Dal leaders had been arranged with Prime Minister Indira Gandhi on October 14 when Sant Bhindranwale was in Ferozepur jail. The Akali leaders who were part of the delegation included Tohra, Badal, Longowal, Ravi Inder Singh and Balwant Singh. Tohra expressed the view while sitting in Kapurthala House where the Akali leaders had gathered that meeting the Prime Minister at the time when Sant Bhindranwale was in jail would be inappropriate as he headed a Sikh organization. His logic was that in case the government hardened its stand about the Sant, it is the Akali leaders who would be accused of complicity with the government. Longowal concurred with this view and he immediately contacted R. K. Dhawan to reschedule the meeting. He got back after a few minutes saying Sant Bhindranwale would be released on October 15 and the meeting could take place on October 16 to which the Akali leaders agreed. The meeting had been arranged to discuss the Akali demands.

A distinct pattern had started emerging in militancy-related violence as the targets were Nirankaris, Hindus, Sikhs suspected to be informers, police officials and the government establishments. The pattern continued till Operation Bluestar. The two main militant outfits at time were Dashmesh Regiment having links with the AISSF and Babbar Khalsa. The functioning of Dal Khalsa was somewhat different as it was not directly involved in such killings.

Soviets expose of CIA design on Operation Khalistan

The situation in Punjab was being closely monitored by international intelligence agencies. By the end of 1981, the Soviets had come out openly to expose what was described as the designs of the CIA in Punjab and the North-Eastern states. A UNI report from Moscow on December 30 said: "The Soviet Union has accused the US Central Intelligence Agency of fomenting trouble in Punjab and the North-Eastern states. The official Soviet news agency Tass said in a communication today that although there was a distance of more than 2,000 kms between Punjab and the north-eastern region, reports from these two areas were alike."

"The similarity of these crimes is not surprising. All of them have an anti-India slant and endanger the country's security and territorial integrity. These were directed from one place – the headquarters of the CIA at Langley, near Washington. It is there that all kinds of subversive operations, including the one code named 'Gibraltor' and 'Khalistan' are reportedly planned with the aim of separating from India some of its territory. The methods, directions and code names of the conspiracies against India have been changing over the years. However, their anti-India slant remains unchanged. The CIA also tried to overthrow the government of Jawahar Lal Nehru. The CIA seems to have shifted the emphasis of its subversive work to the northern regions of India and it is supporting the separatist elements in Punjab and Jammu and Kashmir," The Tribune reported on December 31, 1981. The two main radical organizations active at that time were Chohan's National Council of Khalistan and Dal Khalsa, though without any effective support base. It was Sant Bhindranwale who was creating base for the radical thought and support for militant outfits. The followers of Yogi Harbhajan Singh in US were frequent visitors to Punjab during that period interacting with the followers of the Akhand Kirtani Jatha.

Whatever might be the designs of such forces, Punjab was fertile for radical thought that supported militancy and this was all the more important. What the Soviet Union had said at that time was a warning to the government in Delhi. Keeping in view India's relations with that country, the KGB might have alerted New Delhi much earlier before going to the press. Subsequent events indicated that the policy adopted by the ruling Congress at the Centre also encouraged the forces of destabilization. Rather than opting for a political settlement with the Akalis to isolate the radicals and the militants, it went in for confrontation with the Akali Dal that provided these forces the space to function. Despite the Darbar Sahib complex having been put under constant watch, weapons were being smuggled in. This was not possible against the connivance of intelligence agencies. The Congress Party, which was described as the 'Hindu Congress' in the pre-Partition era, was using the Hindu card for short-term gains to retain power in the next Parliamentary elections.

Forces unleashed to deepen the communal cleavage in Punjab had intensified their activities. Hindu leaders were targeted to ignite the communal spark. Virender, editor of Partap, and Ramesh Chander, editor of the Hind Samachar group, who were perceived to articulate the Hindu view, received parcels containing ears of cows on February 28, 1982. Packets of cigarettes were found near gurdwaras at some places in the state, including the Darbar Sahib complex. The situation was being ignited on both the sides. The Hindu organizations indulging in such activities were never identified.

The throwing of severed cow heads in front of the temples on the night intervening April 25 and 26, 1982, can be seen in this context of provoking communal strife. Dal Khalsa owned responsibility for the cow heads found at two Shiva temples in Amritsar on April 26. The handwritten note recovered from these places said that this action was provoked by the resistance of the Hindus in accepting Amritsar as a holy city. They warned that the incident was first in a series of steps that would be undertaken if the Sikhs sentiments were not respected. The organization demanded immediate ban on smoking in the walled city. During a press conference at Chandigarh on March 17, Dal Khalsa had warned of such actions and threatened direct action. The same day, Jaswant Singh Thekedar, one of the presidium members of this radical outfit, warned that in case liquor, meat and tobacco shops were not removed from near the gurdwaras by April 13 and that if Hindus continued to show disrespect to the gurdwaras, his organisation would throw slaughtered cows into the temples. Dal Khalsa leader Manmohan Singh Bajaj repeated this threat on April 4. The efforts to spark communal tension in the state continued as the Akalis headed towards the Dharamyudh Morcha.

Reacting to the intensified violence, the Centre banned Dal Khalsa and National Council of Khalistan on May 1 despite Giani Zail Singh warning that it would give undue importance to these organizations which lacked mass base.

In the escalating violence, two persons were injured in a bomb explosion in the Central Telegraph Office at Patiala on September 26. Country-made hand grenades exploded on October 6 and 7 at Amritsar, Bhikhiwind and near the residences of the sub-divisional magistrates at Moga, Tarn Taran and Hoshiarpur. There was also an explosion at Moga on October 9. Another such incident was reported from Ghuman village in Gurdaspur district on October 10.

Niranjan Singh, an IAS officer and a close associate of the assassinated Nirankari chief, was fired at in front of the civil secretariat, the seat of the government in Chandigarh, on October 9, 1982. While he managed to escape, his brother died on the spot. He was the Gurdaspur Deputy Commissioner at the time of the Sikh-Nirankari clash. He was the first IAS officer to have been targeted. It was around this period that Babbar Khalsa chief Sukhdev Singh and his associates entrenched themselves in the Darbar Sahib complex.

The first real encounter between the police and the militants during the first phase of militancy was reported from Daheru near Khanna in Ludhiana district on November 19, 1981, where a police inspector and a constable were killed. It was after this encounter that the members of the first two groups of militants got identified during investigation.

A bomb accidentally exploded at Gurdwara Gurdarshan Parkash on November 29 killing three persons but the security forces did not conduct any search at the Taksal headquarters.

The Akali Dal leaders were apprehensive about the designs of certain forces to further vitiate the atmosphere in the state. Both Badal and Longowal, while announcing their civil disobedience movement on April 8, 1982, expressed concern over certain elements that might instigate communal violence to sabotage the Akali agitation. However, while making a statement in Rajya Sabha on April 29, the Union Home Minister blamed the communal clashes in Amritsar that week to the conspiracy aided and abetted by certain foreign powers to disintegrate the country. This was much before Indira Gandhi saw foreign hand in Punjab violence.

In a case of indiscriminate firing on shopkeepers at Patti, four persons were gunned down and seven injured on May 22, 1982. Sacrilege of religious places continued. The designs of the forces were clear by now.

While earlier the Akali Dal resolution on the killing of Nirankari chief had provided some sort of legitimacy to the militant actions, it was now the Akal Takht Jathedar who took up the cases of state repression, especially the police raid on the house of the father of Talwinder Singh, in his letter written to Chief Minister Darbara Singh on December 31, 1981. Jathedar Ajnoha referred to the police raid at village Panchhta on December 22 and alleged that the 80-year-old father of Talwinder Singh was harassed and humiliated. The same treatment was meted out to his father-in-law at village Padhiana under Adampur police station. He equated it with repression on the Sikhs during the Mughal rule, especially by Mir Mannu, the detested Governor of Lahore. He warned that it would lead to anger and rebellion against the police and religious people like him would have to make sacrifices to put an end to this repression. The state repression continued to increase with the intensification of violence by the militants.

A few days earlier, Tohra had virtually extended indirect support to militancy during the Jor Mela conference at Fatehgarh on December 26 when he said the police repression on innocent persons was a challenge to the entire Sikh nation and declared, "We have tolerated enough"[1].

The designs of Sant Bhindranwale had become clear when he exhorted the Sikhs officers and cops not to be a party to the inhuman treatment being meted out to innocent Sikhs including women and children while giving a call not to take state atrocities lying down. He said every Sikh was being treated as a slave and if the situation persists, "Every Sikh would have to become an extremist," though the Sikhs "could never be an extremist historically."[6] This call was later echoed by Jathedar Ajnoha also.

Neither Jathedar Ajnoha nor Tohra can be blamed for taking up the cause of state repression. They had no other choice. Moreover, it was blatant violation of human rights by the state and the central agencies. It was Sant Bhindranwale who came to symbolise the fight against state repression and confrontation with the state. It was the state repression that acted as a catalyst in the intensification of militancy. This had happened in the state earlier during Naxalite movement also. The only difference is that the Naxalites did not have a person of the stature of Tohra who could take up the issue of violation of human rights at that time.

The intensity of violence increased with the launch of the Dharamyudh Morcha though the Akali Dal had nothing to do with militancy. The second hijacking of an Indian Airlines plane coincided with the launching of the morcha. It could not be just a coincidence. The lone hijacker was never associated with Akali Dal. However, violence was part of the design of certain forces not under the control of the party. From day one of the launching of the morcha, the designs of the central government aimed at maligning the Akalis and identifying the party with militancy.

At one stage, Sant Bhindranwale took over the Akali agitation in practical terms as Longowal got marginalised despite support from Babbar Khalsa. I was witness to the comparable scenes between the two camps towards the end of 1983. While Sant Bhindranwale would be surrounded by hundreds of his supporters, Longowal would be alone in his room. People, especially youth, would flock to Sant Bhindranwale to offer their services. These were the times when senior Akali leadership except Tohra deserted Longowal.

The increasing militant violence was provided political content by Sant Bhindranwale who heavily dwelt on the persecution complex but stopped short of raising the slogan of Khalistan directly. His demand was confined to the implementation of the Anandpur Sahib resolution, which was also the demand of the Akali Dal. His role was to see that the Akalis did not backtrack. He also tried to put the Akalis against the Indian state, which was resisted by them. Of course, he would talk of ending slavery without being specific. As Sant Bhindranwale appeared to have emerged as the fountainhead of militancy, on December 20, 1983, Babbar Khalsa tried to trim down him by claiming the responsibility for gunning down 35 Nirankaris since 1981.

NOTES

1. The man with the arrow.
2. Jagtar Singh, The Indian Express, June 27, 1981.
3. Reference to the Nirankaris.
4. The Tribune, November 14, 1981.
5. The Indian Express, December 29, 1981.
6. The Indian Express, February 15, 1982.

3

The Build Up

Operation Bluestar was outcome of the deadly politics being played in Punjab, which was avoidable under normal circumstances. If the idea was to consolidate support for the Congress to win the Lok Sabha elections by projecting the party as saviour of the Indian nation, the cost was too high. But why was the Indian state playing politics that suited those being blamed for inciting the situation? The factors that made Punjab fertile for the politics of violence should also not be overlooked. At one level, these are more important considering the cyclical nature of political violence here.

The Shiromani Akali Dal was never a party to the militant movement for the creation of a Sikh state as it's political goal remained confined to the demand for state autonomy on the basis of the Anandpur Sahib Resolution, the policy programme drafted in 1973 and amended and diluted in 1978. It was at a much later stage that the Akali Dal too supported the demand for Khalistan. Prior to the Anandpur Sahib Resolution, articulating the Sikh concerns, the Akali Dal had demanded Sikhstan, an autonomous state within the Indian federation. This demand for Sikhstan was preceded by the struggles the Akali Dal had launched in free India after the Congress government went into the denial mode.

Till Operation Bluestar, the slogan for Sikh homeland had been raised not by any of the main Panthic organizations but by the minuscule minority represented by some radical outfits without any significant base. The Sikhs are a global Diaspora and this aspect was significant to the Sikh struggle, especially in the context of the demand for a separate state. The proponents of Khalistan advance the logic that the Sikhs are the only notable religious entity without a homeland. Sant Bhindranwale used to say that every bird needs a nest and ever since the Partition of the country in 1947, the Sikhs in Punjab had felt discriminated against and betrayed by successive governments at the Centre. For years, the Akali politics has been thriving on this perceived discrimination syndrome. However, the Akali Dal never came into direct confrontation with the Indian state as such. Of course, the party came under attack for the politics of violence which had been unleashed in the state though the Akali Dal had never supported violence as instrument of conflict resolution.

After the Akali leaders had a meeting with the group of ministers deputed by Prime Minister Indira Gandhi on May 26, 1984, in New Delhi, both Shiromani Gurdwara Parbandhak Committee chief Gurcharan Singh Tohra and Akali Dal President Harchand Singh Longowal arrived at the conclusion about the inevitability of Army action in the Darbar Sahib complex. This is clear from Tohra's testimony in the Supreme Court on December 6, 1994, while deposing in a case filed by the SGPC to claim damages from the central government on account of Operation Bluestar. By that time, the Army had already moved into Punjab from other cantonments also.

"I told him [Sant Longowal] about the talks, which were held in the meeting and told him that the government side was not serious in accepting the demands. I also told him that there was no use of attending the meetings with the representatives of the government in future. Both myself and Sardar Longowal were of the view that the government was only wasting time before conducting raid over Darbar Sahib. Sardar Longowal agreed with me that the then Prime Minister was dealing the Sikhs with mala fide intentions. I also brought to his notice that as per the information received by me, the government had prepared a model of Darbar Sahib at Dehradoon to give training to the commandos for conducting raid over Darbar Sahib. Sant Longowal asked me to call a meeting of the Akali Dal... On 2nd June, 1984, Sardar Longowal tried to contact the then Prime Minister on telephone but could not succeed. On 2nd June, I also wrote a letter to the then Prime Minister in my capacity of the President of the SGPC. That letter was given to the Deputy Commissioner".[1]

All along, Tohra was convinced that Indira Gandhi was personally annoyed with the Sikhs for the sustained agitation that the Akali Dal had launched against the Emergency[2]. He got this impression at the first meeting of a delegation of Akali Dal with her on the party's demand charter on October 16, 1981. This was the time when the revenge psyche had already been unleashed in Punjab.

"We placed all our demands before her for about 45 minutes. She did not give any satisfactory reply to our demands. Rather she expressed the annoyance that we had fought against her during the Emergency and that now we had approached her with demands. We repeatedly told her that during the Emergency days we had staged the morcha in the larger interests of the country.... After hearing us, Mrs. Gandhi expressed her anger," Tohra testified in the Supreme Court on May 18, 1994.

During the meeting, the SGPC chief asked her why was force being used to stop Akalis from staging peaceful protests in Delhi. "On my insistence for a reply, she said that during the Emergency days, Sikhs of Akali Dal had started the morcha after prayer at Akal Takht. In the present case also, they had performed Ardas at Akal Takht before staging a march against her in Delhi and therefore she apprehended trouble... Our Ardas at Akal Takht was that we would remain peaceful and not raise any slogan... From her talks about the Akal Takht and our Ardas there, we got the impression that she was bent upon taking revenge against us and against Akali Dal for holding morcha during Emergency days. Even during Emergency days, we used to hold our morcha after Ardas at Akal Takht. During the Ardas, we always prayed that freedom of the citizens all over India be restored," he had said.

Indira Gandhi first talked to Longowal alone for about 25 minutes. Home Minister Zail Singh was also called to the meeting she had with the Akali delegation after her interaction with Longowal. She denied the Sikhs were being discriminated. Tohra countered her pointing out the harsh treatment meted out to the Akali workers going to Delhi to stage peaceful demonstration.

In another testimony in the Supreme Court on August 25, 1994, he stated: "Prior to 1975, the Sikhs were not so badly treated by any Prime Minister of India and even by Smt. Indira Gandhi. She maltreated the Sikh population after 1975 because she was aggrieved that she was opposed by the Sikhs during Emergency while other political parties did not oppose". This was in the context of the humiliating treatment meted out to the Sikhs in Haryana in 1982 at the time when the Asian games were held in Delhi.

He further said, "Whenever we met Mrs. Gandhi and other ministers of the central government, we told them about tenets of Sikhism and also about the religious demands of the Sikhs. We had also explained that the Sikh religion is a universal religion and had no ill will against any other religion... Since even after understanding and appreciating our demands, she was not accepting them, this created an impression upon us that we were second grade citizens of the country... Several meetings were held with the government... During meetings with the cabinet colleagues of Mrs. Gandhi, we got an impression that these ministers were interested in dragging and prolonging the talks because in every meeting they used to tell us that they were helpless... *During the talks, some of these ministers also used to say that they will change our history*. Mr. P.C. Sethi, then the Home Minister, had said this in a meeting which was held in Punjab Raj Bhavan in Chandigarh which was also attended by Mr. R. Venkataraman and Mr. Shiv Shankar".[3]

By the time the Congress returned to power, first at the Centre and later in Punjab in 1980, certain developments had already taken place in the state and the state was heading towards militancy. In the first ever case, though unregistered, relating to militancy, the first abortive attempt was made on the life of newspaper baron Lala Jagat Narain in December 1979 by two motorcycle riders who chased his car near Rajpura in Patiala.

The fertile ground for the struggle, at one level, was provided by the perceived notion of injustice and discrimination among the members of the Sikhs community at the hands of the successive Congress governments at the Centre. The army attack on the Darbar Sahib complex and some other shrines code named Operation Bluestar was culmination of this confrontation. The hostility had been building up between the Centre and the major section of the Sikhs in Punjab to which the element of militancy had been added much later but not by the Akali Dal that had been claiming to represent the Sikhs. But then it wasn't just the Akali Dal that nurtured regional aspirations. Some other political parties were already articulating such demands in other regions. The major difference was that in this case the Sikhs had been pressing their claim years before the Partition and, during negotiations started by the British government, were considered as the third party after the Hindus and the Muslims.

Within years of the Partition of India, during which this region suffered the most with *lakhs* of Punjabis having been forced to migrate, Sikhs in Punjab were on a path of confrontation with the central government. The Sikhs as a community had decided to be part of India. However, the Sikhs would never have imagined that this confrontation could turn so vicious and brutal at one point. Operation Bluestar had been conceived months before it was launched and was part of a larger design. The Operation targeted to put an end to the militant violence proved to be the biggest provocation as the state passed into a more turbulent and vicious second phase and the violence did not just remain confined to Punjab alone.

If Bluestar was launched to target militants holed up inside the Darbar Sahib complex, why were the dozen other Sikh shrines across Punjab attacked? If Sikh militancy was part of the designs of the CIA and the ISI to destabilize India, Indira Gandhi was playing the same game but to win the support of the Hindus by dubbing Sikhs as secessionists. In the pre-Partition era, the Congress would be described as a Hindu party and the party was playing the same role again. Indira Gandhi herself became a victim of the deadly politics at play. On the other side of the war was a community that had made a major contribution to the freedom struggle. A testimony to the contribution of Punjabis in general and the Sikhs in particular to the freedom struggle is the museum dedicated to the freedom fighters at Port Blair in Andaman and Nicobar islands, better known as Kala Pani.

After the Partition of the country in 1947, which divided Punjab and later trifurcation[4] of the Indian Punjab in 1966, demographic characteristics of the region underwent a major transformation. For the first time, the Sikhs, a minority at the national level, became a majority in their own truncated state, and this national minority, which once ruled this region, had its own ambitions and aspirations. This demographic characteristic also defines the production relations, especially in the predominant farm sector in the state. The agricultural land is owned mainly by the Sikhs while the Hindus comprise the trading block. At the economic level, there is a close inter-dependence through the market system as the Sikh farmer has to sell his farm produce through the trader, who generally is the Hindu commission agent-cum-moneylender. This mutual relationship is of love and hatred and generates tension often. References to this relationship can also be found in the Punjabi folklore. Due to this ethnic composition, politics in the state has been communalized. However, this communalization is issue based.

Despite this distinct communal characterization, the Akali Dal, the party that claims to represent the interests of the Sikhs at large, often depends upon the support of the Hindus (read Bharatiya Janata Party) to come to power. It is a different matter that in both the 1985 and the 1997 elections, the Akali Dal was in majority at its own in the Assembly. But then the 1985 elections could not be termed as normal while in 1997, the party was in alliance with the BJP and what was all the more important was that it was the first outburst of the accumulated anger against the Congress in the Assembly elections. However, in the 2007 elections, it is the BJP that catapulted the Akali Dal to power. Ironically, the Akali Dal had been voted out of power due to the poor performance of the BJP in the 2002 elections whose base had shifted to the Congress. The alternative often debated to the Hindu support is the Dalit section, which constitutes about 30 per cent of the population. This section comprises both Sikhs as well as Hindus.

The Akali Dal leadership in general and Parkash Singh Badal in particular have repeatedly come under attack for this dependence on the Sangh Parivar, which questions the exclusive and independent identity of the Sikhs, treating the community as part of the Hindu mainstream. Badal has always been apprehensive about the leaders like Tohra and he would depend upon the BJP to frustrate possible moves to dislodge him from the government as part of the power struggle within his own party. He had faced this situation even during his third tenure beginning 1997. The Akali Dal captured power in the 2007 Assembly elections only because of the support from the BJP as the party could not get majority at its own. However, by then, Akali Dal had become unipolar in character after the demise of Tohra. The basic character of the Akali Dal of representing the collective Sikh consciousness, however, has now been diluted with the party abandoning the plank of minority politics and the issues which used to articulate the Sikh agenda. It is not just the Sangh Parivar which has been attacking independent identity of the Sikhs. The Sikhs have been clubbed with the Hindus under Section 25-B (II) of the constitution. It is the Congress which used to be referred to as Hindu Congress in pre-1947 period.

Partition and the Sikhs

Within no time after the Partition of the country, the Sikhs started feeling discriminated against, betrayed and persecuted as the Congress, after coming into power at the Centre, backtracked from the promises it had made before Independence. The Akali leadership too had realized that it could never come into power through the ballot on its own in Punjab. The Sikhs were a minority in the state; even culturally, the area that comprised Punjab was not homogenous. The Sikhs have also been facing the threat of hegemonisation from the fundamentalist Hindu organizations from time-to-time, which treat Sikhs as part of the extended Hindu family. The Sikhs have repeatedly confronted this threat by hammering the exclusive identity thesis.

The first in this series of assurances and promises referred was the resolution adopted at the Lahore session of the All India Congress Committee in 1929. The resolution states: "The Congress assures the Sikhs that no resolution in any future constitution will be acceptable to the Congress that does not give them full satisfaction"[5]. Pandit Jawaharlal Nehru also made a promise to the Sikhs at a press conference in Calcutta after the AICC session on July 6, 1946: "The brave Sikhs of Punjab are entitled to special consideration. I see nothing wrong in an area and a set up in the North wherein the Sikhs can also experience the glow of freedom"[6].

However, the attitude of the ruling Congress towards the Sikhs changed within no time after the Partition. It even opposed the Akali demand for re-organization of Punjab on linguistic basis on the pattern of other states, which further reinforced the persecution complex. The Akali Dal contested the 1952 elections on the issue of Punjabi speaking state. However, then Prime Minister Pt. Jawahar Lal Nehru rejected this demand while addressing an election rally on January 4, 1952 saying he would not allow another partition of the country.[7] Clearly, in his perception, the demand for the re-organization of Punjab on linguistic basis was secessionist though other states were being re-organized on linguistic contiguity criteria.

The Akali Dal subsequently launched an agitation to achieve this and thousands of Sikhs went to jails during those times. Even when the state was finally re-organized in 1966, large Punjabi speaking areas with Hindu domination along with the capital city of Chandigarh were left out, which was unprecedented. Water from the rivers of Punjab was already flowing to non-riparian Rajasthan. The ruling Congress was unsuccessfully trying to intervene in the Sikh religious affairs, with the first such effort made to indirectly contest elections to the general house of the SGPC towards the end of 1954 under the banner of Khalsa Dal.

In Punjab, it is the Congress Party that had been articulating the Hindu interests and not just the Sangh Parivar. The Hindus in Punjab aligned with the Congress to oppose re-organization of the state. The Sangh Parivar had its own role in building up the communal tension in the state, especially on the language issue. The Hindu organizations gave a call to the Punjabi Hindus to adopt Hindi as the mother tongue during census operations in 1961. The Sangh Parivar had the support of a majority of Hindu Congressmen. This was done to oppose the Akali demand for re-organization of the state to carve out Punjabi Suba, which was perceived by the opponents as the Sikh state.

The re-organization of Punjab in 1966 which turned it into a Sikh majority region virtually coincided with the ushering of the Green Revolution which totally changed the scenario of agrarian economy in this region but had some inherent contradictions that manifested later. The initiative provided food security to the country with Punjab becoming the food basket. It brought prosperity initially but later, by and large, pauperization to a major section of the farming community. However, it was the middleman in the food grain trade, mainly the Hindu, who continued to prosper at the cost of the farmer. The political ambition to rule the Sikhs, who lorded over the region at one time, was fuelled by the prosperity brought by the Green Revolution. This was also a time when the Akali Dal leadership passed into the hands of leaders from rural background. The net state domestic product, which, at constant prices, increased from Rs. 1,382 crore in 1970-71 to Rs 2,204 crore in 1980-81, registered a growth of 4.1 per cent. The per capita income at current prices during the same period increased from Rs 1,030 to Rs 2642. At constant prices, the per capita income of the state in 1980-81 was Rs 1,336 as compared to Rs 696 at the national level. However, the income distribution in the state was skewed. As per a survey carried out by the state government in 1980-81, a little less that one-third of the households earned Rs 3,600 or less per annum and 40 per cent of the house holds fell in the income range of Rs 6,000 or below annually[8].

Punjab was heading towards an era of prosperity when the Anandpur Sahib Resolution was adopted by the Working Committee of the Shiromani Akali Dal at its two-day meeting in October 1973 demanding autonomy for the region on the basis of the exclusive and separate Sikh identity. This was also a time when unemployment was on rise in the state. Punjab had already experienced Left radical militancy in the form of the Naxalite movement. The kind of work force that the green revolution needed came from the cow belt comprising Hindi-speaking states of Uttar Pradesh and Bihar, making local labour redundant.

The committee to frame the policy programme of the Akali Dal, which later came to be known as the Anandpur Sahib Resolution, was constituted at the party working committee meeting held on December 11, 1972. Headed by General Secretary Surjit Singh Barnala, considered to be a moderate, the members of the committee included SGPC President Gurcharan Singh Tohra, Jiwan Singh Umranangal, Gurmit Singh, former minister, Dr Bhagat Singh, Balwant Singh, Gian Singh Rarewala, Prem Singh Lalpura, Jaswinder Singh Brar, Bhag Singh, ex-MLA, Maj General Gurbax Singh Badhni and Amar Singh Ambalavi. The committee held 11 sittings, beginning with the one at Amritsar on December 23, 1972.

Significantly, though the original version of this contentious Resolution was still to be adopted as the policy programme formally, its broad political content was incorporated in the Akali Dal constitution in 1974 as the political objective. While the first was religious in nature, the second was political: "To reinforce the exclusive (Sikh) identity and strive for the creation of geo-political environment in which national sentiments and aspirations of the Sikh Panth are fully manifested." This is no different from the political objective specified in the 1973 version of the Anandpur Sahib Resolution which states, "The political goal of the Panth, without doubt, is enshrined in the commandments of the Tenth Lord, in the pages of the Sikh history and in the very heart of the

Khalsa Panth, the ultimate objective of which is the pre-eminence of the Khalsa. The fundamental policy of the Shiromani Akali Dal is to seek the realization of this birth right of the Khalsa through creation of congenial environment and political set up".

This original version was watered down at the general house of the party in 1978. However, the political objective of Akali Dal continues to be the one adopted in 1974 on the basis of 1973 version of the Anandpur Sahib resolution. It was the 1973 version that came to be dubbed as secessionist during the subsequent years. The Anandpur Sahib Resolution flowed from the demand for Sikhstan earlier raised by Akali Dal.

The Emergency once again brought Akali Dal into confrontation with the Congress government at the Centre. By now, the Akalis were too experienced at the morcha (agitational) politics, the first one after the Partition being the Punjabi Suba Morcha in 1955 — agitation for a Punjabi speaking state. The Akali Dal was one of those parties, which launched a sustained stir against the imposition of Emergency and restoration of civil liberties though the government had detained none of the Akali leaders till then. All the Akali agitations have been peaceful.

Tohra happened to be in Amritsar the day Emergency was imposed in 1975. His reaction was that Indira Gandhi should have resigned in the wake of the Allahabad High Court judgment, which unseated her from the Parliament rather than taking such dictatorial decision, which would have far-reaching repercussions. He was the first Akali leader to come on record against the Emergency. He took the initiative of summoning a meeting of the Akali Dal working committee on June 29. Meanwhile, he received an emotional letter from Janata Party leader Yagya Dutt Sharma calling upon the Akalis to lead the country in the fight against Emergency. As the government had not detained any Akali leader by then, none in the meeting favoured launching the agitation. Despite that, Tohra, party President Mohan Singh Tur and former chief minister Parkash Singh Badal were authorised to take the final decision. Later, the three leaders met Jagdev Singh Talwandi. Tohra was in favour of sending only selected leaders and workers to court arrest in case an agitation was to be launched. Later, some leaders alleged that Tohra was in league with Indira Gandhi, a charge he vehemently denied at a meeting with Tur. He was among the first five leaders who courted arrest after offering a prayer at Akal Takht. The agitation launched by the Akali Dal on July 9, 1975 was withdrawn on January 22, 1977. In the Lok Sabha elections that followed, Janata Party conglomerate replaced Congress at the Centre and Akali Dal was an ally to it.

As the Emergency was lifted, the Akali Dal and the Janata Party formed a government in the state too after the Assembly elections held on June 12. This government, however, was dismissed once Congress recaptured power at the Centre in the Lok Sabha elections in 1980. The dismissal of the government once again reinforced the persecution complex. It may be mentioned that the first elected government to be dismissed in free India was the Akali Dal led government in PEPSU (Patiala and East Punjab States Union), the region, which was later merged with Punjab. The Akali Dal came into confrontation with the ruling Congress within months after the dismissal of its government. The Congress party came into power in Punjab the 1980 state assembly elections held on May 31 with Darbara Singh becoming the Chief Minister. The situation provided a fertile ground for the Akalis to start a peaceful agitation in 1982. The centre of the agitation, as usual, was Akal Takht.

However, even before Akali Dal launched the agitation, the situation in Punjab was already getting vitiated. Militancy had been triggered and radical Sikh organizations were trying to appropriate Akali Dal's space. Rather than matching the Akali Dal at the political level, the Congress opted for the policy of confrontation which suited the radical politics.

By the time the Akali agitation was formally launched on August 4, 1982, some significant developments had taken place. Different Akali factions were resorting to competitive politics and the radical tinge was distinctly discernible. Organizations like the All India Sikh Students Federation, separatist Dal Khalsa and Babbar Khalsa provided platform to the radical content. The situation in the state had been heating up since the Sikh-Nirankari clash in April, 1978.

Within weeks of the Amritsar clash, Dr. Jagjit Singh Chohan under the banner of the International Council of Sikhs at Jalandhar on June 11, 1978 accused the ruling Akali Dal of backtracking from the Anandpur Sahib Resolution and spelled the political goal as the sovereign Sikh state. This meeting was also attended by Mahant Sewa Dass and Bibi Rajinder Kaur. A new dimension was being added to the already tense political scene in the border state by raising the secessionist demand for Khalistan which was supposed to be a buffer between India and Pakistan. The Akali Dal government headed by Parkash Singh Badal was also coming under attack from the Sikh radical organizations and a section within the party for soft-pedaling the Nirankari issue.

A section of Jalandhar-based vernacular press, especially the Hind Samachar group, which publishes the Hind Samachar, Punjab Kesari and Jagbani newspapers in Urdu, Hindi and Punjabi respectively, came to be targeted by Sikh organizations for supporting the Nirankaris.

Those criticising this attitude of a section of the media included leaders like Tohra, Talwandi who was then president of Akali Dal and of course, Sant Bhindranwale.

The situation was getting hot for Badal within his own party also. With the factionalism in the party going deeper, both Tohra and Talwandi, on September 27, 1979, submitted their resignations from the offices they were holding to Akal Takht chief Jathedar Sadhu Singh Bhaura, along with a lengthy charge sheet against Badal. The charges against the Chief Minister included backtracking from the Anandpur Sahib Resolution as evident from the cancellation of the meeting of the non-Congress chief ministers Badal had convened on the autonomy issue, adopting soft attitude towards the Nirankaris, opposition to the 'Sikhs are a separate nation' resolution adopted by the SGPC, nepotism, rampant corruption in the state administration and playing into the hands of the Sangh Parivar. The letter pleaded for the intervention of the Akal Takht in affairs of the Akali Dal and demanded Badal's resignation. This was the severest ever indictment of the Badal government and that too by the senior most Akali Dal leaders. Tohra later patched up with Badal and it was Talwandi who became the sacrificial goat. The Akal Takht subsequently declared Talwandi a Tankhaiya — guilty of religious misconduct and in this case violation of the Akal Takht directive — on November 11, 1979. The Akal Takht directive, which he had violated related to maintaining party unity.

Under a situation characterized by growing factionalism, Akali Dal had already lost ground and the party retained only one out of thirteen seats in the Lok Sabha elections held in January 1980. Indira Gandhi dismissed the Badal government in the state on February 15, 1980 before it could complete its term.

In the ensuing Assembly elections in June, Sant Bhindranwale and the radical organizations turned down the request from some Akali leaders to extend support to the Akali Dal candidates on the argument that the party's attitude towards the Nirankaris had been soft. Rather, on May 19, Dal Khalsa gave a call to the Sikhs to boycott elections. With the Congress being the only other major player in the field, one could easily make out as to who was to benefit from this call. The Congress won 63 out of 117 seats and formed the government with Darbara Singh as Chief Minister. Heading the 37-member Akali Dal legislative party, Badal was elected leader of the opposition. The CPI, the CPI (M) and the BJP won nine, five and one seat respectively while two seats went to the independents.

A victim of inner strife, Akali Dal finally split with Talwandi heading a parallel splinter group. Longowal was elected president of the

Shiromani Akali Dal at a delegate session of the party on August 20 at Amritsar. What a coincidence that he was also gunned down on August 20 by the militants. The meeting also approved the expulsion of Talwandi. A day earlier, the Talwandi faction had organised a convention at Manji Sahib in the Darbar Sahib complex where Badal was attacked for disregarding the edict against Nirankaris. This convention had been organised following recommendation of a seven-member committee of the Akali Dal set up on directive from Akal Takht that advocated expelling Talwandi from the party for six years for anti-party activities.

In the competitive Akali politics, the Talwandi faction also opted for the hard line. This faction 'expelled' several leaders including Badal, Atma Singh, Parkash Singh Majitha, Kartar Singh Vaid and Ravi Inder Singh from the party on August 31. Talwandi was to play an important role in queering the pitch for the mainstream Akali Dal later. This faction came out with its own version of the Anandpur Sahib Resolution and took a lead in launching an agitation on this issue.

In a development embarrassing to the Shiromani Akali Dal, Rajinder Singh Sharda, brother of Mahant Sewa Dass, went on an indefinite fast on August 15 in Amritsar demanding transfer of Chandigarh and other Punjabi-speaking areas to Punjab. There was tension in the holy city. He abandoned the fast after a few days against the wishes of certain leaders including Mahant Sewa Dass, who later emerged as a one-man party with direct access to Indira Gandhi and was used against the Akalis and then the militants. The transfer of Chandigarh to Punjab had been a long pending demand of the Akali Dal too.

A pattern of sort was thus already emerging in Punjab. Separatist slogans started appearing across the state. Such slogans were also seen written on the walls of the office of the Hind Samachar group of newspapers at Jalandhar.

Tohra was re-elected President of SGPC on November 20 defeating Nirlep Kaur of Talwandi Akali Dal in the annual elections. The mainstream Akali Dal had asserted itself through the religio-political platform of the SGPC.

This was a time when radical organisations were trying to dictate the mainstream Akali Dal but the party joined hands with the two communist parties to launch a powerful agitation against bus fare hike on December 6. With its pro-people stance, Akali Dal was resisting pressure from the rival Akali factions and the Khalistanis to adopt the radical posture. Joint jathas, contingents of volunteers, from the three parties were sent from the gurdwaras to give court arrest. This honeymoon with the Left continued till the launching of agitation against the construction of the Satluj-Yamuna Link Canal at Kapoori village in Patiala to carry waters to neighbouring Haryana from Punjab rivers. This pro-people combination had the potential of challenging the Congress in the legislative politics. The agitations by the Akali Dal during the pre-partition period had been interpreted by the Left as anti-imperialist in character.

In an attempt to pre-empt the mainstream Akali Dal, the faction led by Talwandi decided to launch an agitation on the Anandpur Sahib Resolution at a convention at Anandpur Sahib on April 13, 1981. Shahi Imam of Jama Masjid, Syed Abdullah Bukhari, also attended this conclave. At another level, Longowal, in his capacity as the Akali Dal President, demanded the acceptance of the separate Sikh nation doctrine by the government and federal set for the country with the states having their own constitution. The Akali factions had already entered the competitive mode.

Going a step further in this competitive Akali politics, Akali Dal (Talwandi) General Secretary Randhir Singh Cheema, on April 19, demanded associate UN membership for the Sikhs on the basis of the 'Sikhs are a separate nation' doctrine. At a meeting on May 1, the action committee of his party formally announced the decision to launch an agitation for the implementation of the Anandpur Sahib Resolution with effect from May 5. As part of this agitation, the party members were to offer court arrest in Delhi once a week.

Akali Dal resolution on Sikh nationhood

Longowal was re-elected Akali Dal president at a meeting of the general house of the party on May 17, 1981. The meeting adopted resolution hammering the 'Sikhs are a separate nation' doctrine and demanded implementation of the Anandpur Sahib Resolution and holy city status for Amritsar. It was the Shiromani Akali Dal, considered to be moderate, which was now pressing for the 'Sikhs are a separate nation' principle to assert exclusive Sikh identity. The resolution to this effect had already been adopted in the general house of the SGPC dominated by the mainstream Akali Dal and as such the options with the party were getting limited, more so under pressure from the radicals. These demands of the Akali Dal had assumed all the more significance in the Sikh religio-political matrix as evident from the mobilization of the Sikhs on the issue of holy city status for Amritsar.

Shiromani Akali Dal reiterated the issue of 'Sikhs are a separate nation' at the World Sikh Convention organized by the party at Amritsar on July 26 while demanding the implementation of the Anandpur Sahib Resolution and duel citizenship for the non-resident Sikhs. However, the party continued to make a clear distinction from Khalistani separatists. By then, it was apparent that though lacking in mass support, the radicals had succeeded in making the sovereign Sikh state an issue. At the Rakhar Punnia conference at Baba Bakala in Amritsar on August 15, leaders including Badal, Tohra and Longowal made the party position on the demand very unambiguous while dissociating the party from the demand for Khalistan raised by one of their associates Sukhjinder Singh. The traditional Akali leaders rather opted for more powers to the states on the basis of Anandpur Sahib Resolution. Despite making this distinction at an early stage, the Akalis were at the receiving end for years on the Khalistan issue.

On Independence Day, Dal Khalsa and National Council of Khalistan activists saluted the Kesari Nishan Sahib, the Sikh religious flag. For the radicals, this flag was synonymous to the Khalistan flag with a slight difference that the emblem on the Khalistan flag had the inscription of Sarkar-e-Khalsa or Khalistan Zindabad on it. The protagonists of Khalistan organised a meeting at Amritsar on August 30, which was attended by leaders like Sukhjinder Singh, Bharpur Singh Balbir, Harsimran Singh, Gajinder Singh and Dr. Sohan Singh. It was perhaps for the first time that a reference had been made by the radicals to the USSR. They said that if the Indian government could seek help from that country, they could solicit intervention of China, USA or Pakistan for the creation of a sovereign Sikh state. The effort was intended at globalising the issue of Khalistan.

The state of affairs had begun causing concern at various levels. Alarmed over the gravity of situation, senior CPI (M) leader Harkishan Singh Surjeet, on September 22, wrote to the Prime Minister: "You are aware that the situation in Punjab is deteriorating rapidly, leading to communal tension and polarization on communal lines. The handling of the situation at Mehta Chowk on Monday has further added fuel to the fire. It is unfortunate that the gruesome murder of Lala Jagat Narain, which was condemned by all sections of public opinion in Punjab irrespective of political affiliations, has been allowed to take a communal turn sheerly by mishandling by the state government and administration... if communal frenzy is allowed to grow, it can have very serious repercussions for the democratic movement as well as the State creating a situation of instability."[9]

It was in the backdrop of this volatile situation that Akali Dal submitted to a list of 45 demands and grievances in September 1981to the government, which was revised down to 15 the next month. The revised demands included unconditional release of Sant Bhindranwale who had been arrested in the Lala Jagat Narain assassination case, special rights to the Sikhs as a separate nation, transfer of Chandigarh and left out Punjabi speaking areas to Punjab, adjudication of river waters dispute on riparian principle, linking the prices of agricultural produce to the index of industrial production and grant of licence to start a bank under the management of the Sikhs. The first meeting of the Akali Dal delegation with Indira Gandhi was on this demand charter. The agitation in August 1982 was launched mainly on these very issues.

The Sikh content in the original 45 demand charter was heavy with 14 out of 45 demands relating to religious affairs. The political content referred to the assurance given by the Congress to the Sikhs in the pre-partition period about an autonomous region. The demand for a Sikh personal law was not part of the religious demands but formed the social content. Thus after joining hands with the Communists for pro-people movement, the Akali Dal had reverted to the religio-political issues with thrust on religious demands and special rights to the Sikhs as a nation. Of course 21 of these demands were economic but the thrust was on Sikh content. But in the religious domain, the man with credibility was Sant Bhindranwale who subsequently who entered the political space by shifting to the agenda of ending slavery by restoring Sikh honour and dignity and implementation of the Anandpur Sahib Resolution seeking special autonomous region for the Sikhs.

The party decided to stage a silent protest march in Delhi on September 7, 1981 against the withdrawal of the river waters dispute case from the Supreme Court and the appeal pending in the Punjab and Haryana High Court against the acquittal of the accused in the case relating to killing of Sikhs by the Nirankaris in 1978. In both these sensitive cases, law of the land was not allowed to chart its own course by the ruling Congress which further provoked the Sikhs. The calculations of the Congress were different due to the forthcoming elections in Haryana. The river water dispute related to apportionment of waters between Punjab and Haryana subsequent to the re-organization in 1966. The Nirankari sect had the patronage of the Congress. Both the issues were very sensitive and the Congress must own the blame for not allowing the law of the land to prevail. If the ruling party abandons the constitutional path, the situation provides justification to those who take to guns for conflict resolution. The Akali Dal queered the pitch to regain its space being appropriated by the radicals and the Congress exploited the situation.

The Akali volunteers were stopped at the railway stations and roads while proceeding to Delhi to stage protest. The police fired on volunteers on the GT Road at Madhuban near Karnal in Haryana in which four persons were killed. Despite all odds, the Akali volunteers who managed to reach Delhi staged a protest march from Red Fort to the Boat Club.

The demand charter listing 45 demands was submitted to the government. The government initiated a dialogue on the demands but never took it to a logical conclusion. The government was repeatedly giving the impression that it favoured a negotiated settlement while the practice was different. The militants and the radicals had begun intensifying their activities by then.

The Akali delegation comprising Longowal, Badal, Tohra, Barnala and Balwant Singh had their first meeting with the Prime Minister in her office on October 16. Cabinet Secretary C.R. Krishnaswamy Rao Sahib, principal secretary to Prime Minister P.C. Alexander and Home Secretary T.N. Chaturvedi were also present. The meeting remained inconclusive. The second round followed on November 11 in Parliament House and was attended by Union Minister P.V. Narsimha Rao. Union ministers Zail Singh and Pranab Mukherjee were also present in the third meeting that took place on April 14, 1982. The Akali delegation also included SGPC Secretary Bhan Singh, R.S. Bhatia, P.S. Oberoi and Ravi Inder Singh. In between, the Akali Dal leaders including Barnala, Balwant Singh, Ajit Singh Sarhadi and Bhan Singh had two rounds of talks on October 23 and 24 with Narasimha Rao. The Akalis were yet to launch the agitation. The Akali Dal working committee, at a meeting at Fatehgarh Sahib on November 30, described the start of dialogue as "a good step in the interest of both the Sikhs and the country". The party also talked of Hindu-Sikh unity while blaming Chief Minister Darbara Singh for the situation in the state getting tense.

At a meeting in Chandigarh in April, the state secretariat of the Communist Party of India expressed concern over the increasing incidents of sacrilege of religious places of both Hindus and Sikhs while demanding a ban on Dal Khalsa.

The Hindu organizations reacted to the vitiating situation by raising provocative slogans like 'Khoon ka badla khoon se lenge' — blood for blood — during a procession taken out at Amritsar on the anniversary of Lord Parshuram on April 26. The information office of the SGPC was also attacked. The SGPC urged the state government on April 27 to declare Amritsar as holy city to avoid further complicating the situation. The same day, leaders of the Hindu organisations including Dr. Kali Charan and others exhorted the Hindus to wear saffron turbans and carry trishuls or lathis for their own protection. Amritsar was brought under curfew on April 27, 1982 following mob violence. The radicals and those playing divisive politics were succeeding in their designs.

Laying foundation of SYL Canal

At a time when communal tension was rising in the state, the laying of the foundation stone of the Satluj Yamuna Link Canal to carry water to Haryana from Punjab rivers at Kapoori village by Indira Gandhi on April 8, 1982 added fuel to the fire, providing immediate provocation to the Akalis to adopt the path of agitation.

Under the Punjab Re-organisation Act, 1966, the sharing of benefits of the Bhakra Nangal and Beas projects was to be agreed upon by Punjab and the successor state of Haryana within two years, failing which the Centre reserved the right to intervene. It was under this legislation that Punjab had been re-organized leading to the creation of a separate state of Haryana and the water dispute between the two states had its genesis in this Act. The Prime Minister gave her first award on this dispute between the two states under this Act during Emergency on March 24, 1976, which came to be dubbed by the Akali Dal as the Emergency Award.

Section 78 (I) of the Re-organisation Act states: "Notwithstanding anything contained in this Act but subject to the provisions of Sections 79 and 80, all rights and liabilities of the existing state of Punjab in relations to Bhakra Nangal Project and Beas project, shall, on the appointed day, be the rights and liabilities of the successor states in such proportions as may be fixed, and subject to such adjustments as may be made, by agreement entered into by the said states after consultation with the central government or, if no such agreement is entered into within two years of the appointed day, as the central government may order determine having regard to the projects; provided that the order so made by the central government may be varied by any subsequent agreement entered into by the successor states after consultation with the central government."

The Beas and the Bhakra Nangal projects have been clearly defined under the Act, which excludes Ravi waters. However, Indira Gandhi, in her award of March 24, 1976, allocated 3.5 MAF (Million Acre-Feet) each to Punjab and Haryana out of total surplus Ravi-Beas waters of 7.2 MAF falling to the erstwhile state of Punjab after setting aside 0.2 MAF for Delhi drinking water supply scheme. This intervention had been made under Section 78. Punjab objected to this allocation. Haryana approached the Supreme Court on April 13, 1979 for the implementation of the 1976 award. Punjab filed a civil suit in the apex court on July 11, 1979 challenging the vires of Section 78 of the Punjab Re-organisation Act, as well as the vires of the 1976 award. Earlier, Haryana had deposited Rs. 1 crore on November 11, 1976 and another installment of the same amount on March 31, 1979 with the Punjab government for starting the construction of the SYL canal.

Interestingly, the Akali government in Punjab had already set in motion the process for the construction of the carrier channel. Badal had personal relationship with his Haryana counterpart Devi Lal and their family ties were very old. The first notifications No. 113/5/SYL and No. 121/5/SYL under Section 4 of the Land Acquisition Act, 1894, for acquiring land for this canal was issued on February 20, 1978 when Badal was the Chief Minister. This notification was part of the White Paper on 1981 Ravi-Beas "Agreement" released by the Darbara Singh government on April 23, 1982. The land to be acquired was in Rajpura tehsil bordering Haryana as last 30 km portion of the SYL Canal in Punjab territory was to run parallel to Narwana branch of the Bhakra Main Line. There was no compulsion to initiate the process for the construction of this canal by going ahead with the acquisition of the land.

Tohra had the key to this approach of the government on the SYL Canal issue. He himself made the disclosure during later years. He claimed Badal had agreed to the suggestion from his friend Devi Lal to jointly lay the foundation of the canal at the point where it was to enter Haryana. It was to be a joint function of the two states. However, he intervened and cautioned Badal about the repercussions of such a suicidal move. Badal acted on his advice. And when it was pointed out at a press conference when he was no more the chief minister that the first notification for the land acquisition of land had been issued during his tenure, he tried to wriggle out saying the bureaucrats might have done it at their own. It is ironic that the process for the construction of this career channel was initiated during the Badal government and the work speeded up when the next Akali Dal government headed by Surjit Singh Barnala came to power in 1985.

Earlier, Punjab Chief Minister Giani Zail Singh at a meeting with his Haryana counterpart Banarsi Das Gupta on November 5, 1976 had agreed to start work on this canal in the reach on which there was no difference of opinion among the chief engineers of the two states. Subsequent to this meeting, the Haryana Chief Minister wrote a Demi-official letter about the release of the first installment of Rs. 1 crore to Punjab for setting up the organization to start work.

Haryana proceeded with the legal remedy seeking Supreme Court intervention after the construction process got struck and Punjab followed to protect its interest. It was not Punjab which had taken the initiative of approaching the apex court. Haryana had already started construction of this canal in its territory on war footing after the 1976 award.

While the case was pending, the Prime Minister intervened again and the chief ministers from Punjab, Haryana and Rajasthan were made to sign an agreement on dotted lines on December 31, 1981 on the basis of what was claimed to be the revised flow series. Under this agreement, Punjab was allocated marginally enhanced share of 4.22 MAF, Haryana 3.50 MAF, Rajasthan 8.60 MAF, Delhi 0.20 MAF and Jammu & Kashmir 0.65 MAF. Punjab was allowed to utilise the waters surplus to Rajasthan's requirement, which increased Punjab's share to 4.82 MAF. It was the executive intervention in the process which should have been allowed to be settled through the judicial exercise.

Rajasthan had been allowed 8.0 MAF from Punjab rivers in 1955 by the central government. This had been done on the basis of requirements of the states concerned. The meeting called by the Centre on January 29, 1955 for this purpose was attended by representatives from Punjab, Pepsu (then not merged in Punjab), Rajasthan and Jammu and Kashmir on the basis of 1921-22 to 1945-46 flow series. There is nothing on record that either the Punjab government or Akali Dal disputed the allocation of share from the state rivers to Rajasthan for it's being a non-riparian state at that time. The Centre had Rajasthan in mind at the time when Harike barrage was conceptualized even before the 1955 allocation as provision had been made for the proposed canals. The Rajasthan Feeder takes off from Harike barrage and is known as the Indira Gandhi Canal in the desert state. Rajasthan, a non-riparian state, was allocated waters from Punjab rivers subject to the condition that Punjabis would be settled in the command area of the canal, which was never met. During the pre-Partition days, Rajasthan used to pay royalty for the Gang Canal waters to Punjab. Rajasthan was also allocated 1.43 MAF from the Bhakra Nangal project in Punjab in 1954 against the riparian principle.

The dispute on river waters mainly arose when Haryana was carved out from Punjab in 1966. Under the Indus Water Treaty of 1960 signed with Pakistan, the waters of Satluj, Beas and Ravi had become available for unrestricted use by India after March 31, 1970.

It was under this 1981 "agreement" that Prime Minister Indira Gandhi laid the foundation of the SYL Canal at Kapoori in Patiala district. She forced Chief Minister Darbara Singh to sign the "agreement" with his Rajasthan and Haryana counterparts as he faced the threat of removal from office. It was under this pressure that the suit from the Supreme Court was withdrawn by the Punjab government. It was election year in Haryana.

The Akali Dal manifestos for the 1967, 1969 and 1972 Assembly elections are silent on the apportionment of river waters. It was in 1977 manifesto that the party demanded "annulment of arbitrary division of Ravi Beas waters which had been done in complete detriment to the state of Punjab" and restoration of control of "Bhakra dam, Satluj project etc". There was no mention of allocation to Rajasthan.

Akali Morcha Against Canal

The Akali Dal decided to resist the digging of the canal and supported by the Communist Party of India (Marxist), launched a civil disobedience movement from Ghanaur near Kapoori on April 8 as the Prime Minister laid the foundation stone of the SYL Canal. Longowal announced that the second stage of this agitation would be the refusal by the farmers to repay co-operative loans. Significantly, he made it clear that his party was not against waters flowing to Haryana but favoured allocation on 60:40 basis. This ratio was supposed to be the notional basis for division of assets between the two states, though no such mention had been made in the Punjab Re-organisation Act.

Badal asserted that the fight with the Centre had begun and neither the Army nor the police would be able to contain the Akalis. At the same time, he expressed apprehension that the government might try to influence the course of the fight covertly. However, going a step further, it was Tohra who advocated strong action saying that the issues concerning the state could only be resolved by making sacrifices and the use of force.

Communist Party of India MLA Raj Kumar during discussion on river waters in the Punjab Assembly on March 31, 1982 had described the Indira Gandhi award as Emergency award and said the Prime Minister should postpone the foundation stone laying ceremony. Sarwan Singh Cheema from the CPI(M) said riparian principle should have been followed while making the allocations.

Canal water for irrigation is one of the most important inputs in Punjab, the most agriculturally advanced state in the country. It is the canal water over which maximum murders have been committed in Punjab next to property. Ironically, while about 60 per cent of the land is being irrigated by tube wells, more than 50 per cent of the waters from the state rivers have been diverted to the neighbouring non-riparian states. Water table has drastically gone down in Punjab due to intensive tubewell irrigation. The villages Punjab, in the olden days, used to have a person designated as Mir-aab for the distribution of canal water. These were times when clocks were a rarity in the countryside. A young boy who could run fast would sprint from the house of the Mir-aab after getting the signal and start shouting from a distance to make a cut in the water distributory.

In a historic speech at Kapoori, Indira Gandhi said:

"Certain friends from Punjab are agitated on the waters issue. Is it credible to suggest that harm to Punjab can come from me whose grandmother belonged to this state? I have been a frequent visitor to this area from my childhood. I have deep personal ties with Punjab. I am also appreciative of the spirit of bravery and industry of its residents...

"Rajasthan after all is economically weak. It no doubt has rich soil, which is sandy. That state was given certain amount of water under the 1955 agreement. In any case, Rajasthan cannot use its share for about eight to ten years. This water can be used by Punjab for that period.

"What after ten years? I have an answer to this also. If the man can land on the moon, which was inconceivable sometime ago, it is possible to harness new technology in the next ten years to raise water and other power resources. So long I am at the helm of affairs, I am determined to achieve that objective, provided people let me work."[10]

In Chandigarh, Badal had earlier announced in the Assembly on March 31 that digging of canal would not be allowed and this despite the fact that the first notification to acquire land had been issued during his government.

The Shiromani Akali Dal, at a meeting of the party MLAs, members of the SGPC and district jathedars at Jalandhar on April 11 discussed the issue of the SYL canal. It was decided to send a contingent of volunteers to Kapoori on April 24 to block the digging of the channel. It was to be followed by a delegation of MLAs. Other options discussed included *gherao* of the offices related to the carrier channel and resignations by the MLAs to force dissolution of the state Assembly. Longowal, on April 16, directed the MLAs and the SGPC members to enroll 1,000 volunteers each for the agitation to block the digging of the canal. On the other hand, the Prime Minister ruled out a fresh look at the water accord as demanded by the Akalis.

The volunteers from the Akali Dal and the CPI (M) staged a joint protest at Kapoori village on April 24 to block the digging of the canal. Within days of launching the agitation, the CPI (M) was in a quandary as Akali Dal named it Dharamyudh Morcha, an agitation for justice with religious overtones, and added nine more demands including autonomy to the state on the basis of the Anandpur Sahib Resolution, and the setting up of a transmitter at Darbar Sahib for the live transmission of Gurbani. The demand for the setting up of the transmitter was earlier queered by the Revolutionary Akali Dal, a radical Akali faction, which had successfully installed a symbolic transmitter in the complex in 1980, the signals from which could be picked up in the immediate vicinity of the complex only. The CPI (M) protested the inclusion of other demands. The CPI (M) did not oppose the digging of the canal per se but wanted the apportionment between Punjab and Haryana in 60:40 ratio.

The situation in the state had started deteriorating with more and more communal incidents and those of militancy-related violence being reported. It was not the Akali agitation that vitiated the atmosphere. The situation had already worsened so much that a BJP delegation demanded dismissal of the Darbara Singh-led Congress government and the imposition of President's rule to restore normalcy from Governor Dr. M. Chenna Reddy.[11]

State repression was on an increase. It was the state's answer to the increasing militancy. "Instead of finding a solution to the long-pending problems, the state government started picking up the most committed innocent young Sikh and killing them in broad day light and in the vicinity of their villages to instill terror among the Sikhs," Longowal said in his letter to the Members of Parliament. The action of the state government further provided legitimacy to the Akali agitation. Both central and state governments had opted for the policy of confrontation instead of going in for a political solution.

In a knee jerk reaction, Centre banned Dal Khalsa and National Council of Khalistan on May 1, 1982. The ban, however, failed to check the escalating violence. Four persons were killed and seven others injured in a shootout in a market at Patti in Amritsar district on May 22. Reports of desecration of religious places were coming from all over. Cigarettes were found in the Darbar Sahib complex at Amritsar on May 2, while the tail of a cow was recovered from a temple at Kotkapura on May 18.

To counter the state repression against the Sikhs, Sant Bhindranwale, on June 20, gave a call to the community to gherao police stations where Amritdhari – baptized — Sikhs had been detained.

As the situation became volatile, the Amritsar police arrested Sant Bhindranwale's associate and AISSF President Amrik Singh and Gurdwara Gurdarshan Parkash manager Thara Singh on July 19. Amrik Singh and his associates had gone to the Civil Lines police station in Amritsar to enquire about two other associates of Sant Bhindranwale. All of them were arrested under the Arms Act. Amrik Singh was also charged with conspiracy to assassinate Amritsar Nirankari leader Joginder Singh Shant who had survived assassination attempt on June 27.

Sant Bhindranwale launched an agitation to press for their release. He reached the Darbar Sahib complex from his headquarters at Mehta Chowk around 2.30 PM and the first group of volunteers was out to protest at 5.00 PM. The agitation against state repression had been launched within two and a half hours. He never left the Darbar Sahib complex after that day. A group of 51 persons was to stage dharna in the Amritsar district courts everyday — the protest was to be democratic and peaceful. A convention was organised on July 25 where Sant

Bhindranwale expressed the resolve to protest the atrocities against Amritdhari (baptized) Sikhs. The agitation was no more confined to the demand for the release of Amrik Singh and his associates. The Sant also sought support from Akali Dal and Tohra attended the convention on the direction of Longowal. The fight against the state repression on the Sikh youth had now come on the agenda of Akali Dal. A year later, Amrik Singh and his associates were acquitted by the courts. However, their arrest had set the process for the shifting of Akali Dal agitation to Akal Takht. Akali Dal was to adopt Sant Bhindranwale's agitation within the next few days.

Akali Dal shifts the Morcha to Amritsar

Late in the evening on July 24, the senior leadership of Akali Dal resolved to intensify the agitation launched from Kapoori at a meeting at Fatehgarh Sahib. Once again, it was Tohra who gave a new direction to the agitation by pressing the party to confront the increasing state repression. This, in a way, also amounted to providing legitimacy to militancy indirectly. Out of power, the Akali Dal had little option under the circumstances and the party had to adopt the agenda being dictated by the SGPC chief. So, it was decided to shift the agitation from Kapoori to Akal Takht from August 4. The agitation launched by Sant Bhindranwale had been taken over by Akali Dal. The secular content of the Akali agitation got diluted with the decision to shift it from Kapoori to Amritsar. Tohra was away to Hazoor Sahib at the time Sant Bhindranwale launched the agitation. The day working committee of Akali Dal was to meet, he was asked by Longowal to proceed to Amritsar to stop Sant Bhindranwale from giving new action programme after July 29. Some Akali leaders in the working committee meeting attacked Tohra for going to Amritsar. Sant Bhindranwale asked Tohra to publicly deliver the message from Longowal to the gathering at Manji Sahib Hall in the evening to which he agreed. Tohra declared that as per the message, the Akali Dal would take over the morcha.

Earlier also, the Akali agitations had been launched from Akal Takht. It was here that the Shiromani Akali Dal had been created on December 14, 1920 with Sarmukh Singh Jhabal as its first president. The Akali agitation provided the political platform to Sant Bhindranwale and he soon occupied the centre stage.

BJP criticized this decision of Akali Dal at its state executive committee meeting chaired by Dr. Baldev Parkash at Ludhiana on August 2. They said it would affect trade and communal harmony in the state. The Akalis defended by saying that the party was adopting the morcha launched by Sant Bhindranwale to get his followers released.

At a press conference in Chandigarh on August 3, Badal specified the demands on which the agitation was to be launched. These demands included transfer of Chandigarh and Punjabi-speaking areas to Punjab, justice in the sharing of river waters with Haryana and Rajasthan, more powers to the states through the federal system, second language status to Punjabi in Delhi, Haryana and Himachal Pradesh and Sri Ganganagar district of Rajasthan, end to the eviction of Punjabi settlers in Terai and release of innocent persons. The religious demands included enactment of All India Gurdwara Legislation, live broadcasting of Gurbani from Darbar Sahib, holy city status for Amritsar and non-interference in the religious affairs of the Sikhs by the government. However, there was no reference to the Anandpur Sahib Resolution in the press note issued by Badal. The following day, the Indian Express reported: "Mr. Badal did not mention the Anandpur Sahib resolution but later took pains to explain that these demands were contained in the Anandpur Sahib resolution. He was evasive about the special status to the Sikhs as demanded in the resolution".

But Longowal had set the agenda of the Anandpur Sahib Resolution on the same day in a statement issued from Amritsar arguing that the demands contained in the Resolution were in the interests of Punjab. Subsequently, this resolution became the main theme of the morcha and that of Sant Bhindranwale. The first contingent of about 1,000 volunteers, led by Badal, offered arrest on August 4.

The Politics of Hijack

As an Indian Airlines plane on the Delhi-Srinagar flight via Amritsar was hijacked, a new dimension was added to the Akali agitation on Day One itself. Certain forces—not under the command or control of Akali Dal—whose design was to marginalise the party had also hijacked the agitation. The prevailing socio-economic forces provided the necessary space for these elements to operate and the persecution complex served a catalyst in that situation. This was the second hijack relating to Punjab militancy.

The lone hijacker Gurbax Singh—a simple middle-aged granthi (priest) from Kurukshetra district in Haryana—later surrendered as the plane was brought back to Amritsar on Lahore's refusal to let it land. During negotiations, he came out with demand of Rs. 50 lakh compensation for Sant Bhindranwale, release of Amrik Singh and declaration of Amritsar as a holy city. He was carrying a rubber ball wrapped in a piece of cloth, which was taken for a bomb. The government never came out with the forces that had planned the hijack to coincide with the launching of the morcha. The hijacker had never board an aircraft earlier. He belonged to an ordinary family and was married having kids.

Chief Minister Darbara Singh briefed the Prime Minister in Delhi on August 7 about his perception of the situation. He told her that the morcha had failed to stir the Sikh masses and quoted figures of those coming forward to court arrest to reinforce his argument. He said that while 1,100 persons courted arrest on the first day, the number came down to 65 on the following day and on August 6, it was 11.[12]

The politics of reaction of the Hindu organizations was also at play. A section of the Hindus observed fast and wore black badges in Patiala on the call given by the Vishal Hindu Sammellan on August 7 and pressed for acceptance of their demands.[13]

The Akali leadership was aware of the designs to create communal divide. Tohra took pains to clarify in Chandigarh on August 17 that the morcha was not against any community but only against the government. He explained the lack of support from other political parties on the logic that these parties had always been ranged against the Akalis right from the Punjabi Suba agitation and had joined hands with the Akali Dal only to gain power. He was hinting at the BJP.

Within days, yet another Indian Airlines aircraft flying from Jodhpur to Delhi was hijacked on August 20. Being refused permission to land in Lahore, it returned to Amritsar where the lone hijacker Manjit Singh, hailing from Putlighar locality in Amritsar, was shot dead.

A Bombay-Delhi hopping flight was hijacked shortly after it took off from Jodhpur and diverted to Lahore at gunpoint. Pakistan refused permission to land and the plane was brought to Amritsar after circling over Lahore for about an hour and a half. The demands put up by the hijacker included installation of a high power transmitter at Darbar Sahib, release of Sikh granthis, arrest of police officials involved in the murder of Kulwant Singh Nagoke and Amarjit Singh in fake encounters, control over Ravi and Beas waters and installation of Badal as chief minister. Nagoke was the first militant having been gunned down in a fake encounter ever since the militant movement started in the state. In this case also, the hijacker was an ordinary person belonging to an ordinary family. The mystery as to who financed him or who briefed him about the functioning of the aircraft was never solved. This was the third hijacking relating to militancy in Punjab. The hijacking coincided with the futile attempt on the life of Darbara Singh at Rahon near Nawan Shahr.

Bhindranwale appeals for communal amity

While refusing to comment on the incident of hijacking and the attempt on the life of the chief minister, Sant Bhindranwale said that he condemned any sort of violence and appealed to the people to remain peaceful. He pleaded for Hindu-Sikh unity and cautioned the people to be wary of designs of those who wanted to sow the seeds of dissension between the two communities. This appeal was contrary to the general perception about the man. He also allayed the apprehensions about his differences with the Akali leadership saying that the morcha was "combined and we are making all efforts to succeed in it".[14]

The government resorted to the police methods to crush the morcha by arresting the Akali leaders even at the lower level. At the same time, the chief minister ruled out any possibility of police entering the Darbar Sahib complex to arrest the leaders putting up there, including Longowal. Earlier, during the Punjabi Suba agitation, the police had entered the complex and the rulers had to pay a heavy cost for it.

Though the Akali morcha and the militant violence had no direct correlation, both were being mixed up. While commenting on the situation in Punjab, the editor-in-chief of The Tribune, Prem Bhatia talked of an "obvious sense of insecurity and fear about the future, especially in the urban centres" in his article dated September 3. The peaceful agitation launched by the Akalis was being perceived as a threat to peace. The Akali leaders were trying their best to remove such apprehensions.

Badal, Longowal oppose Khalistan

The Akali leaders were conscious of the forces at work and it was for this reason that both Badal and Longowal repeatedly distanced themselves from the radicals and dissociated from the demand for Khalistan. "We categorically state that we are opposed to Khalistan. What we want is a true federal structure in the country in which all the states enjoy more autonomy to ensure faster development", they declared in separate interviews at Amritsar and Ludhiana.[15]

The interviews Longowal and Sant Bhindranwale gave separately to senior journalist Kuldip Nayar for The Tribune on September 19 were again significant. Longowal talked of transfer of power on a substantial scale from the Centre to the states and pleaded for the setting up of a high-powered commission to recommend ways of making the constitution federal in real terms and ensure autonomy not only to Punjab but all the states. He was obviously trying to clear the misconception about the Anandpur Sahib Resolution being secessionist. While feigning ignorance about the political matters, Sant Bhindranwale threw the ball in the court of Akali Dal saying that he would abide by whatever the Akali leadership decides. Till the very end, he never wavered from this line. Longowal repeatedly said that he was opposed to the concept of Khalistan and alleged his party had been linked with the demand by the Congress to give the Sikhs a bad name. However, he talked of re-demarcation of the boundaries of Punjab incorporating the adjoining Punjabi-speaking areas as stated in the Anandpur Sahib Resolution.

NOTES

1. Quoted from the transcript of Gurcharan Singh Tohra's recorded statement in the Supreme Court.
2. She had imposed emergency in 1975 after having been unseated from the Lok Sabha by the judiciary.
3. Quoted from the transcript of recorded statement of Gurcharan Singh Tohra in the Supreme Court.
4. Punjab was trifurcated in 1966 leading to the formation of Haryana and Himachal Pradesh.
5. Young India, March 16, 1931, as quoted by Harchand Singh Longowal in his letter to the Members of Parliament.
6. The Statesman, July 7, 1946.
7. Sarhadi, Ajit Singh: Punjabi Sube Di Gaatha, Lok Geet Parkashan, Sirhind, 1992.
8. Economic Survey, 1981-82.
9. Surjeet, Harkishan Singh: Happenings in Punjab, pp. 1-2.
10. The Tribune, August 8, 1981.
11. The Times of India, June 20, 1982.
12. The Tribune, August 8, 1982.
13. The Tribune, August 7, 1982.
14. The Indian Express, August 23, 1982.
15. The Indian Express, September 10, 1982.

4

At War with India

The agitations launched by the Shiromani Akali Dal since Partition of the country were never against the Indian state but the government at the Centre. Now, for the first time, a new dimension had been added to the situation and it was no longer just an Akali agitation. It was being projected as the Sikh struggle, not just for more shares in the spoils of power but a sovereign state, though this had not been the explicit agenda in the first stage. Sant Jarnail Singh Bhindranwale, who had brought about this new dimension, never raised the demand for a sovereign Sikh state formally but this was the basic character of his radical politics that had had the traditional Akali leaders marginalized. Apparently, his agenda was to restore the lost dignity and honour of the Sikhs and end slavery, whatever that meant. On the surface, he talked of Anandpur Sahib Resolution of the Alkali Dal and his refrain would be that he was a watchdog to see that the party does not waiver from the demand for implementation of the Resolution and that he himself nurtured no political ambition. This added to his credibility among the Sikh masses. From the very beginning, he had love-hate relationship with the Akali leaders.

Though it was Sant Bhindranwale who had emerged as a symbol of the militant struggle aimed at ending "slavery of the Sikhs", Babbar Khalsa had been active all along resorting to target killings. Sukhdev Singh, a semi-literate person from Amritsar headed this militant organization but maintained a low profile and did not interact even with the media. His only public appearance used to be when he would leave Guru Nanak Niwas to pay obeisance at Darbar Sahib along with his armed to the teeth associates. The Babbar Khalsa at a later stage few months before Operation Bluestar came out with the agenda of Khalistan but not much notice of it was taken at that time. Both the groups were initially staying in the same complex managed by the Shiromani Gurdwara Parbandhak Committee.

In the context of Sant Bhindranwale and his supporters and other radicals staying in the Darbar Sahib complex, the role of the SGPC should be seen in the wake of the extraordinary relationship the complex shares with the Sikh community. This relationship cannot be explained in just the religious framework. It has played a crucial role in the religio-political sphere relating to the Sikh community all along. Ever since its inception in 1920, the Akali Dal was been functioning from the shrine complex until the mainstream Akali Dal adopted the agenda of Punjabiat and then degenerated into an ordinary political party hankering after power and the party headquarter was shifted to Chandigarh some years back.

All the Akali agitations have been launched from Akal Takht located just opposite Darbar Sahib. However, this special relationship would not justify the activities of the fully armed militants holed up there, nor the Army action. Such a situation had never developed earlier. The militant activities in the complex during the second phase of the struggle were all the more shocking. The concept underlying this shrine whose foundation stone was laid by a Muslim sufi saint Sain Mian Mir, stands on secular pillars, with doors on all the four sides open to all. The content of the Akali Dal agitation was secular. However, by the time the Akali Dal launched the Dharamyudh Morcha, the radicals had begun deepening the communal divide in the state by design.

The efforts of the radical organizations, particularly of the Dal Khalsa, to polarize the Punjabi society should be seen in the context of the strategy to consolidate the militant struggle for the establishment of a sovereign Sikh state while marginalizing the traditional Akalis who were not confronting the Indian state. Interestingly, this Sikh struggle, however, was not being identified with the Babbar Khalsa, the Dal Khalsa or the National Council of Khalistan but with Sant Bhindranwale who had not formally raised the demand for Khalistan. Though the Akali Dal and the SGPC had been hammering the issue of exclusive and separate Sikh identity, it was necessary, though not the sufficient condition, to carry forward the struggle for the Sikh state on the basis of that doctrine. The Akali Dal demand was confined to a special geo-political environment for the Sikhs in this framework of exclusive identity but the party did not press for it during negotiations with the Centre.

Historically, Sikhism evolved from the Hindu society. That's why the Sikhs and Punjabi Hindus continue to be closely-bonded communities sharing strong cultural links, though at times, some sections from both the sides have adopted the confrontationist attitude as happened with the advent of the Arya Samaj that started the efforts at hegemonisation of the Sikhs. The Rashtriya Swayamsewak Sangh too follows the same approach while treating the Sikhs as part of an extended Hindu family. The RSS efforts towards hegemonisation are resented to by the Sikh organizations. Article 25 B of the Indian constitution treats Sikhs as Hindus.

The communal divide being engineered by the radical organizations emphasized on the exclusivity of the Sikh religion. In their perception, this struggle for an independent Sikh state could not be carried forward without making the distinction between the Sikhs and the Hindus very explicit and breaking their cultural bonds. The Muslim organizations did not confront this problem at the time of the formation of Pakistan. The objective of the Dal Khalsa was very obvious and the communal politics of the radical organizations on both the sides was getting the desired communal response.

At another level, Congress too nurtured the same objective of communalizing the situation. In a way, the radical Sikh organizations, PM Indira Gandhi and the foreign forces seemed to be working in tandem towards this. Gandhi was to emerge as a saviour of the Hindus, the card that was to be played in the next Parliamentary elections. The PM's provocative threat about the fate of the Sikhs outside Punjab and the belligerent response of Sant Bhindranwale to attack Hindus should be seen in this perspective of divisive politics. The Sikhs as a community were dubbed secessionists as part of this design of the then rulers.

With the situation deteriorating, the Gandhi Peace Foundation dispatched a three-member team consisting of Rajmohan Gandhi, Dr. Sushila Nayyar and S.M. Joshi to study the deepening communal cleavage. Rajmohan Gandhi proposed: "Two political solutions are prescribed for the polarization: a Congress Akali coalition in Punjab or an Akali-BJP alliance for the future government. The first solution carries a hazard. A large number of Sikhs may disown those who accept office alongside Congressmen. Will the risk be less if partnership is attempted after a spell of President's rule? I do not know, but there is no doubt that Akali leaders will take great care before inviting the charge of being Congress' fellow travelers.

"...something very akin to the second solution was attempted in the late sixties and again in the late seventies. The flow of water down Punjab's rivers since then has weakened the foundations of any projected Akali-BJP alliance... Such an alliance may be politically wise. It may also perhaps serve the national interest. But Akali and BJP leaders would find it very hard to carry their rank and file towards it. If they push hard, the BJP leaders may find their followers drifting towards the Congress. A political solution may therefore, remain elusive..."[1]

Years later, the Akali Dal opted for an alliance with the BJP at the national level at a time when the Sikhs had virtually become untouchables. The alliance with the BJP, in a way, restored respectability to the Sikh community at the national level. It may be mentioned that the Akali Dal had entered into an understanding with the Congress in the late fifties and Akali leaders including Parkash Singh Badal had contested the 1957 elections on the ticket of that party. However, this relationship did not last long.

Earlier, in the beginning of August 1982, Communist Party of India (Marxist) senior leader Harkishan Singh Surjeet had written to Akali Dal chief Harchand Singh Longowal appealing to him "not to allow communal hatred to spread in Punjab. This is totally against the best traditions of the Akali movement, which contributed a lot in the struggle for freedom". In this lengthy letter, Surjeet recounted the anti-imperialist tradition of the Akali Dal and the party's struggle against Emergency while pointing out the dangers inherent in the Anandpur Sahib Resolution. But then maintaining communal harmony was not the responsibility of the Akali Dal alone. Despite the fact that there were no communal overtones in the agitation launched by the party, it suffered trust deficit from the very beginning.

At the same time, Akali Dal (Talwandi) launched a parallel and competitive morcha in Delhi for state autonomy and transfer of Punjabi-speaking areas left out at the time of the reorganization of Punjab. Party President Jagdev Singh Talwandi and 91 of his supporters courted arrest outside the Parliament House on August 30.

In an attempt to bring cohesiveness in the Akali stream, the Akal Takht chief intervened in the political affairs by issuing an edict (Hukamnama) on September 8 that directed Talwandi to join hands with Longowal. Akal Takht Jathedar Giani Kirpal Singh had earlier issued an appeal for Akali unity, which was turned down by Talwandi arguing that this supreme institution never issued an appeal but a directive.

The central government tried to give the impression that it was keen to resolve the Punjab tangle through dialogue. However, on October 7, Longowal rejected the appeal of Union Home Minister P.C. Sethi to suspend the agitation and resume negotiations with the government. The offer was turned down saying the Akali Dal had had five rounds of inconclusive talks with the government during the last year and that the futility of the dialogue had forced the party to resort to agitation. Significantly, the last meeting the Akali leaders had with Indira Gandhi was on April 5, 1982, much before the launch of the Dharamyudh Morcha.

The situation turned grave when four agitating Akali workers were killed in police firing outside the Parliament House in Delhi on October

11. They had gathered at the culmination of the Shardhanjali March from Anandpur Sahib to Delhi organised in the memory of 34 party volunteers in custody who were killed when the bus carrying them collided with a train at a railway crossing near Tarn Taran a month back. In Amritsar, while appealing to the party men to remain peaceful, Longowal said that the government would have to pay for its atrocities on the peaceful volunteers. The leader designated as the Morcha Dictator has to stay in the Darbar Sahib complex till the withdrawal of the agitation or arrest as that has been the tradition of the Akali Dal.

Longowal clarifies Sikh Nationhood

Both the sides, Indira Gandhi through her representatives and the Shiromani Akali Dal, continued to be stubborn on the negotiating table. With the pressure mounting from the radical organizations, the Akali Dal could not afford to dilute its struggle. Even otherwise, it was not easy to wriggle out of the situation without getting some major demands accepted. Longowal reiterated in a statement released in Delhi by Dr. Gurnam Singh Tir that "nothing short of the implementation of the Anandpur Sahib Resolution would be acceptable to the Sikhs. Nobody should unsuccessfully get frightened from the Sikhs if they claim to be a separate nation on the basis of their religion, culture and history. However, the Sikhs have the same nationality as other Indians." He made it clear the Sikhs had no design to secede from India saying they only wanted to live in the country as Sikhs, free from direct and indirect interference in their religion and way of life.

The Akali Dal issued such clarifications several times but the mistrust only grew. The media was being used to portray the Akalis as supporters of militants and secessionists. An international TV channel reporter would go to the extent of encouraging people to raise Khalistan slogans for the added effect.

Earlier, it was Parkash Singh Badal who had tried to clarify the party's position in the face of increasing attack for allegedly supporting radical tendencies. In a letter circulated to all the opposition political parties in August, he stated: "The Akali Dal has stood for communal harmony in the state and integrity and solidarity of the country. The history of the struggle of Akali Dal has always been that its morchas have been peaceful and non-violent and it shall be the strenuous effort of the Akali Dal to maintain tradition during the present struggle also." Badal referred to the demands on the basis of which the agitation had been launched. Significantly, there was no reference to the Anandpur Sahib Resolution and he only talked about "more autonomy and powers for the states throughout the country in accordance with the real federal set up". He had tried to allay all apprehensions about the agitation being communal or violent in character. It may be mentioned that even West Bengal Chief Minister Jyoti Basu had supported the Anandpur Sahib Resolution saying, "This is what has been [sic] our party insisting on and I think time has come to have a second look at the constitution to redefine the Centre-State relations in the light of the experience gained in the past 32 years. The country must accept the federal principle. Delhi is under the erroneous impression that more powers for the states will weaken the Centre. In fact, this would strengthen it."[2]

However, the perception, rightly or wrongly, was that the Akali agitation was providing the radicals the necessary space to function. And ironically, the agenda of the radicals was to marginalize the traditional Akalis. Both the radicals and Indira Gandhi were thus playing the politics to corner the mainstream Akalis. The Akali Dal attracted the charge of being communal when it projected itself as a party articulating the aspirations of the Sikhs, though its practice, especially when in power, has always been by and large secular, contrary to the general perception of its being religion based. This character of the Akali Dal—of being a Sikh-based party—is rooted in its very origin. With this historical character of the Akali Dal, the radicals could not achieve their target.

The Hindu view at that time was articulated in the following words of Virendra, President of the Punjab Arya Pratinidhi Sabha: "Those who want to understand the Punjab problem should know that for the Hindus in Punjab today, the only question is of survival. The Hindus are not interested in whether Chandigarh is given to Punjab or not or whether Punjab gets more water or less. They are interested mainly in knowing whether they can live a free and decent life in the state. During the last year more than a dozen Hindus have been shot dead by the extremists in Punjab. Many others are constantly in danger. It has also been taken for granted that a Hindu can never be Chief Minister of Punjab as also vice-chancellor of any university in the state.... The Hindus of Punjab are not going to commit a harakari. We want a strong and forceful centre. With a fully armed Pakistan across the border, we are not prepared to take any risk. We cannot afford to have 1947 repeated. Hindus in Punjab are a minority. They have every right to get all the protection that any minority in any other state can expect. No solution in Punjab will be acceptable to the Hindus of that state which does not have their consent" [3]. These views only reinforce the issue-based communal approach of one section of the population in Punjab.

Jung Hind Punjab Da[4]

About two months after launching of the agitation, Longowal circulated an open letter to the Members of Parliament in which he traced the historical background of the peaceful Sikh struggle. While recalling the contribution of the Sikhs towards the freedom struggle, he referred to the promises made by the Congress in the pre-Partition days and quoted 1929 resolution of the Congress passed at the Lahore session and the 1946 statement of Pandit Jawahar Lal Nehru in support of his arguments. He summed up the demand saying, "All that we are seeking for the last 35 years is an arrangement to safeguard the hard core of their basic socio-religious and cultural-cum-political rights. It must be emphasized that the rights we seek not only do not impinge against any of our fellow countrymen but actually enlarge their rights as well in as much as we stand for similar rights for all communities in India". Longowal's letter had put the Akali agitation in the context of Sikh struggle while maintaining a safe distance from the demand for a sovereign Sikh state raised by the radicals. And there was no ambiguity.

The demands were specified as listed here in yet another pamphlet brought out in Punjabi by Longowal:

1. End to the state repression and the killing of the innocents.
2. End to government interference in Sikh religious affairs and enactment of all India gurdwara legislation.
3. Holy city status for Amritsar.
4. Transmission of Gurbani live from Darbar Sahib
5. Autonomy on the basis of Anandpur Sahib Resolution and transfer of Chandigarh and left out Punjabi-speaking areas to Punjab.
6. Control of head works to Punjab and adjudication of river water dispute on riparian basis.
7. Second language status for Punjabi in the neighboring states. Priority to Sikhs in Army recruitment and end to injustice in central services.
8. End to the uprooting of Sikh settlers in Haryana and Uttar Pradesh.
9. Adequate central assistance.

Longowal described the morcha in the pamphlet as 'Hind-Punjab Da Jung', the way the Anglo-Sikh wars had been described by Shah Mohammad in his 'Zangnama'. The end to the state repression and the killing of the innocents in fake encounters had already come on the agenda of the party. While Badal had earlier omitted any reference to the Anandpur Sahib Resolution, Longowal talked of state autonomy on the basis of Anandpur Sahib Resolution in his letter to the non-Congress political parties.

By mid October, Sant Bhindranwale, who advocated the 1973 version of the Anandpur Sahib Resolution, seemed to have taken over the Akali agitation in practical terms, though it continued to be led by Longowal till the end. He would mobilize and address the Akali volunteers going to offer themselves for court arrest, calling upon them to remove the shackles of "slavery". At the same time, he continued to focus on the Anandpur Sahib Resolution, saying nothing less would be acceptable. His speeches used to be fiery and his communication with the masses direct. In a way, his struggle was for the implementation of the political objective as defined in the Akali Dal constitution. Of course, he differed on tactics for the implementation of the same political objective.

Several forces had been unleashed in the state by that time. For the first time since the launching of the morcha, there was trouble in front of the Darbar Sahib complex on the Ghanta Ghar side, the main entrance to the shrine, on October 18 as some anti-social elements set ablaze two passenger buses and a jeep. Small groups of people in the attire of the Nihangs moved about burning and looting shops. A Nihang was killed and another received bullet injuries when the police opened fire to disperse the unruly mob.

Later during that day, tear-gassing and baton charge took place in the district courts complex when a 300-strong jatha of Akali volunteers led by Harbhajan Singh Sandhu stormed the DC office. Six Akali workers were hospitalized. Longowal blamed the state government for engineering the trouble to discredit the morcha. The situation turned so fragile that shoot-at-sight orders were issued in Amritsar the next day.

Sikh Shanti Sena for Hindu localities

Alarmed by the incidents of arson, violence and looting near the Darbar Sahib complex, Longowal announced the decision to constitute a 50-member Shanti Sena (Peace Corps) to patrol the adjoining Hindu-dominated localities and markets. Interestingly, the area around the Darbar Sahib complex is Hindu dominated. This was part of the confidence-building measures being implemented by Longowal. However, the deep-rooted suspicion continued. The shrine is located in one corner of the Amritsar Central Assembly constituency, which is characterized by Hindu domination. It is one constituency from where only a Hindu candidate, either from the Congress or the Bharatiya Janata Party, wins always. This has been the usual pattern since the re-organization of the state in 1966.

In yet another turn of events, the Bharatiya Janata Party submitted a memorandum to the Chief Minister on October 23 demanding that injustice done to Punjab on the issue of Chandigarh and Punjabi-speaking areas, river waters and control of head works should be undone. These were some of the main issues the Akalis were fighting for. At the same time, the party "warned and cautioned the government that in the attempt to diffuse the situation, any submission before the separatist and communal demands by the government would be disastrous for the country, the state and the Punjabis as a whole. It will invite vehement opposition from all sections of people. So far as the Akali Party is concerned, it has a never-ending process for political gains. Political history of Punjab of the last three decades confirms it. In the ascending series from the regional committees in 1957 to Punjabi speaking state in 1966 to Anandpur Sahib Resolution of 1978, it is not difficult to anticipate the next move."[5] The BJP, to some extent, echoed the line of the Congress.

The state government offered what was projected as an escape route for the Akalis. Thousands of jailed volunteers were released on October 18 with an appeal from the Chief Minister to the Akali leadership, urging them to abandon the path of agitation and respond positively to the offer of talks by the PM. However, it was the compulsion of the government to release the Akalis as the jails in the state were already overflowing with thousands of Akali agitators. However, the Akalis could not withdraw the agitation without even a single demand having been accepted. Moreover, the pressure from the radicals was increasing every day, making it difficult for the traditional Akali Dal leadership to relent.

The PM once again tried to give the impression that the government favoured conflict resolution and deputed former Foreign Minister Swaran Singh to hold parleys with the Akalis. He met former Finance Minister Balwant Singh at Jalandhar on October 21 late in the night who rushed to convey the proposed package to Longowal the next day.

As the much-awaited process of negotiated settlement between the Akali Dal and the government was initiated, Devi Lal, leader of the opposition from neighbouring Haryana, threw a spanner in the dialogue process. He issued a warning on October 22 that the entire state would rise like one man to protect its rights, including the claim on Chandigarh, the Hindi-speaking areas in Punjab and the Ravi-Beas waters. He threatened to launch an agitation if the Centre tried to appease the Akalis at the cost of Haryana. Arya Samaj leader and former Minister of State for Defence Professor Sher Singh, who was also from Haryana, said that the Arya Samaj would not accept any anti-national or anti-Haryana decision.

Following the meeting with Swaran Singh on October 24, Longowal set up a five-member committee to give and seek clarifications on the party's demands. The panel members included Badal, Tohra, Balwant Singh, Talwandi and Sukhjinder Singh. Swaran Singh, who described the meeting as a good beginning, accompanied by Balwant Singh and SGPC Secretary Bhan Singh, also had a 75-minute encounter with Sant Bhindranwale. Later Sant Bhindranwale said at Manji Sahib Hall that he did not accept Swaran Singh as a mediator as "he is known for prolonging discussion without conceding anything".

Swaran Singh also met the BJP delegation led by its president Dr. Baldev Parkash at Jalandhar on October 15. The party leaders conveyed that while conceding the religious demands of the Sikhs like transmission of Gurbani live from Darbar Sahib and declaring Amritsar a holy city, interests of other religions should also be kept in mind. However, the religious demands of the Akali Dal infringed upon the interests of any other religion in no way. Still, parties and organizations claiming to articulate the interests of the non-Sikhs were expressing reservations.

In a telephonic talk with Darbara Singh, the former Foreign Minister suggested the release of Amrik Singh and Thara Singh, associates of Sant Bhindranwale. He had a long discussion with the five-member Akali panel at Fatehgarh Sahib on October 28, followed by another meeting at Chandigarh the next day. He denied making any concrete proposals to the Akalis on behalf of the PM but advised them against sticking to the Anandpur Sahib Resolution.

Every time parleys started between the Centre and the Akali Dal, the Haryana leaders would become hyperactive to oppose any proposed settlement. Rather, the shape of things to come could be assessed from the reaction in the neighbouring state. Haryana Chief Minister Bhajan Lal asserted on October 25 that the 1970 award on the transfer of Chandigarh to Punjab and Fazilka and Abohar in lieu of Chandigarh to Haryana and the 1981 award on river waters could not be reopened. He clarified that Haryana could stipulate leaving Chandigarh only if the state was provided Rs 100 crore to build its new capital along with the transfer of Fazilka and Abohar areas.

In 1970, Indira Gandhi had awarded non-contiguous Fazilka and Abohar areas to Haryana in lieu of transfer of Chandigarh to Punjab. The contiguity was to be provided by an 8-km long and 100-meter wide corridor through the Punjabi speaking Kandukhera village. The decision was unprecedented as nowhere in the country had the non-contiguous areas been transferred to a neighbouring state linked through a corridor. The 1970 award had some deeper ramifications. The transfer of this territory would have accorded riparian status to Haryana over rivers in Punjab as river Satluj flows through Fazilka area to Pakistan.

The Akali Dal panel held three more meetings with Swaran Singh in Delhi in the beginning of November. After his first engagement with the panel in Delhi, Swaran Singh had a meeting with the cabinet sub-committee comprising four senior ministers including Home Minister P.C. Sethi, Finance Minister Pranab Mukherjee, Defence Minister R. Venkataraman and External Affairs Minister P.V. Narasimha Rao, set up by Indira Gandhi to go into the inter-state issues and suggest a solution. CPI(M) leader Harkishan Singh Surjeet met Indira Gandhi to discuss the Punjab situation. Haryana leaders led by Bhajan Lal met at the residence of Agriculture Minister Rao Birendra Singh to put pressure on the Centre to protect the interests of their state. The Haryana delegation met the cabinet sub-committee. Bhajan Lal also called upon the PM and Sethi. Darbara Singh also met Sethi the same day. The members of the Akali Dal panel rushed back to Amritsar to brief Longowal. Sant Bhindranwale was also invited to the second meeting Longowal had with the panel. Badal and Balwant Singh had left the meeting by that time.

The parleys with the Centre, as usual, remained inconclusive. In that situation, the only option with the Akalis was to intensify the peaceful agitation. The situation in the state was to further deteriorate. Narasimha Rao happened to be the main negotiator on behalf of the government in most of these meetings with the Akalis.

Akalis and the Asiad: Conspiratorial distortion

The situation took an unexpected turn with the Akali Dal's announcement from the Manji Sahib stage on November 4 to send volunteers to Delhi to give court arrest everyday from November 19 onwards. The arrests were aimed to coincide with the Asian games to bring world attention to the issue and intensify the agitation. It was also decided to gherao Darbara Singh whenever he visited Punjab and not to allow him to enter the villages. Longowal said, "We will put up our case before the world and inform it about the deliberate impediments being put in the way of acceptance of our just demands."[6] The agitation in Delhi was to continue till the games were over.

However, a Chandigarh based newspaper carried a different version of the Akali Dal decision, which changed the course of events. It said, "The Akalis plan to disrupt the Asian games commencing at Delhi on November 19 in protest against the Union government's refusal to accept the morcha demands."[7] The headline of The Tribune story screamed: 'Akalis plan to disrupt Asiad'. The version had also been filed by a wire service. Both the newspaper and the wire service had deputed senior staff from Chandigarh to cover the developments at Amritsar that day. The Akali Dal had never planned to disrupt the games. This version, however, added fuel to the fire and changed the entire course of events. The Sikhs passing through Haryana were to be humiliated and harassed. The clarifications issued by Longowal the next day failed to undo the damage this malicious distortion had caused.

The media's reaction was as expected. The Indian Express commented on November 6, "It would be tragic if the Akalis have decided to abandon the negotiating table and enter the Asiad arena. This would be the path of extremism and inviting avoidable trouble.... the authorities will have to ensure that extremist action does not disrupt the Asiad and this could well necessitate stopping the jathas outside the capital." The stage had been set for humiliation and alienation of the Sikhs as a community and ultimately Operation Bluestar.

Slogans on Khalistan were raised at this convention when party leader Bibi Rajinder Kaur took the mike at Manji Sahib Hall where the decision to stage demonstration in Delhi during the Asiad was announced. She alleged that the Hindu community was on the offensive all over the country. Years later, she was gunned down by the militants on February 5, 1989. Pro- Khalistan slogans became louder and louder when former minister Sukhjinder Singh addressed the mammoth gathering. He was a former Punjab police officer who had joined politics.

Significantly, Sant Bhindranwale intervened and counseled the audience against departure from Akali Dal's programme and raising Khalistan slogans in the presence of Guru Granth Sahib. It may be mentioned here that no such slogans can be raised in the presence of Guru Granth Sahib. It is a different matter that this maryada (code of conduct) is violated frequently by raising even leader-specific slogans by the Akalis. Sant Bhindranwale and Talwandi regretted the tendency among some people to plough the lonely furrow, thus attacking Sukhjinder Singh who had been a minister in the Badal government. The stage managers switched off the mike to stop Sukhjinder Singh from raising Khalistan slogans. The traditional Akali leaders used to be very cautious about such elements raising Khalistan slogans.

Almost all the speakers pressed for acceptance of the Anandpur Sahib Resolution as a condition for the withdrawal of the agitation. Sant Bhindranwale, Longowal, Talwandi and Badal pledged their allegiance to the Resolution from the stage.

Sant Bhindranwale repeatedly used to assert that he would not allow the Akalis to backtrack from the Anandpur Sahib Resolution. At the same time, he would maintain that the resolution was not his personal agenda but the policy programme of the Akali Dal and he would see to it that it was implemented.

Reacting to this warped version of the decisions taken at this meeting, Haryana Chief Minister ordered searches of Sikhs passing through the state in trains, buses and cars, which humiliated and tarnished the entire community. Even the Sikhs in defence services who were traveling through Haryana were not spared. Longowal issued a clarification next day that the Asian games won't be disturbed. He said, "We will send jathas to New Delhi to tell the people assembled there from all over the world about our demands and the Sikh grievances. Our purpose is not to disturb the games." He regretted that such distortion of news had occurred despite the appeal to the press to be objective and truthful. Referring to the Khalistan slogans raised at the November 4 meeting, he said that everybody including the radicals condemned it. "What further proof of our patriotism does the country want?"[8] he asked. The distortion of the facts was part of the larger design as to what subsequently happened in Haryana had far-reaching consequences.

The problem that the Sikhs faced in Haryana did not end with the Asian Games. This, in fact, was the beginning. Sikhs became target of a hate campaign all over the country. I was assigned to cover Haryana in 1985. While covering a press conference of then Chief Minister Bhajan Lal in his office, I was the only journalist to be frisked by the security personnel. One of them stood near me with his automatic gun. A senior colleague from a wire agency objected to this degrading attitude. The Chief Minister was indifferent. This humiliating attitude towards the Sikhs in Haryana continued for sometime and brought Bhajan Lal on the hit list of the militants.

Reacting to the scenario in Haryana, Longowal wrote to Indira Gandhi demanding expulsion of Bhajan Lal from the National Integration Council. He said Bhajan Lal had launched a tirade and let loose the reign of terror and naked atrocities against innocent Sikhs. The Akali Dal chief had received complaints that the Sikhs who even produced interview cards, marriage invitations or death ceremony letters were not allowed to pass through Haryana.

Bhindranwale Proposes Mass Action

It was around this period that Sant Bhindranwale proposed mass action to protest against the humiliation of the Sikhs in Haryana and acceptance of demands at a meeting with the Akali leadership. He said about four lakh Sikhs should be mobilized who should march to Delhi via Haryana and gherao Parliament. He offered to seek the support of religious leaders (Sikh saints) also for this mobilization. He wanted senior Akali leaders to lead the procession. He said he himself was willing to go to Delhi along with the procession. It was a two pronged strategy. It would be a direct challenge to Bhajan Lal through this mass action and the gherao of Parliament would force the Centre to accept demands of the Akali Dal. At his meetings with the Akali leaders, he opposed the formation of 5-member committee to hold talks with the Centre as he was of the view that the Prime Minister should hold talks with the Akalis at Amritsar. "If Indira Gandhi can go to Srinagar to talk to Sheikh Abdullah, why can't she come to Amritsar", he said at the meeting.[9] The Akali leadership rejected the proposal of mass action. Acting against his advice, the Akali Dal also set up the committee to hold parleys with the Centre.

Forces dictating the political discourse were trying to portray the Sikh community secessionist; the Haryana Chief Minister was an instrument in its implementation. In Haryana, the political parties put up a united show at a November 11 meeting chaired by Bhajan Lal and gave a call to the people in the state, especially in the border districts of Sonepat, Rohtak, Gurgaon and Faridabad, adjoining Delhi, not to allow the Akalis (read Sikhs) to reach Delhi for disturbing the Asian Games. Addressing a gathering near Sonepat, he reiterated his government's resolve not to allow passage to Akalis through the state at any cost. The Sikhs and the Akalis had become synonymous. Bhajan Lal warned that the demands of the Akali Dal had provoked people in Haryana so much that it might result in some unpredictable retaliation. This statement was highly provocative.

Meanwhile, a deputation of the BJP from Punjab led by state unit President Dr. Baldev Parkash met the PM on November 4 and urged her to impress upon the Akalis to renounce the Anandpur Sahib Resolution. Sethi appealed to the Akalis to withdraw the morcha and come to the negotiating table. However, all along, the effort was to paint Akalis as villains. The Akali Dal had already renounced the 1973 version of the Anandpur Sahib Resolution.

The same day, in Delhi an official spokesman expressed regret and disappointment over the decision of the Akali Dal to spurn the offer of negotiations. He said that the PM had gone out of her way to accommodate the religious demands of the Akalis though some of these were not justified and clashed with the personal freedom of the members of other communities. The spokesman clarified that the government had also agreed to reopen award on river waters and offered to hand over Chandigarh. He alleged that the Akali leaders had rejected the government offer under pressure from the extremists. The government continued to give the impression that the Akalis, under pressure from the militants, were in no position to enter into a negotiated settlement. However, the Akali leaders questioned the sincerity of the central government all along. As the subsequent events indicated, even Sant Bhindranwale was not averse to a settlement between the Akali Dal and the government in Delhi, provided it was 'honourable'.

On November 6, Longowal averred there was still time for the government to reconsider its stand and added that the Sikhs must be treated as equal citizens and justice be given to Punjab before it was too late. He warned the government of grave consequences if it continued to stick to its "communal and obstinate" attitude[10]. Next day, he made it clear that there was no need to give further clarifications as all aspects had already been discussed with Swaran Singh.

At another level, On November 14, Chief Minister of Jammu and Kashmir Dr. Farooq Abdullah initiated a move to prepare fresh grounds for a negotiated settlement. That, however, did not generate much optimism within the Akalis. He had an hour-long meeting with the Akali high command represented by Longowal, Badal, Tohra and Balwant Singh at Amritsar where he impressed upon them to sit across table while stressing the need for flexible postures on both the sides. Later, he met Sant Bhindranwale and was optimistic that if sincere goodwill was created on both the sides, the outcome could be positive. He told Sant Bhindranwale that all should live together in India to which he responded positively. Anyway, it was his photo session with Sant Bhindranwale on the roof of Guru Nanak Niwas, which received all the more prominence in the newspapers.

The Hindu Interest

As efforts were on to find a solution to the conflict, Punjab Hindu Sangathan convener Virendra urged the Centre to take the Hindus into confidence before arriving at a settlement with the Akali Dal, arguing that the "Akali agitation" was not only a law and order problem, it had also strained relations between the Hindus and the Sikhs. Pawan Kumar Sharma and Ramesh Kumar Bhardwaj, president and general secretary respectively of the Punjab Hindu Suraksha Samiti, warned the government that the Samiti would not remain a silent spectator if the interests of the Hindus were sacrificed in a bid to appease the Akalis. They said the Samiti would not consider any sacrifice too great for the protection of the interests of the Hindus of Punjab. The representatives of the Samiti were to tour the neighbouring states in order to mobilize public opinion against the injustice perceived to be inflicted upon the Hindus in Punjab. However, it was never explained as to how the

Hindu interests were going to be affected by conceding the Akali Dal demands.[11]

The BJP's views, naturally Hindu centric, were summed by former Industries Minister Balramji Dass Tandon in a statement issued on November 8, which advised the Akalis to shun the path of agitation and confrontation and take the people of Punjab and all other political parties into confidence for achieving economic and political aims of the state and abandon the Anandpur Sahib Resolution (secessionist, communal and against the national integration), which in his perception, was a stepping stone towards Khalistan. The statement said, "The present agitation and attitude of the Akali party is doing incalculable harm to the economic and political interests of the state. No one in the state or any major political party of the state is opposed to the religious demands of the Sikhs in fundamental if their acceptance does not interfere with the followers of other religions or in their private practices.

"So far as the political and economic demands are concerned, the Akali party is not at all prepared to talk to the other political parties of the state. Unfortunately, they put every demand in the shape of discrimination against the Sikhs to which no political party of the state is going to accept. It is really strange that the Akali party is now demanding the inclusion of the major portion of Haryana and Himachal Pradesh areas they themselves have lost at the time of formation of Punjabi Suba. They have also done incalculable harm to the Punjabi language themselves."[12]

He asserted that all the major political parties in the state including BJP, Janata Party, Lok Dal, CPI and CPI (M) "are one so far as economic and political interests of the state are concerned." He summarized these interests as transfer of Chandigarh to Punjab while retaining Fazilka and Abohar areas, transferring control of head works and appropriate share in the river waters, inclusion of Punjabi-speaking areas from the neighbouring states, setting up of big industry and more financial assistance from the Centre. The problem was that it was mainly the Akali Dal, which had been taking up such demands concerning the state. Such attitude reflected issue-based communal polarization in the Punjabi society of the Indian Punjab.

At the same time, Tandon targeted the Akali Dal for allegedly helping extremists in their militant activities by offering them shelter and honouring them with siropas. At least this was his perception.

Prior to this, the BJP had submitted a memorandum to the PM and the Home Minister on November 3 demanding a round table conference of all the sections involved, political or otherwise, to diffuse the situation and create a consensus. It said, "The solution arrived at should have firm commitment from the Akalis dissociating themselves from the secessionist and communal part of the Anandpur Sahib Resolution and a seal of finality to bring a lasting peace to the state. Grab this and ask more policy of the Akalis should be put to an end... by communalizing these purely political and economic demands the Akalis did more harm to the state than good." The party also submitted a memorandum to the Chief Minister of Punjab on October 23, 1982 pressing for the acceptance of economic and political demands concerning the state. The Akali Dal had many times made a clear distinction from the radicals still the party was under the cloud.

A year back, on November 2, 1981, BJP had submitted a memorandum to then President of India N. Sanjiva Reddy stating: "Punjab is rocked with waves of turmoil threatening to destroy its peace, communal harmony and national solidarity. Demand of Khalistan, an independent sovereign state for the Sikhs, is being raised by a microscopic minority of religious fanatics. In the absence of any solid base and popular public support, its protagonists have resorted to terrorism to highlight and obtain publicity.... The demand for Khalistan is rank communal, secessionist and treason against the country.... any soft peddling of the issue and indifference to the problem which the government has been doing till now would be suicidal. Time has come when it should be dealt with heavy hand and should not be allowed to do any further harm." The political climate was being already generated for Army action.

Dr. Abdullah's intervention remained futile. In his views expressed in Delhi on November 17, an impasse had been created because of the refusal of the PM to accept the Akali demands "at gunpoint" and the unwillingness of the Akalis to withdraw their morcha without getting something tangible. The Akali Dal needed some face saving, which Indira Gandhi was not willing to provide. The design was slowly unfolding.

At the same time Surjeet, Amarinder Singh and Harvinder Singh Hanspal continued their efforts for a negotiated settlement. The problem with the Akalis was that they were caught in a vicious circle not of their making. The need at that time was to strengthen the Akalis by providing them a face saver to confront the radicals. However, the Centre's strategy was only marginalising the Akali leadership further.

The Settlement that never was

It appeared at that stage that the government was likely to arrive at a negotiated settlement with the Akalis. Senior Akali leaders Badal and Balwant Singh and Union Home Secretary T.N. Chaturvedi along with

Amarinder Singh were to fly to Amritsar at night by a special plane with the draft of the proposed agreement. The two had already informed Longowal about their visit. Quoting sources, a newspaper report said the government had accepted all the religious demands, including the arrangement for the transmission of Gurbani live from Darbar Sahib on All India Radio for two hours daily. The demand for the All India Gurdwara legislation was said to have been accepted in principle. The Centre had agreed to refer the issue of apportionment of river waters to the Supreme Court. On the territorial issue, the PM was to convene a meeting after the Asiad to give a fresh award. A commission on the territorial dispute was to be appointed following the award on Chandigarh. The Akalis did not insist on the Anandpur Sahib Resolution. However, a committee of legal experts was to be set up to go into the Centre-State relations.

Surjeet and Amarinder remained active for about 48 hours to hammer out the agreement. The PM had a meeting with the political affairs committee of the cabinet on the morning of November 18 to consider the Punjab situation. Later, she held consultations again with the 4-member committee on Punjab. Some clarifications were considered necessary by noon. Amarinder Singh was asked to contact the Akali leaders. Surjeet had a separate meeting with them. The Home Ministry had instructed the Border Security Force to keep a plane ready to fly to Amritsar anytime after 5 pm. The draft was finalised by the PM around 6 pm and it was decided to send the Home Secretary along with the Akali leaders to Amritsar to make the announcement.

However, the plane never took off. Indira Gandhi had changed her mind. Perhaps her mind had already been made and she was going ahead with the design. A major opportunity had again been wasted. The only option with the Akali Dal was to further intensify the agitation.

Earlier in the day at Amritsar, Longowal directed 37 MLAs and MPs of the party to resign from their seats before November 30 as a protest against the "cruel and authoritarian attitude of Mrs. Gandhi towards the Sikhs and their demands". He issued a statement saying, "The fundamental rights of the Sikhs to function as free and equal citizens stand denied and we cannot move freely outside our homes, villages, towns and the state.... We have been denied even ordinary freedom of movement because we happen to be a minority community. The Constitution of India has failed to provide protection to the minorities and the democracy has been set to naught." He called upon the Khalsa Panth to be ready to "make greater sacrifices as it is better to die with honour than to live in humiliation. In view of the fact that our approach to Delhi has been sealed, I call upon the Sikhs of Delhi in particular and people of minority communities and justice loving people in general to join hands and lodge a peaceful protest by organising demonstrations around the Asiad stadia so that the people gathered there may know our woes.... We want to live as part of India but the government itself is provoking us time and again to get separated."[13]

He, in the presence of Badal and Balwant Singh, denied the reports about any accord having been arrived at. Balwant Singh said, "We have given clarifications to the PM's emissary on our demands, now it is for the Centre to accept our demands."

The talks had once again ended in fiasco. The Akali leaders were taken aback when they read the draft handed over to them in the evening. The wording of the draft was materially different from what they had been conveyed verbally. The merger of Chandigarh had not been de-linked from the incorporation of Fazilka and Abohar areas into Haryana, and the findings of the high-powered linguistic commission to be specially set up for re-demarcation of the disputed areas had not been made binding on the parties concerned. Only the 1970 award had been rephrased. After about three hours of discussion, the talks broke off and the Akali leaders returned to Punjab Bhavan. Surjeet and Amarinder resumed their efforts early next day. They met Badal and Balwant Singh, members of the cabinet sub committee on political affairs and the Home Ministry officials to iron out the differences. The Akali leaders left for Amritsar by the Indian Airlines flight. Surjeet was of the view that wittingly or unwittingly, the government was feeding Sikh fundamentalism and extremism by its obstinacy and while this policy might bring the centre some dividends over a brief period, it would prove extremely dangerous to the country's integrity and sovereignty in the end.[14]

Longowal had an hour-long meeting with Sant Bhindranwale after these developments. Amarinder air dashed to Amritsar to pursue discussions with the Akali leaders. Accompanied by Rajinder Singh Bhatia and Ravi Inder Singh, he reached Amritsar on Friday night by a special plane and met Longowal. Balwant Singh confirmed that the parleys with the Centre were continuing. Meanwhile, Tohra was arrested in Delhi on November 23.

In an effort to resume the dialogue process, Swaran Singh was asked by the PM to re-establish contacts with the Akalis on the night of November 23. However, Tohra said in an interview in Tihar Jail that the mediators had no more roles to play. He left it to Indira Gandhi and Longowal to settle the issues at their own level. He declared that the agitation would continue till all the demands, including the implementation of the Anandpur Sahib Resolution, were accepted. He supported the statement of Longowal that nothing short of Anandpur Sahib Resolution would be acceptable. However, Longowal ruled out any possibility of meeting the PM until an announcement on specific demands was made unilaterally. For him, the ball was now in her court.

"The responsibility for breaking the talks does not lie with the Akalis. They had completely demarcated themselves from the extremists and their slogans," observed Surjeet.[15]

Darbara Singh met the PM on December 1 and impressed upon her the need to solve the Punjab tangle. He told her that any future negotiations with the Akalis should be conducted by a duly-authorised person like Swaran Singh. He was obviously targeting Amarinder Singh. He pressed for immediate transfer of Chandigarh to Punjab.

NOTES

1. The Indian Express, August 25, 1982.
2. The Tribune, August 18, 1982.
3. Another View of Punjab, The Indian Express, October 15, 1982.
4. Jung Hind Punjab Da (War between India and Punjab) – Shah Mohammad had described the Anglo-Sikh wars in 'Zangnama' in these words.
5. Quoted from the original memorandum.
6. The Times of India, November 5, 1982.
7. The Tribune, November 5, 1982.
8. The Times of India, November 6, 1982.
9. Quoted from the video recorded interview of Sant Jarnail Singh Bhindranwale.
10. The Indian Express, November 7, 1982.
11. The Tribune 17, 1982.
12. Quoted from the original press release.
13. The Indian Express, November 13, 1982.
14. The Tribune, November 20, 1982.
15. Surjeet, Harkishan Singh: Happenings in Punjab, p. 5.

5

Call for Armed Struggle

By now, Sant Jarnail Singh Bhindranwale had become the pivot of Sikh struggle. He would never be spotted alone and was always surrounded by his admirers and associates. Gun culture had taken over the Darbar Sahib complex. In April 1983, the assassination of Deputy Inspector General of Police Avtar Singh Atwal right in front of the main entrance of the shrine shocked everyone. I happened to meet Sant Bhindranwale in one of his rare solitary moments in the evening on the roof of Guru Nanak Niwas, which was his abode those days after a few days of this killing. He was, as usual, sitting on a cot. A few minutes into the discussion, the gruesome killing came up. I asked him what had been gained from the murder, that too at the main entrance of this holiest of the holy shrines of the Sikh faith whose interests he claimed to protect. Sant Bhindranwale was candid. He looked straight into my eyes and denied any role in the killing as was being made out at that time. His expressions could not be disbelieved. His face would normally betray his thoughts and emotions, especially during informal interactions.

The government had preferred against police entry into the shrine to nab the killers and wasted the opportunity. The situation would have been different in case the security forced had entered the shrine that day.

The build up was allowed to continue.

With the phenomenal rise of Sant Bhindranwale and the radical tinge in the Sikh political matrix becoming more and more distinct, Shiromani Akali Dal's sticking to peaceful methods was in the process of becoming irrelevant. Prime Minister Indira Gandhi adamant attitude had virtually left the Akali Dal with no soft options, which was getting increasingly marginalized and could not withdraw agitation without some tangible results despite the situation deteriorating in the state. The only choice with them was to intensify the agitation within the democratic framework. The activities of the radicals, on the other hand, were getting the desired response at every level. Centre's indifference to even the legitimate demands of the Akali Dal was creating a situation where even Akali rank and file started looking to Sant Bhindranwale for a radical action programme.

The radical struggle has its own romanticism and Sikh history is replete with examples of individual heroism. On the other hand, the martyrdom of Guru Arjan Dev and Guru Tegh Bahadur are unparalleled examples of peaceful struggle and supreme sacrifice. The Sikh religio-political history is characterized by these two extremes – peaceful and militant.

By this time, tremors of the developments in Punjab were being felt in other states too. If the design of the radical forces was to consolidate the Sikhs in Punjab by isolating them from the Hindus and what is described as the mainstream, some Hindu leaders and organizations were catering to it. Radical slogans were getting more and more space in the Sikh religio-political domain and the media. The feeling of being second-class citizens among the Sikhs was getting further reinforced. The situation was providing all the more credibility to the bucolic logic of Sant Bhindranwale. However, the interests of the Sikhs outside Punjab were different and they did not support the radicals. Even after Operation Bluestar and the mass killing of the Sikhs in November, 1984 in Delhi and some other states, there was not much change in the situation though the community got alienated from the Congress for some years. Of course, the funding from the Sikhs settled in other countries to the radicals increased manifolds. Several radical and other Sikh leaders came under attack for misusing these funds.

The statement of Haryana Congress leader Swami Adityavesh on December 3, 1982 asking Sikhs living in the districts bordering Punjab to leave the state fuelled the radical propaganda in Punjab further. In a damage control exercise, he was later suspended from the primary membership of the Congress. Haryana Congress chief Chaudhry Sultan Singh described Swami's statement as utterly irresponsible. However, what was happening in Haryana was a signal that the Centre was in no mood to accept the demands of the Akali Dal. Pressure was mounting on Akali Dal from all sides.

As SAD President and Morcha Dictator Harchand Singh Longowal called the party leadership to meet on December 10 at Amritsar to intensify the agitation, Home Minister P.C. Sethi, in a pre-emptive move, wrote to him on December 7 expressing hope that the issues will be sorted out through parleys to the satisfaction of all concerned and in the framework of the national interest. His two-page letter stressed the need for settlement of Akali grievances through a dialogue. He pleaded them not to rake up the past and felt that an amicable settlement was always possible. The letter was in reply to the communication Longowal had addressed to the Prime Minister complaining against the Haryana government. Longowal rejected the offer of resumption of talks on December 9 saying no useful purpose would be served by sitting at the negotiation table. As part of the intensification of the agitation, it was decided on December 10 that all the party MLAs and MPs would resign on January 26, 1983. The Akali Dal already had given enough time to the Centre.

Meanwhile, continuing his initiative, Swaran Singh had a long discussion with Balwant Singh at Jalandhar late in the evening on December 6. On the other hand, fed up with the delaying tactics adopted by the Centre, Shiromani Gurdwara Parbandhak Committee President Gurcharan Singh Tohra on December 8 advised the mediators to sit back home as they had no further role to play. It was for the Prime Minister to take the initiative and announce the acceptance of demands, he said.

Bhindranwale's call to get Armed

The intensification of militancy will have to be viewed in the context of the obstinate attitude of the Centre despite the fact that the Akali Dal wanted an appropriate and honourable escape route. The feeling was already growing among a section of the Sikhs that peaceful struggle alone would not produce the desired results. Sant Bhindranwale's call to get armed will have to be seen in this background. This was the first such public call by him. However, he continued to be vague about the political goal of the struggle as the militant struggle could not be just for the implementation of the Anandpur Sahib resolution that was otherwise the agenda of the Akali Dal.

The call for armed struggle was given at the convention of ex-servicemen convened by the Akali Dal at Manji Sahib. It was a chilly afternoon of December 23. The turn out was huge—much more than the organizers had expected. Among those attending the convention were two retired Major Generals, 23 retired Brigadiers and 70 retired Colonels from the Army. Sant Bhindranwale called upon the Sikhs to arm themselves and urged them to be ready to fight the repression of the government. "Eat only once a day and cut down on all your needs to get arms but these arms are not to be used against the innocent," he said.

It was for the first time since the launch of Dharamyudh Morcha that Sant Bhindranwale had given such a call and that too from the Manji Sahib Hall, which had been the Akali Dal's platform. Akali Dal's peaceful methods were not producing results and Sant Bhindranwale was emerging as the rallying point and becoming more and more relevant. The de facto leadership had passed into the hands of the young maverick leader who was getting unprecedented mass support, something that had not been witnessed in the recent years. As the call had been given at the convention organized by the Akali Dal, under the given situation, the party increasingly came to be identified with radical politics.

Several retired Sikh defence officers had already got associated with the Sikh struggle. The most notable among them was Major General Shabeg Singh who had played a key role in the dismemberment of Pakistan in 1971 leading to the creation of Bangladesh. He was the senior-most military strategist in the immediate circle of Sant Bhindranwale. From the Dharamyudh Morcha of the Akali Dal, which had been launched to get religio-political demands of the community and Punjab accepted, the situation was heading towards armed struggle for an independent Sikh state. However, none of those leading the armed struggle had given a thought as to how to confront the might of the Indian state. The topography of Punjab is not suitable even for guerilla warfare. It was not for the first time that an armed struggle had started in this state. But this time it was characteristically different. The Akali Dal, however, adopted a laid-back attitude to the call.

It is debatable whether specifying the unambiguous political goal would have made any difference to the armed struggle at that stage.The Morcha had been peaceful but a new dimension had been added to get the demands accepted through the barrel of the gun and that too by the leader who was not even a primary member of the Akali Dal.

Despite being vague at times, Sant Bhindranwale continued to hammer the Anandpur Sahib Resolution. It was only later that he began talking of Haleemi Raj (Benign state based upon the teachings of Guru Nanak) under Nishan Sahib, the Sikh flag, which is always erected on a raised platform. His refrain would be that rather than making any compromise, he would prefer to die for the cause of this Resolution. He had his own logic for the armed struggle and drawing from Sikh history, he would point out that never have two generations followed the peaceful struggle. He would cite the supreme sacrifices made by Guru Arjan Dev, 5th in succession and Guru Tegh Bahadur, 9th in succession in the most peaceful manner. Both these supreme scarifies were followed by armed struggle. He would say that the history of the Akali Dal was an exception to this tradition. He would refer to such examples from the Sikh history while calling upon the Sikh youth to form motorcycle borne armed squads in every village to seek justice.

Col Joginder Singh Mann, father of Simranjit Singh Mann who later resigned from the coveted Indian Police Services, proposed at the convention that Sant Bhindranwale be appointed to the exalted office of Akal Takht Jathedar. Longowal agreed to recommend the proposal to the SGPC, which was later supported by the AISSF at its convention on January 2. The AISSF also threatened to launch Assam-type agitation in case the problem in Punjab was not resolved by January 26. The AISSF too was ambivalent on the political goal though at an early stage, the organization supported the demand for Khalistan.

The Armed Struggle

The government continued to give an impression that it was sincere in sorting out the Akali demands. The year 1983 started with Swaran Singh having an hour-long meeting with Pranab Mukherjee, P.C. Sethi and R. Venkatraman on the night of January 3. Sethi again invited the Akalis for talks and was sent to Longowal on January 6. He said that either Longowal or his nominee could interact with the members of the cabinet sub-committee either at Delhi or Chandigarh. As usual, Balwant Singh and Amarinder Singh were also active behind the scene during this period.

The convention of ex-servicemen was followed by a meet of Sikh intellectuals on January 9, 1983, who assured Longowal that they would stand by him in pursuit of his mission. The convention was again a big draw. Sant Bhindranwale shared the stage with Akali leaders including Badal, Tohra, Talwandi, Barnala and Sukhdev Singh Dhindsa. While demanding federal structure for the country, the convention expressed concern at what was described as gradual erosion of fundamental rights of the people. Through another resolution, it demanded dual citizenship for the non-resident Indians. The Akali Dal was trying to mobilize support of various sections of the Sikh community, including the global Sikhs.

Sant Bhindranwale symbolized the radical stream in the Sikh political matrix and at the same time, he shared the stage with leaders who differed with him on the means of achieving the common political objective, which, till then, was the Anandpur Sahib Resolution. However, though the Akali leaders preferred to maintain stoic silence on the approach of Sant Bhindranwale towards common issues, their presence with him provided him legitimacy. Of course, Sant Bhindranwale did not raise the slogan of Khalistan and traditional Akali leaders repeatedly distanced themselves from this slogan raised by some radical organizations. His relevance was increasing among the masses with every passing day. His down-to-earth logic was convincing and his simple lifestyle added to his credibility.

While Sant Bhindranwale's popularity was on the rise, the Centre continued the exercise of parleys with the Akali leaders. The prospects of a solution seemed to have brightened after two rounds of talks extended over five hours on January 11 between members of the cabinet sub-committee and the Akali leaders in Chandigarh. The Akali team included Badal, Tohra, Barnala, Talwandi, Sukhjinder Singh, Balwant Singh and Ravi Inder Singh. The discussion centered on a nine-point plan including four religious demands, the main agenda being the Centre-State relations, river waters dispute and the transfer of Chandigarh. The team offered to refer the river waters dispute to a serving or retired judge of the Supreme Court with suitable terms of reference. The Punjab government also submitted a note to the central team on the territorial and other issues. Mediators such as Swaran Singh and Amarinder Singh had prepared ground for the meeting. Amarinder also attended the meeting. On the Akali Dal demand for the transmission of Gurbani live from Darbar Sahib, the members of the cabinet sub-committee talked about similar demand from some other communities to which the Akalis said they had no objection. Regarding the enactment of the All India Gurdwara Legislation, the central ministers favoured seeking views of other states also. On the river waters issue, the alternate proposal considered was allocating one MAF of water to Rajasthan from river Narmada in exchange for the reduction of Rajasthan share from the Punjab river waters.

On the transfer of Chandigarh, the central team was for implementing the 1970 award of Indira Gandhi, which was subject to the condition of transfer of Fazilka and Abohar areas to Haryana. Another proposal to divide Chandigarh between the two states was rejected by the Akali leaders. The central team made it clear that the chief ministers of the states concerned would be consulted before finalizing any settlement with the Akalis. The talks again remained unproductive.[1]

In none of these rounds did the government talk to the representatives of the radicals who provided the vital third dimension to the situation in the state. As the talks resumed, a spurt was observed in the activities of the militants. Bomb explosions rocked the state and the intensified violence put a question mark on conflict resolution by talking to the Akali leaders alone. This pattern was to continue through the coming months. Whenever the dialogue process started, a sudden spurt in violence was observed.

The violence did not suit the Akalis and the militants were not under their control. Their strings were being pulled from elsewhere. The Indian Express noted January 11, 1983: "There is a discernible pattern in the activities of the terrorists and similar incidents occurred earlier whenever there was any effort to resolve the Punjab crisis. And there is no guarantee that terrorism will abet once the agreement is reached between the Centre and the Akalis." Sant Bhindranwale symbolized the radical stream but his refrain was that he was only a religious leader and the government should hold talks with the Akali Dal leaders.

The same day at Amritsar, Longowal warned that the country would be on fire in case the Centre rejected the Akali demands. He said the Centre had no option but to grant the genuine rights of the Sikh community. On resuming talks with the Centre, he said, "There is no question of compromising on the genuine Akali demands and the Sikhs' grievances".[2]

Another round of inconclusive talks between the cabinet sub-committee and the Akalis ended on January 18 in Chandigarh. The central team consisted of Sethi, Energy Minister Shiv Shankar, Venkataraman and T.N. Chaturvedi. Apart from Badal, Tohra, Talwandi, Barnala and Balwant Singh, the Akali team included Ravi Inder Singh. Amarinder Singh accompanied the central team to Chandigarh but did not participate in the parleys. On the territorial issue, the central team referred to the need for dividing Chandigarh between Punjab and Haryana to compensate the latter for the notional "loss" of Fazilka and Abohar areas. The proposal was rejected by the Akalis in no uncertain terms who maintained that linguistic principle should be upheld in keeping with the Congress Working Committee resolution on the reorganisation of the states. The Akali Dal representatives suggested that Haryana could be given some Hindi-speaking areas from Uttar Pradesh or Delhi. The central team cited the example of Berlin in favour of the proposal to divide Chandigarh. The Akalis countered this argument saying that the division of Berlin was between two countries and that too, caused by war.

AISSF General Secretary Harminder Singh Sandhu, on January 17, threatened to stage protests on January 26 in case the Centre continued with the delaying tactics, which did not prove just rhetoric as three bomb explosions were reported in Amritsar on the Republic Day. Earlier on November 30, 1982, this organization had given the call to gherao ministers and disturb their public meetings in case they continued to oppose the Akali agitation.

The behavioural pattern of a section of population in Punjab and the deepening communal divide during that period could be observed from the attitude of the Punjab Hindu Surakasha Samiti, which opposed transfer of Chandigarh to Punjab and favoured status quo. At the same time, Samiti chief Pawan Kumar Sharma, who belonged to Patiala and had links with some Congress leaders, talked of the "old Punjab".[3] He demanded enactment of Punjab Mandir Act on the pattern of the Sikh Gurdwara Act. The Samiti submitted a memorandum to Governor M. Channa Reddy seeking an end to the alleged discrimination against the Hindus in the state. The memorandum demanded proportional representation to the Hindus in the state services and warned that the Hindus would be forced to take up arms for self-defence if the government failed to protect them.

Competitive communalism was brewing. The Samiti did not spell out its objections to the transfer of Chandigarh to Punjab but was being used against the Akalis.

Tohra's Resignation

The talks with the Centre were deadlocked once again. The Akali leaders began subscribing to the prevalent view that the Prime Minister was in no mood to accept their demands. Tohra made his views on the situation public in Patiala on January 19. He said there was no hope left for a negotiated settlement. Earlier in the morning, he had submitted his resignation from the presidency of SGPC to Longowal who had sought resignation of its executive members by January 25.

The air was thick with pessimism, especially in the domain of the moderate Akali politics. In an attempt to mount pressure on the Centre, Longowal announced from the Manji Sahib Diwan Hall on January 20 that the resignations of all the party MLAs and the MPs would be forwarded to the authorities concerned on January 27, 1983. The effort was to avoid a showdown on Republic Day, the day when the resignations would be forwarded.

As the Akali Dal continued to resort to the democratic methods of protests and agitation, from the same stage, Sant Bhindranwale repeated his call to the Sikh youth to arm themselves as a crucial battle was in the offing.[4] Sant Bhindranwale was repeatedly giving such calls but the government did not initiate any action against him. Arms and ammunition were also being smuggled into the shrine. There were no checks. It was at a much later stage that a consignment was confiscated. It is this situation which raises questions about the role of then ruling Congress in the build up to Operation Bluestar. This situation should have been thoroughly investigated to find out the truth. However, this was never done. Almost all the intelligence agencies had their sources in the Darbar Sahib complex. Amritsar was the only district in Punjab which had the post of Superintendent of Police (Intelligence) of the state intelligence wing. The Intelligence Bureau and the Research and Analysis Wing had their own set ups. Being the centre of Sikh politics and close to international border, Amritsar had always been under close watch of the intelligence agencies.

Two divergent political tendencies had distinctly emerged in the Sikh political matrix by this time.

The cabinet sub-committee had an hour-long discussion with Haryana Chief Minister Bhajan Lal and his Rajasthan counterpart Shiv Charan Mathur in Delhi on January 20 on the territorial and the river waters issues. As expected, the leaders strongly opposed the reopening of river waters issue. At the same time, Bhajan Lal reiterated the demand for the implementation of the 1970 award on territorial dispute. Darbara Singh was also invited to join the futile exercise but he did not attend the meeting.

On January 21, Gandhi consulted the opposition parties in Delhi and the dominant view was that an invitation be sent to the Akalis to a tripartite meeting for considering the problem arising out of their demands. The 10 opposition parties were represented by Charan Singh (Lok Dal-C), Atal Behari Vajpayee (BJP), Indrajit Gupta (CPI), Harkishan Singh Surjeet (CPI-M), K.P. Unnikrishnan (Cong-S), Ramvilas Paswan (Lok Dal-K), G.M. Banatwallah (Muslim League), Harikesh Bhandari (DSP), Piloo Modi (Janata) and Satyavani Muthu (AIADMK). From the government side, Venkatraman, Mukherjee, Sethi, Narasimha Rao, Shiv Shankar and Parliamentary Affairs Minister Bhishma Narain Singh attended besides the Prime Minister.

Amarinder flew to Amritsar with Ravi Inder Singh and handed a formal invitation to Longowal on January 22. The Akalis once again decided to respond positively to the invitation. The team deputed for the talks included Barnala, Balwant Singh and Ravi Inder. It was evident from the constitution of the team that the top Akali leadership had some reservations about the outcome of the meet. Senior leaders would have been assigned the job in case there had been signals that the issue would be clinched. It was because of this apprehension that Sant Bhindranwale advised the Morcha dictator against sending the team to Delhi.

First round of the talks on January 24 remained inconclusive. A solution to at least two demands was in sight in the five-hour meeting the next day. The government postponed the discussion on the territorial issue to the next meeting the date for which was to be decided later. It was agreed upon to appoint a high-powered committee compromising jurists and constitutional experts to review the Centre-State relations and make suggestions for ensuring a truly federal form of government for the country. However, this was agreed to only after the Akali team was persuaded to give up its insistence on specific reference to the Anandpur Sahib Resolution. The Akali team was being flexible.

Reopening the issue of sharing of river waters was also settled. The government agreed to invite the chief ministers of Punjab, Haryana and Rajasthan to the next tripartite meeting.

Akali leaders said that reopening the agreement on river waters was a big gain. Both Barnala and Balwant Singh expressed satisfaction. Indira Gandhi had consultations with her cabinet colleagues and senior officers to prepare a draft. Congress General Secretary Rajiv Gandhi and Alexander were also involved in the exercise. The effort was to avert the January 27 crisis relating to the submission of resignations by Akali legislators.

The legislators and MPs submitted their post-dated resignations effective from February 21 to Longowal on the night of January 26 for forwarding the same to the authorities concerned. The post-dated resignations aimed at giving more time to the Centre in view of the tripartite talks. Sant Bhindranwale, on the other hand, wanted them to quit immediately. The resignations, dated January 27, were handed over to Assembly Secretary Partap Singh by Badal the next day at 4.45 pm.

A statement issued on the occasion said, "We are left with no other course except to resign our seats in the legislature with a strong sense of anguish and protest. We owe this to our electorate and the people of Punjab before whom we pledged to fight for the protection of the rights of the state and the Sikhs... For more than a year, the Akali Dal has been agitating for the acceptance of the demands that are just, genuine and patriotic.... The government chose to adopt ambivalent attitude. Consequently, our agitation passed through various phases and it saw endless stream of people marching to the jails, merciless killings by the Punjab police and infliction of humiliation on the Sikhs on the national highway No. 1. While the Akali demands relate to the undoing of the wrongs done to Punjab over the years, especially on matters like the distribution of river waters, Chandigarh, Punjabi-speaking areas and the Sikh minority rights within the framework of the Indian constitution, the government complicated the matters by bringing in other states in a big way and dubbing these demands as separatist through their media." In Delhi, four Alkali MPs submitted their postdated resignations to the presiding officers of the two houses of the Parliament.

The decision to submit the resignations was taken at a meeting of the senior party leaders, which was ratified by the legislators and the district jathedars on January 26. The party also decided to boycott the elections to the Delhi Metropolitan Council and the Delhi Municipal Corporation where the Sikhs have a sizeable population.

Yet another round of futile talks began in Delhi on February 8. As expected, Bhajan Lal and his Rajasthan counterpart Shiv Charan Mathur, at separate meetings with the cabinet sub-committee, did not agree to the reopening of the 1981 agreement on the sharing of Ravi-Beas waters. This was followed by the tripartite meeting, which again remained inconclusive. On the territorial issues, the perception of senior BJP leader L.K. Advani was that the Akalis were demanding areas from the neighbouring states to unite the Sikh-dominated areas and the demand was not just aimed at merging linguistically contiguous regions. It was clear that some leaders in the country felt the demands of the Akali Dal were a step towards the setting up of a Sikh state. Ironically, most of the Punjabi-speaking areas in the neighbouring states of Haryana, Himachal Pradesh and Rajasthan, being sought to be transferred to Punjab, were Hindu dominated, as such, the apprehensions of leaders such as Advani were unfounded. Still, the demand aroused suspicion against the Akalis. The proposal to refer the issue of transfer of Chandigarh to Punjab and Fazilka and Abohar tehsils to Haryana was opposed to by the Akalis as a quid pro quo to a commission.[5] The Akali Dal would have never come to power at its own if these areas had been transferred to Punjab. The Sikhs would have been reduced to a minority in that Punjabi state.

For the next round of negotiations, the Akali delegation had Balwant Singh, Barnala and Ravi Inder Singh on board. Members from the opposition included Advani, Madhu Dandvate, Chandrajit Yadav, Surjeet, Gulam Rasool Kochak, Dr. Sarup Singh and Harikesh Bahadur. Both Badal and Tohra were also present in Delhi for on-the-spot consultations. The thrust was on resolving the territorial dispute. Bhajan Lal and leaders of other political parties also had a two and a half-hour meeting with the cabinet sub-committee in the morning. These leaders included Chaudhary Sultan Singh, Dr. Sarup Singh, Devi Lal, Mangal Sein, Chandravati, Om Parkash Malik, Baldev Tayal, S.C. Mahanta, Rao Nihal Singh and Irrigation Minister Shamsher Singh Surjewala. The Haryana delegation pressed for the implementation of 1981 agreement on river waters.

Chief Minister of Rajasthan and the state opposition leaders also opposed reopening of the river waters issue. Mathur was accompanied by his Irrigation Minister Paras Ram Maderna and leaders from the political parties in opposition in the state, who included Raj Bahadur, Bhairon Singh Shekhawat, Lacchu Ram, Virendra Partap and Megh Ram.

The differences on the formulation of the draft for a fresh review of the river waters issue stalled the progress of the tripartite talks on February 10. The differences continued to persist on the territorial issue also. Sethi told the meeting that the Haryana and Rajasthan chief ministers who met him earlier during the day had opposed the reopening of the river waters issue. He presented the draft proposing that water dispute be referred to an inter-state tribunal. Status quo should be maintained with non-riparian Rajasthan on the 1955 agreement and the digging of the SYL canal should continue. All the three states should continue getting waters according to their present allocation till the tribunal gave its verdict and the 1981 agreement be scrapped and the 1976 notification withdrawn. The Akalis objected to the inclusion of the clause protecting Rajasthan's share under the 1955 agreement. They pleaded that if the 1955 agreement was retained, then the 1981 agreement could not be reviewed because Rajasthan got extra water under the 1981 accord on the basis of the 1955 agreement. The government reminded the Akalis that they had earlier given an assurance against reopening of the 1955 agreement. Almost all the opposition leaders told the Akalis they had changed their stand on this issue. The Akali leaders quoted another draft presented by Surjeet at one of the earlier meetings, which envisaged the reopening of the waters issue on the same lines as put forward by Sethi without any reference to the 1955 agreement. The attitude of the Akali leaders to the draft prepared by Surjeet was positive. The opposition leaders made it clear to the Akalis that they would not support them on this issue in case they pressed for the reopening of the 1955 agreement also. The agreement had been engineered by the Centre as a precursor to the signing of the Indus Water Treaty with Pakistan. This agreement had not been signed at the level of the chief ministers but at the lower level.[6]

There was no breakthrough even at the third round of the talks held on February 15. The Akali delegation proposed setting up of a tribunal by scrapping 1976 and 1981 agreements while maintaining that Rajasthan, a non-riparian state, did not have any legal rights over Punjab river waters. Balwant Singh insisted that after abrogating the 1976 and the 1981 agreements, the dispute should be referred to the Tribunal to be set up under the Inter-State Waters Disputes Act, 1956. "We want to go before the Tribunal as citizens and not with fetters or as criminals. We are patriotic people and believe in the integrity of the country," he said. The Akali leaders argued that it was the duty of the Centre to see that the law of the land was enforced and if any chief minister stood in the way, he should be bypassed. As per the constitution of the country at that time, such a tribunal could be constituted only to resolve a dispute between co-riparian states. However, neither Haryana nor Rajasthan were co-riparian to Punjab rivers. The Act was later amended while setting up the Eradi Tribunal under the Rajiv-Longowal Accord in 1985.

The Akali representatives reiterated that under the 1955 agreement, erstwhile East Punjab and Pepsu were allocated 7.2 MAF of water and

Rajasthan 8 MAF and Haryana was not covered by the agreement not because it did not exist at that time but because part of that region lacked gravity flow and was considered more suitable for lift irrigation. The Akali leaders argued that the 1976 award allocating 3.5 MAF each to Punjab and Haryana was neither legally tenable nor ethically correct. The Akali leaders also refused to accept the revised figures on the water flow under the 1981 accord saying they were inflated.

The Akalis continued to oppose the allocation to Rajasthan on two counts. One that Rajasthan was not a riparian state according to the universally-accepted definition of the term, the second being Rajasthan's failure to honour another part of the 1955 agreement under which it was to give five acres of land each to about 25,000 Punjabi families to be settled in the area to be irrigated by the Rajasthan canal. The participants proposed that the 1981 agreement be reopened provided it was agreed to ensure not less than 6.5 MAF of waters to Rajasthan. This proposal was rejected by the Akalis.

In a significant shift in the stand of his party, BJP leader Dr. Baldev Parkash said in Amritsar on February 17 that the river waters accords and awards were political in nature and not based on principles of equity, justice and fair play. The Centre should not hesitate to perform its duty merely because the chief ministers of Haryana and Rajasthan did not want to undo the wrong done to Punjab. On the territorial issue, he said Chandigarh should be transferred to Punjab without further delay and a commission of legal experts should be constituted to demarcate the remaining Punjabi-speaking areas. Abohar and Fazilka could not be transferred to Haryana, he said, as the very concept of corridor between the two states was preposterous. He advocated more powers to the states to ensure rapid development and greater administrative efficiency.[7]

The territorial and the river waters issues were discussed in a meeting of the Cabinet sub-committee on February 17, chief ministers of Punjab, Haryana and Rajasthan, leaders from the opposition in Haryana and in the Parliament. Haryana CM was accompanied by Devi Lal, Dr. Mangal Sein and Chandravati, Rajasthan Chief Minister was present along with Irrigation Minister Paras Ram Maderna and the Cabinet committee consisted of Sethi, Venkataraman, Shiv Shankar, Buta Singh, Alexander and Chaturvedi. The opposition leaders included Dandvate, Advani, Unnikrishnan, Surjeet, Dr Sarup Singh, Harikesh Bahadur, S.C. Mohanta and Ghulam Rasool Kochak.

Bhajan Lal opposed the reopening of the waters issue and pressed for the 1970 award to settle the territorial dispute. He said that in case the issue was to be reopened, Haryana's share should be raised from

3.5 MAF to 3.86 MAF in accordance with the 1976 award under which Punjab and Haryana were to be given an equal share. He pointed out under the 1981 award, Punjab's share was raised to 4.22 MAF but Haryana's share was kept at 3.55 MAF. He proposed that the capacity of the SYL canal be increased to 4 MAF. On the territorial issue, he suggested in case the Centre did not want to implement the 1970 award, the entire dispute including the areas of Kharar tehsil, Chandigarh, Fazilka and Abohar should be referred to a judicial commission. Rajasthan Chief Minister initially opposed the reopening of the agreements on river waters but later agreed, provided its share was protected. Dandvate, Surjeet and Yadav pointed out that the present leadership of the Akalis belonged to the moderate section and it would be in the interest of all to come to some settlement with this leadership. The consensus was that the Akalis should be persuaded to agree to the reference of waters dispute to a tribunal without disturbing the 1955 apportionment.

Five proposals were discussed on the territorial dispute at the over 3-hour tripartite meeting on February 18 out of which two were mooted by Yadav and Unnikrishnan, two by two other opposition leaders and the fifth was informally mooted by the government representatives. Yadav's proposal suggested that Chandigarh should be awarded to Punjab, which should hand over 17 villages to Haryana as compensation. All other territorial disputes, including Fazilka and Abohar, should be referred to a high-powered commission for adjudication. Unnikrishnan suggested that the Centre should award Chandigarh to Punjab immediately and all formalities about its transfer be completed by April 13, 1983. The Centre should give an outright grant of Rs. 25 crore and a loan of the like amount to Haryana to construct its new capital. A one-man boundary commission should be constituted to examine the census revenue records till January 1, 1983 regarding the linguistic composition of Punjabi- and Hindi- speaking villages transferred to the Union Territory in 1966, of Fazilka and Abohar and all other villages along the Punjab-Haryana border, which the two states claimed as their own. The report should be submitted by March 31 and that the government should announce its award on the basis of the report of this commission and the principle of contiguity by April 5. Division of Chandigarh on 60:40 proportions was also suggested. The informal suggestion from the Centre was that the representatives of the two states should sit across the table to arrive at some amicable solution or authorize the Centre to appoint non-North Indian linguistic experts to re-demarcate the disputed contiguous areas. The Akalis favoured the Yadav formula with a slight modification that instead of referring the territorial dispute to a commission, the views of the village panchayats should be respected; Bhajan Lal, however, opposed this. The CPI was then being represented by Yogendra Sharma.

Another meeting was held on February 19 and before that meeting, the Haryana delegation proposed division of Chandigarh and the reference of the other disputed areas to the commission. Chandravati and Mangal Sein pressed for implementation of the 1970 award.

It again turned out to be an exercise in futility. The talks ended on February 20 without arriving at any settlement. Even an attempt to involve Rajiv Gandhi, MP, could not end the stalemate. The territorial and the waters issue were discussed by Balwant Singh and Ravi Inder Singh with Gandhi for more than an hour where Krishnaswami Rao Saheb, Alexander and Amarinder Singh were also present. It was Amarinder who had taken the two Akali leaders to the PM.

At the tripartite meeting, the first session was spent on informal discussions as Sethi had gone to Assam and joined the talks only in the second session. Only Mukherjee and Buta Singh were present along with the officials. The Akalis made it clear that a solution could be found to the territorial dispute provided their demand on the waters issue was accepted. The Rajasthan leaders who were invited to the meeting later reiterated their stand that the 1955 division should not be disturbed. They pointed out Punjab's dispute was with Haryana and till 1979, Punjab had never mentioned Rajasthan's name in this dispute. The Akalis disagreed but on the opposition's persuasion, agreed not to disturb Rajasthan's share.

Next, differences cropped up on the formulation of the draft on river waters. The Akalis, the government and the leaders from opposition had agreed to the clause of the draft, which proposed that the 1981 agreement should be rescinded, the 1976 notification withdrawn and the dispute between Punjab and Haryana referred to a tribunal. On the last clause, which stipulated that till the tribunal's award is given, the present "allocation" of water should be protected, the Akalis said that instead of allocation, it should be "utilization". The opposition also pleaded with the government not to insist on allocation. Sethi said he would have to consult leaders from Haryana before accepting the draft. This bogged down the talks again. Haryana was not in a position to utilize its entire allocation in view of the limited capacity of the carrier channels. The Akali Dal, at the time of its signing or even during the immediate succeeding years, had never objected to the 1955 agreement, which allocated share to Rajasthan.[8]

Surjeet had perhaps anticipated the situation in the wake of the deadlock. In a letter dated February 22, he urged the Prime Minister to end the standoff. He wrote: "The deadlock in the talks will be helpful only to the extremists and everybody else feels concerned about it." He also referred to the clear demarcation made by the Akali leaders from separatist tendencies. With reference to the tripartite meeting, he said, "As was seen in the talks, the Akali representatives were reasonable and accommodative. After having agreed on the reference of the water dispute between Haryana and Punjab to a tribunal, the talks broke on the issue whether in the interim period, the existing supply should be allowed to continue or the allocation made in 1981 agreement should remain. The first proposal was originally made by me and accepted by the Akalis and Opposition parties. But in practice, it does not make any difference even if the second proposal is accepted because the digging of the canal will take two years and till then, Haryana cannot use the surplus waters and the government can ensure that the tribunal does not take more than a year to decide... Therefore, I request you to take the initiative to solve the tangle so that the divisive forces can be isolated and the game defeated."[9] There was no response from the Prime Minister.

Akali Dal MP Rajinder Kaur quit the Rajya Sabha on February 21 as a peaceful protest against the rejection of demands of the people of Punjab by the Centre. She said that the courting arrest by 82,000 persons during the last nine months had gone to prove that the agitation was legitimate. Even during the Quit India Movement, not more than 62,000 people had courted arrest in the country. She regretted that even the law of the land had been denied to the Sikhs. The denial was basically with reference to the river waters dispute as in case of other water disputes in the country, it was the riparian principle which had been followed till then. In this case, both Rajasthan and Haryana were non-riparian states, though Haryana was a successor state.

In an effort to break the impasse, the Punjab Chief Minister reached Delhi on February 25 with a new formula. He met Sethi and other members of the sub-committee individually. Later, he discussed the latest situation with six Congress (I) MPs from the state including Sat Pal Mittal, H.S. Hanspal, (both from Rajya Sabha), Rajinder Singh Sparrow, Gurbrinder Kaur Brar and Sukhbans Kaur Bhinder. He proposed: (a) Chandigarh should be transferred to Punjab; (b) Ghaggar, a seasonal rivulet, should be the dividing line between Punjab and Haryana; (c) If Ghaggar is accepted as the natural boundary between the two states, about 75 Punjab villages would go to Haryana; and (d) These villages should be regarded as compensation to Haryana for the loss of Chandigarh and for giving up its claim over Fazilka and Abohar. The PM rejected this too.

Acceptance of Three Religious Demands

Prime Minister Indira Gandhi announced unilateral acceptance of three religious demands of the Akali Dal on February 27. These demands included removal of liquor, tobacco and meat shops from specified areas around the Darbar Sahib complex, direct transmission of kirtan from the Darbar Sahib by Jalandhar station of the All India Radio and permission to the Sikhs to carry a nine-inch kirpan with a six-inch blade on the Indian Airlines flights. She also announced the removal of liquor and tobacco shops around the Durgiana Mandir on the pattern, which was not part of the Akali Dal demands but had been done to placate the Hindus. The demand for the enactment of All India Gurdwara Legislation was accepted in principle. She made the announcement at a huge gathering at Gurdwara Bangla Sahib in Delhi. The visit had been organized purportedly to thank the Sikhs of Delhi for their support to the Congress in the recent elections of the Delhi Metropolitan Council and the Municipal Corporation. She said that while certain portions of the historic kotwali in which Guru Tegh Bahadur was detained had been handed over to the Delhi Sikh Gurdwara Management Committee, the remaining portion would be transferred within three months. About 75,000 Sikhs had gathered there that day. The Sikhs in Delhi had been traditional supporters of Congress till November 1984.

However, the announcement failed to mollify the Akalis. Party MPs and MLAs submitted a memorandum to President Giani Zail Singh on March 2 in Delhi pleading him to resign from office in protest against the humiliation of the Sikhs. The Akali Dal had voted for him in the presidential elections.

Meanwhile, the state executive of the BJP, at its meeting at Pathankot on March 7, reiterated that the waters accord should be scrapped and the dispute referred to a tribunal. The party had echoed the Akali stand on these issues earlier also.

Longowal Calls for Decisive War

The situation was heading towards total confrontation. It was in this context that Longowal gave a call to the people on March 13, 1983 to be ready for a long-drawn, decisive war. He said though more than 95,000 volunteers had courted arrest and 120 sacrificed their lives, the union government, under its "communal thinking", had been dilly-dallying the acceptance of legitimate, constitutional and legal demands. The Punjabis in general and the Sikhs in particular had no other alternative but to wage a decisive war. Perhaps since independence, in no other political agitation in the country had so many people gone to jail. This had perhaps been an unparalleled example of a peaceful agitation in the post-Partition period.

Ever since the Akali Dal came up as a political party during the Gurdwara Liberation Movement, their agitations had been one of the most peaceful. Historically, the Sikh matrix has been characterised by both peaceful and radical streams. The morchas launched by Akali Dal had been examples of peaceful agitation even in the face of the brutal state repression. The Dharamyudh Morcha was in the same tradition. However, the activities of the radicals and the Dharamyudh Morcha were being mixed up and such a situation suited the forces behind the grand design. Bhajan Lal, on March 16, suggested the division of Chandigarh along the Madhya Marg, with the Capitol Complex side going to Haryana.

As part of the implementation of the design, support was being mobilised for attacking the Darbar Sahib complex. In the absence of the Akali members who had resigned, Punjab Assembly adopted a resolution on March 25 expressing concern over the growing tendency in the state to defile and desecrate the sanctity of religious places and desired that the SGPC should hand over criminals taking shelter in the Darbar Sahib complex to the police.

The resolution had unconditional support from the CPI while the CPI (M) was critical with its legislator Balwant Singh taking the line that the state government was trying to sidetrack the main issue of deteriorating law and order situation by focusing only on the misuse of gurdwaras by the extremists. He alleged it was the state government, which had propped up Sant Bhindranwale. He was apprehensive that the government might order the police to enter the shrine after getting the resolution passed and warned of serious consequences if such an action was taken. He traced the root of the problem to the delay in accepting the demands of Punjab. CPI group leader Raj Kumar proposed that the resolution be adopted unanimously. It was the Amritsar district unit of the CPI, which later passed a resolution demanding the deployment of Army in the border district later in early 1984. This resolution was subsequently withdrawn at the intervention of the party's central secretariat.

Sant Bhindranwale on Khalistan

Within two days of the resolution having been adopted by the Punjab Assembly, on March 27, Amritsar police registered a case against Sant Bhindranwale under section 506 IPC for delivering inflammatory speeches. According to the FIR, the Sant had named some local police officers and called upon the people to take revenge against them. Earlier in 1981, a case against him had been registered in connection with the murder of Lala Jagat Narain, owner and editor-in-chief of the Hind

Samachar group, in which he was acquitted and another under the Arms Act.

By then, Sant Bhindranwale had assessed the situation and the grand design was clear to him. His historic speech at Manji Sahib on March 27 about Khalistan has to be seen in this context. "If the police enter the Golden Temple, nobody would be able to stop the creation of Khalistan," he warned. This was the only instance when he had referred to Khalistan, though he did not raise the demand as such. It was this speech of Sant Bhindranwale, which provided the militant struggle whatever ideological content was there during the second phase of militancy in the post-Bluestar period. The immediate provocation for this reaction was the heavy deployment of police around the shrine. In that very speech, he had said the Sikhs would now not repeat the blunder committed in 1947 saying, "We are neither for nor against Khalistan but in case the Queen (Indira Gandhi) gives it we will definitely accept but this is not our demand as yet". He also gave a call to the Sikhs to give a befitting reply by killing anti-Sikh people in case of attack on the Darbar Sahib complex. He had also referred to the peaceful methods advocated by Longowal. [10]

From that very stage and the same day, Longowal hammered the Anandpur Sahib Resolution. There was no meeting point for the two distinct political streams in the Sikh matrix. Sant Bhindranwale repeated the call to take revenge even at the village level during his speech on April 13 in case Darbar Sahib Complex was attacked by the security forces. Both the sides were heading for a show down.

At the general house meeting of the SGPC on March 30 at Amritsar, Delhi Akali Dal President Harcharan Singh raised the demand for appointing Sant Bhindranwale as Jathedar of the Akal Takht. He was hooted down by members; it was for the second time that such a proposal had been mooted.

As the PM continued with the grand design, the Akali Dal continued to mobilize people through democratic means. They organized political conferences in the Assembly constituencies of the Congress MLAs to expose their anti-Punjab role and to build pressure on them to submit their resignations.

Yet another dimension was added to the otherwise peaceful Akali agitation when 21 persons were killed and 61 injured as the police fired at various places in the state during the 'rasta roko' (road blockade) agitation on April 4. Akali workers squatted on the highways and road traffic remained suspended all over the state throughout the day. Longowal demanded resignations from Indira Gandhi and Darbara Singh for the police repression. He rejected Sethi's offer for resumption of talks made in the Parliament on April 5. "We cannot hold your hand when you are holding a rifle in your other hand," he had said on April 6. The fact-finding committee set up by the Communist Party of India blamed the police for the excesses during road blockade. The state government was forced to order judicial inquiry into the April 4 incidents.

Taking Oath as Marjeewadas

The agitation entered a crucial phase on April 13, 1983 with about 31,500 Akali workers taking oath at the Akal Takht and offering their services to the Panth. This was the creation of corps of what came to be known as Marjeewadas or self-sacrificing squads. Longowal administered the oath in the presence of Sant Bhindranwale. The squad was to be trained for a peaceful struggle. Sant Bhindranwale, who took the pledge too, renewed his call to the Sikhs to arm themselves for removing the shackles of slavery at the ceremony.[11] The oath read: "I solemnly pledge that from today onwards, I offer my services to the Panth and will make every sacrifice at the call of the President of the Akali Dal for the glory (chardi kala) of the Panth."

The oath only reinforced the commitment to the Akali Dal and the Sikh Panth and as such, there seemed to be nothing wrong about it. However, the action received flak from the other political parties as this move was seen as another step in what had came to be perceived as the fight for Khalistan. The volunteers later came to be clubbed with the militants by other political parties, especially the Congress. It was the call given by Sant Bhindranwale to avenge attack on Darbar Sahib which had added this dimension to the otherwise innocuous move of the Akali Dal.

It was around this period that reports started appearing in the press about the communal cleavage in the state becoming more and more palpable. "In this city or, for that matter, in Punjab, where the Sikhs and Hindus, who have lived there as friends for years, have become distant to one another... They do not meet as often as they used to. Social contacts have become strained. Fewer Hindus now visit gurdwaras. Both Hindus and Sikhs prefer not to intermingle. In clubs and bar rooms in many towns, Hindus sit in one corner and the Sikhs in another... villages are not yet affected but the hot wind of communalism has blown so strongly in the urban areas that even the best of liberals in both the communities have been swept off their feet.... Hindus are unsure about their and the State's future..."[12]. The content of the Akali Dal agitation was not communal yet some forces were working towards sharpening the divide.

Another position was coming forth from Sardar Hukam Singh, former Lok Sabha Speaker, who wrote, "Tension between Hindus and Sikhs in Punjab is certain to continue unless the communal Hindus see wisdom and retrace their steps by acknowledging Punjabi as their mother tongue. If the Punjabi Hindus had not disowned Punjabi and isolated the Sikhs, then a sense of Punjabi nationality would have grown and suppressed Hindu and Sikh communalism. The same approach has been adopted towards the present Morcha. The demands that were dubbed separatist, unpatriotic and dangerous in the beginning are after great suffering and sacrifice being conceded gradually. But care is being taken even then that the Congress does not lose its pool of traditional Hindu supporters in Punjab and that the Congress ministries in the neighbouring states do not suffer in any case. Justice will never be done on any issue if authority is influenced more by political considerations rather than by merit. In such a case, the minorities will continue to be a torment in the country."[13]

As the situation continued to deteriorate, Rajiv Gandhi rushed to Chandigarh and met party legislators and senior Congress leaders individually on April 19 to elicit their views on the situation. Giving his perspective of the Akali agitation, he is reported to have said that he had his doubts whether the acceptance of Akali Dal's major demands relating to religious matters, territorial issues and the river waters would lead to an end to the impasse; the problem was essentially political. His felt things the situation would not normalize that easily. It was perhaps this perception of the Congress Party and the design to play the Hindu card, which finally led to Operation Bluestar. All these months, ever since the launch of the Akali Morcha, the Congress had failed to counter the agitation at the political level.

Meanwhile, Akal Takht Jathedar Giani Kirpal Singh, on April 24, denied reports appearing in a section of the media about a ban on carrying of firearms in the Darbar Sahib parkarma (walkway) and said: "Rather in most of the gurdwaras, we adorn ourselves with weapons." The Sikh code of conduct is very clear on the issue of weapons in the parkarma. Akal Takht is part of the Darbar Sahib complex and the very first directive issued by Guru Hargobind from this seat to the Sikhs was to bring horses and weapons. But then those were the formative years of Sikhism. These weapons however, are not carried into the sanctum sanctorum that is Darbar Sahib.

DIG Atwal shot

In the first ever such action, Deputy Inspector General of Police, Jalandhar Range, A.S. Atwal, was gunned down in front of the Darbar

Sahib complex at the main entrance on the Ghanta Ghar side on April 25. He was the first senior police officer to have been shot since the beginning of the militant violence in the state. Amritsar was part of the Jalandhar Range. Both Sant Bhindranwale and Longowal condemned the killing. "I condemn the killing of DIG Atwal in very strong words. The Golden Temple is a common place of worship for all. People of all communities come to the Golden Temple to pay homage," Longowal said.

Sant Bhindranwale said, "I condemn the incident especially as it has taken place just outside the main gate of the shrine. We are not in favour of violence at all." He alleged that the state government was behind the killing and it was part of the conspiracy to prepare ground for police entry into the complex. AISSF General Secretary Harminder Singh Sandhu demanded judicial inquiry into the killing.

The circumstances around this killing are very significant. Atwal had gone to the shrine for some specific purpose – reportedly, Brigadier Tejinder Singh Grewal from the Army Intelligence had called him there. Accompanied by Indian Police Service officer Jarnail Singh Chahal then posted as the Senior Superintendent of Police, Gurdaspur, Brig Grewal had met Longowal on April 23 and the two were in Amritsar for three days. Before going to Amritsar, they had a meeting with Governor A.P. Sharma, in Chandigarh. They had ostensibly gone to Longowal to discuss some sort of settlement.[14] The CBI questioned Brig Grewal and Chahal during investigation of this case. "It has been established that Brigadier Grewal had rung up Mr Atwal at Jalandhar and called him to Amritsar. They had met outside the Golden Temple," the Indian Express reported on June 1, 1983. The report further stated: "According to some important sources, it is established that Brigadier Grewal and the IPS officer had two meetings with the Akali Dal chief, Sant Harchand Singh Longowal, on April 23 and 24 just before the murder of Mr Atwal and the Brigadier offered his services to mediate between the government and the Akalis on their demands. The Brigadier had told the Akali Dal chief that politicians were not telling him the truth and since his office was very close to the Prime Minister's office, he knew certain things and could arrange a settlement. According to some Akali sources, Sant Longowal had asked the Brigadier to see him again on April 25 at 11 AM when he would call some other party leaders also for further discussion. Accordingly, the Sant had sent urgent messages to some important party men to reach Amritsar on April 25 for some important consultations."

There's another version to this killing. The plan to attack Ludhiana district police chief D.R. Bhatti got leaked out to Atwal, who, accompanied by his source from the inner circle of Sant Bhindranwale, reached the office of Amritsar Senior Superintendent of Police S.S. Bains where a strategy was chalked out to nab the persons who had been assigned the task.

Seated in a private vehicle near the Sindhi Hotel, Superintendent of Police (City) Joginder Pal Birdi along with that source, waited for the militants assigned the job to move out of the serai complex from the gate towards the Brahmbuta Akhara. They were to be ambushed near the Mananwala drain bridge on the G.T. Road a few kilometers from Amritsar by a police party under the command of Superintendent of Police A.P. Pandey. Birdi followed the jeep while maintaining a safe distance and stopped his vehicle near Doburji from where the Mananwala Bridge was visible. Suddenly there was smoke; a grenade had hit the jeep. He rushed along with the force and found Pandey lying injured. Later, it came to be known that the jeep had made a detour and reached Khadoor Sahib from where the dead and the injured were transported to the Darbar Sahib complex in an SGPC bus. One of the militants had also been killed. Sant Bhindranwale could make out as to who had leaked the information and his body was found from the gutter the next day.

A few days later, Brig Grewal and Chahal advised Atwal to strike a compromise with Sant Bhindranwale and offered to intervene. It was under this operation that Atwal was advised to reach the Darbar Sahib Complex. As he was coming out after paying his obeisance, he was fired from behind.

Some information on the planned attack had reached a senior police officer at the headquarters. He tried to contact Atwal and alerted the Amritsar police but it was too late. Within minutes, the news of Atwal being shot reached the district police. Birdi was rushed to the Kotwali police station. He gathered his men and headed for the Darbar Sahib Complex. He was about to enter the shrine when he got a message against police intervention. However, the Home Ministry had clarified in a message to Chief Minister around 11.40 that day that the security forces could enter the complex in hot pursuit in such a situation. That day, an opportunity to nab the militants holed up inside the complex was lost. The designs were different.

The Union Home Minister announced in the Rajya Sabha on April 28 that the SGPC had been given one week to hand over the killers of Atwal. He confirmed reports that the Punjab government had sent a registered letter about criminals taking shelter in the Darbar Sahib Complex to the SGPC and that the letter had been returned. Minister of State for Home P. Venkatasubbaiah clarified Sethi's statement the next day saying that the government had not given any "ultimatum" to the SGPC. The Amritsar district authorities handed to the SGPC a list of about 40 persons allegedly involved in various acts of violence and suspected to be hiding in the shrine. Significantly, Sant Bhindranwale's name was missing from the list.

At the political level, on April 27, Punjab Vidhan Sabha Speaker Brij Bhushan Mehra, rejected the resignations of all the 36 MLAs submitted earlier on January 27. He observed the resignations were not voluntary. The Akali Dal Legislature Party had the strength of 37 members and Dr. Bhagat Singh was abroad. In the political circles, this was considered as a goodwill gesture to create an atmosphere congenial to conflict resolution. Longowal reacted by saying that the Akali legislators did not consider themselves as members of the state Assembly anymore and they would not enter the House till the acceptance of their demands.

Janata Party MP Dr. Subramaniam Swamy visited Guru Nanak Niwas in the complex on May 6 and met both the Sants. Significantly, he denied that the office of Khalistan functioned from Guru Nanak Niwas. National Council of Khalistan General Secretary Balbir Singh Sandhu was functioning from a room there and that room had got projected as office of Khalistan. He crossed the border during Operation Bluestar.

The Foreign Hand

For the first time, the Prime Minister came out with the foreign hand theory in Punjab and Assam on May 8. She suspected considerable foreign interference in the country. Interestingly, the reports about CIA being active in Punjab had appeared much earlier. According to an October 21, 1982 UNI report datelined Moscow, the Soviet Union had, on October 19, blamed the Central Intelligence Agency for instigating trouble in Punjab. Soviet news agency Tass, in a commentary on the Punjab situation, had accused the US secret service for having established special camps for military training of secessionists. "The tasks of the agents recruited from among the Sikh extremists are to assassinate political and religious leaders, provoke communal clash," it said. The news agency said that Kashmir was another place that had become one of the main areas of operation of foreign agents under the patronage of CIA.

It had become all the more necessary to strengthen the Akali Dal to frustrate the designs of the forces of destabilization. This could have been done by conceding some of the Akali demands, which was done much later in 1985, though that accord was ultimately consigned to the dustbin of history, never to be implemented.

At the national level, S.N. Singh's left radical faction of the Communist Party of India (Marxist-Leninist) extended moral support to the Akali agitation in May. Earlier, this group had backed the Anandpur Sahib Resolution at its Ludhiana convention in 1981. Singh, in one of the articles in the party organ, blamed the Centre for the present situation. It was as part of this understanding of the situation that some of the Naxalite leaders had made their way to the Darbar Sahib complex in an attempt to give secular orientation to the Akali agitation and counter the All India Sikh Students Federation. These leaders, including Jasjit Singh Khaira, a former Punjab Students Union leader, extended support to Longowal in the setting up of a parallel youth wing.[15]

Meanwhile, communal tension continued to be on a rise with the Sikh radical and Hindu fundamentalist organizations working in the same direction. Communal clashes were reported in Patiala on May 2. Members from the two communities indulged in looting, arson and violence. To control the situation, police opened fire at two places. Three cases of arson were reported from Patiala on May 7. In Amritsar, iron gates, the legacy of communal violence during the Partition in 1947, had again been put up at the entrances of several narrow lanes in the walled city.

On May 13, the PM offered to meet both Longowal and Sant Bhindranwale when Akali Dal (Master Tara Singh) President Jathedar Santokh Singh met her with the request that she should invite them for talks. At the same time, she reiterated that certain foreign powers were trying to weaken the country.[16] These foreign forces were, however, not being identified.

Indira Gandhi toured Punjab on May 29 and signaled that she did not believe in confrontation and preferred amicable settlement of all disputes. Addressing meetings at Nabha, Ludhiana and Gurdaspur, she said that while all religious demands had been conceded, the remaining demands concerned other states and a settlement could be arrived at only in consultation with them. She advised the Akalis to withdraw the Morcha and start negotiations. Denying that the Sikhs were suspects, she eulogized the bravery of the Punjabis in defending the motherland. Clearly, she was in no mood to concede the main demands of the Akalis.[17] However, after sending thousands of workers to jail, the Akali leadership could not afford unconditional withdrawal of the Morcha.

In another development, Sant Bhindranwale took a strong notice of the publication of a calendar by the Hind Samachar Group of newspapers and threatened its editor-proprietor Ramesh Chander demanding his apology within four days. Chander disclosed this at a news conference at Delhi on June 1. It was a two-page calendar of six months each, first page having a picture of Lord Krishna and the second, a portrait of Guru Gobind Singh. On the left hand side of both the pages was a picture of Lala Jagat Narain, earlier gunned down by the militants. According to the management, the calendar was published with the objective of promoting communal harmony in the tense atmosphere in the state. Sant Bhindranwale objected to the picture of Lala Jagat Narain having been published along with the portrait of the 10th Guru. On appeal from Ramesh Chander, Sant Longowal referred the matter to the Dharam Parchar Committee of the SGPC. Ramesh too was later gunned down by the militants.

NOTES

1. The Indian Express, January 12, 1983.
2. The Indian Express, January 12, 1983.
3. The Indian Express, January 18, 1983.
4. The Tribune, January 20, 1983.
5. The Indian Express, February 9, 1983.
6. The Indian Express, February 11, 1983.
7. The Tribune, February 18, 1983.
8. The Indian Express, February 21, 1983.
9. Surjeet, Harkishan Singh: Happenings in Punjab, pp. 61-62.
10. Quoted from his speech.
11. The Indian Express, April 14, 1983.
12. Kuldip Nayar, The Indian Express, April 18, 1983.
13. The Indian Express, April 11, 1983.
14. The Indian Express, May 16, 1983.
15. Jagtar Singh, The Indian Express, May 19, 1983.
16. The Indian Express, May 14, 1983.
17. The Indian Express, May 30, 1983.

6

Media and Akalis

It was in the second week of October 1983 that the Indian Express team was detailed to cover the construction of bunkers and digging of trenches in the Darbar Sahib Complex after a two-line story to this effect had appeared in a paper. The first trench had been dug in the serai area in front of the Teja Singh Samundari Hall housing the offices of the SGPC and had been covered with a tin sheet and sand bags. Gun position had also been constructed on the roof of Guru Nanak Niwas, the abode of Sant Jarnail Singh Bhindranwale. Gun-totting youth could be seen moving around in the area as we reached the complex. It was considered safe to click the pictures from a distance and incidentally, it was from the window of the third floor office of Harbir Singh Bhanwar, Public Relations Officer of the SGPC, that one could have a clear view. Himself a journalist also stringing for a news agency, Bhanwar could make out the purpose of the visit. Within a few minutes, a messenger came with the message that there was a call for me in the office of Abinashi Singh, the all-powerful personal assistant to the SGPC chief.

Having spent two years in Amritsar, I fully understood the import of the message. As we reached Abinashi Singh's office, Amrik Singh, president of the All India Sikh Students Federation, was also waiting for us. Both of them tried to persuade us against using pictures of the fortification. They were very polite but I was firm and clear that we were on that very assignment and there was no question of not using the pictures. "We can only request you," said Amrik Singh. We came out. The first picture of the fortification appeared on the front page of the Indian Express along with the story about the preparations.

After finishing the assignment, I went to meet Sant Bhindranwale on the roof of Guru Nanak Niwas where he was sitting surrounded by a large number of people. He counseled to wait for sometime and have lunch with him in his room. And the lunch was the simple dal and roti from the langar. Amrik Singh was also present. None of them broached the subject of assignment. And though the count down for the final armed confrontation had started, there was no tension in the air and Sant Bhindranwale was relaxed. The two main players at that time, Sant Bhindranwale and Indira Gandhi, seemed to have already made up their mind.

Interestingly, Punjab Police chief Pritam Singh Bhinder said in Hoshiarpur in July that the state government had no evidence of extremists taking refuge in the Darbar Sahib complex. He said such stories were spread by inefficient officers in order to save themselves and that it was his firm belief that no political party would give refuge to criminals.[1]

Even a few months before the bunkers came up, Congress' designs on Punjab were already getting exposed with the impression gaining ground that the Centre was out to play the Hindu card in the Lok Sabha elections and hence not keen to enter into a negotiated settlement with the Akalis, which could have isolated the militants. The tragedy of the Akali Dal was that despite repeatedly making its position clear on the sovereign Sikh state issue, the party continued to be deliberately mixed up with the radicals by some sections. This included a part of the media too, a major section of which had become an instrument in the implementation of the grand design. For years, this section continued to play a partisan role in the state, thanks to media management by the rulers.

With each day, the situation in the state was getting vitiated. Two persons were killed when a pencil bomb exploded in the office of Partap, a Hindi daily in Jalandhar, on June 24. Bomb explosions were also reported from other parts of the state the same day. Police officials and Nirankaris continued to be targeted during this period.

As the political temperature continued to rise, the Centre expressed the pretension of initiating a process of conflict resolution. On the evening of May 31, Union Home Minister P.C. Sethi extended an invitation to SAD President Harchand Singh Longowal for resumption of talks. The letter stated: "As you know, the government has been having a series of discussions on the demands of the Shiromani Akali Dal in which some progress has already been made, but some things need to be discussed further. The government's readiness to find an amicable solution has already been conveyed through those who were in touch with you. From the press, we understand that you will be willing to continue the talks. It would be appropriate to resume the talks directly. I, therefore, invite you and your representatives to meet me and my colleagues in Delhi. As soon as I hear from you, the date and time mutually convenient will be finalised."

Longowal sent his reply on June 11 through a special messenger seeking some further clarifications. Sethi exchanged yet another letter with Longowal on June 14 providing the clarifications Akali chief had sought.

To convey its seriousness on solving the conflict, on June 7, the government, in accordance with Prime Minister Indira Gandhi's earlier statement in the Parliament on March 24, formally constituted a commission headed by retired judge of Supreme Court Justice R.S. Sarkaria to review the Centre-State relations. June 30, 1984 was fixed as the deadline for submitting the report. The announcement, however, failed to end the deadlock. The Akali leaders were far from convinced about the mindset of the PM.

In an effort to exert more pressure on the government, the Akali Dal, on June 12, gave a call to block rail traffic in Punjab on June 17. Sant Bhindranwale supported the call. The stand taken by the Communist Party of India at the national level was significant. Party chief C. Rajeshwara Rao said the call should not be treated as a law and order problem and the mass action planned by the Akalis should be allowed to pass off peacefully. He also expected the Akalis to counter any move by the extremists within the party to enact violence.[2] The government faced the challenge by suspending rail and bus traffic in the state for a day.

Conceding yet another demand, the government handed over the remaining portion of Kotwali in Delhi to the Delhi Sikh Gurdwara Management Committee on June 14 in the presence of MP Rajiv Gandhi, Delhi Lt Governor Jagmohan and SGPC President Gurcharan Singh Tohra. The Ninth Guru of the Sikhs, Guru Tegh Bahadur, had been detained in that building during the Mughal period before his martyrdom.

However, these steps failed to convince the Akali leadership about Indira Gandhi's sincerity as the government was not addressing the main demands. Longowal rejected Sethi's invitation on June 21 saying the government was not interested in doing justice to Punjab. He said that, after deep consideration, "I have come to the conclusion that the government is not serious about the constitutional, legal and clear cut demands of the Akali Dal and about a solution to the Punjab tangle." He added that the attitude of sacrificing the demands for the sake of personal and party interests was unfortunate for the country and for "all of us".[3]

Here goes the text of the letter written by the Union Home Minister to Longowal, dated June 15, 1983:

"I am in receipt of your letter.

"You may recall that in your letter of June 2, you had asked for the identification of the issue for discussions. As you are aware, the Prime Minister made an announcement on the religious issues some time ago. A commission under the chairmanship of Justice R.S. Sarkaria has also been set up. Various view points pertaining to the relations between the Centre and the states can now be placed before it. In view of the above, I had referred only to the two pending issues, namely, the distribution of Ravi-Beas waters between Punjab and Haryana and the territorial disputes between these two states. A number of formulations have been put forth in respect of these matters on different occasions. As you will appreciate, solutions to these problems have to be found with the concurrence of the government of Haryana and new formulations, if any, from your side have to be discussed with representatives of that government also. We are prepared to arrange such discussions after knowing your suggestions on these matters and shall try to find a solution satisfactory to all parties.

"I may point out that the government was not trying to bring in any extraneous elements or being provocative while mentioning the reported misuse of holy places whose sanctity we all cherish and want to maintain. This issue was raised earlier in our discussions. This is the cause for anxiety to us and indeed in the public mind.

"I may add that it is unfortunate that immediately after sending your reply to my communication, you should have given a call for rail roko. This cannot but lead to tremendous inconvenience and needless suffering to innocent people. I do hope that you will still reconsider your stand.

"I once again reiterate my earlier invitation to you for further talks in Delhi and request you to suggest dates that you may find convenient for the purpose."

Supporting Longowal, Tohra and Balwant Singh separately rejected the offer of talks on June 24. Balwant Singh turned down the proposal to set up a tribunal to go afresh into the territorial dispute. He, however, was not averse to the setting up of a tribunal under the Waters Dispute Act if it was done without conditions. Referring to the territorial dispute, Tohra clarified the Akali Dal had never accepted that the transfer of Chandigarh was linked to the barter of Abohar and Fazilka with Haryana.

Conspiracy to Attack Gurdwaras

On June 28, Longowal alleged that the Hindu Suraksha Samiti and the Hindu Rashtriya Sanghathan had held secret meetings to plan attacks on gurdwaras and appealed the Sikhs to remain vigilant. The two Hindu organizations had organized a successful Punjab bandh a day earlier in protest against the intensified activities of the Sikh radicals. The politics of Sikh radicals and the Hindu chauvinists had the common target and that was to whip up the communal passions further.

Chandra Shekhar met Longowal on June 29 and expressed the view that no decision on Akali demands was possible until Indira Gandhi made up her mind. However, the government was still dealing with the situation mainly as a law and order problem. This was evident from the ordinance promulgated on June 29, arming executive magistrates with judicial powers.

By now, the suspected role of the Congress party had come to be questioned at various levels. "The Congress has assumed the mantle of the saviour of the Hindus to oust the BJP among Hindu voters in Punjab and the Lok Dal from Haryana... That is why the Government of India is dragging out the negotiations over the demands and pulling them back every time they come to the brink of a settlement, while it makes completely false charges against the Akali Dal of shifting its ground or rejecting counter offers. Its only aim now is to win Hindu support and isolate the Akali Dal (which now means isolating the Sikhs) from the national mainstream by calling them secessionist," Pran Chopra wrote in The Indian Express dated July 3, 1983. It was the Congress, which was out to play the communal card to win the forthcoming Lok Sabha elections. It was perhaps part of this design that the distinction was not being made between the Akali Dal agitation and the activities of the radicals. The thrust of both the Akali agitation and the militant movement got projected by and large as anti Hindu in the media.

The resolution adopted by the Punjab state committee of Communist Party of India (Marxist) at its two-day meeting at Jalandhar from July 2 onwards also suspected some design of the rulers. It stated: "The present situation in the state is a direct result of the selfish and the anti-people policies pursued by the Indira Gandhi government. This perilous situation could have been easily avoided had the Indira Gandhi government dealt with the demands raised by the movement applying democratic norms and putting the interests of the Indian people in the forefront... The opportunism of the ruling party has given full scope to the Sikh communalist agents to set one community against another."

Once again, Longowal tried to prove the patriotic credentials of the Shiromani Akali Dal in a statement issued on July 20 while demanding a separate personal law for the Sikhs. Though at the beginning of the agitation, the issue of ethnicity was not that important on the Akali Dal agenda, it was being increasingly emphasised now, apparently to out compete the radicals. While stressing that the Sikhs were not Hindus, he questioned as to why they were being governed by the Hindu personal law. At the same time, he stressed that the Akalis believed in the unity and integrity of the country and were prepared to make the greatest sacrifice to preserve it. He attacked the BJP for criticizing the Anandpur Sahib Resolution. The Akali Dal was time and again making a clear distinction from the radical agenda.

Sant Bhindranwale and the Sikh Nation

On the other hand, Sant Bhindranwale, while addressing a congregation on July 20, urged the government to recognize the Sikhs as a separate nation and provide constitutional guarantee to that effect. At the same time, he reiterated that Sikhs wanted to live with dignity and as equal citizens in the country, adding the Sikhs were neither against nor for Khalistan but if it was given to them, they would not repeat the mistakes committed by them in 1947.[4] He had made his position very clear, though it was also contradictory. He was talking of the Sikh homeland without directly raising a demand for it while also talking of constitutional guarantee. He had expressed similar views in March also in the presence of Longowal. In the process, he was limiting the options of the Akali Dal and dictating the agenda. He had a two-hour meeting with Longowal before he addressed the congregation.

At the time when Sant Bhindranwale was raising the pitch, the Akali leaders' making a clear distinction from the agenda of the radicals was not going unnoticed. It was in this context that Rajmohan Gandhi gave certain suggestions to the Akalis: "Condemn every Punjabi killing, no matter who is murdered. Condemn it at once. Condemn it in the press. Condemn it at street corners. Let your foes know you have condemned it. Let your followers know it likewise... It is noteworthy that, from time to time, the Akali leaders disown or disavow the Khalistan slogan. The latest to do so is the SGPC chief Mr. G.S. Tohra... This sort of disavowal is precisely the thing that Sikh extremists object to. It should be freely acknowledged".[5]

The Rajya Sabha debated the Punjab issue for nearly four hours on July 25 with the members pressing the government for a settlement, as the delay in the matter could be disastrous. The leaders warned that Punjab was on the tip of a volcano with communal tension building up in the cities and villages. A small spark could ruin the state and the country. They urged the government to give up the policy of drift. Surendra Mohan (Janata) charged the Congress with encouraging radicals led by Sant Bhindranwale. He said that the recent speeches of the PM had worsened the law and order and communal situation in the border state. Indira Gandhi was trying to exploit the situation by whipping up a sense of insecurity amongst the Hindus with an eye on the mid-term polls. On the other hand, Satpal Mittal (Congress) alleged that several foreign powers including the USA and Pakistan were supporting the Akali agitation.

Harkishan Singh Surjeet of CPI (M) attributed the situation to the conspiracy hatched by the US government to harm the unity and integrity of the country. At the same time, he wondered as to what was the hitch in enacting the all India gurdwara legislation and handing over the territorial and river waters dispute for adjudication. Khushwant Singh, however, disputed the charge that foreign powers were behind the Akali movement and demanded proof.[6]

On July 22, the Akal Takht summoned Jagdev Singh Talwandi to appear on July 26 for convening a meeting of the district presidents, MLAs and MPs at Amritsar on July 28, thus posing a direct challenge to the leadership of Longowal. However, the summons was withheld as he cancelled the meeting the very next day.

Pakistan Denies Involvement

In a significant development, for the first time, Pakistan denied involvement in India's internal problems in a statement issued in Delhi on July 27. It said that the country adhered to a "policy of non-interference in the internal affairs of other states and has been making every effort to promote the cause of friendly relations with India"[7]. But despite denials, accusing fingers continued to be raised at Pakistan. Rajiv Gandhi raised the issue of Pakistan's involvement in Punjab while addressing a public meeting at Sri Ganganagar in Rajasthan on October 18. However, some newspapers decided to take precaution while hinting at Pakistan's involvement.

It was during this period that a group calling itself "Secessionist de Khalistan" opened its office in Belgium's capital Brussels.

Longowal once again distanced his party from the Khalistanis, saying, "The Shiromani Akali Dal has never made a demand for Khalistan. We are rather openly opposed to the idea of Khalistan." He reiterated the charge that National Council of Khalistan chief Dr. Jagjit Singh Chohan was a creation of the Congress. The 58-page pamphlet he released that day stated that whenever there was any significant progress in finding an amicable solution to the tangle, Punjab Chief Minister sabotaged the negotiations by fomenting communal trouble and by resorting to police repression on the Sikhs.[8]

Meanwhile, Amrik Singh and Thara Singh, associates of Sant Bhindranwale, were finally acquitted in the two different cases on August 6. It was their arrest a year back that had provoked Sant

Bhindranwale to launch the agitation, which was later taken over by the Akali Dal. Longowal demanded Darbara Singh's resignation because he had been morally defeated on their acquittal. Sant Bhindranwale declared that the agitation would continue till the release of all innocent Sikhs and the acceptance of the Anandpur Sahib Resolution.

Indications seemed clear — the Centre was unlikely to concede to the demands of the Akali Dal. In her Independence Day speech from the ramparts of the Red Fort on August 15, the Prime Minister categorically stated that the Centre would not accept any more demands without consulting the states likely to be affected by the decision. She refuted that she was blocking a solution to the problem. These demands included the river waters and the territorial disputes.

The reaction to her statement in the Akali Dal was on expected lines. Longowal threw the ball in her court on August 19 again saying that the Akali Dal would have no objection to Gandhi's unilateral announcement regarding the acceptance of demands. He specified the parameters of the unilateral announcement as referring the river waters dispute to the Supreme Court, transferring Chandigarh to Punjab and constituting a commission to decide respective claims of Punjab and Haryana on the principle of linguistic contiguity. At the same time, the Akali Dal gave a call to gherao the offices of the deputy commissioners in the state on August 29. The Akali Dal was pressing for a constitutional solution to the river waters dispute through the Supreme Court from where the case had been withdrawn by the Congress government in Punjab under pressure from Gandhi.

Media and the Akalis

The media, especially the so-called national ones in Delhi, had, consciously or unconsciously, mixed up the Akalis with the radicals and the militants. Here is what appeared in the magazine section of The Indian Express: "*The Akali hit list exists:* It is no invention. Piara Singh, the police sub-inspector who was attacked and killed in the train, had been part of the police operation that had gunned down the Sikh hijacker, Museebat Singh, at Amritsar. D.R. Bhatti, Ludhiana's Senior Superintendent of Police, had once arrested Sant Bhindranwale. One morning, assassins shot at him. Bhatti's bodyguard died but Bhatti escaped with wounds. And in each case, the assassins disappeared into the nearest gurdwara. In the last two years, *Akali extremists have killed over 80 people, hijacked two planes, looted two armouries and several banks, thrown grenades at Punjab ministers, and planted time bombs in public places..........So how is the Akali terrorism to be countered?*"[9] This is just one example.

Yet, a new dimension was added to the already highly-volatile situation with the threat issued by Sant Bhindranwale on August 16 to the Hindus in the state. The threat was in reaction to the police detention of the mini bus, which had been sent to fetch the parents of Amrik Singh from Muktsar. On August 19, The Indian Express quoted him as saying: "When I came to know that the mini bus had been detained, I sent a word to the police that if the bus is not released by 5 pm, Hindus (5,000) would be killed within one hour.... The Prime Minister is a Hindu, Sethi is a Hindu and the Mahasha press is also Hindu." It was in this context that Longowal made yet another attempt to clarify his party's stand on the killings of the innocents saying that the killings were against the traditions of the Sikh religion and that a person attacking innocent people was a traitor to the Sikh Panth. This clarification was in the context of the threat issued to the Hindus in Punjab by Sant Bhindranwale.[10] Significantly, Sant Bhindranwale himself had been repeatedly telling his supporters not to use arms against the innocents.

However, this warning echoed in both Houses of the Parliament on August 24. The Parliament expressed deep concern over *Sant Bhindranwale's threat to kill 5,000 Hindus "to press the Akali demands"*. The threat had been issued in an entirely different context and had nothing to do with the Akali agitation. The Home Minister announced in the Lower House that a case had been registered against Sant Bhindranwale. L.K. Advani demanded imposition of President's rule in Punjab. The Akali Dal was getting isolated at the national level, despite Longowal's repeated assertions making a clear distinction from the militants.

On August 24 in Jalandhar, the little-known Punjab Hindu Sangathan, held the Akalis responsible for the "persecution of Hindus in Punjab" while welcoming the condemnation of the killing of the innocent by Longowal. Sangathan President Amar Nath Sharma demanded proportional representation to the Hindus in the state government services.

As part of the intensification of the peaceful agitation, on August 29, Akali workers gheraoed the offices of the deputy commissioners in response to the "Kam Roko" (stop work) call. As per the state government's assessment, about 40,000 workers participated in the agitation that day. The police and Akali workers clashed at several places in the state.

Sant Bhindranwale again queered the pitch for the Akalis at a meeting of the 'clean hearted Sikhs' organized on September 4 at Amritsar in which he set the agenda for settlement with the Centre. He made it clear that there would be no settlement without getting the demands including the Anandpur Sahib Resolution, the 'Sikhs-are-a-separate-nation' doctrine and enactment of separate Sikh personal law on the basis of this doctrine, accepted. The settlement would be acknowledged only after endorsement from the Sikh masses. He warned that in case the Centre persisted with its policy, the agitation would not remain confined to the acceptance of the Resolution. He said, "Iss ton agge vee jaaya jaa sakda hai (We can go further)," provided the Sikhs got united. His argument was that in case the Sikhs got united, Indira Gandhi would herself come to Amritsar to negotiate with the Akali Dal.[11]

There was no umbrella organization of the agitating Sikhs as such and the radicals were not part of the Akali Dal mainstream. It was in this context that the proposal had been mooted to elevate Sant Bhindranwale as the Akal Takht Jathedar so that the Sikh struggle could be carried forward under the direction of this supreme Sikh institution for prayer and politics.

In an unprecedented move, the CPI legislature party staged a dharna in the state assembly on September 6 and demanded immediate convening of tripartite talks by the PM and impress upon the ruling party to pass a unanimous resolution to this effect.

Mrs. Gandhi is Communal: CPI

In a significant development at the national level, the Communist Party of India sharply attacked Indira Gandhi for her alleged communal designs to win the next Lok Sabha election. "For short term political gains, Mrs. Gandhi is pandering to a certain communal sentiment in the majority community and it has become part of her electoral strategy to win the next Lok Sabha election," the national council said in a resolution. Party General Secretary C. Rajeshwara Rao said that the policy of the Congress (I) was to have confrontation with minorities — Muslims, Christians, Sikhs — to appease the Hindu communalists. He claimed that twice an agreement on Punjab was very near but the government "sabotaged it". The Punjab problem could have been solved within no time had Indira Gandhi desired so but she did not want that. The council, in its resolution, expressed surprise at the continued hobnobbing with Sant Bhindranwale by the Congress.[12] However, despite the designs of Indira Gandhi getting exposed, it was the Akalis who were increasingly at the receiving end. This resolution of the CPI was very significant because at one stage the party had been mainly blaming the imperialist forces for militancy in the border state. The Russians had earlier pointed fingers at the CIA.

Intensified militant activity was observed during this period. Ludhiana district police chief D.R. Bhatti was attacked near his office on

September 21. He survived the attack but his gunman and one of the assailants were killed in the exchange of fire. Bhatti's name had been associated with the raid conducted at Chando Kalan in Haryana to arrest Sant Bhindranwale after the assassination of Lala Jagat Narain. One Nirankari was shot dead at Amritsar on September 10. Morning walkers were fired upon at Jagraon near Ludhiana on September 28 while a police head constable was gunned down at Amritsar. Municipal Councillor Dr. Sudarshan Tandon was shot dead at Patti on September 30. Hindus were targeted at Jalandhar, Tarn Taran and Batala on October 5.

While strongly criticizing the Akalis, the Punjab Suraksha Samiti, in an open letter to the members of Parliament released on September 30, demanded the enactment of Punjab Mandir (Hindu temple) Legislation on the pattern of the Sikh Gurdwara Act, direct transmission from Durgiana Temple in Amritsar, ban on export of cows from the state and a commission headed by a Supreme Court judge to go into the alleged discrimination against the Hindus. The Samiti had raised these demands in reaction to the Akali agenda.

Meanwhile, Akali leaders Jagdev Singh Talwandi, Sukhjinder Singh and Bharpur Singh Balbir were detained under the National Security Act on October 4.

Darbara Singh Government Dismissed

Amidst intensified violence, the Darbara Singh government in the state was unceremoniously dismissed on October 6 following the gunning down of eight bus passengers near Dhilwan in the first of its kind incident in the state. The private bus had started from Amritsar late in the evening and was forced to divert near river Beas. For years, this case remained untraced. None of the militant organisations claimed responsibility for the action. Darbara Singh was credited with the view, which he used to share privately much later that it was an agency operation. Significantly, both Sant Bhindranwale and Longowal condemned this incident. I was sitting with Bhindranwale when his personal assistant Rachhpal Singh broke the news of the bus killings.

Though for different reasons, the dismissal of Darbara Singh government was interestingly welcomed by leaders from across the political spectrum including Longowal, Amarinder Singh from the Congress and BJP leader Atal Behari Vajpayee. Sant Bhindranwale, during his speech at Manji Sahib Hall on October 16, expressed the apprehension that the dismissal of Darbara Singh government was another step advanced by the Centre to attack Darbar Sahib Complex. He was bitter in his speech saying all this time the Centre had not reacted despite the fact that more than 150 Sikhs had been killed and thousands went to jail while the Darbara Singh government was dismissed within no time of the killing of eight 'Topiwale' (Hindu) bus passengers.

The situation was heading towards total chaos with incidents of violence being reported almost every day. Hindus were also being increasingly targeted to provoke communal violence.

As Governor A. P. Sharma took over the reigns of the administration in Punjab, both Punjab and Union Territory of Chandigarh were declared disturbed areas on October 7 providing unlimited powers to the security forces. The Centre also decided to replace Sharma by B.D. Pande, then Governor of West Bengal.

This ordinance, declaring Punjab and Chandigarh as disturbed areas under Section 4, empowered the security personnel not below the rank of sub-inspector to "fire upon or otherwise use force, even to the causing of death against any person who is acting in contravention of any law or order for the time being in force in the disturbed area, prohibiting the assembly of five or more persons or the carrying of weapons or of things capable of being used as weapons or of fire arms, ammunition or explosive substances." Section 6 stated: "No suit, prosecution or other legal proceedings shall be instituted except with the previous sanction of the state government against any person in respect of anything done or purporting to be done in exercise of the powers conferred by Sections 4 and 5." The security forces had been licensed to kill.

Yet another ordinance known as The Armed Forces (Punjab and Chandigarh) Special Powers Ordinance was promulgated by the government on October 15, conferring similar powers on defence forces. It also empowered the armed forces to arrest, without warrant, any person who had committed a cognisable offence or who it was suspected would commit one. The AISSF organized protest against these ordinances with the students observing a strike on October 26.

The imposition of President's rule and the Disturbed Area Act failed to check the escalating violence. Bus passengers were again fired upon near Patti on October 17 in which two policemen were killed. Retired Deputy Superintendent of Police Giani Bachan Singh was attacked at Amritsar on October 29. A Punjab Roadways bus of Moga depot was hijacked near Khabbe Dogran village on November 18 and four Hindu passengers were gunned down.

As the radical tinge became more dominating in the Sikh political spectrum, communal tension also became further manifest. The Akali Dal started getting isolated and the party began coming under increasing attack for its failure to resist the radicals. To counter this criticism, the party started focusing on Hindu-Sikh amity. In a resolution on October 10, the Akali Dal Legislature Party declared that the most important political task in Punjab was to restore Hindu-Sikh amity and mutual trust, which had come under heavy strain because of the acts of omission and commission of the sacked Darbara Singh government. The party strongly condemned the violent incidents and killings and appealed to all Punjabis to maintain communal harmony at all costs. The resolution demanded an "open inquiry by a sitting judge of the Supreme Court into the role and responsibility of the outgoing Congress ministry in actively promoting conditions of communal tension leading at several places to riots, encouraging violence against peaceful citizens, sponsoring fake encounters to kill its political opponents and in general creating a fear psychosis to justify adoption of draconian measures to suppress civil liberties."[13] However, the Akali Dal failed to carry forward this offensive against the Congress to a logical conclusion.

A joint meeting of the district presidents of Akali Dal MPs and MLAs at Amritsar on October 11 rejected the opposition's plea to suspend the agitation in view of the bus killings. It was decided to make earnest efforts to maintain communal harmony. The party resolved to convene a meeting of the opposition parties not only to find a solution to the Punjab problem but also to strengthen the forces of communal amity. Longowal offered to resign in case the party men were dissatisfied with his performance. Sant Bhindranwale welcomed the Akali Dal decision to continue the morcha.

While the Akali Dal had made its stand clear, even Sant Bhindranwale refuted some of the allegations against him, including the Prime Minister's remark that he had prepared a hit list of his opponents. He challenged that he would leave Guru Nanak Niwas if Indira Gandhi proved her allegations; otherwise, she should resign. [14] The Prime Minister did not accept his challenge.

Longowal accused the Prime Minister of complicating the problem with her rigid and stubborn attitude. In a statement issued on October 18, he criticized the "communal and anti-people policies" of the government. Condemning the incidents of sacrilege at places of worship, he alleged that the government was engineering such activities to create differences among the Sikhs and the Hindus as Congress stood to gain in an atmosphere of violence.

On the other hand, the Prime Minister reiterated in Chandigarh on October 29 that the resolution of the problem was possible only through a negotiated settlement and again offered to hold talks with the Akalis. Addressing a joint meeting of her party workers from Punjab, Haryana and Chandigarh, she rebutted the charge that the Centre was dishonest in resolving the issues. She offered to entrust the territorial dispute including Chandigarh to a tribunal if the earlier award was not acceptable to the parties concerned. At the same time, she maintained that retaining the union territory status was in the best interest of the city. She said it was perhaps not a correct decision to have associated the opposition with the talks on Punjab because these parties also kept changing their stand, adding to the confusion. Longowal rejected the offer to refer the territorial dispute to the tribunal.

Governor on Foreign Hand

Governor Pande gave a further twist to the foreign hand theory by saying that the state government had no evidence to that effect. Addressing a news conference at Jalandhar on November 15, Pande said that there was great deal of suspicion about the foreign hand but his government had not come up with anything specific so far. About the allegation to this effect having been made by Rajiv Gandhi, he said some reports directly go to the Centre.

However, the PM asserted the very next day in the Lok Sabha that the government had circumstantial evidence of foreign elements trying to destabilize the situation in Punjab. Subramaniam Swamy had raised the issue in context of what Pande had said. The Prime Minister maintained that it was not always possible to prove foreign involvement. The government felt handicapped as it did not have sophisticated equipment to prove foreign involvement. She said that not only Pakistan but other agencies too were involved. "I feel personally that very grave danger exists not only just for us. Look at what happened in Cyprus and Grenada and other countries," she said, adding that she was prepared to repeat hundred times that Pakistan and other agencies were involved. The same day in Chandigarh, Pande denied the Jalandhar report credited to him saying that he had been misunderstood and misquoted.[15]

Though Sant Bhindranwale had emerged as the supreme leader, the militants lacked a monolithic command. Militant outfits like Babbar Khalsa and Dal Khalsa were not under his control — they didn't just lack common command, even their actions needed coordination. It was under such a situation that Ranjit Singh, assassin of Nirankari chief Gurbachan Singh, fell out with Sant Bhindranwale and managed to negotiate his surrender through a moderate Akali leader, who handed him over to the Central Bureau of Investigations in Delhi. Sant Bhindranwale had announced that the assassin of the Nirankari chief would be weighed against gold. This was stated to be one of the points of contention with Ranjit Singh. Reacting to his arrest, Sant Bhindranwale said in Amritsar on November 26, "When Ranjit Singh is a free man, he will be weighed against gold." He denied a spat with

Ranjit Singh. Interestingly, Babbar Khalsa demanded his release saying he had been framed up in this case. The statement was attributed to a Babbar Khalsa activist Manmohan Singh.

In another effort to internationalize the Sikh issue, Longowal circulated a four-page letter to the Commonwealth heads of government in Delhi alleging a campaign of ruthless repression of Sikhs and compared the situation to that of Jews suffering at the hands of Hitler. Longowal urged the CHOGM delegates to save the Sikhs. This was in the last week of November.

Sant Bhindranwale on Threat to Sikhs in Rajasthan

In Rajasthan, a Gurdwara was burnt at Churu while the so-called Jai Hindu Sangh threatened the Sikhs to leave the state by December 5. Reacting to these developments, Sant Bhindranwale said on December 1 that if the Sikhs were uprooted in Rajasthan, Hindus would have to pay a heavy price. He described the call given by the Hindu Sangh as another attack on the Sikhs. He warned that if the Sikhs living in other states were evicted, the Hindus in Punjab should be prepared for the worst.

The warning whipped uproar in the Lok Sabha. Members equivocally condemned the threat to "massacre" Hindus in Punjab and told the government very bluntly that it should muster courage to arrest him for endangering national security or quit. Lok Sabha Speaker Balram Jakhar told the Home Minister that he should act firmly. "There is serious danger to the country, you will have to do something," he said, adding, "The more you are afraid, the more critical the situation will become. You have to face the situation." Satyasadan Chakraborty (CPM) and Jagpal Singh (Lok Dal) wanted the government to arrest the Sant under the National Security Act. Buta Singh and Rajesh Pilot, while tracing the genesis of the statement, said that there was no gurdwara in Churu and the report about setting it on fire was baseless.[16] The reporting was again one sided. In various newspaper reports that day, there was no reference to the threat to the Sikhs in Rajasthan to quit the state by December 5, which had provoked Sant Bhindranwale issue the threat.

Significantly, while talking to the media persons on December 5, Sant Bhindranwale offered to face any punishment if it was proved that he first made the provocative statements on any occasion. "I am a true Sikh. I never hit first with tongue, sword or bullet. History had proved that the Sikhs are not aggressive," he asserted. He said that real harm to the country came from persons like Indira Gandhi who had warned the Sikhs living outside Punjab. He also referred to the statement by Jai Hindu Sangh. Longowal regretted Parliament's silence over threat to the Sikhs in other states and called upon the Sikhs to observe December 16 as protest day.[17]

On December 5, the Home Minister, while speaking at a six-hour debate in the Lok Sabha on the camps reportedly training Punjab extremists in the neighbouring areas, appealed Longowal and Tohra to ask Sant Bhindranwale to leave Guru Nanak Niwas and surrender to the authorities. He requested the Akali Dal to dissociate from the extremist groups. Sethi reiterated government's willingness to resume dialogue with the Akali Dal, provided it was a "meaningful dialogue and not a one sided affair". He made it clear there could not be any unilateral decision and all the concerned parties would have to be consulted. He disclosed that six training camps were organized to impart training to the militants in Jammu and Kashmir, three in Punjab, two each in Himachal Pradesh and Uttar Pradesh, and one in West Bengal. The next day, he assured in the House that Punjab government would take action against Sant Bhindranwale at the appropriate time. He said that eight cases had been registered against him.

Next day, both Longowal and Tohra turned down the request to persuade Sant Bhindranwale to surrender saying that the government wanted to implicate him in false cases to suppress the Sikhs. The SGPC chief said in Delhi that there had been a tradition in Sikh history that anyone who takes shelter in the Darbar Sahib premises is not handed over to the authorities. He maintained that Sant Bhindranwale had committed no criminal offence. It was an indirect support to Sant Bhindranwale at a very critical juncture. Of course, historically, both Longowal and Tohra were correct. However, in this case, Sant Bhindranwale was not just taking shelter in the shrine.

Sant Bhindranwale Shifts to Akal Takht

The simmering differences among the militant groups came to the fore with Sant Bhindranwale shifting to Akal Takht on the evening of December 15. The provocation was Babbar Khalsa men's forcible occupation of the two rooms in Nanak Niwas where he was staying. This militant organization supported Longowal. When Sant Bhindranwale's associates objected to this, SGPC authorities expressed helplessness. The Sant directed his followers to vacate all the 29 rooms they were occupying in the Niwas. Tohra met him the next day with an appeal to return. Sant Bhindranwale apprehended a conspiracy to engineer a clash, blame him for it and then summon the police. Tohra also met the Babbar Khalsa men staying there. Babbar Khalsa Chief Sukhdev Singh, on December 19, denied that his organization had been given money to force Sant Bhindranwale to vacate Guru Nanak Niwas.

A day earlier, he had described the decision of Sant Bhindranwale a mere drama saying he had started staying at Akal Takht for the night much earlier.

While Sant Bhindranwale had come to symbolize the militant movement, in a move aimed at challenging his supremacy, the Babbar Khalsa, on December 20, claimed the gunning down of 35 persons over the period, mainly the Nirankaris. In general perception, these incidents were being attributed to Sant Bhindranwale's associates. Longowal lost no time in denying his links with this militant organization. The Babbar Khalsa chief clarified that his outfit was opposed to the killing of innocent Hindus and had also condemned the killing of bus passengers at Dhilwan and Naushehra Pannuan. Power struggle was on among the militant outfits. The Babbar Khalsa, that very day, had also announced its political target as Khalistan. However, this announcement was not given any importance by the media. It was Sant Bhindranwale with whom the militant movement had come to be associated.

Months before this development, Amarjit Kaur, widow of Fauja Singh who had led the protesters to the Nirankari meet, in a private talk with this author, had claimed that most of the killings being attributed to the associates of Sant Bhindranwale were in fact carried out by Babbar Khalsa men. She also talked of some sort of understanding with Longowal including financial support. Till then, she had not talked to any media person. It was after much persuasion that she opened up in off the record interaction which lasted more than an hour. Here was a new dimension to the militant movement. Now Babbars had come on record to claim credit for the killing of Nirankaris.

On December 19, initiating a damage-control exercise, the SGPC chief issued an appeal to various militant groups and organizations staying within the complex against making any comment, which could be detrimental to the cause of the Akali struggle or encourage factionalism. He said that any violation of that code of conduct would be contrary to the sentiments of the Sikhs. He met both Sant Bhindranwale and Longowal separately. Tohra was perhaps the only senior Akali leader who commanded influence among the radicals also.

Bichhu Ram, Station House Officer of Police Station Guru Har Sahai in Ferozepur district was shot dead on December 19. This action was considered significant as Sant Bhindranwale repeatedly referred to him in his speeches for torturing Sikh youth and denigrating Sikh religion. The Station House Officer of Police Station Sultanpur Lodhi in Kapurthala district, Bhagwan Singh, was gunned down on December 30.

Bhindranwale Rejects Peaceful Struggle

With the peaceful agitation by the Akali Dal getting prolonged without any tangible results, Sant Bhindranwale made a qualitative shift. On December 31, he rejected the idea of a peaceful agitation by the Akalis in the face of oppression and torture of Amritdhari Sikhs while making a significant departure from his earlier stand on Khalistan. "Earlier, we did not ask for Khalistan, but had no objection to accepting it if the government offered it. Today, it is different. It is for the government to make up its mind on the question of whether to remain with us or not." Moreover, he defined the character of the ongoing agitation as the decisive war between the 'turban' (representing the Sikhs) and the 'topi' (the cap representing the Hindus) for obtaining the rights of the Sikhs. For him, the Indian state represented the 'topi'. The occasion was the weeklong religious training camp organised by the AISSF.

In yet another significant development, perhaps for the first time, he made a scathing attack on the Akalis who, he alleged, had started a character assassination campaign against him. He also sounded a note of warning against those who wanted to grab political power by exploiting the name of the Sikh Panth and the Sikh martyrs. He had unfolded his agenda in unambiguous terms. The unresponsive attitude of the Centre towards the demands of the Akali Dal was providing the necessary space for this agenda. There was no more any hidden agenda. However, he was too cautious in defining the political goal as the sovereign Sikh state in explicit terms.

With the radical tendencies dominating the political space, the silent majority of Punjabis residing in Delhi, including retired defence, IAS and IFS officers, authors, artists and journalists, made an intervention by issuing an appeal to confront such tendencies. The appeal read: "The situation in Punjab is more than disturbing. The rapid escalation of tension between Hindus and Sikhs can be dangerous for the state and for the nation as a whole. The protracted delay in facing the problems, in taking decisions, has led to a deep frustration, which in turn has given birth to extremism of the most virulent kind. Action, therefore, has to be immediate if peace and stability are to return to the state.... to allow the state to be paralyzed or torn apart by communal frenzy would be suicidal. Therefore, it is imperative that the demands voiced in Punjab be demarcated as demands not of a particular community but of a region as a whole. This is the context in which they must be seen and pressed. We have to cut through the legacy of the past when Punjabis were divided on the basis of languages. The disowning of the mother tongue by some and the aggravation of other problems by inexplicable delays in the formation of a Punjabi-speaking state have created a schism between the Hindus and the Sikhs, which can be disastrous for both communities, for Punjab, and indeed for the whole of India."

It further said, "There have been enough talks and discussions. Agreements have been reached on several occasions. These have not been honoured or implemented. The Union government owes the Indian people an explanation for inaction and drift. We call upon all men and women of goodwill – the silent majority, which is the real backbone of the country – to recognize the dangers inherent in the Punjab situation and give clear expression of their concern and dismay at this inaction. We also call upon them to:

(*i*) Condemn all actions of terrorism, violence and communal killings,
(*ii*) Support each other in maintaining the peace of a secular society,
(*iii*) Respect the sanctity of every place of worship, and denounce any attempt by anyone to desecrate any such place, and
(*iv*) Oppose attempts by anyone to use places of worship of any community as a refuge from the law, for that is the worst form of desecration."

The signatories included I.K. Gujral, who later rose to be the Prime Minister, Air Marshal Arjun Singh (retd), Karuna Ahmed, Sheila Bhatia, Pran Chopra, K.S. Duggal, Lt Gen Jagjit Singh Aurora, Khushwant Singh, Harji Malik, Inder Malhotra, Kanwar Mohinder Singh Bedi, N.K. Mukherjee, who was later appointed Governor of Punjab, Amrita Pritam, Aroon Purie, Romesh Thapar, Romilla Thapar and Rajinder Sareen.[18] The designs of the Centre had also come to be questioned from such elite sections of the society and not just the political parties.

By the beginning of 1984, the Darbar Sahib complex had been completely taken over by various militant groups. Young boys moving about with automatics dominated the shrine complex. Such was the scare that the local Sikh population had virtually stopped going to the shrine. The situation was very tense. Shopkeepers from the area around the shrine complex went to Sant Bhindranwale in a deputation. The issue was of extortion by some people considered close to the Sant. They had come with the keys of their shops, which they said they were willing to hand over to him. The complaint was against Satinder Singh P.T., the person who could not manage his escape from Darbar Sahib Complex during the Army attack. Atop the langar building, the Sant thrashed him with a lathi in full public view.

This was one extreme. There was another one too. Some followers of Sant Bhindranwale objected to women wearing make up into the shrine. Either it was over enthusiasm or some method in madness. The

Morcha dictator expressed helplessness in controlling this situation. By that time, he was a loner as few people visited him. At the same time, there used to be heavy rush in the Bhindranwale camp. That was also a period when Sant Bhindranwale and Longowal were publicly distancing from each other.

Under increasing tension, the first delegate session of the newly-constituted Akali Dal youth wing was held at Manji Sahib on January 22, 1984 where Longowal gave a call to the youth to plunge into the battlefield. This was aimed towards setting at rest the apprehensions in the minds of the AISSF leaders about the genesis of this organization in competitive politics. Denials apart, the youth wing of the Akali Dal had been set up as part of the efforts to strengthen the hands of Longowal.

Significantly, the authority of Longowal was challenged that very day as anonymous leaflets posing six questions to him were distributed in the Darbar Sahib complex at the youth wing convention. This was aimed at accusing him of betraying the cause of Sikh struggle. He was asked why were Akali demands being bargained with Centre in a clandestine manner; with whose permission did Parkash Singh Badal meet Rajiv Gandhi in Moscow and Indira Gandhi in New York; why did he ask the PM to detain Sikh leaders Jagdev Singh Talwandi, Sukhjinder Singh and Bharpur Singh Balbir, under the National Security Act; who was behind the conspiracy to get Sant Bhindranwale arrested by engineering a feud between Babbar Khalsa men and his (Sant Bhindranwale's) supporters in Nanak Niwas; who had permitted Badal to start a 'rasta roko' agitation on January 31; on what basis were Nirlep Kaur, Jiwan Singh Umranangal, Harchand Singh Fattanwala, Surjit Singh Sokhi, Talib Singh Sandhu, Sucha Singh Chhotepur, Hari Singh Zira and Jaswant Singh Bathinda, who were hobnobbing with the government, dubbing Sant Bhindranwale an agent of the government; and lastly, what was Longowal and his associates' motive behind getting Bhai Ranjit Singh arrested?

Longowal cautioned people against forces opposed to the Panth. Badal's alleged meetings with Indira and her son were never substantiated. It was an effort to add to the atmosphere of mistrust that was increasing with the agitation getting prolonged.

Confrontation between the Longowal-led section and Sant Bhindranwale's associates had come into the open. The situation was forcing Akali Dal to move towards the extreme to save party leaders from getting marginalized under the onslaught of the radicals and the adamant attitude of the PM.

In order to assert an exclusive and separate Sikh identity and compete with the radical sections, the Akali Dal on January 27, 1984 raised the demand for amendment in Article 25(2) (b) of the constitution, which clubs Sikhs with the Hindus. They announced an agitation including the burning and mutilating this section of the Constitution. Badal opposed the move to burn the section at the party forum. However, he did not defy the party decision once it was arrived at and was among the first to implement it.

The party threatened to observe 'Panth Azad Week' from April 2 to hammer the exclusive and separate Sikh identity. The Centre responded with the offer to amend the relevant provisions of the Constitution after consulting representatives of the Sikh community. The SGPC constituted a 21-member committee to suggest amendments to the section. Longowal, in a pamphlet brought out on this, quoted the promises Congress made to the Sikhs before Independence, including the resolution moved by Pt Jawaharlal Nehru in the Constituent Assembly on December 9, 1946 that states: "Adequate safeguards would be provided for minorities in India." He had said, "By recognising the individual identity of the Sikhs by conceding them a separate personal law based upon their own customs and traditions in harmony with their socio-cultural heritage and by extending concessions to the weaker sections of all religious denominations, the government would be removing a basic anomaly in the fundamentals of the Constitution of the country". The party also gave a call for Punjab Bandh on February 8, 1984.

Secret parleys were on between the Akalis and the Centre in January with Tohra playing the role, one of the channels being Buta Singh. During several meetings with Tohra, Sant Bhindranwale conveyed that he was not averse to any settlement but the Akalis should not relinquish any of the demands. The surrender of Ranjit Singh, facilitated by a senior Akali leader, was part of the strategy to convey that Sant Bhindranwale could also be taken care of by the Akali leadership.[19]

On February 1, Longowal publicly admitted to his fundamental differences with Sant Bhindranwale on the policy matters for the first time. He disclosed that Sant Bhindranwale had suggested him that motorcycles and arms be purchased on a mass scale for killing people of a particular community. The Akali Dal chief asserted that he was firmly committed to communal harmony and peace and did not approve of the line of action suggested by Sant Bhindranwale as it ran counter to the canons of Sikh religion.[20]

On the other hand, the militant Sikh leader deprecated the soft line being pursued by the Akali leadership. He said that those who advocated non-violence were overlooking Sikh history. Addressing the day-long convention of the AISSF, Sant Bhindranwale said that the Akali morcha was a rare example that rejected use of force to wreak vengeance on enemies of the Panth. He also rebutted the charge of his being a Congress agent. "If I am a Congress agent, why are arms licences of my associates being cancelled by the government and why my supporters are being rounded up?" he asked. He alleged that a section of the Akalis was in league with the Congress, trying to sabotage the Akali morcha for personal political benefits. He also cautioned against government attempts to create rift among various sections of the Sikhs to weaken the movement. Part of the Darbar Sahib complex occupied by militants came to be equated by some Akali leaders with the Chambal ravines in Central India, which sheltered dacoits.

However, the very next day, Longowal refuted the agency report about his differences with Sant Bhindranwale. Sant Bhindranwale too denied having suggested to Longowal that motorcycles and arms should be purchased for intensifying the morcha.

Significantly, Longowal sought the co-operation of all Hindu organizations for making Punjab bandh on February 8 a success. The call for the bandh had earlier been given on January 27 to press for amendment of Article 25. Letters were sent to all parties, employers' organizations and trade unions soliciting their support. The letters to the Hindu organizations were written in Hindi. Longowal tried to clarify that the Akali demands were neither communal nor of one section of the population in the state. He once again tried to make the distinction from the politics of the militants.

BJP General Secretary L.K. Advani welcomed this distinction made by Longowal as the first earnest attempt, though belated, to dissociate the Akali leadership from the radicals. He asked the Akali leaders to condemn the killing of Nirankaris.

After Longowal, it was Sant Bhindranwale who came under attack from some sections. A militant organization had earlier posed some questions to Longowal. Now, it was Babbar Khalsa's turn to pose eight questions to Sant Bhindranwale on February 2.

The questions were: why did the person who propagated use of motorcycles and fire arms failed to protect the sanctity of Guru Granth Sahib and flee from Chando Kalan near Sirsa in Haryana in 1981 leaving the holy book behind; why did he go back on the solemn pledge he took before Akal Takht in April 1978; were not certain office bearers of the AISSF involved in smuggling and other anti-social acts; was not Rajinder Singh Mehta, who allegedly placed severed heads of cows in temples, acquitted in the case with the connivance of the government; what punishment should be meted out to those close associates of his who indulge in drinking and love making within the holy precincts of the Darbar Sahib Complex and was performing the betrothal ceremony of an AISSF activist at Akal Takht, a gross violation of the traditions of the highest Sikh seat [The weddings of some of the associates, including his soft-spoken personal assistant Rachhpal Singh and AISSF General Secretary Harminder Singh Sandhu were performed at the Akal Takht].

The Punjab Bandh on February 8 was unprecedented and peaceful. "The like of this had perhaps never happened in Punjab. An eerie silence enveloped the countryside. The only sound one could hear on the highways was the chirping of birds. The press vehicles breaking this silence were looked upon with curiosity."[21] The bandh was peaceful and signaled the government at the Centre as to who was in command in the border state. The Centre once again invited the Akali Dal to participate in tripartite talks. However, the politics of violence was again to sabotage these talks.

Communal Clashes in Punjab

The success of Punjab bandh was perhaps a provocation to some forces to engineer clashes using the Hindu Suraksha Samiti, which had called for a bandh in Punjab, Haryana and Himachal Pradesh on February 14. The call had been given to press for the release of its President Pawan Kumar Sharma who had earlier been detained under the National Security Act. The law and order situation in the state took a turn for the worst during this bandh as communal clashes rocked several places in the state. Amritsar, Jalandhar, Ludhiana, Patiala, Ferozepur and Khanna were placed under curfew. At least 14 people were killed and about 200 injured in one of the worst waves of group clashes in Punjab since Partition. The model of Darbar Sahib at the Amritsar railway station was smashed. The BJP also supported the call for bandh and some party leaders were involved in the violent incidents at the Amritsar railway station. The BJP leaders involved in these incidents included Harbans Lal Khanna who was later gunned down. Incidents of violence were also reported from Haryana where Sikhs traveling by road were attacked. "Vicarious communal reprisals of this kind are a shame in much the same way as the murder of innocent bus travelers in Punjab last year," The Tribune commented on January 16, 1984. Apparently, the clashes were pre planned. The harassment of Sikh passengers in Haryana continued for a couple of days. The communal backlash was an indication of the coming events.

Ironically, Sumit Singh, editor of the progressive Punjabi monthly Preetlari who escaped the Hindu fundamentalists in Haryana during those turbulent days because he was clean-shaven, was shot by the militants in his native village near the international border in Amritsar district on February 22.

A Times of India edit on February 16 stated: "The moderate Akali leadership, in particular, must realize that neither universal denunciation nor the security forces by themselves can sufficiently curb the Hindu backlash unless they make a clean break with Sant Bhindranwale and his diehard followers". At the same time, it said, "The polarization of communal extremism in Punjab, betokened by Tuesday's riots, is, however, not irreversible. There can be no doubt that the vast majority of the Punjabis, Hindus and Sikhs, wish to live in harmony, as they have done for centuries, and have a profound stake in peace. This is why the leaders of the state unit of the BJP in Punjab, as also of the Hindu Suraksha Samiti, have been quick to condemn the disrespect shown to religious places during the bandh and the smashing of the replica of the Golden Temple at the railway station in Amritsar, as also of the portraits of some gurus and saints elsewhere".

It was the timing of the violence which was all the more important. The violence took place on the eve of the tripartite talks. The target of those instigating violence was to sabotage any chance of settlement.

Expectedly, the tripartite meeting held on February 15 was adjourned after unanimously condemning violence in Punjab and with an appeal to the people in the state to stand for unity, solidarity, brotherhood, communal harmony and peace. The Home Minister referred to the eruption of violence and said that certain elements tried to vitiate the atmosphere in the state. The meeting was adjourned on Surjeet's suggestion to enable all to work for restoration of peace. Badal said that all should join in restoring communal harmony in the state. The ministers present at the meeting, apart from Sethi, included Venkataraman, Buta Singh, Mukherjee and Narasimha Rao, besides Krishnaswami Rao Sahib, Alexander, Chaturvedi and Special Secretary P.P. Nayyar. The Akali delegation consisted of Badal, Tohra, Barnala, Balwant Singh and Randhir Singh Cheema. The Opposition leaders present included Chandra Shekhar, Madhu Dandvate, Biju Patnaik, Jagjivan Ram, Surjeet, Samar Mukherjee, Inder Deep Sinha, Chitta Basu, G.R. Kochak, C.T. Dandapani, Dr Sarup Singh, S.N. Mishra, S.C. Mohanta, L.K. Advani and Lok Nath Joshi. The Cabinet Committee on Punjab Affairs also heard the views of Bhajan Lal and Prof Sher Singh from Haryana.

The Hindu view was summed up after the February 14 bandh in the following words, "We feel that they are talking in the same way as the Muslim League did in 1947 and because this has happened with us once, we will not let it happen again; this is what we are preparing ourselves for.... They are never satisfied and we feel that ultimately what they want is what they say in their prayer everyday 'Raj karega Khalsa'

(The Khalsa will rule)."[22] Those who had all along been trying to portray the Akali agitation as secessionist had succeeded in the design. This perception had virtually justified what happened in the region on February 14.

Later, Surjeet sharply attacked the Centre for this stalemate and commented: "On February 7, when Prime Minister accepted the suggestion of the opposition for tripartite talks, we were hopeful of finding a solution. And on February 14, when we met again we had hoped to succeed, but it seems the extremists and the government succeeded in their game. What happened in Haryana from February 14-21 could not have happened without the connivance of the government. It shocked everybody. Sikh extremists also intensified their activities to further poison the atmosphere."[23]

The Central Reserve Police Force exchanged fire with the militants holed inside the Darbar Sahib complex for about five hours on February 17 in which two persons were killed. The firing started at 11.30 am and continued till about 5 pm. The exercise aimed at assessing the firepower of the militants and also the strategic locations of their fortifications. The area was under curfew.

NOTES

1. The Indian Express, July 7, 1983.
2. The Statesman, July 15, 1983.
3. The Indian Express, June 22, 1983.
4. The Indian Express, July 21, 1983.
5. The Indian Express, July 26, 1983.
6. The Tribune, July 25, 1983.
7. The Indian Express, July 28, 1983.
8. The Indian Express, August 4, 1983.
9. Arvind Kala, The Indian Express, October 26, 1983.
10. The Indian Express, August 19, 1983.
11. Akali Patrika, September 5, 1983.
12. The Indian Express, September 23, 1983.
13. The Indian Express, October 11, 1983.
14. Quoted from his speech of October 16, 1983.
15. The Times of India, November 17, 1983.
16. The Indian Express, December 3, 1983.
17. The Tribune, December 6, 1983.
18. The Tribune, January 23, 1984.
19. The Indian Express, February 1, 1984.
20. The Times of India, February 2, 1984.
21. The Indian Express, February 9, 1984.
22. Virendra, The Telegraph, February 22, 1984.
23. The Telegraph, March 28, 1984.

7

Last Meeting with Sant Bhindranwale

It was around 9 am on May 25 and Akal Takht was already over crowded. All India Sikh Students Federation President Amrik Singh was holding his court, settling disputes of the people in a corner on the upper floor. At this time he had also come to slip into Sant Jarnail Singh Bhindranwale's role in some respects, especially in making interventions in dispute management. Sant Bhindranwale had been making such interventions for the last few months and providing quick justice to people. It was the shortest cut, bypassing the long and tedious judicial process. People would come to him even with land disputes.

Sant Bhindranwale was sleeping, his room locked from inside. He had woken up very early and was now taking a nap in the hot and sultry morning. His associates from the Damdami Taksal were oiling their guns in the adjoining room. Amrik Singh, donning the role of Sant Bhindranwale in resolving disputes of the people, was not to the liking of many as it was being interpreted as over ambitiousness. This was conveyed to me by Rachhpal Singh, the soft-spoken personal assistant of Sant Bhindranwale who tried to impress upon me to talk to the Sant about it.

After waiting for about an hour, I decided to leave. I had gone to Amritsar to cover the Akali developments and the assignment was over. However, Rachhpal persuaded me to wait for some more time as Sant Bhindranwale would be annoyed with them in case I left without meeting him. He opened the door after some time to go to the toilet, people waiting there rushed into his room. He returned to his room and on spotting me in one corner, signaled me to wait. After about half an hour, only Amrik Singh was left with him. I told Sant Bhindranwale that I wanted some time with him alone. Amrik Singh left. What followed was about one-hour interaction during which the possibility of Army attack had also come under discussion. I asked him what could the way out be in such a tense build up. He answered, straight and simple, "Let the government enter into an honourable solution with the Akali Dal on the demands. All those in jail including those relating to the militant activity should be given general amnesty. I will return to my headquarters at Mehta Chowk". The air was filled with apprehension but Sant Bhindranwale was calm.

For a moment, I could not believe what he was saying. However, after Operation Bluestar I came to know that he had made the same proposition to an interlocutor who called on him on May 28 and the conversation was tape recorded. According to highly-placed sources in the Congress, the cassette was taken to Prime Minister Indira Gandhi.

This was my last interaction with Sant Bhindranwale. While traveling from Chandigarh, I had seen Army convoys moving to Amritsar. Operation Bluestar was on. Operation Bluestar had to be there. The story based upon this interaction was filed after the Army action was spiked.

Years after Operation Bluestar, Capt Kanwaljit Singh, one of the saner voices in the Shiromani Akali Dal, looked back and drew conclusion that this extreme confrontation could have been avoided had any of the two sides taken the initiative. Capt. Kanwaljit was one of those who had taken the initiative but he was not considered an important leader then. However, he had visualized the ramifications of the frightening situation. He shared this with me once while discussing the situation prevailing prior to Operation Bluestar. With the situation deteriorating all over, including in the Darbar Sahib complex, he had suggested suspension of the agitation for a few weeks to Harchand Singh Longowal in early April. This could have provided a breather but Longowal was silent to the proposition. He held that in case Indira Gandhi was resorting to deadly politics, the Akali Dal could still have avoided the June action by suspending the agitation. Moreover, the suspension would have made a clear distinction between the Akalis and the militants.

The reports about Centre's decision to invade the Darbar Sahib complex appeared in as early as the last week of February, 1984 giving the militants a lot of time to prepare for the show down with the Indian state. It referred to the Centre's plans to launch a decisive action to flush out the militants from the holiest of the holy Sikh shrine. According to this report, the PM had an unscheduled meeting with Chandra Shekhar and Bharatiya Janata Party leader Atal Behari Vajpayee. Both these leaders later rushed to consult Communist Party of India General Secretary C. Rajeshwara Rao to know the Left's reaction to what they had heard from the PM. Later, neither Chandra Shekhar nor Vajpayee, at any stage, hinted that Indira Gandhi had taken them into confidence on Operation Bluestar.[1] Shekhar was the only senior leader who later strongly reacted against the Army action.

The same day, The Telegraph carried a hard hitting editorial under the caption 'Cowards of Punjab', excerpts from which are reproduced here: "There are a handful of men inside, some with sophisticated semi-automatic weapons, who are misusing the sanctity of this holy place to challenge not only the law but also the spirit of the nation. These men, and their leader, Sant Jarnail Singh Bhindranwale, are cowards of course, who, unable to face either the people or the authorities, are hiding from the law by misusing the respect, which this nation gives to Sikhism and holy institutions of that religion. If these pretenders like Bhindranwale had any courage, or if their spurious passions had any genuine popular support, they would not need such sanctuaries. No leader who has wrought change in his or her country through a popular movement, armed or unarmed, has needed the protection of walls; the crowds have ensured what protection from authority the leader may need. Since Jarnail Singh Bhindranwale does not have the real support of Punjab's people, he brandishes the guns of a few fanatics so that the country might be impressed with his display of silly bravado. Tragically, this game is being conducted by adolescents who do not know the price of life or the meaning of anything larger than their pathetic need for self-promotion. And so the extremists, each day, shame their own glorious Sikh martial traditions by behaving like bullies and thugs, killing an innocent here and an innocent there. What does Jarnail Singh Bhindranwale, whose intellect and grasp of national affairs would be laughable were it not so frighteningly simplistic and dangerous, hope to achieve behind the sandbags piled on the roof on which he spends the winter days within the precincts of the Golden Temple? A revolution? Somebody should tell Jarnail Singh, since it is impossible to believe that he will ever realize it himself, that revolutions are not made by hit and run cowards like him.

"The sadder part of this story is that this leader of cowards is a consequence of degenerate democratic politics, which the state of Punjab has had the misfortune to undergo since the coming of the Congress (I) in 1980. The nation has had to pay a heavy price for this. It is now time that mollycoddling stopped. However, Delhi should be wary of one thing. First it made Jarnail Singh an extremist; it should not now turn him into a martyr. The opposition parties might have a point when they say that since it was the Congress (I), which created the mess in Punjab, the same party should try and untangle it. But that would, in the end, be a purely destructive attitude. The majority of the

Akali Dal obviously is eager as anyone else to be rid of extremism of Sant Bhindranwale. It is those parties who still have some credibility with the Akalis who must take the lead in creating the conditions for the return of normalcy. We need violence neither in Punjab nor in Haryana (where incidentally, the government of Bhajan Lal is not without sin either). We all have to work together to prevent an irritation from becoming a cancer". The politics might have been degenerate but the conviction and the commitment of the militants led by Sant Bhindranwale could not be overlooked. The media was being used to build public opinion in favour of the Army action. The role of the media not only in relation to the militant movements in Punjab but in other regions of the country, including the Naxalite movement, is a subject matter of study in itself". They proved to be mavericks, not cowards.

Sant Bhindranwale had a military strategist in Major General Shabegh Singh, who had planned the fortification of the complex. However, it was a small yet dedicated group pitted against the might of the Indian state.

Provocative posters were brought out by the BJP in Delhi while calling for a bandh against violence in Punjab. The posters showed dead bodies only of the Hindu victims in Punjab and Haryana with a heading saying, "How long will you watch the situation?"[2] The call for bandh coincided with the Akali call to burn Article 25 of the Constitution. On February 27, the call saw response from Akali workers at Chandigarh and some other places in Punjab.

The situation was signaling the communal build up outside Punjab. It could be part of the grand design of the rulers to mobilize public opinion in favour of the planned Army action. The BJP was already pressing for decisive action.

In the aftermath of the February 14 communal violence, CPI (M) leader Harkishan Singh Surjeet wrote to Longowal in March pleading him to withdraw the agitation. He argued: "The dominant feature of today's situation is that a growing polarization on communal lines is taking place threatening not only the unity of the Punjabi people but also the values of secularism, patriotism and nationalism created during the struggle for independence through the sacrifices of thousands and thousands of our people.... at this juncture, it was expected of you as a believer in Hindu-Sikh unity to suspend the movement and work for Hindu Sikh unity.... I appeal to you to give up the agitation against Article 25 of the Constitution, to sharply denounce the activities of the Sikh extremists as anti-national and to declare that gurdwaras will not be allowed to be used to harbour criminals. By these bold steps, you will be able to force the unwilling hands of the central government to concede the just demands".

Surjeet further observed, "Your call for observance of Azad Panth Saptah can only add fuel to the fire. The concept of Azad Panth can only provide grist to the mill of Sikh extremists from whom you have been trying to demarcate yourself.... The new slogan of Azad Panth that you have raised now is nothing but a slogan to provide a theoretical basis for Khalistan. Whether you realise it or not, your movement which was against the central government is being converted into anti-Hindu movement. I do not want to minimise the role of Hindu communalists to divide and disrupt the unity of not only the Punjabi people but also in creating a feeling of hatred against the Sikhs in other parts of the country as well". However, it was the stubborn attitude of the government at the Centre and the apprehension of getting marginalized, which had forced the Akalis to raise the demand.

At a time when the countdown had already started for the decisive state action, Sant Bhindranwale reiterated the call for armed struggle. Leaders including Sukhjinder Singh, Harinder Singh Kahlon and Amarjit Singh Chawla at a political conference near Kartarpur in Jalandhar district called upon the Sikh masses to march towards the Darbar Sahib complex in case the security forces raided the shrine. At another conference at Patiala on March 13, the AISSF leaders threatened retaliation against the Hindus in case the security forces attacked the shrine complex. The BJP observed Protest Day by staging dharnas at the district headquarters in Punjab on March 25 against the killing of innocent persons.

AISSF banned

The AISSF was finally banned on March 19, 1984 for indulging in subversive and anti-national activities. A few days later, on April 3, Punjab and Chandigarh were declared "dangerously disturbed" areas under Section 3 of the Armed Forces (Punjab and Chandigarh) Special Powers Act. The National Security Act was also amended on April 5, making it more stringent. It sought to extend the detention period to six months without obtaining the opinion of the advisory board in Punjab and Chandigarh. The ordinance to amend the Act was issued at a time when the Lok Sabha was in session, inviting strong reaction from the opposition. The Home Minister, as he laid the copy of the ordinance on the table of the House, assured the agitated members that the provisions would not be misused, especially against the political opponents. The members who opposed this procedure included Ram Vilas Paswan, Prof. Madhu Dandvate and Subramaniam Swamy (All

Janata Party), Chitta Basu (Forward Block), Somnath Chaterjee (CPI-M) and M.A.R. Kabuli (National Conference). Chatterjee said it was strange that the government had not hinted at it a day earlier during a discussion on the situation in Punjab.

Political violence related to Punjab continued to escalate during this period. Delhi Akali leader and President of the Delhi Sikh Gurdwara Management Committee Harbans Singh Manchanda, a protégé of Indira Gandhi, was gunned down on March 28 in the national capital.

Yet another dimension was added to the militant violence when the protagonist of Panjabiat and Rajya Sabha member Prof. V.N. Tiwari of Panjab University was shot in Chandigarh on April 3. This was one incident, which shocked everyone. He was considered close to the Prime Minister. Alleging that the murder of Prof. Tiwari was the sequence of a conflict between the Arya Samaj and the Congress (I) leaders over the appointment of the next Vice-Chancellor of Panjab University, Longowal demanded probe by the Central Bureau of Investigation, which was never ordered.

The Prime Minister held consultations with the cabinet committee thrice on April 3 while Home Secretary M.M.K. Wali was sent to Amritsar in the wake of violence during BJP's bandh against April 2 killing of former party MLA and district President Harbans Lal Khanna. Wali returned in the evening. Krishnaswami Rao Sahib also held discussions with Special Secretary Prem Kumar, Chief Security Advisor R.N. Kao and heads of the intelligence agencies and paramilitary forces. Violence had broken out in Amritsar during the funeral procession of the BJP leader on April 3 where eight people were killed and nine injured. The violence was communal in nature as Sikhs were the target.

Longowal, on April 7, wrote to President Giani Zail Singh demanding a judicial inquiry into the killings. He protested against what he described as the rabid communal attitude of the CRPF against the Sikhs, especially in the context of violence during the funeral procession on April 3. He pointed out that all the eight persons killed were Sikhs and all of them were killed in firing by the CRPF during the procession. Two Sikh policemen from the Punjab Armed Police were lynched to death by the mob aided and abetted by the CRPF. Subsequently, on April 10, the Border Security Force and the Punjab Armed Police replaced the CRPF at strategic points in the walled city. Patiala was also brought under curfew on April 12 as violence erupted there.

As the spurt in violence continued all over Punjab, Wali discussed the law and order situation with Governor B.D. Pande, Haryana Chief Minister Bhajan Lal and the senior officers from the two states and Chandigarh.

Demand to ban Akali Dal

Taking extreme position, the Hindu Suraksha Samiti had earlier, on April 3, submitted a memorandum to the Governor of Punjab demanding a ban on Shiromani Akali Dal. It alleged that its leaders had turned anti-national and seditious and demanded that they should be punished and the party MPs and MLAs disqualified for insulting the Constitution of the country. The Akali agitation should be declared illegal and anti national as it had destroyed trade and shattered communal harmony. The Samiti also demanded special recruitment of Hindus in the police force in proportion to their population and carbine licenses for its office bearers.

In another significant development, the followers of Sant Bhindranwale and Longowal again exchanged accusations and counter accusations in the Darbar Sahib complex on April 13. Both the groups came out with pamphlets, a four-page leaflet bearing the photograph of Sant Bhindranwale questioned Longowal. It read: "When the Sikh youth tried to avenge the indignities heaped on the Sikhs in Haryana by annihilating the tyrant police officers and anti-Sikh forces, several Sikh leaders in league with the Hindu communalists started dubbing Sant Bhindranwale and his followers as extremists, separatists, terrorists and robbers... the dictator of the Dharamyudh Morcha started criticising those Sikh youth who had annihilated the enemies of the Sikhs by terming them as agents of the government. Sant Longowal, by terming the demands of the Sikhs as demands of the Punjabis, tried to dishonour and belittle the sacrifices made by the Sikh youth." The Akali Dal was under attack from two fronts, a section of the Sikh radicals as well as a large section of the Hindus.

In a counter attack, Sucha Singh Chhotepur, Hari Singh Zira, Talib Singh Sandhu and Jaswant Singh, presidents of the Gurdaspur, Ferozepur, Ludhiana and Bathinda district units of Akali Dal respectively, dubbed Sant Bhindranwale not only as a Congress agent but also a traitor. These leaders alleged that Longowal's critics were speaking the language of the government for creating a wedge between the Hindus and the Sikhs. Asserting that the Akali Dal could not sacrifice the interests of 50 lakh Sikhs living outside Punjab to please one man's ego, the party made it clear that it stood for the welfare of the entire humanity.

The politics of bullet took yet another unexpected turn when Surinder Singh Sodhi, a close associate of Sant Bhindranwale and a proclaimed offender, was gunned down by one Surinder Singh Chhinda and his accomplice Baljit Kaur at a dhaba opposite the Darbar Sahib complex on April 14. The incident gave a jolt to Sant Bhindranwale whose personal assistant Rachhpal Singh blamed Akali Dal Secretary Gurcharan Singh of hatching a conspiracy to assassinate the militant leader. The allegation was based on the questioning of Baljit Kaur, which was tape recorded.

Baljit Kaur, dazed and holding a revolver in her hand, rushed towards Sant Bhindranwale shouting that she had killed Sodhi as he had misbehaved with her. She was overpowered a few feet from Sant Bhindranwale. She was interrogated in a very brutal and barbaric manner. She confessed that the plan to eliminate Sant Bhindranwale and some of his associates was finalised in Guru Ram Das Serai three days back and that Gurcharan Singh had paid Rs 2 lakh to Chhinda for the job. Her body, which was recovered later from a gutter, bore marks of inhuman torture. Ironically, those who had tortured her in the Darbar Sahib complex itself justified their action. The militants themselves did not care for the sanctity of the shrine. Human rights activists talked of torture only by the security forces. Chhinda's body, hacked to seven pieces, was found next day near Mananwala in Amritsar district. Gurcharan Singh later resigned.

There is another dimension to this incident. Baljit Kaur carried revolver and she entered the shrine without getting noticed. This was the situation despite the fact that the shrine complex during that period was under close watch.

In the continuing violence, Malak Singh Bhatia, an Akali leader associated with Jagdev Singh Talwandi, was gunned down in public view in the Darbar Sahib complex on April 16, indicating further deterioration of the situation in the shrine complex. He was alleged to be one of the conspirators in gunning down Sodhi.

In a major action on April 15, the militants set on fire 31 railway stations across nine districts of Punjab. Dashmesh Regiment, the militant wing of the AISSF, owned responsibility. There is a significant aspect of this action as the government had advance information about it from Research and Analysis Wing. "S.K. Tripathy, the RAW man who was in-charge of Amritsar from mid 1982 to May 3, 1984 had sent a coded telegram to Delhi with details of an impending attack on more than 40 railway stations in Punjab and the government chose to do nothing about it," Surya, a monthly magazine, reported in its September 1984 issue. Deterioration in the situation was perhaps part of the grand design.

Suspension of Morcha Suggested

It was in view of the situation getting out of hands of the Akali leadership that Capt Kanwaljit Singh, comparatively a junior leader at that time, suggested Longowal to suspend the Morcha by at least two months. The logic was that forces out of Akali Dal control had virtually hijacked the situation. It was for the first time during this movement that killings had taken place inside the complex.

Taking belated initiative to control the situation, the SGPC constituted an 11-member committee on April 22 to check the antecedents of all those staying in various serais in the complex. However, it was an exercise only on paper as by that time, the SGPC had ceased to have effective control over the shrine complex.

Times were bad and Chandigarh, for the first time in its history, was placed under curfew on April 18. Angry mobs protesting against the gunning down of Hindu Suraksha Samiti chief Inder Pal Gupta turned violent. This violence was communal in nature.

It was during that period that Communist Party of India senior leader Arjan Singh Mastana, who hailed from Patti in Amritsar, planned an armed counter offensive against the militants, though in a limited area. The idea was to arm the Left cadre who would provide protection to the people in rural areas, especially in one of the worst-affected Patti-Tarn Taran belt. He also approached a former Naxalite activist in Chandigarh to coordinate the operation. This proposal, however, could not be taken to logical conclusion. He was later gunned down during the post-Bluestar period. Such a proposal had also been mooted at a party meeting at the state level also but it did not find much acceptance. The central secretariat of the party also turned down the suggestion. It was around this period that the Amritsar district unit of the CPI adopted a resolution demanding deployment of the Army, especially in the border district, which was later withdrawn at the intervention of the party high command.

Centre's Offer, Revolt against Longowal

To allay the apprehension that the government had some other designs in Punjab, the Indira Gandhi government, in the Rajya Sabha on April 24, offered to refer the river waters dispute to a tribunal provided there was an overall agreement to resolve the Punjab tangle. Home Minister P.C. Sethi made the offer at the fag end of his reply to the three-hour discussion on the situation in Punjab in which 15 members participated. The offer was conditional and hence rejected by the Akali Dal.

Sources, however, hinted at secret parleys between the Centre and the Akalis during this period. According to a report, the Centre maintained contact through its sources with Longowal in Amritsar, Tohra lodged in Chandigarh jail and Badal in Tihar jail. The Centre succeeded in organizing two secret meetings between Badal and Tohra in Chandigarh. Badal was secretly flown to Chandigarh twice in Air Force plane for this. A member of the cabinet committee had accompanied Badal to Chandigarh.[4]

In yet another development in the Panthic politics, more than 40 members of the SGPC from the Akali Dal and a number of party activists including former ministers and district and circle presidents, on April 27, revolted against Longowal's leadership and announced their allegiance to Sant Bhindranwale. They announced at Akal Takht in the presence of Sant Bhindranwale that Longowal was not giving the right directions to the Panth. Earlier, these rebels led by Darshan Singh Issapur had walked out of the Akali Dal meeting after charging Longowal with pursuing a weak policy.

Sant Bhindranwale welcomed the rebels but made it clear he was not in favour of a parallel Akali Dal. He appealed to them to keep working for the Dharamyudh Morcha. However, those who revolted against Longowal's leadership were not considered mainstream leaders. Describing the walkout as pre-planned, the Morcha Dictator, while offering to step down, proposed that the Akal Takht Jathedar and chiefs of other Takhts find a way to forge Panthic unity.

The Akali Dal warned of disastrous consequences if the Centre failed to find a solution to the problem in Punjab. The party demanded lifting of the ban on the AISSF. It was resolved to organize meetings at the village level from May 1 to May 13 followed by prayer meetings for the glory of the Panth on May 14. The district-level meetings were to be organized from May 15 to May 22. The Akali Dal was trying to exert moderate intervention without openly coming into confrontation with the radicals.

Bhindranwale a Religious Leader: Rajiv

While the Akali Dal was trying to make democratic and moderate interventions, the Congress leadership, in a way, tried to subtly neutralize their interventions and encourage tendencies associated with the line of Sant Bhindranwale. The inevitability of the Army action was already being discussed in the political circles at that time. All India Congress Committee General Secretary Rajiv Gandhi visited Chandigarh on April 29 and held discussions with the party men. He held that pressure from within the Akali ranks was blocking a settlement. He reiterated that the doors were always open for a dialogue with the Akalis. It was during this visit that he made his startling and the oft-quoted statement on Sant Bhindranwale.

Q. Is Bhindranwale an extremist?

A. This is for you to evaluate.

Q. Do you think he is a political leader?

A. He is a religious leader and has not shown any political inclination so far.[5]

He admitted that Sant Bhindranwale represented a powerful pressure group. This comment of Rajiv Gandhi is often quoted to substantiate the charge that the Gandhi family encouraged Sant Bhindranwale to pursue its deadly and degenerate politics for narrow political ends.

The Congress legislators submitted a memorandum to Rajiv Gandhi demanding early transfer of Chandigarh to Punjab and expeditious resolution of the remaining issues. He also met Bhajan Lal. The Congress in Punjab decided to launch a mass contact programme from May 15 to mobilize support against militancy and confront the Akali Dal. This was Congress' first organized move to confront the situation head on.

Top Sikh clergy including Akal Takht Jathedar Giani Kirpal Singh, Takht Keshgarh Sahib Jathedar Giani Harcharan Singh Mahalon, Takht Damdama Sahib Jathedar Giani Lakha Singh, head priest of Darbar Sahib Giani Sahib Singh and head priest of Akal Takht Giani Pritam Singh, on April 30, issued a 'directive' to maintain peace within the Darbar Sahib Complex. The directive stated that no firing should take place in the Darbar Sahib area, nor should anybody be punished or tortured or beaten in any manner or killed. The clergy asked for an end to the war of attrition going on among various Sikh organizations.

However, it was too late.

The upward trend in the graph of violence continued unabated. Giani Bachan Singh, the Deputy Superintendent of Police (retd), his wife and daughter, were gunned down in Amritsar on April 30. He was on the militants' hit list for a long time. Squadron Leader Paramjit Singh, posted at Raja Sansi Airport near Amritsar, was shot on April 22. Earlier, Punjab Shiv Sena President Bhupinder Kumar was shot and injured at Ferozepur on April 10 while two Hindus were gunned down at Rahon in Hoshiarpur district the same day.

It was in this backdrop of intensified violence that the security forces laid siege to the gurdwaras in Moga and Vajidpur in Ferozepur district. Longowal, giving an ultimatum to the government to lift the blockade within 48 hours, gave a call to the Sikhs to form self-sacrificing squads and march to the two gurdwaras. The SGPC also served a notice on the government. The Jathedars of the five Takhts decided to lead the shaheedi jatha (self-sacrificing squad) in case the siege continued. It was perhaps for the first time that the Takht chiefs had donned such a pro-active role ever since the Akali Dal had launched the agitation. Sant Bhindranwale supported the decision of the Jathedars. A day earlier, they had warned the government against the continuing siege of these gurdwaras. Longowal also took up the issue with Sethi and Buta Singh. The Border Security Force lifted the seven-day siege of the three gurdwaras at Moga on May 3. This siege was part of the exercise to assess the situation likely to arise following the Army action in the Darbar Sahib complex.

In another incident that had the potential to unleash communal violence, Romesh Chander, proprietor and editor-in-chief of the Hind Samachar group, was gunned down at Jalandhar on May 12. Incidents of arson following his killing were reported in the area. Curfew was imposed in Jalandhar, Amritsar and Patiala in view of the bandh call. His father Lala Jagat Narain had been gunned down earlier in 1981.

The law and order situation in the state further dipped. Former Akal Takht Jathedar Giani Partap Singh was assassinated on May 10. He had been highly critical of the activities of the militants. Four Hindus in a Ferozepur-bound bus were shot dead near Moga on May 21 while two more Hindu passengers were gunned down near Faridkot the same day. Three persons were killed in the grain market at Mari Megha in the Khalra sector in Amritsar district.

Foodgrains as Weapon

In the region, which is the food basket of the country, strategic use of foodgrains can be one of the most potent weapons during a peaceful agitation in the context of food security. It was the success of the Green Revolution in Punjab, which made India self-sufficient in wheat and rice. This state was contributing about 60 per cent of the rice and 50 per cent of the wheat to the central buffer stock at that time. The agitating students in Assam had resorted to blockade of petroleum products to other states as an effective weapon. The Akali Dal also decided to make strategic use of this weapon.

A crucial meeting of the Akali Dal high command, party legislators and district presidents was held on the night of May 22 at Amritsar to formulate a new strategy. They decided to launch a non-cooperation agitation and block the movement of foodgrains out of the state from June 3. The wheat procurement season had just got over and most of the stock was lying in the state. This strategy was finalised by Longowal, Tohra and Badal on the morning of May 23 after four hours of discussion with other leaders earlier. The triumvirate had been authorized to take a final decision.

It was a sensitive move. The impact would have been felt at the national level as the buffer stock would have lasted just a few weeks. The SAD workers were to gherao the godowns and block the movement of the special trains transporting wheat to other states. The Akali Dal had the main support base in the rural areas. The ranks of the radical sections were also drawn mainly from this section. Sant Bhindranwale himself was from a family of marginal farmers. The Sikh peasantry at large was coming into such direct confrontation with the government at the Centre for the first time, though such sections had launched agitations earlier also, including in the pre-independence days. However, it was the Green Revolution, which had enabled the farmers to produce such huge marketable surplus.

The non-cooperation movement was to be confined to non-payment of land revenue and abiana (canal water cess) in the first phase. Under the banner of the Bharti Kisan Union, the farmers had already demonstrated their strength in March by laying siege of the Punjab Raj Bhavan in Chandigarh for about a month in a peaceful manner to press for their demands. Ever since the launch of the Dharamyudh Morcha, the Akali Dal had come out with one of the most powerful weapons in its armoury. It was this decision that was cited by the Centre as one of the immediate provocations for the Army action.

Interestingly, while giving the call for the blockade of foodgrains movement, the party demanded bonus on wheat at the rate of Rs. 20 per quintal sold in the open market, mainly to the government procurement agencies for the central pool.

Other decisions taken at the meeting but not announced included blocking of power and river water flowing to other states and stoppage of the excavation of the SYL Canal. The meeting expressed full faith in the leadership of Longowal, who had offered to resign. This expression of faith was in the context of the revolt earlier by a section of the Akalis against him.

Nine resolutions were adopted in the meeting. The party appreciated the appeal issued by the Sikh clergy to create congenial atmosphere in the Darbar Sahib complex. While demanding lifting of the ban on the AISSF, the meeting warned the government against erecting fortifications around the shrine.

A section of the media had strong reservations even about this non-cooperation movement as it was perceived to have dormant tendencies of violence. This was clear from the editorial in a leading daily. "The Akalis are about to launch what they euphemistically describe as a non-cooperation movement but which has in it the seeds of violence arising from an intensified challenge to governmental authority."[6] By that time, the Army units, which were to implement Operation Bluestar, had already been garrisoned at Amritsar. The call for non-cooperation proved to be the flash point for the Army action and the call had not been given by Sant Bhindranwale.

According to classified information from sources, Longowal was delivered a letter from Indira Gandhi towards the end of May, at the time when the armed forces had been moved to Punjab for the decisive action. The letter was handed over by an emissary of the Centre to Abinashi Singh, the all-powerful personal assistant to Tohra for passing it on to the Morcha dictator. The emissary did not know its contents as the letter was sealed. Longowal never talked about the letter till his death. Abinashi Singh fell prey to the politics of gun with the revival of militancy in the post-Bluestar period. The content of the letter remained confidential.

A delegation of Arya Samaj called on Indira Gandhi on May 30 urging her to take strict action to deal with the situation in Punjab. Led by Ram Gopal Shawlwale, President of the International Arya Samaj League, the delegation expressed the view that the situation had assumed dangerous proportion and was threatening the sovereignty of the country. The delegation suggested that either the state should be handed over to the Army or emergency be declared. Public opinion was already being mobilised in the country in favour of Army action.

Secret Meetings

The Akali leaders had altogether nine secret meetings with the government at the Centre since the launch of the Morcha till Operation Bluestar. Two rounds of talks were held at 27, Safdarjung, on November 16 and 17 1982 by Badal, Balwant Singh, Ravi Inder Singh and R.S. Bhatia with Union Ministers including R. Venkataraman, P.C. Sethi and Shiv Shankar. Also present were Congress MP Amarinder Singh and bureaucrats P.C. Alexander and T. N. Chaturvedi. Another meeting was organized at the same venue on January 17, 1983. The participants on the Akali side included Badal, Tohra and Ravi Inder Singh while the Congress side was represented by Rajiv Gandhi, Amarinder Singh, Krishnaswami Rao Sahib and P.C. Alexander. These very Akali leaders had another meeting with the same set of people on January 24, 1984. Tohra, Barnala, Balwant Singh Ramoowalia and Randhir Singh Cheema explored the possibility of resolving the Punjab tangle with Narasimha Rao in Chandigarh on March 27. The meeting was also attended by Rao Sahib, Alexander and Home Secretary M.M.K. Wali. This was followed by a meeting between Badal and Narasimha Rao in Delhi the very next day with the same set of officers also present. Narasimha Rao returned to Chandigarh on March 29 to meet Tohra, Badal, Barnala and other leaders he had met earlier. This time, Special Home Secretary Prem Kumar was also there.

In one of these meetings, the Centre tried to give the impression that Chandigarh could be transferred to Punjab and the issue of the rest of the Punjabi-speaking areas be entrusted to a commission. This was subject to the settlement of the river waters dispute. One of the Akali leaders proposed that the Centre should allocate one MAF additional water to Punjab rather than going in for a tribunal. Held at Alexander's residence, the meeting was also attended by Balwant Singh, Amarinder Singh, Ravi Inder Singh, Narasimha Rao, Shiv Shanker and T.N. Chaturvedi. According to one of the participants, the Prime Minister seemed to be favourably inclined to this suggestion.

An aircraft was kept ready to fly the Akali leaders to Amritsar. The understanding was to make the announcement of acceptance of demands and the withdrawal of the Morcha simultaneously, by the government in Delhi and by the Akalis in Amritsar. However, that Akali leader again changed his mind on the river waters issue in favour of the tribunal. Surjeet was also invited to the venue of the meeting. The plane never took off as the final word never came from the Prime Minister. After waiting for a long time, when Indira Gandhi was contacted, it was conveyed that the parleys were off. In between, Haryana Chief Minister Bhajan Lal, who was camping in Delhi, had got wind of the proceedings of the meeting and called on Indira Gandhi. The talks appeared to have been sabotaged. However, Bhajan Lal could not have dictated a powerful leader like Gandhi and the decision against settlement was part of her own calculations.

Some more meetings were held prior to Operation Bluestar. Chandigarh Airport's lounge was the venue of one such meeting on April 21. The central team including Narasimha Rao and Mukherjee along with a team of officers was there to interact with Tohra, Badal, Barnala, Ramoowalia and Cheema. This was followed by another meeting at a guest house in New Delhi on April 26. This meeting with Narasimha Rao, Mukherjee and Shiv Shankar was attended by Tohra, Badal and Barnala. At one of the secret meetings as deposed by Tohra, Badal was to be brought from Tihar Jail (where he was lodged in early 1984) to Burail Jail where both Tohra and Barnala were detained. Narasimha Rao and Alexander were to attend that meeting on behalf of the government. However, Badal could not be brought to the venue of this secret meeting for some reasons. The emissaries of Indira Gandhi discussed the proposal to divide Chandigarh with the two Akali leaders.

Very sorry, Madam does not agree

In the January 24, 1984 meeting at New Delhi, Rajiv Gandhi sought views of Tohra as to what should be done. Tohra shot back saying that the Centre had linked the Punjab problem to the forthcoming Lok Sabha elections. His apprehension was that the Congress would play the Hindu card and that the elections to the Delhi Municipal Corporation were just an experiment in this regard. The second experiment had been done in Jammu and Kashmir. Tohra gave the example of Indira Gandhi addressing public meetings at Gurdaspur and Batala in Punjab during Jammu and Kashmir Assembly elections to give the impression that she was fighting against Khalistanis while projecting herself as a saviour of the Hindus. Tohra said that under the given situation, he did not expect any solution. It was at this point that Rajiv Gandhi, unconsciously, hinted at the future plans regarding Punjab. He said that in case Congress was determined to play the Hindu card, then Hindus would be the happiest if Army was sent into the Darbar Sahib complex. Tohra reacted by saying his doubts had been confirmed as that exactly was the design. Rajiv Gandhi vehemently denied any such move. He gave the impression that come what may, the Army would not enter Darbar Sahib. Within a few days, Tohra's worst fears came true.

The Akali leaders had their last meeting with the Centre on May 26. The Akalis were represented by Tohra, Badal and Barnala, and the government's representatives included Narsimha Rao, Mukherjee and Shiv Shankar. The Akali leaders were air lifted from Chandigarh and taken to a guest house at R.K. Puram in Delhi. The formula discussed included the transfer of Chandigarh to Punjab within eight days, setting up of a commission for the left-out Punjabi-speaking areas, referring the river water dispute to the Supreme Court and the Anandpur Sahib Resolution to a commission.

The Akali leadership proposed that the adjudication of the river waters dispute by the Supreme Court should be within the framework of the established riparian principles. The Akali leaders also pressed for declaration of Punjabi as second language in neighbouring Haryana and Delhi and enactment of the All India Gurdwara Legislation. Shiv Shankar wanted assurance on behalf of Sant Bhindranwale of which Tohra took the responsibility. The Akali leaders also suggested that Haryana could be given some areas from Uttar Pradesh in case the Centre had any apprehensions on that score. The meeting continued for more than four hours. It was for the first time that negotiators from the government had not raised many objections to the Akalis's suggestions. The negotiators from the government side said they would meet them again after consulting the Prime Minister. It was around 4.30 in the evening when they returned and said, "Very sorry. Madam does not agree." Indira Gandhi had rejected the formula. Operation Bluestar was on. Tohra shared the contents of these meetings years later.

After these meetings, the SGPC chief conveyed to Longowal that the government was not serious. Both the leaders were convinced that it was a subterfuge to gain time for the Army action and that the PM's intentions were mala fide. He also shared that the Army had prepared a model of the Darbar Sahib complex at Chakrata near Dehradun to train the commandoes. On June 2, Longowal instructed Tohra to call a party meeting to discuss the situation.

It is significant that the Prime Minister did not have any direct interaction with the top Akali leadership after April 5, 1982.

Of course, Tohra was approached by Buta Singh and Darbara Singh sometime in 1983 for secret talks with Indira. Buta Singh had met Tohra at the dera of Baba Harbans Singh near Gurdwara Bangla Sahib in Delhi. Tohra was of the view that it would not be possible to keep meeting with the PM a secret. The meeting could materialize only if Longowal gave him clearance. Later, Darbara Singh met him at night at the official residence of Tohra in Delhi. He also made the similar offer. Tohra again gave the same reply that the direction for the meeting should come from Longowal as meeting Indira Gandhi in secret would be suicidal. Giani Gurdit Singh also met him with the offer to arrange his meeting with Giani Zail Singh.

Governor Requisitions Army

It was Tohra's meeting with Governor B.D. Pande that generated a lot of controversy and it was after this meeting that he was accused of giving a green signal for the Army action. Here is Tohra's own version. He had suggested to Badal to meet the Governor with the demand to lift ban on the AISSF. However, later he himself sought an appointment and the meeting lasted about 45 minutes. Pande put the pre-condition of an incident-free week for accepting the demand. Suddenly, Tohra told the Governor that it seemed he was not taking him seriously. It was at this stage that Tohra expressed his apprehension of the Army attack. The Governor was categorical in saying that as long as he was in the office, Army action could be ruled out. This was later conveyed by him to Longowal as well as Sant Bhindranwale.

Sant Bhindranwale's opinion, expressed in the presence of Major General Shabeg Singh, was that maintaining peace was not under his control. At the same time, he told Tohra not to worry about the ban saying that the government would be forced to lift it within 24 hours the day the Taksal decided on it. His meeting with Sant Bhindranwale lasted about half an hour. Amrik Singh, who was also present, said it would be seen as to how Tohra succeeds in getting the ban lifted. The SGPC chief said it was all in his hands. Despite the opposition to the

Army action expressed by the Governor, Tohra continued to be apprehensive.

The security forces assessed the strength of the militants and position of the fortifications inside the Darbar Sahib complex in the heaviest ever exchange of fire on June 1 lasting more than five hours. The Akali Dal and the SGPC lodged strong protests with President Giani Zail Singh and the Governor against the firing. Curfew was imposed in the walled areas of the city. Akal Takht Jathedar Giani Kirpal Singh and Darbar Sahib Head Priest Giani Sahib Singh reacted to the firing saying it was a "challenge to the Khalsa Panth and the Sikh organisations". They appealed to the Sikh masses to give a befitting reply to the paramilitary forces for violating the sanctity of Darbar Sahib complex.[7] In the views of the SGPC chief, this firing was the beginning of assault on the shrine complex. Repeated attempts from Chandigarh to establish telephonic contact with Sant Bhindranwale late in the evening that day did not succeed despite efforts by the men in the telephone exchange who were also curious to know as to what was happening in Amritsar as the lines to the Darbar Sahib complex were not getting through.

At a meeting of the senior officers at Kotwali, Amritsar Deputy Commissioner Gurdev Singh Brar questioned as to on whose orders had the CRPF opened fire on the shrine. In protest, he proceeded on leave and was replaced by Ramesh Inder Singh. However, before proceeding on leave, he attended a meeting on June 3 at the Army headquarters at Amritsar presided over by Major General Kuldip Singh Brar, the local commander of Operation Bluestar. The DC made it clear that Sant Bhindranwale would not surrender to which the Major General retorted, "When tanks roar, planes zoom and guns crack, even generals tremble in pants." Incidentally, Sant Bhindranwale also happened to be a Brar.

On June 1, the state government had denied reports about a likely Army action while asserting that the movement of the troops was not related to the requirement of the law and order situation. An official spokesman in Chandigarh said the state government had not requisitioned more central forces as the existing force comprising about 150 companies of the CRPF and the BSF were considered sufficient to deal with the situation. This denial had come despite the fact that heavy Army movement had been observed in the last week of May in the state. Convoy after convoy moved into Punjab.

The government, however, announced the deployment of Army in Punjab the very next day. Also, Punjab and Chandigarh were declared restricted areas for foreigners. Lt General Ranjit Singh Dayal, Chief of Staff, Western Command, took over as Adviser (Security) to the

Governor. Punjab Governor was made administrator of the Union Territory of Chandigarh also. Army had also been deployed on the second line of defence along the border with Pakistan. The Army action was on.

Punjab and Chandigarh were formally handed over to the Army on June 2. An official announcement said, "In view of the escalating violence by terrorists in Punjab, the Governor of Punjab has asked the central government for the assistance of the Army to help in restoring law and order. The Government has accepted the Governor's recommendation. The Army has been called in aid of the civil authority and Lt Gen Ranjit Singh Dayal, Chief of Staff, Western Command, has taken over as Adviser (Security) to the Governor of Punjab. The paramilitary forces deployed in Punjab will continue their work but under the over all command of the Army. In order to ensure coordinated action against terrorist activities, which in recent days, have extended to the Union territory of Chandigarh, the Governor of Punjab has been appointed Administrator of the Union territory of Chandigarh also, as a temporary arrangement for two months."[8]

For the record, the Army had been deployed on the recommendation of the Governor, who, a few days earlier, had very categorically assured Tohra against it. Normally, it is the district magistrate who is supposed to requisition the army. However, in this case, that formality had been done at the higher level, by the head of the state, the Governor. The army action was not confined just to the Darbar Sahib complex.

Indira Gandhi came out with her final words on the situation in Punjab through her broadcast to the nation over the All India Radio in the evening of June 2. She said, "The reality that has emerged is not the adequacy or otherwise of the terms of settlement offered by the government on the various Akali Dal demands, but the fact that the agitation is now in the hands of a few who have scant regards for the unity and integrity of the country or concern for communal peace and harmony or the continued economic progress of Punjab. Every three or four months a new morcha is started, and Punjab is torn by a senseless and tragic strife. Terrorists and anti-social elements have gained the upper hand. Innocent people, Sikhs and Hindus, have been killed. There is arson, looting and sabotage. Holy shrines have been turned into shelters for criminals and murderers. Their sanctity as places of worship has been undermined. A deliberate and systematic campaign is spreading bitterness and hatred between Hindus and Sikhs. And worst of all, the unity and integrity of our motherland is being openly challenged by a few who find refuge in holy shrines".

The hint was clear about the impending action. About the Akali demands, she said, "Whenever the demands did not affect the rights of other states or where they could be fitted into a wider framework, the government had no hesitation in accepting them." As she was advising the Akalis in her broadcast to continue the talks with an appeal to call off their proposed non-cooperation agitation, the Army was out for the decisive action. Ironically, her speech ended with the appeal: "Don't shed blood, shed hatred." She herself became victim of the deadly politics reinforcing the Sikhs' belief that anyone who orders attack on Darbar Sahib does not survive.

The Prime Minister got the necessary support including from the media. "Not to mince words, the war on the terrorists cannot be won so long as their leaders can continue to function from within the sanctuaries of various gurudwaras, especially the Golden Temple in Amritsar. And the war has to be won if India has to live. This means that it is not desirable to delay for long an operation to flush out the criminals."[9] The media behaved as if the Army was to attack a foreign country. Punjab was virtually treated as a foreign land by the armed forces.

Longowal and Tohra reacted to the Army deployment calling it "a terrible blow to the peaceful and the democratic agitation of the Akali Dal" and convened a meeting of the party MPs, MLAs, district unit presidents and the executive committee on June 4 to discuss the situation. They said the Akali Dal was fighting against injustice and discrimination and it would continue to do so till the end. They declared that they would face "all the atrocities, oppressions and aggressions boldly". Tohra had gone to Amritsar to attend the June 3 meeting of the party working committee convened by Longowal to discuss, among other things, the situation arising out of the CRPF firing on the shrine complex. The only other leaders to reach Amritsar included Balwinder Singh Bhunder and Sukhdev Singh Dhindsa. They informed Longowal that Badal had left for Uttar Pradesh. It was decided to hold the meeting on June 4. Both Dhindsa and Bhunder went back while Tohra stayed put in Amritsar.

Longowal tried to contact the PM to lodge his protest over the June 1 firing but could not succeed. Tohra wrote a letter to her the same day, which was delivered to the DC. Later the DC conveyed that the letter had reached the Prime Minister. Hundreds of devotees had started gathering in the complex for the Martyrdom Day of Guru Arjan Dev on June 3. The electricity and water supply to the shrine were cut in the night and telephones disconnected. Indira Gandhi had decided to attack Darbar Sahib on the Martyrdom Day of Guru Arjan Dev, whose peaceful sacrifice is unparalleled in the history of the region.

President Giani Zail Singh put off his 10-day visit to Himachal

Pradesh. Earlier, the PM had a discussion with him, their longest meeting ever since Giani Zail Singh had been elected the President.

The Akali Dal, on June 3, rejected PM's appeal to call off the non-cooperation agitation while describing her broadcast as a distortion of facts. The Morcha Dictator made it clear that there was no change in the party programme. He demanded that his party should also be allowed to broadcast its views on the All India Radio for the same amount of time as the PM.

In Delhi, the situation in Punjab was reviewed at a high-level meeting that was attended by Krishnaswamy Rao Sahib, Alexander, security adviser to the Prime Minister R.N. Kao, Wali and Prem Kumar.

On June 3, Punjab and Chandigarh were placed under 36-hour curfew from 8 pm onwards and all train and bus services were suspended. The curfew was extended later. Not only the movement of private vehicles including trucks, cars, jeeps, mobikes, but animal and hand driven carts and bicycles were also banned. Communication links with Punjab were snapped. The telephones in the entire city of Amritsar went dead, including those of the district police chief and except that of the DC and the local Intelligence Bureau chief. Publication of newspapers in the region was suspended in view of the curfew.

The Chandigarh administration issued a notification banning media coverage of the Akali agitation and operations of the security forces for two months on the logic of maintaining communal harmony and public order. The government in Punjab had already issued this notification the previous night. Due to the censorship, people in Punjab started depending upon Radio Lahore and the BBC.

Wali said in Delhi on June 4 that the militants hiding in religious places would be served with the notice to come out and surrender. The Army had been assigned the task of restoring complete normalcy in the state. The action to be taken was to be decided by the Army commander in consultation with the local authorities.

As per Tohra's deposition in the Supreme Court, he went to the sarovar in the early morning of June 4. It was at that time that heavy firing started targeting the complex. He returned to his room in the Teja Singh Samundari Hall. Longowal, Balwant Singh Ramoowalia, Abinashi Singh, Bhan Singh, Darshan Singh Issapur, Nachhattar Singh and Jagir Singh had also gathered there. The firing continued incessantly. Tanks and armoured vehicles entered the shrine on June 5 through Gate No 2 on the langar side. The Army men came out of the armoured personnel carriers and entered Guru Ram Das Serai where pilgrims were staying. They started breaking the doors of the rooms and lobbing hand grenades without any warning. A large number of devotees died. Medical aid was refused to the injured. Tohra also said that he saw Army personnel looting and setting the Sikh reference library on fire from the SGPC office complex where his room was located.

It was after the imposition of curfew that Tohra had a meeting with Sant Bhindranwale who advised him to leave the complex and go abroad to undertake political work to carry forward the Sikh struggle. He assured that his escape would be managed by his supporters. However, Tohra said Sant Bhindranwale would be the best suited for the purpose and he should escape. Sant Bhindranwale refused.

It was on June 6 that a Major accompanied by some soldiers went to Tohra saying he was under arrest. Others arrested with him included Longowal and Amarjit Kaur. They were taken to a room in Guru Ram Das Serai. It may be mentioned that the office of the SGPC is located in Teja Singh Samundari Hall next to Guru Ram Dass Serai. Longowal conducted the morcha from a room on the first floor of the Teja Singh Samundari Hall. The rest room of the SGPC President is also located in a corner of this complex. About 15 officials of the SGPC were already there in that room. They were taken to the cantonment around 5 pm.

Tohra had claimed in his testimony that he complained to a Colonel in the camp about the looting of the Darbar Sahib treasury by the Army men. The treasury (toshakhana) having costly jewellery and other items had four keys and could be opened only when all the four persons authoriszed to keep the keys were brought there. One of the persons was Bhan Singh who was with him in the camp. The said officer agreed for inspection by the authorised persons provided he gave in writing that these people were his representatives. Abinashi Singh was also sent with Bhan Singh. They were back after about two hours as the inspection could not be carried out due to the presence of Defence Minister R. Venkataraman and Army chief General A.S. Vaidya. They told Tohra that the Defence Minister and the Army officers were going about in the complex with shoes on. They also saw a number of persons with their hands tied at the back towards the Ghanta Ghar side. They also saw the bodies of the dead being carried away in the trucks used for carrying night soil.

Neither the district administration nor the Army authorities had contacted the SGPC authorities for conducting a search of the complex before the action. The Army action should have been ordered after exhausting all other avenues. But it had not been done so.

In none of the briefings in the days preceding Operation Bluestar, had the government raised the apprehension that the Khalistan government was to be announced by Sant Bhindranwale from inside the shrine around that time. The argument advanced by the Centre to justify the Army action was this apprehension. Sant Bhindranwale had never given any such signal. Of course, he had started advocating armed struggle to achieve the goal without using the term Khalistan.

In fact, there was nothing new about the demand for Khalistan. The issue had been raised in the Punjab Assembly as far back as on March 25, 1982 through a non-official resolution listed in the name of Communist Party of India group leader Raj Kumar, which dubbed the demand as secessionist, anti-people and anti-national. In his absence, Babu Singh of the CPI moved the resolution on authority from Raj Kumar. Speaker Brij Bhushan Mehra disallowed the discussion on it after about a 40-minute debate on the issue of desirability of taking up the subject. The ruling Congress members had divergent views. However, Chief Minister Darbara Singh favoured the debate.

NOTES

1. The Telegraph, February 25, 1984.
2. The Telegraph, February 25, 1984.
3. The Telegraph, March 28, 1984.
4. The Indian Express, April 27, 1984.
5. The Indian Express, April 30, 1984.
6. Prem Bhatia, The Tribune, June 1, 1984.
7. The Indian Express, June 3, 1984.
8. The Indian Express, June 3, 1984.
9. The Times of India, June 4, 1984.

8

Courage of Conviction

Western Army Commander Lt General K Sundarji admitted during the first press briefing after Operation Bluestar at Chandigarh that the militants had confronted the Army with unprecedented courage, determination and dedication. Such fortitude could only be attributed to deep conviction and unflinching faith in the leadership. Those entrusted with the responsibility of the action had clearly miscalculated this courage of conviction, which motivates a person to make the supreme sacrifice and differentiates militancy from other forms of violence. The loss suffered by the Army was too heavy. And never in the history of free India had such large number of innocent men, women and children been killed in a state operation of this magnitude. The country was to pay a still higher cost in the years to come. Though the intelligence agencies had rightly given the assessment that the Army action in the Darbar Sahib Complex would alienate the Sikh community for at least 10 years, this was not the only cost the country had to pay. The tremors of Operation Bluestar continued to be felt for years. The Sikh issue had now been globalized.

The government charged those arrested from the Darbar Sahib Complex during the Army action with waging war against the Government of India, conspiracy, sedition and promoting enmity among various communities. Those arrested also included women and children (read terrorists!), all enemies of the Indian state. The First Information Report No. 182 was registered at Amritsar on June 10 under sections 121, 121-A, 122, 123, 124-A, 153-A, 153-B, 307, 302 and 333 IPC on the basis of the report lodged by an Army brigade commander. It stated the brigade was posted outside the Darbar Sahib Complex. There were AISSF and Dal Khalsa members, extremists led by Sant Jarnail Singh Bhindranwale, Kuldip Singh Kohla of Amritsar and Major General Shabeg Singh (retd.) holed up inside the shrine. These people took measures to wage war against the Indian Union and establish an independent state known as Khalistan. The terrorists, instead of responding to the appeal to come out, opened intensive firing from automatic firearms, anti-tank weapons and grenades. They also raised anti-national slogans. Ironically, the formal announcement by the militants about Khalistan from the shrine complex was made about two years later. Several other outfits like the Dal Khalsa and the National Council of Khalistan whose political objective was the establishment of Khalistan had been active for years. In this context, the reasons for the immediate Army intervention advanced by the government were far from convincing. Kohla was some unknown person till then, stated to be a small time smuggler.

An official statement issued in Delhi said an independent Khalistan fully supported by the neighbouring and the foreign powers was the obvious goal of the Punjab terrorists trained in Pakistan occupied Kashmir. Had the Army action not been resolute and determined, the terrorists' campaign would have moved towards full-scale insurgency which would have crippled the armed forces in any future confrontation across the borders. The terrorists led by Sant Bhindranwale were perhaps only cogs in the wheel. The Home Ministry statement said the government decided to deploy the Army in the state after all other methods failed and escalation of terrorist activities continued under Sant Bhindranwale's command from the Darbar Sahib Complex. However, no other method had been resorted to by the government to flush out the militants.

Giving details of the Army operation, the statement said: "From 1630 hours on June 5, 1984 onwards, continued appeals were made on loudspeakers to all within the premises of the Golden Temple to come out and hand themselves over to the authorities. 120 men, women and children came out. Similar actions took place in a number of places in Punjab. Full opportunity was given to all the inmates of the Golden Temple and other holy gurudwaras, which the terrorists had usurped, to avoid bloodshed. From 2230 hours, Army units commenced moving to the Golden Temple precincts. This drew heavy fire from the terrorists into the narrow streets at close range. Despite causalities, troops closed in and slowly commenced movement into the area around the Temple, after overcoming initial resistance. Very heavy fire had to be faced from the Akal Takht, which stood like a fortress, sweeping all avenues of approach with a deadly volume of machine gun fire, causing heavy causalities. At 1.00 am on June 6, Sant Harchand Singh Longowal and G.S. Tohra surrendered near Guru Nanak Niwas with about 350 people, including some women and children. At about 4.10 am on June 6 some troops attempting to close in with Akal Takht in an armored personnel carrier were fired by anti-tank rockets which damaged the APC. By the morning of June 6, the troops had effectively engaged all loopholes in Akal Takht. Room to room fighting continued in Akal Takht till it was cleared by 12.30 pm on June 6, though some resistance continued from the ground floor..... We must ask ourselves where all this was leading to. What were the eventual aims of this movement? They had support and encouragement from some foreign countries and had effectively controlled the Punjab countryside by ruthless terrorism."[1]

The statement further said the Akali morcha passed into the hands of Sant Bhindranwale who started the terrorist movement with active encouragement, connivance and assistance of certain foreign powers. However, the statement did not explain why the action coincided with the martyrdom day of the fifth Sikh lord, Guru Arjan Dev, when thousands of people go to the shrine to pay their obeisance or why some other strategy was not put into operation, as recommended by a central agency. Of course, at the national level, Prime Minister Indira Gandhi emerged as the saviour of the Hindu nation. The Sikhs as a community had been painted as anti-national.

These women and kid 'terrorists' were released months later, but only at the intervention of the Supreme Court on the petition filed by some human rights organizations.

The Prime Minister, while calling for a healing touch on June 8, justified the action as unavoidable and expressed her regret at what had happened. At the same time, she said no government could tolerate the continued massacre of innocent people by the terrorists. However, the subsequent events proved her wrong as the situation further worsened, the state virtually faced insurgency and was pushed into senseless violence for many years.

President Giani Zail Singh, who visited the shrine on June 8, was surprised as to how heavy weapons like the medium machine guns could be smuggled into the shrine without anybody's notice. No inquiry has ever been instituted into this aspect, not even by any subsequent Akali Dal government in the state.

Rubbing salt on the brutally wounded Sikh psyche, the government announced a compensation of Rs lakh and liberalized pensionary benefits to the Army personnel killed during Operation Bluestar.

It was during this period that Congress General Secretary Rajiv Gandhi claimed in an interview published in Sunday Times of London that the "terrorist activity and unrest in Punjab" would end in the next two to three months. He might have been echoing the official perception.

An 11-member deputation of the Shiromani Akali Dal met Governor

B.D. Pande on June 8 demanding immediate withdrawal of the Army and the handing over the complex to the SGPC so that the "interrupted maryada is resumed". Led by Surjit Singh Barnala, the deputation submitted a memorandum demanding that no repair work or reconstruction of the Akal Takht and other building be undertaken by the government and the bodies of those killed during the action should be handed over to them. The deputation included Sukhdev Singh Dhindsa, Gurdarshan Singh Grewal, Joginder Singh Sawhney and Manjit Singh Khaira.

The five Jathedars (high priests), for the first time after the Operation, met on June 17 and resolved to reconstruct Akal Takht without any change in the original design. Baba Harbans Singh and Baba Karnail Singh were entrusted with the Kar Sewa of Akal Takht. They demanded the withdrawal of the Army to restore maryada of the shrine including from the langar building (community kitchen) also. Other demands included handing over the shrine to the SGPC and opening it to the devotees, end to harassment of the Sikhs traveling in trains and buses and the release of SGPC staff including Bhan Singh, Mit Singh, Dyal Singh, Gurdarshan Singh and Narinder Singh Nanda against whom there was no case. The video film shot in the Darbar Sahib Complex should not be screened without their permission. All the Sikh soldiers who had deserted their barracks should be given general amnesty. The names of all those killed and arrested should be made public. Those who participated in the meeting included Akal Takht Jathedar Giani Kirpal Singh, Darbar Sahib Head Granthi Giani Sahib Singh, Takht Keshgarh Sahib chief Jathedar Harcharan Singh Mahalon, Akal Takht Head Granthi Giani Pritam Singh and Takht Damdama Sahib head Jathedar Lakha Singh. The government refused to hand over the complex to the SGPC for Kar Sewa.

It was the team from Jalandhar Doordarshan led by News Editor Jagdish Vaidya, which had been assigned the task of filming the situation in the complex immediately after the action was over. This assignment of the Doordarshan team was exclusively for the Army. Years later too, Vaidya would shudder over what he had seen there. The Doordarshan team was not allowed to take out any recording. The ban on the movement of vehicles in Punjab imposed on June 3 was finally lifted only on June 21.

The Prime Minister visited Darbar Sahib on June 23. Giani Sahib Singh submitted to her a memorandum demanding withdrawal of the Army and opening of the shrine at least for fixed hours and according holy city status to the entire walled city and not just 200 metre area around Darbar Sahib Complex. Ironically, he appreciated the role of the generals and the Army who, in his perception, exercised restraint and did not fire at the main shrine. She did not make any comment.[2] He subsequently came under attack from the militants.

The shrine, for the first time after the Army action, was opened to the public for two hours on the morning of June 25. Many people cried on seeing the damage inside the shrine. Several curious onlookers could be moving around in the shrine with their heads uncovered, which is violation of the Sikh code.

The Central Intelligence Agency again figured in a PTI report, which said this agency and Pakistan intelligence were actively involved in the training of anti-India terrorists in specialized camps in Pakistan. The report stated the terrorists were being trained in camps at various places in Pakistan by the Pakistan intelligence under the direct supervision of American CIA agents. Muslims in the guise of Sikhs were being trained in Kasur near Lahore by a Brigadier of the Pakistan artillery. This report was purportedly based on the interrogation of the persons by the Army arrested during Operation Bluestar.[3]

Another Hijack

In the first such major incident after Operation Bluestar, an Indian Airlines air bus from Srinagar to Delhi was hijacked to Lahore on July 5. The hijackers demanded withdrawal of Army from Punjab, handing over the shrines to the SGPC and reopening of the Darbar Sahib Complex to the general public. As the hijackers threatened to blow up the plane, Lahore gave permission to land on the request of the Indian authorities. Other demands included ransom of 25 million dollars and release of all the arrested Sikhs. They also demanded that those arrested in connection with the assassination of veteran journalist Lala Jagat Narain, his son Ramesh Chander and Nirankari chief Gurbachan Singh should also be released. The hijackers who surrendered to the Pakistani authorities later included Paraminder Singh Harfanmaula, Gurinder Singh, Harbhajan Singh, Ravinder Singh Pinka, Dalip Singh, Harminder Singh, Manjit Singh, Malagar Singh and Gurdip Singh.

Significantly, former Jammu and Kashmir Chief Minister Dr Farooq Abdullah pointed a finger at Indira Gandhi for this hijacking. He said in an interview, "Isn't it just too much of a coincidence that just three days after my removal from office this hijacking takes place? I read accounts of the hijacking given by the passengers, and all of them had said that the security had been so tight that every article of theirs was checked. So where did these weapons come from? They were obviously placed on board even before the plane landed in Srinagar. And I hold G.M. Shah and Indira Gandhi responsible for planning out this hijacking to malign me. They are behind it."[4]

At the political level, in its so called first major reaction, the 11-member ad hoc committee of the Akali Dal constituted to manage the party affairs in the absence of the senior leaders met at Chandigarh on July 8 and decided to send shaheedi jathas (self-sacrificing squads) to Amritsar from July 16 if the Army was not withdrawn from Darbar Sahib Complex by then. The party called upon the Sikhs all over the world to start akhand paths (uninterrupted recitation of entire Guru Granth Sahib) in gurudwaras from July 13 to perform bhog on July 15, which was to be observed as Martyrs' Day. By giving this call, the Akali Dal had accorded the exalted status of martyr to all those who had been killed during the Army action in the Darbar Sahib Complex, including Sant Bhindranwale. Ironically, Sant Bhindranwale was formally declared a martyr by the Damdami Taksal only years later.

Commenting on the situation in the state, Nirmal Mukarji, who was later appointed Governor of Punjab, wrote, " For normalcy to return, what is most crucially required is the building up of a new consensus between the Sikhs and the Hindus and between the Sikh sub-nationalism and the federal Centre."

Operation Bluestar was one part of the strategic plan chalked out by the Army to check militancy in the state. Its second part was code-named Operation Woodrose, which was launched in the countryside under which village after village, especially in the border belt, was searched and the common Sikhs, both men and women, harassed and humiliated. The entire village would be made to stand outside under the burning sun. It was this dreaded operation, which mainly triggered migration of the young Sikhs to Pakistan across the border. Hundreds of others went missing. What was strange was that this was the period when the government claimed that the border had been completely sealed by the Army. These boys got training in the use of weapons in the camps across the border. The state repression was one of the factors, which contributed to the resurgence of the militancy months later. Majority of those who crossed over to the other side were initially kept in jails and later provided training in the use of arms and explosives. Of course, their leaders were kept in private accommodation. Only junior officials from the Inter-Services Intelligence of Pakistan used to interact with the militant leaders.

State repression was one aspect of the situation. The other was again the revenge psyche. Here is a case of a young Sikh, student of Khalsa College at Amritsar, who crossed over not due to the fear of state repression but motivated by the desire to take revenge from the Indian state. He was just 19 years old and one of those whose psyche had been badly hurt due to the Army action. Some of his other class fellows were also thinking on similar lines. They discussed the situation and the talk also focused on as to how to avenge the action of the Indian state. They decided to cross over to Pakistan. They had to spend the first six months in jail and later after some messages were exchanged by the militant leaders with the ISI that they were taken out and sent to the training camp. Later one of them rose in the hierarchy of the militant group he had come to be associated with at that time, the Babbar Khalsa.

Reports appeared in a section of the media on July 6 about the mood in the Akali Dal to preserve Akal Takht in the damaged state. However, the predominant view was that the final decision on this sensitive issue should be left to the Sikh community. The same was conveyed by the senior Akali leaders managing the affairs and to the members of the clergy. Buta Singh, who had already explored the possibility of reconstruction of the Takht by the government, reacted caustically to these reports and sought explanation from Abinashi Singh.

Ironically, while the government repaired the Akal Takht, even the Akali Dal dominated SGPC decided not to leave most of the visible marks, which could recall the Army action for posterity. Years later, moves were initiated to preserve a few of such marks. A few hundred metres away, the bullet marks are till date preserved on the walls of Jallianwala Bagh reminiscent of the biggest ever massacre of the innocent men and women during the freedom struggle when peaceful and unarmed protesters organizing a rally were fired upon on the Baisakhi of 1919. Only history would judge this decision of the SGPC.

Reacting to the reports about the possibility of Akal Takht being preserved, the Prime Minister, on July 24, made it clear in the Rajya Sabha the building would be repaired despite threats by the Akalis. "We will leave it as we found it," she said adding in case it was to be left in the damaged state, the seeds of bitterness would go very deep. She made this observation during discussion on a White Paper on Punjab. She made it clear she would not entertain the demand for Khalistan and expressed the resolve to deal firmly with communal forces while not allowing any place of worship to turn into an arsenal. She continued, "I am not only the butt of attack of opposition in the country, but also of some most powerful forces in the world". However, she did not identify these forces. At the same time, she maintained these forces had always been against India but now they were against her personally. The Russians had been hinting at the CIA design to foment trouble in this region for a long time.

In the Rajya Sabha, former Punjab chief minister Darbara Singh alleged that both the CIA and Pakistan President General Zia-ul-Haq helped the militants through Dr Jagjit Singh Chohan to destabilize India.

However, the Prime Minister observed that getting information about foreign involvement always took time while maintaining it might not be in the national interest to divulge the entire information, the Times of India had reported on July 25, 1984.

Meanwhile, in an effort to frustrate the move to preserve Akal Takht, the Indira Gandhi government entrusted its Kar Sewa (construction through voluntary labour) to repair the damage to the complex to Nihang Chief Baba Santa Singh who started the work on July 17 amidst controversy and tight security. This decision of the Centre dealt another blow to the bleeding Sikh psyche. The Sikh religious places are constructed through voluntary labour by the community itself. This decision of the government violated this age old tradition.

Akal Takht Jathedar Giani Kirpal Singh, SGPC General Secretary Major Singh Uboke and Akali Dal acting President Parkash Singh Majitha condemned the launching of government sponsored Kar Sewa and described it as a second attack on the Sikhs. In a strong reaction, Baba Santa Singh was ex-communicated from the Panth by the Akal Takht for this action of his on July 22. Reacting to his ex-communication, he is reported to have said the Akal Takht Hukamnama was not binding on him as he was neither a member nor an employee of the SGPC. Moreover, he said he was not even baptised. As per The Tribune dated July 23, 1984, being the head of the "Azad Khalsa Panth", he was above the five high priests. He challenged the authority of the high priests to declare him a Tankhaiya (guilty of religious misconduct) or order his social boycott. The directives issued from Akal Takht are considered to be binding on the entire community and the Nihang chief was distorting the historical Sikh tradition with the statement that it was not applicable to him. The Nihang chief blamed Tohra for the build-up in the Darbar Sahib Complex which led to the Army action saying the SGPC chief nurtured political ambitions and was willing to go to any extent for that. It was to boost Tohra's political interests that Sant Bhindranwale was encouraged to stockpile arms and fortify the complex. "Had their evil design to divide this country succeeded, Mr. Tohra would have had high office in the new dispensation", he said. The Times of India on July 22, 1984 had reported that he favoured disbanding of the SGPC, arguing it was a political organization. Ironically, it was years later that he sought forgiveness at the Akal Takht and was re-admitted into the Panth.

Major General Kuldip Singh Brar, while leaving the Darbar Sahib Complex on July 18, expressed his "repentance" to the high priests and said, "As a soldier, I had to obey the orders and do my duty. I regret my mistake, if any. I cannot say much"[6].

In New York, a convention of the Sikhs organized in protest against Operation Bluestar on July 28, pledged to work for the establishment of Khalistan. The resolution adopted at the conclave said the unprecedented genocide of the Sikhs and the assault on Akal Takht had caused irreparable damage and alienated the Sikh community from India for ever. The convention at the Madison Square Garden was attended by about 2500 persons. The Khalistan issue was getting globalized, though the demand had not till then had formally been raised by any major Sikh organization. This was the fallout of Operation Bluestar.

Baba Santa Singh formally launched the Kar Sewa on August 1 and one of the Panj Piaras who performed ardas (prayer) for this purpose was Baba Nihal Singh Harianwelan who had earlier been arrested by the security forces on June 27 and arms and ammunition recovered from his headquarters at Hakimpur village in Hoshiarpur district.

Akali Decision to Raise Shaheedi Fund

Now it was the turn of the leaders like Giani Zial Singh and Buta Singh to feel the heat. The Akali Dal and the SGPC, on August 8, gave a call to the Sikhs to socially boycott Giani Zail Singh, Buta Singh, Lt Gen R S Dayal and Major General Brar. The party decided to observe August 15 as a protest day to express its "anguish" against the Army action and the starting of Kar Sewa by Baba Santa Singh. It was also decided to constitute a committee of retired defence officers to defend those Army men who, in the heat of the moment, deserted the barracks without any intention of mutiny. It was also resolved that those journalists who deliberately wrote against the Panthic leaders should be socially isolated. However, such newspapers and media persons were not identified.

The Akali Dal, at its meeting, decided to raise a shaheedi fund to provide financial assistance to the families of those killed during the Army operation. It was also decided to arrange for free legal aid to those facing false cases. Through another resolution, the Akali Dal condemned the Sarbat Khalsa convened by the Budha Dal on August 11. On August 9, 1984, The Tribune reported Party Secretary General Sukhdev Singh Dhindsa saying after the meeting, "The Sikhs should decide whether to stay with India or not. We are not going to be slaves." The Army action had provoked the moderate leaders like Dhindsa to take such a radical stand. However, it was only another form of democratic protest and it was nothing more than an emotional outburst against the Army action. The decision to raise a shaheedi fund was soon to be forgotten. The Akali Dal did not take the trouble even to enumerate those who had died during the Army action despite the fact that the party formed the government in 1985.

This "Sarbat Khalsa" organized by the Nihang sect at Amritsar on August 11 with the support of the government, while "ex-communicating" Tohra from the Panth, ratified the Kar Sewa undertaken by the Nihang Chief and favoured changes in the laws governing the gurudwara administration. The resolution ex-communicating Tohra held him directly responsible for the damage done to Darbar Sahib Complex and other Sikh shrines. The convention, held at Burj Akali Phula Singh outside the walled city of Amritsar, was attended by Bhai Man Singh, Jathedar of Takht Patna Sahib who presented siropa (robe of honour) to Baba Santa Singh. It was Bihar Chief Secretary S S Dhanoa who had been instrumental in the participation of Bhai Mann Singh in this conclave. Dhanoa was later appointed Advisor to the Punjab Governor.

The resolutions at this convention were moved by Rachhpal Singh, President of the Delhi-based Akali Dal (Master Tara Singh), and seconded by Bir Devinder Singh, chief whip of the Congress Legislature Party, and Buta Singh. It was essentially the show of the Sikhs aligned with the Congress. Delhi Mayor Mohinder Singh Sathi, again a Congressman, came in his official car. Bhai Man Singh was also brought to the venue in a government car and escorted to the podium by Amritsar Senior Superintendent of Police Bua Singh, The Indian Express reported on August 12, 1984. It was a futile exercise to give the impression that the Sikh community was with the government.

It was clear that instead of countering militancy at the political level, the Congress was joining issue with the Akalis who were not the main party in this bloody confrontation. Several Akali leaders themselves became the victim of militancy. One of the resolutions at the convention stated that after the loss of power in 1980, the Akali Dal took up the Anandpur Sahib Resolution at the instigation of some anti-national forces. An attempt was made to damage the entire Sikh community. Efforts were made to provoke communal riots in the state. The Akali leaders, crossing all limits, encouraged the extremists and separatists. The Akal Takht was converted into a fortress. The thrust of the resolution "ex-communicating" Tohra was that the religious places would not be allowed to be used for political purposes. Though adopted by the Akali Dal working committee way back in 1973, the Anandpur Sahib Resolution did not become an emotive issue till it was vociferously taken up by the party in 1982. The Congress was to contest the next Lok Sabha elections with the attack on the Anandpur Sahib Resolution as the main poll plank.

The response from Sikh leaders to this show was on expected lines. Amarinder Singh, scion of the former royal family of Patiala who was now emerging as the Panthic leader, on August 13, rightly described this Sarbat Khalsa as the Congress (I) convention with Baba Santa Singh as the show boy and Buta Singh as the front boy.[7] Earlier, SGPC acting President Rajinder Singh Dhaliwal had dubbed it as a Congress sponsored 'Bhaiyya sammellan' (gathering of migrant workers from the Hindi-speaking states)[8].

USSR blames CIA

Significantly, the USSR backed the Army action in Punjab as per the PTI report of August 12 datelined Moscow. This was the first official pronouncement after the Indian Prime Minister had written to Soviet President Konstanin Chernenko. The pronouncement was made by Lev Rovnin, Minister of the Russian Federation, at an Indian Embassy function.

It said: "It has been irrefutably proved that behind the extremists who made the sacred Golden Temple their base, is the Central Intelligence Agency of the United States and the aggressive imperialist circles of Washington". This statement accusing the CIA assumes importance in the context of the alert issued by the KGB in 1982 about the designs of this US agency in Punjab and Jammu and Kashmir. Significantly, External Affairs Minister P V Narasimha Rao at a meeting of the Parliamentary Consultative Committee on June 27 had referred to the involvement of foreign hand which he did not identify.[9] However, even if militancy in Punjab was the design of the CIA, how come that Indira Gandhi also played the same game? There could have been some other methods to isolate Sant Bhindranwale and his supporters holed up in the Darbar Sahib Complex, as was done later during another action by the security forces, Operation Black Thunder.

Taking the initiative at his own level, Amarinder Singh, on August 13, announced the setting up of anti-repression and legal defence committee to fight the cases of those arrested by the security forces, with renowned jurist V M Tarkunde as its chairman. The members included Ram Jethmalani, Soli Sorabji, Khushwant Singh, Hardev Singh and S.N. Kacker. It was also decided to set up such committees at the state and the district level.

Yet another Hijack

A Delhi-Chandigarh-Jammu-Srinagar flight of Indian Airlines was hijacked over Pathankot on August 23. The drama ended 38 hours later at Dubai as the UAE authorities promised a seven-day political asylum to the Sikh hijackers before their departure to the USA. It all started when the hijackers shouting pro-Khalistan slogans seized the plane over

Pathankot and directed the pilot to land at Lahore. The hijackers included Kamaljit Singh Sandhu, Amarinder Singh, Devinder Singh, Tejinder Singh, Avtar Singh, Man Singh and Surinder Singh. The plane was first taken to Lahore and then Karachi from where it was flown to Dubai. Initially, the hijackers demanded compensation at the rate of Rs 50,000 per passenger. The plane carried 79 passengers.

It was for the second time within a few months that Commander V K Mehta had been confronted by the Sikh hijackers. He was commanding the plane which Manjit Singh alias Museebat Singh had tried to hijack earlier. Initially, the Pakistan government did not concede was the demand of the hijackers for refueling. The hijackers had announced that their destination was United States. The hijackers threatened to shoot one passenger every 30 minute in case their demand for refueling was not conceded. At one stage, they offered to surrender in case Pakistan agreed to grant them political asylum. The Lahore control tower gave permission to land only after the commander threatened to make an emergency landing as the plane was left with fuel for 27 minutes only. The hijackers had taken over the aircraft within minutes of its take-off from Chandigarh. They abandoned the plane on the assurance of seven-day political asylum in UAE following which they would be allowed to fly to USA. However, they were sent back to India after nine days where they faced legal action.

At the religio-political level, in an attempt to counter the state-sponsored Sarbat Khalsa, the high priests announced the decision to convene a World Sikh Convention at Amritsar on September 2. The state government preferred to ban it and ordered raids all over the state to arrest the Akali leaders. Senior party leaders were already in jail. An official spokesman said on August 27 the step had been taken in the interest of peace and public order. The government also objected to the posters issued under the signature of the high priests that exposed the atrocities committed by the government against the Sikhs. Union Home Minister P.V. Narasimha Rao clarified that the convention had not been banned and only permission refused, which practically, amounted to the same. With the entire senior Akali Dal leadership in jail, the role of leading the community fell on the high priests, which was not unprecedented, though rare.

However, the government at the Centre, keeping up with its posture at conflict resolution, made another offer to the Akalis to resume talks on the eve of the convention provided they denounce secessionism and terrorism, which they had been denouncing all along. The Akali Dal had neither supported secessionism nor political violence and the party had been repeatedly making its position clear on this issue before

Operation Bluestar. Till then, there was not a single resolution by the party or speech by any senior Akali leader including Tohra, Badal or Longowal supporting such tendencies ever since the launch of the Dharamyudh Morcha. Despite the extreme provocation that was Operation Bluestar, the Shiromani Akali Dal had not raised this secessionist demand, even as a slogan of protest. Even when such slogans were raised at a later stage, the practice of the party continued to be democratic.

While extending the offer of negotiated settlement, Narasimha Rao said no settlement could be a one-sided affair and it had to be on the basis of some commitments and acceptance of certain obligations by the Akali Dal in the overall national interest. He added: "It follows, therefore, that the leaders of the Akali Dal should denounce in unambiguous terms secessionism in any form, agree that the gurudwaras will not be used for political purposes, undertake that the places of worship will not be allowed to store arms or harbour persons wanted by law and order authorities and condemn all forms of terrorism and violence including sabotage, hijacking of planes, arson and looting... It is for the Akali Dal to assure the nation of their agreement to these points in the larger interests of Punjab and the country." The Akali Dal continued to be under attack from the ruling Congress. The response from the Akali Dal under such a situation was on expected lines.

The World Sikh Convention, organized at Gurudwara Shaheed Baba Deep Singh at Amritsar on September 2, declared President Giani Zail Singh and Buta Singh 'tankhaiya' (guilty) and served ultimatum on the government to withdraw Army from the Darbar Sahib Complex by September 30 or face a massive march under the leadership of the high priests the next day to liberate the shrine. As per the Hukamnama issued by the five high priests and endorsed at the convention, Giani Zail Singh was found guilty of religious insolence by visiting Darbar Sahib under the cover of an umbrella, which is prohibited, by the Sikh traditions and tenets. Buta Singh was punished for his utterances against the high priests. The high priests warned that 10 lakh Sikhs would march to the shrine on October 1 in case the complex was not handed back to the SGPC by then. The convention organized under the aegis of the Akal Takht called upon the Akali factions and Sikh organizations to unite under the banner of the Shiromani Akali Dal, as that alone could "break the shackles of subordination". It demanded immediate stoppage of Kar Sewa of Akal Takht being undertaken by Baba Santa Singh.

The resolution adopted at the convention condemned the use of armed forces for the resolution of political conflicts within the country and said this would prove dangerous for democracy and secularism.

The Sikh soldiers, who had deserted their barracks, were praised for their love for religion and the government was urged not to take any action against them. It sought protection for the Sikhs settled in other states and abroad. The turnout at the convention was massive. The focus was on the need to fight against the onslaught on Sikh religion and identity in the context of the Army action.

Significantly, the only political leader allowed to address the convention was Amarinder Singh.

Giani Kirpal Singh said in his address that the Centre was trying to weaken the Sikhs religiously, politically and economically with the aim of eliminating the Sikh Qaum (Sikh nation). He described the Army action as part of this conspiracy and accused the government of creating the monster of extremism and separatism and then resorting to killings of the Amritdhari (baptised) and other innocent Sikhs. For him, the Army attack was a challenge to the honour and pride of the Sikhs.

Amarinder Singh clarified the Sikh struggle was not against any other religion or people, but against the authoritarian actions of the government and offered to make any sacrifice for the Panth. He was directed by the Akal Takht Jathedar to lead a jatha from Patiala to Darbar Sahib on October 1 to liberate the shrine.[10] By describing the Sikh struggle as just a form of protest against the authoritarian actions of the government, he had diluted its content. The Sikh struggle had its origin elsewhere.

The members of the outlawed AISSF took out a procession near the convention venue and shouted "Khalistan Zindabad" and "Bhindranwale Zindabad" slogans. This youth brigade was critical of the organizers for adopting a soft line. Some of those members of the high clergy who took soft line became the target of the militants subsequently.

Zail Singh Distressed

Giani Zail Singh expressed his displeasure with the political rulers on the issue of continuing confrontation with the Sikhs and the handling of the situation by the government. He conveyed his feeling to Narasimha Rao and Cabinet Secretary Krishnaswami Rao Sahib, following which Indira Gandhi had a 30-minute meeting with him. They discussed the implications of the resolution passed at the World Sikh Convention at Amritsar. The President told both Rao and the Cabinet Secretary: "It is President's rule in Punjab but the President does not know what major decisions are being taken. The President is not consulted about his home state."[11]

On September 5, the high priests dispatched 'hukamnamas' to Giani

Zail Singh and Minister for Parliamentary Affairs Buta Singh, declaring them guilty of religious misconduct. In the edict sent to Giani Zail Singh, the high priests said that on the orders of the President, who is also the Supreme Commander of the armed forces, the security forces attacked Darbar Sahib and 30 other gurudwaras in Punjab from June 4 to 6. Tanks were deployed in that operation and bullets hit Darbar Sahib while Akal Takht was destroyed. Bullets pierced Guru Granth Sahib in the Darbar Sahib and about 2500 manuscripts preserved in the Sikh reference library in the parkarma were reduced to ashes. Innocent persons who had come to the shrine to pay obeisance were killed or captured. A reign of terror had been let loose by the government against the Sikhs. The Hukamnama also referred to the umbrella controversy relating to the visit of Giani Zail Singh to the Darbar Sahib Complex.

The government had not provided the details about the people captured from the Darbar Sahib Complex during Operation Bluestar. It was much later that startling information started coming out. Many of those arrested did not have anything to do with militancy. Even kids were not been spared; such was the brutality of the state.

One and two-year old 'terrorists'

Ten boys, aged 10 to16 years, arrested from the Darbar Sahib Complex during the Army action, were released in September from the Ludhiana jail following a petition filed in Supreme Court by well-known social worker Kamladevi Chattopadhya. They said after the release they were beaten with rifle butts, hung upside down and tortured by the Army and the police personnel to find out their connection with Sant Bhindranwale. Two of them happened to be Bangladeshis. The migrants from Bangladesh used to reach Amritsar to illegally cross over to Pakistan as the border till then was open with cultivated fields on the two sides of the Radcliffe Line.

The apex court, on September 21, ordered the release of another batch of four women and nine children. These children were between one and 14 years of age. Yet another group of children released was in the age group of 2 and 16 years. The petitioner was the same. The detainees included Swaran Kaur with her one-and-a-half-year old son and a three-year-old daughter, Surinder Kaur with four sons aged 14, 12, 9 and 5 and Jamila Khatoon from Bangladesh with two sisters and two brothers, all arrested from the Darbar Sahib Complex.[12] The Sikh boys were on a pilgrimage while the Bangladeshis had gone to have langar and as curfew had been imposed, they could not come out. These boys included Dalip Singh (15), Kuldip Singh (15), Rajinder Singh (15), Harsaran Singh (10), Jaswant Singh (12), Lakha Singh (16), Kewal Singh

(16), Tarsem Singh (15), Chuttan Mian (15) and Ali Akbar (14). Their release was ordered by the Supreme Court on September 21. Earlier, the Supreme Court had directed district judges of Amritsar and Ludhiana to visit the jails in their areas to investigate the charge of detention of innocent women and children.

While the government had not immediately provided the identity of those taken into custody at the time of the Army action, even the Akali governments which came into power in the later period did not make any effort to identify those who had been killed in the Darbar Sahib Complex in the Army action. The law and order is otherwise a state subject. The state government could at least prepare a list of all those who had gone missing during that period. Many of those killed were part of the Akali Dal squad, which had come to court arrest.

Within a few months of Operation Bluestar, the militants struck in a big way to make their presence felt when they mowed down 20 Hindu passengers of a bus near Batala in the border district of Gurdaspur on September 12. This was the first time since militancy had raised its head in the state that so many people and that too from a single community had been targeted. Nothing could come as a bigger shock to the ordinary people. Bomb explosions at some places were also reported that day. Clearly, Operation Bluestar had failed to root out militancy, which was touted as the main aim of the brutal and unprecedented Army action in Punjab. This single incident raised questions about the desirability of the Army intervention. The Army action was aimed more at harvesting political benefits.

Army Withdrawal

The Army was finally withdrawn from the shrine on September 25 after the Prime Minister announced the decision in her broadcast to the nation.

Here goes the full text of the broadcast: "I spoke to you on Punjab on the 2nd June. Later, on various occasions I made it clear that at no time did the government have any intention of retaining control over the Golden Temple, or for that matter, any place of worship. In fact, 36 temples were handed over almost immediately after the June action. In the Golden Temple, we had the problem of repairs to the Akal Takht and a couple of other buildings. Obviously, these repairs had to be undertaken with the utmost dispatch and devotion. Unfortunately, no agreement about this could be reached with the priests and others who were approached initially. Other devotees came forward and the work proceeded. The Akal Takht has been restored to its original resplendence. We had to introduce some restrictions on entry, merely to ensure that the repair work continued unimpeded. Over the last several weeks, the

Army presence has been thinned down. Lately, a couple of guards were kept only for the protection of the Toshakhana. As the work progressed, the hours of public entry were also increased. The government have taken note of the public statement made on behalf of the head priests that they are against any misuse of the Temple, and the taking in and storing of arms in holy places. Now that the repairs are complete, even the token presence of the Army in the Golden Temple can be withdrawn. Thus we have decided that as soon as the necessary arrangements have been made, the present governmental regulation of entry will cease. The nation's sole concern is that places of worship should not become centers of secessionist, terrorist and anti-social activities. Dynamic Punjab has always been a source of strength and pride for the country as a whole. I am sure that with our present decision, a new phase will begin in Punjab in which all sections will again work together in harmony and trust. I convey my good wishes to all devotees of the Golden Temple. Jai Hind".

There were certain developments that preceded the decision of the government to withdraw Army. The high priests had conveyed that they were against the carrying of weapons inside the shrine. Only the traditional weapons were permitted. Jathedar Harcharan Singh of Takht Keshgarh Sahib had made the position clear through a statement on September 18. The high priests had also condemned the killing of the bus passengers near Batala.

The very next day of the Army withdrawal, the high priests exonerated Giani Zail Singh after scrutinizing all the relevant documents submitted to them on behalf of his two emissaries - former minister Ravel Singh and his personal assistant Kulwant Singh. They said they were satisfied with the explanation and the clarifications and as such, no further action was required to be taken. The President had earlier been declared guilty of ordering the Army action in his capacity as the Supreme Commander of the defence forces and carrying an umbrella over his head in the shrine parkarma. The decision to exonerate him was taken after extensive deliberations spread over two days.

Giani Zail Singh visited the shrine again on September 27 and sought forgiveness from the Sikh Gurus and the sangat for the tragedy. He said he felt unhappy whenever such an unpleasant task had to be undertaken in the country but as head of the state, he was responsible for all the actions of the government. He prayed to the Almighty to forgive him and his countrymen for the damage and the desecration of the Darbar Sahib Complex. His prayer was greeted with "bole so nihal" which virtually put the seal on the decision by the high priests to exonerate him. He also prayed to God to pardon acts of omission and commission of all those who, during the Army action, laid down their lives, irrespective of the fact whether they were security personnel, terrorists or secessionists, visiting pilgrims, helpless women or innocent children. The highest dignitary of the state, for the first time, though indirectly, had conceded that innocent pilgrims, women and children had been killed during the Army action.

According to one account, Giani Zail Singh, when he visited the shrine soon after the Army action, was too shocked but could not express his anguish. It was then that he silently prayed to God to forgive him and his countrymen who were responsible for the devastation either by their direct or indirect complicity or by being indifferent spectators to the ugly developments which ultimately led to the Army action. He promised to see that all cases of alleged harassment of innocent Sikhs were investigated by highly responsible officers. He assured the Sikhs that the guilty would be punished.[13] On behalf of the SGPC, he was received only by Abinashi Singh. About 200 slogan shouting youth staged a demonstration near the Darbar Sahib Complex during his visit.

Giani Kirpal Singh, in his address, warned the government against continued harassment of the Sikhs and said under such a situation, the government should be prepared to face threat to national unity. The Sikhs as a community had become suspect and even ordinary Sikhs were being harassed by the security forces, especially in the border districts.

Amarinder Singh, however, on October 15, questioned the exoneration of Giani Zail Singh and displayed photographs of the President showing his staff carrying umbrella over his head in the parkarma. He pleaded for the review of the exoneration in the light of the evidence submitted by him.

The government formally handed over the control of the Darbar Sahib Complex to the SGPC, withdrew the Army and threw open the shrine to the public on September 29. R V Subrahmanian, senior adviser to the Punjab Governor, handed over the keys of the Toshakhana (the shrine treasury where precious artifacts are kept) to SGPC Secretary Bhan Singh in the presence of the high priests. The process of handing over started when Baba Santa Singh, after the completion of the Akal Takht, left along with his about 1,000 followers. He had undertaken the repair on July 17. The proposed liberation march to be led by the high priests was called off. Apart from Subrahmanian, Lt Gen K Gowri Shankar, Union Home Secretary N.N. Vora and other officers were also present. The high priests directed the Sikhs against raising anti-national slogans in the shrine. The very next day, Darbar Sahib Head Priest Giani Sahib Singh received a threatening letter.

While appealing to the Sikhs to observe October 1 as Thanksgiving Day, the high priests said in a statement, "We appeal to the Sikh community to observe October 1 as Thanksgiving Day. The Sikh history is a history of sacrifices and patriotism which is known all over the world. History shows that the Sikhs have always conducted peaceful struggle. That is why the Congress leaders had also appreciated the peaceful struggle for gurudwara reforms. We appeal to the Sikh community, which wants to live with honour and dignity in India, to act in conformity with history and the tradition of unity and amity. It should live in peace with every one. The duty of the government is that it should treat people of all religions with equal respect. We appeal to the Sikhs not to raise anti-national slogans. Nothing should be done against the dignity and sanctity of this pious place. We condemn all anti-national activities". The appeal issued by the high priests was meaningless as they had ceased to be any moral force. These ordinary people pitted against this unprecedented situation were not expected to rise to the occasion.

This dark chapter in the recent Sikh history seemed to be over. However, it was not to be.

Security Forces re-enter Darbar Sahib Complex

The security forces re-entered the Darbar Sahib Complex within 48 hours of the withdrawal on October 1 to flush out about 200 youth who had forcibly occupied Akal Takht, raised pro-Bhindranwale and pro-Khalistan slogans and hoisted the Khalistan flag at Darshani Deori. As the bhog ceremony to commemorate the handing over of the complex to the SGPC was on, the youth who claimed to be the supporters of the banned AISSF, moved near the stage to present a questionnaire to the high priests. They proclaimed the formation of Khalistan with headquarters in the Darbar Sahib Complex. A resolution to this effect was adopted by them who took control of the Takht for about three hours. Through another resolution, this group of youth threatened to dismantle the Akal Takht rebuilt by the Nihang chief. The high priests and Akali Dal ad hoc committee convener Parkash Singh Majitha criticized the action of the youth describing them as anti-social and anti-national elements. These youth were flushed out by the Army and security forces and several were detained. The SGPC described as unfortunate the entry of the security forces in the complex to flush out these elements saying it was part of a conspiracy. The high priests announced the handing over of the Kar Sewa of the sarovar (holy tank) to Baba Kharak Singh.

The high priests the very next day blamed the government for this incident which was suspected to be part of the conspiracy to erode their supremacy and that of the Akal Takht. Giani Kirpal Singh said the government did all this to create hurdles in the way of handing over of the remaining three buildings to the SGPC which included the residential areas. The high priest, on October 3, took strong exception to Governor K T Satarawala's statement that the police entered the Darbar Sahib Complex on their request. They asserted the police entered the complex on their own. The priests blamed the factional fight in the Congress for this mischief. This was the first indication about the turn the situation was to take with the militants holding a complete sway over the shrine complex once again.

Akali Dal for Bluestar Memorial

In a significant development in consonance with the Panthic traditions, the Akali Dal ad hoc committee, at its meeting at Amritsar on October 7, resolved to raise a suitable memorial to those killed during the Army action in June at Darbar Sahib Complex and at other shrines.[14] The meeting was also attended by the party MPs, MLAs and the district presidents. This was the first such formal resolution adopted by the party. However, this resolution was soon to be forgotten. The issue was revived only about two decades later when the Akali Dal was again trying to revert to the Panthic agenda close to the Assembly elections. The Akali Dal talked of building such memorial when the 5-year rule of the Akali Dal government, which came into power in 1997 was about to end and the party faced the prospects of defeat from the Congress in the Assembly elections. Harping back on the Panthic issues seemed to be the compulsion at that time, despite the agenda of Punjabiyat having been adopted in 1996. The SGPC executive at its meeting at Anandpur Sahib on May 27, 2005, again adopted a resolution to build a memorial to those killed during the Army action.

The meeting also demanded immediate pullout of the security forces from the remaining buildings in the complex. The resolution adopted at the meeting urged the Sikh youth to exercise restraint and strengthen the hands of the high priests and described the hooliganism in the complex on October 1 as unfortunate. The meeting condemned the indiscriminate arrests of the Amritdhari Sikhs and the Akalis. Through another resolution, the party demanded that the government adopt a lenient attitude towards the Army deserters as they revolted in the wake of their religious sentiments having been hurt. Those who attended the meeting included Sukhdev Singh Dhindsa, Balwinder Singh Bhunder, Basant Singh Khalsa, Gurdev Singh Badal, Baldev Singh Mann and Nirlep Kaur.

The remaining three buildings in the shrine complex were handed over to the SGPC on October 8. The announcement to this effect was made by Subramanian after going around the Teja Singh Samundari Hall, Guru Ram Das Serai and Guru Nanak Niwas. Reports hinted at a tacit understanding having been arrived at among the government, the high priests and the SGPC against the misuse of these buildings. It had also been agreed upon that in case of anti-national activities within the precincts, the security forces would take necessary steps to arrest the trouble makers. The SGPC was to devise a fool-proof method of allotting rooms to the pilgrims and devotees. It was also decided that gates would not be put up on either side of the passage in front of the three buildings which separated them from the main complex. Present at the meeting with Subramanian were Giani Kirpal Singh, Darbar Sahib Head Priest Giani Sahib Singh, Takht Keshgarh Sahib Jathedar Giani Harcharan Singh Mahalon, Akal Takht Head Priest Giani Pritam Singh, SGPC Secretary Bhan Singh and Assistant Secretary Abinashi Singh. The Army finally vacated the three buildings on October 9.

The Kar Sewa to de-silt Darbar Sahib sarovar started on October 12 in which lakhs of devotees participated. It was a sea of humanity. Those present included Amarinder Singh and Biju Patnaik. The Kar Sewa in a way turned out to be the catharsis for the community feeling hurt, humiliated and betrayed by the unprecedented Army action. It was a historic occasion. After the ceremonial inauguration with golden spades by the Panj Piaras, thousands of devotees entered one-half of the sarovar to remove silt with their bare hands. The Panj Piaras included Baba Harbans Singh (Delhi), Sant Kartar Singh (Patna), Baba Darshan Singh (Jhabal), Baba Daya Singh (Sur Singh) and Baba Diwan Singh (Khan Chhabri). This Kar Sewa of the sarovar was the devotion personified of the Sikh community, which had gone through the trauma of Operation Bluestar. The last time this exercise had been undertaken was in 1973. However, the present Kar Sewa was under entirely a different situation. This was not just to remove the silt but at a higher level, it was a purification exercise. According to one estimate, about 10 lakh devotees participated in this week long Kar Sewa.

Janata Party President Chandra Shekhar, who participated in the Kar Sewa, demanded immediate release of the detained Akali leaders and a solution to the Punjab problem to restore normalcy in the state. He criticised the incompetence and callousness of the government in handling the Punjab situation.

Pro-Khalistan and pro-Bhindranwale slogans, which had again appeared in the complex, were erased by the SGPC authorities. The basement of the Akal Takht was locked as pro-Khalistan slogans were found to be written there also when the complex was handed over to the SGPC. The SGPC displayed notices at prominent entry points prohibiting carrying of weapons inside. The ban on carrying of the weapons was part of the agreement the SGPC and the high priests had entered into with the government. However, within months, this ban came to be violated with impunity. The role of the government had also come under question.

Giani Kirpal Singh, for the first time, said the Akal Takht reconstructed by Baba Santa Singh was not acceptable but left the final decision to the Sikhs. However, he refused to spell out the time frame for the community to take this decision.[15]

Longowal Equates Indira Gandhi to Abdali

The Akali Dal, on October 21, released the contents of the meeting the two Supreme Court advocates, Gajinder Singh Cheema and Rani Jethmalani, had with Longowal lodged in jail at Udaipur. Longowal was categoric that there would be no compromise with the government on the basic demands. "We will come out of jails after securing our rights and demands and not on the basis of any compromise", he reportedly said. He compared the approach of Indira Gandhi towards the Sikhs with the foreign invaders saying following in the footsteps of Ahmad Shah Abdali, the Afghan invader of the 18th century, she was out to finish the Sikhs, Sikhism and their places of worship. It was Abdali who had brought down the Darbar Sahib Complex and filled the holy tank with cow heads. He repeated the demand for an inquiry by a Supreme Court judge to uncover those behind the killings and other violent incidents in Punjab. "We will prove the Congress hand behind these events," Longowal reportedly said. Ironically, the successive Akali Dal governments never ordered any inquiry into the genesis of militancy, despite the poll promises.

NOTES

1. The Indian Express, June 14, 1984.
2. The Indian Express, June 23, 1984.
3. The Indian Express, June 26, 1984.
4. Surya, August 1984.
5. The Indian Express, July 14, 1984.
6. The Tribune, July 18, 1984.
7. The Indian Express, August 14, 1984.
8. The Indian Express, August 12, 1984.
9. The Indian Express, August 13, 1984.
10. The Indian Express, September 3, 1984.
11. The Indian Express, September 5, 1984.
12. The Telegraph, September 11, 1984.
13. The Tribune, September 28, 1984.
14. The Tribune, October 8, 1984.
15. The Indian Express, October 15, 1984.

9

The Retribution

It is rooted in the collective Sikh psyche that nemesis visits the person responsible for the attack on Darbar Sahib, the holiest of the holy Sikh shrines and this belief is supported by history. When a few months after Operation Bluestar, her own security men, who happened to be Sikhs, gunned down Prime Minister Indira Gandhi there was sense of utter shock and disbelief all over the country. However, for the followers of the Sikh faith, it was the continuation of that very historical phenomenon. She had personally paid the price for Operation Bluestar and become the victim of the deadly and degenerate politics being played in Punjab of which she happened to be one of the key players. The other security men mysteriously fired upon her assassins, Beant Singh and Satwant Singh, though they had surrendered immediately. Beant Singh died on the spot while Satwant Singh was seriously injured and was hanged to death years later.

Her assassination on the morning of October 31 while walking down to her residential office was followed by a planned genocide of the Sikhs in Delhi and other places in the country to teach them a bitter lesson. Even the cavalcade of President Giani Zail Singh was not spared when he entered the All India Institute of Medical Sciences where the body of Indira Gandhi had been brought. Thousands were killed in this worst form of violence perpetrated against the Sikhs in the post-independence period. Men were burnt to death with burning tyres around their necks and women raped. Rajiv Gandhi's comment justifying the violent reaction saying the earth trembles whenever a big tree falls is now part of the history. He was sworn in as the Prime Minister thus continuing the dynastic rule.

The SGPC's publicity wing issued a signed statement on behalf of the high priests expressing shock at the assassination of Indira Gandhi and appealed to the countrymen to maintain peace, communal harmony and amity. Significantly, Deputy Commissioner Ramesh Inder Singh read out this statement at a meeting of the district peace committee. However, Akal Takht Jathedar Giani Kirpal Singh within no time rang up several journalists to convey that the high priests were not a party to the statement. Within minutes, a news agency flashed the denial. Apparently, the denial had been issued under pressure from the militants. Akali Dal ad hoc committee convener Parkash Singh Majithia and SGPC acting President Rajinder Singh Dhaliwal also condemned the assassination.

Across the Border, Pakistan announced three-day state mourning.

The Times of India, Delhi, reported the widespread violence against the Sikhs breaking out in the aftermath of the assassination of the PM thus on November 1: "In a spontaneous manifestation of their wrath, hundreds of youths took to the streets this evening following the news of the death of the Prime Minister, setting fire to the shops, vehicles and other property belonging to Sikhs." Going by the pattern of anti-Sikh violence, the manifestation of wrath was not spontaneous but pre-planned. The same paper commented on the edit page: "Once again the light has been sniffed out. Once again the country has been plunged into darkness. The blow is even heavier and crueler this time than on January 30, 1948. Then there were other stalwarts, Jawaharlal Nehru and Sardar Patel, who could steer the nation to safety. Now there is no one to step into her place. Indira Gandhi was not just India's Prime Minister. She was the hope of the country in the turbulent period ahead. So much hinged on her. Independent India has never been so orphaned".

A more balanced Indian Express editorial dated November 3 was blacked out in the paper's Chandigarh edition due to censorship and was reproduced on November 30. Excerpts:

"Yesterday we mourned for Indira Gandhi. Today we mourn for India. Ever since Wednesday night, but more so on Thursday, rampaging mobs have been indulging in an orgy of violence aimed against Sikhs, in Delhi and several other cities in a number of states. This is totally wrong. Indira Gandhi's assassins were not representatives of any community and taking revenge against Sikhs is unpardonable folly. What started out seemingly as sporadic outbursts of community anger steadily degenerated into a mindless frenzy, causing the most grievous loss of life and property, with arson and loot as significant motif. Curfew was declared in some places and the Army called out in others. But the machinery of law and order totally collapsed in the capital with mobsters and looters enjoying virtually a free run of the city while the police stood by pleading helplessness. The Army already on alert was tardily summoned to the aid of civil authority. There was no curfew until evening, only the most trivial show of force and lack of command and strategy for dealing with an extremely delicate and dangerous situation. Key posts seemed to be unmanned as frantic and pathetic appeals for assistance by beleaguered and terrorized groups in scattered areas went unheeded. Some senior officials and political figures appeared to be trapped in Teen Murti House where huge, milling crowds had gathered to pay homage to Indira Gandhi as her body lay in state.

"Whatever the factors, the administrative breakdown in the capital is dangerous portent. One surmise for its passivity was that the Delhi police was on the defensive as Indira Gandhi's assailants were from its fraternity and it possibly wished to keep a low profile. However, whatever the psychology at work there was a failure of leadership at all levels when ever a determined show of force and vigorous patrolling could have deterred the hooligans and lumpen elements whose cowardly demeanour was apparent whenever opposed but whose appetite grew on what it fed. Delhi Doordarshan too allowed some provocative slogans to go on the air.

"Reports of attacks on places of worship and assaults have come in from many places. In exasperation the victims have sought to defend themselves with firearms and other weapons. The marauding hoodlums have done the crudest violence to the memory of Indira Gandhi and are playing into the hands of Punjab extremists and others who want to see India bleed. Unless the rioting is put down ruthlessly there is risk of spreading panic, refugee movements and retaliatory strikes and reprisals elsewhere. Hundreds have already been ruined and their rehabilitation must be a charge on the nation. The attack on the Delhi residence of an opposition MP from Bihar is ominous and hints at political forces at work. The new government cannot appear supine. The holocaust must be ended. Else the nation could be torn apart in fratricidal strife and exposed to great peril."

It was The Indian Express that took the lead in exposing this pre-planned violence.

A report from as far away as Ranchi, then in Bihar, on violence against the Sikhs was very significant. Col M.S. Duggal, in charge of the Army operations in Ranchi, Bokaro and Daltonganj, told media persons that the Army had been alerted on the very day the PM was assassinated but not called out to curb the violence till 7 pm on November 1. Similarly, the Army was rushed to Bokaro where 60 Sikhs had been killed on November 2. He said the first request to the Army was to send out two columns for a flag march. Though the Army moved in immediately, no authority was given till the evening to effectively curb violence, The Telegraph reported on November 8, 1984. The same report quoted Parhlad Singh, a local Sikh leader, alleging that a particular magistrate had encouraged anti-social elements to attack the Sikhs, apart from two local Congress leaders. Everywhere, the administration was conniving with the mobs led by Congressmen to attack the Sikhs. The situation was worst in Delhi and adjoining areas, including parts of Haryana.

The situation in Delhi was described thus by Arati R. Jerath and Sanjay Suri in The Indian Express' Delhi Edition, "For three days, mobs prowled the streets, killing, looting and burning, unchecked and often aided by the police and local Congress (I) workers." This report, due to appear in the Chandigarh edition on November 9 was carried almost a month later on December 5 due to censorship.

A deputation of the Sikh leaders including Delhi Mayor M.S. Sathi, G.S. Dhillon, President of Guru Tegh Bahadur Foundation, Prof Harbans Singh, General Secretary of Guru Nanak Foundation, Jathedar Rachhpal Singh, President of Akali Dal (Master Tara Singh), Jaswant Singh, President of Delhi Sikh Gurdwara Management Committee, Gurbax Singh, Vice-Chancellor of Delhi University and Harvinder Singh Hanspal and Charanjit Singh, both MPs, called on the Prime Minister on November 6 to condole the death of his mother. He gave them the certificate of patriotism.

While addressing the congregation at Gurdwara Sis Ganj in Delhi on Guru Nanak's birthday, Amarinder Singh commented on the situation, "It is not just their fault. We must look into ourselves also. Who asked us to drag out innocent people from buses and kill them? Who told us to shoot down poor people in villages? We must share the blame for what has happened today." He also felt that by assassinating Indira Gandhi, the Sikhs had alienated themselves. "We have moved in wrong direction. And this is what happens when hate and revenge rule the mind," he said.[1]

In his first party reaction to this genocide of the Sikhs, Bharatiya Janata Party President Atal Behari Vajpayee, on November 9, held the Congressmen "squarely responsible for the anti-Sikh violence". He said that this violence was engineered by Congress (I) workers and MPs and the entire government was responsible for the collapse in administration that allowed the violence to take place.[2] In the December Lok Sabha elections, BJP's strength was reduced to just two seats in the Lower House. Congress had emerged as the saviour of the Hindus. It was time to re-define the so-called secularism of the Congress. But then it was the BJP, which had earlier extolled Operation Bluestar.

Several prominent Sikhs including academicians, doctors, businessmen and journalists in Delhi condemned the assassination of

Indira Gandhi. They issued a statement saying, "The assassination of Mrs. Gandhi is both a heinous crime and an act that is against all tenets of Sikhs and abhorrent to all who cherish the norms and values of a civilized society. We believe that those who follow in the path of Guru Nanak feel deeply the condemnable nature of this crime and we are moved to express it on their behalf. This senseless act has precipitated senseless violence, which must be condemned. It threatens the very values for which India stands". The signatories included Dr. Gurbaksh Singh, Vice-chancellor of Delhi University, Khushwant Singh, Air Chief Marshal Arjan Singh, Dr. Amrik Singh, Raunak Singh, Bhai Mohan Singh, Dr. Isher J. Ahluwalia, Tawleen Singh and S.S. Duggal.[3]

The pre-Operation Bluestar period had been characterised by increasing communal tension in Punjab. The reaction to the Army operation too had by and large been on communal lines as a section of the Hindu population had distributed sweets after the action. A section of the Sikhs too distributed sweets following the assassination of Indira Gandhi, not just in Punjab, but across the globe. However, there was no communal backlash in Punjab to the planned massacre of the Sikhs in Delhi and other places in the country. The Punjabi society did not get fractured despite the tension and this was the most positive aspect of the situation. Of course, the genocide was one of the main contributory factors to the revival of militancy on a much bigger scale in the post-Bluestar period. In far away England, protest rallies by Hindus against the assassination and by Sikhs against the genocide were banned in the aftermath of the assassination due to rising tension in Southall having heavy concentration of Indians in general and Punjabis in particular.

Within a few months of the Army action and a few weeks prior to the assassination of Indira Gandhi, a concerted move had been initiated to revive the militant movement now synonymous to Sant Jarnail Singh Bhindranwale. The move to piece together the remnants of the pre-Bluestar militant movement and bring the radical political activists together was initiated during this period. The first meeting was held at a gurdwara near Jalandhar Cantonment railway station. Twenty-odd persons including Dalbir Singh, a journalist who had been close to Sant Bhindranwale and had gone underground, Manbir Singh Chaheru, Dhanna Singh and Harinder Singh Kahlon attended the meeting. The only discernible common thread was their proximity to Sant Bhindranwale. Kahlon later headed the All India Sikh Students Federation while Dhanna Singh was included in the Panthic Committee, the first five-member apex committee of the militants.

It was also around this time that Baba Joginder Singh, 83, father of Sant Bhindranwale, was brought to the scene to provide leadership. In the absence of any ideological content, the remnants of the militant movement looked towards the families of the martyrs for leadership. This proved to be a major blunder as the families of Sant Bhindranwale or Amrik Singh or even others for that matter as most of such families lacked stature and maturity needed at that time. A convention of the families of the martyrs was organized at Damdami Taksal. It was this convention, which paved way for the revival of radical politics through re-organization of the AISSF as the front organization of the militants.

The assassination of Indira Gandhi was a violent reaction by a section of her Sikh security persons to Operation Bluestar and these people were not linked, even remotely, to any militant organization. However, the assassination could be part of some grand design to destabilize the country. The foreign hand became more and more pronounced during the post Operation Bluestar period in the second phase of militancy. Before the Army action in the Darbar Sahib complex, there could have been a design of the Congress to play the communal card, apart from the other factors. However, the forces of destabilization dominated the region later.

While the entire Sikh community was shell-shocked, the Akali Dal leadership was involved in petty politics, ignoring the larger issues facing the Sikhs. Of course, at that time, the entire senior traditional Akali leadership was in jail. But then this leadership had already become irrelevant. It was the second rung leadership that was in command with its entirely different priorities and concerns and an indication of power struggle. This leadership landed the party in crisis at one of this most crucial junctures in the recent history on the eve of the annual election to the office bearers of the SGPC. Ironically, the main concern of a section of the party was to oust Gurcharan Singh Tohra, who was in jail, from the presidency of this body. The high priests replaced Parkash Singh Majitha by Surjan Singh Thekedar as ad hoc chief of the party on November 7 and dissolved the ad hoc committee.

On November 11, Majitha held a parallel meeting claiming he was still the convener of the ad hoc committee. The high priests had earlier postponed the meeting that was, however, attended by leaders including Ravi Inder Singh, Vaid Kartar Singh and Ranjit Singh Brahmpura, all opposed to Tohra. Ravi Inder Singh held Tohra responsible for Operation Bluestar arguing he had encouraged Sant Bhindranwale to shift to Akal Takht, the main battlefield during the Army action. A group of people gathered in front of the Teja Singh Samundari Hall and raised slogans against the high priests describing them as stooges of Giani Zail Singh. Later, the high priests, Thekedar and some senior Akali leaders met separately.

What triggered Majitha's removal was his alleged secret meeting with Buta Singh in October. There were other reasons also for the drastic action. Majitha was blamed for his failure to meet the Sikh detainees and arrange legal aid for them. He failed to go to Delhi along with a team of the Akali leaders to assess the situation after the assassination of the Prime Minister. According to the high priests, Majitha could not arrange even about 2,000 volunteers on Diwali when Baba Santa Singh threatened to visit the Akal Takht. Prominent Akali leaders and the district presidents extended their cooperation to the high priests. Balwant Singh, Sukhdev Singh Dhindsa and Balwinder Singh Bhunder appreciated the decision. Balwant Singh Ramoowalia produced a letter from Parkash Singh Badal asking party men to extend cooperation to the high priests.

Despite the move to dislodge him, Tohra, while in jail, was re-elected SGPC chief at the general body meeting on November 30, 1984.

This was a time when the migration of Sikhs from other states to Punjab had started. Camps had been established at various places to re-settle the migrants. The only notable incident of backlash to the migration was a poster circulated in Ludhiana carrying the photographs of Indira Gandhi, Rajiv Gandhi, Beant Singh and Satwant Singh asking Hindus to leave Punjab within one month.

It was during this period that Jasvir Singh Rode, semi-literate nephew of Sant Bhindranwale, who was working as a carpenter in Dubai, appeared on the scene. He was taken to London but was not allowed to leave Heathrow airport by the authorities and deported to Dubai on December 22. His change of clothes from pant-shirt to a long robe was managed at Heathrow by Dr Jagjit Singh Chohan, who was the one to arrange his visit too. The authorities at Dubai refused him entry but allowed him to take another flight after a few hours. Denied entry into Thailand, he landed in Manila where he was again detained at the airport. Earlier in November, he had visited Nankana Sahib in Pakistan. A case had also been registered by the Central Bureau of Investigations in Delhi against Rode for his objectionable activities and inflammatory speeches at Nankana Sahib. He had left for Dubai in the pre-Bluestar period. His only qualification was that he was Sant Bhindranwale's nephew.

Attack on Giani Kirpal Singh

Intensifying their activities, the militants made an abortive attempt to gun down Giani Kirpal Singh on January 16, 1985. Jagjit Singh Anand commented in the Patriot on January 25, 1985: "The stark reality is that there are more Bhindranwale men stalking Punjab at present than he was alive, despite all the tall claims by the establishment to the contrary. The only difference is that their operations command has shifted from Akal Takht to across the international border. They are led by competent operators of the CIA and Pak intelligence, whose sole aim is to destabilize and dismember India." Apart from other factors, what had made the Jathedar controversial was his dubious statement on Akal Takht immediately after Operation Bluestar.

On the surface, Operation Bluestar was targeted against Sant Bhindranwale and his associates holed up in the shrine complex and many of them were eliminated. However, despite the army action, the situation in the state had started deteriorating within months. In that sense, Operation Bluestar had already become counterproductive. If the aim was to capitalize upon the Hindu sentiments, it had, of course, been achieved, as proved in the December Lok Sabha elections. The apprehension of the Congress using the Hindu card had been expressed by Gurcharan Singh Tohra at one of the meetings the Akali leaders had with the Centre in which Rajiv Gandhi was also present.

Congress, the oldest political party in the country, had contested this Lok Sabha election with Anandpur Sahib Resolution as the main poll plank. The Congress having so-called secular credentials had played the communal card to the hilt, targeting the Sikhs. If that was the grand design of Indira Gandhi, the target had been achieved but at an enormous cost. Commenting upon the post Lok Sabha poll scenario, Communist Party of India (Marxist) leader Harkishan Singh Surjeet observed: "The leaders of the ruling party must be very happy over the election victory, but at what cost? Imperialism succeeded in encouraging extremists to assassinate the former Prime Minister in order to destabilise the country. This was followed by riots which reminded one of the partition days. Secularism has become the worst victim, the Sikhs are further alienated, a feeling of insecurity exists among the Sikhs through out the country, further communalisation has taken place in Punjab and its impact can be felt in other states as well. This situation suits the imperialists and enemies of the country most. This has to be changed. Any exploitation of this situation for narrow partisan gains can prove disastrous[4]."

For the Communists in India, she had become victim of the grand design of Imperialism from the very beginning and the KGB had been accusing the CIA of fomenting trouble in this region. It may be mentioned that during the pre-Partition period in particular, the Congress was described as the Hindu party. The party would use Hindu symbolism at every level.

It was in a statement that appeared on January 15, 1985 that Chief of Amy Staff General A.S. Vaidya claimed that the army had, more or less, successfully completed the task of clearing the militants from various villages in Punjab and unearthed most of the weapons and explosives. The situation which developed later belied this claim. This also showed lack of understanding of the psycho-political dynamics of this region.

Amarinder floats Sikh Forum

After two days of deliberations by 32 prominent Sikhs, Amarinder Singh floated the Sikh Forum on February 7 with Lt General Jagjit Singh Aurora as the co-convener to take up issues concerning the community and develop national pride among its members. It was to be a non-political body, the members of which were not to participate in the activities of any political party. Amarinder announced that the Forum would welcome negotiations between the Akalis and the government, provided the negotiators kept in mind the youth who were rotting in jails without trial and the victims of the November violence against the Sikhs. The setting up of the Forum followed the constitution of a five-member committee in December in Delhi comprising Lt General Aurora, Justice R.S. Narula, Manmohan Singh, Sukhjit Singh and Amarinder Singh to prepare a blueprint for launching a new organisation of the affluent Sikhs. The meeting was attended by Air Chief Marshal Arjan Singh (retd), Lt Gen Aurora, Major General Gurbax Singh (retd), Raja Malvinder Singh, Sukhjit Singh, Justice Narula, Justice Gurdev Singh, Manmohan Singh of Delhi, Bishan Singh Samundari, former Vice-chancellor of Guru Nanak Dev University, Amritsar, Dr Bhagat Singh, former Vice-chancellor of Punjabi University, Patiala, Gurdial Singh, retired Inspector General of Police, Kirpal Singh, President, Chief Khalsa Dewan, Rachhpal Singh Gill, former chairman of the Punjab State Electricity Board, Ajmer Singh, advocate, Gurdarashan Singh Grewal, advocate, Gurpreet Singh of Delhi, Prof H.S. Deol, S.S. Gill, former IG (Prisons) , Prof Gursewak Singh, former DPI, Kulraj Singh, former IT Commissioner, retired IFS officer Gurbachan Singh, Inderjit Singh Jaijee, Wg Cdr Hazara Singh, former IAS officer Daljit Singh, Bhai Ashok Singh, Capt Amarjit Singh Jaijee, Bhai Shavinder Singh and advocate Amrik Singh Chhina.

It was the Sikh Forum that came out in defence of the Anandpur Sahib Resolution with an open introductory letter to Rajiv Gandhi in a full page advertisement in the newspapers, which appeared under the signature of Amarinder Singh. It was the 1978 version of the resolution. The letter referred to the issues including the November massacre of the Sikhs, the Sikhs arrested during and after Operation Bluestar, the

Sikh Army personnel who left their barracks, the Anandpur Sahib Resolution and the river waters and the territorial disputes. The Forum emphasized that inquiry should be instituted into the November massacre or the Sikri report be accepted and the Sikh detenus released to normalize the situation and pave the way for a dialogue.[5] It is the 1973 version of the Anandpur Sahib Resolution which is considered to be controversial.

The ad hoc committee of the Akali Dal at its meeting chaired by Surjan Singh Thekedar at Amritsar on February 11, 1985 held the Rajiv Gandhi government responsible for the carnage after the assassination of Indira Gandhi and described it as a deep-rooted conspiracy. The turning down of the demand for a judicial inquiry by the Prime Minister was cited as proof of the complicity of the government. Through another resolution, the party warned the government that if the Panthic leaders and innocent Sikhs were not released and those guilty of committing atrocities on the Sikhs not punished, special courts not abolished, all black laws under which Punjab had been declared a disturbed state not revoked, the Akali Dal would be constrained to take some "harsh" steps. Yet another resolution said extremism and secessionist tendencies had emerged because of the inhuman policies of the government, which had curbed the fundamental and democratic rights of the Sikhs and denied them justice. The Akali Dal took a serious note of the government's action against Sikhs donning Kesari turbans. However, the party did not make any reference to the abortive attempt on the life of Jathedar Kirpal Singh.

Akali Dal decision to observe June 6 as Black Day

The Shiromani Akali Dal in this meeting decided to observe the first anniversary of Operation Bluestar on June 6 as 'Black Day'. It is significant to note that originally it was a decision by the moderate Akali Dal and was not an intervention by the radical sections as was later made out to be in a section of the media and political circles. This decision was ratified at a February 27 meeting at Amritsar. However, the Akali Dal subsequently distanced itself from the Bluestar anniversary and the event came to be associated mainly with the radicals. The meeting also demanded judicial inquiry into the November carnage.

Commenting on this move, the Times of India commented on March 4, 1985, "Should the Akali Dal go ahead with its move to observe June 6 as a 'Black Day' in Punjab to mark the first anniversary of Operation Bluestar, it would be doing something needlessly and recklessly provocative... Operation Bluestar was very specifically aimed at destroying the main stronghold of Sikh terrorists who had long been sowing death and destruction at will throughout Punjab and elsewhere. It was by no means aimed at the Sikh community as a whole, or at their faith. It was, moreover, resorted to only when no other option was available. Had it not been carried out, the consequences of allowing the terrorists free rein would have been immeasurably worse. To mark the day on which it was undertaken as a 'black day' for all Sikhs would be to try and portray it as an assault on the Sikhs. Nor can the Akalis be oblivious to the fall out of such an observance on the communal situation in Punjab, which remains at best uneasy and at worst subterraneanly tense. Should they try to polarise feeling in the state and elsewhere in the country on wholly religious lines by burning into Sikh consciousness that Operation Bluestar was an anti-Sikh, instead of anti-terrorist action, they will be working to harden the community against any conciliatory resolution of the Punjab problem."

After 1986, Parkash Singh Badal attended this function only in 2005.

Kesari turbans dominated the scene those days. In an unprecedented move, the Akali Dal started selling these turbans as the shopkeepers hiked the price with an increase in their demand. As the security forces started targeting the Sikh youth wearing Kesari turbans, students of Khalsa College, Amritsar, on February 12, observed strike and resolved that boys would wear Kesari turbans and the girls would don Kesari duppattas. The resolution passed to this effect said that the colour signified sacrifice and martyrdom and they would continue to wear it.

During this period, reports also appeared about even the incensed school students trying to cross over to Pakistan, despite the border having been "sealed" by the security forces.

The situation in the state was back to square one, despite the Army action spread over a couple of months, beginning Operation Bluestar. Ironically, Operation Bluestar, Operation Woodrose and subsequent actions of the government were now providing support base to militancy. "The Punjab politics is back to square one in more than one sense, despite the various initiatives taken by Prime Minister Rajiv Gandhi to defuse the situation. The most important aspect of the current scene in Punjab is the escalation of extremist activity.....Punjab is again at the cross roads. The emotional injury suffered by the Sikhs, which has partly some objective basis though artificially painted on the minds of this community, would be further exploited to create instability in the state."[6] The state repression produced equal and opposite reaction.

As the state ushered in the new year, the renewed militant activity included setting some school buildings on fire and bomb explosions near the Hindu temples. Three explosions were reported from the communally sensitive area near the Debi Talab Mandir in Jalandhar on January 30, 1985.

Another form of protest began against the government actions in the Sikh stream. A section of the Akalis started Amrit Parchar campaign. Hundreds of Sikhs, both men and women, were partaking Amrit at such functions.

The ad hoc committee of Akali Dal, which met at Anandpur Sahib on March 7, threatened to embark on protest action to press the acceptance of the seven-point charter of demands by April 12, which included judicial inquiry into the November genocide, release of Akali leaders and others arrested during and after Operation Bluestar, withdrawal of armed forces from the state, release of the detained Army personnel who had deserted their barracks in the wake of Operation Bluestar, withdrawal of the black laws under which Punjab was declared disturbed area along with the abolition of special courts set up at Ajmer and Jodhpur, release of all youth implicated in false cases and lifting of the ban on the AISSF.

Longowal, Talwandi Released

The government, on March 11, released several Shiromani Akali Dal leaders including President Harchand Singh Longowal, Jagdev Singh Talwandi, Surjit Singh Barnala, Atma Singh, Randhir Singh Cheema, Ujagar Singh Sekhwan, Dalip Singh Pandhi and Baldev Singh Brar. Simultaneously, Union Home Minister S.B. Chavan renewed the offer for talks.

After his release, Longowal, in an interview appearing in The Tribune on March 13 responded to the offer from Chavan and put up five demands as preconditions for negotiated settlement with the Centre. These included judicial inquiry into November violence against the Sikhs and arrest of the guilty, humane treatment to the Sikh Army personnel who had deserted their barracks and stern action against all those Army men who indulged in "wanton vandalism" from June 6 to 8 in the Darbar Sahib complex, killed innocent men, women and children and set on fire the Sikh Reference Library and the SGPC office. He said in the interview that the desecration of the Darbar Sahib and the destruction of Akal Takht stood between the Hindus and the Sikhs. It was perhaps for the first time that he had talked about the Sikh-Hindu divide in this harsh tone. He said that had the government heeded his advice and ordered judicial inquiry into terrorist activity from September 1981 onwards, all those responsible would have been identified and exposed. Longowal later entered into an unconditional accord with Rajiv Gandhi for which he had to pay the ultimate price. On reaching Amritsar, he said the government did not regard Sikhs as Indians and wanted to wipe them out. He admitted that Buta Singh and R.V. Subramanian, senior advisor to the Punjab Governor, had called on him in jail, though separately.

The Akali Dal delegation headed by Balwant Singh, on March 12, submitted a memorandum to Governor K.T. Satarawala against state repression in the Border areas. The memorandum cited specific instances where innocent persons had been victimized and even small children not spared. The delegation also demanded withdrawal of TADA and lifting of the ban on the AISSF.

The high priests and a representative gathering of the Akali Dal, at a meeting held on March 19 at Amritsar, authorized Longowal to lead the party and dissolved the ad hoc committee that had been set up during his detention.

Bhindranwale not Pakistan agent: Longowal

Mollifying the hurt Sikh psyche was not on the agenda of the government at the Centre. President Giani Zail Singh, in a provocative move, presented bravery awards to the Army officials who had participated in Operation Bluestar. The Akali Dal reacted on March 24 saying it mounted to rubbing salt in the wounds of the Sikhs. The government action was described as highly offensive and uncalled for.

A two-page detailed interview of Longowal by Kuldip Nayar appeared in an English paper in which he tried to clarify the Akali Dal position before the Army action and the subsequent events. He said: "Whenever the government wanted to have negotiations, we always welcomed it. But after every meeting, our conviction got strengthened that the government wanted to serve its own ends and would sacrifice the interests of the people. Then we resolved that it was no use talking to them. Then the opposition parties forced us to resume the dialogue. My party was not really for it, but I forced it to respond. Nothing came out of these meetings. Then there were four other meetings which are now called secret. They too were of no use. Then we came to the conclusion that the government wanted only to put us to shame.... It meant humiliating us after inviting us. Then there was a meeting on February 14. The opposition forced us to attend the meeting. I agreed because we did not want the people to get the impression that the government wanted to settle the problem but the Akalis did not. The meeting started on February 14. The government, the Opposition and we participated in it. While this meeting was taking place, Mr Bhajan Lal, with his force, was dragging Sikhs from the vehicles and killing them – at Karnal and Panipat and other such places. The Akali Dal representatives said to themselves that it was the government which humiliated the Sikhs. They left everything and came back..."

About his meeting with Subramanian, advisor to the Governor, while in jail, he said: "I asked him whether he had come to find a solution or to further humiliate me. I told him that there should first be a judicial inquiry to punish those who killed Sikhs in Delhi, Kanpur and the rest of India and the victims should be rehabilitated. I said release all the Sikhs, whether they are Akali workers or others, students or soldiers who started going towards Amritsar to express their anger against Operation Bluestar, also treat (the Sikhs) who hijacked the planes on par with those who had been rewarded with seats in the Parliament and the Assemblies. Also abolish the special courts; withdraw the army from Punjab. Only after that come and ask me...."

On Khalistan and Operation Bluestar was: "Two persons said they had gone to Bhindranwale and asked him to announce the birth of Khalistan over the loudspeaker, and they had been directed to me. I said I would not announce that, adding that my policy was the same as that of the Akali Dal. Later, those persons came to us again and asked us to announce the birth of Khalistan. They said they had been to Bhindranwale. We asked them to tell us what the Sant had told them. They said the Sant had told them that if Harchand Singh Longowal was to announce it, he would support it.... *Bhindranwale had no links with Pakistan or the CIA. The real thing is that RAW was working there; the government of India had planted some people; they were neither Bhindranwale's men nor ours...*

"On June 1, we complained to the Governor about the firing at the Golden Temple. He said he had no hand in it and whatever happened, it was at the Centre's instance. We told him that he was responsible for Punjab. He then did make efforts. He contacted the local Deputy Commissioner, the Superintendent of Police, the Inspector General and the Deputy Inspector General of Police, and informed us that the firing had stopped. We told him that the firing was continuing. He said it was from inside. I told him it was my responsibility if it was so. No firing was taking place from inside. After several hours, he was able to have the firing stopped. On June 2, Sikhs found Harmandir Sahib pockmarked by bullets; it had been hit by 36 bullets fired from three sides. On the evening of June 2, Mrs Gandhi made a statement over All India Radio; on the next day, all Punjab was sealed off. Till then, no one, neither the Punjab government, nor the militants, had told us that the authorities wanted to arrest any one; they did not say: "if you do not allow us to arrest, we shall fire". The government did not say it wanted to arrest Sant Jarnail Singh Bhindranwale...

"On June 4 at 4 or 5 am, the first bomb fell on Akal Takht – a big bomb. After that, there was continuous firing with machine guns and sten guns. The firing was so heavy for three hours that nobody could hear anything. All the people stayed where they were. Many of them had come from outside; that was the day of the Gurpurab of Guru Arjan Dev Sahib. There was firing on 4th and 5th June at night; there was a heavy firing on the 5th. In the evening I went to Teja Singh Samundari Hall. There were about 500 people – the satyagrahis who had come for the Morcha. After getting them together, I went to Tohra's room. There were seven or eight other Sikhs. The sun set at that time. Tohra Sahib said prayers. Then there was such a heavy firing that no one could move out. On June 5 there was no water, no food. The tank had been destroyed; no one could go out to fetch anything because there was continuous firing. I think that by the 5th night by 10 o' clock, the Army had occupied the entire area. Their tanks were stationed on the middle road. They were continuously firing at Teja Singh Samundari hall, Guru Nanak Niwas and Guru Ram Das Serai. Then they went to the parkarma and occupied Akal Takht. That day at about 3 pm, they occupied Guru Ram Das Serai... they arrested me on the morning of June 6. Later, they arrested all the volunteers in Teja Singh Samundari Hall. After that they came near our room and threw a bomb. They said we were to be arrested and asked us to offer ourselves for arrest.... None of Bhindranwale's men asked us not to offer arrest. Harminder Singh Sandhu, Mehta and Manjit Singh, Sant Bhindranwale's men, were sitting with our men till the evening. If they had wanted to harm us they could have done it any time. Really, this was a rumour spread by RAW; the government wanted to kill and attribute the killings to them. This propaganda had been done by the government. Tohra Sahib, I and others told the Army authorities that we were prepared to face arrest or bullets: "Do whatever you want to do." Then they took us to the executive's room. In the process, two of our Sikh colleagues were hit by bullets. They posted guards armed with machine guns. This again created an ugly situation. The volunteers, including women of the jatha, stood between us and the Army men, thinking that we were facing a firing squad. They almost came to a fight. We intervened and told them to allow us to offer ourselves for arrest. "If they want to kill, let it be so. Everyone has to die. After killing us, they will kill you. Now you should not do anything." They were pacified. After 15 minutes, the troops said that buses had come and the Sikhs of various jathas would be taken out. Tohra Sahib, I and seven or eight others were confined to a room. We were not allowed to go out, nor was anybody allowed to meet us. At that time, about 600 people were there. After half an hour, they gave a fauji sign that they would throw a bomb. Some people were lulled by bullets and some by bombs. Some were arrested and shot while under arrest. And subsequently, it was given out that boys of the AISSF had thrown bombs from outside, but those boys were sitting with us. We did not know the details because we were at a distance from the place of the incident and there was a lot of noise.

"Then at 11 PM, there was a big noise. Some people came running to us; we also shouted and told the colonel who came there that he should be ashamed of himself. If they wanted to kill us, we were all ready; but was the Army meant to kill the public of their own country? "You are committing a crime by killing people after arresting them." This had the effect; the firing stopped. Down below in the basement, many bhaiyas stay, 2,000 to 3,000 of them. They eat at the langar and spend the night. Because of the emergency they stayed there. They too were shot. They were not Akalis, Sikhs and extremists. They were beggars, laborers or rickshaw pullers. We asked the Army men why they were killed. They said they had to fulfill their quota. In the evening at 5 pm, we were arrested and taken to a bungalow at troops' headquarters and guards were posted. We were warned not to stir out because their instructions were to kill anyone who came out. We stayed in the room. This was on June 6. We were kept there also on the 7th. On the 8th, we were told that we would be taken to jail. We asked them where; they said they could not say. They took Tohra Sahib to Jodhpur and I was taken to Udaipur. None of us met Bhindranwale during those days. There was continuous firing all around. If anyone stirred out, he was killed there and then.... Our belief is that so many weapons could not have been brought into the place. There were three barriers - one at the gate, one at Jallianwala Bagh and one before that. In the same way, there were other checks also. Every person was searched. Whether man or woman. So also were all suitcases, luggage and vehicles. This continued for one year. Why could not the government catch even one pilgrim with weapons? If the government could not catch anyone, how should be we say that the weapons were found within the Golden Temple premises? In reality, to malign us and create hatred towards our religion the government brought in the arms... those who died in front of me did not have any weapon. They would have offered themselves for arrest peacefully.... Yes. Arms should be kept in gurdwaras. We worship them. We do it at Akal Takht and Keshgarh Sahib. Even in gurdwaras in England this is done. In the olden days, there were swords. Now the time have changed the quality of the weapons has been improved. There is nothing bad in possessing arms; only misusing them is bad...." Longowal had said it all.[7]

On April 2, the high priests ex-communicated Buta Singh for flouting the Akal Takht Hukamnama. Earlier, he had been declared a Tankhaiya at the World Sikh Convention on September 2, 1984 and directed to appear at Akal Takht.

Continuing with the confidence building measures after the release of some Akali leaders, the Centre, on April 11, announced the decision to order judicial probe into violence against the Sikhs in November 1984, release detenus and lift the ban on the AISSF.

Tohra for Bluestar memorial

The only option with the Akali leaders after the tragic events of June and November was to take a hard line. Tohra, who was also released on April 19 from the Jodhpur jail, was credited with the view after coming out that the Punjab problem did not relate to the state as such but was ethnic in character, relating to a minority community which had sacrificed a lot for the preservation of the freedom of the country. At the same time, he eulogized the assassins of Indira Gandhi and justified honouring of their relations. Talking to the journalists at New Delhi a day after his release, he made it clear the Akali Dal had always been in favour of a peaceful settlement and stood for the unity and integrity of the country. The party had never demanded Khalistan or raised secessionist slogans. It was the Congress that had been projecting the Akalis as separatists.

His stand on the assassination of Indira Gandhi would have to be seen in the context of Sikh history. The attack on Darbar Sahib has always been avenged. It was in this framework that he said that Indira Gandhi might be a martyr for the majority of the country but ardent believers of the Sikh faith would describe Beant Singh, her assassin, as martyr. He maintained the Akali Dal had always opposed the politics of violence. However, the Sikh sentiment was such that whenever any ruler had attacked Darbar Sahib, the revenge psyche had come into operation. He regretted that the Parliament had not taken notice of the genocide of the Sikhs following the assassination of Indira Gandhi. But then this was never done even when the Akali Dal shared power at the Centre.

Tohra announced in Amritsar on April 22 that the Akal Takht would be rebuilt as the structure constructed by the government was not acceptable and reiterated the decision of the Akali Dal to raise memorial to the victims of Operation Bluestar in the Darbar Sahib complex.[8]

Security forces raided the Darbar Sahib complex again on April 20 following the assassination attempt on the life of AICC General Secretary R.L. Bhatia at Amritsar a day earlier and searched the serai area. SGPC acting President Prem Singh Lalpura condemned the action of the government. He had been one of the conduits between Indira Gandhi and Sant Bhindranwale.

Next to be released was Badal on April 25 who was brought to Chandigarh the next day where his release orders were served to him at the airport.

Addressing a press conference on April 28, Badal called upon the government to take bold steps to regain confidence of the Sikhs which had been completely shattered. The desecration of the holy shrine and the systematic massacre of the Sikhs in the wake of the assassination of Indira Gandhi left deep scars on the Sikh psyche. The Congress and Rajiv Gandhi had maligned the Sikhs during the Lok Sabha elections and painted them as secessionists and traitors. The community had felt alienated. It was in the national interest to bring the Sikhs back into the mainstream. He took strong exception to the awards given to the Army men for Operation Bluestar saying this was tantamount to rubbing salt into the wounds of the Sikh community.

Mann Appointed Party Chief

Renewed activity was observed in the Akali political stream after the release of the senior Akali leaders. Baba Joginder Singh announced the merger of all Akali factions on May 1 and constituted a nine-member ad hoc committee under the leadership of Simranjit Singh Mann, former Indian Police Service officer then in jail, to run the party affairs. He had been arrested while trying to cross over to Nepal. Baba Joginder Singh claimed he had acted following the confidence reposed in him by Longowal and Talwandi. Longowal and Talwandi had written to him on April 3 reposing full confidence in his ability as mediator of the Panthic unity. The members of the ad hoc committee included former IAS officer Gurtej Singh, former Indian Foreign Service officer Harinder Singh Khalsa, Bhai Manjit Singh, Bhindranwale's brother Jagjit Singh Rode, Longowal, Talwandi, Tohra and Badal with Inderjit Singh Khalsa, considered close to Giani Zail Singh, as its general secretary. Baba Joginder Singh was to oversee the party affairs till Mann's release.

Longowal, however, rejected the ad hoc committee the very next day calling it illegal and unconstitutional. He made it clear that the delegate session of the Akali Dal at its meeting on May 17 in Amritsar would consider Baba Joginder Singh's proposal. He denied having offered his resignation to Baba Joginder Singh saying he had only expressed his willingness to accept mediation on Panthic unity. Immediately after his release, he had submitted his resignation to the high priests who had rejected it. He had a close-door meeting with Badal and Tohra at Jalandhar.

Longowal and Badal submitted their resignations from the party posts on May 11 and announced they would continue to serve the party as ordinary members. Longowal declared, "I have now decided that in future I will not hold any office, nor will I remain a member of any committee." However, he was again later entrusted with the responsibility of heading the party.

SGPC Decides to Rebuild Akal Takht

In another significant development, the executive committee of the SGPC, at its meeting at Amritsar on May 11, announced the decision to rebuild Akal Takht and authorized Tohra to make arrangements and formulate modalities. The executive committee stated, "The glorious and self-respecting Panth cannot accept the shrine built on contract basis by an ex-communicated Sikh." It was also decided to give Rs 10,000 each to the families of those killed during the Army action in June. However, the SGPC never ever compiled a complete list of those who had died in the complex during the Army action.

The Executive Committee, as expected, rejected Tohra's resignation from SGPC presidency submitted earlier. The reconstruction of Akal Takht after demolishing the structure constructed by the government was the one issue on which the views of the traditional Akalis, the radicals and the militants converged. The move provided the necessary platform to facilitate the takeover of the shrine by militants and subsequently, the agents of the government agencies under the garb of the militants, which led to another entry by the security forces under Operation Black Thunder.

Baba Joginder Singh convened a meeting of the merged Akali Dal on June 6 to pay homage to the martyrs and discuss Panthic unity. This decision was taken at a meeting of the ad hoc committee of this new Akali outfit attended by only four members. The resolution passed at the meeting stated that the district jathedars of the Akali Dal (Longowal) had no right to summon a meeting to decide the fate of its President. It said that the merged Akali Dal was the only representative party of the Sikhs. Talwandi and Jagjit Singh Rode were the only two original members of the nine-member ad hoc committee who attended the meeting. Gurdev Singh Shant represented Harinder Singh Khalsa. The meeting called upon the Sikhs to observe June 2 as a day of prayers. The ad hoc committee also decided to give time limit till May 25 to Longowal, Tohra and Badal to join the ad hoc committee.

The Akali Dal (L), on May 24, cancelled the Panthic convention convened at Longowal without assigning any reason. It was rather decided to convene a meeting of the district jathedars to review the situation arising out of the unity move initiated by Baba Joginder Singh, who, on May 25, announced a 51-member panel. The working committee members nominated included Prof Darshan Singh, Major Gen Narinder Singh (retd), Brig Mohinder Singh (retd), Harminder Singh Sandhu, Dr Bhagwan Singh, Rajinder Singh Mehta, Sant Singh Teg (Jammu & Kashmir), Delhi unit chief Harcharan Singh, Ranjit Singh Brahmpura, former MP Mohinder Singh, Ujagar Singh Sekhwan, Parkash Singh Majitha, Atma Singh, Mohinder Singh Sarupwali, Natha Singh Dalam, Randhir Singh Cheema, Gurbachan Singh, Satwant Kaur Sandhu, Jaswinder Singh Brar, Harbans Singh Jalal, Jagdev Singh Khudian, Toga Singh, Baldev Singh Brar, Dr Harinder Singh Gill, Darshan Singh Issapur, Angrez Singh, Amar Singh and Ajmer Singh Boparai.

Longowal came under sharp attack for not responding to the unity initiative of Baba Joginder Singh and he was charged with playing into the hands of the government. United Akali Dal ad hoc committee member Randhir Singh Cheema alleged on June 3 that Governor Arjun Singh had persuaded Longowal to withdraw his resignation which he had handed over to Baba Joginder Singh following a secret meeting held at the Raj Bhavan on May 22. He alleged that the government had been trying to scuttle the Akali unity and the purpose of the May 22 meeting was to perpetuate the existence of two Akali Dals. He said a secret meeting between Tohra and Buta Singh a day earlier at a farmhouse somewhere along the Patiala-Nabha highway was also arranged for the same purpose and it was on the basis of the report of Buta Singh that a meeting between Longowal and Arjun Singh was arranged. Tohra denied such a meeting. The Raj Bhavan also denied the secret meeting saying it was a figment of imagination and totally baseless.

The Terrorist and Disruptive Activities (Prevention) Bill was introduced in the Parliament on May 18 and it provided death penalty for terrorist acts. It was adopted by a voice vote two days later.

NOTES

1. The Times of India, November 1, 1984.
2. The Telegraph, November 8, 1984.
3. Arati R. Jerath and Sanjay Suri in The Indian Express, Delhi edition.
4. The Telegraph, November 8, 1984.
5. The Telegraph, November 10, 1984.
6. The Indian Express, November 11, 1984.
7. Jagjit Singh Anand, The Patriot, January 25, 1985.
8. The Patriot, February 6, 1985.
9. The Indian Express, March 18, 1985.
10. Times of India, March 4, 1985.
11. Chopra; V. D., The Patriot, February 18, 1985.
12. The Tribune, April 1, 1985.

10

The Betrayal

Much before he set upon the path of confrontation with the Indian state, Sant Jarnail Singh Bhindranwale was fully aware about the end result. However, even after he had realized the inevitability of the bloody confrontation with the Indian state, he did not take any step to set up some sort of command structure to continue the struggle. Though he himself symbolized the Sikh militancy, there was no homogenous command system to steer the militant organizations even when he was alive as the Babbar Khalsa, the other main militant organization, functioned independently.. This was a tactical blunder. This situation posed serious problems immediately after Operation Bluestar period, even at the political level.

This was not a problem with the radicals alone as the Akali Dal was also virtually in a mess. Operation Bluestar, the severest of the trauma the Sikhs endured during the 20th century, had failed to bring about cohesiveness in the Akali political matrix, what to talk of Sikhs as a community. Tragically, even one year after the army action in the Darbar Sahib complex, the contending and competing Akali factions were engaged in the same old petty game of leveling allegations and counter-allegations against each other. Perhaps some of these factions and leaders continued to function as instruments of some other forces. Even the first anniversary of the army action had failed to bring them on a single platform even for a day to pay tribute to those who had become victim of the brutality of the state resulting from the degenerate and deadly politics. This was perhaps the biggest misfortune of the Sikhs at that time.

The United Akali Dal headed by Baba Joginder Singh organized a Panthic convention in the Manji Sahib Hall in the Darbar Sahib complex on June 6 to observe the first anniversary of Operation Bluestar. The stage had been set for the ascendancy of Baba Joginder Singh, a novice in political affairs. At one level, this was the compulsion of the radicals who did not look beyond the families of the martyrs for leadership and at the other, yet another part of the design which was to unfold later. Baba Joginder Singh was opposed to Pritam Kaur, wife of Sant Jarnail Singh Bhindranwale, to be brought into the limelight and pursued her not to participate in the June 6 function. He exchanged heated arguments with some of the organizers on this issue. So long as her husband was alive, she would visit the Darbar Sahib complex as an ordinary devotee, attend the congregation addressed by her husband and leave for her village. She would take a rickshaw to the bus stand from the shrine. A simple woman, she could be seen bargaining with rickshaw pullers over the fair to the bus stand. When it was pointed out by a well wisher to one of the AISSF leaders, his stock reply was that Sant Bhindranwale would get angry if conveyance was arranged for his wife to be dropped at the bus stand. The family was not a priority for Sant Bhindranwale.

Baba Joginder Singh did not favour honouring sons of Sant Bhindranwale either. He had his own logic. He, along with another senile person Thakar Singh, acting chief of Damdami Taksal, had taken the stand that Sant Bhindranwale did not die during the army action and would re-appear at an appropriate time, the line which suited the government. The government much more dreaded Bhindranwale the Martyr who would be the source of inspiration to others. Baba Joginder Singh was thus implementing the designs of the agencies from day one by denying the status of the martyr to his son, the status which the Akali Dal and the leaders like Parkash Singh Badal had already bestowed upon him and others who had been killed during the army action.

Baba Joginder Singh could not even read his address himself and it was read out by his office secretary Surat Singh Khalsa. It was clear that Baba Joginder Singh was totally incapable of providing the much needed leadership and that too at one of the most crucial juncture in the recent Sikh history. At the time when effective leadership was lacking, money from overseas had started pouring in. This had its own effect on the so called leadership which could not stand upto the situation and ultimately, on the movement also which was far from being appropriately organized. This very first convention after Operation Bluestar had exposed the chinks. However, lessons were not to be learnt. Money acted as the spoiler and this had not been the case with Sant Bhindranwale who was above all such considerations. Only two leaders stand out in this context in the period under discussion and the other was Gurcharan Singh Tohra.

Of course, the spirit of Sant Bhindranwale dominated the

convention which eulogized the assassins of Indira Gandhi. It gave a call to the Sikhs to get baptized and arm themselves to defend their religion, honour and dignity. The convention adopted eleven resolutions. It demanded immediate withdrawal of army and other security forces from the shrine complex and alleged the security forces had terrorized people in the rural areas. Another resolution demanded the prosecution of the Congress leaders responsible for November massacre of the Sikhs. Rich tributes were paid to those who died in army action while defending the Darbar Sahib complex under the leadership of Sant Bhindranwale. The convention accused the government of using mass media for anti-Sikh campaign and called upon the community not to be misled by the mischievous propaganda.

Those who addressed the convention included Jagdev Singh Talwandi, Ranjit Singh Brahmpura, Parkash Singh Majitha, Gurdev Singh Shant, Randhir Singh Cheema, Sant Makhan Singh, Didar Singh who was an uncle of Amrik Singh, Harcharan Singh from Delhi, Surinder Kaur Grewal, Baldev Singh Brar and Ujagar Singh Sekhwan. The mother of Major General Shabeg Singh and wife and child of Amrik Singh were also introduced to the congregation.

This convention also did not specify the political goal which continued to be shrouded in ambiguity. The refrain was to follow in the footsteps of the martyrs. The appeal was emotional. Significantly, the convention sought support from the minorities in the country for the "Sikh struggle". The Akali Dal had also been earlier harping on the minority syndrome.

Khalistan slogans were repeatedly raised by the young participants. Yet another slogan which dominated was "Sikh qaum de tin gaddar, Badal, Tohra, Longowal". (Badal, Tohra and Longowal are three traitors of the Sikh nation).

It was also the time for the traditional Akalis to assert themselves and carve out their own space in the Sikh political matrix. The signals emanating from the June 9 convention of the Akali Dal (Longowal), which was also held at Amritsar, were loud and clear and the choice exercised was in favour of the unity and integrity of the country and the only form of protest registered by the party against the army action was the line that it would have no negotiations with an "evil and dishonest government" till it ensured the dignity and self respect of the Sikhs. However, the Congress, especially till the December Parliamentary elections, did not make any distinction between the radicals and the moderates and virtually the entire Sikh community was targeted as secessionist supporting militancy, overtly or covertly. Clearly, the traditional Akalis were in no mood to confront the Indian state even after Operation Bluestar and the attack was only targeted against the government at the Centre. However, by that time, Longowal and some of his associates had opened their channels with the Rajiv Gandhi government and the thrust on unity and integrity of the country would have to be seen in that context.

Longowal had already written to Rajiv Gandhi the first formal but secret letter on June 2 which paved the way for what came to be known as the Rajiv-Longowal Accord. Ground work had been done for the opening up of the line of communication formally by former finance minister Balwant Singh, one of the main architects of the accord.

A resolution was also adopted at this convention reposing faith in Longowal's leadership. The government was to be conveyed the impression that it was Longowal who continued to be the most dominant leader. Significantly, the convention paid homage to the "martyrs of Operation Bluestar" and the Dharamyudh morcha while condemning the anti-Sikh violence in Hoshiarpur. The resolutions were moved by Surjit Singh Barnala.

Communal clashes had broken out in the communally sensitive town of Hoshiarpur following the gunning down of Lok Dal leader Chandhary Balbir Singh on May 10. Parts of the town remained under curfew for about a month. The Hindu outfits like the Shiv Sena and the Parvati Sena, a women outfit, were active during this period. Both the communities had their fanatics. The district administration seized 142 trishuls, a crate of acid and empty bottles from the Shakti Mandir while petrol, spears and lathis were recovered from a gurdwara in the troubled town.

Those who attended the convention included Gurcharan Singh Tohra, Badal, Balwant Singh and Balwinder Singh Bhunder. Akal Takht Jathedar Giani Kirpal Singh was also present. The speakers demanded the restoration of the Sikh dignity, a pre-condition towards return to normalcy. Longowal regretted the Akali Dal had got discredited despite expressing full faith in the unity and integrity of the country. The Sikhs were being tarnished the world over and the Prime Minister, during his trips abroad, was letting slip no opportunity to malign them.

Reacting to the offer of negotiations from the government, Longowal took the stand that it was impossible for the Sikhs to consider any kind of agreement with those who had attacked Darbar Sahib, instigated the massacre of the Sikhs, defiled over 500 gurdwaras and incarcerated thousands of innocent youngsters on trumped up charges. Nothing could have been more farther from truth in the context of the June 2 letter to the Prime Minister. Interestingly, he said doors of his party were open for Baba Joginder Singh and his associates to join them and work against the common enemy – the government, with whom he was already negotiating.

Badal also ruled out dialogue with the government which had humiliated the Sikhs, defiled their religion and demolished their self-respect through state terror. Ironically, Longowal entered into an accord with Rajiv Gandhi the very next month which was never implemented and attacked by many sections of the Sikh society. What was came to be described as the 'great betrayal' cost him his life.

Some youth said to be the AISSF activists raised pro-Bhindranwale slogans and threw pamphlets into the hall where the convention had been organized. The pamphlets attacked Longowal, Tohra and Badal as "traitors" and "murderers".

Earlier on June 1, prayers were organized in the gurdwaras to observe Operation Bluestar week as the Ghallughara Week (Holocast/Genocide Week) during which tight security arrangements were made by the security forces apprehending violence. However, no incident of violence was reported during the period. A section of the media had apprehended threat to peace during the Genocide Week. "The provocatively so-called 'genocide week', being observed to commemorate the army action forced last year to liberate the Golden Temple of Amritsar from terrorists, is a renewed threat to communal amity and thus to the cause of national unity", commented The Patriot on June 1. Yet there was another comment on the situation: "Bhindranwale is no more. He was shot dead in Akal Takht. But his ghost continues to haunt Punjab. He is a hero for the youthful and aggressive members of the community – almost a legend and larger in death than in life".[1]

Here is yet another summing up of the situation one year after Operation Bluestar: "One year after Operation Bluestar, where do we stand? The problem of terrorism and its ability to hold the nation to ransom has increased. Bhindranwale dead has turned out to be an even more potent source of militant inspiration than Bhindranwale alive. Far from solving the Punjab crisis, Operation Bluestar and its aftermath may have even more complex".[2] And Punjab was to pass through years of unprecedented violence, perpetrated both by the militants as well as the state agencies. The objective of Operation Bluestar was not to curb militancy but project Indira Gandhi as the saviour of the Hindus. The Sikh radicals raised the accusing finger against the Soviet Union and charged Indira Gandhi with playing the game of that country. It may be mentioned that the AISSF, a few weeks before the army action, had included the Indian Communists in the list of enemies. And the KGB, all along, had been describing the Sikh struggle as the imperialist design hatched by the CIA and implemented through the Inter-Services Intelligence of Pakistan. Indira Gandhi had been warned against the attack on the Darbar Sahib complex, the advice which she had preferred to ignore.

Adopting legal tactics in this political battle against the government, the Shiromani Gurdwara Parbandhak Committee served a legal notice on the Centre on June 10 demanding compensation of Rs. 1,000 crore for the loss of property in the Darbar Sahib complex and 40 other gurdwaras during Operation Bluestar. The two month notice under section 80 of the CrPC stated the SGPC would file a civil suit against the Union and the Punjab governments after the expiry of the notice period. The notice was served to the Centre through the Ministries of Defence and the Home Affairs and to the Punjab government through the Amritsar Deputy Commissioner. The SGPC also sought unqualified apology from the chief functionaries of the governments at the Centre and in the state responsible for the Army action.

The comments of Amarinder Singh during this period on the situation in Punjab were significant: "The Sikh community today stands at the cross roads. Feelings are deeply hurt and bitterness still persists. In Punjab, they are more vocal while self-preservation forces those outside to speak in a subdued manner. Delhi must understand this... anyone who has read Sikh history or has made a study of the community, must know that to deal with the Sikhs, one must do so with tact and understanding. To try and subdue the community by force is foolish, as it will only evoke a similar response. That is the Sikh psyche. That is our heritage and has been our way of existence since the Khalsa was created in 1699.... It is time that the Prime Minister realized that the Sikhs will not bow to pressure and all that delay is creating more bitterness. Unless he makes a determined effort to break the impasse, the voice of reason will once again be pushed aside. We have made our stand known. We have said how the matter can be resolved. Yet there is inaction. If Delhi agrees to what Sant Longowal and the Sikh Forum have reiterated on a number of occasions, this will be accepted by the Sikhs. It will not only pave the way for normalcy in Punjab but will also begin the slow process of healing and emotional integration among those who have been alienated by the past events.

"The issues in question are: The release of all innocent youth and other detenus held in the past year. They should be released forthwith. The remaining who the government feels have broken the law should be tried under the normal law of the land if the Sikhs are to feel that justice is being done. The laws introduced in the past years applicable to Punjab should be withdrawn. They amount to a denial of justice and prevent the detenus getting a fair trial, resulting in heavy convictions.

"The Sikh soldiers who reacted to the extreme religious provocation must be dealt with leniently. They reacted to the destruction of the Akal Takht. Soldiers of any religion would have reacted in similar manner if it had happened to their supreme place of worship..... ban on the AISSF having been lifted, all those who were arrested only because they were members of this banned organization must be released...

"The Sikhs too must decide on one of the two options. We can either revert to the 18th century style of functioning or extricate ourselves from the plight in which we find ourselves in, in a way that redeems Sikh honour. We live in 20th century and are about to pass into the 21st. 18th century tactics suited those times. Today, if we have to achieve anything, we must get the support of the people in the country and indeed the world. Nobody will support violence and all that we shall achieve by the first option is to isolate ourselves further and invite military intervention, possibly incalculable harm to the community and destroy Punjab. The second option demands that the community stands united and speak with one voice. The Sikh leadership must realize that this is not the time for bickering and promoting one's ego or for scrambling to fill a leadership vacuum. Today personal egos are secondary to the supreme interests of the Sikhs. If the present trend continues, the community must push leaders aside as nobody's interests come before that of the Khalsa.... The Sikhs want peace, probably more than people realize. It is their homes and the future of their children that are in jeopardy. Nobody would wish his home to be in state of perpetual crisis affecting his livelihood. The Sikhs want a settlement, but a settlement with honour. The ball is now squarely in Delhi's court".[3]

It was in this background that initiating the moves to bridge the Sikh-Hindu divide, Longowal organized a joint meeting of the representatives from the two communities at Sangrur on June 16 where he offered to review the Anandpur Sahib resolution to remove the apprehensions, while maintaining it was neither separatist nor aimed at creating a Sikh state. In the backdrop of the parleys going on with the Prime Minister, he was addressing the Hindus all over the country from the platform of that meeting. The Hindu leaders assured him of full support in the mission. The meeting was chaired by Ram Sarup, district president of the Janata Party. Later on June 25, while speaking in Delhi, he made an impassioned appeal for preserving Hindu-Sikh unity saying, "Let us take the challenge together and resurrect and restore the traditional values of human life and brotherhood". He blamed the policies of the ruling Congress for the situation.[4]

As the secret parleys were on between Rajiv Gandhi and a section of the Akali leadership, one of the most shocking tragedies took place on June 23 which came to be linked to Punjab militancy, though none of the Sikh militant organizations ever owned responsibility for it and those tried for the crime were ultimately declared not guilty after about two decades. It was the mid-air bombing of Air India's Kanishka, the Air India flight 182 from Montreal to Bombay (Mumbai), which crashed into the Atlantic off the Irish coast, killing all the 326 persons on board. Years later, the suspects, who happened to be Sikhs, were acquitted by the Canadian court after a lengthy trial. Accusing fingers were also pointed towards the Indian intelligence agencies as part of the operation to discredit the Sikh militant movement. The movement was just reviving after Operation Bluestar. The tragedy continues to be shrouded in mystery.

In the Punjab political scene, Santokh Singh Randhawa resigned from the presidency of the Pradesh Congress Committee on June 29 following allegations of his links with the militants. This incident reinforced the allegations which were being leveled by a section of the Akalis against the Congress for aiding and abetting secessionism.

The Rajiv-longowal Accord

A new chapter was now about to be opened in the Punjab tragedy.

In a move to strengthen the hands of Longowal, the Punjab government announced partial amnesty for those detained since 1982 under charges other than sedition, murder, dacoity and arson. The announcement was made by the Governor on the death anniversary of Maharaja Ranjit Singh at Amritsar on June 28. Baba Joginder Singh, however, demanded that all the detainees should be released if the government was sincere. Again, this has to be seen in the context of the behind the scene parleys between Sant Longowal and Rajiv Gandhi in which Arjun Singh played a crucial role. He was considered to be one of the architects of the Accord.

Longowal too, like Balwant Singh, was convinced that the Sikhs would be in for bigger trouble in case the situation was allowed to linger on. He had revealed his mind to this writer at a meeting after his release at his native village, Gidriani, near Lehragaga in Sangrur district. A posse of police guarded his ordinary house in the village. He went to the extent of saying that he was aware of the danger to his life and was prepared to make the supreme sacrifice. His dera was at Kaimbowal village adjoining Longowal a few kilometers away in the same district.

The formal negotiations followed the 4-page letter Longowal wrote to the Prime Minister on June 2 presenting the case of the Akali Dal following the ground work done by the intermediaries who mainly included Arjun Singh and former finance minister Balwant Singh. Strangely, he did not list any pre-conditions. Taking note of the offer by the Prime Minister for negotiated settlement, Longowal said in this secret letter that his party had always been committed to the unity and integrity of the country and those suspecting the Sikhs and the Akali Dal were the real enemies of the Sikhs. He clarified that the Akali Dal had never supported secessionism or the separatist forces. Projecting the Sikhs as anti-national was part of the conspiracy to disintegrate the country. Defending the Anandpur Sahib resolution, he sought state autonomy. Immediate transfer of Chandigarh and setting up of a commission to identify the Punjabi speaking areas in other states and referring the river waters dispute to the Supreme Court were the other issues. The other concerns he referred to included the enactment of all India gurdwara legislation, second language status to Punjabi in the neighbouring states, recruitment in the defence services on merit alone and holy city status for Amritsar.

Longowal specified the demands of his party in this so far unpublished correspondence. Referring to the issues concerning Punjab, the Sikhs and the Akali Dal, he started with the situation arising out of Operation Bluestar. In this context, he sought an end to the state repression, release of detenus, withdrawal of cases against the army men who had deserted their barracks in protest and other government employees, compensation to the next of kin killed during the army action, punishment to the guilty of November, 1984 massacre of the Sikhs and setting up of special courts for the protection of human rights of the Sikhs and withdrawal of all black laws. He ended the letter with the suggestion that the procedure and medium to settle these issues to be finalized through personal contacts while maintaining that the party would welcome the "constructive initiative to resolve the issue".

He started the letter saying, "For the last some time, the Prime Minister has repeatedly announced that the Government of India was willing to settle the issues concerning Punjab and the Sikhs within the framework of the unity and integrity of the country. The Shiromani Akali Dal which has always articulated the Sikh view point and the interests of Punjab has always been committed to the unity and integrity of the country. The party has also been of the considered view that the real threat to the unity and integrity of the country were those who had been raising doubts about the loyalty of the Sikhs to the country.... We have never supported the secessionism and terrorism. If despite this commitment of the Akali Dal the party is dubbed as anti-national, then it is very unfortunate and part of despicable conspiracy to strike at the unity and integrity of the country".

Rajiv Gandhi was quick to respond and in his letter dated June 3, he appreciated "your overriding commitment to the integrity of India; your concern for communal harmony; and your opposition to violence, secession and terrorism" while taking note of the fact that "there are no preconditions in your latter". He further said, "I am asking the Governor of Punjab to get in touch with you regarding your letter and I shall follow up with him on my return from my foreign tour".

Longowal, in his letter dated June 6, appreciated this gesture of the Prime Minister expressing satisfaction that "You have conceded that the campaign raising apprehensions about the commitment of the Akali Dal to the unity and integrity of the country is part of the conspiracy to disintegrate the country". He said it would not be relevant to talk of pre-conditions in the context of the issues raised by him in his earlier letter.

The Governor took the initiative on June 8 and wrote to Longowal saying "I would request to kindly indicate whether it will be convenient for you to come over personally to meet me or you would like to nominate someone on your behalf to do so at the earliest possible opportunity so that further action may be initiated in the light of the letter exchanged between the Hon. Prime Minister and your goodself".

The very same day, Longowal wrote to Arjun Singh authorizing Balwant Singh for the talks. He wrote, "In the context of the correspondence exchanged between the Prime Minister and myself, I authorize Mr. Balwant Singh as my representative to contact you". He did not trust any other Akali leader for this purpose including Badal and Tohra who were senior to Balwant Singh. He had ignored these two senior leaders at this very stage itself. This was perhaps one of the reasons as to why Badal and Tohra did not accompany Longowal to Delhi to sign the accord and stayed back. And ironically, both these leaders ratified the accord when it was made a condition for the allotment of the tickets for the Assembly elections. Of course, the reasons given out by them later for not joining Longowal in Delhi were different.

An unsigned and undated note purportedly scribbled by Arjun Singh on the letter head of Raj Bhavan stated: "We are in contact with the Akali Dal leadership to work out the modalities for negotiations to arrive at an amicable solution to the Punjab problem. This is an internal problem of the country and we shall solve it without any outside help. The Sikhs are as patriotic as any other Indian citizen and they occupy a place of pride in our national polity".

At the time when the parleys had already started, Longowal, commenting on certain statements of the Prime Minister about negotiated settlement, said, "Such moves were like a person who after killing your child, twirls his moustache and declares that he is ready for negotiations....we don't want a sarkar (government), we want 'izzat' (honour), 'insaaf (justice) and 'dharam' (religion)". He was categoric that there could be no negotiations for a settlement unless the government took steps to improve the atmosphere in the state.[5] However, the reality was different.

The Prime Minister sent the formal invitation to the Akali Dal chief on July 2 "to come to Delhi at your earliest convenience for a meeting with me so that we could discuss and decide the manner in which further steps are to be taken".

This invitation to Longowal was discussed at a meeting of the senior leaders including Longowal, Tohra, Badal, Barnala and Balwant Singh. Tohra insisted that release of all the Sikh detainees should be the minimum precondition. He said, "We should have patience. Entering into a dialogue is the compulsion of the government, not ours. We have already gone through the worst. The government must release the Sikh army men who left their barracks and the Sikh detenus to pave way for the talks".

The issue of talks also cropped up at a meeting of senior leaders, district jathedars and ex-MPs and ex-MLAs at Anandpur Sahib on July 8. It was decided to list some pre-conditions which included abolition of all black laws and special courts, withdrawal of false cases against the Sikh youth and Akali workers, judicial inquiry into the November 1984 massacre of the Sikhs and withdrawal of warrants issued against Akal Takht Jathedar Giani Kirpal Singh for appearing in a Ludhiana court in the case relating to the attack against him. The meeting authorized Longowal to revive the Dharamyudh morcha and lead it as and when it was re-launched. It was also decided that the party leaders would visit other states to remove misgivings about the Anandpur Sahib resolution.

Longowal had also approached Babbar Khalsa on the issue of negotiations with the Centre but the militant organization opposed such moves. It was senior Babbar Khalsa militant Anokh Singh, a former employee of the Shiromani Gurdwara Parbandhak Committee, who was then organizing secretary of the outfit with whom Longowal had held discussions. Anokh warned him about the consequences of any deal with the government at that juncture which was considered to be a defining moment for the Sikhs as a community which was still to come out of the trauma of Operation Bluestar and the November massacre. This was the only militant organization with which Longowal had his channels of communications.

However, Longowal accepted the formal invitation for talks in his letter to the Prime Minister on July 16. The letter was again vague about the preconditions. Longowal said in his reply that he shared the anxiety of the Prime Minister to arrive at some settlement in the interest of the country and Punjab.

Another letter from Rajiv Gandhi was received a few days later in which it was stated that the release of the army deserters would be given priority at the talks. Tohra tried to impress upon Longowal that once they went for the talks without pre-conditions, the demand for the release of detainees would not be conceded. He was of the view that it was the compulsion of Rajiv Gandhi to enter into negotiations and not of the Sikhs who had already suffered the worst. He tried to impress Longowal that in case the government agreed to the release of army deserters and other detenus, the party would not mind settling for less in case of other issues. According to Tohra, Longwal initially agreed to his suggestions. Longowal shared the second letter from the Prime Minister first with Tohra.

A meeting of the senior leaders was again summoned to discuss the second letter in the SGPC sub-office at Chandigarh. Prem Singh Chandumajra, comparatively a junior leader, who was also present that day, also insisted on pre-condition of the release of the detainees. However, he got a snub following which he left the place. At the meeting, Tohra and Badal again pressed for the pre-condition. At that stage, Balwant Singh brought out the proposed draft, each and every point of which was discussed. As per the draft, Chandigarh was to be transferred to Punjab on January 26 next. Only Barnala supported Balwant Singh. Tohra expressed the apprehension of betrayal by the Centre under the cover of the accord and dubbed the proposed draft as fraud and play of words. Chandigarh was to be divided with Sector 26, industrial area and Mani Majra to be kept out. Longowal agreed to write another letter to the Prime Minister. Balwant Singh offered to get the letter typed from his office. However, Tohra got a shock in the evening when he heard over the All India Radio in the Punjabi bulletin that the meeting between Longowal and the Prime Minister was scheduled for the next morning at 9.00 AM. It was also given out that a messenger had delivered the invitation to Tohra also to reach Delhi by 8.00 AM the next day at the residence of Delhi Akali Dal leader Paramjit Singh Sarna. Tohra decided not to go and gave company to Badal in Chandigarh the day Longowal signed the accord in Delhi.

Longowal and Rajiv Gandhi met for about half an hour on July 23. The spadework for the meeting had already been done by the Arjun Singh. Swaran Singh had also made his own contribution. This was the first meeting at that level after Operation Bluestar. The meeting was followed by another meeting between two aides of Longowal and members of the Political Affairs Committee of the cabinet. Longowal drove to the Parliament House along with Balwant Singh and Barnala. Arjun Singh was also present in the Prime Minister's office but withdrew after escorting Longowal to Prime Minister's office. Both Balwant Singh and Barnala waited in the ante room.

The Political Affairs Committee of the Union cabinet had more than two hour meeting with the aides of Longowal. Those present at the meeting included Home Minister S. B. Chavan, Finance Minister V. P. Singh and Defence Minister P. V. Narasimha Rao. Longowal wanted the government to enlarge the scope of the judicial inquiry into the November 1984 violence against the Sikhs by including violence at other places also along with Delhi, rehabilitation of the victims and punishment to the culprits and abolition of special courts and special laws. He stressed that the honour and dignity of the Sikhs must be restored. Arjun Singh earlier had several secret meetings with the top Akali leaders prior to the signing of the accord. Longowal met Arjun Singh for the first time on June 26.

An aircraft kept waiting for Badal at the Chandigarh airport to airlift him to Delhi to be part of the Akali delegation. Tohra landed at the residence of Badal early in the morning and gave him the company for several hours. They stayed back.

The Punjab Accord was signed between Rajiv Gandhi and Longowal on July 24 after 36 hour round the clock discussions at various levels. The Akali Dal chief said after signing the accord that he was fully satisfied with the agreement which, for him, marked the end of the confrontation with the Centre. The accord envisaged the transfer of Chandigarh to Punjab by January 26, 1986, setting up of a commission to identify Hindi speaking areas to be transferred out of Punjab and setting up of a tribunal to go into river water dispute with Haryana while protecting the usage by the two states as on July 1, 1985. The Anandpur Sahib resolution was to be referred to the Sarkaria Commission on Centre-State relations.

It was presumed that the accord would put an end to the violence. But then the already marginalized Akali Dal (Longowal) did not dictate the situation at that time. This was one of the reasons, besides the intentions of the Centre, for the non-implementation of the accord. It met the fate it was destined to. The accord was to be consigned to the dustbin of history. Moreover, the fight was between the militants and the Centre and the Akali Dal (Longowal) was not a party to this bloody confrontation. The accord, to be effective, should have been signed with those who were spearheading the Sikh struggle. The accord failed to take off.

In Amritsar, a small group of the United Akali Dal and the AISSF activists staged demonstration against the accord in front of the Darbar Sahib complex. The ad hoc committee of the United Akali Dal, on July 25, passed a resolution rejecting the accord saying it was a sell out. The resolution said Longowal, Barnala and Bawant Singh had no right to represent the Sikhs. The three leaders, by becoming party to the accord, had justified Operation Bluestar, the desecration of the Darbar Sahib, burning of the religious books in the Sikh reference library and the attack on other Sikh shrines. The slogan given by the Darbar Sahib based militants was: "Sikh qaum de tin gaddaar, Balwant, Barnala te Longowal". Within a few weeks, Longowal had to pay the highest cost for entering into the accord.

A representative meeting of the Akali Dal (L) held at Anandpur Sahib on July 26 ratified the accord amidst criticism from Badal and Tohra. Longowal announced the withdrawal of the Dharamyudh morcha. Tohra said, "It (accord) is not an achievement but ruination". Badal commented, "We had taken a pledge at Akal Takht about our demands. As these have not been accepted, we should withdraw this pledge... we have lost our wealth, our religious places and honour". The two leaders who did not ratify the accord by raising their hands were Tohra and Badal.[6] A total of 52 persons voted in favour of the accord and 19 against it.

While commenting upon the accord years later in private talk, Tohra was of the view that Longowal was sincere towards the Panth but lacked political maturity and would not go into the depth of the issue. He was not greedy and would easily trust people. He did not use the word naïve for him.

The reaction to the accord in Haryana was on expected lines. The opposition parties decided to launch agitation. Twenty nine members of the Haryana Assembly from the Opposition, on July 27, handed over their resignations to their leaders to be submitted to the Speaker on August 9. The opposition parties included the Lok Dal, the BJP, the Janata Party, the Congress (S) and the Congress (J). Former chief minister Devi Lal gave a call for Haryana Bandh on July 31. Rajasthan also adopted aggressive attitude as the accord envisaged adjudication of the river waters though that state had been excluded from the water dispute. Rajiv Gandhi had assured that the interests of Haryana and Rajasthan would be safeguarded. The Haryana Lok Dal and the Bharatiya Janata Party described the accord as surrender to terrorism and demanded the resignation of Bhajan Lal for having failed to protect the interests of the state.

It was Badal who had been first approached by Arjun Singh for initiating the dialogue. The bait was the office of the chief minister after the Assembly elections which were proposed to be managed in favour of the Akali Dal. He was assured that dummy candidates would be put up by the Congress to facilitate the exercise. However, while he declined the offer, both Barnala and Balwant Singh took the bait. Badal was against entering into any agreement without some concrete steps having been taken by the Centre to restore the confidence of the Sikhs. Earlier also, Badal had been approached by the emissary from the Centre while in jail after Operation Bluestar but he had refused to meet him. As the Centre decided to release him, he was brought to Delhi and the special aircraft carrying him was parked in one corner of the airport. He was given the signal that an emissary from the Centre was to hold discussions with him. He declined again. He was flown to Chandigarh and dropped at his residence.

The hostile reception to Longowal in the Darbar Sahib complex on July 30 was an indication of the mood of the forces dictating the political discourse. Rival Akali activists clashed at the arrival of Longowal. Shots were fired in the air and swords, iron rods, lathis and brickbats were freely used. He was to preside over a meeting of his party's district jathedars. The situation provided an excuse to the security forces to intervene. The SGPC lodged a strong protest the next day with the Governor over the entry of the security forces into the shrine complex. But then after the army action, entry of the security forces had ceased to be an issue.

The assassination of Congress leader Lalit Makan and his wife Geetanjali in Delhi on July 31 within days of signing the accord was an indication that it was not the anti-dote to militancy. The assassination was revenge for the massacre of the Sikhs in Delhi in November. The accord had thus already been rendered redundant within days of its signing.

Longowal met Tohra a few days later to impress him the need to start political activity and assured that all the Sikh detenus would be released within two months. Tohra suggested to him that the Assembly elections announcement should be delayed till then as it was not possible to go to the people otherwise. Longowal's response was positive. However, the elections were announced the very next day. Longowal, who was under attack for betraying the Sikhs, had himself been let down by the Centre on this issue.

Longowal Gunned Down

The Akali Dal President convened a meeting of the party at Longowal to discuss the allotment of tickets for the Assembly elections. Both Tohra and Badal were conspicuous by their absence. He sent them a message to meet them. They conveyed that they would be present at Nadampur rest house in Sangrur district on August 20. Tohra protested that he had again kept them in the dark. Longowal extended the excuse that he did not get time to take up the issue of poll postponement with the Centre. Tohra was of the view that the notification was still to be issued and as such, the elections could be deferred. Longowal, on the suggestion of Tohra, constituted a two member committee, including Badal, to talk to Baba Joginder Singh to contest the elections on a single platform. The tickets were to be allotted by the Parliamentary Board of the Akali Dal(L).

However, within few hours the very same day, Longowal, 53, was gunned down around 5.30 PM by the militants at a gurdwara in Sherpur village in Sangrur district. The doctors at the civil hospital, Sangrur, announced his death at 9.32 PM. Tohra, Badal, Barnala and Sukhdev Singh Dhindsa had reached the hospital by that time. Teams of doctors were rushed from Patiala and Chandigarh. One of his assailants was shot on the spot by the security men while his associate, Gian Singh Leel, was overpowered. Longowal had been provided security by the Punjab police apprehending threat to his life from the militants for signing the accord. He was aware of the risk involved even before the signing of the accord.

A day earlier while addressing a gathering at a Hindu temple (Luxmi Mandir) at Sunam, he had said that he was prepared to make the supreme sacrifice for the unity and integrity of the country and stoutly defended the accord.

The United Akali Dal, while condemning the assassination, appealed to the Akal Takht Jathedar to convene Sarbat Khalsa to seek mandate on the accord while stressing the need for unity in the Panth which was passing through a "deep crisis". The signatories to the statement included Atma Singh, Ujagar Singh Sekhwan, Parkash Singh Majitha, Ranjit Singh Brahmpura and Satwant Kaur Sandhu. The Sikh Forum headed by Amarinder Singh described the assassination as the "most shameful act" while maintaining that expeditious implementation of the accord would be the most befitting tribute to Longowal. The offices of the SGPC remained closed for two days as a mark of respect to the assassinated leader.

Amarinder Singh finally joined the Akali Dal (Longowal) on August 23. Announcing this decision, he said the Panth and Punjab were confronted with a grave situation. Well wishers of the Panth must unite to face it. He appealed to all Akali leaders to fight for the interests of the community and Punjab under the banner of the Akali Dal as division in the community would lead to chaos and instability.

Barnala took over as the acting president though the dominant view in the party was that a committee be set up to run the party affairs. However, both Amarinder Singh and Ravi Inder Singh did not favour the idea. Finally, the name of Barnala was proposed by Tohra and seconded by Ravi Inder Singh. Both Tohra and Badal were included in the Parliamentary Board which was dominated by the Barnala associates.

Assembly Elections 1985

In accordance with the unwritten parameters of the Rajiv-Longowal accord, Punjab went to the polls on September 25 which facilitated the coming into power of the Akali Dal (Longowal). The Akali Dal (Longowal) made it clear that tickets would be given only to those leaders who ratified the accord. Badal fell in line and got the ticket.

The call given by the United Akali Dal to boycott the polls did not get the desired response. The voter turn out was 66 per cent as compared to 64 per cent in 1980. The Akali Dal won a record 73 out of a total of 117 seats while the Congress had 32 seats in its kitty with 10 seats going to other political parties. Elections had been held to 115 seats in a House of 117 as elections to the Jalandhar Central and Jalandhar North had been countermanded. The Akali Dal polled 38.40 per cent of the votes as compared to 37.31 per cent in favour of the Congress, with 24.29 per cent going to the others.

In the then districts of Bathinda and Sangrur, all the seats (9 and 10 respectively) went to the Akalis. The Akali Dal won from nine seats out of 16 seats in Amritsar and five seats out of 11 seats in Gurdaspur. The police repression during Operation Woodrose was the worst in the border districts of Amritsar and Gurdaspur. Some of the semi urban Assembly seats in Gurdaspur district are Hindu dominated.

The Akali Dal (L), in its election manifesto, had promised to release all the "innocent youth" under detention and their rehabilitation. A judicial commission headed by a High Court judge was to probe the killings and action to be taken against guilty politicians and officials. The accord was described as "vindication of Akali Dal stand" which "restores to the Sikhs a place of pride and dignity in the Indian mainstream".

Barnala was elected as the Chief Minister on September 27 and his name was proposed by Badal and seconded by Sukhjinder Singh. His was sworn in on September 29. The ministers in the first lot included Balwant Singh, Amarinder Singh, Sukhjinder Singh, Basant Singh Khalsa and Major Singh Uboke.

Though the traditional Akali leadership had compromised with the Centre, the Sikhs at the global level continued to feel hurt and humiliated and the sentiments of this section were articulated by the radicals. For them, contesting elections under the Indian constitution would have amounted to virtually justifying Operation Bluestar.

And as the designs later unfolded, it was the Barnala government which subsequently provided legitimacy to Operation Bluestar with contribution from a section of the militants who also functioned as instruments in this game and provided the much needed excuse for the Akali Dal government to raid the Darbar Sahib complex. The build up within the shrine complex during the post-Bluestar period would have to be studied in this framework.

Badal wanted to be inducted in the cabinet with number two status but it was Balwant Singh who was Barnala's choice. Badal's case was hesitatingly pleaded by Tohra who proposed that the former chief minister be included in the cabinet with number two status in place of Balwant Singh. An upset Balwant Singh questioned the proposal and asked whether he was being denied the status simply because he was non- Jat. Tohra clarified that was the general perception in the party and not just his personal view. At the same time, he said in Badal's place, he would not have opted to join the ministry because a person, who had already been the chief minister, should not accept number two position. However, Barnala was not favourably inclined to have Badal in his cabinet. Badal declined the offer to take over as Speaker of the Assembly. Next day at a meeting, Badal suggested the alphabetical order should be followed in the matter of protocol rather than going in for number two position in the cabinet. Brnala decided against inducting Badal as a minister.

The Barnala government, in the policy statement, again promised to set up a commission of inquiry to probe the "association, connivance and support of political elements with the activities of terrorists and extremists". Ironically, a similar poll promise was made by the Shiromani Akali Dal at the time of the 1997 elections. Neither Barnala nor the 1997 Badal government ordered such a probe. Badal took the plea that it would reopen the raw wounds of Punjab which had returned to normalcy. The priorities of the Barnala government listed at the formation of the government included the implementation of the Rajiv-Longowal accord.

Barnala said in his policy statement, "My government will pursue the policies of constructive cooperation rather than that of confrontation pursued by the previous government.... The mandate is to heal the wounds of the past and to revive the spirit of Panjab deriving its strength and inspiration from the Sikh Gurus, saints and visionaries, culminating in the concept of Sarabat Da Bhala."

The statement further said: "The government has assumed office at a time when the state's finances are in a shambles, its industrial, commercial and economic growth was stagnating and employment opportunities were shrinking..... it would be our utmost duty to restore sanity to the state's finances and rebuild its economic strength by reviving and promoting in a big way, its industry, commerce and agriculture . The government would undo the anti-rural policies of the previous government in matters of agriculture growth, integrated rural development schemes and modernization of education in rural areas. The government would take all possible measures to provide our Hindu, Harijan, Muslim and Christian brethren who have extended their electoral support to us, opportunities for fullest sense of participation and self-realization.

"We are aware that the youth of Punjab feel hurt and alienated. No state or society can truly make progress without the youth being in the vanguard in all activities. Immediate steps would be taken to end the rule of suppression and repression. A high powered committee would be set up to immediately start the process of releasing the youth from jails and their rehabilitation".[7] The problem with the Barnala government was that it lacked credibility and within no time came into confrontation with the radicals who were in the process of getting re-organized.

Within days of the Barnala government taking over, some militant leaders re-surfaced in the Darbar Sahib complex. The group of Sukhdev Singh Sakhira from Tarn Taran was spotted in early October. The report appearing in The Indian Express about this development seemed to have upset the officers concerned in the state government who vainly tried to deny it. It is a different matter that sporadic incidents of militancy related violence were continuously being reported all the time. Transistor and pen bombs were also introduced in the state during this period. Delhi and some other places had already been hit by transistor bombs in May. Tarn Taran municipal committee President Ram Labhaya was gunned down on October 16. Fatehgarh Churian block Congress President Raj Kumar, was shot on October 19. Hindu Shiv Sena president of Phillaur Vijay Kumar was assassinated on November 11. Punjab had already ushered in the second phase of militancy which was to be deadlier than the first phase. Though it could just be coincidence, the revival virtually coincided with the efforts to re-organize the radicals at the political level. It was this build up in the shrine complex which was important in the context of the Barnala government providing legitimacy to Operation Bluestar.

The only action of the Barnala government which was venerated was the setting up of a committee headed by Justice A S Bains (Retd) to go into the cases registered in the state relating to militancy, including police encounters. Hundreds of Sikhs in detention were released on the recommendations of this committee and cases withdrawn against many others who had gone underground apprehending arrest.

The Damdami Taksal and some militant groups separately opened channels with the Barnala government. One of the emissaries deputed by the Taksal had cases pending against him and he wanted to meet Barnala as a free man. The talks failed to take off. The cases against him were withdrawn later on the recommendations of the Bains committee.

Within days of the democratic intervention in Punjab, Delhi was rocked by series of bomb blasts. More than 70 persons were killed in these serial blasts triggered by transistor bombs in Delhi on October 29, two days before Diwali. These blasts demonstrated the capacity of the militants to strike anywhere. It was the revenge psyche in operation to avenge the genocide of the Sikhs in November last year. The Babbars were in action.

As part implementation of the Punjab Accord, the Centre set up the Mathew Commission in October to resolve the territorial dispute with Haryana. The Prime Minister, however, on October 11, admitted there had been a drafting error in its terms of reference. He described the mistake as unintentional and unfortunate but said it would be difficult to amend the same as the Commission had already started functioning. As per this controversial term of reference, the Commission could take into account any other factor in determining territorial claims in addition to language, contiguity and village as a unit.

AISSF as Front for Radicals

However, such steps did not help in restoring peace in the troubled state and the build up was going on. The AISSF which provided the much needed platform to the radicals to start their political activity held a meeting of its executive committee and other office bearers on October 5 in which it was resolved to rebuild Akal Takht and press for the replacement of its Jathedar Giani Kirpal Singh. The reconstruction of Akal Takht later became the rallying point for the militants. The dominant leadership of the SGPC was attacked for betraying the Sikhs and being in league with the government. The political resolution was kept intentionally vague about the goal while maintaining that the AISSF would continue the struggle for the freedom and dignity of the people and maintained the Sikhs were slaves in India. The priority was given to reviving the political activity. Though critical of the Akali leadership, the resolution commented on the Assembly elections stating it was the defeat of Hindu communalism in the state. The mandate to the Akali Dal was described as the reflection of the anger of the Sikhs against the Congress and the Hindu communalism and rejection of the anti-Sikh policy adopted by the rulers in Delhi. At the same time, the resolution warned the youth against pinning much hope on the Barnala government. Through another resolution, the AISSF opposed the move to revive the Upper House.

The main demands included holy city status for Amritsar, more time to Punjabi programmes on state run TV Doordarshan and All India Radio and use of Punjabi in state government offices, and extending financial help to the families of those under detention. The AISSF called for adjudication of the disputes at the local level rather than approaching courts. Initially, Baba Joginder Singh tried to cold shoulder the proposal to organize this meeting and refused to provide financial help. Money was raised from the shopkeepers of Bazar Kaulsar by some sympathizers of the radicals, including a few journalists. Baba Joginder Singh was already getting money from abroad.

The AISSF, on October 31, observed first anniversary of the death of Beant Singh, the assassin of Indira Gandhi, at Manji Sahib Diwan Hall in the Darbar Sahib complex. The event was part of the resurgence of the radical politics. It reiterated the resolve to rebuild Akal Takht after bringing down the structure constructed by the government with the help of Baba Santa Singh. The conclave once again rejected the Rajiv-Longowal accord saying it did not restore the rights of the Sikhs snatched away by the Centre but rather put a seal on the killing of the Sikhs. It was described as a betrayal by Longowal with the Panth.

It was decided to set up a committee to provide financial relief to the families of the martyrs and those under detention. The members included Baba Thakar Singh, Harnam Singh, Pritam Kaur, widow of Sant Bhindranwale, Bibi Naranjan Kaur, mother of Bhai Amrik Singh, Bibi Bimal Kaur Khalsa, widow of Beant Singh and the president of the AISSF. Yet another resolution called upon the government at the Centre to end to the policy of confrontation and discrimination against the Sikhs. With this function, the AISSF again became the centre of the radical politics.

The symbolic Kar Sewa of the Akal Takht to pull it down was performed by the selected leaders and activists of the AISSF after this conclave. This operation was kept a secret till the end. Five amritdhari (baptized) Singhs including Swaran Singh Khalsa and Jasbir Singh Malhi, presidents of the Kapurthala and Gurdaspur districts respectively and three persons from Damdami Taksal comprised the Panj Piaras who were entrusted with the responsibility of symbolic demolition in accordance with the Sikh Maryada. The core group behind the move had consulted Mohkam Singh of Damdami Taksal about Maryada on this sensitive issue. The prayer (Ardas) before demolition was also performed by Mohkam Singh at Akal Takht. It was announced from the Manji Sahib hall stage that after the main programme, the families of the martyrs would go to Akal Takht to pay obeisance. It was a camouflage to keep the SGPC in the dark about this sensitive move. After the symbolic demolition, it was AISSF President Harinder Singh Kahlon who briefed the Sikh devotees present about the operation.

The idea behind Kar Sewa was to take over the control of Akal Takht again for which Harminder Singh Sandhu was also consulted in jail who did not react favourably to this strategy. Baba Joginder Singh was also opposed to the move. Militant leader Sukhdev Singh Sakhira was brought in for intervention who talked to the Baba in the presence of Mohkam Singh and Dhanna Singh and succeeded in persuading him.

However, the SGPC took strong reservation to the move and described the symbolic action as desecration of Akal Takht. It was a direct challenge to its authority. The spokesman clarified that the SGPC had already taken a decision to rebuild Akal Takht and the Sant Samaj was being contacted for this purpose. The misguided youth, acting in haste, had violated the Sikh traditions and were interfering in the functioning of the SGPC. Those at the helm of affairs at that time in the radical stream avoided yet another immediate confrontation with the government at the Centre.

The AISSF submitted a memorandum to the Barnala government on November 1 at Chandigarh after the bhog ceremony of Beant Singh organized at his native village Maloya on the outskirts of Chandigarh. Earlier, a march had been organized from Amritsar to Maloya village. The AISSF activists raised Khalistan slogans during the march. Barnala assured sympathetic consideration of the demands which included release of the Sikh youth and re-instatement of the army deserters.

The AISSF parted company with the United Akali Dal on November 2 and gave a call to the Sikh masses to unite under Damdami Taksal. The AISSF chief, a day earlier, had objected to the organization being described as a wing of the United Akali Dal. The AISSF had been distancing itself from Baba Joginder Singh. The AISSF had been revived to function as the front organization of the radicals and the militants and not a wing of any Akali faction. The Darbar Sahib complex was once again becoming the epicenter of radical political activity.

The Hindu communalism was also competing with the Sikh radicals. The Shiv Sena distributed 51 trishuls to its volunteers at Mukerian in the communally surcharged Hoshiarpur district on November 16.

Panth Rattan for Longowal

Tohra was re-elected President of the SGPC at its general body meeting on November 29, 1985. The general house conferred the title of "Panth Rattan" on Longowal. Ironically, it was Tohra who had opposed the signing of the Rajiv-Longowal Accord and it was under his presidency that Longowal had been honoured with this title. The general house demanded release of all Sikh youth and made a strong plea for the re-instatement of the Army personnel who had left their barracks and adequate compensation for the victims of the November massacre. The general house described the repair of Akal Takht by the government as violation of the Sikh tradition and an insult to the Sikhs and endorsed the announcement made by Tohra earlier that it would be re-built.

And in an effort to discourage the militant activity, the executive committee of the SGPC at its meeting on December 10 at Amritsar decided to ban the pasting of posters of all types inside the Darbar Sahib complex.

After the revival of the AISSF as the political wing of the militants, the first major initiative to mobilize the scattered sections of the militants and the radicals was undertaken in December from the Damdami Taksal platform. It was as part of this initiative that a Shaheedi (Martyrs) conference was organized at the Damdami Taksal headquarters towards December end. The response was overwhelming, more than the expectations of the organizers. The families of those having been killed by the security forces were honoured at that conference. The conclave rejected the SGPC decision to start Kar Sewa of Akal Takht on January 27. Money virtually poured at the convention. This convention paved the way for organizing a Sarbat Khalsa conclave at Akal Takht on January 26.

With this Shaheedi conclave, the radical politics had come to occupy its earlier space again. Tohra had constituted a 5-member committee consisting of Baba Thakar Singh, Baba Harbans Singh, Baba Jagtar Singh Tarn Taran, Baba Uttam Singh Khadoor Sahib and Baba Dewan Singh to supervise the Kar Sewa. Baba Thakar Singh and Bhai Mohkam Singh of Damdami Taksal had a meeting with Tohra on January 21 in which it was resolved that the Kar Sewa would be undertaken by a committee of religious leaders under the supervision of Damdami Taksal from January 26.

As the radical politics revived in the Sikh political stream, the future of Chandigarh also came to be speculated upon as part of the implementation of the Rajiv-Longowal Accord. Reports appeared in the press on January 11, 1986 that Chandigarh would be transferred to Punjab on January 26 and Haryana would get approximately 40 villages of Patiala district. The Mathew Commission, on January 14, ordered a linguistic survey of Kandukhera village in Muktsar tehsil. It was through Kandukhera village that Indira Gandhi had proposed a 100 feet wide and eight kilometer long corridor to link Abohar and Fazilka areas of Punjab with Haryana in her 1970 award to resolve the territorial dispute between the two states. The entry of political workers, including ministers, was banned in Kandukhera for two days during the survey which created a lot of tension between Punjab and Haryana. Describing the survey as against the national integrity and unity, Badal said on January 16 that it would lead to far reaching consequences. The transfer of Fazilka and Abohar would have cut off Sri Ganganagar district of Rajasthan which Punjab claimed as Punjabi speaking while according riparian status to Haryana so far as the Punjab rivers were concerned.

The Mathew Commission submitted its report to the government which the Home Ministry forwarded to the Prime Minister on January 24. The government also decided to set up a river waters tribunal.

The transfer of Chandigarh to Punjab on January 26 was deferred on January 25 ostensibly on the logic that the Mathew Commission had failed to identify the villages to be transferred to Haryana. The commission upheld the criteria of contiguity on the transfer of Abohar and Fazilka areas. Bhajan Lal and Barnala met Union Home Minister S. B. Chavan for the second time on January 26 but failed to identify the areas to be transferred to Haryana. Bhajan Lal did not agree to the principle of linguistic contiguity. The main obstruction coming in the way of the transfer of Chandigarh was the forthcoming Assembly elections in Haryana. The Prime Minister telephoned Barnala on January 24 expressing the inability of the Centre to transfer Chandigarh to Punjab at least for four months in view of the forthcoming elections to the Haryana Assembly.

Finance Minister Balwant Singh advised Barnala to resign in protest against the failure of the Centre to transfer the city to Punjab saying sooner or later, the government, anyway, would have to go. Barnala did not agree. The Barnala government had made all preparations for the big show slated for midnight and journalists from Delhi had also descended on the City Beautiful to cover the transfer which eventually ended as a non-event. The state government had also sent out invitation for the ceremony. The situation would have taken a new turn in case the Barnala government had resigned on the issue. Barnala seemed to be under some kind of pressure from the government in Delhi. He was later suitably rewarded by appointing him as Governor. However, he had once again betrayed the Sikhs.

The Centre decided to appoint another commission consisting of Justice E. S. Venkataramiah, a judge of the Supreme Court to determine the Hindi speaking areas to be transferred to Haryana from Punjab. Both Bhajan Lal and Barnala welcomed the setting up of the new commission. Barnala, on April 3, reaffirmed his government's commitment to complete the construction of the Satluj-Yamuna Link Canal. He said the remaining construction of the carrier channel would be entrusted to a public sector undertaking in consultation with the Planning Commission (The Indian Express, April 4, 1986).

Justice Venkataramiah submitted his report on June 12 and awarded an area of 70,000 acres to be given to Haryana. Interestingly, he proposed the setting up of another commission to identify this area. It was also proposed that Haryana should build its own capital. The Haryana government accepted the recommendations after a cabinet meeting chaired by Chief Minister Bansi Lal. The government constituted Justice D A Desai Commission on June 20 for this purpose. This commission was asked to submit report by June 21 forenoon. Meanwhile, it was announced in Delhi that the transfer of Chandigarh to Punjab had been postponed to July 15. This followed the meeting Barnala had with Gandhi. On Barnala's suggestion on June 21, the Centre amended the terms of reference of this commission. The decision to amend the terms of reference was taken by the political affairs committee of the cabinet following night long consultations between the Prime Minister, Home Minister Buta Singh and Barnala.

The operative part of the original terms of reference said: "Having regard to the award of Shri Justice Venkataramiah and also having regard to the Government of India's resolve to transfer Chandigarh to Punjab on June 21, 1986, simultaneously with the territories in lieu thereof to Haryana, the Government of India have decided to refer the question of specifying the territories consisting about 70,000 acres to be transferred from Punjab to Haryana in lieu of Chandigarh to hon'ble Shri Justice D A Desai, retired judge, Supreme Court of India and Chairman, Law Commission of India whose name has been recommended by the hon'ble Chief Justice of India. All the relevant materials including the report of Shri Justice K N Mathew and the report of Shri Justice E. S. Venkataramiah are being placed at the disposal of Shri Justice D A Desai".

The amended terms of reference said, "Hon'ble Shri Justice D. A. Desai should keep in view the parameters stipulated in para 7.2 of the memorandum of settlement and consider the 30 villages measuring about 45,000 acres identified by the Justice Venkataramiah Commission, provided they fall within the purview of para 7.2 of the memorandum of settlement". The deadline for the transfer was now July 15, instead of June 21, 1986. Justice Desai was to submit his report by that date.

Punjab had earlier on June 21 rejected this commission taking objection to its terms of reference. The resolution adopted at a meeting of the cabinet stated that the appointment of higher legal authority was not warranted even by the Venkataramiah Commission which had suggested the appointment of another commission and not a higher legal authority. The resolution said the appointment of Desai Commission was aimed at slicing away large Punjabi speaking areas of Punjab in utter disregard and utter violation of the letter and spirit of the Accord. Barnala, on July 7, formally informed the Desai Commission of his government's decision to boycott it as the terms of reference were not in consistent with the Punjab accord.

Consequently, Barnala sought postponement of the transfer of Chandigarh to Punjab slated for July 15. He gave this indication at a joint meeting he had with Buta Singh and his Haryana counterpart Bansi Lal on July 10. He proposed the setting up of yet another commission on territories on the terms of reference mentioned in the Punjab accord. The government later extended the date of submission of report by the Desai Commission. The decision was taken by the political affairs committee of the cabinet which met twice on July 14. The Prime Minister reviewed the situation earlier in the day with Buta Singh and the senior Home Ministry officials.

The report of the panel on territorial dispute headed by Justice Venkataramiah submitted on June 10, 1986 was discussed by the Political Affairs Committee of the cabinet. Home Minister Buta Singh also consulted BJP President L K Advani, Congress (S) leader K P Unikrishanan, Harkishan Singh Surjeet from the CPM and Inder Deep Sinha from the CPI on the recommendations of the panel. The commission identified about 45,000 acres to be transferred to Haryana while 25000 acres were to be identified by another commission or the Central government.

The Eradi panel on river waters dispute submitted its interim report on May 20, 1987. Broadly, the Eradi Commission recommended the allocation of 5 MAF and 3.68 MAF of surplus Ravi-Beas waters respectively to Punjab and Haryana. Punjab was to get 0.78 MAF more water than allocated to the state under the 1981 award. Haryana was to get 0.33 MAF more water than the 1981 allocation. The final report is yet to be submitted.

Within weeks of the Barnala government taking over, there was sudden escalation in the incidents of militant violence, especially beginning 1986. The Barnala government was determined to confront the radicals. The activists of the Youth Akali Dal and the Damdami Taksal exchanged fire in front of the Akal Takht on January 19, 1986.

Tension had been mounting in the complex between the Taksal and the SGPC on the issue of Kar Sewa of Akal Takht. The effort of the Youth Akali Dal activists was to oust the militants from the Darbar Sahib complex. Barnala's son Gaganjit Singh, who later became an MLA on the Akali Dal ticket, led the attackers.

NOTES

1. Subhash Kirpekar: The Times of India, June 5, 1985.
2. Chandan Mitra: The Statesman, June 6, 1985.
3. The Indian Express, June 11, 1985.
4. The Indian Express, June 26, 1985.
5. The Indian Express, June 22, 1985.
6. The Indian Express, June 27, 1985.
7. The Indian Express, September 30, 1985.

11

Akali Legitimacy to Bluestar

Unambiguous political goal is the pre-condition for the liberation struggle to be sustained and inspire the cadre. Unlike the first phase of the militant struggle which started with the revenge psyche and zeroed in on the Anandpur Sahib Resolution which falls far short of sovereignty, the second stage had its well defined political aim, though it took sometime before this objective could be formally specified. Moreover, the implementation of the Anandpur Sahib Resolution was the demand of the Akali Dal taken over by Sant Jarnail Singh Bhindranwale.

But then merely specifying political goal is not the end in itself. The goal and the corresponding strategy and tactics should have the support from the masses. Punjabi society at large is not homogenous so far its demographic structure is concerned. But then the struggle did not have the level of support even from within the community for the liberation of which it was stated to have been launched. Moreover, the militant struggle must have leadership which can inspire. Unlike the first phase, this aspect was utterly lacking in the second phase. Sant Bhindranwale provided leadership during the first phase. Although he continued to be the main source if inspiration during the second phase, the lack of competent unified command was perhaps the biggest limitation in the second stage. Most of these so called leaders were just hit men. Agencies, both domestic and international, were to perform yet more active role during this phase. The second stage also suffered from some inherent contradictions.

Operation Bluestar was aimed not just at the militants holed up in the Darbar Sahib complex but what was more important was the attack on the institution of Akal Takht symbolizing synergy of temporal and the spiritual and sovereignty of the Sikh doctrine. The re-organization of the radicals in the post-Bluestar period started with the recapture this very sovereign institution which articulates the ambition to rule and this was done systematically. The setting up of the institution of Akal Takht by Guru Hargobind was the watershed in the articulation of political ambition of this most nascent religious community.

Initially, given the then political situation characterized by brutal state repression, the political goal was not fully defined deliberately. What was considered to be more important at that time was mobilizing the sympathizers of the militant struggle to start with which mainly included their immediate families. The meeting of the remnants of the All India Sikh Students Federation which was being re-organized under Harinder Singh Kahlon had set the stage for the action. The meeting of the AISSF office bearers on October 5 in 1985 paved the way for organizing the first anniversary of the martyrdom of Beant Singh, one of the assassins of Indira Gandhi. The Shaheedi convention which followed at Mehta Chowk was part of the strategy which led to organizing Sarbat Khalsa at Akal Takht. It was with this Sarbat Khalsa that the militants got consolidated again in the Darbar Sahib complex, thus going back to the situation from where it all had started in the pre-Operation Bluestar period.

Significantly, the radicals started dictating the situation in the Darbar Sahib complex at the time when the Akali Dal government was in power in the state and law and order is a state subject. This situation added a new dimension as till Operation Bluestar, Congress ruled both at the Centre and in the state (indirectly through President's rule). Of course, the militants were now also getting the necessary training across the border, along with the supply of unlimited arms and ammunition. And it was the Akali Dal government which, falling into the trap, virtually justified Operation Bluestar. The role of the militants which invited the action by the security forces in the second stage and defiled the sanctum sanctorum is not only questionable but also highly condemnable. The downfall of the second phase had started with a section of the militants resorting to killing, rape and extortions within the shrine complex. The harrowing experience of the victims of extortion, mostly Sikhs, by the militants holed up in the Darbar Sahib complex also needs to be recorded along with the cases of state repression. This was the dark side of the militant movement.

It was the Sarbat Khalsa organized by the Taksal on January 26, 1986 at Akal Takht which marked the revival of organized militancy and the radical politics. The militant and radical leaders met at the Taksal headquarters on the night of January 25 to finalize the resolutions to be adopted for the January 26 conclave. The proposal to include the demand for Khalistan did not find favour with a section led by Dalbir Singh, a journalist associated with Sant Jarnail Singh Bhindranwale, and it was finally rejected. It was at this meeting that the name of Jasvir Singh Rode was suggested in place of one Dalip Singh for appointment as the Akal Takht Jathedar. Mohkam Singh, a Taksal leader, formally proposed the name. Technically, the appointing authority in case of the Akal Takht Jathedar is the Shiromani Gurdwara Parbandhak Committee. The forces to marginalize the Akali Dal and the SGPC had been unleashed with this Sarbat Khalsa. Though the demand for Khalistan was not raised at this conclave, moves had been initiated to consolidate the communal divide in the state.

The Sarbat Khalsa constituted a five member Panthic Committee which was to function as the umbrella organization for the militant outfits as part of the effort to intensify the armed struggle. Members of the first Panthic Committee included Wassan Singh Zaffarwal, Arur Singh, Dhanna Singh, Gurbachan Singh Manochahal and Gurdev Singh, their common qualification being the proclaimed offenders and proximity at one time or the other to Sant Bhindranwale. Manochahal had acted as his double when Sant Bhindranwale escaped from Mumbai to evade his arrest in 1981. The Panthic Committee was to take all the decisions under the supervision of the Akal Takht Jathedar, in this case the one appointed by the militants and not the SGPC.

It was clear from day one that the members of the Panthic Committee lacked vision, perspective and the quality of leadership needed at that crucial juncture and that some other forces were pulling the strings. These people who were brought into the frontline to lead the Sikh struggle did not have ideological grounding. At the ideological level, the Khalistan movement was a catastrophe. The second phase of Sikh struggle already seemed to have been hijacked by some forces.

The Sarbat Khalsa conclave 'sacked' Akal Takht Jathedar Giani Kirpal Singh and 'dissolved' the SGPC. Rode was 'appointed' Akal Takht Jathedar and in his absence, Gurdev Singh Kaonke was brought in to officiate. In the beginning of the second phase of the struggle itself, the radicals targeted this statutory Sikh institution for the creation of which the community had made many sacrifices during the movement for the liberation of the Sikh shrines. The fight was misdirected.

The militant leadership came into direct confrontation with the traditional Akali leadership by making the announcement to 'dissolve' the SGPC which is a statutory democratic institution constituted under the Sikh Gurdwara Act, 1925 and as such, cannot be dissolved without nullifying the Act which is in the jurisdiction of only the Parliament. What is all the more important is that this body is elected by the Sikhs residing in Punjab, Haryana, Himachal Pradesh and Chandigarh through adult franchise and as such, to a large extent, reflects the collective will of the community, though at times, this collective will gets distorted under diktats from those controlling it.

Those who were trying to revive militancy had either bungled at the very first stage itself or there was a method in it. No militant movement can survive for long without a political front and ideological content. Rather than coming into direct confrontation with the SGPC and the Akali Dal, the support of at least a section of the Akali Dal should have been managed for this purpose. Perhaps the militant leadership could not realize at that stage the need for a political front. The revived AISSF lacked capacity to function as a political front organization at that level involving the Sikh masses. It was years later that the need was felt to have a political front but that was too late and by that time, irrevocable damage had already been done to the movement. Rather than confronting the Indian state, the tone and tenor of the resolutions at the Sarbat Khalsa was directed more at the traditional Akali Dal then in power in Punjab.

The convention 'ex-communicated' from the Sikh Panth President Giani Zail Singh, Union Agriculture Minister Buta Singh, Giani Kirpal Singh and Darbar Sahib Head Priest Giani Sahib Singh. The remaining three Jathedars including Giani Harcharan Singh Mahalon of Takht Keshgarh Sahib, Sant Lakha Singh of Takht Damdama Sahib and the Akal Takht Head Priest Giani Pritam Singh were directed to submit their resignations. Giani Bakhshish Singh, the chief priest of Gurdwara Gurdarshan Parkash, Mehta Chowk, was appointed the new Head Priest of Darbar Sahib. The secretariat of the Panthic Committee was to function from the office of the Akali Dal located in the Darbar Sahib complex which was under the occupation of the United Akali Dal and the AISSF at that time.

The Gurmata (resolution) adopted at the convention portrayed Harchand Singh Longowal, Parkash Singh Badal, Gurcharan Singh Tohra, Surjit Singh Barnala, Balwant Singh, Sukhjinder Singh and Balwant Singh Ramoowalia as traitors of the Panth. Amarinder Singh was described as "bukkal da sapp" (serpent in fold).

The convention rejected the Rajiv-Longowal accord describing it as a betrayal with the Sikhs as it fell far short of the declared aim of the implementation of the Anandpur Sahib Resolution, implying this resolution continued to be the political goal. At that time, the demand for Khalistan had not been formally raised by the radicals trying to revive the movement. In the pre-Bluestar period, this demand had been raised mainly by the Dal Khalsa and Dr. Jagjit Singh Chohan. The Babbar Khalsa had also made a passing reference to the creation of Sikh state as the political goal in December, 1983. The Sikh struggle till then had revolved around the 1973 version of the Anandpur Sahib Resolution incorporated as the political objective in the constitution of the Akali Dal.

Significantly, while Longowal had called off the Dharamyudh morcha launched on August 4, 1984 after the signing of the accord, this convention declared that the Sikh struggle was on for the achievements of their rights and for this purpose, cooperation would be sought and given to all those fighting for their liberation. The Gurmata said, "This Sarbat Khalsa convention makes it clear that the Sikhs are slaves in India and freedom is their fundamental right". The parameters of this right to freedom were not defined. This resolution provided the much needed political backing for the armed struggle which also marked a slight shift from the Anandpur Sahib Resolution.

This convention also settled the issue of the death of Sant Bhindranwale by according him the status of "Anmol Shaheed" (Great Martyr). However, there were second thoughts later in a section of the militant leadership and the controversy was allowed to linger on. Others who were similarly honoured posthumously included Amrik Singh, Major General Shabeg Singh, Thara Singh, Rachhpal Singh, Sant Sujan Singh, Upkar Kaur and Beant Singh. The Taksal later backtracked from the issue while maintaining that Sant Bhindranwale was alive. Finally, he was declared a martyr by the Taksal in 2005.

The Gurmata called upon the Sikhs to socially boycott those who had worked against the interests of the Sikhs and Punjab. This part of the Gurmata was also targeted not only just against the Akalis but also against those members of the Hindu community (dubbed as communal) in the state who had disowned their mother tongue at one stage and were considered to be in league with the forces working against the interests of Punjab. As per this Gurmata, the Akali Dal and the SGPC also connived with the Centre to attack the Darbar Sahib complex and perpetrate atrocities on the Sikhs in and outside Punjab. It said the Akali Dal government in the state was determined to please the Delhi durbar.

The Gurmata specified some conditions for the Kar Sewa of Akal Takht. The devotees were to contribute only from their hard earned money, not the black money. The Golak (cash box) was always to be kept in public view, to be opened in public. Only those Sikhs were to be allowed to participate in the Kar Sewa who maintained their true form. Women putting on cosmetics were to be barred. This condition was later misused by the younger element who humiliated women putting on cosmetics who would come to Darbar Sahib to pay their obeisance. Others who were barred included those taking intoxicants, those who had violated the oath taken at Akal Takht during Dharamyudh morcha (thereby meaning the traditional Akalis who had taken the oath of Marjeevadas) and others who had supported the army action.

Within minutes of the announcement of the SGPC having been 'dissolved' almost the entire senior staff of this mini-Parliament of the Sikhs left the offices. The Teja Singh Samundari Hall and the ground floor of the Guru Nanak Niwas housing the SGPC complex were completely deserted, such was the immediate impact. The employees of the SGPC were too scared to come into confrontation with the radicals despite the fact that it was the Akali Dal government ruling the state. The control of the shrine had been allowed to pass into the hands of the radicals once again, thus nullifying the so called gains of Operation Bluestar.

A day later, the Taksal announced that the Akal Takht building, except the original Takht (Throne of Almighty) the foundation stone of which was laid by Guru Hargobind and constructed by Baba Buddha and Bhai Gurdas, would be pulled down. At the time of its construction, no other person had touched the Throne of Almighty except these two close associates of the Sixth Guru. This perhaps is the only original structure in the Darbar Sahib complex from that period. The pulling down of the building followed this announcement. The Taksal had started operating from the Darbar Sahib complex, despite an abortive attempt by Barnala men to throw out the radicals. The police entered the complex in plain clothes to search the rooms during that operation.

Pulling down the government constructed Akal Takht was the immediate task of the people who had earlier initiated the moves beginning with October 31 function to honour the family of Beant Singh and other martyrs of the Sikh struggle.

Avoiding any direct confrontation, Tohra, at a meeting with Taksal acting chief Thakar Singh, had earlier resolved the controversy over Kar Sewa on January 21 and it had been decided to set up a committee of Sikh religious leaders. The Akali Dal, at its meeting the next day at Amritsar, endorsed the decision taken by Tohra. It may be recalled that originally, it was the SGPC which had taken a decision on May 11, 1985 to rebuild Akal Takht.

The radical leadership believed that the Sikh struggle would revolve round the Kar Sewa of Akal Takht and as the building starts going up, the movement would also intensify. However, distortions had crept in at the very beginning itself of the second phase of the militant movement.

Earlier on January 6, 1986 the ruling Akali Dal at a joint meeting of the district jathedars, MLAs and MPs had chalked out a three pronged strategy to confront the militants and take a tough stand against what was described as "nefarious designs of forces of disruption and destabilization". It was decided to organize district level meetings to launch political offensive. The SGPC executive committee which met at Anandpur Sahib the same day discussed the Kar Sewa of Akal Takht. The underlying idea of the party meeting at Chandigarh was to devise strategy to meet the challenge posed by the call given by the radicals to jam traffic on January 10 to press for the release of the Sikh detenus and rehabilitation of the army men who had left their barracks in protest against Operation Bluestar. The Akali Dal government should have taken these steps at its own rather than virtually handing over this agenda to the radicals.

The resolution passed at the meeting stated: "The Sikh Panth does not sanction terrorism as a moral or political weapon. On the other hand, the Sikh Gurus laid before us the ideals of brotherhood, peace and sacrifice. Attacking or killing innocent people is the most heinous crime against humanity and a cardinal sin". The radicals and the traditional Akali leadership had not come into such direct confrontation during the first phase of the Sikh struggle. Of course, the situation was now different as the Akali Dal had now been facilitated into power in the state as unwritten part of the Rajiv-Longowal accord.

The traditional Sikh leadership initiated measures at the political level to deal with the situation. The general house of the SGPC, which met at Anandpur Sahib on January 28, decided to request the Akal Takht Jathedar to convene Sarbat Khalsa at the earliest to end the occupation of the Darbar Sahib complex by the militants and the radicals. The meeting was attended by 97 out of 139 members of the general house. The SGPC asserted only the Akal Takht Jathedar could convene Sarbat Khalsa and this right could not be usurped by any other individual or organization. The resolution passed at the meeting stated the Sarbat Khalsa organized by the Taksal on January 26 was not attended by any representative Sikh body. The suggestion for a counter Sarbat Khalsa had been made at a joint meeting of the Akali Dal district jathedars, MPs and MLAs at Chandigarh a day earlier which was also attended by Tohra. The general house is traditionally convened at Teja Singh Samundari Hall, the SGPC headquarters, in the Darbar Sahib complex. In the normal times, Sarbat Khalsa also traditionally used to be organized only at Akal Takht.

The radicals came into direct confrontation with the Barnala government as the United Akali Dal and the Damdami Taksal at a meeting at Amritsar on January 29 decided to gherao district courts on February 26, block supply of milk and fodder to the cities and gherao the state Assembly during the budget session. It was decided to constitute a 151-member committee to assist the Panthic Committee to run the Sikhs affairs and the administration of gurdwaras.

Sarbat Khalsa at Anandpur Sahib

To counter the radicals, the Sikh clergy convened Sarbat Khalsa, not at Amritsar but at Anandpur Sahib on February 16, 1986 which directed the SGPC to end what was described as the unlawful interference by the radicals in the Darbar Sahib complex and restore Maryada (religious code of conduct) being violated by them. The resolution passed at this gathering stated the forcible take over of Akal Takht constituted anti-Panthic activity and assault on the Sikh religion. It further alleged these forces were hatching a dangerous conspiracy to bring about a permanent division in the Panth through civil war and fratricidal violence. It was for the first time that the SGPC had decided to confront the radicals. However, in a way, the ruling Akali Dal had already accepted its defeat by not organizing the Sarbat Khalsa at Akal Takht.

At the same time, Tohra, in a subtle tactical move, announced his resignation from the presidency of the SGPC at the conclave as earlier demanded by the radicals. He forwarded his resignation to Chief Minister Surjit Singh Barnala, who was not competent to accept it and directed it to the SGPC executive. Apparently, going by his offer to resign, Tohra was trying to avoid show down with the radicals. He unequivocally attacked the militants only in the run up to the elections to the general house of the SGPC in 1996.

The meeting discussed the options available to counter the radicals who had entrenched themselves in the complex. While asserting that he was against militancy, Badal made it clear that he would never approve of the entry of the police into the Darbar Sahib complex, all the more so during the Akali regime. However, he did not spell out as to what should be the approach in this case. Barnala, while reacting to Badal, made it clear something would have to be done when arms were being smuggled into the shrine and the people were shot. Intriguingly, arms were being smuggled into the shrine despite surveillance by the central and state intelligence agencies and the security forces.

It was Tohra who suggested that jathas (groups) of Sikh leaders should be sent to the Darbar Sahib complex to persuade the militants to act according to the Sikh Maryada. That would have been the right approach. He offered to lead the first such Jatha. However, this plan was never put into action.

The convention of the Akali Dal youth wing organized at Patiala on February 18 also resolved to confront militancy at the political level. Tohra was present.

Reconstruction of Akal Takht

The reconstruction of the Akal Takht under the supervision of the Taksal after demolition started on February 16. The resolution adopted on the occasion stated the struggle for freedom of the voice of their conscience and against the atrocities by the "Barnala-Brahmin" government would continue. The looting of the natural resources of Punjab must stop. The looting of natural resources was with reference to the diversion of Punjab river waters to neighbouring non-riparian states of Haryana and Rajasthan. The claim of the neighbouring states on Punjab river waters was rejected in the resolution. Justice to Punjab in the apportionment of river waters had been on the agenda of the Akali Dal all these years. Further, the resolution stated the endeavor would be to protect the Sikh way of life, including the right to carry arms. It was also emphasised that Chandigarh was essentially a Punjabi speaking area and along with it, the Punjabi speaking areas in the neighbouring Haryana and Rajasthan should be transferred to Punjab, again a long standing demand of the Akali Dal. Interestingly, these areas are Hindu dominated. Ironically, these were the same issues on which the Akali Dal had launched the agitation in 1982.

Commenting on the Akali Dal convened Sarbat Khalsa at Anandpur Sahib, the resolution stated it was attended by only the well-to-do Sikhs, cowards, liars, greedy and those who had given up the Sikh principles. It reiterated the demand for the release of detenus, reinstatement of the soldiers who had deserted their barracks in the wake of Operation Bluestar and withdrawal of black laws.

Significantly, the Panthic Committee opposed the killing of the innocents and incidents of looting. By that time, such incidents were already being increasingly reported. It was becoming clear that such incidents could lead to the isolation of the militants. People used to be summoned in the two rooms from where the militants used to operate in the Darbar Sahib complex for extortion. The intelligence agencies had already infiltrated their ranks.

As the demolition of the government repaired Akal Takht started, none would have anticipated that its debris would become the dumping ground for the dead bodies, victims of the militants holed up inside the Darbar Sahib complex. More than 35 bodies were dug up when operation clean up started two years later after Operation Black Thunder. The militant groups never offered any public explanation for this state of affairs.

With the situation deteriorating fast, Barnala, while speaking at a bhog ceremony at Ghuman Kalan village near Batala on February 21, sought the cooperation of the people to curb terrorism and warned if it continued unchecked, the state might face the imposition of martial law. In his perception of the situation, Pakistan was supplying weapons to the militants to avenge the 1971 defeat which led to the creation of Bangladesh.

Along with the fresh build up by the militants, the communal tension continued to rise in some areas in the state. The Shiv Sena and the AISSF activists clashed at Batala on February 19 as the Shiv Sena activists tried to force closure of shops to protest the killing of one Chaman Lal at Jandiala Guru. Curfew was imposed in the town as three persons were killed and four others injured in the clash. Activists from the two sides clashed again on March 16 following which the AISSF appealed to the Sikhs not to supply milk and fodder in the town till March 20. The town remained under siege of the AISSF activists for several days as all the approach roads to Batala were blocked. It was first of its kind mass action ever since the start of militancy in the state. People from the villages around Batala participated in the action.

As per the programme announced earlier, the United Akali Dal workers marched to the state Assembly in Chandigarh on March 21 and gheraoed the complex. Two persons were killed as the police opened fire on the procession. A memorandum was submitted to the Chief Minister.

Violence also marred the Hola Mohalla celebrations at Anandpur Sahib that year. The plan was to stage a protest against the Satluj-Yamuna Link Canal by undertaking its symbolic filling up by the activists of the United Akali Dal and the AISSF. However, everything went hay wire as the activists suddenly rushed towards the venue of the ruling Akali Dal (L) conference. The police opened fire in which five persons were killed and 18 others injured. In the original plan, there was no move to march to the venue of the ruling Akali Dal conference. It could never be known as to which force had sabotaged the original plan.

The situation in the state was taking a downward plunge and the Centre brought in J. F. Ribeiro, a Maharashtra cadre IPS officer, as police chief in Punjab who joined on March 28, 1986. It was Ribeiro who advocated the bullet for bullet policy to deal with the militants. Though Punjab had a democratically elected government, the situation in the state was being directly monitored by the Centre with Barnala government having little say in the decision making at the Delhi level. The state government was not even consulted in the appointment of Ribeiro.

The militants organized yet another Sarbat Khalsa in the Darbar Sahib complex on Baisakhi on April 13, 1986 but stopped short of making categorical commitment to the Khalistan demand while giving a call to the people to "break the shackles of slavery and strive for the concept of Raj Karega Khalsa (Khalsa shall rule)". The Gurmata (resolution) adopted at the convention reiterated the demand for the implementation of the Anandpur Sahib resolution. At the same time, the Gurmata referred to the statement of Sant Bhindranwale that attack on the Darbar Sahib complex would amount to laying the foundation for Khalistan.

Dubbing the Barnala government as traitor, the Sarbat Khalsa conclave gave a call to the people to boycott ministers and gherao Akali MLAs and seek their resignations as the government had failed to keep the election promises which included the release of all the detained Sikhs, rehabilitation of Army deserters and action against the guilty police officials. These promises had conveniently been swept under the carpet. The Gurmata also called upon the people to force the SGPC members to resign as their term had expired and forward the panel of names to the Panthic Committee from each SGPC constituency to constitute a new House of this mini-Parliament of the Sikhs. The election to the general house of the SGPC was last held in March, 1979. The five year term was over in 1984. However, the house continues to function till the next election.

Kaonke offered to quit as the acting Jathedar of Akal Takht at the conclave which was rejected by Baba Joginder Singh. His offer of resignation was the culmination of crisis which had hit the AISSF following the announcement of five member presidium by its detained leaders Manjit Singh and Harminder Singh Sandhu from the Jodhpur jail two days earlier. This was not to the liking of the dominant Kahlon group. The Panthic Committee also did not support this announcement.

The convention passed a resolution appealing to the United Nation to constitute a special court to try all those responsible for conspiring to annihilate the Sikh nation and destroy its culture, religion, symbols and history. Those named guilty in the resolution included Giani Zail Singh, Indira Gandhi, Rajiv Gandhi, P. V. Narasimha Rao and Barnala. This resolution aimed at seeking international support.

Differences cropped up among the radicals during this period as AISSF convener Harinder Singh Kahlon attacked Baba Joginder Singh for misappropriating funds sent by the sympathizers from abroad and appealed to the Panthic Committee to restrict his activities to religious affairs only.

Panthic Committee member Wassan Singh Zaffarwal was declared a Tankhaiya by the Akal Takht on April 25 for using derogatory language against militants' appointed Jathedar Gurdev Singh. He later headed the Khalistan Liberation Force and now is a free man staying in his native village practicing Homeopathic system of medicines.

Panthic Panel Declares Khalistan

The militant leaders spearheading the armed struggle wanted the political goal to be specified which, till then, had been vague. The political goal had not been categorically defined even in the Gurmata adopted at the Sarbat Khalsa on April 13. The militant leaders' poser to the Panthic Committee was simple: what were they fighting for. This poser dictated the choice in favour of Khalistan. Leading this section of the militants was AISSF President Gurjit Singh, who was underground and in touch with Pakistan. It was also said that defining the political goal was the pre-condition put up by Pakistan for the supply of sophisticated weapons. The sophisticated weapons surfaced mainly during the second phase of militancy in the post Bluestar period. Yet there is another significant dimension as it was this announcement from the Darbar Sahib complex which was to provide retrospective legitimacy to Operation Bluestar and that too by an Akali Dal government in the state.

The Panthic Committee, on April 29, finally announced the setting up of sovereign state of Khalistan and sought recognition from all countries of the world, including India. The announcement was made at a news conference by all the five members of the panel without specifying the territory of Khalistan but quoted Sant Bhindranwale that the Sikhs would unfurl their Kesari flag atop the Red Fort in Delhi. The declaration said Khalistan would have its own constitution based on Sikh laws and religion. It called upon the Sikh men to wear saffron turbans and women saffron dupattas. The Panthic Committee announced the war with India had begun (Jang Hind Punjab Da), the slogan once used by Harchand Singh Longowal, coined by Shah Mohammad to describe Anglo-Sikh wars.

The declaration stated: "The Five member Panthic Committee constituted by the Sarbat Khalsa convened by the Damdami Taksal, today hereby declares the formation of Khalistan. This declaration of the Khalistan is made before the Khalsa Panth as well as the Sikh community (comprising of every Sikh; male, female, mother, brother etc.) so that all of us may, in accordance with our individual capacity, contribute to its cause physically, mentally, and financially... Today the five member Panthic Committee calls upon the entire Sikh nation to be ready for all types of sufferings and scarifies". The Sikhs living outside Punjab were invited to migrate to Khalistan.

The political resolution stated, "The policy of Khalistan will be as per the Guru's wish, Sarbat Da Bhala (welfare of all) and a policy of encouraging a civilized life, of promoting the sense of brotherhood of mankind and a sense of involvement. The segregation of humanity based upon caste, creed (jati), birth, locality and colour will not be permitted, and such divisions will be abolished by the use of political power. Likewise, such other cruel and distasteful practices ascribed to social-inequality, especially between Sikh males and females will be removed through the use of political power".

The Panthic Committee also sacked all the five secretaries including Kahlon (AISSF), Gurdarshan Singh Bahia (Panthic Committee), Bimal Kaur Khalsa (Women wing), Ajaib Singh (Kar Sewa) and Mohkam Singh (Damdami Taksal). However, this action was part of the strategy to allow them space to function and facilitate their over ground movement after the Panthic Committee members went underground.

The proclamation about Khalistan was nothing more than just a slogan. It was not for the first time that such slogans had been raised by the Sikh organizations, the only difference being that the radical streak in the Sikh political matrix had never been so distinct. Moreover, the raising of the Khalistan slogan was not unexpected in reaction to the gruesome Operation Bluestar in June, 1984 and the massacre of thousands of Sikhs following the assassination of Indira Gandhi. It was the apprehension about the declaration of Khalistan which had been advanced by the government as one of the reason for Operation Bluestar.

Tohra and Barnala were in Delhi the day the Panthic Committee made the announcement. They met at a common place late in the night over dinner. The same night, Barnala, accompanied by Minister of State for Internal Security Arun Nehru, flew to Amritsar to review the situation. Director General of Police Ribeiro expressed the opinion at the meeting that those who had made the announcement had already gone underground and as such, no useful purpose would be served by sending security forces into the shrine. However, it was Nehru who insisted on this line of action. After all, Operation Bluestar had to be justified and that too when the Akali Dal government was in power in the state. Perhaps the build up was again part of the design to that end. Barnala was just one character in the drama which unfolded during the post Bluestar period.

The Barnala cabinet, on April 30, affirmed the resolve to launch a fight to finish against secessionist elements, who, it asserted, could not be allowed to challenge the sovereignty of the country. The resolution adopted at the meeting strongly condemned the declaration of Khalistan made by the Panthic Committee saying the action of the radicals exposed the sinister designs of the foreign forces who sought to destabilize and disrupt the unity and solidarity of the Indian people through the mercenary mafia of murderers and marauders in unauthorized possession of the Darbar Sahib complex.

The logic extended by the Barnala cabinet was no different from what the Indira Gandhi government had said on the eve of Operation Bluestar. The only difference was that the Barnala government also suggested a long term political solution through the speedy implementation of the Rajiv-Longowal accord and the logic was that it would strengthen the resolve of the people to deal firmly with the anti-national forces who had launched the "phoney movement of Khalistan" to cover their sacrilegious and criminal acts against God and the man.

The entire moderate stream reacted against the declaration of Khalistan. Describing the declaration as shocking and against the interests of the Sikhs, Badal averred the Akali Dal had always opposed this demand and would continue to do so.

The reaction from the Hindu organizations was again on the expected lines. The Rashtriya Swayamsewak Sangh demanded that anti-national elements be thrown out of the holy places, which meant sending security forces to the shrine again. The RSS had earlier fully backed the ruling Congress at the Centre in taking army action in the Darbar Sahib complex in June, 1984. BJP General Secretary in Punjab Hit Abhilashi said raising the demand for Khalistan was an act of treason and calculated provocation. The leaders of all the major political parties in the advisory group constituted by Governor S. S. Ray met him to discuss the situation. They expressed the view that the declaration of Khalistan made from the Darbar Sahib complex was an anti-national and treasonable act. They expressed full support to Barnala in the fight against the Khalistanis. The meeting was attended by Manjit Singh Khaira (Akali Dal), Hit Abhilashi, Gurbir Singh (Cong) and Avtar Singh Malhotra (CPI).

Barnala Govt Provides Legitimacy to Bluestar

The security forces entered the Darbar Sahib complex around 4.50 PM on April 30, a few hours after the announcement had been made, to flush out the militants, thus in a way providing the retrospective legitimacy to Operation Bluestar. The Centre, in a subtle move, had got the justification from an Akali government. The National Security Guards commandos were assigned the task of clearing the complex. History had repeated itself. The security forces also raided Gurdwara Shaheedan at Amritsar and Gurdwara Darbar Sahib, Tarn Taran. Giani Puran Singh, Head Granthi of Darbar Sahib, negotiated the surrender of the militants. The government decided to continue the police deployment, both inside and outside the complex. The members of the Panthic Committee had already escaped after making the announcement and the action of the security forces proved to be an exercise in futility. However, the state action changed the course of Akali politics once again.

Facilitating the installation of the Akali Dal government as unwritten part of the Rajiv-Longowal accord could have been part of the design to get legitimacy for Operation Bluestar and the militants also became instruments in this design by converting the Darbar Sahib complex once again into the centre of the Sikh struggle. This was the beginning and the worst was to follow. The Barnala government knew that the members of the Panthic Committee had already escaped but still security forces were deputed to search the shrine complex.

The state government was dictated to send security forces in the complex at a high level meeting in Delhi which, among others, was attended by Union Home Minister P. V. Narasimha Rao, Congress (I) Vice-president and the former Punjab Governor Arjun Singh and Barnala.

Expectedly, the Prime Minister congratulated Barnala for the action. It may be recalled that Barnala had made clear his attitude towards political violence in the state earlier on January 2 while addressing a gathering at Harchand Singh Longowal's native village Gidriani. Mincing no words, he had said: "Do not give them any shelter and hand them over to the police whenever you come by terrorists as the only fit place where they can live is jail.... Those who gunned down the Sant (Longowal) in a gurdwara and made an attempt on the life of Giani Sahib Singh, Head Granthi of the Golden Temple within the temple complex on the birthday of Guru Nanak, could not be Sikhs". Barnala was now a national hero, to be reduced to zero later.

The action triggered immediate reaction in the Akali political stream which turned highly turbulent. Agriculture Minister and scion of the former royal family of Patiala Amarinder Singh and Education Minister Sukhjinder Singh were the first to resign from the cabinet in protest, describing it as the mini Operation Bluestar while Tohra and Badal quit the party working committee. These leaders accused Barnala of taking action at the behest of the Centre without taking them into confidence. Amarinder Singh had earlier resigned from the Congress in protest against Operation Bluestar. Years later after his five year stint as the Congress chief minister, he regretted the decision to quit that party.

Amarinder Singh said in his resignation: "You are aware that the Akali Dal of which you are the President, has always been for the preservation of the sanctity of our gurdwaras and has consistently taken a stand against the police entry into them... at the cabinet meeting on Wednesday, you did not take your council of ministry into confidence even though the entry of the paramilitary forces began an hour and a half later at 4.50 pm. From this, it was obvious that you lack confidence not only in your ministers but also you did not think it fit to take a senior cabinet colleague into confidence when a decision of the magnitude affecting the future of the government and the party and each individual was concerned". He made it clear he would continue to remain a member of the Akali Dal and work for preserving the unity and integrity of the country.

Even Finance Minister Balwant Singh, considered to be close to the Chief Minister and one of the co-architects of the Punjab accord, came to know about the entry of the security forces into the Darbar Sahib complex only after the action had started. He later alleged that a day before Amarinder Singh resigned from the cabinet, he had breakfast meeting with Arun Nehru in Delhi. Nehru was considered close to Rajiv Gandhi and so was Amarinder Singh. Barnala justified the action of his government on the logic that he had done the duty assigned to him by the Sarbat Khalsa earlier organized at Anandpur Sahib.

For Punjab Congress General Secretary Gurbir Singh Baku, the resignations of Amarinder Singh and Sukhjinder Singh were a confirmation of their collaboration with seditious and secessionist forces and a cover for more sinister plan.

Amarinder Singh said in an interview: "After the extremists took over the Golden Temple in January, I offered to lead several thousand peaceful volunteers to liberate it. I am completely opposed to Khalistan and stand for country's unity. I resigned from Parliament and from the Congress (I) when the security forces moved into the Temple during Operation Bluestar, and I could not, in all conscience, act differently on this occasion. Furthermore, what was actually achieved? No terrorists were caught, hardly any weapons seized. In fact, at the cabinet meeting, we were told that those who made the Khalistan demand had already escaped".[1]

The AISSF (Manjit) gave a call to the Akali Dal MLAs and MPs to resign to register their protest against the entry of security forces into the Darbar Sahib complex. Protest day was observed in the state at several places on May 7 on the call given by the radical outfits.

Hand written posters were found pasted on the walls of a temple at Moga on May 23 threatening the Hindus to leave the state within five days. Such posters were part of the design to create fear psychosis to trigger migration from the state. The situation in the state was getting further polarized.

Curfew was imposed in the Fatehgarh Churian area of Gurdaspur district as the communal violence broke out following the gunning down of Ram Lubhaya, former member of the municipal committee. The Shiv Sena workers set on fire some shops in the area.

Split in Akali Dal Legislature Party

As the confrontation within the Akali matrix turned more acrid, Tohra met the clergy with a proposal that Barnala be directed to keep only one office, either of the party President or the Chief Minister. It would be better if he resigned from both the offices and in that case, there would be no objection to his getting re-elected as the Chief Minister.

The Akali Dal Legislature Party finally split on May 8 with the dissidents forming a separate group of 27 MLAs, reducing the Barnala government to minority. As Speaker Ravi Inder Singh recognized it as a separate group, the Barnala faction decided to remove him. The strength of the Barnala supporters was reduced to 45 in a House of 117. The Congress, the BJP and the CPI having 31, six and one member respectively in the House rushed in to the rescue of the Barnala ministry. Barnala had come to be projected as crusader against militancy by these political parties.

Both Badal and Sukhjinder Singh were of the view that Barnala and his colleagues responsible for the police action would have to apologize from the Sikh Panth for their sins. The MLAs who broke away from Barnala included Tara Singh, Bachittar Singh, Kirpal Singh, Hardyal Singh, Raja Narinder Singh, Jasdev Singh, Satwant Singh Mohi, Sukhdev Singh Dhindsa, Inderjit Singh, Balwinder Singh Bhunder, Amarinder Singh, Jasmel Singh, Sujan Singh, Badal, Mohinder Singh Brar, Giani Arjan Singh, Devinder Singh Garcha, Sukhdev Singh Dhillon, Talib Singh Sandhu, Kuldip Singh Wadala, Jagdish Kaur, Sukhjinder Singh, Dr Rattan Singh Ajnala, Prem Singh Lalpura, Sucha Singh Chhotepur and Kulwant Singh.

Barnala again defended the action of his government on May 11 saying his conscience was clear and had no hesitation in presenting himself at the Akal Takht if this could bring about unity in the party but at the same time, expressed the view that this may not be the only thing that the dissidents might be looking for. He left the decision to the Akal Takht Jathedar in this regard. Prem Singh Chandumajra, cabinet colleague of Barnala, decided to mobilise the youth wing of the party to educate the people about the party policies by organizing district level meetings. He accused the dissident leaders of trying to weaken the Akali Dal and the government.

Hukamnama Against Barnala

It was time for the religio-temporal leadership of the Sikhs to assert by way of intervention in the political affairs of the Akali Dal. Barnala was summoned by the high priests for the police action in the Darbar Sahib complex on May 17 and awarded the religious punishment. He was directed to dust the shoes of the devotees for one week as atonement. The Hukamnama issued in this regard said, "Mr. Surjit Singh Barnala, Akali Dal President and the Chief Minister, Punjab, presented himself before the Akal Takht in the presence of Guru Granth Sahib and read out his explanation for the police action in the Golden Temple complex and gave it to us. The five high priests considered the explanation and have decided that though the action was taken by him in accordance with the directive of the Sarbat Khalsa of February 16 under particular compulsions, we are of the view that the police action was painful and unfortunate and unpleasant incidents have taken place. Therefore, we order Mr. Barnala to undertake five services". Going by Barnala's action to provide retrospective legitimacy to Operation Bluestar, the action announced against him was mild. Perhaps the deeper meaning of sending security forces in the shrine had not been realized at that time as none of the Akali leaders raised this aspect.

The Chief Minister pointed out in his explanation that the Sarbat Khalsa held at Anandpur Sahib on February 16 had been called by the high priests. The resolution adopted at that conclave had directed the SGPC and the Akali Dal to take immediate remedial steps to end the unwarranted meddling by the militants and restore maryada of the shrine which stood violated. It had also been assured that whatever steps were to be taken for the purpose would have the cooperation and endorsement of the entire Panth. He pointed out the situation took a dangerous turn when the Panthic Committee declared the battle for Khalistan which shocked 50 lakh Sikhs living outside Punjab. The deep wounds of the November 1984 violence had still not healed and to ignore such a repugnant declaration from the Darbar Sahib complex was to invite further deterioration in the Punjab situation. The danger inherent in the situation was more horrible than the one at the time of Operation Bluestar. He was exonerated on May 26 after his week long atonement. However, the atonement did not bring back his estranged party colleagues.

The justification extended by Barnala was no different from the logic advanced by the Indira Gandhi government at the time of Operation Bluestar, the only difference being the so called mandate in this case from the Sarbat Khalsa to take action against the militants who had defiled the sanctity of the shrine through their actions. However, mobilization of the people could have been the right answer in such a situation. At the time of Operation Bluestar also, in case the Centre had some apprehension about the threat to the territorial sovereignty from some forces located inside the shrine, some other methods could have been used, rather than sending in the army.

Badal Joins Bluestar Anniversary

The action of the Barnala government effected new permutations and combinations in the Sikh matrix as the section of the Akali Dal leadership which had brought about the split in protest shifted closer to the radical stream. This new found opportunistic relationship was demonstrated at the time of the second anniversary of Operation Bluestar.

This had not happened earlier. Political exigencies made the leaders like Parkash Singh Badal, Gurcharan Singh Tohra and Amarinder Singh to join hands with the Damdami Taksal and the AISSF to observe the anniversary of Operation Bluestar at Manji Sahib in the Darbar Sahib complex on June 4, 1986. That was the only time in about two decades that Badal participated in the Operation Bluestar anniversary function. He recalled the anniversary again only in 2005. The conclave passed a vote of no confidence against the members of the Sikh clergy and Barnala. It was also perhaps for the first time that the leaders like Tohra and Badal were in the company of the people who had posed a challenge to the Sikh clergy.

Akal Takht Jathedar Giani Kirpal Singh and his four colleagues were called upon to submit their resignations since they had betrayed the faith reposed in them by the Sikh Panth by stage managing atonement of Barnala. The convention adopted a resolution removing Barnala from the party presidency and expelling him from the primary membership of the party. The resolution called for his social boycott and also of his 'power hungry' supporters.

The resolution recalled that the sanctity of the holiest of the holy Sikh shrine had been violated on 36 occasions earlier but it was for the first time in the history that the shrine had been "attacked" when the "Panthic" government was ruling the state. Both the Taksal and the AISSF leaders expressed the hope that the dissident Akali leaders present at the stage would not betray the faith of the Sikh masses (sangat). However, this honeymoon was short lived.

What was perhaps all the more important was the endorsement in the presence of these leaders at the conclave of the announcement made earlier by the Taksal appointing militant leader Gurbachan Singh Manochahal as the acting Jathedar of the Akal Takht in the absence of Gurdev Singh Kaonke, who had been arrested on April 30. It may be mentioned that Badal was later also party to the appointment of Jasvir Singh Rode from the ranks of the radicals as the Akal Takht Jathedar.

The Damdami Taksal spokesman and Tohra in their hard hitting speeches at this function, castigated Barnala on the issue of police entry into the shrine saying "either the Guru will pardon Barnala or some 'Guru Ka Lal' (man of God) would avenge the action".[2] The speech of

Tohra was clearly inflammatory. The radicals, at that crucial stage, were getting legitimacy from a section of the traditional Akali leaders. In the early days of militancy, it was the Akali Dal which had legitimatized the revenge psyche through a resolution on the killing of Nirankari chief Gurbachan Singh. History was repeating itself within a span of about six years. The radicals hoped that these dissident Akali leaders would not betray the Sikh cause now. The resolutions had been read out by Akali leader Manjit Singh Calcutta. Badal was the last to address the congregation who wanted Barnala and Balwant Singh to resign to pave the way for Akali unity.

The ruling Akali Dal (Longowal) retaliated at a convention at Maur Mandi in Bathinda district on June 8 and attacked Badal and Tohra for ratifying the appointment of Manochahal as the Akal Takht Jathedar. The resolution adopted at the meeting took strong notice of the threats issued to the Sikh leaders from the stage on June 4 where Badal and Tohra were also present. This convention called upon the Sikhs not to have any relationship with anti-Panthic and anti-national elements. This was the fourth such convention organized by the party to mobilize the people against radicals and militancy.

Yet another convention was organized by the Akali Dal (Longowal) the next day at Samrala in Ludhiana district which gave a call to the Sikhs to boycott Tohra and Badal for their alleged support to the militants and the appointment of Manochahal as the Akal Takht Jathedar. It was also demanded that both these leaders should be summoned at Akal Takht.

At the time when the Sikh religio-political stream was highly turbulent, communal tension was again rising in the state. One of the militant outfits issued a warning to the Hindus on June 24 to leave Gurdaspur district within 15 days. Five Hindu occupants of a car and another person standing nearby were gunned down under Mamdot police station in Ferozepur district on July 2. Within days of this incident, a Chandigarh bound bus starting from Muktsar was hijacked on the Sadiq road on July 25 and 14 Hindu passengers gunned down while 6 others injured seriously. Earlier on June 8, indiscriminate firing was resorted to by some people at Chohla Sahib in Amritsar district in which two persons were killed. On the same day, six persons were gunned down in an ice cream factory at Tarn Taran. A new pattern had emerged in the killing by the militants.

Earlier, in the clash between the task force, deployed by the SGPC to maintain security in the shrine, and the members of the AISSF in the first week of June, a member of the task force was killed. The AISSF and the Taksal supporters were led by Bimal Kaur Khalsa, widow of

Beant Singh, the assassin of Indira Gandhi. The security forces again entered the complex and made some arrests.

Split in Akali Dal (L)

The split in the Akali Dal (Longowal) was formalized on July 5 when Badal was elected President of the new Akali Dal at the convention held at Anandpur Sahib while Barnala was expelled from the primary membership of the party. This expulsion did not matter as it was a new Akali faction and he was the President of the original Akali Dal. Amarinder Singh, who could not attend the convention as he was seeking legal opinion in Delhi about dissident MLAs who were facing disqualification, favoured the name of Badal for party presidency in his message. Badal's name for President was formally proposed by Tohra and seconded by Prem Singh Lalpura and Surjan Singh Thekedar. It was for the first time that Badal, who had been the chief minister twice, had been entrusted with this organizational responsibility.

Badal said in his speech that Barnala had become irrelevant to Punjab and was Chief Minister only in name. He reminded Barnala of Sikh history which never forgave a leader who aligned himself with the government in Delhi. Tohra assigned three reasons for summoning the delegate session to replace Barnala as party president. These included Barnala's treachery with the Guru by way of sending police into the Darbar Sahib complex, masterminding the defeat of the party candidate Simranjit Singh Mann in the Rajya Sabha election and the traitor's act of agreeing in principle to cede 70,000 acres of land to Haryana in lieu of merger of Chandigarh with Punjab.

The resolution seeking Barnala's expulsion from the primary membership of the party stressed that he, as president of the party and the leader of the Akali government, had committed the heinous crime of sending security forces in the holiest of the holy Sikh shrine which created a vertical ideological split in the Akali Dal and thus cast a slur on the glorious traditions of the party. He was also charged with betraying the Panth by helping the Congress (I) candidate win the Rajya Sabha election in preference to Mann.

The political resolution reiterated that the Anandpur Sahib Resolution was the panacea for the Sikhs and regretted that the Barnala government had gone back on this resolution and betrayed the basic programme and policy of the Akali Dal. The resolution said the post independence history of the country was one of discrimination against Sikhs and they were given a truncated Punjabi Suba in 1966. The Akali agitation that followed was aimed at having a separate national, linguistic, cultural and religious entity for the Sikhs in a multi-lingual multi-national India. The convention rejected the reports of various commissions on territorial dispute.

The convention alleged the Barnala government had declared war on the Sikhs by branding them secessionists and extremists. Significantly, the resolution called upon all Panthic organizations and individuals engaged in the battle for the survival of the Sikhs to unite under the command of Guru Granth Sahib and the Kesari flag. It also demanded immediate release of the Sikh detenus and the rehabilitation of army deserters.

The revenge psyche in the context of Operation Bluestar did not stop operating with the assassination of Indira Gandhi. Retired Army chief General A. S. Vaidya was gunned down in a daring action at Pune in Maharashtra by Harjinder Singh Jinda and Sukhdev Singh Sukha on August 10 to avenge Operation Bluestar. He was the army chief at the time of the army action in the Darbar Sahib complex. Both of them were later hanged to death. The justification they gave for their action is one of the rare political documents the Sikh militant movement has produced. They went to the gallows raising the Sikh slogan of "Bole so nihal sat sri akal".

The situation in Punjab was now heading towards insurgency. Operation Bluestar and the succeeding Operation Woodrose had completely failed to normalize the situation in the border state. Were those operations necessary? The Barnala government acting as instrument of the Centre was also clueless.

In a single biggest retaliation during the Barnala regime, the security forces shot ten militants in an 'encounter' near Dera Baba Nanak in the border district of Gurdaspur on August 30. They were reportedly returning from Pakistan.

With the Leftist leaders increasingly becoming the target of the Sikh militants, the Communists once again thought of organizing their cadre on militant lines. After the gunning down of senior CPI leader Darshan Singh Canadian near Garhshankar in Hoshiarpur district, the party leadership was under pressure from the young cadre to adopt the line of armed resistance. However, this line of thinking was rejected at the decision making level in the CPI. The radical Revolutionary Communist Party of India (Jaikara group), CPI (M-L) Chandra Pulla Reddy group and the CPI (M-L), S N Singh group, joined hands to give a call for mass mobilization combined with armed resistance. The platform of theatre was also used by the Leftists to mobilize people against the fundamentalists. The CPI (M-L) central committee in its resolution adopted on Punjab in April had stated: "Terrorism cannot be defeated by counter-terrorism. Instead, the political and ideological roots of the terrorists should be thoroughly exposed and the people should be organized on their immediate issues. The only alternative is mass resistance by all the sections of the people".[3]

Prime Minister Rajiv Gandhi survived an assassination attempt at Raj Ghat on October 2. Days before the attack, Karamjit Singh, the lone assailant from Sunam had met some radical leaders in the Darbar Sahib complex while disclosing his intentions. He pleaded for a weapon. However, he was not taken seriously. The weapon which was recovered from him was a twelve bore country made pistol which could fire a single shot and was ineffective from that distance. He had hidden himself on a tree during the night and fired from there. He spent a couple of years in jail.

In Punjab, Director General of Police Ribeiro and his wife Melba survived a gun attack at Jalandhar on October 3.

Amarinder Singh, who had been elected leader of the Akali Dal (Badal) Legislature Party, proposed on October 27 a round table conference involving militants to pave the way for normalcy in the state. He said the government should invite the ruling Akali Dal, Akali Dal (Badal), the United Akali Dal, two factions of the AISSF and the Damdami Taksal. He was of the view that decline of the state terrorism would lead to decline of individual terrorism. While strongly condemning the killing of bus passengers, he said the note left behind by the killers in one such case indicated that it was an act of vengeance against state terrorism. He attacked both the forms of terrorism, state and the militant.[4]

Sarbat Khalsa Excommunicates Barnala

Meanwhile, the gulf between the Sikhs and the Hindus continued to widen despite the so called moderate stand of the Congress supported Barnala government, a government which had ceased to be of any relevance. "The growing mistrust between Hindus and Sikhs has created a gulf between the two communities which had been living in peace and harmony over the years. Hindu-Sikh relations have worsened during the past one year with little hope of improvement in the foreseeable future. The perception differs vastly: If Punjabi Hindus look up Mr. J. F. Ribeiro as a "saviour", he is a pain in the neck to large sections of the Sikhs. Hindus accuse Mr. Surjit Singh Barnala of pursuing "communal" policies but appreciate his police action against pro-Khalistan elements lodged in the Golden Temple complex. The Sikhs, by and large, feel that the Barnala government has not done enough for the community and criticize the "Sacrilege" by sending commandos into the Golden Temple complex".[5]

Continuing with the religio-political onslaught against the soft liners represented by Barnala and the like, yet another Sarbat Khalsa was organized by the radicals at Akal Takht on the Diwali of November 2 of 1986. This congregation "excommunicated" from the Sikh religion Barnala, his Finance Minister Balwant Singh and the five high priests, including the Akal Takht Jathedar. The reason cited for the ex-communication of the high priests was their absence at the April 13 Sarbat Khalsa. Referring to the excommunication of Barnala and Balwant Singh, the resolution said they had repeatedly indulged in anti-Panthic activities, including sending security forces to the Darbar Sahib complex on April 30, staging fake encounters at the behest of the Centre and causing hurt to the Sikh honour and psyche. "No Sikh should have relations with the two politicians. Cut off the relationship of roti and beti (socio-economic relations) with them in future", it said.

One of the resolutions passed at this convention endorsed the Khalistan announcement and warned of serious consequences if harm was done to any of the five members of the Panthic Committee. With his elevation as the Akal Takht acting Jathedar, Manochahal was replaced by Subheg Singh on the Panthic Committee. Udhey Singh was co-opted in place of Aroor Singh who had volunteered to quit.

The resolution called upon the Sikhs to be ready to make any sacrifice for the struggle launched by Sant Bhindranwale to achieve the goal of a separate Sikh homeland and to break the shackles of slavery. It condemned the Centre and the Akali government for having let loose a reign of terror and perpetrating atrocities on the Sikhs. It demanded the release of the detained Sikh youth, rehabilitation of army deserters and end to the killings in fake encounters. An appeal was made to the international organizations to speak up for the Sikhs who were facing tyranny at the hands of the government.

Though the Khalistan slogan had been given by the Panthic Committee in April, no move had been initiated by the radicals to involve the Sikh masses in the struggle for the achievement of this goal. It was the politics of the gun which continued to dominate.

On the other hand, Giani Kirpal Singh ridiculed the Sarbat Khalsa convention describing it as a gathering of a group non-representative of the community. He refused to recognize the Sarbat Khalsa on the logic that it is only the Jathedar of Akal Takht who is the convening authority. Such a congregation should have the participation of all sections of the Panth, including the representatives of the SGPC, the Akali Dal, Chief Khalsa Dewan, Kendri Singh Sabha, Delhi Sikh Gurdwara Management Committee, the Nihangs, the Udasis and Sikh saints and others as had happened during the World Sikh Convention.

The resolution passed by the militants could not be described as Gurmata, he said.

The first test of strength between the two main Akali factions was the annual election of the office bearers of the SGPC. The ruling but marginalized Akali Dal (Longowal) lost to the Akali Dal (Badal) in this test on November 30 as Tohra was re-elected it's President who announced that the task force entrusted with the responsibility of maintaining discipline within the Darbar Sahib complex would be disbanded. This task force was deployed after Operation Bluestar. His shift was closer to the radicals, though he had never supported the Khalistan demand.

In the biggest ever killing spree till then, the militants on November 30 gunned down 24 Hindu bus passengers and injured eleven others near Khudda village in Hoshiarpur district after segregating them.

Badal, Tohra Arrested

As the violence further escalated, the state government decided to get tough with the leaders of the Akali Dal (Badal) and the United Akali Dal. Badal and his associates were not supporters of the militant violence. Rather than putting pressure on the Rajiv Gandhi government to provide some legitimacy to his government by implementing at least some of the clauses of the Rajiv-Longowal accord, Barnala opted for confrontation within the Akali matrix. He had exercised the wrong choice. Tohra, Badal and Kuldip Singh Wadala were among about 100 activists and leaders from these two parties detained in the crackdown on December 2 and charged with supporting militancy. Badal said before his arrest, "It was weighing on my mind that we were moving about freely while thousands of our young men have been rotting in jails for over two years".[6] Badal wanted the community to unitedly fight for the demands which included release of the Jodhpur detenus, re-instatement of the Army deserters and a solution to the Punjab problem to the satisfaction of the Punjabis. Significantly, within months of providing some sort of legitimacy to the radical politics by attending the Operation Bluestar anniversary on June 4, he again talked of the Punjab problem in the context of the Punjabis.

For Tohra, this was going to be his longest detention and that too, on flimsy grounds. This was one confinement he remained bitter about. He had been incarcerated by the Congress supported Akali Dal government. He spent a total of about 16 years in jail in free India as part of various Akali agitations. He was also critical of the role of Capt. Kanwaljit Singh who was the Minister of State for Home in the Barnala government.

Though virtually functioning as an instrument in the hands of the Rajiv Gandhi government, Barnala denied that the Akali Dal (Badal) leaders had been arrested at the behest of the Centre or out of political vendetta. The Chief Minister was of the view that Tohra's decision to disband the SGPC task force responsible for maintaining law and order within the Darbar Sahib Complex amounted to an open encouragement to the militants. He claimed the state cabinet had endorsed the steps taken to confront the challenge of militancy. He had met the Prime Minister a day earlier. However, the radicals had retrenched themselves in the Darbar Sahib complex much earlier during the year.

It was during this period that reports appeared about the conspiracy to shoot down the plane of the Prime Minister. A petition was filed in the Allahabad High Court by Major D V Singh posted at Dehradun in which it was alleged that Lt Col A. P. S. Sandhu, commanding officer, called him in his office and sought his cooperation to shoot down the plane carrying Rajiv Gandhi. The petitioner alleged that Lt Col Sandhu went to Canada to meet some hard core terrorists and returned on June 26, 1986. He stated he was again called by Lt Col Sandhu seeking his cooperation in the operation shoot down. Subsequently, he was arrested and shown as insane and not fit for duty. But when Major Singh rejoined duty, he was harassed by the said officer who threatened him saying if General Vaidya could be killed, he was a small fry. Later, he was forced to take pre-mature retirement.[7]

It might not be out of place to refer to a news item published on the front page of a Hindi daily from the Jalandhar based Hind Samachar group, Punjab Kesari, a year earlier on September 15 relating to militancy during that period. It is a classic example of irresponsible journalism. Datelined Jagraon, the report talked of the plan of a group of militants active at the international level to bomb Delhi using fighter- bombers, preferably F-16. The bombs were not to be ordinary ones but chemical weapons. These bombers were to take off from some secret location in Sri Lanka. The report went to the extent of saying that these bombers were already conducting exercises and the route detailed was from Israel to Sri Lanka and then back via Pakistan. These planes were to be flown by suicide bombers. It was also mentioned that Israel had already trained about 500 Sikh militants at some secret camp in that country.

The Punjab government was given sweeping powers to curb militancy under Terrorist and Disruptive Activities (Prevention) Rules, 1986 which was tabled in the Parliament on December 4. Simultaneously, the state government the same day declared Amritsar district and 16 other sub-divisions as the disturbed areas. The notification said certain areas in eight out of 12 districts were in such a dangerous condition that the use of armed forces in aid of civil power was necessary. The Union Territory of Chandigarh was also declared as "disturbed" the same day.

The working committee of the Barnala faction of the Akali Dal, at a meeting at Chandigarh on December 4, endorsed the decisions taken by the state government for maintaining law and order, which meant the arrest of the leaders like Tohra and Badal. The working committee expressed the view that the growing alienation of the Sikh community from the national mainstream could be checked only by the implementation of the Punjab accord. The resolution at the meeting was moved by Cooperation Minister Prem Singh Chandumajra and seconded by Balwant Singh. It was Tohra who had been instrumental in introducing Chandumajra to the Akali Dal.

Meanwhile, Prof. Darshan Singh was appointed acting Jathedar of Akal Takht by the executive of the SGPC at a meeting on December 24 after accepting the resignation of Giani Kirpal Singh. Giani Puran Singh was appointed officiating head priest of Darbar Sahib in place of Giani Sahib Singh who was sacked. The appointment of Prof Darshan Singh was a significant development in this militant struggle.

Drifting along the radical stream, the Akali Dal (Badal), at its Jor Mela conference at Fatehgarh Sahib on December 26, demanded amnesty for the assassins of Indira Gandhi. Most of the senior party leaders were in jail at that time. The demand was voiced by party's acting president Gurdev Singh Badal in the presence of Amarinder Singh. The conference was also attended by leaders of the AISSF, Damdami Taksal and the United Akali Dal.

The conference called upon the Centre to release Jodhpur detenus or face direct action, which, however, was not specified. The party adopted 11 resolutions. It also demanded the release and reinstatement of the army deserters. Another resolution demanded the release of Tohra, Badal and other Akali leaders. The conference asked the state government to declare the martyrdom days of the sons of Guru Gobind Singh and his mother Mata Gujri as holidays. It condemned fake encounters and atrocities against Sikhs. The conference also demanded that the agricultural prices be linked to the price index. The party was not ignoring the economic interest of its main support base, the farmers.

A partial bandh was observed in the state on December 29 called by the radicals to protest against the confirmation of death sentence awarded to the assassins of Indira Gandhi.

NOTES

1. The Indian Express, May 4, 1986.
2. The Tribune, June 5, 1986.
3. The Indian Express, October 3, 1986.
4. The Indian Express, October 28, 1986.
5. The Tribune, October 28, 1986.
6. The Indian Express, December 3, 1986.
7. The Indian Express, November 21, 1986.

12

Beginning of the End

As Chief Minister Surjit Singh Barnala presented himself at Akal Takht in the afternoon at the appointed time in response to the summons for sending security forces into the Darbar Sahib complex, the shabad (hymn) being recited at Darbar Sahib was "Kutta raj bahaliye phir chakki chatte" (a lowly person even if exalted to high position, would not desist from his wicked actions). It was not just a coincidence. In a way, he had already been pronounced guilty.

In this religio-political context, the revolt against Barnala within the ranks of Akali Dal (Longowal) was quite natural as although he was being projected as the national hero who was confronting the militants, for the majority of the Sikh community he was a traitor who had played into the hands of the government at the Centre. Here was an Akali Dal government which had implemented the design of the Rajiv Gandhi government to provide retrospective legitimacy to Operation Bluestar by sending security forces into the Darbar Sahib complex. However, this was the first step in this grand design.

Ironically, despite the police action, the build up within the Darbar Sahib Complex was continuing and the situation was getting out of control for the state government as the radicals again started dictating terms. Yet another chapter of the Punjab tragic drama was to be enacted as the events unfolded. The continued build up within the shrine complex provided the stage for the next act. The militants who had taken over the Darbar Sahib complex and converted it into the base for the struggle were either functioning as instrument in this grand design or had committed a blunder. The actions of the militants were to discredit this movement and this situation suited only the government. Certain forces had already been triggered to sabotage the second phase of this movement when it was in the process of getting consolidated. The militant leaders lacking vision and perception were more and more banking on the borrowed brains. Some of these borrowed brains were working for the agencies. It was a strange situation as this was the period when the radicals were getting consolidated and receiving wider support. After retrospective legitimacy to Operation Bluestar by the Barnala government, stage was now being prepared for another full scale intervention by the security forces in the Darbar Sahib complex. Now this holiest of the holy shrine was to be defiled by the militants themselves.

Continuing with its policy of appeasement of the radicals, the executive committee of the SGPC, at its January 23, 1987 meeting at Amritsar, decided to relieve Takht Keshgarh Sahib Jathedar Giani Harcharan Singh Mahalon and Takht Damdama Sahib Jathedar Sant Lakha Singh, who were respectively replaced by Sawinder Singh and Jaswant Singh while Kashmir Singh was given the charge of acting priest at Darbar Sahib. All the three appointees were associated with Damdami Taksal. In a resolution, the executive committee strongly condemned the entry of the police into the buildings in the Darbar Sahib complex.

Earlier, former minister and Congress (I) leader Joginder Pal Pandey was gunned down at Ludhiana on January 19.

Yet another Sarbat Khalsa, called by the radicals on January 26, 1987, endorsed and reiterated the announcement for Khalistan, arguing it was necessary in view of the situation created by the Centre. It was attended by the Prof. Darshan Singh and all the newly appointed members of the clergy. The Sarbat Khalsa accepted the resignation of Gurbachan Singh Manochahal from the office of the Acting Jathedar of Akal Takht and ratified the appointment of Prof. Darshan Singh in his place. Prof. Darshan Singh announced his advisory committee which included Ajaib Singh, who was spokesman of Damdami Taksal, Jagdev Singh, Manjit Singh, Dr. Harinder Singh and Avtar Singh. Manochahal was again nominated to the Panthic Committee in place of Dhanna Singh who had been arrested earlier It was stated that all such appointments henceforth would be made at the Sarbat Khalsa.

The political resolution held the "communal" government at the Centre and its "puppet" Barnala-Balwant government in Punjab responsible for repression against the Sikhs. It proposed a front of minorities comprising Sikhs, Muslims, Christians, Parsis and Dalits to confront the government at the Centre. An appeal was made to the Akal Takht Jathedar to raise suitable memorial to commemorate the memory of those who had sacrificed their lives in the present Sikh struggle. Earlier, it was the Akali Dal which had earlier adopted similar resolution to this effect and though supported by the SGPC which was to be the implementing agency, it was never implemented. The conclave, while criticizing lootings and snatchings, appealed to the Sikh organizations to take action against such elements.

It was not for the first time that the radical Sikh organizations had initiated the move to seek the support of other minorities. Earlier, uniting minorities used to be the agenda of the Akali Dal.

The Barnala cabinet the very next day condemned the endorsement of the call for Khalistan saying it was a conspiracy of the foreign powers seeking to destabilize unity and integrity of India through their agents and called upon the people of Punjab to unitedly isolate these anti-national forces and fight them to the finish. The cabinet resolution said the government could not remain silent spectator of secessionist and seditious declarations from any platform what so ever, nor could any individual or foreign power be permitted to challenge directly or indirectly, the sovereignty of the country. The Akali Dal (L) working committee, at its meeting the next day, criticized the manner in which Jathedar Mahalon and Sant Lakha Singh were removed by the SGPC executive.

Operation Bluestar and Operation Woodrose had failed to instill confidence among the members of the Hindu community who continued to have sense of insecurity. A 101- member squad of the Rashtriya Suraksha Samiti left Durgiana Mandir at Amritsar for Delhi on February 1 to meet the Prime Minister to demand protection to life and property of the Hindus in Punjab.

Akali Factions Dissolved

Within days of the Khalistan resolution having been endorsed by the Sarbat Khalsa, the Akali politics took another turn when in a major development, the Sikh clergy, on February 3, 1987, while intervening in the political affairs, dissolved the Akali factions through a directive (Hukamnama) issued under the signatures of Akal Takht acting Jathedar Prof. Darshan Singh, Giani Jaswant Singh of Takht Damdama Sahib, Giani Sawinder Singh of Takht Keshgarh Sahib, Giani Puran Singh, Head Granthi, Darbar Sahib and Giani Kashmir Singh, Head Granthi, Akal Takht. The directive warned that any faction using the name of Akali Dal would be considered as violating the directive and flouting the Panthic interests. It was not for the first time that the Akal Takht had intervened in the affairs of the Akali Dal, the party claiming to articulate the religio-political aspirations and concerns of the community. The intervention from Akal Takht in the Akali Dal affairs draws legitimacy from this very character of the party which is rooted in its very origin.

The Hukamnama said: "The Akali Dal is not only a political party, but it is an organization of the Sikh Panth. For some time past, due to political situation and due to acts of selfish elements, the party was divided into many small units which resulted in erosion of the strength and it was a matter of concern to the Sikhs". It was made clear that interests of all sections would be safeguarded. The directive warned that any faction using the name of the Akali Dal would be considered as violating the directions and flouting Panthic interests. It was also made clear that the clergy had no intention of interfering in the Barnala government. All the office bearers of the factions using the name of Akali Dal were directed to send their resignations to Akal Takht. The political agenda for the newly constituted Akali Dal was also set by the clergy.

This move was seen as an effort by the militants to gain control over the Akali factions. The necessity of having a strong political front to achieve the political goal was being discussed in the militant circles at that time.

The Akali Dal (Longowal) working committee at its meeting on February 4 at Chandigarh discussed the directive and decided to hold talks with Prof. Darshan Singh. Barnala set up a 7-member committee headed by Amar Singh Nalini with Balwant Singh, Natha Singh Dalam, Harbhajan Singh Sandhu, Dr. Gurnam Singh Tir, Tota Singh and Hari Singh Zira as members to hold parleys with the Akal Takht Jathedar. This meeting was also attended by the party MLAs, MPs, SGPC members, advisers and the district presidents. The resolution passed at the meeting made it clear that the unity of only those organizations could strengthen the Panth which believed in the basic principles, political objectives and democratic structure of the Akali Dal. "We always wanted Panthic unity and are ready to make any sacrifice for bringing back factions and individuals who have broken away, to the mainstream under the discipline of the Akali Dal. But there is no question of any unity with any faction which does not have faith in the party's principles, constitution, political objectives, unity and integrity of the country and a democratic set up... any effort to weaken the glorious traditions of the Akali Dal, which had fought and won battles for political interests of the Sikh community and political, economic and cultural interests of Punjab during the past 70 years, would tantamount to a blow to the Panth", the resolution said. It was clear from the resolution that the ruling faction of the Akali Dal was in no mood to join hands with other factions to constitute a unified Akali Dal. The compulsions of Barnala were different. For some inexplicable reasons, he was totally under the control of the government at the Centre.

Mann Appointed Akali Dal Chief

The Sikh clergy, on February 5, merged the Akali factions and appointed Simranjit Singh Mann, then in jail, as the president of the re-organized Akali Dal. It was for the first time that the former police officer had been entrusted with such an enormous political responsibility, though, being in absentia only in name. It was considered to be a move to provide some sort of radical framework to the Akali Dal so that the party could function as a front organization of the underground militant organizations engaged in the armed struggle for the creation of a sovereign Sikh state.

The Akali Dal (Longowal) had not out rightly rejected the directive from the Akal Takht. The 7-member committee of the party reached Amritsar but failed to meet the high priests as Swaran Singh Khalsa, General Secretary of the AISSF (Gurjit faction), issued a statement earlier during the day warning the Finance Minister against meeting the high priests as he had already been excommunicated. There was a design behind issuing this statement as he was given this task by some other leaders functioning from within the shrine complex. That some such statement was being issued by the AISSF General Secretary was known to many including some journalists, even before it was released.

The high priests constituted a 13-member committee, including a 5-member presidium, to run the party affairs in the absence of Mann. The presidium included Baba Joginder Singh, Parkash Singh Badal, Jagdev Singh Talwandi, Surjan Singh Thekedar and Gajja Singh. Gurdev Singh Badal and Prem Singh Lalpura were nominated to function on behalf of Badal and Thekedar who were in jail. Other members of the committee included Manjit Singh Calcutta, Ranjit Singh Brahmpura, Major General Narinder Singh (Retd), Sukhjinder Singh, Gurcharan Singh Tohra, Ujagar Singh Sekhwan, Harcharan Singh Rode and Sant Ajit Singh. Bimal Kaur Khalsa, Shaminder Singh and Bachittar Singh were asked to function in place of Major General Narinder Singh (Retd), Sukhjinder Singh and Sant Ajit Singh who were also in jail.

The high priests released a summary of the party programme which was essentially the re-assertion of the 1973 version of the Anandpur Sahib resolution with some additions and changes in the rules and regulations of the party. This party programme should have been in the context of the Khalistan resolution passed by the Panthic Committee and endorsed at the Sarbat Khalsa subsequently. Prof. Darshan Singh had already made the move to blunt that demand in a subtle way. He also asserted that the new programme in no way was in contradiction with the unity and integrity of the country.

The aim of the new outfit was to maintain the exclusive and independent identity of the Panth and create a geo-political environment which could reflect the aspirations of the Sikh nation. It maintained that the Khalsa Panth was a separate and independent nation and the party would fight for a special status for the Sikhs. This policy programme was no different from the one stated in the party constitution which was adopted by the party working committee at its meeting on September 2, 1974. Section 2 under the title 'Main Aims' of this constitution defines the political objective as: "To preserve and keep alive the concept of distinct and independent identity of the Panth and to create an environment in which national sentiments and aspirations of the Sikh Panth will find full expression, satisfaction and growth". Still, Prof. Darshan Singh came under attack for pandering to the radicals.

The new rules and regulations barred one person from holding two offices. The party president would not contest the Assembly or the Parliamentary elections. No member of the party high command during the tenure of 2 years would hold office of minister. No Akali leader would negotiate with the Centre without written permission from the party high command. The SGPC president was made ex-officio permanent member of the Akali Dal high command but barred from becoming the Akali Dal chief. Under the new policy, it was made obligatory for the Akali Dal government to oppose the entry of security forces into the Darbar Sahib complex.

The high priests clarified that the members of the 7-members committee of the ruling Akali Dal (Longowal) could approach them to submit their resignations but not to seek clarifications. The SGPC also assured full security to the committee in the shrine complex for this purpose. The SGPC officials waited for the committee at the main entrance of the shrine till the expiry of the time limit but none of its members turned up. Justifying the intervention of the clergy in the Akali Dal affairs, Prof. Darshan Singh argued the Akali Dal was not just a political party but a religio-political organization and as such, Akal Takht could rightly intervene in its affairs. The Akali Dal (Badal) working committee, which met the same day at Amritsar, expectedly, appreciated the unity move.

Barnala reacted by rejecting the directive and said, "It seems to be the unity against the Shiromani Akali Dal and its government. The Shiromani Akali Dal and the government stand". He said the United Akali Dal consisted of those who were opposed to him and it appeared the Darbar Sahib and the Akal Takht were under the control of the forces of disunity. He had come into direct confrontation with Akal Takht.

Interestingly, years later, the reaction of the Shiromani Akali Dal headed by Parkash Singh Badal, then the ruling Akali Dal, was no different to a directive from Akal Takht to maintain semblance of unity to celebrate the 300th anniversary of the birth of the Khalsa in 1999. This reflects the behaviour pattern of the Akali Dal in power and the faction not in power. The behaviour of the same Akali faction when enjoying power and when struggling for it can be contradictory and the Akali politics is characterized by this political opportunism. Now was the turn of Minister of State for Health Sukhdev Singh Dhillon to resign in protest against Barnala's attitude towards the Sikh clergy.

Prof. Darshan Singh, on February 6, strongly reacted to the posture adopted by Barnala saying it was against the spirit of the Akal Takht directive. The high priests directed the Akali Dal (L) MLAs, MPs, party office bearers and workers to offer their services to the re-organized Akali Dal by February 8. The acting Jathedar made it clear the Akal Takht was not interfering in the political matters per se and would dissociate itself from it the day the Akali Dal was declared only a political outfit.

The Akali Dal (Master Tara Singh) in Delhi rejected the directive terming it open interference by the religious authority in the political process. But then Akal Takht is not just a religious institution as such but the one associated with the religio-political affairs of the Sikh community.

The ruling Akali Dal (L) working committee appealed to Prof. Darshan Singh to review the decision and not to take any step which might add to the turmoil, weaken the Panth and harm the unity and integrity of the country as any decision taken by the Akal Takht acting Jathedar without taking into account the stand of the ruling Akali Dal would tantamount to his becoming partisan. Unity of only those organizations having faith in the same political objectives, fundamental structure and character could strengthen the Panth. The resolution reposed faith in the supremacy of the institution of Akal Takht but regretted that the seven member committee of the party which was sent to Amritsar to present the case was prevented from meeting Prof. Darshan Singh.

There was very strong reaction in the media over the move to re-organize the Akali Dal which was seen as an endeavor by the radicals to take over the reigns of the oldest regional party in the country. "Mr. Tohra and the extremists are therefore the ones who are directing the events. They are the ones whom Mr. Barnala and the country have to contend with. Their aim is clear: Khalistan. And the Hukamnama etc are but a device to replace Mr. Barnala by a government of their nominees, a government that will help them towards establishing Khalistan".[1] Tohra had no role to play in these developments as the subsequent events indicated. Moreover, he never subscribed to the radical ideology though he had always played a key role at every critical juncture in the Sikh religio-political affairs of his times.

The Times of India commented the same day: "A new crisis of unknown magnitude has arisen in Punjab. And it is reasonably clear that the Barnala government cannot surmount it. Indeed, the question is whether it can survive the crisis". But then it was Operation Bluestar which had provided legitimacy to the radical politics. This party programme, seen in the framework of the 1974 Akali Dal constitution, could not be termed as radical. And the constitution had not been amended till then. Still the reaction in the media was adverse.

One of the reasons for this type of reaction perhaps was the warning to the Akali leaders from the Panthic Committee coinciding with the unity move against working for the political objective less than Khalistan. However, the day the clergy dissolved all Akali factions, the leaders from the militant factions kept on denying in private their role in these development.

Submitting to the edict, Chandumajra dissolved the Youth wing. The Chandigarh unit of the Akali Dal also accepted the directive. Akali Dal (Badal) Legislature Party leader Amarinder Singh placed the services of his legislative group at the disposal of the Akal Takht. He called upon all the Akali MLAs and MPs to offer their services to Akal Takht by February 8.

The high priests, on February 7, rejected the appeal of the Akali Dal (L) to reconsider the decision with Prof. Darshan Singh extending the logic that the Akali factions had been merged on the basis of a party programme on which the party won elections and as such, there was no need for a review. The manifesto for the 1985 elections referred to the Anandpur Sahib resolution and the new policy programme was within the framework of that resolution. The manifesto defined the character of the Akali Dal in these words; "Shiromani Akali Dal can take genuine pride in the fact that it is the only party which has stood as the guardian of the interests of Punjab in general and the Sikhs in particular". It is this Sikh character of the party which justifies the intervention of Akal Takht. The very first objective of the party as per its constitution is defending the religion.

The high priests said the leaders dubbing the decision as anti-national were setting the Panth against the country and as such, they were loyal neither to the Panth nor the country. The Akal Takht acting Jathedar argued that had the Darbar Sahib complex been under the control of the militants, he would not have been able to reinvent the Akali Dal whose principles and programmes stood for the unity and integrity of the country. At the same time, the high priests effected some minor changes in the policy programme.

Agriculture Minister Harbhajan Singh Sandhu handed over a letter from Barnala to Prof. Darshan Singh on February 8 which stated: "We appreciate your efforts to bring about Panthic unity and have full faith in the supremacy of Akal Takht. In his regard, the two resolutions passed by the working committee are already at your kind notice. These resolutions clearly express our feelings about the Panthic unity... We wish to reiterate that the Shiromani Akali Dal advocates Panthic unity, but we want that this unity be based on the principle for which the Shiromani Akali Dal has been struggling for the past 70 years and should be attained through a consensus among the concerned parties. Our services are always available for the attainment of the above said goal". The Legislative wing of the party, at a separate meeting, reposed confidence in Barnala's leadership, who asserted on February 8, "My government stands and I have neither resigned as ruling Akali Dal President nor dissolved the party".

Barnala ex-communicated

The confrontation with the clergy proved to be too costly for Barnala who was awarded religious punishment (declared Tankhaiya - guilty of misconduct) by the clergy on February 9 and directed to present himself at Akal Takht on February 11. He was charged with violating the Akal Takht directive on dissolving the Akali factions and also accused of denigrating the high priests. The high priests decided to take the drastic action after a long wait for Balwant Singh who was to meet them with a message from the Chief Minister.

Barnala described the action against him as action taken in haste. Even after the Akal Takht onslaught, the Akali Dal (L) Legislature Party expressed faith in his leadership and resolved to maintain separate identity of the party. The party leaders advised him against appearing at Akal Takht. The legislative wing met thrice on February 10 defended Barnala arguing what he had said and done in response to the directive was not in an individual capacity but on behalf of the party. As such, he personally did not deserve any punishment.

Barnala, who opted for the policy of confrontation, sent a letter to the Akal Takht instead of presenting himself. At the same time, he called for a party convention at Longowal on February 20 to take the issue to the people's court. He described the charges against him as baseless and requested the Jathedar to review the "whole situation". The letter said, "You were desirous of bringing about unity among parties which differ vastly from each other on matters of principles. Our party follows the path of national unity and integrity and human love and brotherhood on the lines of Sant Harchand Singh Longowal and has faith in electoral process while others boycott elections and rejoice in the brutal killing of the Sant..... Some forces had been sparing no effort to dislodge the Akali government. Nothing should be done that leads people to believe that the Singh Sahiban have taken a decision under the influence of these forces".

Barnala was finally ex-communicated from the Sikh Panth on February 11 for having failed to present himself at Akal Takht. It was for the first time that such an extreme action had been taken against a Chief Minister, of course in this case in his capacity as the party president. The high priests directed the MPs, MLAs, organizational leaders and workers of the Akali Dal (L) to appear at Akal Takht to express allegiance to the institution and offer their services by February 14. Barnala was found guilty on five counts. One, he did not resign from the presidency of the party. Second, he denigrated the high priests by leveling baseless and false allegations against them about the unity efforts. Third, he deceived and betrayed the Akal Takht by going back on his commitment about offering the services of his faction to the supreme temporal institution. Fourth, his refusal to appear before the Akal Takht and lastly, creating rift among the Sikhs by continuing to claim himself to be the party President. The assertion by the supreme Sikh institution for prayer and politics was absolute, though not unprecedented.

The Akal Takht edict ordered socio-economic boycott of Barnala (roti beti da rishta) and directed that he should neither be allowed to speak from the Panthic platform nor the members of the Sikh community interact with him and offer any cooperation. Barnala sent another letter to the clergy which was consigned to the dust bin.

Akali Dal (Master Tara Singh) President Rachhpal Singh was also ex-communicated on February 14. Reacting to his ex-communication, he described it as a pre-planned conspiracy.

Balwant Singh, accompanied by state Advocate General G. S. Grewal, met Prof. Darshan Singh on February 12 to discuss the political crisis faced by the Akali Dal (L) following the ex-communication of Barnala. He said on February 14 that the Akal Takht verdict had become controversial as it lacked proper procedure. Never in the history of Akal Takht had the Jathedar given a verdict on matters not referred to him by the parties concerned. In this case, the verdict was unilateral, premeditated and against all norms of justice and fair play. He said the Chief Minister was acting as the country's shield against terrorism and foreign conspiracy to destabilize the country and appealed to the Jathedar to review the decision.

But then earlier in history, Akal Takht Jathedar Akali Phoola Singh had taken a suo motto notice of the misconduct of Maharaja Ranjit Singh and pronounced him guilty who accepted the verdict in all humility. The Jathedar had sentenced him to be whip lashed in front of Akal Takht. The sentence was waived when Maharaja Ranjit Singh presented himself to undergo the punishment. The functioning of Akal Takht till then represented the democratic ethos of Sikh religion the parallel of which would be difficult to find anywhere else. That was the might of this supreme Sikh institution. It is a different matter that slowly, this character of democratic functioning of Akal Takht got eroded during the times of Maharaja Ranjit Singh itself. One sovereign would not accept another institution symbolizing sovereignty. Operation Bluestar was also an attack on this very character of Akal Takht.

Revolt in Akali Dal (L)

Expectedly, the ex-communication of Barnala triggered a chain reaction who was confronted with the attack from within the party as about 30 delegates gave notice for requisitioning the meeting of the general house on February 22. The logic advanced was that the ex-communication had created a serious and unprecedented situation as an ex-communicated person could not continue to be member of the Akali Dal. Till then, the membership of the Akali Dal was not open to other communities, of course with some exceptions like the Muslims of Malerkotla and Sehajdharis (Hindus having faith in Sikh doctrine).

Barnala tried to confront the Akal Takht at a different level. His supporters organized a convention at Sangrur on February 20 with the support of the government machinery in an attempt to project his so called mass base in the community. This convention 'rejected' his ex-communication describing it as a wrong decision which violated the Panthic traditions. Barnala was projected as the "General of the Panth" by Balwant Singh.

The resolution passed at the convention portrayed the Chief Minister as a true Sikh and a servant of the Panth. It said: "Some divisive forces have been active in attempting to bring down the legally and constitutionally elected Akali government since its inception. Some persons had even boycotted the elections to the Vidhan Sabha. The combined effort of all these forces could not succeed in toppling the government. Now under the garb of Panthic unity, these very forces have connived with the Jathedar of Akal Takht Sahib to destabilize the Panthic government. Shiromani Akali Dal which has a glorious record of service of 70 years was abolished with one stroke. The President of the Shiromani Akali Dal was summarily ordered to tender his resignation. Another parallel party was constituted with a new president, new office bearers and a new constitution overnight. It constituted a coup which proved to be counter productive. A new constitution was also framed. SAD working committee repeatedly asked for time to present its case which was denied. The President of the SAD was asked to submit a written reply to the charge against him before Sri Akal Takht. Much before the written explanation reached the hands of Jathedar Sahib, order of indictment had been written, typed and cyclostyled. The elements determined to topple the legally and constitutionally elected government by foul means did not even pause to consider that their action would tarnish the image and glory of Sri Akal Takht Sahib in public mind. These disruptive forces and frustrated elements perhaps could not even visualize the dire consequences that followed the removal of a representative government and imposition of the army rule in the state. This convention representing the Sikhs from all over India strongly condemns the activities of the extremists and secessionists and all the forces working against the interests of Punjab and the country and pledges to fight them as one man. It appeals to all the Punjabis, all the political parties in the country and the whole nation to extend their whole hearted support to meet this national challenge. SAD reiterates that it believes in the supremacy of Akal Takht Sahib and will religiously follow the traditions established since the times of Guru Nanak Dev Ji. SAD will always strive for the Charhdikala (well being) of the Sikh Panth. It firmly believes in the Panthic unity. This mammoth gathering assures Sikhs all over the world that any suggestion for unity based upon democratic principles and in consonance with Sikh traditions will be accepted".[2]

In Amritsar, the requisitioned meeting of a section of the Akali Dal (Longowal) general house on February 22 removed Barnala from the primary membership of the party. The delegates elected Harbans Singh Ghuman, senior vice –president, who was earlier expelled from the Akali Dal (L), as president, who offered services of the faction to the Akal Takht.

The Finance Minister, on February 27, advised the high priest to confine themselves to the religious activities rather than jumping into the political arena. His logic was that for the first time, a clear distinction had been made between the functioning of Akal Takht and the Akali Dal while terming the confrontation between the two as unfortunate.

The ruling Akali Dal (L) chalked out a strategy to confront the new Akali Dal in the religious domain and accordingly, decided to start Amrit

Parchar (Baptism) campaign. This decision was taken at a meeting of the party working committee at Chandigarh on March 3. It was also decided to organize workers camps to educate them in religio-political affairs.

Earlier on February 12, in one of the biggest bank robbery during militancy, an amount of about Rs 5.70 crore was robbed at Ludhiana. Senior Communist Party of India (Marxist) leader Chanan Singh Dhoot was gunned down in Hoshiarpur district on February 15. In Patiala, BJP executive committee member Shambu Parsad was shot on March 17.

Abinashi Singh, personal assistant to the SGPC chief and Dr Baldev Singh Brar of the SGPC run Guru Ram Dass Hospital, mysteriously disappeared from Amritsar on April 1 and their bodies remained untraced. Both of them were taken together to some undisclosed place by some militants. All the militants involved in this case were subsequently killed by the police one after the other. Unaware of his involvement, the last of the survivors who knew the place where their bodies had been buried was also killed by the police within hours of having been caught. The message from the police headquarters reached Tarn Taran too late in this case.

Meanwhile, thespian Sunil Dutt entered Punjab on April 2 on a Mahanshanti Padyatra which was to culminate at Darbar Sahib. The peace march had started from Mumbai.

Militants' Social Code of Conduct

This was the time the militants started enforcing what came to be known as the social code of conduct governing the life of the people which finally plunged the state into fear psychosis of unimaginable magnitude and triggered the countdown for the withering away of militancy. The consumption of liquor and meat was banned as part of this code and the number of members of the marriage party was restricted to 11 persons. The code covered almost every aspect of the social life. This forced social metamorphosis started from the Malwa belt. The movement was kicked off from the area around Moga from where Sant Bhindranwale had started his Amrit Parchar campaign after his release from the Ferozepur jail in 1981. Despite being the traditional support base of the Akalis, religion had comparatively lesser grip on the people in Malwa region as compared to the Mazha area.

The village panchayats started adopting resolutions against the opening of liquor vends in their respective areas. This was the area where addiction was high and as such, this part of the social code was initially welcomed by the people at large in general and women in particular. Cigarette vends and barbers' shops also started disappearing. Even giddha (a traditional girls' dance) was banned in girls' schools. Panthic dress code was prescribed for the school students. In the townships, the shopkeepers were directed to paint their sign boards in specified colours (yellow and blue).

The legitimacy to this so called social reforms movement was indirectly provided by the high priests at a convention organized by the United Akali Dal on April 7 at Baba Bakala in Amritsar district. At this convention, the village panchayats were called upon to provide the names of the dowry seekers while those who had deserted their wives due to insufficient dowry were asked to bring them back. Earlier at Humbran village in Ludhiana district, directive was issued against the sale of tobacco products on March 21. Such directives were issued virtually at every function organized by the radicals, especially in the rural areas.

This was too strict a discipline which the people finally refused to comply with. This moral policing by the militants was not acceptable to the Sikh masses in general who revolted against the way the code was being thrust upon. Social reform movement was a direct intervention in the private lives of the people. Perhaps this was not the concept of the sovereign Sikh state for the common man in the rural areas which was the main support base for the armed struggle. The rural Punjabi society, by and large, is accustomed to a different life style where drinking is common, though it used to be looked down upon around 50 years ago when even cooking meat on the stove in the kitchen was also considered to be a taboo, especially in the Malwa area. Men used to wash their utensils after enjoying the non-vegetarian feast. The Sikh struggle was already being sabotaged. The idea to start this reform movement had come from the borrowed brains.

Meanwhile, in an effort to dictate the political agenda, the AISSF (Manjit) announced the launching of the struggle for the 'Khalsa Raj' at Hola Mohalla convention at Anandpur Sahib on March 15 and warned that any Akali leader negotiating for anything less than this demand would meet Longowal's fate. However, there was no clarity about 'Khalsa Raj' at the conceptual level. Ironically, the resolution carried a warning that in case the creation of Khalistan was further delayed, the country would disintegrate. Going by the logic of this warning, the Khalsa Raj was to be just an autonomous state within India, not radically different from the demand for the implementation of Anandpur Sahib Resolution. At the same time, the convention stated that it was attack on the Darbar Sahib complex in 1984 which had laid the foundation of Khalistan. The resolution as such was full of contradictions. Another resolution alerted the Sikh masses against the Akali leaders suspected of bartering away the interests of the Sikh community.

Through a resolution, the convention authorized the Khalistan Commando Force to punish according to the Sikh traditions all those attempting to harm the institution of Akal Takht at the instigation of the Centre. However, as the subsequent events revealed, it was too subjective an issue as to who were the people defiling and desecrating the Darbar Sahib complex which includes the Akal Takht. The Unified Akali Dal at its Hola Mohalla convention stuck to the Anandpur Sahib resolution. The ruling Akali Dal preferred to stay away from Anandpur Sahib.

At the time when the state was gripped by fear psychosis, a number of political parties joined the ruling Akali Dal in observing the Martyrdom Day of Shaheed Bhagat Singh, Rajguru and Sukhdev on March 23 at Khatkar Kalan. The convention resolved to fight extremism and terrorism. It was the red colour of the Left which dominated the convention, not the blue of the ruling Akali Dal. This function at Khatkar Kalan is organized by the state government every year.

Noted film personality Sunil Dutt who had started his padyatra from Mumbai, reached Amritsar on April 13. He had a 90-minute talk with the high priests. Earlier, Baba Amte had undertaken a similar goodwill visit of Punjab.

Sushil Muni Negotiates with Darshan

The Centre gave the impression of taking yet another initiative to restore peace in the troubled state. The main actor this time was Acharya Susheel Kumar, a controversial Jain Muni, who, accompanied by Tarlochan Singh Riyasti, a Congress (I) leader and former minister, met Prof. Darshan Singh on May 6 to pave the way for a renewed dialogue. The Central Reserve Police Force pickets in the vicinity of the Darbar Sahib complex were removed for the first time that day since Operation Bluestar to give the signal that he had the backing of the government in Delhi. The removal of pickets was the pre-condition set by Prof. Darshan Singh for talks. However, the pickets were re-deployed late in the evening. A joint statement was issued after the talks which said, "We are attempting to pave a way to bring about peace in the state and end the present stalemate".

The third round of talks between the Acharya and Prof. Darshan Singh ended on a note of grave concern over the attempts being made by certain vested interests to sabotage the talks. The Acharya condemned the state government for registering a case against Prof. Darshan Singh for the alleged seditious speeches made by him on February 27. A case was registered against Prof. Darshan Singh on May 8 under Section 4 of the TADA and Sections 124-A and 505 IPC in the Sadar police station, Amritsar, on a complaint filed by district police chief Mohammad Izhar Alam. Acharya Muni said the real danger to the country's unity and integrity was not from Prof. Darshan Singh but from the state government which had registered a case against him.

A few months later, the charred body of Riyasti was recovered from his car on January 9, 1988 from near Ludhiana. He had alleged in July that the talks between the Acharya and Prof. Darshan Singh had been sabotaged by a powerful central minister. He was hinting at Union Home Minister Buta Singh. It may be recalled that he was one of the last non-Akali politicians to meet Sant Bhindranwale before Operation Bluestar. His tape recorded conversation with the Sant had been taken to Indira Gandhi. He was one of those leaders from Punjab who had access to Indira Gandhi. He also had the distinction of being the one Congress leader who had started wearing black turban after Operation Bluestar in protest against the army action.

The outcome of the talks between Prof. Darshan Singh and the Acharya was circulated as a 4-page document among the high priests, the Damdami Taksal, the Unified Akali Dal and the two factions of the AISSF. The crux of the draft was to grant unconditional general amnesty to the Sikh detenus with 1978 as the base year. It covered persons wanted in criminal cases also, including murders. The general amnesty was also to be given to those who were suspects but had not been arrested, those against whom no criminal case was pending but somehow were wanted by the police and those who had been arrested on political ground but no criminal case was pending against them.

The territorial and the river waters disputes were also on the agenda of the two leaders. Other subjects which came up for discussion included bridging the gap between the two communities, Kar Sewa of the Akal Takht and pull out of the para-military forces from the state. It was decided that the negotiations would be within the framework of the constitution. Prof. Darshan Singh did not agree to unconditional surrender of arms by the militants at that stage. The document had envisaged such a surrender followed by trial in special courts, especially of the proclaimed offenders. In respect of persons under training in Pakistan, it was resolved that they would be given complete asylum and kept in a reformatory. This experiment had already been successfully done in Gurdaspur district without making any announcement. These persons had been divided into three categories: between 18 and 20 years, between 21 and above and lastly, the students. The government was to review their cases sympathetically and rehabilitate them according to their capacity and ability.

Barnala Government Dismissed

The Barnala government was finally unceremoniously dismissed and Punjab brought under President's rule on May 11, 1987. The state Assembly was placed under animated suspension. This followed the Governor's report which said the Barnala government was incapable of running the administration according to the constitution, the law and order situation was deteriorating day by day and was beyond its control. After having been alienated from his own community, Barnala, once a national hero, had been reduced to zero. Earlier, the Union Home Minister had written three letters to Barnala impressing upon him the need to take remedial steps to control the situation. In these letters, the Centre had expressed total lack of confidence in the Barnala government which had failed to realize the gravity of situation and properly utilize the atmosphere created by the all party campaign for communal harmony and against terrorism. In the weeks preceding the dismissal of the Barnala government, campaign was on to baptize the Sikhs all over the state, especially in the countryside. Here was a government which did not have any say even in the appointment of the police chief which is the prerogative of the state government.

Barnala was of the view that his government had been made the sacrificial goat mainly to promote the interests of the Congress in Haryana. But then this had not happened for the first time. The Akali Dal Legislature Party at a meeting the next day deplored the partisan role played by Governor S. S. Ray. The resolution said the Governor had been misused to help the Congress poll prospects in Haryana. The party called for an end to the communalization of politics in the country. It said the Punjab problem was political and only a sincere political initiative could solve it. The party strongly felt that an attempt had been made to mislead the nation on law and order as also on the state government's vigorous efforts to fight the challenge on behalf of the nation. The Centre never allowed a democratic and political solution to be worked out. The political atmosphere in the state was vitiated with the Centre's refusal to implement the main clauses of the Punjab Accord. The Centre had chosen to follow the path of confrontation with the Sikhs and Longowal had been murdered once again. Punjab was in tears and blood -spattered. The state was also hurt. The tears had to be wiped, blood cleansed and efforts made to remove the feeling of hurt, the resolution stated.

A state wide crackdown followed the imposition of President's rule in which activists of the AISSF, Damdami Taksal and some Akali factions including Chandumajra were arrested. A Delhi court issued arrest warrants on May 25 against Prof. Darshan Singh in connection with a sedition case. The Prime Minister made it clear the President's rule would continue in Punjab till terrorism was wiped out. It proved to be the longest spell which ended in February, 1992.

That the Barnala government had been sacrificed on the altar of the Haryana Assembly elections became clear during the campaign in the neighbouring state. Addressing election rallies in Haryana on June 7, Prime Minister Rajiv Gandhi assured Chandigarh would not be transferred to Punjab without adequate compensation to Haryana. He recalled he resisted pressure to hand over Chandigarh to Punjab without the transfer of 70,000 acres of land to Haryana. On the SYL Canal, he claimed while the Haryana Sangharash Samiti was demanding 3.5 MAF waters for this canal from the Punjab rivers, the centre had succeeded in getting 3.83 MAF for Haryana. The Punjab government had been instructed to expedite the construction of the carrier channel. The focus of his speeches was Punjab.[3] He also said the construction of this canal would be entrusted to the National projects Construction Corporation. Ironically, the Congress lost the elections in Haryana.

The mass contact campaign launched by the Communist Party of India in Punjab on June 28 to mobilize people against militancy ended on a bloody note with the militants gunning down a member of its state council Sukhminder Singh, his two sons, one daughter, a relative and his police guard near Moga.

The Centre's rule failed to check increasing violence. The militants gunned down 40 bus passengers near Lalru on the Chandigarh –Ambala road on July 7 followed by killing of 36 bus passengers near Hisar in Haryana. In the Haryana incident, the killers first stopped a Delhi bound bus coming from Ferozepur and shot dead 32 passengers while injuring 30 others. In the second incident which followed soon after, they stopped another bus and gunned down four passengers. All the victims were Hindus. The massacre had strong reaction in Haryana where four Sikhs were lynched by the mobs during bandh the next day called in protest against the bus killings.

Significantly, a few days before the dismissal of the government, Finance Minister Balwant Singh had a spat with Ribeiro who had complained to the Union Home Ministry that the Finance Minister was pressurizing him to release a top militant, Jagtar Singh, operating from the Mand area in his constituency. The police had arrested him from the Shahkot police station area. Balwant Singh shot off a strongly worded 5-page letter to the Chief Minister alleging that the DGP had not only politicized the office but also communalized it.

"Mr. Ribeiro is no doubt an honest and dedicated police officer but the problem with him is that he believes in authoritarianism and police absolutism which have no place in a democratic set up. Moreover, he gives impression of self-righteousness and places himself beyond answerability to the elected government. His methods are out of date and out of tune with the demands of democratic polity. If there is one reason why terrorism continues to be a problem in Punjab in spite of allowing Mr. Ribeiro a free hand, it is because of his refusal to allow the district administration any say in the working of police as a para-military force which owes no obligation to the government but has all the claims of support and resources. This had led to the alienation of the commissioners and the district magistrates from their basic job to maintain law and order and has in return isolated the police not only from the general administration but also from the general masses. Quite understandably, this has led to cultivation of contempt for the police force in constitutional, political, legal and administrative arrangements. His demand for complete autonomy for the police force is fraught with grave dangers. In a democracy, there is no alternative to combining political and ideological fight against terrorism with the administrative measures aimed at isolating the terrorist rather than turning them into martyrs and heroes which precisely has the policy of Mr. Ribeiro achieved", he wrote. He started with the comments that DGP's attempt at one upmanship had earned him the title Director General Propaganda.

This was followed by a letter to Ribeiro on May 7 which referred to the news report about the DGP complaining to the Union Home Ministry and asking him to deny or substantiate the report while denying any knowledge about the said militant leader. The DGP had bypassed even the Chief Minister while bringing it to the notice of the Home Ministry. The elected government did not have any say on the issue of handling militancy though law and order is a state subject.

The fact that the security agencies in the state were reporting directly to the Centre was indicated earlier in yet another case taken up by Balwant Singh in October, 1986 regarding the inquiry into an encounter. Joginder Singh and Baldev Singh were killed by the Central Reserve Police Force on the night intervening June 21 and 22 in Jalandhar district. The inquiry was conducted by the Jalandhar Senior Superintendent of Police which held the CRPF guilty. A murder case under Section 302 was registered at police station Shahkot. The arrest warrant was issued by the judicial court. However, none of the accused was arrested. Balwant Singh brought it to the notice of state Home Secretary R. P. Ojha in writing saying "This is causing a lot of tension in the area. It is not only having political ramifications but also direct impact on our law and order enforcement machinery. People have started doubting the intentions of the top police officers in this connection". The area of incidence fell in the Assembly constituency of Balwant Singh.

And the confidential letter written by Amritsar Deputy Commissioner Ramesh Inder Singh dated March 12 earlier to the state Home Secretary was a telling commentary on the functioning of the security forces. He wrote that "The approach and attitude of the police is one of highhandedness. The general feeling among the officers, particularly the judicial magistrates, is that they have to fear for their lives not only from the terrorists but also from the 'uniformed terrorists', i.e. the Amritsar police".

The letter was in the context of the complaint from three judicial officers, N. S. Kundra, Judicial Magistrate, Tarn Taran and his two colleagues J. S. Chawla and Kuldip Singh who called on him on March 1 to express their apprehensions to their lives from the local police. They complained to the Deputy Commissioner that Sita Ram, incharge of Tarn Taran police station, had threatened to eliminate them. They also stated that the police official concerned was getting tacit support from his superiors. They had earlier brought it to the notice of the District and Session Judge on March 4. The Session Judge contacted the Deputy Commissioner seeking protection for the judicial officials. The Deputy Commissioner also referred to another case relating to the Vice-Chancellor of Guru Nanak Dev University who had complained against the Station House Officer, Sadar police station. The Vice-Chancellor had been directed to report and "surrender" at the police station in connection with the murder of a student on the campus.

The Deputy Commissioner, in this communication, also referred to yet another case in which the Sub-Divisional Magistrate, Tarn Taran, complained on February 27, 1987 that the home guards posted at his residence had been withdrawn his personal gunman was called to the police station and ordered to deposit his weapon and not to report for duty with the SDM. The SDM approached the local home guards commandant to depute some persons for the night but they were also recalled by the SHO. It was at the intervention of the Deputy Commissioner that the security of the SDM was restored.

NOTES

1. The Indian Express, February 7, 1987.
2. Quoted from the original resolution.
3. The Times of India, June 8, 1987 .

13

Design Exposed

The militant movement, during both the pre and the post-Bluestar period is characterized by one common denominator and that is the allegations and counter allegations of being instruments of the government. Sant Jarnail Singh Bhindranwale himself had come under such attack towards the end of 1983 and several political parties and even a major section of the media continue to portray him as a man who was propped up by the Congress (I). A news magazine in the post Bluestar period carried a detailed write up pointing an accusing finger at Raw and Intelligence Wing for masterminding the operations during the build up to Operation Bluestar. There has never been any proof of such operations and collaborations till the hand of the Intelligence Bureau was exposed by a retired officer in his memoirs. It is the broader analysis of the political discourse that can only provide the clue. However, nothing could have been more embarrassing for the government and those entrusted with the handling of the situation than the allegations leveled to this effect by none other than a senior police officer entrusted with controlling the situation during the second build up and it was Inspector General of Police Chaman Lal who exposed the designs of the Centre. The legitimacy managed by the Centre to Operation Bluestar through Surjit Singh Barnala is very significant in this context.

At the ground level, militancy and radical politics in Punjab were getting consolidated during this period. The militant organizations had deputed young women and unsuspecting old men to distribute press notes in Amritsar.

Certain developments during this period were significant in this regard. Continuing with the pro-active role in the religio-political affairs of the Sikh community, the clergy organized a convention at Amritsar on August 4, 1987 the call for which was earlier given by Akal Takht

Jathedar Prof. Darshan Singh. The political goal of the Sikh Panth was defined at this convention as the creation of an area and a political set up in North India where Sikhs could experience the glow of freedom. This political goal was in consonance with the new policy and programme of the party adopted at the time of the merger of the Akali factions earlier during the year in February. It was later clarified that such an area and a political set up would be within the country. The demand was justified as being strictly in accordance with the promises made by Pandit Jawahar Lal Nehru in July, 1946. The demand was also in tune with the Anandpur Sahib resolution of 1973 and the political goal of the party enshrined in the party constitution in 1974. It was just a repetition and such, a subtle move to dilute the militant struggle.

The launching of peaceful struggle under the leadership of the high priests was proposed to achieve this aim. It was during the pre-Bluestar period that the proposal had been mooted to carry forward the struggle under the banner of Akal Takht with the rider that Sant Jarnail Singh Bhindranwale should be appointed its Jathedar. However, it remained a non-starter.

The representatives of the militants disagreed both with this political goal as well as the means as they continued to advocate the use of the bullet and not the ballot for the attainment of the goal that was Khalistan which had already been endorsed at the Sarbat Khalsa congregation earlier on January 26. The political goal proposed in this convention did not synchronize with the demand for Khalistan. They warned that those who proved to be hurdles in the war for the attainment of Khalistan would be eliminated, thereby attacking the high priests. Prof. Darshan Singh asserted the "shastra and the shaster" (arms and logic) would have to join hands. He offered to hand over all the religious, political and social institutions of the community to the militants if they considered him to be a hurdle. He deputed Punjabi novelist Jaswant Singh Kanwal, a former Leftist turned supporter of Sikh struggle, to have talks with the militants so that the Panth could jointly fight for its honour and dignity. The Panthic Committee proposed that another Sarbat Khalsa be summoned if the high priests had doubts about the political goal of the Panth. The gulf between the clergy and the militants widened with Prof. Darshan Singh finally leaving the field open to the militants.

A joint statement on behalf of the Khalistan Commando Force and the Khalistan Liberation Force was read out by an unidentified young man maintaining the sovereign Khalistan was the political objective of the Sikh Panth which had earlier been approved by the Sarbat Khalsa. He appealed to the foreign countries to recognize Khalistan. "We have taken to the gun not as a hobby. It has been thrust upon us. The war will end with our victory. There is no other alternative," he thundered. A spokesman of Gurbachan Singh Manochahal, who was now heading a new militant outfit Bhindranwale Tiger Force of Khalistan, also chided the high priests for the confusion they were trying to create about the political goal and warned against such attempts.

Unified Akali Dal acting President Ujagar Singh Sekhwan stuck to the Anandpur Sahib resolution as the goal and proposed the Akal Takht acting chief should lead the movement for its achievement and if need be, a committee constituted to assist him.

The convention was attended by representatives of the five Takhts, the Unified Akali Dal and the Babbar Khalsa, both factions of the AISSF, Bhindranwale Tiger Force of Khalistan, Khalistan Commando Force, Khalistan Liberation Force, the Sikh International Council and the Dalit Front. The Akali Dal (L) had been barred from participating in this convention.

The AISSF headed by Gurjit Singh was to move the Khalistan resolution at this convention but the plan failed. Satpal Singh, General Secretary and Surinder Singh Kishanpura, executive member of the AISSF respectively, who were handed over the written resolution by Gurjit Singh, were detained by the police at a picket on the GT road near Tarn Taran bypass on way to Amritsar from Chandigarh. They managed to dodge the police but they could not reach the convention in time.

The Panthic Committee rejected the resolution adopted at the convention which was termed as merely the reiteration of the demand for Punjabi Suba (reorganization of the state on linguistic basis demanded by the Akali Dal before 1966). Moreover, it amounted to acceptance of the Indian constitution. The statement issued by the committee was a strong indictment of Prof. Darshan Singh. It stated: "Prof Darshan Singh is killing Sikh youth with the jugglery of his words". The committee warned the Akali leaders saying those who indulge in the vote bank politics would face serious consequences. The radical umbrella outfit also alleged connivance between the Akali leaders and the rulers in Delhi.[1]

Reacting to the Panthic Committee outburst, Prof. Darshan Singh announced his retreat on August 8, saying he had no desire to enter into conflict or confrontation with the youth. He pointed out that two distinct thoughts had emerged at the convention: one for and the other against Khalistan. While the majority favoured negotiations with the government, the militants subscribed to the politics of the gun. The former was a positive approach to clinch any issue whereas the latter only snuffed out life. He felt there was some hidden force out to engineer a confrontation with the youth and denigrate Akal Takht. These very forces which had earlier used Surjit Singh Barnala to defy Akal Takht were now instigating the youth to challenge this supreme institution. The blame game was on. Both sides were accusing each other of playing into the hands of the government.

During Operation Bluestar, it was the Akal Takht building which was attacked but now this supreme temporal institution of the Sikhs itself was under attack and that too, from a section within the community. The design was slowly unfolding.

Later, Prof. Darshan Singh blamed the "internal forces" for dividing the Sikhs to harm not only them but also the country as in case some outside force was at work, rather than weakening the Sikhs, would rather strengthen the community to fight against the government. His hint was very clear as he was blaming a section of the militant leadership.[2]

The AISSF (Gurjit) posed 10 questions to the Akal Takht Jathedar. Was it a fact that in May last, he sounded the Federation to be a party to the talks to be initiated with the Centre, but this suggestion was turned down and he was cautioned against such talks; the killing of the militants by the government increased after the AISSF turned down the proposal. While a number of Sikhs had been killed in fake encounters, he did nothing. Referring to the goal adopted at August 4 convention, the AISSF asked whether he had forgotten the goal of Khalistan and reminded him of the support he had assured to the struggle for Khalsa Raj when his appointment was endorsed by the militants. Further, was he not dividing the militants by issuing statements against them and thus working as Centre's instrument? The role of Prof. Darshan Singh had also come under the scanner.

The high priests, on September 9, announced the amalgamation of at least 16 militant organizations. The priests, Jaswant Singh, Jathedar of Takht Damdama Sahib, Sawinder Singh, Jathedar of Takht Keshgarh Sahib, Puran Singh, Head Priest, Darbar Sahib and Kashmir Singh, Head Priest of Akal Takht, said a new programme would also be announced shortly. The priests called upon the Sikhs to lend the militant youth their whole hearted support in their struggle for "breaking shackles of slavery" as after the Akali leadership having become irrelevant, only the youth could pull the Sikhs out of the woods. They maintained the Sikhs were slaves in India and would strive to achieve freedom at all costs. These high priests were playing the role assigned to them under the garb of providing leadership to the Sikh struggle.

It was apparent that the demand for Khalistan was being watered down. The high priests clarified that it was for the government to decide whether the Sikhs were to be granted "freedom" within or outside the country. Further, they said "The demand for separatism has grown out of the oppression let loose by the government" which was deliberately maligning the Sikhs, their religion and their places of worship. The high priests were not confronting the Indian state but only blaming the government. For them, the demand for a separate Sikh state was just a form of protest in reaction to the oppressive and discriminatory policies of the government and not legacy of the earlier Sikh rule which continue to nurture the ambition to rule.

They warned against the entry of security forces into the shrine saying it would be the last nail in the coffin of the government. This apprehension of entry by the security forces was the reason for the attack on the Akali leadership which was sharp and bitter. They said, "The Akali leaders should wear bangles, don women's clothes and stay at home" while women should come forward. They called upon the Sikhs to reject and boycott the Akali leadership. They did not spare even Prof. Darshan Singh, who, they said, had fled from the battlefield. His so called retreat from the scene was described as a foolish act.[3] However, Giani Puran Singh met Prof. Darshan Singh at his residence at Zirakpur near Chandigarh on September 14 and dissociated himself from this statement.[4] The SGPC executive committee, at its meeting at Fatehgarh Sahib on September 20, questioned the authority of these high priests appointed by the radicals to issue such statements. In an attempt to assert itself, the executive did not confirm the appointment of Jaswant Singh as the Akal Takht Head Priest. The SGPC seemed to be determined to meet the challenge from the militants. Unified Akali Dal acting Chief Ujagar Singh Sekhwan also attended the meeting to extend moral support to the SGPC against the militants. However, the writ of the SGPC had ceased to run in the Darbar Sahib complex.

It was not only the SGPC which seemed to be in a mood to take upon the militants. The Youth Akali Dal headed by Sher Singh Doomsheri, at a meeting at the SGPC sub-office in Chandigarh on September 25, posed a direct challenge to the Panthic Committee with the resolve to 'reinstall' Prof. Darshan Singh before Diwali. The resolution adopted at the meeting announced that Prof. Darshan Singh would be taken to Amritsar in a procession. He was urged to launch a peaceful agitation from 'black Diwali' for the 'removal of shackles of slavery'. The resolution made it clear the Youth Akali Dal would not tolerate any criticism of Akal Takht by the Panthic Committee. The Panthic Committee could not challenge the decisions of the SGPC which was considered to be the Parliament of the Sikhs. The youth wing alleged

Prof. Darshan Singh had been attacked on August 4 at the instigation of the Centre. Doomsheri had the backing from the Babbar Khalsa. He was subsequently gunned down, not for opposing the Panthic Committee, but fell victim to the rivalry among militant groups.

Prof. Darshan Singh hit back at the Panthic Committee on September 30 questioning its locus standi. The Committee, a day earlier, had issued a statement saying it did not recognize Prof. Darshan Singh as the Akal Takht acting Jathedar and issued a charge-sheet against him. He asserted he would not allow any confrontation in the Darbar Sahib complex. Those issuing death threats from the shrine could not be called true Sikhs. "I want to tell those who want bloodshed in the complex that if by killing me they can strengthen their leadership; I am prepared to come to any place they want, unarmed and unescorted, so that they can quench their blood thirst. For the sake of God, do not destroy the Sikhs through fratricidal war and spoil the sanctity of the religious places", he said. It was for the first time that the Akal Takht chief had taken such a tough stand against wrong doings of the militants and that too within the shrine complex.

The same day, Sekhwan and SGPC acting President Harinder Singh Tarn Tarani charged the Panthic Committee with playing into the hands of the government. Tension was already building up in the Darbar Sahib complex which was to invite another intervention by the security forces.

Prof. Darshan Singh, on October 2, alleged the letter heads of Akal Takht were being misused to extort money and that the presence of unwanted persons in the Darbar Sahib complex was a challenge to the Sikh religion. People were being killed in the Darbar Sahib complex itself and the bodies dumped in the debris of Akal Takht in front of the Manji Sahib hall. Such killings could not be part of the struggle for the attainment of the independent Sikh state. The situation was pathetic. Even the government did not move to dig out the bodies.

Queering the pitch for the radical politics, the Panthic Committee, on October 7, announced the formation of an 11-member Council of Khalistan "to direct the Sikhs in religious, political, social, economic and administrative affairs, besides looking after the foreign affairs of Khalistan". Headed by US based Sikh leader Gurmit Singh Aulakh, its members included Arjinder Singh Sekhon (USA), Tajinder Singh Babbar (Canada), Tej Pal Singh Dhami (Canada), Harinder Singh (Norway), Shamsher Singh (Akal Federation), Satnam Singh (Dal Khalsa), Gurnam Singh Bundala, Wadhawa Singh Babbar, Resham Singh Malmohri and Sakattar Singh (AISSF). One representative each from the Khalistan Liberation Force and a UK based Sikh organization were to be nominated later. The statement made it clear the council would have no truck with the individuals and the political organizations which try to push the Sikhs in the lap of the Indian constitution. Instead, it would strive to throw out the Indian forces from the soil of Khalistan. The Panthic Committee listed 10-point agenda to be followed by the Council: all council members were to be Amritdhari and Shashtardhari (Baptised and armed); all Sikh youth who had made sacrifices for the cause of Khalistan were to be honoured at Akal Takht; the council would form a sub-committee to smoothly run the affairs of Khalistan; no government would be allowed to be formed in Khalistan if it subscribed to the Indian constitution or owed allegiance to the Indian government; the Panthic Committee had the right to convene Sarbat Khalsa and reconstitute the council in case it violated the Sikh tenets; all council members would have equal rights and powers; in case the council failed any policy decision, it would be referred to the Panthic Committee; the Committee will call for bi-annual reports and present the same at Sarbat Khalsa; the council would help the militant organizations. The Panthic Committee sought the cooperation of all foreign governments to safeguard the interests of Khalistan. This panel never held any meeting. The move aimed at further marginalizing the traditional Akali leadership. This agenda again reflected contradictions as Khalistan was not supposed to be an autonomous region but a sovereign state and hence it could not be within the Indian Union. The Council remained non-functional.

The moderate stream of the Akali politics was also turbulent. Two sets of leaders belonging to the Unified Akali Dal and the Akali Dal (Longowal) respectively were "elected" as office bearers at the general house meeting of the SGPC held at Anandpur Sahib on October 16. The Akali Dal (Longowal) was left in minority with 48 members. Tohra was re-elected as President by the dominant faction with Harinder Singh as the Senior Vice-President while the other faction, at a separate meeting, elected Harcharan Singh Hudiara as the president. The SGPC is an elected statutory body constituted under the Sikh Gurdwara Act, 1925 and cannot be split as was the impression given about this meeting by a section of the media out to implement the grand design of the forces trying to damage the Sikh institutions one after the other. The media put up stories about the split in this statutory body. Columnists even commented upon the "split" in the SGPC. In the article captioned "Lessons from the SGPC split", Senior Communist of India leader from Amritsar Satyapal Dang commented, "Notwithstanding frequent splits in the controlling Akali party and mutual mud-slinging, split in the SGPC has come as a shock and something very painful for all devout Sikhs".[5]

Police Admit Fake Encounters

Though the first fake encounter relating to Punjab militancy dated back to 1981, the police for the first time, admitted to using such tactics to eliminate the militants. And it was a public admission. This was the time when the state government had launched Lok Shakti Samagams (people's empowerment conferences) to mobilize people against militancy in Amritsar district. These functions had earlier been organized at Mattewal, Khilchian and Mudhal in the district. It was at the Patti function that Amritsar Senior Superintendent of Police Mohammad Izhar Alam, for the first time, admitted resorting to fake encounters when he said that the terrorists who had committed five or more murders were killed by the police after they were caught. He justified such actions on the logic that the police had to resort to killing of terrorists as there was remote possibility of their being punished by the law in the absence of evidence against them.[6] Such functions were organized all over the state, especially in the rural areas.

Badal, Tohra 'ex-communicated'

The security forces thwarted an attempt by the Panthic Committee to organize a Sarbat Khalsa at Amritsar on October 22. However, the militant outfit, in a statement, 'ex-communicated' Prof. Darshan Singh, Badal, Tohra and Kabul Singh. It was asserted that nothing short of Khalistan would be acceptable. The Panthic Committee sought the intervention of the United Nation to end the massacre of the Sikhs in Punjab. The Committee nominated Manochahal as Jathedar of Akal Takht, Nirvair Singh as Jathedar of Takht Damdama Sahib, Dalip Singh of Takht Keshgarh Sahib and Darshan Singh as Head Granthi of Akal Takht.

The decision of the security forces not to allow Sarbat Khalsa raises one very pertinent question. The government could have taken similar steps to stop the build up inside the complex earlier also, even during the pre-1984 period. The irony is that the situation inside the complex worsened at the time when the Akali Dal government ruled the state. The law and order is a state subject but Barnala was just a figure head. Punjab militancy was tackled just by treating it as a law and order problems though the means adopted were questionable and undesirable.

The United Akali Dal leaders, at a meeting at Chandigarh on October 24, maintained the Panthic Committee had no authority to ex-communicate Badal and Tohra. However, this ex-communication was to influence some major decisions of these Akali leaders later, including the appointment of Jasvir Singh Rode as the Akal Takht Jathedar by the

SGPC. It is a different matter that this ex-communication otherwise did not have any meaning as only the Akal Takht can take such a decision.

The Babbar Khalsa had earlier opposed the Panthic Committee decision to convene Sarbat Khalsa. This militant outfit was refusing to fall in line with the Panthic Committee. Similarly, the Akali leaders, like Shaminder Singh and Manjit Singh Calcutta, who met at the residence of Badal in Chandigarh on October 19, also opposed the decision.

Prof. Darshan Singh finally announced his resignation from the office on November 17 after a meeting of the religious leaders summoned by him at Fatehgarh Sahib to discuss the crisis in the Panth, including the occupation of the Darbar Sahib complex by the security forces, and to chalk out a concrete programme of action. Announcing his resignation, he said he would not be able to perform his duties as acting Jathedar of the Akal Takht as he was entering into the struggle for the cause of the Panth, and was not sure when he would return. The meeting decided to stage a "march for justice" led by eleven religious leaders, including Prof. Darshan Singh, on December 4 from Fatehgarh Sahib to New Delhi to protest the inhuman state repression against the Sikh youth, maintaining the sanctity and freedom of religious places, action against culprits of November 1984 mayhem, release of Jodhpur detenus and the restoration of the honour of the Sikhs. The Akal Takht chief issued an ultimatum to the Centre to accept the demands by December 2. The march was to be followed by indefinite dharna outside the Parliament from December 5. The religious leaders coming forward to take over the command of the Sikh struggle was a new development in the Panthic politics, though the proactive role was not unprecedented. This march was part of the normal democratic political activity.[7]

Five Unified Akali Dal legislators welcomed this decision taken by the religious leaders. Satwant Singh Mohi, Arjan Singh Litt, Raja Narinder Singh, Jasdev Singh Sandhu and Rattan Singh said Amarinder Singh had all along been advocating democratic means. All these legislators happened to be supporters of Amarinder Singh.

However, even such democratic political activity, that too by the religious leaders, was not palatable to the government. The Punjab government on December 3 banned the 'March for Justice' after putting Prof. Darshan Singh under house arrest.

Badal, was released from his detention on December 2. In a statement on December 12, he demanded general amnesty for the Sikh detenus, repeal of black laws, end to fake police encounters, punishment to the guilty of November 84 massacre of the Sikhs and the re-instatement of the army deserters. Later on December 18, he gave a call to observe

January, 1988 as the anti-repression month by staging dharnas at the district headquarters.

The struggle for the establishment of Khalistan was already going astray as even women and children were being targeted by the militants. Entire families were being eliminated which triggered the migration of even the Sikhs families from the rural areas to the cities. The vigilante groups patronized by the security forces had successfully penetrated the ranks of the militants. The services of the militants were also being used to settle personal scores. Alarmed over the situation, the Panthic Committee, on December 17, warned the militants against the killing of women, children and innocent persons. For the first time, the Panthic Committee also came out against the killing of the Sikhs saying, "Whatever their political ideologies are, they are all Sikhs and we as Sikhs are up in arms against the government which, we believe, is bent upon eliminating the community". By then it was too late. It was such killings of innocents, extortions and molestation of women which isolated and alienated the militants, finally giving the upper hand to the security forces, apart from other factors. The so called militants would not even spare women in the house where they would take shelter for the night.

Khalistan Resolution in Presence of Moderates

In an unprecedented development in the Panthic politics since the start of the struggle, resolution demanding Khalistan was adopted in the presence of Badal and Amarinder Singh at the United Akali Dal conference at Fatehgarh Sahib on December 27. Moved by Gurnam Singh of the AISSF (Gurjit group), it was endorsed by show of hands. The AISSF spokesman made it clear that the objective of the Sikhs was Khalistan and the so called Akali leaders who come in their way would meet the fate of Harchand Singh Longowal. Of course, these leaders neither opposed nor supported it. However, their presence itself amounted to providing legitimacy to the radicals. Prof. Darshan Singh was also present on the stage. Significantly, eminent jurist Ram Jethmalani, then vice-president of the Bharatiya Janata Party, who also addressed this conference, pleaded with the militants to abandon the demand for Khalistan as by raising this demand, the Sikhs were playing into the hands of the government.

Besides demanding Khalistan, the ten resolutions moved by Gurnam Singh eulogized the sacrifices of Sant Bhindranwale, lauded the role of the Panthic Committee, warned the Akali leaders against betrayal, called for revenge against the police officials, appealed to the overseas Sikhs to extend support to the cause and demanded the release of the AISSF leaders.

Addressing this conference, Amarinder Singh called upon the Sikhs to be prepared for a long drawn struggle against the Centre in which they would have to make great sacrifices to achieve their objective. Badal said Punjab problem was not that of the Sikhs alone but of the entire country and the dishonest government at the Centre was not serious in solving it. His stance continued to be anti-government rather than anti-state, the line he had adopted ever since the launch of the Dharamyudh Morcha. Prof. Darshan Singh said some forces were determined to harm the Sikhs and their agents had infiltrated the Sikh organizations. His hint was very clear.[8]

The executive committee of the SGPC, at its meeting on January 1, 1988, rejected the resignation of Prof Darshan Singh. The meeting also decided that no one would be allowed night stay in the rooms in the Darbar Sahib area (rooms along the walkway). These rooms were occupied by the militants. However, this resolution could never be implemented.

The mass contact programme launched by the Congress to mobilize the people against the Sikh radicals during this period evoked poor response.

Apprehending isolation from the Sikh masses, the Babbar Khalsa, in early 1988, reacted to the crimes being committed by some sections of the militants by way of issuing threats to extort money or torturing people to death in the Darbar Sahib complex. The organization set up a reporting room in room No. 26 of the parkarma to receive complaints. Babbar Khalsa chief Sukhdev Singh said the decision was taken after a meeting with other militant organizations in which the disturbing situation was discussed. The Babbars viewed with concern the reports of entire families being wiped out in the villages on the pretext of their being police informers. There were also reports that turning mercenaries, the militants were becoming party to personal feuds and killing innocent persons for a price. The resolution adopted at the secret meeting posed several questions and issued warning. The Babbars directed that no one should be killed on the suspicion of being police informer without proof or without the sanction of the village panchayat. But then there were several militant outfits functioning independently.

The Council of Khalistan also later strongly took up the issue of the wiping out of the entire Sikhs families and administered a stern warning on March 31. The Council appealed to the militants to put an end to the killing of women and children as it was against the Sikh tenets. The warning was issued in a statement signed by Resham Singh Malmohri, Gurnam Singh Bundala, Shamsher Singh and Sukhpal Singh. The Council suspected government hand behind the killing of women and children. The AISSF, Khalistan Commando Force, Khalistan Liberation Force and the Babbar Khalsa had earlier issued such warnings. The council asked the Panthic Committee and the AISSF to launch movement to stop the killing of innocent Sikhs. It appealed to the high priests to expose all such elements. Militant leader Sukhdev Singh Jhamke also directed his associates not to kill Sikh families or extort money.[9]

Subsequently, the AISSF and four main militant outfits, on April 25, also joined the Council of Khalistan in condemning the killing of women and children and extortions. This condemnation was issued by its newly appointed convener Gurjit Singh while talking to select journalists. He carried a reward of Rs. 1 lakh on his head at that time. He talked to select media persons in the hockey stadium in Sector 18 adjacent to the Tagore Theatre in the heart of Chandigarh. The information leaked out to the security agencies a little too late. The modus operandi of organizing such conferences was simple. Only select news persons used to be invited and the name of neither the leader nor the venue would be disclosed. The journalists would either be picked up from their places or a particular point.

Release of Jasvir Singh Rode

A new chapter in the Greek tragedy that was Punjab was now unfolding as Jasvir Singh Rode was released in early March after about four years of detention. Talking to the newsmen at Amritsar the next day, he articulated the political goal of the ongoing struggle as "Puran Azadi" (complete freedom) and left it to the government to decide whether such an area was to be within the country (autonomous?) or have a sovereign status. Other priests who were also released with him included Takht Keshgarh Sahib Jathedar Sawinder Singh, Takht Damdama Sahib Jathedar Jaswant Singh, Akal Takht Head Priest Kashmir Singh and Akal Takht acting Jathedar Gurdev Singh. All four of them were flown to Amritsar from Delhi in a special government plane. In an attempt to establish the credibility of Rode and his associates, the government also released 40 Jodhpur detenus. He had watered down the demand for Khalistan in accordance with his brief immediately after his release. He had been given some specific agenda by the intelligence agencies which was to unfold later.

Rode himself was too cautious of the role which he had been assigned. "There was no understanding or pre-conditions with the government for our release. It did not find any substantial charge against us, and having realized its folly to keep us in jail, it decided to release us", he clarified. The priests, however, conceded having met Acharya Sushil Muni on more than one occasion in jail. The other priests had been detained under the National Security Act after they announced their support to Khalistan in September.

That their simultaneous release was part of the designs of the Centre was exposed later by none else than then Inspector General of Police (Border Range) Chaman Lal within a few weeks.

The state Assembly, under suspended animation ever since the dismissal of the Barnala government, was finally dissolved during the first week of March. The Unified Akali Dal, the Janata Party and the CPI assailed this decision of the Centre. Interestingly, it had coincided with the release of Rode. Reacting to the dissolution, Badal said, "The condemned prisoner has been hanged".

Within days of his release, the executive committee of the SGPC, at a meeting at Chandigarh on March 8, 1988, formally and unanimously appointed Rode as the Akal Takht Jathedar. It may be mentioned that till then, he was not an appointee of the SGPC. It was at the Sarbat Khalsa convened by the militants that he had earlier been designated the Akal Takht Jathedar. Significantly, Badal hailed the appointment in whose presence the announcement was made by SGPC Secretary Bhan Singh. The executive committee accepted the resignation of Prof. Darshan Singh who had been officiating as the Jathedar.

Badal had given his consent to the appointment following certain assurances given to him on behalf of Rode. Even otherwise, he had little say in that situation. Kuldip Singh Wadala and Satnam Singh from the UAD had met Rode at Amritsar a day before the meeting. He assured the two leaders that he would withdraw the 'excommunication' of Badal from the Panth and the 'dissolution' of the SGPC. His ex-communication along with Tohra had earlier been announced by the Panthic Committee. Amarinder Singh had also met Badal before the executive committee meeting of the SGPC.

Rode reiterated the 'Sikhs-are-a-nation' doctrine on March 10 after taking over as Akal Takht Jathedar saying the Sikhs were a separate "qaum" (nation?) and the government should take the initiative to honour the commitments made to them at the time of independence. He said the foundation of the Sikh goal had already been laid and only the manner as to how to construct the building remained. He refused to be drawn into controversy over the issue of Khalistan. He had formally taken over a day earlier. On the issue of parleys with the government, he said only the militants were the legitimate authority but the conditions for talks would be finalized by the community. He strongly opposed the killings of the innocents and extortions.

Expectedly, the release of Rode and other priests raised apprehensions among the parties in Opposition at the national level, which were not without substance, as the subsequent developments indicated. In Parliament, the Centre's move on Punjab came under sharp criticism. Indrajit Gupta from the CPI asked whether the government proposed to fight the terrorists and secessionists by rehabilitating them in the Darbar Sahib complex and legitimizing the status of the people who themselves were the supporters of Khalistan. Lt General Jagjit Singh Aurora (retd) said the government had lost its credibility. Balwant Singh Ramoowalia (Akali Dal-L) wanted to know whether the understanding with the priests would strengthen the secular forces or undermine them.[10] The designs of the Centre were later exposed by those who had been entrusted with the responsibility of implementing it. Significantly, Badal had reacted to the release of Rode and his associates saying, "We are the happiest lot. We have won the battle but the war is on and the fight would continue till the war is won".[11]

Rode addressed the budget session of the SGPC held at Anandpur Sahib on March 30. This development had its own significance as he had provided legitimacy to the body which had been 'dissolved' by the militants. The Akal Takht Jathedar is ex-officio member of the SGPC general house. Going a step ahead, he assured the general house that bottlenecks would be removed in summoning its meetings at Amritsar. He also charged that the agents of the government were indulging in killing of the innocents and extortions. This meeting was significant at another level also. The Akali Dal (L) group of SGPC members who had elected their own set of office bearers attended the meeting, thus recognizing Tohra's presidency.

It was becoming increasingly evident that Rode had sharp differences with one section of the militants. The Panthic Committee, on April 11, warned against negotiations with the Centre on an agenda which did not include Khalistan. "The fight for Khalistan is well organized and being fought in a well planned manner", said the statement which was issued a day after Rode expressed his willingness to do the spadework for a dialogue between the government and the militants. Rode had not committed himself to the demand for Khalistan. He had been assigned to confront the militants from within for which he was to be provided all the assistance by the government. The Khalistan Liberation Organisation headed by Atinderpal Singh who was later elected to the Parliament from Patiala in 1989 also sought clarification from Rode on the difference between the demand for "Khalistan" and "Puran Azadi". At an interaction with the media, Atinderpal Singh also denied the allegation by the Panthic Committee of the KLO being a government sponsored organization.[12]

Punjab BJP leader Hit Abhilashi, on March 23, demanded redeployment of the army in the border districts of Amritsar and Gurdaspur as the law and order situation was getting out of control. Congress leaders including Dr. Kewal Krishan, Sewa Ram Arora and Santokh Singh Randhawa urged the government to declare emergency in view of the manifold increase in killings. The Hindu Suraksha Samiti also called for handing over of the state to the army.

Political exigencies again brought the radical Khalistanis and the traditional Akalis on a single platform at the Baisakhi conference at Talwandi Sabo. Rode announced the merger of both the factions of the AISSF under the leadership of Gurjit Singh at this convention on April 13 and declared the Dharamyudh would continue till the Sikhs rid themselves of the shackles of slavery. The members of the ad hoc committee of the AISSF included Sher Singh Sher, Gurjit Singh Kaka, Surinder Singh Baba and Kulwant Singh Khurana. In a message read out on his behalf, Gurjit Singh said no settlement with the government which aimed at anything less than Khalistan would be accepted. He also warned that any Akali leader who ignored the warning would meet the fate of Harchand Singh Longowal. UAD leaders including Badal were present. However, the leaders of the Akali Dal (Longowal) were conspicuous by their absence. Rode's main thrust was on Panthic unity.

Addressing the gathering, Badal called upon the Sikhs to get ready for a long struggle for the fulfillment of their political goal. "We should get rid of every wish to form the government", he said.[13]

K. P. S. Gill replaced J. F. Ribeiro as the Director General of Police on April 20. Ribeiro was posted as Advisor (Security), a post that was virtually his marginalization. The timing of change had a meaning, as evident from the coming events. The government needed a high profile Sikh officer as a front man. He had been on deputation with Punjab earlier also as Inspector General of Police.

Operation Black Thunder

This was the time when the differences among the militant organizations had started getting more defined. The Panthic Committee, on May 5, came out against AISSF chief Gurjit Singh, accusing him of being in collusion with the intelligence agencies. The differences arose on the issue of the demand for Khalistan. The Panthic Committee had opened an office of the Khalistan in room No. 14 in the parkarma of the shrine. Rode also came under attack from Khalistan Commando Force chief Labh Singh on the charge of siding with the government. He alleged in a statement on May 6 that both the Akal Takht Jathedar and Gurjit Singh were the instruments of the government. He warned that anyone deceiving the Sikh community and deviating from the demand of Khalistan would be dealt with severely. A day earlier, Rode, while addressing a religious function on the campus of the Guru Nanak Dev University, had called for introspection by the militant organizations as to why the movement was losing support among the Sikh community.

The migration of Hindus from the rural to the urban areas within the state and to other states had intensified. Even the rich Sikh farmers started shifting their families to the safe places in the urban areas as the women were not safe. The most affected areas included the border districts. The Hindu Suraksha Samiti demanded deployment of army in the state for the protection of Hindus and financial assistance to the migrants. It was around this time that the idea of fencing the border with Pakistan was mooted by the Centre.

The build up inside the shrine led to its fortification again. All this time, the security forces had their pickets around the shrine complex. Yet, the smuggling of weapons was going on unchecked. The design of the government was clear. Most of the weapons with the militants now were the automatic assault rifles starting with AK-47. Though no inquiry has ever been held into various aspects of militancy in Punjab including the smuggling of weapons, some of the retired officials from the intelligence agencies have made startling disclosures as to how the smuggling of weapons was facilitated and people planted there.

The situation had reached the flash point and the provocation for the direct action was provided by the militants themselves. Deputy Inspector General of Police S. S. Virk was fired upon on the Western side of the shrine on May 9. What provoked the militants was the objection raised by the CRPF to the construction of a bunker. Virk had rushed to the spot at being informed about the construction activity. The firing continued for several hours and the walled city was placed under curfew. Unlike Operation Bluestar, the pilgrims this time were evacuated to safety. The strategy was to tire out the militants holed up inside the shrine. The recitation of kirtan and other religious activity in the sanctum sanctorum had to be discontinued in the afternoon of May 10. The action had begun. The devotees were allowed to come out from one gate the next morning. Amritsar Deputy Commissioner Sarabjit Singh had a meeting with Rode. A group of journalists had also been trapped on the first day. The operation was subsequently taken over by the elite National Security Guards. Rode along with three other priests and 26 of their aides were arrested on the morning of May 12 for violating the curfew as they tried to march towards the shrine from Gurdwara Santokhsar side.

The authorities made an announcement on May 15 for those inside the shrine to come out by raising their hands during the ceasefire. A number of people started coming out of the rooms into the parkarma. However, suddenly, about 50 of them rushed to the sanctum sanctorum of the shrine after crossing the Darshani Deodi opposite the Akal Takht. Rode was contacted in jail about the developing situation who advised the authorities to get in touch with Thakar Singh, the senile acting chief of Damdami Taksal. The situation was very tricky. The authorities announced ceasefire the next day again and repeated it several times. In the meantime, Thakar Singh was approached at Mehta Chowk. Another ceasefire was announced on May 18. This had the desired response. Karaj Singh Thande, one of the militant leaders, consumed cyanide while coming out. As he staggered out of the single file of the militants who were coming out, he was shot. Militant leader Malkiat Singh Ajnala and Nirvair Singh, a spokesman of the Panthic Committee, were among those who had surrendered. Jagir Singh, another Panthic Committee spokesman, had died during the action. Both Nirvair Singh and Jagir Singh had the common qualification of being hit men. The operation was over. Operation Black Thunder was in full view of the media, both national as well as international. A total of 46 militants surrendered, three committed suicide while several others were killed in cross firing. None of those arrested from inside was later convicted in the court.

The holiest of the holy Sikh shrine had been desecrated by those who claimed to be fighting for the dignity and honour of the Sikhs. The utensils kept inside the shrine were full of human excreta. The sanctity of the shrine stood defiled beyond imagination, not by the security forces but by the militants. The design had succeeded and Operation Bluestar had got legitimacy once again. This raises the basic question of using the Darbar Sahib complex for armed struggle, beginning with the pre-Bluestar period. Of course, the shrine had been the centre of political struggles by the Akali Dal.

Badal, Dhindsa and other leaders warned the government on May 12 to lift siege of the Darbar Sahib complex failing which they would stage a march on May 14 to liberate it. The government ignored the threat. Unlike Operation Bluestar, there were no mass protest demonstrations against the action by the security forces. This time, the so called militants had taken shelter in the sanctum sanctorum of the shrine and defiled it, provoking revulsion among the devotees. Nothing could have been more shocking than this. And the focus of the government propaganda was more on this aspect. The defiling of the sanctum sanctorum had been video graphed. The purpose had been achieved. Not only just that. Operation Bluestar had once again been justified and this time, there was no reaction from the Sikh community in view of the horrendous activities of those holed up inside the shrine. Extortions, rapes and killing of the innocents had already eroded whatever sympathy the militants had among the common Sikhs. However, though the operation was over, militancy continued for some years more with even the moderate leaders supporting the radical tendencies at one time or the other.

The state government sought 10 assurances from the SGPC for handing over the Darbar Sahib complex. These included demolition of the doors and windows of the rooms in the parkarma, concrete steps to prevent misuse of the shrine in future, formation of an effective force to check anti-national activities within the complex and the undertaking that the shrines would be maintained as per the law. The SGPC was to render cooperation to the government to check the entry of arms and weapons and set up police pickets on the road between the residential and office area and the main shrine. Maryada was restored in the shrine on May 21 which was opened to the devotees the next day.

Badal, Sukhjinder Singh and Kuldip Singh Wadala, who were arrested on May 14 while protesting against the operation, said in a statement released from Chandigarh's Burail Jail:

"The present situation has caused deep anguish and agony among the Sikhs all over the world. The recent invasion of Sri Darbar Sahib in succession to Operation Bluestar reminds Sikhs of their miserable plight and deplorable existence in this country. The Sikhs see no future in the present situation.

"The recent assault is in series of process of systematic and calculated design of the erosion and defacement of the Sikh value system, religion and ethics and tradition. The government instead of taking recourse to statesman-like solution to the impasse has taken to the extreme of suppressing and subjugating Sikhs.... The pre-conditional threat from the government to the SGPC is a challenge to the self-respect, dignity and the basic concepts of the Sikh life and also their right to administer their own religious affairs. The entire exercise is aimed at the usurpation of the control of gurdwaras from the SGPC, which the Sikhs attained after making unprecedented sacrifices."

The executive committee of the Akali Dal (L) adopted a critical attitude while holding the Congress responsible for militancy and desecration of Darbar Sahib. The party threatened to gherao Raj Bhawan to protest against the action of the security forces. Barnala and his associates were rounded up as they tried to proceed towards Raj Bhawan on May 16 in Chandigarh. The SGPC also expressed concern over siege of the shrine.

While in the aftermath of Operation Bluestar, the people had marched towards the shrine despite curfew and faced bullets, the situation was different this time. The reaction was mainly from the militants through the barrel of the gun. The militants opened fire in Rajpura killing five and injuring 19 persons on May 15. In a shootout near Samana, 17 persons were shot and 30 injured on May 16 while three persons were killed and 12 injured in Mukerian and six persons gunned down in Jalandhar district. In yet another shootout on the banks of Satluj Yamuna Link Canal at Majat village on the Chandigarh-Fatehgarh Sahib road, 30 migrant labourers were killed and 12 injured. There were spates of shoot outs all over the state during that period. As a sequel to the Majat shoot out, hundreds of migrant workers left the state.

The executive committee of the SGPC, which met at Amritsar on May 25, resolved that only the general house was competent to take the final decision on the letter containing pre-conditions received from the Deputy Commissioner for restoring the control of the Darbar Sahib complex to the this body. The general house could be convened only if the President and other members of the executive, high priests and other Akali leaders were first released. At the same time, it was asserted that that there could neither be any compromise on Sikh traditions nor any written assurance furnished. This was conveyed to the Deputy Commissioner by SGPC acting President Ujagar Singh Rangretta. The executive, in a letter to the state government, warned against creating obstacles in the smooth functioning of the SGPC saying some concrete steps would have to be taken as the Sikhs would not tolerate any more repression. Earlier in his letter of May 21, Rangretta had conveyed to the state government that the SGPC would extend all help to the administration to check the smuggling of weapons into the shrine. The SGPC executive had also passed a resolution giving approval to the demolition of the doors and windows of the rooms on the parkarma.

The executive, in a resolution, held Baba Uttam Singh and his associates responsible for the fortifications in the shrine complex and the stockpiling of arms. All this was done with the aim of defaming the SGPC and getting it disbanded. It said checking the smuggling of arms was the sole responsibility of the government because these weapons were being smuggled from across the border, transported on public roads and crossed numerous police check points and the security cordon around the Darbar Sahib complex. Such smuggling was not possible without the connivance of the government. The resolution decried the "dirty" politics being played by the government. It may be mentioned that a group of 'boys' associated with the dera of Baba Uttam Singh who were staying in the complex were allowed safe passage by the authorities during Operation Black Thunder.

Reacting to the increased killing of Hindus, the Punjab Hindu Shiv Sena decided to enroll 10,000 workers to gherao the Prime Minister in Delhi to demand protection.

Meanwhile, the Centre, on May 26, promulgated an ordinance prohibiting the misuse of religious places for political and other such purposes by issuing The Religious Institutions (Prevention of Misuse) Ordinance. The ordinance also prohibited the putting up of any construction or fortification, including basements, bunkers, towers or walls without permission. It was made obligatory for the management of the religious institutions not to allow the entry of arms and ammunition and the persons carrying such material into the religious places. The use of religious places for carrying on unlawful or subversive acts which promoted or attempted to promote disharmony between different religions, regional groups or castes or communities was also banned.

Akali Dal leader and Patiala royal family scion Amarinder Singh described the ordinance as blatant interference in the religious affairs of the Sikhs.

Sgpc Sacks Rode

In a bid to re-assert its authority, the SGPC executive committee, on May 29, sacked Rode and his associate priests. He was replaced by Harcharan Singh while Balbir Singh was appointed Jathedar of Takht Keshgarh Sahib in place of Sawinder Singh, Jagir Singh Poohla of Takht Damdama Sahib and Sohan Singh Head Priest of Darbar Sahib in place of Puran Singh who had replaced the Akal Takht Head Priest Kashmir Singh who was transferred to Tarn Taran.

In a resolution, the executive held these sacked high priests responsible for the sordid happenings inside the complex leading to the unprecedented desecration of the shrine. The SGPC expressed unqualified apology to the Sikh Panth for the revolting and inhuman activities inside the shrine complex and promised that the shrine would not be allowed to become a sanctuary for terrorists and anti-social elements. It was decided to recruit its own security force to maintain law and order within the shrine complex.

The government design was exposed through certain actions of the administration. This decision of the SGPC created a dramatic situation with the state government exerting pressure for the retention of the sacked priests. Before the SGPC could make the announcement regarding replacement of the high priests, the administration swooped on Guru Ram Das Hospital, the venue of the meeting, and whisked away all the nine executive members and its Secretary Bhan Singh. They included acting President Rangretta, General Secretary Mal Singh Ghuman, Shiv Singh Khushipur, Puran Singh Josh, Hari Singh Aarewala, Gurdial Singh Roranwali, Thakar Singh Khamanon, Hardial Singh Brar and Harjinder Singh Jagraon. They were taken to meet K. P. S. Gill. On return, Ghuman said the government put pressure on them against the removal of high priests.

Deputy Commissioner Sarabjit Singh, on May 31, on behalf of the SGPC, sought to deny the sacking of the pro-militant high priests. He produced a 3-page statement which made no mention of the high priests having been replaced. It was signed by five executive committee members of the SGPC. He said the SGPC people had no mind of their own and took decisions under threat.

The Deputy Commissioner advised the SGPC to concentrate on such matters like maintaining the sanctity of the shrine rather than entering into the controversial areas like the replacement of the high priests. The government's undue interest in the meeting was also indicated from the fact that some of the members were picked up in the night from their places and taken to Gill again. Rangretta was brought from Ramdass, Khushipur from Gurdaspur district and Ghuman from Ludhiana. The discussion continued till early morning. The administration failed to persuade the members to withdraw the decision sacking the high priests.

While the government was keen on maintaining the status quo by allowing the same earlier set of high priests to continue, the Panthic Committee added another dimension by appointing its own nominees. Khalistan Commando Force chief Gurbachan Singh Manochahal was re-appointed Jathedar of Akal Takht, "General" Labh Singh of Takht Keshgarh Sahib and another militant leader Avtar Singh Brahma of Takht Damdama Sahib. However, this was only an announcement which could never be implemented, thus making mockery of the functioning of this militant organization.

The Panthic Committee, on June 12, also branded Rode and his ousted associates as the government agents and accused them of misleading the Sikhs. It stressed that as the SGPC had been "dissolved" by the Sarbat Khalsa, these sackings and appointments had no meaning. The committee also appointed Darshan Singh Sahnewal as Head Granthi, Darbar Sahib and Dilbagh Singh as Head Granthi of Akal Takht.

The sacking of the priests had its immediate repercussion on the Akali politics. The Unified Akali Dal split at a meeting at Alamgir near Ludhiana on June 26 on the issue. The party expelled Shaminder Singh, MP, Manjit Singh Calcutta, General Secretary and five members of the SGPC executive who had signed their sack. The expelled members included Rangretta, Ghuman, Khushipur, Aarewala and Josh. Harcharan Singh Rode was appointed the new General Secretary of the party in place of Calcutta.

The meeting of the Unified Akali Dal presidium and council, while defending Rode, unanimously challenged the removal of the priests and charged Shaminder Singh, Calcutta and five members of the executive committee of the SGPC with playing into the hands of the government. The meeting alleged the SGPC had taken the decision in connivance with Union Home Minister Buta Singh, who had been excommunicated from the Sikh Panth. The meeting, among others, was attended by Baba Joginder Singh, Gajja Singh, Sant Ajit Singh, Harcharan Singh Rode and Baldev Singh Lang. Badal was under detention at that time. The meeting clarified that the priests were appointed at a Sarbat Khalsa convention and their appointment was approved by the SGPC general house and other Sikh organizations. A few agents of the government had no right to sack them. Sucha Singh Chhotepur and Jagdev Singh Khudian attended as special invitees while Mann was represented by his father Joginder Singh. Ironically, it was the government which was opposed to this decision of the SGPC.

The meeting, through a resolution, opposed any move by the government to dissolve the SGPC and threatened agitation in that eventuality. Through another resolution, the party warned against any attempt to eliminate the Sikhs, insult Sikh women and kill Sikh youth in fake encounters. The meeting condemned Operation Black Thunder and the ordinance separating religion from politics.

Mann Dissolves Akali Panel

Mann, on August 5, while under detention, dissolved the Unified Akali Dal council and all other bodies and appointed a 7-member presidium to run the party affairs. The presidium included Baba Joginder Singh, Parkash Singh Badal, Jagdev Singh Talwandi, Surjan Singh Thekedar, Gajja Singh, Charanjit Singh Walia and Sucha Singh Chhotepur. Walia was also appointed its Secretary General. The move was seen as an effort to end the Akali factionalism.

In yet in another significant move, Prof. Darshan Singh was reappointed the Akal Takht Jathedar and Calcutta the Secretary of the SGPC at its executive committee at Tarn Taran on August 13. Akal Takht Jathedar-designate Harcharan Singh was in jail at that time. Puran Singh, who had been released on bail earlier, presented his case to the executive committee for re-appointment. Satnam Singh staged a walk out from the meeting protesting against re-appointment of Prof. Darshan Singh without seeking the resignation of Harcharan Singh.

The Sikh political affairs continued to be turbulent. Despite the unity initiative launched by Mann, the Unified Akali Dal suffered split on August 25 with the dominant Badal-Tohra faction electing Talwandi as the president. The meeting was attended by three MPs, 18 ex-MLAs, 11 members of the SGPC executive, district jathedars and the council members. The meeting was presided over by Harcharan Singh Dilli which was also attended by Gurdas Singh Badal, Tohra's wife Joginder Kaur and Sukhpal Singh, son of Sukhjinder Singh. Shaminder Singh and Bachittar Singh proposed Talwandi's name. Calcutta said the decision had been taken in consultation with the jailed leaders. He said, "We have great respect for Simranjit Singh Mann but under the circumstances, we are left with no alternative but to replace him with Mr. Talwandi," who was requested to "leave aside his personal inhibitions and difficulties and come forward to lead the Panth again at the present critical juncture". The provocation for the split was the sacking of Rode and four other priests. Baba Joginder Singh had been insisting that the SGPC had no right to sack the high priests.

It was around this time that AISSF General Secretary Harminder Singh Sandhu wrote a letter to the Prime Minister from Jodhpur jail on the situation in Punjab while laying down conditions for a dialogue. He wrote: "Beware of myopic assessment of your computer assessed aides... no Operation Mand or Operation Black Thunder can quell the Sikh spirit or marginalize the Panthic ascendancy in Punjab. The more you kill, the more we flourish... after every police encounter death of Sikh youth, ten more Sikhs jump in the militant columns to replenish the cadres". He maintained the dialogue could be initiated only after certain preconditions were met which included end to draconian laws, withdrawal of corridor plan around Darbar Sahib complex, end to state repression and release of detenus etc. He said talks could be held with the government only by the nominees of the Akal Takht. Operation Mand was the action by the security forces against the militants holed up in the riverine areas of Amritsar and Kapurthala districts.

IG Chaman Lal exposes Rode, government

For the first time, the designs of the government were getting exposed by the very people who were supposed to implement them. This was with reference to the activities of Rode and his associates. Nothing could have been more embarrassing than Chaman Lal, Inspector General of Police, Border Range, questioning the actions of the government in Punjab.

In a move targeted at confronting the traditional Akalis, Rode, who had been released earlier, entered the Darbar Sahib complex on October

10 at the end of his 10-day march originating from Takht Damdama Sahib at Talwandi Sabo and declared that the political goal of the Sikhs would be decided at the Sarbat Khalsa to be convened by him on Diwali. He specified the agenda for the Sarbat Khalsa which included the Sikh crisis and the growing factionalism in various Sikh organizations, the working of the SGPC, the controversy over the dismissal and appointment of high priests by the SGPC, growing political interference and the political goal of the Sikhs. He marched to the Darbar Sahib from the samadh (memorial shrine) of Baba Naudh Singh on the Tarn Taran road, a distance of about 10 kms from Amritsar. The march was organized to get thrown open all entry points to the Darbar Sahib complex, removal of timing restrictions on paying obeisance and withdrawal of security men from the complex. The marchers literally gate-crashed the security barricades facing the clock tower entrance.

For the first time at the official level, an accusing finger was raised towards the role of the government in perpetuating the crisis in Punjab when Chaman Lal, on October 10, applied for leave following his differences with Gill over the handling of the march from Bathinda to Amritsar. And significantly, he aired his differences at a press conference. He also requested the government to repatriate him to the Border Security Force, his parent organization. He had been sent on deputation to Punjab.

"To me, the handling of Mr. Rode's march has nullified the gains of Operation Black Thunder. What was achieved then has been substantially eroded by allowing Mr Rode to enter the complex", he said adding the march should not have been allowed from Takht Damdama Sahib in the first place and the problem of allowing the march to enter the Darbar Sahib should have been foreseen. "But we were asked to wait for the orders from above", he continued.[14] This was the first ever exposure of the designs of the government by a senior officer.

From the day Rode's contingent reached Harike, Chaman Lal was keen on arresting the marchers but he was not given permission. He requested the DGP not to call him back. "I have no respect for such senior officers as cannot take the decision on their own". He said the DGP wanted him to let loose reign of terror. "My very consciousness does not allow me to harass the public who are basically peace-loving".

Chaman Lal was appreciated by Ribeiro after his retirement when he said, "I would go out of my way to find more Chaman Lals". He said this while clarifying his perception according to which he favoured more thrust on winning the hearts and minds of the Sikhs rather then depending purely on police operations to end terrorism.[15]

Rode and the Panthic Committee withdrew the calls given

separately for convening the Sarbat Khalsa on Diwali. The Committee also 'removed' him from the office of the Akal Takht Jathedar and re-appointed Manochahal in his place. The statement charged Rode with playing into the hands of the government and dividing the Sikh youth.

Talwandi survived an attack on November 29, a day ahead of the SGPC general house meeting. The attack was seen as an attempt to sabotage the meeting. The general house met at Amritsar on November 30 in the backdrop of the order of the Punjab and Haryana High Court prohibiting the body to elect new executive committee for which the elections are held annually in October or November. The general house allowed the outgoing executive committee headed by Tohra to continue while authorizing Talwandi to nominate the new body after the legal tangle was resolved. The house passed a resolution reiterating the supremacy of Akal Takht for resolving differences among various Panthic organizations. The House expressed full confidence in the leadership of Tohra. The meeting strongly condemned the Bill passed by the Parliament separating religion from politics and described it as a direct interference in the basic tenets of Sikhism.

Barnala Seeks Exoneration

There might have been a design to denigrate the institution of Akal Takht but within no time, this supreme temporal institution of the Sikhs asserted itself again. This was regarding the re-admission of Barnala back into the Sikh fold. Barnala finally presented himself at Akal Takht on December 5 to seek exoneration after dissolving Akali Dal (L). He also resigned from the presidency of the party. He was tied to a pillar with a rope with a plaque hanging around his neck which read: "Hum apradhi saad bhultay, tum bakshanhaar" (I am sinner. You are the forgiver). He was awarded 18 day religious punishment. He was ordered to organize five Akhand paths and sit through himself, clean utensils and shoes and sweep floors in a gurdwara for seven days. Ex-communicated from the Panth on February 11, 1987, he was finally readmitted on December 25, 1988 after undergoing religious punishment. He presented himself at the Akal Takht for readmission with the same plaque around his neck. After announcing his re-admission, Akal Takht Jathedar Prof. Darshan Singh took off the plaque from around the neck of Barnala.

It was not for the first time that the Akal Takht had asserted its authority in this manner. The only Sikh emperor, Maharaja Ranjit Singh, also accepted the punishment awarded to him in all humility. However, his punishment was then waived. The Nihang chief, Santa Singh, who was ex-communicated from the Sikh Panth for undertaking Kar Sewa of Akal Takht after Operation Bluestar, presented himself to seek exoneration years later. Questions can be raised about the practice of excommunication but not on the authority of this sovereign religio-political institution. The Akal Takht symbolizes the synergy of religio-political affairs of the Sikh community, the seat where the community used to take all the important decisions democratically till the coming into power of Maharaja Ranjit Singh. Ironically, the democratic ethos of this institution got eroded during the first, which also happened to be the last, Sikh Raj (Sikh rule).

The Akal Takht Jathedar strongly criticized the Members of Parliament who had taken strong exception to the punishment given to Barnala saying it was direct interference of the religion in the political affairs.

NOTES

1. The Tribune, August 7, 1987.
2. The Indian Express, August 10, 1987.
3. The Tribune, September 10, 1987.
4. The Indian Express, September 14, 1987.
5. The Indian Express, October 24, 1987.
6. The Tribune, October 2, 1987.
7. The Indian Express, November 18, 1987.
8. The Indian Express, December 28, 1987.
9. The Tribune, April 1, 1988.
10. The Tribune, March 13, 1988.
11. The Indian Express, March 9, 1988.
12. The Tribune, April 10, 1988.
13. The Indian Express, April 14, 1988.
14. The Tribune, October 11, 1988.
15. The Times of India, July 16, 1989.

14

Heading Towards Insurgency

Punjab was heading towards insurgency despite Operation Bluestar in 1984 followed by Operation Black Thunder four years later. On the surface, the situation seemed to be getting out of the hands of the government. Having been flushed out from the Darbar Sahib complex, the militants moved to other safer sanctuaries, including the riverine tracts in the districts bordering Beas and Satluj rivers, mainly parts of Amritsar, Kapurthala and Ferozepur districts which is also known as the Mand area. The plains of Punjab are not suitable for the guerrilla warfare.

Earlier in the late sixties and early seventies, Punjab was witness to the Left radical Naxalite movement which was also a sort of guerrilla warfare, hit and run, though the terrain was not suitable for it. The Naxalites resorted to target killing in Punjab but there was no place to hide. The activists were over the period picked up by the police and shown to have been shot in encounters, many of them after brutal torture. In the pre-independence era, parts of Punjab, especially the Doaba area, were rocked by the Babbar Akali militant movement which also adopted the guerilla tactics. In this background, the militant movement starting in eighties was not a new phenomenon in the context of political violence and similar tactics of target killing. The Sikh militants had also resorted to target killing during the first phase. But then political violence associated with this movement did not remain confined to just Punjab or target killings.

The state witnessed spurt in extortions, contract killings and unreported rapes during this period. The infiltration of the state agencies in the ranks of the militants was almost complete and this was one of the reasons for spurt in such crimes along with the criminalization of a section of the militants. What is all the more significant is that despite such distortions, militancy was gaining ground in more areas including some pockets of Malwa, especially in the Moga-Jagraon belt despite the fact that the movement was far from being well organized and lacked a central command and a charismatic leader who could inspire and motivate. Moreover, it had already started degenerating. Notwithstanding all these inherent weaknesses, the Kesari (saffron) being identified with the radicals had come to dominate the Blue of the traditional Akalis almost at every level in the Sikh political matrix. At the same time, certain developments brought the two streams closer like never before.

Satwant Singh and Kehar Singh were hanged to death on a wet and chilly morning of January 6, 1989 at 8.00 am in the Indira Gandhi assassination case. Their last words were "Bole So Nihal, Sat Sri Akal" and they were in high spirits. Their ashes were not handed over to their families. The structures erected for their cremation in the Tihar jail were also demolished immediately. Kehar Singh walked to the gallows with prayer on his lips. The capital punishment to Kehar Singh evoked strong reaction from the senior political leaders at the national level as there was no evidence of his direct involvement. He had been sentenced for his alleged involvement in the conspiracy to assassinate Indira Gandhi.

Four senior Opposition leaders, including Atal Behari Vajpayee (BJP), K. P. Unnikrishnan (Congress-S), Lt General (Retd) Jagjit Singh Aurora (Akali Dal) and Surendra Mohan (Janata Dal) came out against the hanging of Kehar Singh hours before the execution of the death sentence. They tried to reach Prime Minister Rajiv Gandhi to prevent what they said would be "senseless, inhuman and judicial murder". They wanted to meet the Prime Minister to ask him to convene an emergency meeting of the cabinet to review the earlier decision rejecting the mercy petition of Kehar Singh, as President R. Venkataraman had made it known that he was bound by the advice of the council of ministers. Rajiv Gandhi was out of Delhi. As they tried to contact Home Minister Buta Singh, they were told that he had already gone to sleep. They sent a letter to the Home Ministry seeking stay on the hanging of Kehar Singh. The government did not respond. "Everyone I have had occasion to talk with about Kehar Singh case says there is no evidence against the man, that what the Supreme Court and the lower courts have read into the so called evidence is a string of non-sequiters... in the Delhi high court today, Ram Jethmalani was at his logical persuasive best. But it was logic, it was persuasion, it was eloquence before a wall.... The court, but not just the court, the court on behalf of society, was just going through the motions", wrote Arun Shourie.[1] Jethmalani had pleaded the case of Kehar Singh.

The last futile battle to save Kehar Singh was fought in the Supreme Court. The apex court that heard two petitions during the working hours and a hurried last minute plea found no merit. "I am arguing under the shadow of two hangmen", pleaded Jethmalani. For two hours, Jethmalani and Shanti Bhushan tried to impress that the President had not applied his mind on the mercy petition. Their plea was that the evidence on which he was to be hanged was circumstantial. The five judge bench headed by the Chief Justice refused to intervene. These were the last words of Jethmalani: "If this court can't intervene then it is not just my client who will hang tomorrow. Something much more vital will die. It will not be Kehar Singh who will be hanged; it will be decency and justice". Shanti Bhushan said, "In fact, the court must decide whether a man should ever be sentenced to death on the basis of circumstantial evidence alone. Circumstantial evidence can never remove that last lingering speck of doubt about a man's guilt".[2]

In the adjoining court, R. S. Sodhi, counsel for Satwant Singh, argued that with his hanging, a vital piece of evidence would be lost for ever. Two Indo-Tibet Border Police commandoes had opened fire killing Beant Singh on the spot and injuring Satwant Singh immediately after the attack on Indira Gandhi. He only wanted the execution to be stayed till his evidence against the commandos was recorded. The court refused to grant relief. It was around 4.00 pm that a lawyer ran into the court of the Chief Justice, huffing and panting. He wanted to file petition on behalf of Satwant's parents to prove that the entire case stood vitiated. The petition was dismissed within a minute after the lawyer stopped arguing.

At another level, the International Commission of Jurists pleaded with Venkataraman to grant clemency to Kehar Singh. Commission Secretary General Niall Macdermot said he was profoundly disturbed by the rejection of pleas for mercy. Here goes the text of the appeal:

"The International Commission of Jurists is profoundly disturbed by the rejection of pleas for mercy which have caused deep concern among the jurists throughout the world. As appears from the judgment, the only substantial evidence on which his conviction was based was that he had talks with Beant Singh on various occasions but there was no evidence as to the contents of those talks. We beseech you to exercise your right and power to have regard to the merits of the case in order to prevent what might be a terrible error of justice".

Kehar Singh told his son on the eve of his hanging, "This has happened with the Sikhs before, it is happening today, it will continue to happen...there is nothing new in what is happening to me...And if by my 'Qurbani' the Panth can be strengthened, it is for the good.... I did nobody any harm".[3]

Inder Kumar Gujral, who later rose to be the Prime Minister, A. G.

Noorani, Kuldip Nayar, Patwant Singh, Rajinder Sachar and Rajni Kothari strongly reacted to the hanging saying, "All right thinking people in our republic must reflect with infinite sadness on the pass to which this land of sages and savants has been brought by those in political power. It is a particularly appropriate day for such introspection, since a man whose guilt was in grave doubt was sent to the gallows by the government incapable of making a distinction between right and wrong, between compassion and vindictiveness, between the majority and the law and the arrogance of power. It will take India a long time, if at all, to live down the President's inability to exercise his powers which the Supreme Court had clarified for him in its historic opinion of December 16. Through his inaction and his indifference to our appeal two days ago – and to the appeals of countless others – he has shown the world that India's head of state lacks the stature to step back and look at the responsibilities dispassionately and not – as he has done- with a desire to fall in with the voices of unreason".[4] (The Indian Express, January 7, 1989)

Shourie, in his article "This alone is repentance", described Kehar Singh's hanging as murder. He wrote, "A life has thus been extinguished because no one who could save it had the courage, the audacity to seize the main point. Even this is not accurate. It isn't just that no one who could save it had the courage or audacity to reach out. It is that no one who could have such courage, such audacity is these days anywhere along the line....And therefore, two three sentences will live on, long after the murder of Kehar Singh".... "The only judge is Rajiv Gandhi", said the shocked Rajinder Singh as he came out of the court room. "His mother was killed. By whom we do not know. And he wants to take revenge on Sikhs, on all Sikhs".....At last what had been the struggle to get this heartless system to heed the innocence of a man had once again become a Hindu-Sikh question. What a great tragedy. And the fools in this government don't have sense enough to see even this". [5]

However, in obscure Mustafabad, the native village of Kehar Singh about 10 km from Bassi Pathana on the Chandigarh-Sirhind road, his relatives were calm on the day of hanging. The relatives had heard the news broadcast by Radio Pakistan in the 9.00 AM bulletin. His nephew Gurmail Singh was reported saying, "People started coming to our house. Hindu brothers came to us. There is no difference between the Sikhs and the Hindus here".[6]

Yet there was another reaction in these words: "Why did the government act in this perverse way? Why did it refuse to draw a distinction between Satwant Singh and Kehar Singh? In a sense, the answer should be obvious. It was not for lack of sensitivity or moral conscience. All these considerations are secondary, if not irrelevant, in what is called politics. Kehar Singh had to die not because his guilt was incontestable. He was hanged because those who run the country were of the view that this is what would suit their political strategy".[7] The hanging of Kehar Singh was one case where leaders cutting across ideological and political barriers had join hands to save the man.

In accordance with the Sikh traditions, both Satwant Singh and Kehar Singh were declared martyrs by the SGPC and the Unified Akali Dal on January 8. This status was bestowed upon them by SGPC Secretary Manjit Singh Calcutta in the presence of Akal Takht Jathedar Prof. Darshan Singh saying, "We recognize them as martyrs because whatever they did was the direct result of the attack on the spiritual and temporal seats of the Golden Temple and the Akal Takht". They are now the forgotten heroes.

At the time when the radical factions had appropriated most of the Akali space, the marginalized sections of the Akalis were carrying on with the normal activity for survival. The priority for these factions was unity of the moderates to make effective intervention in the normal legislative politics. The Akali Dal (L) proposed to the Akali Dal (Talwandi) to constitute the working committee giving proportionate representation to all the factions. Under this unity move, assassinated Akali leader Harchand Singh Longowal was to be accorded the status of martyr. What influenced the activity of various Akali factions was the assessment that the Assembly elections were likely to be held by May that year.[8]

Unified Akali Dal leader Amarinder Singh met with Akali Dal (L) leader Surjit Singh Barnala on January 11 at the residence of Capt. Kanwaljit Singh to set the unity ball rolling. Barnala had earlier explored the unity moves with Jagdev Singh Talwandi.

Barnala, after his re-admission into the Panth, met Parkash Singh Badal in Coimbatore jail in February to discuss the Akali unity. The Akali Dal (Talwandi), at its meeting at Ludhiana on February 27, specified that the unity could be achieved only on the basis of political ethics and the framework of the Akali Dal for the last 70 years of its existence. A 4-member delegation from the Akali Dal (L) led by Balwant Singh also called on Talwandi. The resolution adopted at the meeting on the current situation stated that the party had always favoured peaceful and democratic stance in its struggle for fulfillment of the legitimate political objective and aspirations but the government had resorted to dictatorial and fascist methods to stifle the voice of the Sikh conscience by imprisoning front rank Akali leaders, Sikh youth and others. "The government is determined to sell out national interests of the Sikhs and jeopardizing the prospects of a lasting peace in the subcontinent", it added while blaming the Congress for creating Hindu-Sikh divide which was not only unpalatable to the Sikhs but also repugnant to their socio-religious philosophy.

The government released most of the Jodhpur detenus on March 7 following the announcement to this effect by the Prime Minister in the Parliament.

Balwant Singh Expelled from Dal (L)

Taking belated action, the Akali Dal (L) expelled Balwant Singh from the party for writing a letter to Indira Gandhi soon after Operation Bluestar on June 9, 1984. In the purported letter, he had given the undertaking to "refrain from active Akali politics", while supporting the army action in the Darbar Sahib complex. The decision to this effect was taken at a meeting of the party's district presidents on March 6 in which this action of Balwant Singh was dubbed as a cardinal sin. He, however, took the plea that the letter had been fabricated and he was in England at that time. Officiating President Tota Singh chaired the meeting as Barnala had resigned in December at the time of his re-admission into the Panth. The party, at a meeting on January 3, had rejected his resignation but he refused to take over the reigns of the party.

Continuing the unity process, Amarinder Singh, on March 12, announced the merger of the Mann, Talwandi and Longowal factions of the Akalis at Ludhiana. Talwandi was to head the merged Akali Dal with Mann as its patron. Talwandi was also authorized to nominate his working committee. However, the move fell through the very next day as the Akali Dal (Mann) refused to accept Talwandi as the president saying the announcement was not only misleading, baseless and ridiculous but also against the sentiments of the Sikhs. The statement issued by the party said Talwandi was a traitor who had toppled the Akali government headed by Badal in 1980. The Akali Dal (L) also backtracked from the merger.

Barnala was re-elected as the party president of the Akali Dal (L) at the delegate session at Longowal on March 20. This meeting also endorsed the expulsion of Balwant Singh. The party decided to organize dharnas at the district headquarters for three days beginning June 2 on the issues concerning Punjab.

Talwandi announced party working committee on March 30 which included Parkash Singh Badal, Gurcharan Singh Tohra, Sukhjinder Singh, Surjan Singh Thekedar, Harcharan Singh Dilli, Bachittar Singh, Arjan Singh Litt, Nirmal Singh Kahlon, Kuldip Singh Wadala, Ujagar

Singh Sekhwan, Balwinder Singh Bhunder, Sukhdev Singh Dhindsa, Jaswinder Singh Brar, Randhir Singh Cheema, Janmeja Singh, Amarinder Singh, Ravi Inder Singh, Balwant Singh, Harbhajan Singh Sandhu and Amar Singh Nalini. Parkash Singh Majitha was appointed the senior vice-president with Gurdev Singh Badal as the vice-president. The general secretaries included Dhindsa, Bhai Shaminder Singh and Manjit Singh Calcutta with Mewa Singh Gill as the chief advisor and Harinder Singh Tarn Tarani as the secretary.

Badal, while in jail, was appointed chairman of party's Parliamentary Board at a meeting of its working committee at Ludhiana on June 14. Talwandi was authorized to nominate members of the board. The party also constituted a Sant Sipahi (Saint -Soldiers) Forum to fight state repression and corruption. However, this forum remained a non-starter.

An Akali unity conclave was organized at Mann's native village Talanian near Fatehgarh Sahib in June which brought into open the differences among various factions as the supporters of the militants attacked leaders associated with Tohra and Badal. The members of the Akali Dal (T) and the Akali Dal (L) left the meeting midway.

Joginder Singh Mann, father of Simranjit Singh Mann, carrying forward the unity initiative, on July 1, constituted a 9-member committee which included Kuldip Singh Wadala and Surjan Singh Thekedar from the Akali Dal (T), Baldev Singh Hothian and Dharamvir Singh from the AISSF, Gurtej Singh and Sucha Singh Chhotepur from Akali Dal (Mann), Inderjit Singh Jaijee from the Punjab Human Rights Organisation and Jagmohan Singh Saini, an advocate.

Yet another attempt was made by certain forces to provoke communal violence when 20 activists of the Hindu fundamentalist Rashtriya Swayamsewak Sangh were gunned down at Moga on June 25. A bandh was observed in the state on June 30 which was called by the AISSF against fake encounters and state repression.

For the first time, the penetration in the ranks of the militants by the police cats and the extortions and rapes indulged in by them were exposed with one of these persons allegedly from the police hit squad having been accidentally shot in Batala police district in September. Jaswinder Singh Kala, was killed while trying to loot a family in Kaler Khurd village near Batala. A day earlier, K. P. S. Gill had announced that Kala had been dismissed from service after it was known that he was resorting to lootings. However, as per the police record, he was still working as special police officer till his accidental death. Kala had earlier disclosed in an interview that he and his 11-member gang had nabbed or killed about a dozen militants. His gang was provided assault rifles by then Batala Senior Superintendent of Police Gobind Ram, who was subsequently killed in a bomb explosion.[9] Kala case was part of the modus operandi which the security forces adopted to counter militancy in the state.

November Lok Sabha Poll

Continuing with its authority assertion, the SGPC installed Prof. Manjit Singh as Jathedar of Takht Keshgarh Sahib, Anandpur Sahib on September 22. Earlier, the AISSF (Manjit) at a convention had questioned the authority of the SGPC where the demand for Khalistan was also reiterated. Akal Takht Jathedar Prof. Darshan Singh strongly attacked those who had challenged the authority of the SGPC, saying it was part of the conspiracy to destroy the Sikhs. SGPC Secretary Manjit Singh Calcutta said the decision of the radicals to appoint their own jathedars was part of such conspiracy and those confronting the SGPC were challenging the entire Sikh community.

Punjab entered yet another significant phase as the Centre announced the Lok Sabha elections to be held in November. This was the first test of democracy to be faced by the radicals and their supporters. The result threw up surprises. This phase once again is to be seen in the context of degeneration of the militant movement while the radical politics appropriated virtually the entire space earlier occupied by the Akali factions. The radicals dominated the space at the time when the militants were getting alienated from the Sikh masses in general due to criminalization of the movement. Traditional Akalis faced total marginalization in these elections.

The AISSF, on October 19, announced the decision to boycott the Lok Sabha elections and then the Assembly elections as and when held but extended selective support to Simranjit Singh Mann, then under detention, and human rights activist Ajit Singh Bains. Rejecting the electoral process, AISSF General Secretary Harminder Singh Sandhu and the Organizing Secretary Rajinder Singh Mehta in a statement released from Sangrur jail said Operation Bluestar, November 1984 Sikh carnage, false encounters, torture of women and the black laws had forced the organization to fight for liberation on the pattern of the Palestinian Liberation Organization. At the same time, the two leaders maintained that the AISSF would try to use its influence to send Sikhs of high character to the Parliament and warned against interpreting it as a back door approach. The two leaders also appealed to the Damdami Taksal to unite the Sikhs to defeat the Congress (I).[10] While announcing the boycott, the Federation had virtually kept its option open to support to the Non-Congress Sikh candidates. The rejection of electoral process was just on paper as the first part of the call was totally ignored in practice.

In the Lok Sabha elections held on November 26, 10 out of the 13 candidates who got elected were supported by the radicals. Former Haryana Chief Minister Devi Lal contested the elections from Ferozepur and lost to radicals supported independent Dhian Singh Mand, though he won from a seat in Haryana. He was at third position after Jagmeet Singh Brar of the Congress. Devi Lal was in a way the candidate of the Badal family. Badal himself was in jail at that time. His wife Surinder Kaur was quoted as saying during the election campaign that the victory of Devi Lal could pave the way for the release of her husband.[11] At the personal level, the two families are considered to be close and that relationship continues to be maintained.

Mann, who won this election with a massive margin getting 89.16 per cent of the votes polled, the highest in the state, from the Mazha hinterland of Tarn Taran then considered to be the liberated zone, dissipated the mandate by taking up the issue of entry into the Parliament while carrying his sword. He contested the election while in jail and was released subsequently. Atinderpal Singh, former Khalistan Liberation Organization chief, who won from Patiala, also contested from jail. This election witnessed total marginalization of the traditional Akalis who were subsequently pushed towards radical politics to regain some of the lost base. Though no untoward incident was reported from any part of the state during the election campaign, the situation was characterized by fear of the unknown.

Here is one example of the harassment of the traditional Akali campaigners by the AISSF activists: "This reporter was a witness to the harassment of the Akali Dal (B) campaigners in the Rampura Phool Assembly segment of the Lok Sabha constituency (Bathinda) on Tuesday. AISSF activists came up in jeeps whenever the Akali Dal (B) caravan with 25 vehicles and under heavy escort, neared meeting venue in villages. They would then shout slogans for about ten minutes and leave. These incidents took place near the villages of the in-laws of former chief minister and Akali Dal (B) leader under detention, Mr. Parkash Singh Badal. Spearheading the party's campaign on Tuesday was Mrs. Surinder Kaur Badal, wife of Mr. Badal. She maintained her cool despite grave provocation".[12]

Sucha Singh Maloya, father of Indira Gandhi's assassin Beant Singh, who could not speak even a single sentence, had been fielded by the radicals from Bathinda. This author met him during campaigning who was being carried around by the AISSF activists. He did not utter a single world, what to talk of a sentence, even after much cajoling and he appeared to be sick. His campaigners joked that the old man would be all right after he got elected. They seemed to be sure of his smooth passage to the Lok Sabha. He defeated his nearest rival from the Congress by a margin of more than two lakh votes while Gurdev Singh Badal put up by the Shiromani Akali Dal could mange just about 35,000 votes. Rajdev Singh in the adjoining Sangrur constituency was again an unknown face, a lawyer who also won by a margin of more than a lakh votes.

Mann never entered the Parliament during the entire tenure. That was the time when his presence was needed the most in the Lok Sabha to take up the issues concerning the Sikhs and Punjab. That was an opportunity wasted which amounted to betrayal with the people who had reposed unflinching faith in him. It continued to be a matter of debate even years later as to whose design it was to keep Mann away from the Parliament. That was the time when he had emerged as the most powerful leader of the community. He got bogged down under the heavy weight of the confidence the community had reposed in him. And that mandate was unprecedented. He failed the Sikhs at a very crucial juncture.

Others who made it to the Lok Sabha included Kirpal Singh from Amritsar, Inder Kumar Gujral from Jalandhar who rose to be the Prime Minister some years later, Harbhajan Lakha of the Bahujan Samaj Party from Phillaur, Bimal Kaur Khalsa, widow of Beant Singh, from Ropar, Atinderpal Singh who earlier headed the Khalistan Liberation Organisation from Patiala, Rajinder Kaur Bulara from Ludhiana, Jagdev Singh Khudian from Faridkot and Dhian Singh Mand from Ferozepur. Within no time, most of these MPs became irrelevant to the religio-political scenario in the state, to be dumped by the people in the absence of any contribution made by them and went into oblivion. Khudian met a mysterious end as his body was recovered from a canal. The Congress returned Sukhbans Kaur Bhinder (Gurdaspur) and Kamal Chaudhary (Hoshiarpur).

Despite having marginalized the traditional Akalis and won with massive margins, these leaders miserably failed to consolidate their positions in the political matrix. Ironically, this was the first mass support to the radicals without any organized mass front organization and that too at the time when the ranks of the militants had been penetrated by the security forces and extortions and rapes were on the rise. Till three days before the elections, there did not seem to be any wave in support of these candidates. The situation changed dramatically in the next 72 hours. The traditional Akali stalwarts who faced humiliating defeat included Sukhdev Singh Dhindsa from Sangrur, Charanjit Singh Atwal from Phillaur and Gurdev Singh Badal from Bathinda.

At one level, the massive victory margin of these MPs was an indication of the consolidation of Sikh sentiment as the Hindu majority in the urban areas did not show much enthusiasm.

The post-election scene at the residences of the Shiromani Akali Dal leaders used to be interesting. The house of Parkash Singh Badal in Chandigarh would be deserted with only a couple of leaders personally loyal visiting him. His bedroom on the ground floor used to have an ordinary double bed and two cheap folding iron chairs. This scene was to change later for luxurious life style. The only senior party leader the originality of whose house, barring some minor alterations, was maintained till his death was Gurcharan Singh Tohra. His native house was the mirror reflection of his Spartan life style and corruption free politics.

The Akali Dal (Mann) rejected the suggestion from the AISSF that the newly elected MPs should not take oath till the government conceded some of the demands. The idea was to translate the consolidated Sikh sentiment into some sort of action to put pressure on the government at the Centre through the democratic process. However, in Parliament, these MPs miserably failed to use the democratic forum to project the issues concerning the Sikhs and Punjab for which struggle had been going on in the state all these years.

With the change of government at the Centre, Tohra, Mann and Badal were finally released on December 2. The radicals had appropriated the Akali space at the time when the two main moderate leaders were in jails. In the political circles, it used to be said that it was Ram Jethmalani who had lobbied with Rajiv Gandhi for the release of Mann and this was one of the last decisions of that government. Jethmalani had been fighting the case of Mann in the court. Immediately after his release, the Akali Dal (Mann) watered down the demand for Khalistan, though the slogan was raised time and again later.

The AISSF reiterated the demand for Khalistan at its meeting at Amritsar on December 5 while the Akali Dal (Mann) talked of autonomous Sikh region at its working committee meeting held there on December 11. This region was to include Dalhousie and Nalagarh from Himachal Pradesh, Ambala, Sirsa, Karnal, Guhla, Chika and Ratia from Haryana and Sri Ganganagar from Rajasthan. Akali Dal had been demanding this region ever since the re-organization of the state in 1966. The only difference was that in the revived demand, the government of this autonomous region was supposed to have the right to frame its own constitution. The party said the demand was based on the 1946 recommendations of the Cabinet Mission. The resolution passed at the meeting said the Sikhs of India were historically recognized as a political nation. The meeting dissolved the party working committee, district units and the frontal organizations.

A section of the Punjab militants made an effort to coordinate their activities with their counterparts in Jammu and Kashmir with the setting up of the Kashmir Khalistan Liberation Front, the announcement regarding which was made on December 2. It was claimed that an executive committee representing six Sikh and five Muslim organizations had been constituted for this purpose. However, this coordination was not carried forward at the ground level.

V. P. Singh Visits Darbar Sahib

With the Congress having been voted out of power at the Centre in the Lok Sabha elections, the conflict resolution process was initiated afresh. Under the changed scenario, the priorities of the rulers were supposed to have changed. Immediately after the elections, Prime Minister V. P. Singh visited Amritsar on December 7 to pay obeisance at Darbar Sahib, raising the hopes of the people for settlement. He was accompanied by Deputy Prime Minister Devi Lal, Home Minister Mufti Mohammad Sayeed and Foreign Minister Inder Kumar Gujral. He virtually created history when he addressed a mammoth gathering in front of the Akal Takht. He said, "I know the hearts of the people of Punjab are wounded. We have to balm them. We have to see the wrong that has been done to the people and the state and to correct it... I pray from my heart that the Almighty gives me strength so that with your support, we are able to solve the problem of the state.... Your love and my faith in you is my security. So I will not leave the temple in a closed car but would go back in an open jeep.... Our attempt is to carry all the people and the political parties with us. Dialogue is the only way".[13] Exhibiting moral courage, he moved through the streets of Amritsar standing in an open jeep. However, not much headway was subsequently made and it remained at best an emotional endeavor.

An all party meeting was held in Delhi on Punjab on December 17 in which V. P. Singh favoured step by step approach to normalize the situation in the state. However, Badal and Mann factions of the Akalis preferred to stay away saying some steps should first be announced to create an atmosphere conducive to negotiations.

Tohra, who resumed the office of the President of the SGPC on December 17 after about three years following his release from the jail, welcomed the gesture of the Prime Minister. He had been arrested in December, 1986 during the Barnala regime. Detained under the National Security Act, he was later charged with waging war against the state. This was his longest jail tenure and that too over non-issues. This was one detention about which he remained bitter. This also exposed the brutal face of the Indian state as there was no evidence against him, nor had he indulged in such activities. He disclosed later that an emissary of the Centre met him in Raipur jail and suggested to him to resign from the presidency as a pre-condition for the withdrawal of the case in which he had been framed. It was also conveyed that the SGPC would be replaced by a board in case he did not resign. Tohra told the emissary that he would resign provided Badal was brought there to be a witness. The matter ended there.

After taking over, Tohra tried to settle the controversy about the appointment of the Takht chiefs. He made it clear after his release that the appointing authority was the SGPC but suggestions from the Sikh organizations were welcome.

The Jor Mela conference at Fatehgarh Sahib on December 26 was significant as it saw the first major public appearance of Mann. He made it clear in the presence of Badal that he would strive for the achievement of the goal set by the Sant Jarnail Singh Bhindranwale. However, he did not spell out what that goal was while preferring to be evasive. At the same time, pleading for democratic intervention, he demanded elections to the Assembly, Shiromani Gurdwara Parbandhak Committee and the panchayat bodies. Of course, he favoured Assembly polls under the supervision of the United Nations peace keeping force.

All India Sikh Students Federation General Secretary Harminder Singh Sandhu reiterated the demand for Khalistan at the conference. Sandhu later became a victim of the politics of the gun. Badal stuck to the Anandpur Sahib resolution.

Making a paradigm shift in the matrix of radical politics, Mann expressed the opinion that the conflict would have to be resolved through the ballot box and the Centre should initiate the moves to take militants into confidence. Here was a total departure from the politics of gun.

From a separate stage, the Khalistan Commando Force, the Khalistan Liberation Force and the Bhindranwale Tiger Force hammered the demand for Khalistan. Resolutions were read out on behalf of these organizations from the stage controlled by the AISSF. Badal later left the company of Mann, who at the Talwandi Sabo Baisakhi conference on April 13 next year, announced the Akali Dal (Mann) would approach the United Nations for plebiscite in Punjab to find out whether the Sikhs wanted to live in this country. He said he had given in writing to the Prime Minister that "we will not live under the present set up and we do not accept your constitution". He reiterated that his party would carry on the struggle launched by Sant Bhindranwale.

The Akali politics was in a flux with no clear cut political agenda. Senior leaders continued to waver.

Demand for plebiscite

The government at the Centre was continuing with the process to evolve some sort of concensus and as part of this process proposed to have another all party meeting at Ludhiana. However, the Akali Dal (Mann) MPs, former members of the working committee and the former district presidents, who met at the Bhog ceremony of Jagdev Singh Khudian at Khudian village on January 10, 1990, decided against participation in the all party meeting which was to be held the next day. Mann demanded the dismantling of the oppressive apparatus in the state which was responsible for violence as a pre-condition. Earlier, as part of this exercise, an all party meeting had been organized at New Delhi on December 17. Mann received the Prime Minister at Halwara airport but did not attend the meeting, which was organized at Guru Nanak Stadium. Most of those who attended were the supporters of the Akali Dal (Longowal).

It was during this period that a section of the people from the academics including Dr. Pramod Kumar, Director of the Institute for Development and Communications in Chandigarh, Prof. Manoranjan Mohanty from Delhi University and others stressed the need for democratic intervention in Punjab. The February 16, 1990 statement issued by them said: "While early elections are a must, elections should not be seen as the only democratic exercise nor should they be restricted to sending representatives to the Lok Sabha and the state Assembly. Every other elected body, right upto the village level, should choose their own representatives, in what can only be a statewide gigantic but vigorous and health giving democratic exercise. Incidentally, any opposition to holding elections now or in the immediate future suffers from an inbuilt flaw and also contains a danger. The danger comes from stalling a democratic process and reverting back to the days when the crisis was compounded by shutting out popular participation. For this, it is imperative to restore people's confidence and create conditions for removing fear psychosis for holding free and fair elections".

While the November elections had reflected the consolidation of Sikh sentiment, the situation in the state continued to vitiate at the other level. In a belated damage control exercise, the Damdami Taksal, on January 9, 1990, issued a stern warning to the people who were resorting to kidnappings for ransom and extortions. Its acting chief Thakar Singh said such elements were misusing the name of the Taksal. The statement also called upon the militant organizations to deal firmly with those indulging in killing of the innocents and lootings.

The Akali Dal (Mann) announced at the Baisakhi conference at Talwandi Sabo on April 13, 1990 that the party would approach the United Nations for plebiscite in the state to find out whether the Sikhs wanted to live in this country. During his recent visit to Delhi, he had given in writing to the Prime Minister that "We will not live under the present set up and we do not accept your constitution". It was under this very constitution that he had earlier contested the Lok Sabha election.

He gave a call to the people to observe May 11 as black day in protest against the extension of President's rule in the state. The party decided to stage a march from Amritsar to Chandigarh on May 25 and organize a rally in front of the Raj Bhawan to protest against murder of democracy. At the same time, he continued to reiterate that his party would carry on the struggle launched by Sant Bhindranwale.

At a separate conference at Talwandi Sabo, Badal said his party was for giving more time to the National Front government to arrive at some settlement on Punjab and assured full cooperation of his party for this purpose. He was for early initiative as the delay would further worsen the situation. He specified the political agenda of his party as the implementation of the Anandpur Sahib resolution. He had already started demarcating his political agenda from that of Mann.

However, it was left to Tohra to lambast Mann and a section of the militants, the exception being the Babbar Khalsa and three other militant organizations, which, in his perception, were sincere, though he did not subscribe to their ideology. He threw a challenge to Mann saying a five member committee be set up to determine as to who the government agents were and also to go into the veracity of Mann's allegation that it was Tohra who had given the green signal to the government to go ahead with Operation Bluestar. He alleged it was Rajiv Gandhi who had propped up Mann. He recalled that Governor S. S. Ray used to say that he would produce a leader who would pose a challenge to the established Akali leadership. He charged Mann with playing into the hands of the government. His obvious interpretation was that it was part of the design of the state agencies to prop up militant leaders to marginalize the traditional Akalis in the 1989 Lok Sabha elections.

Holding former Akal Takht Jathedar Jasvir Singh Rode responsible for Operation Black Thunder, he said on the one hand, his party leaders spent long time in jails while protesting against this operation and on the other the Akali Dal (Mann) leaders were released within days. He described the so-called militants as thieves in the religious garb and regretted that the Centre was still supporting such elements. At the same time, he proposed that let Badal and Mann chalk out the programme for the restoration of peace and end to bloodshed. This was the bitterest ever attack on the militants by Tohra so far.

In a major action, former finance minister Balwant Singh was gunned down by the militants in Chandigarh in his car in broad day light on July 10. His two security guards and the driver were also killed in the shooting. Four militant organizations in a statement issued on the letter head of the Khalistan Liberation Force took responsibility for the assassination of the former finance minister. He was targeted for his role in the signing of the Rajiv-Longowal accord. An abortive attempt had also been earlier made on the life of Tohra on May 14 near Sahnewal in Ludhiana district.

The Akali Dal (Badal) organized a convention at Barnala on July 17 after these two attacks where Badal, while expressing total dissatisfaction with the National Front government at the Centre, announced the party would launch an agitation, as the issues concerning Punjab which the Akalis had been taking up all these years were not on the agenda of the government. The party announced the decision to stage dharnas at the district headquarters as part of this agitation.

The Akali factions were again in competitive mode. Within days of the Badal faction convention at Barnala, Mann, on July 24, served an ultimatum on the National Front government at the Centre to solve the Punjab problem within three months failing which the party would announce a new programme of action in October. He asserted a strong Sikh struggle was the only answer. He expressed his disillusionment with the NF government saying V. P. Singh, like his predecessors, was using the Punjab card to keep himself in saddle and to thwart democracy in the country. And interestingly, the party made it clear that the Assembly elections would be boycotted if held under the given situation.

The Akali Dal (Mann), on August 9, submitted a memorandum to US Ambassador in India William Clarke reiterating the demand for right to self-determination under the aegis of the United Nations. In the 19-page memorandum, the party dwelt upon the historical background of the struggle and the state repression. The party also submitted a list of missing persons (involuntary disappearance). In the 9-page open letter to the Members of Parliament also, Mann had appealed to them to "exert your moral and constitutional pressure on the government to enable the Sikhs to exercise their right of self-determination so that they can decide for themselves their future political set up".

Fourth Estate Under Threat

The fourth estate in Punjab was in for perhaps the biggest shock when the militants released a long letter written in Punjabi issued in the names of Sukhjinder Singh Sukha and Harjinder Singh Jinda lodged in Pune jail addressed to the President of India and directed the media to carry its full text. This letter was an endeavor to provide the badly needed ideological content to the militant struggle. The statement in Punjabi was drafted by the people who were well versed with both Gurbani as well as Marxist thought. At the ideological level, this was perhaps the only masterpiece which the militant struggle produced. This statement carried warning letters to individual journalists, providing microscopic details as to what they had been doing and writing. The warning had the desired effect.

Excerpts from the warning sent to one of the editors in Chandigarh: "Carrying each and every word of this historic letter is your responsibility....we have noted that you deliberately down play the reports related to the Panthic Committee. It is very unfortunate as you have the right to resort to constructive criticism but from where have you got this right not to give the deserving display to our news items. You are a Punjabi but victim of Hindu communalism. This is clear from your writings. We appeal to you to carry the letter of Bhai Sukha and Bhai Jinda verbatim in all your editions. In case you tried to ignore this warning, you might be safe under the protection of your gunmen but your reporters would have to face the consequences". It appeared that the covering letters were dictated by a person who had intimate knowledge of the activities of these journalists in Chandigarh and was part of the fourth estate. Such threatening letters had been sent to 14 journalists in Chandigarh.

Though the militant leaders themselves lacked any deep understanding of the phenomenon, it had become evident that some people from the academics and the fourth estate were trying to inject ideological content to the struggle. The 9-page statement in English issued in the name of the Panthic Committee, Khalistan Commando Force, Khalistan Liberation Force, Babbar Khalsa International and the All India Sikh Students Federation issued in 1989 under the headline "Further to the Khalistan Declaration 1986" provides the insight into this back up.

Excerpts from this statement which had not appeared in any of the main English papers: "The Punjab scene is a better description of the Punjab problem, which is itself only a segment of the anatomy of the problem-India and a specimen of pseudo-speak. It goes one better on George Orwell's New-Speak. Pseudo-speak is derived from Albert Schewitzer's finding that a 'brahmin has the courage to be inconsistent'. The caption of the book 'The Thought of India and its Development' is equally significant. Pseudo-speak achieves its multiple effect through double talk and separate sensatisation of different audience- groups... Thus when a terrorist is called, the Sikhs take it to mean, only the militant; his Hindu counter part, all Sikhs. Pseudo-speaks represents the inner most covering of the mystery, the Brahmin-hegemony which has still other coverings to beat Winston Churchill's, 'mystery wrapped in a dilemma inside an enigma'....

"There is a lot of confusion- created deliberately by the hegemonist Brahmin to keep his Sikh prey in a state of mental stupor- about the situation in Punjab. The Brahmin has not made any exception for Sikhs. He is the person who did not inherit the traditions of the ancient sages, of following the intellectual pursuits, shunning the power and the material wealth. He is the descendent of the degenerated Brahmins who established the caste system to divide the society and positioned himself at the most exploitive position. With his cunning manipulations, he fooled the simple masses to believe that no salvation could be achieved without his assistance. He established so many and such superstitions that his generations could live on the society as parasites. During the Muslim oppression most Punjabi families except Brahmins contributed the bravest and the best of their sons to the Sikh Gurus to defend their self-respect and the religious freedom. There is no wonder that there are hardly any Sharmas or Upadhyays amongst the Sikhs".[14] A teacher from Punjabi University, Patiala, was known for this style.

As fear psychosis engulfed the state, the Prime Minister, while addressing a rally at Lopoke in Amritsar district near the Pakistan border on August 19, announced that he would undertake a week long padyatra (walk) of Punjab to understand the problems being faced by the people here. It was V. P. Singh's third visit to the district after he assumed office. Expressing his commitment to restore peace in the troubled state, he said, "In the process if I die, my body should not be taken away from Punjab". He went on saying, "Goli se nahin, pyar se samasya suljhegi". (Not bullets, but dialogue would solve the problem).[15] This emotional approach again lacked in political content. This was the dominant tendency observed during his three visits.

At the time when the government in Delhi appeared to be reconciliatory and soft, Mann, in an interview, favored three choices to be given to the Sikhs while allowing them the right to self-determination under the United Nations supervision which included continuing the status quo, separation from India (Khalistan) and lastly, greater autonomy. He assured that the Hindus would have a place of honour in any future set up. His logic was that the situation had changed for the Sikhs after Operation Bluestar. "We are hurt and humiliated and want to exercise this right (right to self determination). It is for the government to feel the pulse and agree or face this kind of bloody situation. After all, the young men are not dying each passing day for nothing".[16] However, the parameters of autonomy were not defined and moreover, this was not a new demand and the Akali Dal agitation launched in 1982 was for state autonomy.

He was all the time trying to give out signals that he was the only Akali leader who was relevant to the situation in Punjab and acceptable to the radicals. However, the command of the militant groups was elsewhere and again it was not unified. Moreover, his graph had already started falling.

Mann Quits as President

The Panthic Committee, in a statement issued on August 20, made it clear it would not recognize any Akali Dal or individual who followed the Parliamentary path to come to power. In a policy statement, the Committee said it was of the firm view that even those leaders, who had discarded the Anandpur Sahib resolution and demand the right to self-determination, were not clear about the basic difference between the Anandpur Sahib Resolution and this demand. It said in case an honest and unbiased analysis of the approach of the Akali leaders, their political background and their activities was done, it would be clear that adopting hard line was part of their strategy and tactics. With this approach, on the one hand, the militants could be kept on the right side or muted while on the other, the government could be pressured to go in for Assembly elections. The committee regretted that some leaders of the party demanding right to self-determination were active collecting money in foreign countries to contest elections. It was a direct attack on Mann's leadership.

There was a dramatic reaction to this statement of the Panthic Committee and Mann handed over his resignation to this author in the presence of his press secretary M. J. Singh at Punjab Bhavan, the Punjab government guest house in Chandigarh, who requested that two hours be given for reconsideration. However, Mann was adamant. M. J. Singh telephoned exactly after two hours making the final announcement about Mann's resignation. Mann said in an emotional outburst, "Having found myself under attack from the Government of India, the CPI, the CPI (M), the Congress, the Janata Party, stooges of the government within the Panth, the Panthic Committee having questioned my bona fide is the last straw. For an honourable person who has served the Panth selflessly, there is no other option but to tender my resignation". However, the executive committee and the district presidents of the party at a meeting at Chandigarh on August 23, as expected, rejected his resignation.

In yet another dramatic development, the Panthic Committee and the four associate militant organizations, on August 23, clarified they had nothing against Mann. These militant organizations included the Babbar Khalsa, Khalistan Commando Force, Khalistan Liberation Force and the Sikh Students Federation (Daljit). The statement said Mann was sincere but emotional. The statement denounced the MPs including Rajdev Singh, Atinderpal Singh, Rajinder Kaur Bulara, Bimal Kaur Khalsa and party General Secretary Gurtej Singh. It was part of the damage control exercise as Mann was trying to provide some sort of legitimacy to them.

Boycott of Assembly Poll

It was in this background that Akali Dal (Mann) announced the decision to boycott the Assembly elections as and when held, at a meeting of the executive committee and the district presidents at Amritsar on August 29. The resolution said, "If and when the Assembly election is held in Punjab, it would have to be under the auspices of the United Nations and that too for self-determination for the Sikhs". Describing Operation Bluestar as the first war of independence of the Sikhs, the resolution said the Indian state had violated all norms of global law and internationally accepted human rights conventions and covenants. "All options, therefore, have been foreclosed", it said. Another resolution described the proposed move to revive the state Assembly as shameful demonstration of the ill intentions of the government at the Centre which was bent upon killing the democratic process. The resolution stressed that as part of the conflict resolution process and to put an end to bloodshed, the government should initiate peace and friendship talks with the Sikhs as "Punjab cannot remain colony of India". The party also termed the proposed Punjab march of the Prime Minister V. P. Singh as a farce saying the Sikhs were now clever enough to see through the nefarious designs and policies of the government. Pandering to the militants, Akali Dal (Mann) was again opting for the hard line. Though it was the Akali Dal (Mann) which had adoptred the resolution for poll boycott, Mann later used to blame Badal for its implementation as he himself was said to have had a rethink.

While Mann opted for this line, Amarinder Singh, in an article on October 15, 1990, demarcated the traditional Akalis boldly from the radicals. He stated: "The Options before the Sikhs today are two: To follow the path of the 'Panthic Committee' or ours. The time has come for introspection. We can either choose peace in the state that would ensure prosperity and the economic future of our people, and security to the 40 lakh Sikhs living outside Punjab, or succumb to the threats made by the Panthic Committee from time to time, in the hope of subduing dissent...

"Have we forgotten why the Khalsa was baptized? Was it not to fight tyranny and repression, to protect the poor and the weak, to safeguard all who wished to practice their religion in the oppressive and intolerant regime of Aurengzeb. And today these militant organizations, led by the Panthic Committee, who have taken up arms in the name of the Khalsa, are doing exactly the opposite of what Sri Guru Gobind Singhji asked his Khalsa to fight for".

He made this distinction a few weeks after the Panthic Committee had issued an ultimatum to the judges, the lawyers, Amarinder Singh (as his name was being mentioned to head the government in the event of the revival of the Assembly), and to the members of the state Assembly under animated suspension. The Committee threatened them with dire consequences and physical elimination if the judges gave a verdict in favour of revival of the Assembly. The judgment on this issue was being awaited at that time. The Panthic Committee was opposed to the revival of the legislature. The Assembly had been placed under suspended animation at the time of the Barnala government in 1987. A petition had been filed in the Punjab and Haryana High Court for the revival of the Assembly.

He wrote: "The Sikhs have remained quiet spectator for too long. The time has now come out to speak and act. We have never in the past kept quiet in the face of tyranny, and if we do so now we shall be turning our back to the teachings of our 10th Guru. Cowardice is not part of our heritage. Neither is silence in the face of the gun... time has come to recall our heritage and our glorious past and to stand for what we believe in".[17]

The Panthic Committee hit back on November 19, describing Amarinder Singh's views as Brahmanical perspective. Succumbing to the pressure, the newspaper, which had published Amarinder Singh's article, carried full text of the Panthic Committee rejoinder with the heading "We remember our heritage". Excerpts from the rejoinder: "The writing is alienated from the deeper and sensitive springs of human consciousness. Its each invisible layer is infected by spiritual poverty and helplessness because it interprets the present crisis from a Brahmanical perspective. For this reason, the Committee cannot take this article seriously....

"When Amarinder Singh claims that his elders were blessed by the Sixth and the Tenth Guru, he is only explaining the word blessing in the Brahamnical sense, which does not fall within the Khalsa tradition. If any elder of Amarinder Singh did receive the blessings of the Gurus, as he claims, then those should have left their mark on the successors who had been doing all that was forbidden by the Guru. If the blessings always become a monopoly and go by heredity in the family, what will you say of Guru Arjan's brother Prithi born in the same family? Where will one place the relatives of the Guru: Dhir Malis and Ramrayas who throughout their lives kept hatching conspiracies against the Guru...

"When the beloved ones of the 10th Guru were confronting the Afghan invader Abdali head on, Amarinder Singh's ancestor Baba Ala Singh had submitted to the invader already and that also under humiliating conditions...

"When the Khalsa was waging its decisive battle with the British imperial army and needed reinforcement, Amarinder's family was helping the British. When the Praja Mandal movement started, every one now knows, this family unleashed a storm of cruelty to crush the movement....

"All know that Abdali had conferred upon Ala Singh various honours for having betrayed the Khalsa army. He was considered most efficient as an informer and honoured with the title Rajaye-Rajgan-Bahadur. Another king of the family was rewarded with the title 'Daulte-Englishia' by the British. Now Amarinder Singh is restless to manipulate the Nawabi (chief ministership) with the support of Delhi...

"The Panthic Committee is witnessing in the 20th century the form of same Ala Singh in Amarinder Singh. Our question to the Khalsa Panth is: should we absorb the same heritage into our veins! In all humility, we wish to submit that when the soldiers of a nation undertake the task of fighting the struggle for freedom, their guiding centre is the region in which their nation dwells. Our centre cannot be Lahore or Islamabad because in dependence one can last only for a short while, but we have been fighting for the last 10 years and everyday we have become stronger...

"The charming lord of lies is also eager to dispose of the Taksal in his favour. Now by claiming his closeness to the Taksal, he is also preparing to become the liberator of the militants. He acknowledges the Taksal as an 'historical and religious institution' and calls Baba Thakar Singh as supreme religious individual. If he is so devoted and faithful to Taksal, then he should stick to his position and pay attention to us when we say that at the congregation convened by the Taksal on January 26, 1986, at Akal Takht, he was called "serpent in fold" (bukkal da sapp). If Amarinder Singh has suddenly developed such great faith in Baba Thakar Singh, then why does he not do something to get from him a verdict against us?"

Operation Mother Tongue

After making intervention in the social life of the people by way of implementing the social code, the militants turned towards the government. The Panthic Committee, on December 4, forced its intervention directing the Punjab government to use Punjabi in the official work at all levels. All official work was to be done in Punjabi with effect from December 10. Correspondence with the Centre and other states would be done in Punjabi and English translation of the correspondence attached. In an effort to promote Punjabi, the Panthic Committee announced special pay of Rs. 250 to Punjabi teacher in school, Rs. 400 to school lecturer and Rs. 500 per month to the college lecturer. The Punjabi teachers were to be given preference in promotion. All the sign boards were to be painted in Punjabi followed by English. Hindi was not to be used at all. All the universities in Punjab, including the Panjab University at Chandigarh, were "directed" to set up special Punjabi chairs. Every office, school and college library was to subscribe to two Punjabi dailies. Even the courts were to follow these instructions. The study of Urdu was also to be encouraged. The intervention included the policy on education, particularly with reference to the introduction of English, Urdu and Hindi in schools. It had its desired effect.

In an effort to create scare in the administration, All India Radio's handicapped station director in Chandigarh R. K. Talib was shot dead in front of his house. In a statement issued on December 10, the Panthic Committee owned responsibility for this killing as part of "Operation Mother Language" while clarifying that the militant organizations had no personal enmity with Talib or his family and the action was purely symbolic. These five militant organizations maintained they were not opposed to any other language but had only given a befitting reply to the conspiracies of Brahamnism and Arya Samajis to abolish the Punjabi language from its own land. Such actions of the so called Khalistani freedom fighters only invited revulsion.

As per the directive issued by the militants, the Jalandhar and Chandigarh radio stations, the proposed Patiala radio station and any other future station would broadcast all programmes in Punjabi. Punjabi language would have the same status as enjoyed by Tamil in the Southern state of Tamil Nadu. Only those producers were to be recruited who loved Punjabi culture and were fully conversant with its various facets. No announcement from these stations was to be made in Hindi or any other language. Jalandhar Doordarshan would carry only Punjabi captions. The other option was English. The programmes would be impartial. Delhi Doordarshan was also called upon to follow the same code as had been announced for the print media. "The five militant organizations appealed to journalist brethren not to be misled by officers living in the comfortable bungalows of Delhi and their camp followers among journalists as they were preparing the ground for deployment, once again, of the army in Punjab. Dang-Anand-Surjit and the Hind Samachar group were fully engaged in making this conspiracy a success and wanted to use journalists for their narrow ends".[18] The AIR, Chandigarh, switched over to Punjabi overnight.

The Committee issued a statement on December 14 against the deployment of army in the state and called upon the Punjabis, irrespective of their caste or creed to oppose it and appealed to the bureaucracy not to extend any cooperation to the army. Excerpts from the statement: "The Panthic Committee feels that Mr. Rajiv Gandhi has at last succeeded in using Mr. Chandra Shekhar for his nefarious designs. He has made it known to the Sikhs that Mr. Chandra Shekhar has gone two steps ahead of him by deploying the army. Besides the political moves of Mr. Gandhi, something more is being cooked in Delhi. Brahmanism has so much come to dominate in the North that it does not matter as to who is in power in Delhi as the fate and future of dalits and the minorities is decided by the enemies of the human rights. To crush the Sikh struggle with the help of the army is part of this scheme. After coming to power, Mr. Chandra Shekhar has changed. He is no different from Mr. Rajiv Gandhi or Mr. V. P. Singh....The Panthic Committee makes it clear that it has no enmity with the Hindus or others. They are all free citizens of Khalistan and contribute to its achievement as they have roots in this soil. The Hindus should stand up and revolt against their leadership which is a votary of deployment of the army".

Yet another statement was issued on December 16 against censorship imposed in the region by the government. It said, "The Committee has made it clear that if the government tried to project its own point of view only, the five militant organizations would retaliate by imposing complete censorship which would mean that no newspaper would be allowed to be published from the state. Nor would any paper published from outside be allowed in the state. Additionally, the radio and Doordarshan stations would be shut down. Not only this, special sacrifice squads will destroy the entire communication system of the Indian government in the state...

"The newspaper offices would be forced to close since no senior officer of the government would be party to the censorship decision. Nor would he depute any of his juniors to go to the newspaper offices as censors. Radio and Doordarshan staff would not cooperate with the authorities at all and a Jammu and Kashmir like situation would be obtained where there would be no division between the senior officers and the masses...

"The committee commended the action of Mr. Rrajendran Nair, Secretary, Public Relations department, in proceeding on leave and refusing to issue press notes in Hindi and English....no press notes are issued in Tamil Nadu and Andhra Pradesh in Hindi.... The committee appealed to the people not to link language with religion".

The statement was issued in the names of Wadhawa Singh, Sohan Singh, Harminder Singh Sultanwind, Mehal Singh and Satinderpal Singh.

The Panthic Committee also made an attempt to dictate the rural economy when it appealed to the peasantry to go in for crop diversification through a statement issued on December 9, 1990. The cultivation of wheat and paddy was discouraged. However, the farmers owning upto 7 acres of land were exempted from this directive. The farmers with 10 acre holding were to reduce the cultivation of wheat by one acre and that of paddy by half an acre and so on. The effort was to use food as a weapon as Punjab made the biggest contribution to the central food pool. This was to be done in phases. The violators were to be fined. It may be recalled that the Akali Dal had earlier also decided to use food grains as weapon by blocking the movement of trains carrying foodgrains to other states from June 3, 1984 on the eve of Operation Bluestar.

Two different sets of statements were being released in the name of the Panthic Committee, one on the letter head of the 'Panthak Committee' and the other on plain paper. The handwriting on all the press notes issued by the Panthak Committee was identical, so was the case with most of the statements on plain paper. The statements being issued on plain paper were being considered to be genuine as these statements had the same style and polished language as used in the statement issued in the name of Sukhjinder Singh Sukha and Harjinder Singh Jinda. Some people considered to be in the camp of Manochahal were releasing the other set of statements on the Panthak Committee letter head.

Yet another directive was issued by the Panthic Committee on December 18 to the post offices to stamp the post with Khalistan stamp.

Issued in this series in the name of the Panthic Committee was another set of 'guidelines' and 'directives' to the Panjab University and the Chandigarh administration. The militant umbrella organization 'sacked' Panjab university Vice-chancellor Dr. R. P. Bamba for not implementing the earlier directive on the use of Punjabi in official work and ignoring members of the Sikh community in matter of recruitment. Only the Sikhs and the Dalits in 80:20 ratios were to be recruited during the next 10 years to end the distortion in recruitment. The recruitment of Hindus was to be considered only after the balance between the Hindu and the Sikh employees was reached as the University had only about 2 per cent Sikhs. The Committee held the Arya Samaj grip over the University responsible for such distortion in recruitment pattern.

Earlier, the Bhindranwala Tiger Force, Khalistan Commando Force, Sikh Students Federation and the Dashmesh Regiment of Khalistan issued a directive on December 5 that Guru Granth Sahib be installed on the Panjabi University campus at Patiala within 15 days. The Sikh students who had gone apostate were called upon to return to the Sikh fold and start observing maryada. The women students, including in the colleges affiliated to Punjabi University were directed not to wear Western dresses.

The Panthic Committee also took strong notice of the changing demographic pattern of Chandigarh and came out with the 'directive' to the Chandigarh administration to stop this trend. Detailed guidelines were issued regarding the allotment of flats. The Panthic Committee defined the categories priority wise according to which the first preference was to be given to the widows of the November 1984 carnage, second preference to the families of the Khalistani martyrs and those in jails, third preference to those whose lands were acquired to develop Chandigarh, fourth preference to the milkmen supplying milk to the people in the capital city and last preference to those members of the societies who had opted for Punjabi during the last census.

In the same statement, guidelines were issued on promotion of government employees in the Chandigarh administration. First preference was to be given to those who had opted for Punjabi as mother tongue. Every employee was to clear matriculation examination in Punjabi. The recruitment was to be done only from Punjab. The Panthic Committee 'banned' recruitment of B. Ed teachers by the administration as three of the selection committee members happened to be the Leftist card holders. Preference was to be given in the recruitment to the victims of 1984 mayhem, families of the Sikh martyrs and of those under detention. Not only that. The new director of the Post-graduate Institute of Medical Education and Research was to be a Sikh.

The Panthic Committee also issued a code for the press on November 19 to be effective from December 1. The use of the term terrorist, ultra or extremist was completely banned which were to be replaced by militant, Khalistani freedom fighter or Mujahideen. The committee blamed the Editor of a Chandigarh based newspaper group for introducing the term terrorist for the Khalistani freedom fighters. The media was not to use the terms like 'self-styled' or 'so called'. The rank or status of the militant was not to be written in inverted commas. The prefix Sant was to be used with the name of Jarnail Singh Bhindranwale. The particular newspapers not using the prefix pointed out included Hindustan Times, Times of India, the Hind Samachar group (Punjab Kesari in Hindi, Jagbani in Punjabi and Hind Samachar in Urdu), Nawan Zamana and Lok Lehar. The Panthic Committee was not to be described as 'Pakistan based'. The committee also took strong note of some journalists playing the games of the intelligence agencies. At the same time, constructive criticism was allowed. The Panthic Committee made it clear that the journalists would not be allowed to distort and they would have to follow the professional ethics. At the same time, the committee warned that those not following this code would be forced to leave Punjab. The Committee cited the example of some journalist having been forced out of Srinagar in Kashmir.

In these guidelines, no alternate system or ideology was being propounded. The guidelines were within the framework of the existing system. The effort was not to change the system, unlike the earlier Naxalite movement where the target was the system itself. It is the commitment to the ideology which sustains the movement. If the Sikh struggle just petered out, the lack of ideological commitment was one major factor.

Fear stalked the Punjab hinterland with highways getting deserted in the evening. The year witnessed sudden spurt in the killings which were being attributed to the militants. The total such killings in 1990 were 2429, the highest ever since the rise of the militancy in the state. In many of the villages, even dogs had been poisoned to facilitate easy movement of the militants at night.

NOTES

1. The Indian Express, January 4, 1989.
2. The Indian Express, January 6, 1989.
3. The Indian Express, January 6, 1989.
4. The Indian Express, January 7, 1989.
5. The Indian Express, January 7, 1989.
6. The Indian Express, January 7, 1989.
7. Amrik Singh, The Indian Express, January 14, 1989.
9. The Times of India, September 12, 1989.
10. The Indian Express, October 26, 1989.
11. The Indian Express, November 14, 1989.
12. Jagtar Singh, The Indian Express, November 24, 1989.
13. The Indian Express, December 9, 1989.
14. Quoted from the original press note.
15. The Indian Express, August 16, 1990.
16. Hindustan Times, August 22, 1990.
17. The Tribune, October 15, 1990.
18. The Indian Express, December 1, 1990.

15

Akalis back Militant Struggle

This was the time when even the moderate Akalis were inching towards the slogans of the radicals. Punjab was under the shadow of the guns, thick and hot. The state had been gripped by the fear of the unknown. The chances of return to normalcy seemed to be very remote. Even the shutters of the police stations would be down in the evening, especially in the semi-urban and rural areas. These police stations had now been fortified with iron gates and armed pickets at the main entrance. The advice from the police to the people especially in the rural area would be against going out after sun set. A knock on the door in the villages would be dreaded as it meant either some group of militants had come to take shelter or a raid by the security forces. Caught in between was the common man. Sikh farmers living in the farm houses shifted their residences to the village and those who could afford, to the urban areas. Women were not safe. Realizing the gravity of situation, some militant leaders came out to provide protection to both Hindus and the Sikhs in their respective areas. However, irrevocable damage had already been done as a major section of the militants had been criminalized. Moreover, the militants were functioning in groups in their respective areas without much coordination with each other.

Under pressure, the marginalized moderate stream of the Akalis was coming closer to the radicals. Even the Congress leaders in the rural areas opted for understanding with the local militant leaders for survival. The honeymoon of the moderate Akalis with the radicals, however, did not last long.

The Akalis of various shades again shared a common stage at Fatehgarh Sahib Jor Mela on December 26, 1990 where Akali Dal (Mann) President Simranjit Singh Mann was authorized to negotiate with the government. He had earlier received an invitation from Prime Minister Chandra Shekhar who had succeeded V. P. Singh. The spadework for this joint conference was done by Shiromani Gurdwara Parbandhak Committee chief Gurcharan Singh Tohra. Significantly and perhaps for the first time, all the Akali factions supported the demand for self-determination raised by Mann and made it clear nothing less than that would satisfy the aspirations of the Sikhs who were being treated by the government in Delhi as second class citizens which had resulted in the loss of faith in the government.

What was all the more important was that the resolution to this effect was moved by Tohra and seconded by Parkash Singh Badal and Akali Dal (Longowal) acting president Kabul Singh. Having been totally marginalized in the 1989 Lok Sabha elections, the moderate Akalis were either trying to occupy some space in the Sikh political matrix by supporting the demand for self-determination or they were just too scared and buying peace with the militants.

Various Akali leaders expressed the view that a time limit should be fixed for talks and in case the exercise failed, the field should be left open to the militants. Mann specified the demand as a separate state which would act as a buffer between India and Pakistan. The right to self determination was to be exercised for this purpose. The Sikhs were to act as a balancing force between the 'Hindu India' and 'Muslim Pakistan'. According to one point of view, Pakistan had been created less than half a century ago as a buffer state to serve the strategic interests of Great Britain in the region and check the expansionist designs of the Soviet Union. The rise of militancy in Punjab had coincided with the occupation of Afghanistan by the Soviets which was a direct threat to Pakistan next door.

Significantly, Badal appreciated the role of the militants and citing the example of implementation of the use of Punjabi in official work, he said the militants had done it overnight for which they had been fighting for the last forty years. On the holding of talks with the government, he said only those who were fighting the battle should be authorized for this purpose. He made it clear the solution could be found only after talking to the militants.[1] In a tactical move, marginalized Badal had accepted the supremacy of the militants in any negotiated settlement with the government.

The Panthic Committee (Zaffarwal) and the Khalistan Commando Force reiterated the resolve to carry on the fight for a state based upon the Sikh tenets while appealing to the Akali leaders to desist from opportunistic political games.

The Panthic Committee, on December 27, responded positively to the offer of the Prime Minister to hold talks with the militants saying there was no need to shed blood for issues that could be sorted out across the table. The pre-condition was the release of the detained Sikhs, including Harjinder Singh Jinda and Sukhjinder Singh Sukha and the withdrawal of army, not only from Punjab but also from Assam, Kashmir, Nagaland and Mizoram. The government must hand over to the Sikh Panth the Congress leaders including H. K. L. Bhagat, Jagdish Tytler and Sajjan Kumar for their role in the genocide of the Sikhs in 1984. The Committee said the Prime Minister should come forward with a concrete agenda. The venue of talks could be Akal Takht in the Darbar Sahib complex, Geneva or New York at the UN headquarters. The Committee sought at least one month's time to start dialogue and complete security for its members. During the talks, the status of the Prime Minister and the committee members would be equal. The talks would be open in which international observers and nominated news persons could be present for coverage. While appreciating the attitude of Chandra Shekhar, the umbrella militant outfit cautioned him against the design of the people around him and also some newspapers considered to be anti-Punjab, especially those being published from Jalandhar. The militant groups represented by the Panthic Committee included the Babbar Khalsa, Khalistan Liberation Force, Khalistan Commando Force, Bhindranwale Tiger Force of Khalistan and the Sikh Students Federation (Bittu).

The parallel Panthak Committee representing Gurbachan Singh Manochahal, Gurjant Singh Rajasthani and others also welcomed the initiative for a dialogue by the Prime Minister and spelled out the agenda as the sovereign Sikh state. Certain suggestions were mooted to make the atmosphere congenial for talks which included end to press censorship, release of the Sikh detenus, withdrawal of security forces from around the Darbar Sahib complex and action against the police officials guilty of fake encounters.

Following talks with Mann in the December end, the Prime Minister agreed to hold talks with the radicals. The Prime Minister promised the government would favourably consider any offer from the militants. The modalities could be decided when they approach the government for talks. Mann led a delegation of 13 members to the Prime Minister which included Ram Singh, Charanjit Singh Walia, Sucha Singh Chhotepur, Chanan Singh Sidhu, Maninderjit Singh, Kamikkar Singh, Prabhjinder Singh, Roopinder Singh Chahal, Jarnail Singh, Jaspreet Singh and Sharanjit Singh Sharan. The delegation submitted a memorandum listing the demand for self-determination for the people of Punjab under Article 51 of the Constitution. The Prime Minister was closeted with Mann alone for about 20 minutes.[2] Mann later described the meeting as exploratory in nature. He conveyed the Prime Minister that the militants were in command of the situation in the state.

The delegation packed with pigmies and novices lacked capacity and vision to hold parleys on such a complex issue. They were just non-entities. Here was an opportunity wasted. Mann had not associated any other senior and seasoned leader from either the moderate Akali or the radical stream in the parleys with the government. The composition of the delegation remained topic of discussion for a long time, both in the Akali as well as the militant circles.

In the memorandum submitted to the Prime Minister, the Akali Dal (Mann) stated that the "Sikhs have no choice but to safeguard their religious, political and other interests. This is only possible if they invoke the right of self-determination permitted by international law recognized by India. In any case, by framing different laws for Punjab, the nation has accepted Punjab as a separate legal entity. Moreover, the Sikhs had joined the Union on the basis of the Cabinet Mission Plan which gave the right to provinces to change their constitutions after ten years. Even if the format of provinces has changed, the principle remains. After being subjected for years to state repression and discrimination, the people of Punjab wish to invoke this right on which basis the Sikhs joined the Indian Union. On 26th December, 1990, various Sikh parties and religious bodies including the SGPC passed a historic resolution at Fatehgarh Sahib demanding the right of self-determination....

"We meet at a time when Punjab and the Nation stand at the cross-roads of history. This faulty political and economic system evolved by India after independence has collapsed. The inevitable unrest is being exploited by Hindu fundamentalism and suppressed by armed forces with tragic potent.....My mandate is to discuss the right of self determination which is our historic and constitutional right. The Sikhs, though a small minority, have played an important role to secure the rights and freedom of the Indian people. They dream of a peaceful, prosperous and democratic Indian sub-continent. They extend a hand of friendship to all peoples and communities of India".

The memorandum emphasized lasting solution was not possible without involving militants in the parleys saying "Operation Bluestar was a watershed in Indo-Sikh affairs. So great was the trauma that the Sikhs to safeguard the existence are not prepared to accept any political system which does not concede the right of self determination, while the youth we call the militants are shedding their blood daily for a sovereign Sikh state. These are hard realities we must face to find a correct solution. As the militants are an important component in the situation, a formal invitation for talks must also be extended to them. My mandate is to discus the right of self-determination which is our historic and constitutional right. The Sikhs though a small minority have played an important role to secure the rights and freedom of the

Indian people. They dream of a peaceful, prosperous and democratic Indian sub-continent. They extend a hand of friendship to all people and communities of India".[3]

The memorandum also referred to the 59th Constitutional Amendment which had denied the Sikhs the right to life, liberty and expression. He also quoted the Independence Act, 1947 which states: "Power is being transferred to the Indian hand on the clear understanding that the future constitution of India shall provide for special rights and privileges to the Sikhs".

Later, Mann made it clear he would not compromise on the demand for self-determination. The case had, for the first time, been presented to the government which was the first stage of starting negotiations. He was emphatic that the rights of the Hindus would be fully protected in Punjab. They would not be subjected to unconstitutional methods the way the Sikhs have been subjected to. The 10-page memorandum was devoted mainly to the discrimination against the Sikhs by the successive Congress governments at the Centre.[4]

Militants Dissociate from Social Reforms

In the context of the prevalent situation, the announcement by the Panthic Committee on January 2, 1991 dissociating itself from the irresponsible and meaningless statements being issued under the garb of the so called social reform movement was very significant. The Committee said neither it nor the five militant organizations working under it had anything to do with the threats being issued to consumers of eggs and meat, closure of these shops, cutting the plaits of Punjabi women or forcing them to have only a single plait, or forcing them to wear only a particular dress, putting a ban on giddha and bhangra or issuing orders to sing only particular songs and poems, issuing threats to ban a particular language, forcing journalists to publish all sorts of statements, hurting the sentiments of a particular community or pouring scorn on them and putting a ban on tuitions. The committee felt time had come to fight against such stunts. As part of this so called reform movement, even the sign boards of the shops had been ordered to be painted in prescribed colours. [5] The realization of the damage having been done by this so called reform movement had dawned on the Committee too late as the alienation of the militants from the Sikh masses had already started.

However, at the same time, the Committee made it clear that it would like the Punjabi sisters to wear a dress that would promote the state's culture. "If you have been bedazzled by the West, if you like to wear jeans and a top and do not wish to cover your head, and if you have discovered some big truth in such a dress, then Panthic Committee would like to request you to visit in this dress the villages haunted by the souls of your elders. You should also see the delicate phase through which your brethren are passing. You should search your conscience and enlighten us about your role in the Khalsa's struggle for freedom. Only then you will understand the real significance of dress". The committee allowed the school heads to introduce the new dress code from the next academic session. The morning prayers were to include one or two shabads (hymns) but not more than five. The Christian and Muslim schools were given the option to select one hymn from their scriptures. The Sikh girls in these schools were to wear the traditional salwar-kameez and cover their heads with dupatta. The decision about the medium of instruction in the Christian schools was to be taken in consultation with the missionaries.

After enforcing the use of Punjabi in the Punjab government offices, the Panthic Committee targeted the Chandigarh administration and the Panjab University. Chandigarh residents were told to get the number plates of the vehicles painted both in Punjabi and English. The eighteen directives listed in the statement "ordered" the Chandigarh administration to shift its entire official functioning to Punjabi. It asked the public relations department to issue all press notes only in Punjabi, release 90 per cent advertisements to Punjabi newspapers and subscribe to at least two Punjabi dailies, except Jagbani owned by the Hind Samachar group. The administration was told to repaint all milestones and public boards in Punjabi followed by English. In the directive to the Panjab University, the Committee said it would soon frame a common education policy for the land of Khalistan in consultation with the intellectuals.[6]

All schools in Chandigarh were to be affiliated to the Punjab School Education Board from the next academic session and the medium of instruction was to be Punjabi. The official work in all schools and colleges was to be done in Punjabi and English was to be used only for the convenience of non-Punjabis. The use of Hindi was totally prohibited. All the English typewriters were to be replaced by the Punjabi typewriters.

In retaliation, the Chandigarh administration registered cases against the Times of India and Jalandhar based Punjabi daily Ajit for carrying this statement. These cases were booked under TADA, besides sections 124-A, 153-A, 505 and 506 CrPC. The notification issued by the administration said, "The Administration is of the view that publication of such material in newspapers being printed and published at Chandigarh or outside is likely to incite disaffection towards the government and is deliberately and maliciously intended to outrage religious feelings of different communities and is, therefore, accountable under various sections of the law. Therefore, the Administration is pleased to declare every such newspaper containing such objectionable materials to be forfeited to the government".[7]

Continuing the counter-pressure on the media, the Punjab government, on February 18, decided to invoke Section 95 of the Code of Criminal Procedure authorizing the deputy commissioners to confiscate copies of the newspapers carrying objectionable material. The media was feeling the heat from both the sides.

The members of the fourth estate in Chandigarh staged a dharna in front of the Punjab Raj Bhawan (Governor House) on March 4 to protest against the undeclared censorship imposed by the state government. The immediate provocation was the seizure of the copies of Ajit, Aaj Di Awaj and The Hindu and registration of a case under TADA against the Times of India and Ajit and raids on the offices of The Indian Express and The Tribune. An 11-member committee was set up to fight for the rights of the media. The members included T. K. Ramasamy (convener), Jagtar Singh, Kanwar Sandhu, Gobind Thukral, Jagtar Singh Sidhu, Surinder Khullar, Dinesh Kumar, Vidya Sagar, Sushil Bali, N. S. Parwana, A. S. Prashar and Baljit Balli. Communist Party of India senior leader Satya Pal Dang reacted to this action of the journalists in an article in Punjab Kesari in his own style while referring to the killing of 62 people associated with the media, including the hawkers of Hind Samachar group of newspapers against which the Chandigarh based media persons had not staged any such protest. He also questioned the role of the media in carrying verbatim the statements of the militant organizations.[8]

Personal clarifications from the ordinary people under threat from the militants started appearing in the Punjabi newspapers adding to the fear psychosis. Here is one such clarification and an appeal from a liquor contractor which appeared on page 6 of a Punjabi paper: "We have some liquor vends in Khanna. Keeping in view the social reform movement launched by the militants, we have decided against entering this business next year. We appeal to the militant brothers and organizations that we should be allowed to conduct our business till the month end as already, we have incurred heavy losses and clear government arrears".[9] Almost all the Punjabi papers were carrying such clarifications. This was one method of extorting money.

It was around this period that Gurbachan Singh Manochahal became critical of the activities of Mann and issued a lengthy statement. The memorandum submitted by Mann to the Prime Minister was also disapproved of, particularly with reference to the demand for self-determination. It was described as "an eloquent and an ugly picture of the crooked Brahmanical policy".[10] The full text of this statement had earlier appeared on January 11 from Amritsar in a Punjabi paper.

The Panthic Committee, in a separate statement, questioned the Akali unity and made it clear if it became instrumental in carrying forward the struggle for Khalistan in the light of the decisions taken by the Sarbat Khalsa, it should be welcomed but in case it was aimed at paving the way for Assembly elections by using the demand for self-determination, the Khalsa Panth would not allow it. Khalistan could be achieved only through the barrel of the gun and not the ballot box. The intention of the majority of the Akali leaders parroting this demand was to come to power. The Committee said Mann sometimes indulged in unprincipled and irresponsible talk and advised him to desist from claiming that his strategy and tactics had been approved by the Panthic Committee. The basic difference was over the goal as the Panthic Committee was working for the formation of sovereign state of Khalistan while Mann was frequently shifting his stand.[11]

Virtually towing the line of the Panthic Committee, the Babbar Khalsa also separately rejected the demand for self-determination saying it was only a tactic which could not be the political goal. The apprehension was that the demand for self-determination would ultimately water down to the Anandpur Sahib Resolution. In the perception of the Panthic Committee, the demand for self-determination might be used as a stepping stone to come into power without achieving the political goal, the struggle for which would have to be continued under the patronage of the Akal Takht. The resolution adopted against the traditional Akalis at Sarbat Khalsa could be withdrawn provided they carried forward the struggle for Khalistan peacefully by making it a mass movement. This could be done by announcing the boycott of all Assembly and Parliamentary elections in future. Regarding the talks with Chandra Shekhar, the Babbar Khalsa said it was a drama conspired by the stooges of the government. Here was a direct attack on Mann. It was also made clear that the only the goal of Khalistan should be the basis of Akali unity. The Babbar further said that the unification of the Akali factions had made him the chief of the obsolete leaders and fence sitters but not of the militants fighting for Khalistan. They militant outfit warned that any attempt made by the opportunists through Mr. Mann to scuttle the armed struggle would invite death penalty.[12]

The Panthak Committee associated with Manochahal nominated five spokespersons to explain the views of the militants from the Panthic stages on different issues. They included Jassa Singh Sursinghwala,

Baldev Singh, Surjit Singh, Harnam Singh and Satnam Singh. This had been done after it was realized that the lack of communication was harming the militant movement.[13]

Ironically, at the time when Mann should have been the unquestioned leader, a crisis hit his party which provoked the expulsion of party General Secretary Gurtej Singh and working committee member Sukhjinder Singh. The demythification of Mann had started earlier with the two Panthic committees putting question mark on his parleys with the Centre and rejection of the demand for self-determination.

To facilitate the dialogue process, the government, on January 30, offered safe passage to the militants for talks at any place in the country. Minister of State for Home Subodh Kant Sahay said, "We have received some feelers from the Punjab militants after the Prime Minister, Mr. Chandra Shekhar, announced his willingness to talk to them".

However, under pressure from the militant outfits, Mann virtually withdrew from the parleys with the government, saying the matter was now between the Prime Minister and the militants but at the same time, maintained the militants must respond to the offer of talks from the Prime Minister.[14] The Babbar Khalsa, Khalistan Commando Force (Panjwar), Khalistan Liberation Force (Budhsinghwala), Bhindranwale Tiger Force (Sangha) and the Sikh Students Federation (Bittu) rejected the offer of talks saying nothing less than Khalistan was negotiable. "We make it clear that the Sikh demands cannot be accepted within the framework of the constitution". They also said that Mann had no right to negotiate with the Centre. "Mr. Mann's advice to the militants to hold talks in the light of assurance of a safe passage to come over ground is irrelevant and useless".[15] However, earlier, the Panthic Committee associated with Dr. Sohan Singh and Wassan Singh Zaffarwal had appealed to the militants to accept the government offer for talks in two separate statements received in the newspaper offices by post. Both these outfits demanded end to fake encounters and state repression and release of all the Sikh detainees.

While offering an olive branch, however, the government continued to increase pressure on militants by deploying more forces. The strength of the central security forces in Punjab had been increased by about 60 companies by that time. Earlier, the Centre had started fencing the Punjab border with Pakistan. The districts of Amritsar, Gurdaspur and Ferozepur had already been handed over to the army again.

An Army ambush gunned down six farmers in cold blood in the early morning hours near Nathuke Burj village under Sarhali police station on February 26. They were going on a bullock cart around 4.45 AM to get diesel. The army suspected them to be militants. During that period, diesel was in short supply and long queues could be seen at the petrol pumps. Unarmed simple farmers riding a bullock cart could not pose any danger to any body. The army men acted under fear. Irate villagers staged demonstrations at Sarhali against these killings. The way this shocking incident was reported in some papers pointed to the partisan attitude of a section of the media. The impression one got from one such report in an English newspaper was that the bull ignored the signal from the army men and rushed past them! This is the slowest mode of transport. Agitated villagers stage protest against the killings.

Initiating the fresh unity moves, Mann dissolved the Badal and Longowal factions of Akali Dal on February 22. Earlier, both these factions, at a meeting with Mann on January 12 at Chandigarh, had reposed faith in his leadership. Mann, who continued to vacillate, again reiterated the demand for a sovereign Sikh state and said the issue was liberty or death for the Sikhs. He claimed that Tohra and Badal had assured him full support. The immediate provocation was the behaviour of some army men commanded by a senior officer in some border villages (tumhari nasal badal denge- we would change your race) against the Sikhs. Complaints to this effect had poured in from Sarangra, Majh, Panjoo Rai, Lodhi Gujjar, Rai, Kakkar and Alla Baksh village of Amritsar district. The panches and sarpanches had threatened to resign against this insulting behavior of the army personnel. He called upon the Sikhs to cross the border to Pakistan in case they faced genocidal threat. He also sought US intervention to "liberate us" and said USA could not remain a silent spectator to what was happening in Punjab. Mann was so incensed that he used four letter words at the press conference in the presence of the women journalists.

A few days later, he dwelt on the theme of "safe haven" for the Sikhs under United Nations saying the Indian state had proved to be incompetent to carry out its constitutional duty of which the restoration of democracy in Punjab was the most important factor.[16] He announced at the Akali conference at Talwandi Sabo on April 14 that the elections in the state would be fought on the issue of sovereign and independent Sikh state. He echoed the demand of the militants for Khalistan. He reiterated the sovereign Sikh state would act as a buffer between India and Pakistan. For contesting the elections, the candidate has to swear by the constitution of India. It is a different matter that a resolution on a sovereign state can be adopted in the Assembly after the elections in case of majority.

The prolonged spell of the President's rule was not being considered to be conducive to the restoration of peace by one section in Punjab, including some Communist leaders. It was in this background that

Communist Party of India senior leader Avtar Singh Malhotra said, "A solution in Punjab will only be possible if the political forces and the government cooperate and the parties at national level also put aside narrow partisan interests and deal with a national problem with a national approach. Finding the way to restore the democratic process and conduct elections with a moderate degree of freedom to vote will be a good start in search for political solution".[17]

While Mann pressed for elections, the Panthic Committee called for boycott. Some other militant organizations had also earlier given such a call. At one stage, Mann had also expressed reservations about holding the elections under the given situation. However, the AISSF (Manjit), backed by the Panthak Committee (Manochahal), around this time announced the decision to enter the poll fray.

This was the worst year ever since militancy had been triggered in the state. However, despite all provocations, there was no communal flare up. This was the period when entire Sikh families had been eliminated, including kids. Majority of the Hindu families had already deserted the rural areas, especially in the border districts.

The Panthic Committee in its April 24 statement announced the decision against participation in elections, directly or indirectly on the logic that it did not believe in the Constitution of India under which the elections were to be held. The Babbar Akali Dal, front organization of the Babbar Khalsa International, while announcing the decision to boycott elections, took strong exception to the decision of the AISSF (Manjit) and the Panthak Committee (Manochahal) to contest elections. Party President Kartar Singh said these outfits had been misled by the government agents.[18] However, the Khalistan Commando Force (Zaffarwal), on April 24, issued a 3-page statement opting for elections. The statement said the outfit was of the opinion that the Sikhs should not boycott elections as the poll boycott in 1985 by the United Akali Dal representing the militants had led to the Akali Dal (Longowal) government headed by Surjit Singh Barnala coming into power and history should not now repeat itself. The last date for filing of the nomination was April 26. The elections were to be held in June.

Manochahal proposed seat sharing for the Assembly elections with Mann on 60:40 bases. The talks were to be held at Damdami Taksal headquarters at Mehta Chowk with Manjit Singh representing Manochahal. However, Mann left before Manjit Singh reached there, despite having been briefed at Chandigarh about the seat sharing formula before he left for Gurdwara Gurdarshan Parkash, the Taksal headquarters.

The Congress, the two Communist Parties and the BJP had been repeatedly declaring that they would boycott the election under the given situation. The apprehension of these parties was that the candidates supported by the militant organizations would get elected and they might adopt Khalistan resolution in the Assembly.

What added to such apprehensions was the statement issued in the name of Manochahal on May 21 specifying that the election would be projected as a vote for Khalistan and the aim would not be to grab power but tell the world that the Sikhs were anxious to throw away the shackles of slavery. The elections were to be used as one of the weapons in the ongoing Sikh struggle. However, the Babbar Khalsa continued with its poll boycott campaign.

The Panthic Committee associated with Dr. Sohan Singh severed its relations with the Babbar Khalsa in early June. Reacting to this decision, the Babbar Khalsa accused Dr. Sohan Singh of unilaterally taking a decision to enter into negotiations with Chandra Shekhar.[19] It doubted the sincerity and ability of Chandra Shekhar to resolve the Punjab tangle.

Tohra, who had been maintaining low profile even at the time of distribution of tickets by Badal, preferred consensus in the wake of the multiplicity of "Panthic" candidates. He suggested the method of draw of lots in case unanimity eluded the finalization of candidates. He was against division of the Sikh votes. However, SGPC chief Baldev Singh Sibia had given a call for the election boycott, though for different reasons. His poll boycott call was in the context of an incident of sacrilege at Kot Shameer village near Bathinda.

The CPI and the CP (M) announced the decision in Delhi on June 11 to withdraw from the poll fray and called upon all other political parties and democratic forces committed to the unity and integrity of the country to take a similar stand. The Election Commission de-linked the Punjab election from the rest of the country. The BJP, state unit on June 13 announced the decision to go ahead with the election. The CPI reversed the decision following appeal made by the Punjab unit as the state unit opted for elections.

The Panthic Committee associated with Manochahal, on June 18, called upon the other militant organizations to stop the fratricidal war and warned of retaliation in case their activists continued to be targeted. He criticized the killing of candidates while maintaining that the elections would be used as referendum for Khalistan.

The AISSF (Manjit), made it clear the same day that it would work for an independent and sovereign Sikh state to translate the dream of Sant Jarnail Singh Bhindranwale into reality. The organization released a 9-page manifesto. The manifesto promised that the siege of the Sikh religious places would be lifted and all the detained Sikh youth released. All those who had contributed to the Sikh struggle were to be honoured as "qaumi warriors". The manifesto also talked of administrative reforms to put an end to fake encounters and punish the guilty policemen. The farmers or poor from other sections who had taken loans upto Rs. 10,000 upto January 1, 1991 were to be exempted from repayment. The manifesto also promised jobs to those who had lost their family members in Operation Bluestar.

The elections were postponed at the eleventh hour on June 22. The decision to postpone the election was announced around 3 AM, a few hours before the people were to queue up at the polling stations at 8.00 AM. The decision had been taken due to the apprehension that the elections would be used as an instrument by a section of the militants to achieve the goal of a sovereign and independent Sikh state. The Assembly dominated by the members supported by the militants could have adopted the Khalistan resolution with an appeal at the international level to recognize the sovereign state created lawfully through the legislative process.

Punjab Governor General O. P. Malhotra (Retd) was informed by the Union Home Secretary at about 2 AM about the postponement when he had just gone to sleep after interacting with the district police chiefs. He protested over the unilateral decision as Punjab had not been consulted. He decided to leave and bid farewell on August 7.

In the bloody poll campaign, a total of 29 Akali candidates were gunned down. The Babbar Khalsa justified the killing of at least two candidates, Baldev Singh Lang from Samana and Pritam Singh from Nabha saying Mann had been duly informed about their activities. In a statement issued on July 5, they said Amrik Singh Kauli had told Mann that both these Akali leaders had been collecting huge sums from industrialists and resorting to other misdeeds. Mann had assured that these leaders would be expelled from the party. Contrary to the assurance, they were rewarded with tickets. Indulging in extortions was another charge against them. The statement also warned newsmen against making any deletions in the statement.

The Akali Dal held the Congress responsible for the killing of the Akali candidates. The party later substantiated this charge pointing to the elections in 1992 which were boycotted by the mainstream Akalis and not a shot was fired at any candidate. However, the Akali Dal never probed this charge after coming into power.

General Malhotra later disclosed to a newspaper that the Centre had at one stage agreed to de-link the elections in Punjab from the rest of the country to make available adequate number of security forces.

About 60 companies of the security forces were needed for the purpose. However, it was not done. Surprisingly, it was the campaigning period which was extended by five weeks in the state, thus increasing the risk factor for the candidates. According to General Malhotra, all parties had agreed to contest in case Punjab was de-linked from the rest of the country for elections.

Though the elections had been postponed at the last minute, the channels for dialogue between the militants and the government had not been closed. Yet another militant outfit, Akal Federation, which had initiated dialogue with Chandra Shekhar government through a non-descript Christian leader from Amritsar Kailash Samuel, spelled out three parameters in a letter written to him on May 18, 1991. The letter stated the talks would be held on Khalistan issue and these talks would be open. This letter was signed by yet another non-entity, Kulbir Kaur Khalsa, in her capacity as the chief spokesperson for the organization. These were the people without any mass base. She had crossed over to Pakistan with her brother-in-law, Akal Federation chief Kanwar Singh Dhami. She was the only young women to have crossed over to Pakistan which later became a source of embarrassment for the militant leaders already camping there who forced Dhami to adopt her as his wife.

The letter to the Prime Minister begins with reference to Kailash Samuel, Chairman, Christian Forum for Peace in India and the proposed meeting between the militants and representatives of the government on May 2, 1991. The government was to be represented by Anand Ram Jaiswak, MP, M. K. Dhar (from the Intelligence Bureau handling Punjab affairs) who had been described as a Sectional Officer in the Home Ministry and Prime Minister's aide O. P. Pande.

The letter stated: "Many other channels of talks were explored and abandoned in-between. Now you have shown the same mirage to Bhai Manjit Singh and Mr. Gurtej Singh. Your offer of talks is a tablet of sugar coated poison wrapped in golden paper. You have very loudly repeated this offer through all channels of media so as to confuse the people to mislead them into thinking why the militants are not coming forward to talk to such a considerate Prime Minister. But we, by the grace of the Guru, could look through the game. You had become the Prime Minister of this country with only 54 MPs on your side. The Congress party which supported you did not allow you to even present a full budget in the Parliament. How could you amend the constitution which requires two third majority of the House. You sent 4000 army men to Punjab and virtually handed over the districts of Amritsar, Gurdaspur and Ferozepur to them. Your army kill innocent farmers along with their bullocks and no action is taken against them Your Brig.

Sinha threatens to rape Sikh women and no action is taken against him. There have been more fake encounters in your regime than any other.....we could recognize the real nature of the trap laid by you. That is why we had told the honest mediator, Mr. Kailsah Samual, that in the first round, the representatives of the militants would hold only exploratory talks with the envoys of the Sikhs..... the talks can be held in an open atmosphere, on the land of Khalistan and about the establishment of Khalistan".

Dhami himself was a conduit and helped the emissaries from the government side to establish contact with some other militant leaders whose movement to this side of the border was facilitated for the purpose. However, Chandra Shekhar remained in power for a short term and the exercise could not make much progress.

It was during this period that Liberation Tigers of Tamil Elam got in touch with the Punjab militants and the dialogue continued in Chandigarh for four days. The Punjab militants did not agree to the strategy adopted by the LTTE to raise funds through the sale of narcotics. The LTTE established contact with the Punjab militants through Jaspal Singh Dhillon, a human rights activist.

Over a period, confrontation had been going on between the Sikh militants and a section of the Naxalites. Some Naxalite groups had taken upon themselves the role of taking the Sikh militants head on. These groups claimed to have avenged the killing of some of their associates, including Prithipal Singh Randhawa. This confrontation culminated in the gunning down of 18 persons at Sewewala village near Jaito on April 9. Naxalite leader Megh Raj Bhagtuana had been active in the area for about four years under the banner of anti-repression and anti-communal front. This front had organized a cultural programme in the village on April 9 when the militants struck. Megh Raj had come to symbolize the Left resistance against the Sikh militants. The underground cadre of the Naxalites functioned under the banners of Kartar Singh Sarabha Brigade and the Red Guards. These Naxalite groups were also the first to challenge the social code issued by the Sikh militants. The Communist Unity Centre, in a 4-page pamphlet brought out on February 21, 1991 in Bathinda had openly challenged the Sikh militants while giving the slogan of "do or die".

The situation was getting more and more vitiated and the fratricidal killings by various militant groups were just one aspect. Life even for the ordinary Sikh was becoming unbearable in the Mazha belt along the border due to spurt in extortions, lootings, rape and killing of the innocents for ransom. The Babbar Khalsa took strong note of the situation and warned against such heinous activities.[20] The statement issued in the name of the Khalistan Commando Force (Zaffarwal) on July 25 datelined Ludhiana appealing to the doctors and the Hindus not to migrate was also a pointer to the deteriorating situation. The statement tried to clarify that the struggle was not against any particular community but against the government. The statement also condemned the killing of 77 passengers in two trains at Baddowal and Qila Raipur on July 15 in Ludhiana district.[21] Punjab had become the Wild West.

CPI Pleads for Democratic Intervention

Interestingly, within weeks of the cancellation of the elections, the Communist Party of India made a forceful plea for the democratic intervention. State party Secretary Avtar Singh Malhotra said in a 3-page statement issued on August 8, 1991: "Time is running out. We must have faith in the common people of Punjab. They cannot be by-passed. In these ten years of a bloody crisis, they have been subjected to a lot and have learnt much. Secessionist violence continues to take its toll of death. But it has been compounded by protracted bureaucratic rule, draconian laws and powers to the police and security organs and increasing lawlessness and violence. We support talks with all relevant forces but talks to end bloodshed and find a solution but not for an election deal.

"The June election campaign – though not with the normal mass character and mobilization – was nevertheless an eye opener for many. The mass revulsion against all violence and lawlessness, resentment against arbitrary bureaucratic rule and the mass urge for restoring the democratic process and normalcy gushed forth despite the continued terror factor. The people were coming forward as never before to assert themselves. This created real possibilities of a new turn in the situation in this blood soaked state through active popular intervention. Seshan put an end to it, an end to the hopeful prospects. The situation is ripe for a turn provided the centre and the state administrations are ready to face challenges.....

-" the democratic process must be restored at the earliest... Legal enactments- already ample- are not the best way to deal with the secessionist danger. Let such proposals be put before people for full national debate...

-"the centre must take some initiative to establish its lost bona fides. Chandigarh should go to Punjab and appropriate steps taken for settlement of the territorial dispute. The problem is both a Punjab problem and a Sikh problem.

-"the much talked about "healing tough" has to begin with a clear national stand about the Blue-Star army operation and due punishment for the chief culprits of November 1984 killings.

-"the river- waters dispute be settled with due account for the past background in the light of accepted national norms and injustice to none, nor any discrimination. The elected state governments be fully involved in the quest for the solution. Where Punjab and Haryana differ let the Supreme Court decide without any non-judicial interference.

-"the Prime Minister should call all- parties meetings both at state and national levels and open to the press".

Though the election had been postponed at the last moment, the Panthic Committee, in its review of the situation, had decided to use the boycott of future polls as a weapon for the establishment of the Sikh state. The Panthic Committee appealed to the Hindus against participation in any future elections and warned at the same time the violation would be treated as betrayal which could invite retaliation. Those who fell in line would be given protection as the Sikhs had been providing to them historically. The perception was that any government elected in Punjab under the Indian Constitution would be nothing more than a puppet government and as such, the very purpose of the Sikh struggle would be defeated. At the same time, the radical umbrella organization also laid emphasis on the people's movement along with the armed struggle.

Though he was not the first to advocate the line, it was Gurcharan Singh Tohra who set the Akali agenda for shunning the future elections by advocating on July 17 the boycott of the elections as and when held by extending the logic that the elections would not be a solution to the problems being faced by the Sikhs. He had virtually remained passive in the run up to the aborted June elections. For him, the main issue was the state repression on which all the Akali factions could unite.[22] He had already started distancing from Badal.

Akalis back Militant Struggle

For the first time since the start of the armed struggle in Punjab and at the time when the tide had started turning against militancy, various Akali factions and farmers and the human rights organizations, at a convention organized at Anandpur Sahib on August 11, exhibited consolidation in support of the militant movement and resolved that only the militants had the right to negotiate with the government as they had the primary role to play under the given situation. The militants had till then never received such massive support. Chaired by SGPC President Baldev Singh Sibia, this convention against state repression was attended by the representatives from about 30 organizations including Badal, Mann, Longowal, Panthic and Babbar factions of Akalis, Damdami Taksal, Bharti Kisan Union and the human rights organizations.

It was decided to jointly fight the state repression for which an action committee was set up comprising all the heads of the organizations which attended the convention. The convention also appealed to the militants to set up a joint committee in coordination with this action committee. It was resolved that the militants were the principal party in the fight against the government. It was for the first time that all the Panthic organizations had jointly accepted the primary role of the militant organizations. The militant organizations decided to constitute a committee to hold negotiations with the government only if the need was felt for a dialogue.

The convention paid tributes to all the 'martyrs' of the Sikh struggle since 1978. Through another resolution, the convention called upon the Sikhs to be 'Amritdhari and Shastradhari' (baptized and armed) by April 1999, the 300th anniversary of the birth of the Khalsa. It was perhaps for the first time that even the traditional Akalis had been associated with the call to the Sikhs to get armed.

While Tohra himself attended the meeting, other senior leaders including Badal, Mann and Akali Dal (Panthic) President Amarinder Singh were conspicuous by their absence and had deputed their representatives. However, all these leaders were represented on the action committee constituted against state repression.

Apart from the militant organizations which initiated the poll boycott decision, it was the Bharati Kisan Union (Lakhowal), the Punjab Human Rights Organization and the Paigam group which strongly advocated this line of action. The Bharti Kisan Union (Lakhowal) also proposed launching of peaceful agitation followed by a non-cooperation movement for the achievement of the goal set by the radicals. Militant organizations including the Babbar Khalsa, Akal Federation, Khalistan Commando Force (Panjwar), Sikh Students Federation (Daljit Bittu), Bhindranwale Tiger Force of Khalistan (Chhandra), Khalistan Liberation Force (Budhsinghwala) and the Khalistan Liberation Army sent their views in writing which were read out and discussed.

Amarinder Singh and All India Sikh Students Federation (Manjit) General Secretary Sarabjit Singh Jammu initiated fresh unity move and held parleys with Mann. Badal and Tohra had also met Mann separately during the period who advised them to send a joint delegation to President R. Venkataraman to protest against the killing of innocent Sikhs near Pilibhit in Uttar Pradesh by the security forces in a fake encounter. Mann was convalescing after an operation. Earlier, a similar move had been initiated by Ram Jethmalani on the issue of Pilibhit killings.

The militants were now claiming even what were not their actions or what was beyond their capacity. A small three sentence report in a Punjabi daily was a pointer. The statement was issued on behalf of the Khalistan Commando Force regarding a meeting chaired by its chief Wassan Singh Zaffarwal. The outfit claimed to have shot down a fighter aircraft at the Halwara Air Force station near Ludhiana. The news report was datelined Ahmedgarh.[23]

Similarly earlier in the beginning of the year, the Babbar Khalsa, in a statement issued on January 30, had claimed to have set up its first unit consisting of serving army men which was given the name of the Babbar Khalsa Army. The statement issued in the name of Kulwant Singh Babbar also talked of discrimination against Sikh officers in the matter of promotions. The statement claimed that similar units would be set up in the Indian Air Force and the Navy.

Militant organizations also took up the broader economic issues concerning the state as evident from the statement issued on their behalf by Dr. Pritam Singh Sekhon of the Khalistan Liberation Force taking strong note of the adverse credit deposit ratio and the flow of funds to other states through the banking system. He called upon the banks to invest major portion of the deposit from Punjab within the state itself while giving priority to small farmers in the matter of advancing loans. The statement directed the banks in the state to adopt Punjabi as the official language and get the boards painted in Punjabi. The statement was issued in the name of Paramjit Singh Panjwar, Chief General, Khalistan Commando Force, Daljit Singh, President, Sikh Students Federation, Gurjant Singh Budhsinghwala, Chief General, Khalistan Liberation Force and Rachhpal Singh Chhandra (Sangha), Chief General, Bhindranwale Tiger Force of Khalistan.[24]

In yet another significant development, the action committee of the Panthic organizations at a meeting at Anandpur Sahib on September 1 resolved against participation in the Assembly elections. The agenda of the meeting was initially confined to giving action programme to fight repression but the militant organizations dictated the course of events, forcing the Akalis to give this call. The SGPC chief said after the meeting that what influenced this decision was the unprecedented state repression as even the families of militants were not being spared. The committee gave a call for Punjab bandh on September 7 to protest the killing of Gurjant Singh Rajasthani and family members of Babbar Khalsa Malwa commander Balwinder Singh Jatana.

The family members of Jatana were killed and the ancestral house in Ropar district set on fire within hours of the attack on the then Chandigarh Senior Superintendent of Police Sumedh Singh Saini, who had narrowly escaped the bomb attack. The victims included Jatana's

95 year old grandmother, maternal aunt, her teen-aged daughter and his polio ridden cousin. The meeting called upon the militants to unite and check killing of innocents and extortions in their name. The meeting authorized Sibia to constitute a committee and chalk out programme of action against state repression. It was decided to organize bhog of Rajasthani and appealed to the people to attend the bhog of family members of Jatana.

The move to boycott the poll was opposed by Amarinder Singh and his party leader Jasdev Singh Sandhu, who were repeatedly hooted down by the protagonists of this line. It was only the Panthic faction of the Akali Dal led by Amarinder Singh which participated in the 1992 Assembly elections. Badal, who attended the meeting, said earlier the Congress had decided to boycott the poll and now the Akalis followed suit. If the Congress was not dubbed as anti-national for boycotting the poll, how the Akalis could be attacked for similar action.

The election boycott agenda had earlier been set by Tohra, who was credited with the view that the elections should be boycotted as and whenever held and if at all the path of the ballot box was to be adopted, the multiplicity of Panthic candidates should be avoided. He was not in favour of contesting the June elections which were postponed as in his view, the issues facing the Panth were different for which the elections were no solution. It was Tohra, who at critical junctures, used to dictate the political discourse. By the end of July, Tohra had distanced himself from Badal.

The action committee meeting was attended, among others, by the Babbar, Badal, Mann, Longowal and Panthic factions of Akalis, Tohra, Tota Singh, youth wings of various Akali factions, the AISSF (Kahlon), the two factions of the Bharati Kisan Union, Punjab Human Rights Organisation, Movement Against State Repression, Paigam group, Desh Punjab Students Union, Akhand Kirtani Jatha, Sikh lawyers Association, Kendriya Singh Sabha, Sikh Missionary College, Istri Akali Dal, Sikh Intellectual Council, Sant Sipahi Front, Punjab Karamchari Dal, Dalit and Minorities Front, Sikh Pratinidhi Board, All India Muslim Front and the Babbar Sikh Vidyarthi Jathebandi. The AISSF (Manjit) and the Panthak Committee (Manochahal) boycotted the meeting. The Damdami Taksal and the Akali Dal (Baba) also did not participate. However, the Akali Dal (Mann) tried to backtrack from the poll boycott decision the very next day saying the decision was not binding on the party. The logic was that Damdami Taksal and Panthic Committee (Manochahal) had abstained from the meeting and in the absence of these bodies the decision could not be binding on all the Sikh organizations involved in the struggle.

As the security forces started targeting the families of the militants in retaliation, the militant organizations realized the blunder of killing family members of the security men.

In a very significant development pointing to the modus operandi of the police, Senior Superintendent of Ropar Mohammad Mustafa accused Chandigarh SSP Sumedh Singh Saini of ordering the execution of the four members of the family of Babbar Khalsa militant Jatana. Saini was the Punjab cadre IPS officer on deputation with the Chandigarh administration. He leveled the accusation in confidential letter written to Director General of Police D. S. Mangat. The letter also talked of likely reprisals against the family members of the policemen. Mustafa accused Saini of dispatching three jeep loads of plain clothes Chandigarh policemen to Jatana village on the night of August 29. The house was set on fire after the killings. The matter was hushed up. Till August 12 that year, the militants had killed 40 members of the families of serving policemen whereas from September 7 within a month, this number shot up by 79 members.[25]

The Babbar Khalsa condemned the killings of innocent family members including women, children and relatives of the policemen and made it clear the organization was totally against such killings. Babbar Khalsa chief Sukhdev Singh said such indiscriminate killings, setting afire houses of policemen and kidnapping of their children had given a major set back to their struggle and eroded the reputation of the militants in the eyes of the Sikhs.[26] It was the attack on the families of the policemen which was the major provocation for the security agencies to resort to no holds barred tactics against the militants and their families. The realization had dawned too late. However, it was not for the first time that notice had been taken of such distortions in the militant movement.

During this period, Mann also opposed the killing of the innocents and extortions and wanted the militants to purge their ranks. He observed, "It seems the movement is loosing its moorings. Therefore, taking the history of the Sikh struggle into account, anyone who indulges in extortions, seizes weapons of farmers and indulges in the killing of innocent persons is not a militant but one of the vigilante groups of the government". At the political level, he had come around to the view that the Anandpur Sahib Resolution had become irrelevant after thousands of Sikh youth had died for Khalistan.[27] The irony was that the militant movement was petering out at the time when it had started getting support from the Sikh organizations across the board.

In a major such action, a Romanian charge d'affaires in New Delhi, Liviu Radu, was kidnapped on October 9 by the militants. Khalistan

Liberation Force, Sikh Students Federation and two other organizations claimed responsibility for the action. He had been kidnapped to demand release of Harjinder Singh Jinda, Sukhdev Singh Sukha and Iqbal Singh. The responsibility was claimed on October 11. He was later released unconditionally as this action failed to build up pressure on the government.

The Punjab unit of Communist Party of India decided to take up the issues concerning the state by way of organizing dharnas at the district headquarters on November 1. The party had earlier written to all the major political parties to mobilize public opinion on the issues as in the changing perception of the party, Punjab problem was essentially political. The main issues identified by the CPI included transfer of Chandigarh to Punjab, setting up of a commission to identify Punjabi and Hindi speaking areas, solution to the river waters dispute by referring it to the Supreme Court, punishment to the guilty of November 1984 violence against the Sikhs and more powers to the states.[28]

Under pressure from the Panthic Committee associated with Dr. Sohan Singh, Sibia announced the dissolution of the anti-repression committee on October 12, saying the newspapers had carried an ultimatum from the militant outfit directing him to dissolve the committee. The allegation was that Sibia was using the committee to consolidate his position at the time when the elections of the office bearers of the SGPC were near. He said similar views had been expressed by the Panthak Committee (Manochahal). The Punjab Human Rights Organisation described as most unfortunate the threat issued by the Panthic Committee to Sibia. The action committee was virtually functioning as a front organization of the militant organizations. The job of the committee was to mobilize mass support for the militants in the name of fighting against repression. The dissolution had defeated that very purpose. The design behind the threat was to deny mass support to the armed struggle and the purpose had been achieved.

The dissolution of the action committee also provided an escape route to the traditional Akali leaders who had been forced by the situation to extend support to the militant struggle. Panthic Committee clarified its position on the issue later in a statement appearing in the press on October 30 saying though the anti-repression committee resolved to boycott elections, it did not reject the constitution of India. It amounted to going one step forward and two steps back. The leaders of the committee were in a dilemma. The Panthic panel also clarified its position vis-à-vis the SGPC saying it was constituted under the Constitution and as such, could not function independently. It was for this reason that it had been 'dissolved' by the Sarbat Khalsa.

Mann Sticks to Khalistan Demand

The Akali Dal (Mann), on October 17, once again reiterated the resolution adopted at the Sarbat Khalsa convention of 1986 demanding an independent and sovereign Sikh state which would act as a buffer between India and Pakistan. It was also announced that the party would not participate in any future election as it would dilute this demand. Mann said as per the logic of history, Khalistan was going to be a reality and his party had now stopped sailing in two boats as the party executive had specified the demand for Khalistan. However, the goal was to be achieved through peaceful and democratic means. He had completely identified his party with the militants, the only difference being the strategy and tactics.[29]

Mann had heated up the atmosphere in the state with this posture after cooling his heels in the hill resort of Dalhousie in Himachal Pradesh for about two months. He was resorting to competitive politics vis-à-vis other Akali factions, apart from winning over the militants. Though fighting against the government, almost all the main Akali leaders were living under the security cover provided by the police. About half a dozen Akali factions were functioning in the state, leveling charges and counter charges against ach other of being agents of the government. The Akali factions had failed to understand the social reality in the state.

"The green revolution brought a change in the social scene and led to increasing social tensions and pauperization of a section of the peasantry. Over the years, the number of farming families has declined.... Instead of articulating the demands of this section, they went on to raise the demands like the implementation of the Anandpur Sahib resolution. For a household in the remote corner in Faridkot district, which enjoys the facility of running hot and cold water, grabbing political power could be the next ambition, but that was not the case with those marginalized. The increasing prosperity brought in its wake conflict between farm capital which was the result of marketable surplus and the industrial capital, the marginal farmers and the rich farmers. The social dissensions arising out of these conflicting interests have never been understood by the Akalis".[30]

Akal Takht Kar Sewa Resumed

The SGPC set up a 5-member committee on October 27 to resume the Kar Sewa of Akal Takht which had remained suspended since Operation Black Thunder. The members included Baba Thakar Singh of Damdami Taksal, Baba Jagtar Singh Tarn Taran, Baba Diwan Singh Khan Chhabri, Baba Harbhajan Singh Paonta Sahib and Baba Darshan Singh Ghanupurkale. The Kar Sewa started on October 29. The Kar Sewa was mainly Damdami Taksal affair. Devotees turned out in large numbers for the Kar Sewa and such was the rush that security arrangements at the police check points leading to the shrine could not cope up. Ever since Operation Black Thunder, the police had put up pickets near all the main entrances to the shrine.

The Babbar Khalsa dissolved all its zones outside Punjab and re-organized the outfit. A code of conduct was also evolved which was released on November 11 under the signatures of Kulwant Singh Babbar. A 9-member organizational committee was announced which included Sukhdev Singh Chabba, Harbhajan Singh Mand, Harmit Singh Bhaoowal, Dharam Singh Kashtiwal, Harbhajan Singh Delianwali and Amrik Singh Kauli. Sukhdev Singh, Talwinder Singh, Wadhawa Singh, Kulwant Singh and Mahal Singh comprised the high command.

Tohra replaced Sibia as the SGPC chief in the annual elections held on November 13. Mann proposed that the general house of the SGPC should be convened to pass a resolution for a sovereign Sikh state. The run up to the SGPC executive committee elections was marked by intensified political activity in the Akali spectrum. Tohra, who had distanced from Akali Dal (Badal) and stayed away from the party meetings, met with Badal, though he did not attend the working committee meeting of the party held the same day. Sibia was considered close to Tohra. However, the decision of Sibia to remove Manjit Singh Calcutta, a confidant of Tohra, from the office of the SGPC Secretary, had annoyed him. The decision of Sibia was also influenced by the closeness of Calcutta to those at the helm of affairs in the Punjab government at that time. He was known for his proximity to Governor S. S. Ray. It was Ray who used to talk in private about the unwritten agreement arrived at with the SGPC regarding the arrangements inside the shrine when Calcutta was its Secretary. The SGPC, on the directions from the state government, removed all the doors of the rooms opening in the parkarma of the shrine. And every president of this mini-Parliament of the Sikhs respected this unwritten agreement.

It was now the turn of the Communist Party of India to warn the government against the army excesses. Party's national council secretary Chaturanan Misra cautioned the government against any excess committed by the army in the state and said anything like the incidents that occurred in Assam during army deployment would lead to disastrous consequences in the surcharged atmosphere in Punjab. He favoured political solution rather than deploying the army for long period.[31]

The Panthic and Longowal factions of the Akalis finally merged to form the Shiromani Akali Dal with Kabul Singh as President. The announcement was jointly made by Barnala, Amarinder Singh and Capt. Kanwaljit Singh on December 9. Amarinder Singh was nominated chairman of the party's Parliamentary Board. It was after about five years that Amarinder Singh and Barnala had joined hands. Amarinder Singh opted for contesting the forthcoming Assembly elections saying the boycott decision taken at Anandpur Sahib had been undone by the subsequent events. These leaders hoped the Badal and Mann factions would also respond to the unity appeal.

In one of the biggest such action, militants gunned down 52 persons in the Ludhiana-Ferozepur train in the last week of December near Chowki Mann railway station. The militants opened fire after asking members of one community to get down.

Badal, on December 30, proposed a national debate on his party's demand declaring India commonwealth of autonomous states. He justified the demand while arguing that it was based on historical needs and on psychological, political, ethnic and economic factors and that the constitutional framework had been rendered irrelevant and unsatisfactory by the course of events.[32]

The year ended up with the highest ever 2738 people having been gunned down by the militants. The community wise break up of these killings was very significant as more than 1800 persons were Sikhs which constituted about 70 per cent of the killings. This was the peak of the violence which had been registered as crime by the militants. This was also the year when the militants had got support from the Akalis of all shades in the Sikh political matrix. However, this support had nothing to do with violence.

Akalis Decide to Boycott Polls

Four Akali and two factions of the Sikh Students Federation, at a meeting on January 4, 1992, formally decided to boycott the Assembly polls to be held in February. Convened at Mann's initiative, the meeting was attended by Akali Dal (Badal) President Parkash Singh Badal, Akali Dal (Baba) President Joginder Singh, Babbar Akali Dal President Kartar Singh Narang, AISSF President Manjit Singh and Baljinder Singh Gandiwind a representative of the SSF (Mehta-Chawla). The announcement was withheld with Badal saying that the unanimous decision arrived at the meeting would be announced after the poll notification was issued. However, none of the leaders present went on record. Badal told the meeting that he was committed to the poll boycott decision taken at Anandpur Sahib on September 1. Kabul Singh later conveyed to Amarinder Singh to also fall in line and go with the majority.[33] However, the response of Amarinder Singh was far from being positive. Around this period, Tohra was in favour of the talks between the Centre and the militants on the agenda of Khalistan before announcing the Assembly elections.[34]

The Centre announced the Assembly elections in Punjab to be held on February 19. The four major factions of the Akalis and two factions of the SSF formally announced the decision to boycott elections on January 17 at Ludhiana extending the logic they would not become a party to the farce being enacted in the name of democracy and called upon all political parties not to associate with the conspiracy to install a puppet government till a solid and lasting solution to the Punjab and the Sikh problem was arrived at. The decision was taken at a two hour meeting attended by Badal, Mann, Kartar Singh, Capt. Harcharan Singh Rode, Manjit Singh and SSF senior Vice-President, Sukhbir Singh Khalsa. It was decided to organize a rally at Ludhiana on February 2 to mobilize people in favour of the poll boycott and highlight the state repression in the state.

The resolution released after the meeting said holding of elections without finding a "solid and permanent solution" to the Punjab and the Sikh problem would be a futile exercise. These organizations claimed they had always been in the forefront of the Sikh struggle which had reached its peak during the last decade. It would amount to stabbing "this glorious struggle in the back" if they now jumped into the poll fray when not a single genuine demand of the Sikhs and Punjabis had been accepted by the "treacherous Centre". In case any political party decided to participate at this juncture, it would be committing an unpardonable betrayal of the faith with the Sikh struggle, Sikh qaum and Punjabis and will go down as a traitor in history. The resolution further said, "The iron is hot at present and the need of the hour is to strike it unitedly". The time had come to give up the lure of the office and steadfastly guard the Panthic and Punjabi interests.

At the same time, these leaders said they had always been the votary of peaceful and democratic means and preferred a peaceful solution to the problem. However, they could not wear the hollow mask of democracy. They wondered how the elections would be normal under the shadow of the guns of the army. The biggest issue was not the elections but a permanent and respectable political solution to what had come to be known as the Punjab problem.

Mann, in private, later used to hold Badal squarely responsible for the boycott decision which, for him, was historically wrong. What influenced the mind of Badal was the logic advanced by certain leaders including Tohra that in case the Akalis came into power, they would have to confront the militants and this job should better be left to the Congress.

However, while assessing the poll boycott decision later, some of the leaders who were in favour of participation in the democratic process were of the opinion that going by the ambitions of a section of the militants, that decision might have led to embarrassment later. Babbar Akali Dal had been constituted as political front by Babbar Khalsa International. However, other militant leaders were not taken into consideration by Babbar Khalsa leaders while creating this political outfit. It was perhaps for this reason that the Babbar Akali Dal failed to take off. What was intriguing during that period was virtually free movement of some militant leaders across the border as came to be known later.

The Akali Dal (Kabul) of Amarinder Singh, the only Akali faction to enter the poll arena, promised general amnesty in case the party returned to power. The announcement to this effect was made by Amarinder Singh on January 19 before the party formally announced the decision to enter the poll fray. He lambasted those Akali factions which had decided to boycott polls saying it would pave the way for the Congress to come to power and moreover, the solution to the Punjab problem was possible only through the ballot box.

Amarinder Singh was so confident of coming into power that a few days before the polling, he went to the extent of giving signals about the persons who would be part of his cabinet. It was said that he had been given some commitment by the Centre. However, this was an election which was managed at some other level. For Amarinder Singh, the solution to the Punjab problem was possible only through elections and in his perception, there was no logic in boycotting the same.

Mann's counsel B. L. Wadhera made an announcement in Delhi on January 23 that Akali Dal (Mann) was prepared to review the boycott decision provided the Centre assured free and fair poll under the UN observers. As the Centre assured free and fair poll, Mann backtracked from his statement saying he had only written a letter to his counsel to make his stand clear to the representatives of foreign countries and it was not for the press. Mann issued the denial in Badal's presence. The militants launched the poll boycott campaign.

Akali Dal (Badal) senior Vice-president Sukhjinder Singh resigned from the party to float a new outfit to contest the elections. However, he later backtracked. The Panthak Committee (Manochahal) announced the decision to enter the poll fray and released the first list of candidates. In Ludhiana, Talwandi also resigned from Akali Dal (Badal) to form a new party to enter the poll fray. Mann, on the other hand, called upon the Centre to call off the polls saying it would lead to communal strife and bloodshed. The Akali Dal (Kabul) put up candidates for three Lok

Sabha seats only which included Patiala, Ropar and Ferozepur. The two Left parties joined hands with the Akali Dal (Kabul). There were some friendly clashes at some seats which included Barnala, Sherpur, Dhanaula and Guru Harsahai from where the CPM had put up candidates while the CPI candidates had filed papers from Shutrana, Bathinda and Jalalabad also. The two Left parties confronted each other also in Dasuya.

The Congress paved the way for the unopposed victory of Amarinder Singh from Samana by managing the withdrawal of all other candidates. However, he lost from Kharar, the other seat he was contesting from. The Congress returned to power with two third majority, marking the end of the longest ever President's rule in the state. This was a turning point in the history of the state.

On the eve of the anti-poll march which was to start from Anandpur Sahib on February 12, the Punjab government invoked the Terrorists and Disruptive Activities (Prevention) Act against about 60 leaders of the six organizations spearheading the poll boycott. The police arrested Badal, Mann and Manjit Singh. The government also ordered the closure of all government and privately managed schools in the state till February 24 in the wake of the continued killing of the school teachers to deter the government employees from undertaking poll duties.

However, 16 SGPC members who managed to sneak in at Takht Keshgarh Sahib at Anandpur Sahib earlier and stayed put there passed a resolution on February 12 calling upon the people to boycott the elections. Tohra, who later courted arrest, said the resolution had the moral sanctity. The police had cordoned off the shrine. The resolution appealed to all Panthic organizations to rise above narrow interests and boycott the poll which was not only a fraud but a part of the Centre's conspiracy to unleash more repression on the Sikhs. The elections would be meaningless without a political solution, withdrawal of army and the black laws and the release of the Sikh youth. Talwandi also courted arrest along with Tohra.

The government through ordnance issued on January 20, cut down the campaign period from 20 to 14 days while announcing a revised schedule for the February 19 elections.

NOTES

1. The Indian Express, December 26, 1990.
2. The Indian Express, December 29, 1990.
3. Quoted from the original.
4. The Indian Express, January 2, 1991.

5. The Tribune, January 3, 1991.
6. The Times of India, January 16, 1991.
7. The Tribune, January 18, 1991.
8. Punjab Kesari, March 8, 1991.
9. Punjabi Tribune, January 6, 1991.
10. The Indian Express, January 13, 1991.
11. The Indian Express, January 14, 1991.
12. The Indian Express, January 25, 1991.
13. Akali Patrika, January 28, 1991.
14. The Indian Express, February 12, 1991.
15. The Indian Express, February 20, 1991.
16. The Indian Express, April 12, 1991.
17. The Tribune, April 15, 1991.
18. The Indian Express, April 25, 1991.
19. The Times of India, June 6, 1991.
20. Punjabi Tribune, July 5, 1991.
21. The Indian Express, July 26, 1991.
22. The Indian Express, July 18, 1991.
23. Ajit, August 4, 1991.
24. The Tribune, August 6, 1991.
25. The Times of India, October 17, 1991.
26. The Indian Express, October 5, 1991.
27. The Tribune, October 10, 1991.
28. The Indian Express, October 9, 1991.
29. The Indian Express, October 18, 1991.
30. Jagtar Singh, The Indian Express, October 28, 1991.
31. The Indian Express, November 25, 1991.
31. The Indian Express, November 25, 1991.
32. The Indian Express, December 30, 1991.
33. The Indian Express, January 11, 1992.
34. The Indian Express,, January 11, 1991

16

The Fall

Punjab was administered the much needed dose of democracy but in the absence of participation by the majority, the outcome was an illegitimate child. It was this illegitimate child which was the main instrument to curb militancy and this operation was complete within months. Suddenly, it was all over as Punjab emerged out of what at one time was being described as a long dark tunnel without the end in sight. The ordinary people harassed and humiliated by the so called militants finally helped in turning the tide. However, at the political level, this tactical gain by the security forces was neutralized by the unprecedented state repression and violation of human rights. The ordinary people were caught in the grind mill. The militants, alienated from the people and functioning in isolated groups, were hunted down one after the other. Several of them managed to escape to other countries.

The Assembly poll boycott was virtually complete in most of the Sikh dominated Malwa and Majha areas. On the day of polling, it was a silence of the graveyard in the countryside. In Joga constituency in the Malwa hinterland, only 1009 votes were polled out of more than a lakh votes. The winning candidate secured 394 votes, the lowest in the state. And most of these votes were polled in just one village to which that candidate belonged, and that too mainly from the dalit section. At many places, especially in the countryside, bogus votes were polled to increase the poll percentage.

Intriguingly, despite the boycott of the elections by the mainstream Akali Dal supported by the militant organizations, not a single killing in poll related violence was reported from any part of the state unlike the aborted June 1991 elections in which 29 Akali candidates were shot. The Akalis used to draw the parallels to hammer the point that it was the Congress which aided and abetted militancy as when the Congress entered the poll fray, not a single candidate was targeted. The Akali Dal government in 1997 should have at least investigated these killings to unravel the truth. It was not done.

The overall poll percentage was 23.82. While the boycott was almost total in the countryside, the polling was high in the Hindu dominated urban areas of Doaba. Out of the 117 Assembly seats, the Congress won from record 87 while three seats went to the Akali Dal of Amarinder Singh, five seats to the Bharatiya Janata Party, 10 seats to the Bahujan Samaj Party, four seats to the Communist Party of India and a lone seat each to the Communist Party of India (Marxist) and the Janata Dal. The rest of the six seats were captured by the independents. The two Communist parties contested the election in alliance with the Akali Dal (Kabul). For the first time in the history of Punjab, the Bahujan Samaj Party returned as the main opposition in the Assembly. Amarinder Singh very rarely attended the Assembly session.

Punjab had ushered into a new era under a 'democratically elected' Congress government headed by Beant Singh, who had himself received just about 17.15 per cent of the total votes from Jalandhar Cantonment constituency. Such was the situation at that time that even his colleagues had the apprehension about the government lasting more than six months. It was this regime lacking in legitimacy which, on the surface, could rightly claim the credit for restoring the much needed peace in the troubled state after wiping out militancy. However, for the Sikhs in general, the Beant Singh government ended up as a symbol of state repression and hate. The government could never prove its legitimacy. The Beant Singh era is also associated with the politics of unprecedented confrontation in the state at the political level.

Beant Singh himself became the victim of the politics of the gun. He was assassinated by the Babbar Khalsa in a bomb explosion at the main gate of the civil secretariat, the seat of the state administration in the high security zone, in 1995. His was the last major assassination associated with the militancy in the state, though situation had been controlled through police methods by then.

Beant Singh came down very hard against the Akali leaders also. The increasing state repression forced the first such re-alignment in the Sikh political spectrum and that too when the militant movement itself was petering out. The Panthic organizations hardened their stand and the six outfits, including Mann, Badal, Baba and Babbar factions of Akalis and the All India Sikh Students Federation (Manjit) and the Sikh Students Federation (Mehta-Chawla), which had spearheaded the poll boycott campaign, for the first time, completely identified themselves with the militants.

Akalis Support Khalistan Slogan

Within a few weeks of the Beant Singh government assuming office, the organizations which had boycotted the elections, at the Hola Mohalla conference at Anandpur Sahib on March 17, reiterated their goal as the sovereign and independent Sikh state. Adopting the line of total confrontation, launching of non-cooperation movement was threatened in case the Beant Singh government was not dismissed immediately. The legitimacy of this government had come to be questioned from day one itself. Earlier, these organizations had given a call for the boycott of the newly elected MLAs and MPs.

One of the resolutions passed at the Anandpur Sahib conclave stated the Sikhs had been pushed to the wall as a result of the anti-Sikh policies and betrayal by the successive governments at the Centre in general and those of the Congress in particular. The only option for the Sikhs was to struggle for a sovereign state. Through another resolution, the conclave called upon the militants to constitute a coordination committee. These Akali factions and other outfits resolved to function as a front organization for the militants. At last, the militants had the much needed political front and the development was considered to be very significant.

These organizations sought the intervention of the United Nations and the International Human Rights Commission to get Sikhs freedom from India. It was decided to organize district level conferences to thank people for making poll boycott a success. The state government was warned against continued harassment of the panchayat panches and sarpanches who had made the election boycott a success.

Demanding its immediate dismissal, the resolution stated the Beant Singh government which had come into power by getting only about 10 per cent of the votes and that too through rigging did not represent the aspirations of the people.

Those who addressed the conference included Akali Dal (Badal) General Secretaries Sukhdev Singh Dhindsa and Kuldip Singh Wadala, its youth wing President Prem Singh Chandumajra, Akali Dal (Mann) General Secretary Sucha Singh Chhotepur, SSF (Mehtta-Chawla) General Secretary Gurcharan Singh Grewal and Mohkam Singh from the Damdami Taksal. Senior leaders present included Akali Dal (Talwandi) President Jagdev Singh Talwandi, Akali Dal (Baba) President, Baba Joginder Singh and Damdami Taksal acting chief Thakar Singh. Several other senior Akali leaders were under detention at that time.

On the other hand, within a few days, Beant Singh made the truce offer to the militants from Baisakhi provided they laid down arms. He also offered to initiate dialogue with them. He made this offer while winding up the debate on Governor's Address in the state Assembly on March 27. The offer did not elicit any response. At the same time, the security forces went in for the final kill with full backing from the political leadership.

These six Panthic organizations went to the extreme at the Baisakhi conference at Talwandi Sabo in April and reiterated the demand for an independent Sikh state. The conference appealed to the sarpanches and panches to resign from the village local self-bodies (Panchayats) by June 6 and set up Khalsa panchayats. Through a resolution, a call was given to the people to ban entry of ministers, MPs and MLAs in the villages. It also called for boycott of government functions. These organizations also sought support from the United Nations for the Sikh struggle. The BKU (Lakhowal) appealed to the farmers to boycott mandis from May 1 to 7.[1] However, the boycott call of government functions and banning the entry of MPs and MLAs remained confined to the resolutions only.

In a significant development, the Babbar Khalsa, on April 17, condemned the killing of nine persons from the Hindu community in Bhangala village of Majitha police district in Amritsar district and called upon other militant organizations to desist from senseless killings of the members of the minority community.

Khalistan Memorandum to UN

Badal, Tohra and Mann were released from jail on April 17. While both Tohra and Mann expressed their resolve to work for the establishment of a sovereign Sikh state, Badal preferred to be vague saying the goal of the Sikhs had already been decided and there was no need for further debate. At the same time, he stressed the need to be practical and have a viable action plan.[2]

Tohra and Mann, after coming out of Nidampur rest house notified as jail in Sangrur district, said they would launch a peaceful struggle for the establishment of a sovereign Sikh state. Both these leaders were of the view that in any major settlement of the Sikh issues, the militants should be entrusted with the primary role.

Later in an interview, Tohra said it should be a united fight of the Punjabis- Sikhs, Hindus and Dalits- for the creation of a sovereign Punjab. He said the issue was Punjabiat and every body in the state should join the Punjabi mainstream.[3] Tohra had thus tried to add a new dimension to the demand for a sovereign Sikh state. He was not advocating a theocratic but a Punjabi sovereign state. He had set the agenda of Punjabiat which was later to be adopted by the Akali Dal at its 75th anniversary conference at Moga in 1996, though reference to this concept is also available in the earlier election manifestos of the party before the onset of militancy in the state. Of course, there were some contradictions as at the same time, he asserted that Punjab problem was a Sikh problem and should be tackled as such. He pointed out Badal faction was a party to the March 18 resolution adopted at Anandpur Sahib which specified the demand as the independent and sovereign Sikh state.

Badal, on his part, justified the resolution adopted by the six organizations at Anandpur Sahib on Hola Mohalla as the "culmination of deep sense of grievance among Sikhs over constant injustice, betrayal, persecution and continued breach of trust by the treacherous central leaders". He said in a statement that Centre's policies of discrimination and "mulish refusal to listen to even genuine grievances" had left them with no option but to internationally expose the system. At the same time, he expressed deep faith in the democratic and peaceful path while attacking the government for following policy of total confrontation and turning Punjab into a torture chamber. Calling for bold steps to satisfy the political aspirations of the Sikhs, he warned that if it was not done, the Centre would be responsible for the consequences. He referred to the birth of Pakistan which, he said, would never have been created had the Congress respected the sentiments and aspirations of the Muslims.[4] His statement making a clear distinction from the path of armed struggle was delivered on a day when the issue was taken to the United Nations.

In an attempt to internationalize the issue, the Akali leaders submitted a memorandum to United Nation's Secretary General Boutros Boutros-Ghali on April 22 pleading for intervention for the establishment of an "independent and sovereign state to break the shackles of apartheid, slavery, colonialism and a retrograde political system and structure". The memorandum was signed by Mann, Badal, Tohra, and the non-entities like Sukhbir Singh Khalsa, Inderpal Singh Khalsa, Harcharan Singh and Rajinder Singh Monga. However, for Badal, Tohra and Mann, this demand remained only confined to the memorandum though they continued to raise this slogan for some time. All the three leaders later backtracked from this demand at one time or the other.

Badal, Tohra again Ratify Khalistan Resolution

The Hola Mohalla resolution on sovereign Sikh state which was also adopted at the Baisakhi conference was formally ratified at a meeting held at Chandigarh on April 29 which was attended by Badal, Mann, Tohra, representatives from the Bharti Kisan Union and the Delhi Sikh Gurdwara Management Committee. It was decided that a trust should be floated by the SGPC and the DSGMC to rehabilitate the victims of November, 1984 violence against the Sikhs. These organizations supported the appeal to the farmers not to bring wheat to the markets for a week from May 1 to protest against low procurement price. The Badal factions continued to resort to such rhetoric to give impression to the hardliners that the party continued to espouse their cause also. It was for the perhaps for the first time that the DSGMC had become a party to the Sikh state demand.

It was also decided to extend legal aid to those in jails as part of the Sikh struggle and financial help to their families. An appeal was made to the panches and sarpanches to submit their resignations in protest against killings in fake encounters, state repression and harassment of women. It was perhaps for the first time that the demand for a sovereign Sikh state had received such support from the Akali leaders from across the Sikh spectrum.[5] At the political level, the situation was heading towards total confrontation.

It was in March that the Babbar Khalsa International had come out with directives to the bureaucracy in Punjab and Chandigarh on several issues, including the river waters, use of Punjabi in government offices and the teaching of Punjabi and postings, transfers and recruitment. No circular was to be issued in English after March 17. The Public Relations department was to issue maximum advertisements to the Punjabi newspapers and periodicals. The newspapers of the Hind Samachar group and Nawan Zamana (dubbed as traitors) were not to be given any advertisement. No negotiations were to be held on the river waters dispute with Haryana, Rajasthan or the government at the Centre. Earlier, it was the Panthic Committee which had issued the code of conduct for the media.

Yet another statement was issued on the river waters issue on April 16 in which the Babbar Khalsa owned the responsibility for gunning down of two engineers and a contractor who were carrying out the repair of the Bhakra canal. The Babbars had taken the stand that being non-riparian states, Haryana and Rajasthan had no rights over the Punjab river waters. The militant organization threatened that even the families of those working on these canals would not be spared. This included the Satluj Yamuna Link Canal.

Later yet in another statement in April, the Babbar Khalsa "imposed" a complete ban on the wearing of skirts by girls as school dress in Punjab and Chandigarh. The dress prescribed for the girls included saffron dupatta and turban of the same colour for boys.[6] The militants were once again resorting to the tactics which had been rejected earlier due to strong resentment among the people.

The government officials were so scared that the engineers and other employees apologized for repairing the Bhakra main line which carries waters to Haryana and partly to Rajasthan. The apology appeared as an advertisement in a Punjabi daily on April 29. Such ads appearing frequently in the papers, mainly the Punjabi papers, reflected the fear psychosis which had gripped the state during that period.

The Babbar Khalsa, in May, also owned the responsibility for the gunning down of Dr. D. S. Tyagi, chairman of the Agriculture Price Commission which sets the prices for farm produce, in Delhi. The logic advanced was that the Commission exploited the farmers and its policies were aimed at ruination of the Punjab farmers. The militant organization opposed the policy of price fixation by the government saying it should best be left to the operation of the market forces and the farmers should be free to sell their produce in the international market. A plea was also made to the UNO and European Economic Community to study this exploitation of the Punjab farmers. The Babbars were trying to mobilize the support of the peasantry through such targeted killings. It was the Punjab countryside which was the main recruiting ground for the armed struggle. The government intervention in the marketing of mainly wheat and paddy had started after the advent of the green revolution to check exploitation of the farmers at the hands of private traders. However, at a later stage, the Akali Dal and the farmer organizations opposed government intervention and started demanding operation of free market forces to determine the prices. The market intervention ensured assured price to the farmers in Punjab and Haryana, the two states having organized market system for the farm produce.

Yet in another development, the departmental heads of Panjab University, Chandigarh received threatening letters from the militant organizations with a proforma to be filled in by the teachers seeking their views on Khalistan and other issues.[7]

The steep downfall of the militant movement was to start during this period with one of the most barbaric actions by the militant organizations. It was the kidnapping of M. L. Manchanda, station director of the All India Radio at Patiala on May 18 who was later beheaded in a gruesome manner. He was abducted by the Babbar Khalsa. The organization demanded that electronic media adhere to a code of conduct, which included broadcasting in Punjabi rather than Hindi. Negotiations for his release broke down after the government failed to meet the deadline. Manchanda's children appealed to the militants in vain. On May 27, the militants beheaded Manchanda and put his severed head on display at a crossing in Patiala. The operation to kidnap him had been assigned to Babbar Khalsa area commander

Amrik Singh Kauli who was assisted by Gurdial Singh Kauli. He was confined at a secret place by one Gurdip Singh. Earlier, in yet another brutal action, the militants had gunned down handicapped station director of AIR in Chandigarh R. K. Talib.

In the face of tough posture adopted by the government towards the demands of the Babbar Khalsa, one section within the outfit favoured his unconditional release. However, there was another section which was of the view that in case a soft attitude was adopted, the government would never take the militants seriously. Finally, it was decided to adopt soft approach and message was sent accordingly. But then the people who had been assigned the operation to kidnap him did not agree with this line and later feigned the message had reached them too late. Manchanda was shot dead and then beheaded. Within days of this action, police succeeded in laying hands on his kidnappers who were shot dead. The security forces launched the all out offensive against the militants.

Moves were initiated to have joint command of militants among increasing reports of differences leading to even confrontation among some militant outfits. To begin with, the Sikh Students Federation (Daljit Bittu) was dissolved in June to pave way for unity of the SSF factions. The proposed new outfit was to be a front organization of the militants. The leaders of the new federation were to declare their assets and not accept government security for their protection. The government security aspect was very interesting and had many dimensions. Every member of this front organization was to be Amritdhari (baptized).[8] At one stage, the possibility of uniting all the Akali factions under the command of a new leader was also considered and discussed with some leaders including Badal.

After a short honeymoon, now was the time for the traditional Akalis to make a clear distinction from the radical Sikh thought and assert themselves. The Akali Dal (Badal), at its first meeting after the Assembly elections, on May 4, expressed complete distrust in the government as well as the Indian constitution and said the entire system was heavily loaded against minorities, especially the Sikhs. The meeting was attended by the members of the party executive committee, district jathedars, ex-MPs and ex-MLAs and the candidates for the de-notified June, 1991 elections. Chaired by Badal, the meeting expressed full faith in the democratic path and justified the poll boycott as a protest against the denial of democratic liberties of the people in general and the Sikhs in particular. Interestingly, there was no reference to the demand for the sovereign Sikh state. The resolution passed at this meeting stated that the history of the past 45-years had been a chronicle of betrayal, treachery and willful discrimination against the Punjabis and the Sikhs, culminating in the traumatic Operation Bluestar. This had brought the situation to a pass where the community had been forced to take a fresh look at the course it should pursue. The meeting urged the right thinking people in the country and abroad to view the aspirations of the Sikhs in the right perspective. The resolution called upon panches and sarpanches in the state to resign from their offices in protest against government's repressive policies. The meeting marked a paradigm shift from the slogan for Khalistan which the party otherwise had never translated into demand.

Within weeks of identifying itself with the militants and supporting the Khalistan slogan, the party was again in the process of giving out the signals that it was not opposing the Indian state per se and making this distinctions vis-à-vis the militants was very significant. The Shiromani Akali Dal had always been critical of the Congress governments in Delhi rather than attacking the Indian state.

Offensive Against Militants

After administering the first democratic anti-dote to militancy by holding elections to the state Assembly, the state government went in for a major offensive against the militants after the Beant Singh government consolidated its position. The police methods started yielding results. However, the offensive was not accompanied by any socio-economic or political input. It was only police action and the repressive methods and this strategy alienated the Beant Singh government from the people.

Babbar Khalsa chief Sukhdev Singh was killed on August 9 in Ludhiana district within weeks of the barbaric killing of Manchanda. He had been living incognito in Patiala urban estate for four years. His house-"White House"- had all the modern facilities. Posing as a government contractor, he lived with one Jawahar Kaur. They had a son. His earlier wife lived in his native village Dasuwal in Amritsar district. All this time, it was being given out by the intelligence agencies that he was in Pakistan. Babbar Khalsa's area commander Amrik Singh Kauli was also gunned down by the security forces. Gurcharan Singh Tohra carried his ashes for immersion to Kitartpur Sahib. He was very active on such matter during that period. His logic was very simple and according to him, the dead had their own human rights and the dead body should be accorded due respect.

Within days, yet another leader of this outfit based in England, Gurdip Singh Sibia, who had "surrendered", was produced before journalists. The same day, 71 militants, including 31 "listed" militants, laid down their arms at Tarn Taran.

Sibia had been arrested from Ahmedabad where he had been sent by his organization to facilitate the smuggling of weapons from Pakistan via the inhospitable Rann of Kutch area of Gujarat bordering Pakistan. This route was being used after barbed wire fencing came up on the Punjab border. It was a bank transaction from England which helped the security agencies to nab him. He had instructed his bank in England to transfer money in the account of the person with whom he was staying in Ahmedabad. Being Babbar Khalsa activist, his account was already under the scanner of the British intelligence which immediately alerted the Intelligence Bureau in India. The Intelligence Bureau acted swiftly and nabbed him. However, the entire operation was kept a secret affair as it was decided to use him for the bigger operation.

He was put up in a guest house for a few weeks. While in captivity he was deliberately allowed by the Intelligence Bureau operatives to get in touch with his contacts as if nothing had happened but he was not being allowed to convey that he was in custody. The operation worked very well and the Intelligence Bureau succeeded in making some very significant inroads into the Babbar Khalsa network.

While in detention Gurdip tried to convey the state of affairs to Babbar Khalsa leader Mehal Singh in Pakistan who was in charge of outfit there but he could not be interpreted. Unaware of his detention, Mehal singh conveyed to him that weapons would be dispatched from across the border for Punjab operations which were to be delivered to him. Smugglers were used to deliver the weapons to Gurdip via the arduous Rann route. One of the Babbar Khalsa activists also accompanied the consignment. Even before the consignment could reach the Indian side, the leaders from Punjab who went to meet him to take possession of the weapons on arrival smelt that Gurdip was already under detention.

When one of the two leaders met Gurdip at the pre-arranged location near Ahmedabad, a petrol pump, he could make out that the car in which Gurdip had arrived was being driven by a suspicious looking person. Immediately, he asked Gurdip that some thing seemed to be wrong. Gurdip nodded in agreement. The person who had gone to meet him jumped out of the moving car and managed to escape. He informed Mehal Singh through some foreign contact to withdraw the consignment as Gurdip was in police custody. This person was a well known activist of the Babbars in Ropar area. He was not a militant but a transporter and sympathizer of the militant movement. Months later after the militant movement petered out, he was nabbed and shot by the police. His killing was never announced by the police. The local MLA had met the victim in the police station and he was the eye witness in this case. Gurdip had been arrested before Sukhdev was killed.

As the consignment from the other side was still to reach the Indian side, Mehal Singh immediately got in touch with the Inter-Service Intelligence officials who sent a message to the border outpost on the Pakistani side to stop the party carrying the consignment to move further. They were conveyed that a bridge on the way had broken down and they could not proceed further. They understood the meaning. Gurdip had been under custodial observation for about three months before he was formally arrested.

Daljit Singh Bittu while in Pakistan also used this route to sent weapons across. It is the same tribe which inhabits the inhospitable Rann area on the two sides of the border and the main activity is smuggling. The camels used for smuggling are normally highly trained and can smell danger from a distance.

The security forces had started resorting to methods which were not only unprecedented but also inhuman, at least in this part of the region. Innocent persons were used as human shields during 28 hour encounter in Behla village in Amritsar district on June 9 and in the process, seven innocent persons were killed. Militant leaders killed included Surjit Singh Behla and Madan Singh. The militants had been alienated from the people to such an extent that there were no mass protests even against such actions of the security forces. Rather the people harassed and humiliated by the militants in the countryside were coming forward to provide the much needed information to the security agencies.

One of the Babbar Khalsa founders and main architects of the militant movement in the early days, Talwinder Singh Parmar, was killed on October 15 near Phillaur. He was shown to have been killed along five others in an encounter with the police. He had been nabbed earlier from near Pathankot. Two of the dead were identified as Habibulah Khan and Intkhab Ahmad Zia, residents of Lahore in Pakistan. Their passports Nos H-822669 and E-090696 were also shown to have recovered from them.

The militant organizations for years had been aware of the penetration in their ranks. Almost every militant outfit had tried to check extortions, rape and killing of the innocents. The Panthic Committee again came out with a statement on July 29 against such activities and threatened strong action against such elements. The Committee clarified that the militant organizations working under its command had nothing to do with the threatening letters being sent to the people to demand money. Yet another statement released the same day in the name of Gurjant Singh Budhsinghwala, chief general, Khalistan Liberation Force, Satnam Singh Chhina, chief general, Bhindranwale Tiger Force of

Khalistan and Paramjit Singh Panjwar, chief general, Khalistan Commando Force, appreciated the villagers of Gandwa in the Phagwara tehsil of Kapurthala district for getting hold of one of the extortionists who had gone to the village in the name of Khalistan Commando Force. Interestingly, projecting pro-people posture, these organizations directed the panchayat of Bhago village in Gurdaspur district and the district development and panchayat officer to get the encroachment removed on the land allotted to the dalits.

The Akali Dal (Longowal), the two Communist parties and the Republican Party of India, at a meeting on August 7, decided to launch joint struggle against the Centre and the Punjab government demanding justice and restoration of peace in the state. It was decided to set up a joint action committee for the purpose. The action plan was to be announced at the death anniversary of Harchand Singh Longowal on August 20 at Longowal village.

Continuing with its moderate line, Akali Dal (Longowal), at its Shaheedi conference on August 20 at Longowal, served an ultimatum to the Centre to implement the Punjab Accord and end policy of confrontation with the Sikhs by November 2 or face a peaceful and democratic agitation by the Punjabis. The conference was also attended by senior BJP leader Atal Behari Vajpayee, Communist Party of India leaders including M Farooqi, Piara Singh Deosi and Avtar Singh Malhotra, Maneka Gandhi (Janata Dal), Satya Pal Singh Yadav (Janata Dal-Ajit General Secretary), Bhim Singh (Panthers Party) and Mangat Ram Pasla (CPI-M). Earlier on August 5 at a meeting at Chandigarh, the Akali Dal (L), the two Communist parties and the Republican Party of India had constituted a joint action committee to press for the implementation of the Rajiv-Longowal accord. The conference also called upon the militants to do some introspection. It was felt that pressure should be exerted on the Centre to implement the Accord, punish the guilty of November, 1984 anti-Sikh violence and end the state repression.

This conference was seen as an attempt to give new direction to the situation in the blood-splattered Punjab at a time when the state government was confronting the militants and the major Akali factions were more divided than ever in spite of the so-called unity effort. "It is a cry for peace in the Wild West that is Punjab... Even the militants continue to be as divided as ever in spite of the realization by various groups that the division among their ranks would continue to prove counter productive. There are indications that a section of them have been debating for the last some time the futility of sticking to their political goal of Khalistan in the absence of active support from the Sikh masses".[9]

Yet another Akali faction known as the Shiromani Akali Dal (Manjit) was floated by AISSF (Manjit) chief Manjit Singh on August 25 after relinquishing the office of the student's organization. The political goal of the new outfit was to be Khalsa Raj. The meeting demanded immediate election to the general house of the SGPC. His name for the office of the president was proposed by Gurtej Singh, former IAS officer and seconded by Gursev Singh Harpalpur. The meeting demanded immediate elections to the general house of the SGPC and lifting of siege of some gurdwaras. The new outfit accorded recognition to Gurbachan Singh Manochahal as the Jathedar of Akal Takht.

Akali Dal (Mann) President Simranjit Singh Mann at a meeting of Akali workers at Mullanpur near Ludhiana again raised the demand for Khalistan and said nothing less would be acceptable to the Sikhs. Badal said at the meeting that he was contacting the leaders of the national political parties to visit Punjab to have first hand account of the police brutalities.

As the Akalis resorted to the agitational path against the state repression, the Beant Singh government decided to be tough. The anti-repression rally at gurdwara Alamgir in Ludhiana district on August 30 was thwarted with the arrest of Tohra and about 300 odd Akali activists. He was taken into custody when he was addressing a press conference. The police had barricaded the road to the shrine. He offered resistance. Badal was already in jail. Both of them were later released.

Civic Poll

Yet in another attempt to restore power at the grass roots and get legitimacy, the Beant Singh government went in for the municipal elections. In the civic elections held in September, it was a different scenario with full participation by the people. The Congress claimed majority in these elections. However, the civic polls were urban phenomenon and it was the countryside where anger was more discernible against state repression. The normal pattern in Punjab is that the urban local bodies normally go with the ruling party.

Meanwhile, Akali Dal (Badal) decided to launch a peaceful agitation against the state repression, disrespect to women in police stations, detention of the Sikh youth and fake encounters at a meeting at Amritsar on September 12. The first demonstration was to be organized in Delhi at the Boat Club on October 12. The meeting passed a resolution seeking support of the opposition to come to the rescue of the Sikhs. The resolution said the treatment being meted out to the Sikhs and use of state repression to stifle democratic methods in Punjab was the reason the party had decided to stage a demonstration in Delhi. The party retaliated against Mann who had charged the traditional Akali leadership with conniving with the government on Operation Bluestar. The party also demanded the release of Harjinder Singh Jinda, Sukhdev Singh Sukha, Ranjit Singh, Jasvir Singh Rode, Kartar Singh Narang, Amarjit Singh Chawla and Rajinder Singh Mehta.

The Akali Dal (Longowal), at its meeting of the working committee, district presidents, members of the SGPC owing allegiance to the party and the youth wing leaders at Chandigarh on September 14 demanded resignation of the Beant Singh government and fresh elections in the state in the absence of a clear mandate to the Congress in the civic poll. The meeting authorized party president Kabul Singh and Surjit Singh Barnala to chalk out a programme of action in consultation with other political parties to be launched after November 2 for getting the demands accepted.

Disgusted with factionalism, the Akali workers at the grassroots started putting pressure on the leadership to unite and as a first step, Akali factions in Amritsar district dissolved their respective units and set up ad hoc committees to pave the way for unity. In Ludhiana, representatives of various Akali factions decided not to allow the leaders to make use of the gurdwara stage in case they did not unite. Earlier, Akali workers in Faridkot district had forced Badal and Mann to share the same platform at the political conference at Guru Ki Dhab village.

Akali Petition on Sukha and Jinda

The one issue which brought Akalis of various shades on one platform, though for a short while, was the death sentence to Harjinder Singh Jinda and Sukhdev Singh Sukha. As the Supreme Court rejected the plea to stay their hanging in General A. S. Vaidya assassination case, the Akalis, on October 8, submitted a review petition to the President of India which was turned down. The Akalis marched to the Rashtrapati Bhavan to submit a memorandum against the sentence. The memorandum was signed by Mann, Tohra, Badal and Talwandi, besides representatives of Damdami Taksal, Delhi Sikh Gurdwara Management Committee, Babbar Akali Dal, Sikh Students Federation and Akali Dal (Manjit). The Sikh organizations gave a 72-hour Punjab bandh call beginning October 10 in protest against these executions.

The leaders of various Sikh organizations and Akali factions met on October 9 to take stock of the situation. The resolution adopted at the meeting appealed to the Sikhs all over the world to sleep on floor during the bandh period and observe fast on October 10. Another resolution stated the Akali Dal would work for the achievement of the goal for which the duo gave their lives. These two militant leaders had made their ideological position very clear in the letter written in their name to the then President of India R. Venkataraman. The meeting also rejected the constitution of India. Those who attended the meeting included Badal, Tohra, Mann, Mohkam Singh of Damdami Taksal, Talwandi and Ajit Singh Bains from the Punjab Human Rights Organisation.

They were hanged in Pune jail on October 9. The Punjabi daily Ajit paid glowing tributes to the assassins of General Vaidya by describing them martyrs of the Sikh nation who would be remembered for taking revenge for the attack on the Darbar Sahib complex. The editorial said these young men had carved out their place in the history by making this supreme sacrifice. It was said they had attained the same status as Bhai Sukha Singh and Bhai Mehtab Singh in Sikh history who had avenged the sacrilege of Darbar Sahib by the then rulers.[10]

In protest against their execution, the SGPC decided not to illuminate the Darbar Sahib complex on Diwali that year. Their bhog ceremony was performed at Akal Takht on October 18 where they were declared martyrs whose names were to form part of the daily prayer (ardas). Their families were described as the "Families of the Panth". However, no senior Akali leader attended the ceremony. Tohra said at Amritsar on October 20 that Sukhdev Singh and Harjinder Singh were the Sikh martyrs who deserved Panthic recognition. He said anyone who dared to attack Akal Takht would meet the fate of Indira Gandhi and General Vaidya. The traditional Akali leaders, by making such observations, were perhaps trying to seek legitimacy for themselves rather than supporting the cause of the militants.

This opportunism of various Akali factions was exposed by Babbar Khalsa in a 9-page policy statement which laid equal emphasis on the armed and the mass struggle for the achievement of Khalistan. While expressing satisfaction at the armed struggle, the militant outfit regretted that the Akali factions had done nothing to mobilize people on the demand for Khalistan and had only misled them by just supporting the slogan.[11]

The ideological shift in the Akali factions was again discernible at the Jor Mela conferences at Fatehgarh Sahib on December 26. The Akali Dal (Badal) opted for the minority politics and gave a call to the minorities, dalits and secular and democratic forces to launch a countrywide agitation to force the resignation of the P. V. Narasimha Rao government at the Centre on the issue of demolition of Babri mosque at Ayodhya by the activists of the Sangh Parivar. The party said in a resolution that earlier the attack on Akal Takht and now the demolition of Babri mosque had made the minorities realize that their religion, religious places, culture and language were not safe. The party alleged complicity of the government with the BJP and the Sangh Parivar. The party called upon secular and democratic forces to gherao the Parliament for an indefinite period to force the Narasimha Rao government to resign. The resolution blamed the Centre for crushing minorities, dividing the people, sacrilege of religious places and dismissing the state governments without any reason. The party also decided to carry on the agitation against state repression. There was no reference to the demand for the sovereign Sikh state.

It was clear at this convention that the party was in the process of once again going back to the moderate stance in politics. The emphasis was shifting. The parting of ways with Akali Dal (Mann) was complete. Badal compared Akali Dal (Mann) President Simranjit Singh Mann with the Mughal emperor Mohammad Tughlak who is ridiculed for certain flawed decisions.

The Akali Dal (Mann) conference preferred to be silent on political issues and the main agenda was the human rights and the state repression. Of course, the Congress government was criticized for the demolition of the Babri Masjid.

It was after about a decade in 1992 that Congress made its appearance at the Jor Mela by organizing its political conference at Fatehgarh Sahib.

Now was the time for panchayat elections in the state. Contrary to the poll boycott decision during the Assembly elections, all the Akali factions and the militant outfits called upon the people in the countryside to participate in the elections and elect panches and sarpanches unanimously to register their democratic protest against the dictatorial policies of the Beant Singh government. The ruling Congress wanted to seek mandate for the restoration of peace in its first year in office through these elections at the grassroots. Several militant outfits issued policy statements on these elections. The Panthic Committee associated with Dr. Sohan Singh called upon the Akali factions to join hands and confront the ruling Congress from one platform. However, the militants favoured election of candidates supporting the demand for Khalistan in these elections. And the Beant Singh government saw to it that those owing allegiance to the Akalis were not allowed to contest these elections which were held in January, 1993. The Beant Singh government resorted to coercive methods to keep such elements away from the elections to the extent that the potential candidates were framed in false cases. The Assembly elections in the state had earlier been boycotted mainly in the rural areas and the panchayat elections are a rural phenomenon.

Limping back to Normalcy

Punjab started limping back to normalcy in 1993 as the government continued with its no holds barred offensive against the militants, many of them turned criminals, who had already been isolated and alienated from the Sikh masses for indulging in rapes, distortions and killings. Most of the top militant leaders had either been eliminated or fled the country. Here is yet another example of the brutal police methods. A police party headed by Ram Singh, Superintendent of Police, Ferozepur, raided a gurdwara in village 9 GB in Ganganagar district of Rajasthan on December 22, 1992 to arrest a militant Nasib Singh from Mallewala village in Punjab who had taken shelter there. The policemen were in plain clothes and did not inform the local police. As they tried to take away the militant, they were attacked by the gurdwara staff. The policemen then sought the help of the local police and by that time, Nasib Singh had escaped. The Ganganagar police refused to extend cooperation as the team had come without informing the district authorities. Nasib was arrested by the local police the next day and subsequently handed over to the Punjab Police on December 28. The Punjab Police announced his death in an encounter on January 1 near his village Moujgarh where he was shown to have been taken to recover arms.[12]

Despite the Akali factions having supported the demand for the sovereign Sikh state, the militants did not get any mass support. Radical slogans apart, the Akalis continued to adhere to the moderate politics and did not mobilize any support for the cause of Khalistan. Their support to the slogan was just at the level of rhetoric. They too had been the victims of violence. A section of the Akali leadership had come under attack from the radicals right from April, 1978.

There was yet another aspect of the situation. After years of fear psychosis, the state was witnessing the resurgence of cultural activities. These so called cultural activities were promoted, though indirectly, by the police, to instill confidence among the masses at one level.[13] However, this cultural resurgence was taken too far, distorting the Punjabi culture itself. It was this planned multi-dimensional cultural invasion which continues to haunt Punjab. In a way, it was the cultural offensive targeted at the religious sensitivity.

At the Maghi conference at Muktsar, Beant Singh opposed holding of elections to the general house of the SGPC while Tohra expressed apprehensions about the abolition of the Sikh Gurdwara Act to disband the mini-Parliament of the Sikhs.[14]

The Panthic Committee issued a policy statement in February, 1993 on the basis of some introspection in which the importance of political struggle along with the militant line was emphasized. It was made clear that the goal could not be achieved without the proper coordination between the political movement and the militant struggle. The Babbar Khalsa earlier had already come out with such a statement on the strategy and tactics.[15] But then, it was too late.

That the Akali Dal (Badal) had already started demarcating itself from the radical politics was further indicated from the meeting of the party held at Chandigarh on February 19 which was attended by the members of the working committee, ex-MPs, ex-MLAs and the district presidents. The party warned the government against any attempt to dismantle the SGPC. The warning was with reference to the line adopted by Beant Singh that the elections to this statutory body should not be the responsibility of the government. The resolution passed at the meeting said the Sikhs would not tolerate any attempt to tamper with the Sikh Gurdwara Act, 1925 under which this body had been constituted, leave aside abrogating it and threatened a peaceful struggle. The party also demanded the immediate resignation of the government at the Centre. The party took strong notice of the state repression saying: "The party is pained at the grave violations of human rights in Punjab by the power drunken government. Sikh men, women and children are taken away from their homes at the merest suspicion and subjected to all kinds of torture by the police. In many cases, they are released only after extracting huge sums of money from them. What is even more shocking is that even their whereabouts are not revealed and many of them are eliminated and then reported missing by the police. Even the most respected Sikh personages are not spared; the case of Bhai Gurdev Singh Kaonke is painful example of this. Village after village are made the target of state repression. What happened at Beerowali village is an outrage against humanity. The party calls for an immediate end to this butchery in Punjab". There was no reference to the sovereign Sikh state slogan in the 3-page resolution adopted at the meeting.

In the continuing offensive against the militants, Bhindranwale Tiger Force of Khalistan chief Gurbachan Singh Manochahal was shot dead by the security forces in an encounter on February 18. Director General of Police K. P. S. Gill said in Chandigarh, "We have won the battle". The encounter took place at Rataul village under Verowal police station in Amritsar district.[16] At an early morning press conference called by Gill in the police mess in Chandigarh to announce the killing, a senior journalist suggested to him to open a bottle of champagne to celebrate the occasion. He did not like the idea.

After the conference at Muktsar at Maghi, the Congress organized its political show during Hola Mohalla at Anandpur Sahib also on Macrh

8. Beant Singh "rejected" the Anandpur Sahib Resolution at that convention. Akali Dal (Badal), at its political conference the same day there, demanded removal of Beant Singh government, resignation of Prime Minister Narasimha Rao and fresh elections in the country. The resolution stated the Chief Minister was bent upon converting Punjab into a battlefield.

What was perhaps all the more significant trend at the convention was the outburst of Tohra against the militants saying they had gone astray. At the same time, he also lambasted the government for resorting to the policy of bullet for bullet which would not solve the problem as the feelings of the Sikhs who were fighting for freedom must be assuaged. Akali Dal (Mann), from a separate stage, also demanded dissolution of the Assembly and fresh elections while reiterating the demand for a sovereign Sikh state. It was stated that the party would continue its peaceful struggle for the achievement of this goal. Akali Dal (Manjit) also demanded dismissal of the Beant Singh government and elections to the Assembly as well as the SGPC.

Continuing its confrontationist attitude, the Beant Singh government banned the proposed rally of the Akai Dal (Badal) at Jalandhar to be held on March 14 and imposed an undeclared curfew around the venue. His policy was to confront the Akalis while eliminating militants.

The Chief Minister, at the Baisakhi conference of the Congress on April 13 at Talwandi Sabo, demanded ban on communal parties (read Akali Dal) while the Akalis pressed for the dismissal of his government. The Akali Dal (Badal) reiterated the party would continue its drive to mobilize people to force the dismissal of the Congress (I) government which was described as the enemy of the people. The Congress was blamed for the religious, social, economic and political repression of the people. The party demanded that the constitution should be re-written to provide for a real federal structure to meet the aspirations of the people. The farmers should have the right to fix the prices of their produce to end their exploitation. The party was back with its moderate face and started occupying its original space.

The Akali Dal (Badal), under the changing situation, was reverting to its normal democratic activity. The priorities were changing fast. The party, on June 13, submitted a memorandum to Governor Surendra Nath against resuming the construction of the Satluj Yamuna Link Canal saying it could lead to grave consequences in case the government did not desist from playing with the sentiments and honour of the people of Punjab. The party demanded that the entire case of Punjab's river waters should be reviewed strictly in accordance with the provisions of the constitution. Any accord, decision or award or agreement or settlement which violated the provisions of the constitution would be totally unacceptable to the people of Punjab.

The functioning of the state government was exposed at another level. It was the second rung bureaucracy which took upon itself the job of uncovering the misdeeds of the administration. It was the Punjab Civil Service Officers Association which raised the banner of revolt in August against the police methods alleging there was no rule of law in the state. It was a reaction to the arrest of two PCS officers by the police in August. The association admitted the PCS officers had been signing on the dotted lines for many years to justify police actions. They demanded judicial probe into the rise and fall of militancy.

Though the battle had been lost, the radicals continued to confront the traditional Akalis in the religious domain with the Damdami Taksal challenging the SGPC on the issue of Maryada (Sikh religious code). The issue was discussed by the advisory committee of the Akal Takht Jathedar on August 5 which resolved that the Maryada endorsed by the SGPC would continue to be followed. However, the Sikh sants (religious leaders) at a meeting at Mansuran (Ludhiana) convened by the Taksal on August 8 maintained that the Maryada adopted by the Sarbat Khalsa and approved by the SGPC general house in 1988 would be followed. Jasvir Singh Rode was instrumental in affecting a change in the 1988 meeting in his capacity as the Akal Takht Jathedar. The issue mainly related to the recitation of Raag Mala which is at the end of Guru Granth Sahib.

Tohra attended the Shaheedi conference organized by the Akali Dal (Longowal) at Longowal on August 20 thereby raising the hopes of Akali unity. The party gave a call to the people to launch a mass movement to bring pressure on the government to concede the outstanding demands of the Punjabis. The party called upon the people to rally around the policies of Harchand Singh Longowal in order to achieve a lasting and durable peace and restore the honour and pride of the Punjabis and the Sikhs.

The two factions of the Akalis under the leadership of Mann and Joginder Singh merged on September 25 at the intervention of the Damdami Taksal. Under the situation, not much importance was attached to this development as it was the Badal faction which was emerging on the scene to dominate the political space.

As the Beant Singh government continued with its repressive agenda, the police detained Akali leaders including Badal, Tohra, Talwandi, Manjit Singh Calcutta, Surjan Singh Thekedar and others on October 20 to stop them from holding a meeting at Talwandi Sabo to chalk out the strategy for protest march to Delhi on November 1 which was be organized to protest the sacrilege of a Gurdwara at Gujjarwal in Ludhiana district. Asserting that the misuse of religious places would not be allowed, the state government, on October 21, banned the proposed march. The attempt to take out the march from the Akal Takht was frustrated by the police with the arrest of Mann on November 1.

Dr. Sohan Singh, considered to be one of the top ideologues of the militants, was mysteriously shown to have been arrested from Mohali in November. And he was released after questioning. The video of his questioning was played at a news conference which had to be suddenly stopped when he mentioned the name of a senior journalist from a Punjabi newspaper.

The working committee of the Shiromani Akali Dal (Badal) which met at Amritsar on November 23, decided to stage dharna outside Parliament on December 20 in protest against sacrilege by the police of a gurdwara at Gujjarwal in Ludhiana district in mid-September and in support of various demands. The meeting adopted nine resolutions. The working committee condemned the ban imposed by the state government on November 1 Akali march from Akal Takht to Delhi against the sacrilege and described it as open challenge to the Panth. It condemned the misbehavior against Akal Takht acting Jathedar Prof. Manjit Singh by some police officers on November 1 and demanded action against them. The working committee came down heavily against the efforts of the state government to scuttle peaceful struggles and violation of human rights. The meeting also condemned anti-farmer policies of the state government. Yet another resolution took strong note of the rampant corruption prevalent at all levels in the state administration.

The Akali Dal (Badal), while giving a call for "jail bharo" agitation on December 26, 1993 at its Jor Mela conference at Fatehgarh Sahib, decided to enroll about one lakh volunteers to press the Centre to concede the long pending demands of Punjab. Tohra demanded the setting up of a commission to investigate as to which party was responsible for Sikh militancy in the state. This demand was incorporated by the party in its manifesto for the 1997 Assembly elections also. By this time, the guns had become silent. The party had launched its Dharamyudh morcha way back in 1982 precisely as "jail bharo" agitation with the Akali volunteers courting arrest every day till Operation Bluestar on these very demands. The Akali Dal (Mann), from a separate stage, parroted the demand for the independent and sovereign Sikh state.

Ironically, at the time when militancy had been checked, the Sikh issue was getting globalized as evident from the letter US President Bill

Clinton wrote to Congressman Gary A. Condit in which he talked of the Sikh rights and the excesses by the police in Punjab. Earlier, a number of Congressmen had written a letter to the US President on November 17 in which it was stated: "The Sikh nation is facing merciless oppression in its homeland, Punjab, Khalistan. The Indian government has not granted the Amnesty International access to investigate human rights violations in India since 1978.... In the face of such oppression, the Sikh nation declared independence from India on October 7, 1987 forming the sovereign country of Khalistan. Like all Americans, the people of the Sikh nation only desire freedom, democracy, human rights and self-determination". The letter was signed by Condit, Pete Geren, Tom Bliley, Dana Rohrabacher, William J. Jefferson, Phil Crane and others.

However, the Sikh struggle for the sovereign state had already petered out.

NOTES

1. The Indian Express, April 14, 1992.
2. Hindustan Times, April 18, 1992.
3. The Indian Express, April 22, 1992.
4. The Indian Express, April 22, 1992.
5. The Indian Express, April 30, 1992.
6. The Indian Express, April 29, 1992.
7. The Indian Express, May 5, 1992.
8. Ajit, June 28, 1992.
9. The Indian Express, August 22, 1992.
10. Ajit, October 10, 1992.
11. Ajit, November 12, 1992.
12. Hindustan Times, January 6, 1993.
13. The Indian Express, February 29, 1993.
14. The Indian Express, January 14, 1992.
15. Ajit, February 12, 1993.
16. The Indian Express, March 1, 1993.

17

Akali Politics Redefined

With the radicals having been forced out of the space they had been occupying in the Sikh political matrix for about a decade, it was time for the traditional Akalis, who had been wavering from the demand for autonomy to Khalistan during this period, to redefine their politics. The earlier version of this Akali demand for autonomy was Sikhstan. The Akali Dal was not the only regional party in the country which had raised the demand for autonomous states but it was emphasis to the Sikh aspirations in the 1973 version of the Anandpur Sahib resolution which had given a new meaning to this demand which had to be watered down in 1978 to keep out the Sikh content. This transition is very significant as the armed struggle for a sovereign Sikh state had evolved over time and articulation of the Sikh aspirations had been the agenda of the Akali Dal for years. The secessionists took the issue of Sikh aspirations to the extreme. The credibility of the Akali leaders had come to be questioned due to what is described as the politics of opportunism resorted to by these leaders. Sant Jarnail Singh Bhindranwale had come to occupy the space which had become vacant due to this credibility gap associated with the traditional Akalis who had been raising the pitch earlier.

The Sikh issues had come under focus again as the party launched the Dharamyudh Morcha in 1982. With the militants dictating the political discourse by the time the agitation was launched by the Akali Dal, a new dimension had been added to the situation. Now with militancy having been curb, Punjab was entering a new phase with the return of normalcy which brought the much needed opportunity to the traditional Akalis to revert to mainstream politics and chart out a new course but not without resorting to the rhetoric for some more time in the form of Amritsar Declaration. The Maghi convention at Muktsar in January of 1994 provided this break to the dominant Akali Dal (Badal), which after a short honeymoon with the militants, had distanced itself from the radical thought.

Significantly, none of the six resolutions adopted by the Akali Dal (Badal) at this conference referred to the militants or the turbulent period. The allusion to the violation of human rights too was in a milder tone. Rather the effort was to re-establish forward linkage with the national politics. It was in this context that the party gave a call to all the political parties to launch a united struggle for more powers to the states. Yet there was another significant shift. The resolution did not touch upon the demand for autonomy, an issue dear to the Akali Dal all these years, but the thrust was just on more powers. The reference to the Akali struggle on this issue, of course, was there. The resolution said the party had taken up the issue twenty eight years ago. The government retaliated by sending army to attack the Darbar Sahib complex. Thousands of youth, political personalities, intellectuals, women, children and the elders were martyred and thousands of Sikhs were sent to jails. The government tried to isolate the Sikhs by dubbing them as separatists and extremists. It was the Congress which had ultimately got isolated and alienated. It had been proved that the Sikhs were a political force in the country.

The Punjab problem was referred to in the fifth resolution which stated that peace could not be established without resolution of the problems concerning the Punjabis and the Sikhs. The effort was to give the impression that the demands for which the Akali Dal had been struggling were not the issues concerning just the Sikhs alone and thus get out of the isolation which the party had experienced during militancy. The party announced that the peaceful and democratic struggle would continue for the acceptance of these demands and condemned the efforts of the government to ban peaceful and democratic struggles. On the river waters issue, the party reiterated that not a drop would be allowed to flow out unconstitutionally and illegally. However, the party did nothing on the river waters issue after coming into power in 1997 and it was the Congress government headed by Amarinder Singh which returned to power in 2002 replacing the Akali Dal which adopted the historic legislation in the state Assembly to protect the state interests on this issue for which he had to pay the cost for annoying the Congress high command.

At this convention, the party talked about the problems being faced by the peasantry and other sections due to the hike in power tariff, spurious sprays and the like. The party demanded bonus on paddy and announced the peasantry would be mobilized to get justice. The problems of other sections of society including corruption in administration were also referred to. For the traditional Akali Dal, it was going back to the people. The break from the immediate past was almost complete.

Buta at Akal Takht

In yet another noteworthy development in the Sikh religio-political affairs, former Union Home Minister Buta Singh presented himself at Akal Takht on January 25, 1994 to seek forgiveness for his controversial role after Operation Bluestar in the repair of the desecrated and damaged Akal Takht. He repeatedly pleaded, "Main doshi haan, main papi haan" (I am guilty, I have sinned). He had been ex-communicated by the high priests from the Sikh Panth on April 2, 1985. In his letter to the Akal Takht Jathedar, Buta Singh said, "I hereby humbly request your holiness that being Union Minister for Housing and Rehabilitation, the Government of India entrusted the job of repair of the most sacred shrine of the Golden Temple, the Akal Takht and the Darshani Deodi in 1984 which generated a lot of controversy. As a result, the Jathedar of Akal Takht ex-communicated me by the issuance of a Hukamnama. I was not given an opportunity to explain my position. Being a humble Sikh who recites 'nitnem' (prescribed daily prayer) I humbly submit to your holiness that I may be pardoned and taken back into the fold of the Guru Khalsa Panth. I will abide by every directive of yours with full respect and devotion". He was awarded religious punishment (Tankhah) and a plaque hung around his neck which read "God forgive me, I am a great sinner". He was ordered to clean utensils, dust shoes and sweep floors for a period of eight weeks. He was readmitted into the Sikh fold on March 25, 1994. He was one of the guilty men and women of Operation Bluestar.

In yet another related development, Congress (I) MP from Faridkot Jagmeet Singh Brar called upon Prime Minister P. V. Narasimha Rao to tender apology for Operation Bluestar in the wake of Buta Singh presenting himself at Akal Takht to atone for his sins. He said as a long term solution, the Congress Working Committee must pass a resolution apologizing for Operation Bluestar. The promises made to the Sikhs by Mahatma Gandhi and Pandit Jawahar Lal Nehru must be honoured by granting autonomy to Punjab. He maintained the Sikhs were a separate nation and they must enjoy a special status. Commenting upon US President Bill Clinton's observations on the Sikh struggle, Brar said the voice of Punjab had not been heard all these years and it was high times the rulers in Delhi changed the policy towards Punjab.[1] He was the only Congress leader at that time to voice his opinion boldly.

All these months, Shiromani Gurdwara Parbandhak Committee

President Gurcharan Singh Tohra was having differences with Parkash Singh Badal which came to the fore during the Hola Mohalla celebrations at Anandpur Sahib. He preferred to stay away from the Akali Dal (Badal) stage. They reportedly resolved their differences in early April following a meeting at Sirhind.

Moves for Akali Unity At Baisakhi

The Baisakhi of 1994 witnessed another turning point in the politico-religious affairs of the Akalis as it marked the intervention of Akal Takht once again in the efforts to unite the warring factions and leaders. Almost the entire leadership of various factions and the SGPC offered their services to Akal Takht acting Jathedar Prof. Manjit Singh at Talwandi Sabo on April 13. These leaders included Badal, Tohra, Mann, Amarinder Singh, Surjit Singh Barnala, Manjit Singh, Jagdev Singh Talwandi, all factions of the youth wing of Akali factions and the Sikh Students Federation at the concluding function of the Khalsa march.

However, Badal, while submitting his resignation to Prof. Manjit Singh, alleged the march was part of the conspiracy to dislodge him from the presidency of his faction and the offer of their services by various leaders to the Akal Takht was a calculated move to isolate him and it was for this reason that the SGPC spent about Rs 2 to 3 crore on the Khalsa march which had originated from Sri Hargobindpur in Gurdaspur district. Speaking in am emotional tone in a charged atmosphere, he even offered to retire from politics. At the same time, he committed himself to the supremacy of the Akal Takht and every decision taken on Akali unity. He had a brief altercation with Tohra on the stage and said he had always stood by him during the last 20 years but now he was after him. Badal said if he wanted to head the Akali Dal, he should have told him in clear terms. The Akal Takht Jathedar returned the resignation to Badal saying all Akali leaders should send him in writing their views on Akali unity.

However, it was Amarinder Singh and not Tohra who had pleaded for the intervention of the Akal Takht in the Akali unity and the proposal got instant support from Mann who said the unity should be on the basis of principles. However, these factions held their political conferences separately.

Addressing his party conference, Badal called for a decisive democratic movement for political and fiscal autonomy to the states. He said the ethnic, cultural, linguistic, religious and other identities of the people from different regions must be respected and preserved. This was imperative for harmonious co-existence of people with different backgrounds. It was the denial of the legitimate demands and rights which led to extremist and violent trends in the society. His attack was on the Congress policy of divide and rule which was responsible for what had happened in Punjab.

However, within days of this development, Badal wrote to Prof. Manjit Singh advising him to distance himself from the Akali affairs and wait for the mandate of the people to be reflected in the forthcoming elections to the general house of the SGPC which would prove as to which Akali faction enjoyed the support of the Sikh community. In his 2-page letter, he justified his decision against submitting his resignation saying he would go by the statement of the acting Jathedar in which he had clarified on April 14 that he had never sought the resignations. He brought out contradictions in various statements of Prof. Manjit Singh on this issue. While stating that the Sikhs believed in the synergy of religion and politics, he reminded the Jathedar that the Akal Takht did not belong to the Akalis alone but represented the entire Panth.[2]

The crisis in the Akali Dal (Badal) deepened as evident from the walk out staged by the angry supporters of Tohra from the meeting of the dissolved working committee, ex-MPs, ex-MLAs and district presidents called by Badal on April 20 to discuss the unity initiative. The supporters of Tohra protested against the move to get endorsement for the 2-page letter written by Badal to the Akal Takht Jathedar earlier. The resolution adopted at the meeting cautioned Prof. Manjit Singh against the deep rooted conspiracy to weaken the party by accommodating the rejected leaders through the backdoor. It stated it was the high time to frustrate such designs and protect the Akal Takht from conspiracies. Tohra distanced himself from Badal.

Reacting to the letter, the Tohra group appealed to Prof. Manjit Singh to summon Badal and punish him for denigrating Akal Takht. Badal was called upon to withdraw the letter and seek forgiveness, who, however, reiterated that the best course to resolve the leadership issue would be to wait for the SGPC general elections due for a long time. The SGPC poll norm was the democratic alternative to the imposition of unity from the religio-political office of the Akal Takht.

However, within two days of this meeting, Badal, in a tactical move, submitted his resignation from the presidency and constituted a 5-member committee to run the party affairs. He also wrote a letter to the Akal Takht Jathedar apologizing for some portions of his earlier letter which might have hurt him. The resignation followed the signal given by Prof. Manjit Singh to some associates of Badal to withdraw the letter as that amounted to the denigration of Akal Takht. The five member committee, on April 22, announced the decision the next day to suspend political activity of the party. The members of the committee included

Parkash Singh Majithia, Kuldip Singh Wadala, Ranjit Singh Brahmpura, Gurdev Singh Badal and Sukhdev Singh Dhindsa. As part of the strategy, Badal went into hibernation after submitting his resignation.

The heads of all Akali factions, except the Badal faction, wrote to the Akal Takht Jathedar pledging absolute commitment to the supreme religio-temporal seat for prayer and politics. They included Talwandi, Mann, Kabul Singh, Barnala, Kartar Singh Narang (Babbar Akali Dal), Amarinder Singh and Manjit Singh.

The Akal Takht Jathedar, on April 27, directed the Akali leaders who had offered their services to the Takht to undergo religious service for five days. They were directed to listen to gurbani, dust shoes of devotees, clean utensils and participate in washing the parkarma of Darbar Sahib. However, it was not a punishment (Tankhah) but service intended to remove the ego among the Akali leaders and strengthen the feeling of service towards the Sikh masses. Certain legal complications were cited by some leaders with the Akal Takht intervening in political affairs to constitute a party. Tohra consulted legal experts to allay such apprehensions.

The Amritsar Declaration

At the time when the politics and priorities of the up-and-coming Akali Dal (Badal) were being redefined in tune with the changing situation, yet another move was initiated by the other Akali factions to spell out political agenda which turned out to be the last radical document bordering secession adopted by the Akalis minus the Badal faction during the recent Sikh struggle. The document was the Amritsar Declaration and the signatories included moderate leaders like Amarinder Singh and Surjit Singh Barnala. Incidentally, the committee which conceived the Anandpur Sahib resolution in the early seventies was also headed by Barnala. The new agenda was adopted by the new Akali outfit constituted after the merger of the factions minus the Badal group. It was also seen as a subtle move to isolate Badal.

The presidents of the six Akali factions, who had earlier submitted their services to the Akal Takht, on May 1, floated a new unified Shiromani Akali Dal (Amritsar). A six member ad hoc committee was appointed till the election of the president to run the party affairs. This unity was brought about with the efforts of the Sikh clergy spread over five days. The announcement was made from Akal Takht. However, what was more important was the political goal of the party rather than these outfits coming together.

The radical Amritsar Declaration was adopted as the political goal which was specified as an autonomous state for the Sikhs but with a rider. It was stated that in case of non-fulfillment of this demand, the party would be free to launch struggle for the achievement of a sovereign Sikh state. The 6-member ad hoc committee appointed to run the party affairs included Amarinder Singh, Mann, Barnala, Col. Jasmer Singh Bala, Talwandi and Manjit Singh.

The Declaration states: "The Akali Dal being a champion of Punjabi culture based on Guru Granth Sahib reiterates its commitment for waging a struggle within democratic norms for the creation of such a separate region for the Sikhs where they can enjoy a glow of freedom. The Congress had made solemn promises before the partition of the country for the creation of such a region which were never implemented. At the turn of history, when on the one hand, there was unrest in the South-East Asian countries; the European nations were making efforts for restructuring themselves in a changed political scenario. In such a situation, the liberation from political exploitation would be a beacon of light for other cultural entities. The Akali Dal feels that India is a subcontinent consisting of various nations and cultures, each one with distinct heritage. This sub-continent needs restructuring of its polity into a confederation of various cultures, so that each one could make effective development. If the government of India failed to restructure the Indian polity, the Akali Dal would be left with no other alternative but to wage struggle for a sovereign Sikh state".

The Declaration was signed by Amarinder Singh, Jagdev Singh Talwandi, Simranjit Singh Mann, Col. Jasmer Singh Bala, Manjit Singh and Surjit Singh Barnala. Tohra, though present, was not directed by the high priests to sign the Declaration. However, this policy programme was never adopted by the general house of the party and remained on paper only. It was soon to be ditched.

The person who was instrumental in the adoption of the Amritsar Declaration was none other than Prof. Manjit Singh. He was the only person who had the information about such a document being drafted. It was drafted late in the night and handed over to the Akal Takht Jathedar just in time. It was Col. Bala who had authored the new policy programme. Prof. Manjit Singh was handed over the document who had a cursory look and after approving it, passed it on to other leaders who signed on the dotted line. Later, Amarinder Singh made it clear that he would back out in case it was interpreted as a step towards Khalistan. This was the interpretation which he apprehended from Mann. It was also planned to bring about a daily newspaper, the trust for which was to be headed by Prof. Manjit Singh with Parneet Kaur, wife of Amarinder Singh, as one of the five trustees. This plan never took off.

The Anandpur Sahib resolution did not talk of the Sikh state but in case of the Amritsar Declaration, this was the threat. But then some of these factions had earlier endorsed the demand for Khalistan.

The tone and tenor of this convention which adopted the Amritsar Declaration was set by Tohra who was the first speaker. He coined two slogans - "Akal Takht Mahan Hai, Sikh Panth Di Shan Hai" and "Akal Takht Ton Ayee Awaj, Panth Khalsa Zindabad". The target of his attack apparently was Badal. His line of argument was that the Sikhs who had no regard for the institution of Akal Takht were greater sinners than those who had demolished the structure during Operation Bluestar.

Barnala recalled his own confrontation with the Akal Takht leading to his ex-communication from the Sikh Panth and said he could not tolerate the pangs of separation from the community. He appreciated the intervention of Akal Takht to forge Akali unity.

At the national level, the reaction, expectedly, was adverse. Cutting across party lines, members in the Rajya Sabha, on May 2, expressed grave concern over the Amritsar Declaration. The issue rocked the House for about 40 minutes. Home Minister S. B. Chavan articulated the official view saying, "It is very unfortunate that in the name of unity, they have come together and issued the Amritsar Declaration".

Prof. Manjit Singh, while taking this step to unite Akali factions, summoned Badal to appear on May 2 at Akal Takht. The members of the clergy said Badal had sought to distance himself from the Akal Takht and the contradictory statements issued by him had put the Sikh community in a quandary. Earlier, Barjinder Singh, newspaper proprietor and an emissary of Badal, had called on Akal Takht Jathedar and Tohra.[3]

The Amritsar Declaration failed to keep the anti-Badal Akali conglomerate together. Akali Dal (L) General Secretary Capt. Kanwaljit Singh raised the banner of revolt against the Amritsar Declaration as Amarinder Singh came out in its defence. Capt. Kanwaljit Singh dubbed the Declaration as anti-Sikh, anti-Punjab and anti-people and opposed to the true spirit of Guru Granth Sahib saying it would provide fuel to the communal forces and create an atmosphere of tension and hatred. While appealing to Barnala to reconsider the decision, he charged the pro-unity Akalis with trying to disintegrate the country. "The declared intention of a few Akali leaders to lead a movement for the creation of a separate independent state through a process of disintegration of the nation, poses a direct challenge to all right thinking people and the unity and integrity of India. This desperate stand of these leaders will prove to be disastrous for them and reflect adversely on the future of the Sikhs", he said in a statement. He was the most vocal critic of the

Declaration in the Akali matrix. He was competing with Badal in the domain of moderate Akali politics. And he was more articulate. If the Badal family perceived political threat from any leader years later, it was Capt. Kanwaljit Singh.

Amarinder Singh, on the other hand, defended it as the manifestation of cumulative grievances and the Centre's continuing indifference towards Punjab. He clarified it was not much different from the Anandpur Sahib Resolution and moreover, it was only a draft policy programme which would be presented at the general house meeting of the party for approval. He also took strong exception to the comments of the Union Home Minister on Amritsar Declaration. The grievances of the Akalis were known to the Centre all these years but nothing had been done. For this section of the Akalis, the Amritsar Declaration flowed from Centre's inaction on their demands and was nothing more than protest and reaction.[4]

Badal at Akal Takht

Finally, Badal, along with the members of his party presidium, presented himself at Akal Takht and had a 5-hour meeting with the clergy. He withdrew his two page letter written earlier saying he had no intention to hurt anybody's feelings but made it clear the unity could be achieved only after sinking ideological differences and that his party would continue to maintain its independent identity. The unity must be based on mutual trust. The Presidium members made a written representation against joining hands with the leaders with whom they had ideological differences.

The Badal faction, after a long time, was talking of ideological positions. Badal had already chalked out his long term strategy at the time when the radicals were in no position to dictate the political agenda which his faction was forced to support by the situation earlier.

With Badal taking ideological stand in favour of moderate politics and unity on principles, the members of the clergy who had initiated the unity move issued a statement virtually approaching the people's court. They called upon the Sikh masses to force those Akali factions to unite which were still maintaining independent identity. The hint was towards Akali Dal (Badal). Then it was Badal who had the mass base. Despite the long period of marginalization, he was in the process of capturing the centre stage again in the moderate domain. There was no ambiguity in the political course he was to follow.

Reacting to the situation, Tohra said Badal had fallen into the trap of anti-Sikh political parties and the central government by refusing to accept the intervention of the Akal Takht for forging unity. He said from the support extended by the anti-Sikh political forces including the Communists, the Bharatiya Janata Party and the government, it was clear that Badal's line was not in the interests of the Sikhs and he had deviated from the basic concept of Miri and Piri. (The principle of temporal and spiritual, basic to Sikh tenets).

Tohra, at a meeting of his supporters who had deserted Badal, at Patiala on May 16, denied he cherished the ambition to head the Akali Dal and made it clear he was in favour of the Panthic unity under the patronage of Akal Takht to fight a long drawn battle to maintain the independent existence and identity of the Sikh community. Tohra played the wrong card as the situation had changed. He should have taken up the agenda concerning the people at large rather than attacking Badal in the religious domain.

The Akali Dal (Amritsar) constituted under the aegis of Akal Takht at its first political conference organized at Sunam on May 21, gave a call to socially boycott Badal for defying the supreme institution allegedly as part of the conspiracy hatched by the Centre and portrayed him as a stooge of the government.[5] The call did not get any response from the people.

Akali Dal (Master Tara Singh) President Rachhpal Singh was awarded punishment by the Akal Takht on May 24 for violating the directive on Akali unity.

Ajnala Bypoll: People's Assertion for Moderate Politics

That the stand taken by Badal on Akali unity was in consonance with the changing political reality was evident from the result of the Ajnala Assembly bye-election in early June which unquestionably re-established his leadership. A major shot in the arm of the Akali Dal (Badal) was the victory of party candidate Rattan Singh Ajnala from this border area constituency in Amritsar district. This area appeared to be the other Punjab, lacking in roads and all the basic civic amenities with the villages like Bhindi Saidan representing the dark side of what used to be known as the prosperous Punjab. Most of the roads in the area had just disappeared during long period of militancy.

This development was the watershed in the moderate Akali politics in the post-militancy era. This was the area where radical politics also had a strong base at one time. The Akali Dal (Amritsar) had decided against contesting the bye-election as the party did not have a suitable candidate to field. Here was the democratic test to assess the popularity of various Akali factions. Badal did not look back after this bye-election which completely marginalized his rivals in the Akali spectrum in the legislative politics for years to come.

"The candidates fielded by the two sides do not matter in this constituency and the election would be virtually a clash between the two titans – Punjab Chief Minister Beant Singh and Akali Dal (Badal) supremo Parkash Singh Badal", said a newspaper report.[6] The people had exercised a bigger choice in this bye-election. The result was the indication of the rejection of the policies of the Congress by the people.

Close on the heels of this resounding success, Badal resumed the office of the president of his party. The decision to direct Badal to take over the reigns of the party and disband the presidium was taken at a meeting of the party office bearers, district presidents and others at a meeting at Jalandhar on June 6. The party passed a resolution demanding early elections to the general house of the SGPC. While paying homage to the "Martyrs of Operation Bluestar", the party demanded unconditional apology from the government at the Centre for the army action. The resolution said any further delay by the Centre in tendering the apology would deepen the wounds of the Sikhs.

On the other hand, continuing with its anti-Badal stance rather than consolidating its own support base among the masses, Akali Dal (Amritsar), at a meeting at Amritsar on June 15, appealed to the Akal Takht Jathedar to take stern action in accordance with the Sikh traditions against the political leaders and the so-called scholars who were harming the prestige of the Panth and creating confusion. Through a resolution, the party expressed deep concern over such attempts and described the same as deep rooted conspiracy by the anti-Sikh forces. Tohra said the Badal faction of the Akalis posed a grave threat to the authority of the Akal Takht. This meeting had been called to start party's enrolment drive. The meeting expressed concern over repeated violation of the human rights by the government and the harassment of the innocents by the security forces. This conglomerate failed to take note of the signals emanating from the Ajnala bye-election.

The Akali Dal (Badal) got another shot in the arm as a major section of the Akali Dal (Longowal) led by its General Secretary Capt. Kanwaljit Singh, along with his supporters, crossed over on June 18. The district units of the Akali Dal (L), which ratified the merger, included Ludhiana (Rural), Hoshiarpur, Kapurthala, Fatehgarh Sahib and Patiala (Rural and Urban). Capt. Kanwaljit Singh appreciated the bold stand taken by Badal to unite the Punjabis. The resolution adopted at the party convention to announce merger stated that the past decade had been a period of sorrow, pain, violence, bloodshed and utter misery. The people had witnessed with horror the merciless killings of the innocents and the elimination of the youth in fake encounters. The wailing cries of orphans and widows would reverberate for years. The emphasis was on the unity of the Punjabis, the theme which was to dominate the 75th anniversary conference of the Akali Dal later at Moga. For Badal, the Ajnala bye-election result was the manifestation of the unity of Punjabis.

RSS under Scanner

Yet another dimension was added to the Punjab political scene not directly related to what had been going on in the state all these years and it was the activities of the Hindu fundamentalist Rashtriya Swayamsewak Sangh. The role of the RSS once again came under a scanner when Prof. Manjit Singh, for the first time, expressed the apprehension about the Sangh Parivar trying to stage back door entry into the SGPC. He said in Delhi some Sangh Parivar activists were enlisting themselves as voters as Sehajdhari Sikhs. At the same time, he clarified the Sehajdharis, who had faith in Sikhism, were members of the Sikh Panth and entitled to vote in the SGPC general elections. His worry was not the Sehajdharis but the infiltration of non-Sikhs under this guise.[7]

The ad hoc committee of the Akali Dal (Amritsar), on July 26, decided to boycott Independence Day celebrations and observe it as a black day to protest against rampant corruption in the administration and continuing police repression. The committee, at its meeting at Ludhiana, chalked out a programme of political conferences to mobilize the masses to dislodge the Beant Singh government. The Independence Day celebrations are normally official functions and not associated with people's festivities and as such, its boycott does not mean much. At its conference at Fatehgarh Sahib on August 13, the party reiterated that peace could be established in South Asia and the Sikhs get justice and live with dignity only on the basis of the Amritsar Declaration. The party called upon the Sikhs to unite under the leadership of Akal Takht. The party demanded dismissal of the Beant Singh government and fresh elections in the state while warning the Centre against continuing the policy of discrimination and said such policies could deteriorate the situation for which the Narasimha Rao government would be responsible.

The Akali Dal (Amritsar) developed fissures within months of its having been constituted as Mann resigned from the 7-member ad hoc committee of the party in October in protest against the role of Tohra and his associates in the just concluded panachayat samiti and zila parishad elections. The confrontation between the two leaders had started over the selection of candidates. The unity moves initiated by the clergy had thus proved counter-productive.

Prof. Manjit Singh shot off another letter to Badal in November on the issue of Akali unity. He reminded him about the communication sent earlier to all the Akali leaders asking them to sink their differences and regretted that despite the bloody struggle and the huge loss, the community had failed to evolve a concensus on the leadership. The same leadership had come forward which had earlier been rejected by the community. The letter was sort of a warning to Badal. Prof. Manjit Singh said Badal must remove the stigma of being a deserter by presenting himself at the Akal Takht as that would be the last opportunity.

Badal wrote back on November 13 rejecting the directive while reiterating that he was for unity based on principles and pointed out the earlier experiment of re-organizing the party as Akali Dal (Amritsar) had failed as the leaders of that conglomeration were giving different interpretations to the Amritsar Declaration. For some, the Declaration amounted to demand for Khalistan and for others it was confined only to autonomy. He alleged during the Ajnala by-election, Akali Dal (Amritsar) leaders connived with the Congress while the people exercised the mandate in favour of his party.

With the annual elections to the office bearers of the SGPC approaching, Shiromani Akali Dal (Badal) decided to challenge Tohra's leadership. In a statement, the party said, "Sikh Panth has been passing through a crisis for a very long time. One of the main internal reasons is the growing deterioration in the Gurdwara management, coupled with the misuse of Gurdwara funds and resources for factional self-seeking vested interests by the coterie headed by Jathedar Gurcharan Singh Tohra, entrenched in the SGPC... Jathedar Tohra and his small power hungry coterie have appropriated this Panthic organization unto themselves, depriving it of its representative character and deflecting it from its objective of better administration of the gurdwaras and propagation of the Sikh faith..... the SGPC has been politicized in a very narrow, sectarian sense; what is needed is its de-politicisation, that is, liberation from the exigencies of corrupt factional politics". Here was a strong indictment of the functioning of the SGPC and Tohra not by the Congress but by an Akali faction.

While the Ajnala bye-election had seen the re-emergence of Badal in the legislative domain after having been totally marginalized, the religious domain represented by the SGPC continued to be the exclusive preserve of Tohra who was re-elected as the SGPC president by defeating Prem Singh Lalpura put up by the Akali Dal (Badal) in the annual elections of the office bearers in November. The general house adopted nine resolutions demanding revocation of Terrorist And Disruptive Activities Act, elections to the SGPC general house without further delay, immediate release of Ranjit Singh and release of other detainees, punishment to the guilty of November 1984 mayhem and a separate desk in the ministry of External Affairs to deal with the affairs of the Sikh shrines in Pakistan.

The state government foiled the attempt by the Akali Dal (Badal) to take out a march from Amritsar to Delhi on December 1 to press for the demands concerning the state. Badal and a number of his supporters were arrested as they came out from the Darbar Sahib complex. However, the party activists succeeded in taking out a march to Parliament on December 7. More than 500 workers were arrested. They were demanding dismissal of the Beant Singh government and punishment to the guilty of November 1984 violence against the Sikhs.

The race for political power in Punjab had already started. At the annual Jor Mela conferences at Fatehgarh Sahib in December, the demand for an independent Sikh state reverberated from the Akali Dal (Amritsar) stage while Akali Dal (Badal) expressed the resolve to carry on the peaceful struggle to get justice for Punjabis.

The Akali Dal (Amritsar) proposed a front of minorities and regional parties to launch "Desh Bachao" (Save the country) drive. It was also decided to start a "Panth Bachao" campaign in the state from January 1, 1995 to expose the conspiracies of the government to incite anti-Panthic people to denigrate the Sikh institutions. The target, however, was Badal. The party talked of Amritsar Declaration also. Through another resolution, the party demanded immediate elections to the Lok Sabha, withdrawal of TADA and political solution to the Punjab problem. The party warned Badal against playing into the hands of the enemies of the Panth.

The Akali Dal (Badal) reiterated the stand on Akali unity and warned those who were trying to create hurdles in the struggle launched by the party against the governments at the Centre and the state. Through a resolution, the party expressed the resolve to carry on the fight for getting justice to Punjab through democratic and peaceful means. The party also raised the issues concerning the peasantry. Through another resolution, the party demanded general elections to the SGPC in February. Yet another demand related to the release of the Jodhpur detainees.

Traditional Akalis Unite

As part of the normal democratic functioning, the two factions of the Akalis were back to morcha politics in 1995. Akali Dal (Badal)'s Punjab Bachao (Save Punjab agitation) morcha raked up the old issues taken up during the Dharamyudh morcha, the new addition being the demand for punishment to the guilty of November 1984 violence against the Sikhs. The Akali Dal (Amritsar) was relying more on the religious sentiments, arguing that Punjab could be saved only if the Panth was saved. For this faction, the Panth and Punjab were synonymous at that time. Badal was addressing the wider audience.

Despite this politics of competitive opportunism in the Sikh affairs in full play, the unity issue continued to dominate the agenda in the Akali political matrix. The leaders from various Akali factions had a day long meeting with the Sikh clergy at Akal Takht on January 10, 1995 to pave the way for unity. The participants included Badal, Sukhdev Singh Dhindsa, Balwinder Singh Bhunder, Parkash Singh Majitha, Kuldip Singh Wadala, Ranjit Singh Brahmpura and Gurdev Singh Badal from the Badal faction and Tohra, Sukhjinder Singh, Jagdev Singh Talwandi, Surjit Singh Baranala, Amarinder Singh and Manjit Singh Calcutta, all members of the Akal Dal (Amritsar) ad hoc committee. Both factions were given 10 days time and told to appear at Akal Takht again on January 23. Akal Takht acting Jathedar, in a veiled threat to Badal, said the betrayers and detractors of the Panth had always faced ex-communication. However, Badal, on his agenda of Punjab and Punjabiat, was already making assertions in the Akali domain.

At the Maghi conference at Muktsar on January 14, Badal reiterated the demand for the dismissal of the Beant Singh government. The emphasis of the Akali Dal (Badal) was now shifting from the "Sikhs in particular" to the aspirations of the "Punjab, Punjabis and the Sikhs", as evident from the political resolution which sought cooperation from the Punjabis while committing to carry on the fight for getting justice. The party adopted a total of 10 resolutions.

Rejecting the Amritsar Declaration again on January 20, Badal stuck to his earlier stand regarding unity on principles. The decision to dump the Amritsar Declaration was taken at a meeting of the district Jathedars, SGPC members, former MPs and MLAs and the front organizations at Jalandhar. The party reiterated its commitment to autonomy for the states. Badal set up a committee including Dhindsa, Gurdev Singh Badal, Ranjit Singh Brahmpura, Majitha, Wadala and Bhunder to discuss unity issue with other Akali factions. Two resolutions were adopted at this meeting. The first resolution stated that caught in its own problems, the Centre was trying to recreate the demon of terrorism and extract political capital out of it. The party alerted the people against such designs. In the second resolution, the party thanked the people for extending support to the "Punjab Bachao" (Save Punjab) agitation launched to demand the dismissal of the Beant Singh government.

The two Akali factions finally agreed to initiate the process to unite on January 23 at a meeting at Akal Takht and constituted a 7-member committee headed by Ashok Singh Bagrian to evolve the modalities. The announcement was made by Prof. Manjit Singh. Members of the committee, which was to submit its report by February 17, included Wadala, Brahmpura, Dhindsa, Barnala, Manjit Singh and Sucha Singh Chhotepur. Those who attended the meeting included Tohra, Badal, Majitha, Gurdev Singh Badal, Brahmpura, Chhotepur, Talwandi, Barnala, Dhindsa, Bhunder, Sukhjinder Singh, Manjit Singh, Col. Bala and Amarinder Singh. Mann was in jail at that time.

The joint declaration signed by the leaders from the two factions said: "We, all senior Akali leaders, hereby announce the establishment of a 7-member panel to finalize the unity process. This panel will chalk out blueprints of the constitutional, political, economic, social and religious activities of the Shiromani Akali Dal which will represent the Panthic aspirations of the Sikhs. This committee will also discuss the organizational structure of the party.... The members of this committee will take all decisions unanimously with all sincerity on the issues. If it fails to arrive at unanimous decision on any matter, that will be settled amicably by the Shiromani Akali Dal leaders at Akal Takht. We all affirm that whosoever does not agree to accept the report of this committee, he will be declared a fugitive of the Sikh Panth and the Sikh high priests will be the competent authority to take any decision accordingly".

The 7-member committee submitted its recommendations on unity to the high priests on February 17 on the basis of which the two factions decided in principle to merge at a meeting at Akal Takht on February 22. The modalities were to be completed by April 13, 1995. Till then, the two factions resolved to suspend political activity. The announcement was made by Tohra. The high priests distanced themselves from the announcement as a precautionary measure so that the party did not invite disqualification from the Election Commission on the pretext of religious interference in the political affairs. Badal and Tohra were also nominated on the panel. The spadework for unity had been done by Tohra and Badal at a secret meeting earlier at Jalandhar.

Badal was, however, conspicuous by his absence at Hola Mohalla conference at Anandpur Sahib to which invitation was extended by Tohra. The SGPC chief demanded a judicial enquiry by a Supreme Court judge to go into the genesis of militancy at the conference. Significantly, in his continuing onslaught against the militants, he cautioned people against the designs of those raising radical slogans. The dismissal of the Beant Singh government was demanded through a resolution.

The Akali factions finally adopted the 1978 version of the Anandpur Sahib Resolution as the basis for unity in April after several meetings.

The unity was formalized at Talwandi Sabo where these factions organized a joint political conference at Baisakhi on April 14. The unity announcement was made by Bagrian. It was again Amarinder Singh who proposed the name of Badal to lead the united Akalis. Badal and Amritsar factions formally merged at Jalandhar on April 22 with Badal as the president. The organizational set up was announced on June 4 by Bagrian under which a 65-member committee was announced under Badal's presidency. However, within hours, Mann, who was included as the senior vice-president, refused to play second fiddle to Badal.

Ajit Singh Sarhadi, Atma Singh and Amar Singh Ambalavi were honoured as patrons of the new outfit. The vice-presidents included Sukhjinder Singh, Manjit Singh and Gurdev Singh Badal with Dhindsa, Chhotepur and Bharpur Singh as the general secretaries while Manjit Singh Calcutta was appointed treasurer and Bhag Singh the office secretary. The 10-member parliamentary board headed by Bagrian had Tohra, Badal, Sukhjinder Singh, Majitha, Amarinder Singh, Barnala, Wadala and Mann as members. Bagrian also headed the committee on organizational affairs, discipline and party constitution. The members of this committee were Gurtej Singh, Dhindsa, Kasturi Lal, Jasdev Singh Sandhu, Prem Singh Lalpura and Sujan Singh with Bharpur Singh as its secretary.

Members of the working committee included Pritam Kaur, wife of Sant Jarnail Singh Bhindranwale, Jasvir Singh Rode, Tohra, Kabul Singh, Majitha, Gurdev Singh Badal, Nirmal Singh Kahlon, Kasturi Lal, Wadala, Gurdarshan Singh Grewal, Capt. Kanwaljit Singh, Lalpura, Charanjit Singh Walia, Surjan Singh Thekedar, Ravi Inder Singh, Rattan Singh Ajnala, Bhunder, Anwar Ahmed Khan, Amarjit Singh Bhatia, Sujan Singh, Major Singh Uboke, Brahmpura, Rajinder Singh Dhaliwal, Amarinder Singh, Jasdev Singh Sandhu, Narinder Singh, Sukhdev Singh Dhillon, Sant Ajit Singh, Jaspal Singh Dhillon, Gurtej Singh, Sarup Singh, Inderjit Singh Jaijee, Kirpal Singh Libra, Prem Singh Chandumajra, Jagdev Singh Talwandi, Randhir Singh Cheema, Tota Singh, Baldev Singh Mann, Surjit Singh Minhas, Prof. Jagmohan Singh Toni, Major Jagjit Singh, Major Gen Narinder Singh (retd), Gurdarshan Singh Dhillon, Sewa Singh Sekhwan, Bachittar Singh, Manjit Singh Khaira, Karnail Singh Doad, Bagrian, Mohinder Singh Sargodhia, Kartar Singh Narang, Basant Singh Khalsa, Satwant Kaur Sandhu, Rajinder Kaur Bulara and Gur Rattan Pal Singh. This action of Bagrian created further mess as he did not consult the senior Akali leaders while announcing the new outfit. Badal wanted 65 per cent share while Tohra was eyeing the headship of the Parliamentary Board. Though the party had adopted 1978 version of the Anandpur Sahib resolution as the policy programme, the organizational structure did not reflect any ideological cohesion.

As the new outfit was rejected by all the factions within hours of the announcement, Bagrian clarified it was recommendatory in nature and not mandatory as the 9-member committee could make any change. Both Tohra and Talwandi separately dumped the new outfit. Tohra appealed to the party workers to ignore the announcement made by Bagrian as he was neither empowered to constitute the working committee nor announce it. Talwandi charged Bagrian with playing into the hands of anti-Sikh forces.

In an effort to resolve the crisis, the 3-member unity sub-committee headed by Bagrian which included Tohra and Wadala, on July 9, authorized Badal to nominate the working committee. The sub-committee ceased to exist after this announcement. They made it clear only the leaders from the Badal and Amritsar factions would be included in the working committee.

Badal's Clean Break with the Past

Badal brought about a paradigm shift in his party line by making a clean break with the past after dilly dallying for many years. He made a clear distinction from the radical politics while reviving the traditional Akali Dal in early August. The changing political situation with militancy having been curbed facilitated the shift. The Akali Dal had been signing on dotted lines for a long time during militancy under the dictates of the militants. With this distinct ideological position, the polarization in the Akali matrix was complete.

Meanwhile in a significant judgment, the Supreme Court observed in August that the mere raising of slogans like Khalistan Zindabad was neither a terrorist activity nor a seditious act.

In between, the Gidderbaha by-election finally set the course the Akali politics in Punjab was to adopt with the victory of the Shiromani Akali Dal in the polls held in early June. Akali Dal candidate Manpreet Singh, nephew of Badal, was supported by the Bharatiya Janata Party, Bahujan Samaj Party, Communist Party of India, Janata Dal and the Bharti Kisan Union (Lakhowal). The Gidderbara bye-election result was the reinforcement of the line adopted by Badal during the Ajnala bye-election who emerged as the unquestioned leader in the moderate stream. At another level, unprecedented use of money power was the main characteristic of this bye-election. The use of money power in elections in Punjab started from the Malwa hinterland dominated by big landlords. Before his candidature was announced, Manpreet Singh was baptized at Akal Takht.

The unified Akali Dal decided to launch "Punjab Bachao, Congress Bhajao" (Save Punjab, Reject Congress) campaign from August 20, the death anniversary of Harchand Singh Longowal. The decision was taken at the first meeting of the newly constituted working committee of the party at Chandigarh on August 18. The campaign was to be launched from Longowal, followed by a series of rallies in different parts of the state. The issues the party focused on included restoration of democracy, solution to the river waters dispute and restoration of human rights etc. The party also took up problems of various sections of society. The meeting pledged to restore the lost glory and prestige of the Punjabis and the Sikhs by rescuing them from the anti-people Congress government. Through a resolution, the party demanded an inquiry by a high court judge into the alleged conspiracy by the Congress to defame the Sikhs and the Akali Dal.

Badal, for the first time, in 1995, participated in the conference organized every year to commemorate the assassination of Longowal on August 20 at Longowal village. The National Front leaders who attended the convention gave a clear message to the party to shun communal and caste permutations and combinations while forging alliances. These leaders included V. P. Singh and Chandra Shekhar, both former prime ministers and H. D. Deve Gowda and Laloo Prasad Yadav.

To counter the Akali show at Longowal, Beant Singh organized a massive rally at Patiala on August 25 where he announced wide ranging concessions for the peasantry, mainly the Sikhs. This was to wean away the farming community from Akali Dal. He also tried to adopt the Panthic agenda when he said his government would construct Guru Tegh Bahadur Marg on the pattern of earlier Guru Gobind Singh Marg. This was to be the route followed by the 9th Sikh Guru while going to Delhi from Anandpur Sahib to offer himself for arrest.

Beant Singh Assassinated

Beant Singh, who was considered to be the symbol of state repression and politics of confrontation by a section of the population in the state, mainly the Sikhs, was assassinated at the main gate of the Punjab civil secretariat, the seat of the government in Chandigarh, in the evening of August 31 as he got into his bullet proof car. The Babbar Khalsa International claimed responsibility for this daring action. Such was the impact of the explosion that the office of the chief minister on the first floor just above the gate appeared to be the war zone with the windows in the area completely shattered due to to the bomb explosion. The scene outside was ghastly with the bodies of his security men and parts of flesh strewn around. The apprehension expressed at that time was that it might lead to the revival of militancy. However, though very well planned, it turned out to be an isolated incident. This was the last major action associated with that phase of the Sikh armed struggle which otherwise had already petered out. The politics of political confrontation adopted by the Congress government in the state ended with his assassination. His successor Harcharan Singh Brar opted for the politics of reconciliation. However, the damage to the Congress in the state had already been done. Here was a party which had restored normalcy after more than a decade of political violence in the state but in the process had got isolated from the dominant section. The Congress paid the price and the party was wiped out in the 1997 in the worst every defeat in the Assembly elections which restored participatory and vibrant democracy in the state.

The Shiromani Gurdwara Parbandhak Committee organized a 5-day World Sikh Convention at Amritsar in the third week of September where the Akali Dal again expressed its resolve to wage a peaceful and democratic struggle for the achievement of all religious, political, social, cultural and economic demands of the Sikh Panth. Badal said all Sikh institutions were being denigrated, Sikh psyche was grievously wounded and the Sikh identity was under threat.[8] It was proposed to set up a World Sikh Council, a Khalsa centennial fund and an international Sikh university. The convention also adopted a Declaration, besides three resolutions moved by Tohra. The first resolution sought the release of Akal Takht Jathedar designate Ranjit Singh. The second resolution was on violation of human rights all over the world with an appeal to the United Nations and other international human rights organizations to intervene and trace out human rights activist Jaswant Singh Khalra, who had been missing since September 7. It said the UN and the Human Rights Commission should set up a special commission to probe the repeated violation of the human rights of the Sikhs in India. The third resolution sought to constitute a committee of experts and intellectuals to make an in-depth study of the functioning of the SGPC and submit a detailed blueprint. The third resolution was never put into practice.

Later at a "Samman Samaroh" organized at the Manji Sahib hall on September 25 as part of this convention, Sant Jarnail Singh Bhindranwale, Major General Shabeg Singh and Amrik Singh, who died fighting during Operation Bluestar, and the assassins of Indira Gandhi and Gen A. S. Vaidya, were honoured as martyrs by Tohra. Also present on the occasion were members of the Sikh clergy and senior Akali leaders. The function was meant to honour those Sikh personalities who had excelled in various spheres. About 200 personalities were honoured, most of them posthumously. All along, the Damdami Taksal had maintained that Sant Bhindranwale was alive, thus belittling his sacrifice.

Khalra's body was never traced. He had been single handedly working on the cremation of unidentified dead bodies by the police and had recorded hundreds of such cases. His investigations exposed to modus operandi adopted by the security forces to eliminate people suspected to be militants or their supporters. Hundreds of innocent Sikhs were gunned down in the process and cremated as unidentified. His investigation was based on the record maintained at the cremation grounds, mainly in the Amritsar district. The matter later went to the Supreme Court which ordered inquiry by the Central Bureau of Investigations. Compensation was ordered to be paid to the families of the victims by the apex court on the basis of this inquiry. However, nothing has been done to expose the guilty police officials and take action against them. In several cases, some other persons were gunned down in the name of some known militants who were won over to be used against the movement, several of whom have now re-surfaced. This is one of the darkest chapters of the Punjab militancy. Who were those who had been killed in their names? Even the Akali Dal government never ordered inquiry into such gross violations by the security forces.

The excesses, committed both in the name of the militants and the security forces need to be thoroughly investigated. The militants who shifted their loyalties and helped the security forces were given fake identities. Khalra was subsequently forgotten even by the Akali Dal. The party after forming the government in 1997 could have taken Khalra's investigation to the logical conclusion. That was never done and the government did not even order any inquiry into the disappearance of the human rights activist. Even the Khalra Mission Organisation never carried forward the task of the mentor.

The Shiromani Akali Dal proposed a joint front of the like-minded parties against the Congress at its working committee meeting held at Chandigarh on November 13. The party was of the view that the formation of such a front was necessary to end the Congress misrule. This resolution passed at the party working committee meeting on November 12 was endorsed by the political affairs committee the next day. It was this resolution which paved the way for alliance with the Bharatiya Janata Party. Tohra and Amarinder Singh were conspicuous by their absence. Through another resolution, the party reiterated the demand for the implementation of the Anandpur Sahib Resolution arguing that the restructuring of the country on the federal system was the only solution to the problems being faced by the country.

Mann described it as an opportunist and a selfish decision which was totally against the Sikh national interests. He said the ultra nationalist BJP, other Hindu fundamentalist parties and the totalitarian CPI and CPM were responsible for the prolonged spell of President's rule in the state which had deprived the Sikhs and the Punjabis of the democratic rule of law and a civil order. But then the Akali Dal was once again trying to prove its nationalist credentials.

Tohra made the announcement in October that he would neither contest election to the general house of the SGPC as and when held nor of its office bearers which was due. Badal described it as Tohra's personal affair. However, contrary to this announcement, he was re-elected to the post on November 29. His excuse was that he had been pressured by his supporters to continue in that office. The general house of the SGPC at that meeting passed 15 resolutions. It demanded amendment to the Sikh Gurdwara Act to debar Sehajdharis from the voting right, handing over more gurdwaras to this body and according legal status to Takht Damdama Sahib. Any amendment to be passed by the Parliament should first be recommended by the SGPC with a two third majority in accordance with the Master Tara Singh-Jawahar Lal Nehru pact. The general house sought the release of Ranjit Singh and asked the government to disclose the whereabouts of Khalra. This general house meeting was also attended by Badal though he was not its member.

The Akali Dal (Badal) at its Shaheedi Jor Mela conference at Fatehgarh Sahib on December 27 passed a resolution moved by Tohra asserting that only the Sikhs should have the right to vote in the SGPC elections. He also cautioned Badal against going in for alliance with the forces advocating Hindutva. The conference rejected all the awards and accords on the apportionment of river waters and advocated the resolution of this dispute on the basis of riparian principles. Badal favoured launching the movement for autonomy in association with the like minded parties. Through a resolution, the party reiterated its commitment to the harmonious relations among the Sikhs, the Hindus, the Muslims and the Christians and called upon the people to frustrate the Congress conspiracy to divide them. In the context of the disappearance of Khalra, the party appealed to the Commonwealth to cancel India's membership for the violation of human rights.

In the context of forthcoming Lok Sabha election, Mann proposed to Badal in January, 1996 to have seat adjustment among the Akali factions which was welcomed by Tohra. However, the political affairs committee of the Shiromani Akali Dal at its meeting at Ludhiana on February 5 gave a green signal to the party leadership on the issue of electoral understanding with the Bahujan Samaj Party. Badal rejected the suggestion from Mann.

Moga Convention and Punjabiat

With the post Beant Singh period witnessing the politics of reconciliation in place of confrontation, the functioning of the democratic institutions was getting restored. The Akalis were in an aggressive mood. Despite the restoration of peace for which it should have got the credit, the Congress faced hostility from the masses, especially in the countryside, for the state repression and the violation of human rights.

Under the emerging scenario, the refrain of Shiromani Akali Dal at its Maghi convention at Muktsar on January 14, 1996, was getting justice to Punjab while seeking cooperation from all sections of Punjabis. The party targeted the Congress for the mess not only in Punjab but all over the country for which the policy of centralization was identified as the main culprit. The solution, in the opinion of the Akali Dal, was restructuring the Centre-State relations on true federal structure. The party gave a call to the people to remove the corrupt Congress government and facilitate the victory of the Akali Dal in the next elections while demanding an end to the state repression.

On the other hand, continuing with its radical line, the Akali Dal (Amritsar) reiterated the resolve to carry on the struggle through democratic and peaceful means for the implementation of the Amritsar Declaration. The party demanded that the Parliament pass a resolution apologizing for Operation Bluestar and killing of the Sikhs in November, 1984. The party expected the people of Punjab to reject the traditional Akalis.

The Political Affairs Committee of the Shiromani Akali Dal, at its meeting at Ludhiana on February 5, gave a green signal for poll alliance with the BSP for the forthcoming Lok Sabha elections. Earlier during the day, Badal and Tohra had a long meeting with BSP President Kanshi Ram at Chandigarh.

Shiromani Akali Dal's 75th anniversary conference at Moga in February proved to be watershed in the history of the party, especially in the post-militancy period, for the strategic ideological shift. It marked a major qualitative transformation for the party claiming itself to be the representative of the Panth to being the symbol of Punjab, Punjabis and Punjabiat. Though the seeds of this change can be traced to the earlier transitional period as the militancy ebbed out, the shift was formalized at the Moga conference on February 25, 1996. It was a bold attempt to broaden the base of the party. The Moga conference was a show fully backed by the rich and the middle peasantry in the state.

In its new policy and programme released on February 22 on the eve of the conference, the party stressed the need to amend Preamble to the Constitution to incorporate the expression 'federal' to characterize the Republic of India as such, re-draw the Centre- State relations with defence, foreign affairs, currency and communication being in the Union List while transferring all other departments to the State List. The state legislature should have exclusive power and competence to legislate over all subjects in the State List. Article 356 and 365 empowering the Centre to dissolve state Assembly should be dropped. The Centre should not have the power or competence to destroy or dilute the ethnic, cultural and linguistic self-identity of the constituent states. Rajya Sabha should be reconstituted on the basis of equality of the states. The diversity of regional interests and multiplicity of minorities should be adequately reflected in the composition of Rajya Sabha. The party committed itself to the establishment of 'Haleemi Raj' (Benign rule) wherein no community, territory, class or individual would dominate over others. The objective was laudable but remained confined to the paper. The party demanded immediate release of the Sikhs languishing in jails.

The programme stated: "Stressing that the fundamental character of the Indian civilization is its pluralistic nature, reflected in the composite quality and structure of Indian society - enriched by diversity of languages, cultures and religion – and that this is the bedrock of national unity of the country, the Shiromani Akali Dal views with concern the homogenizing challenges to this characteristic of our society – the challenges threatening not only integrity of India but also the minorities as well. The contradiction between the rising Unitarian trends and forces and the pluralist tendencies is becoming acute and critical day by day, disorienting the national policy consequently". But then the Sangh Parivar was no different as the Sikhs faced the challenge of homogenisation from the Hindu fundamentalist RSS as well and Badal had all along come under attack for being a stooge of this organization.

The 2-day Moga convention beginning February 24 was the most impressive show put up by the party in many years. Thousands of vehicles formed the procession on the first day and the highway from Ludhiana to Moga virtually remained jammed for several hours. It was only one way movement of traffic. The party used the opportunity to wash away the charges of aiding and abetting militancy by affirming complete faith in the democratic and constitutional methods and commitment to peace. The slogan of Punjab, Punjabi and Punjabiat formally materialized at this convention. Though no formal resolution was adopted to this effect, the formalization of this shift came to be known as the Moga Declaration. With the slogan of Punjabiat which Badal gave in his presidential address, effort had been made to broad base the party. The metamorphosis of Badal as leader of the Punjabis and not only of the Sikhs was complete. It was after this conference that the Akali Dal came to be ridiculed as the Punjabi party by the opponents in the Sikh political matrix.

The Political Affairs Committee (PAC) of the Shiromani Akali Dal at its meeting on March 4 at Chandigarh kept the issue of alliance during the Lok Sabha elections with the Bharatiya Janata Party and the Bahujan Samaj Party open. Earlier, the working committee had discussed the issue. The dominant view at the political affairs committee meeting on March 15 was to go it alone and if at all an alliance partner was desired, the option should be the BSP. Those who opposed joining hands with the BJP included Tohra, Talwandi, Wadala, Basant Singh Khalsa, Dhindsa and Manjit Singh. The PAC constituted a 3-member sub-committee comprising Badal, Tohra and Wadala to further explore the avenues. The decision to have alliance with the BSP was finally taken on March 20 at the meeting at Ludhiana. The political affairs committee accorded approval to the alliance on March 27.

Significantly, the selling card of all the political parties at the annual Hola Mohalla conferences at Anandpur Sahib on March 6 was peace and prosperity. The theme of the Shiromani Akali Dal was what had already been specified at the Moga convention. Even Akali Dal (Amritsar) swore by peaceful and democratic means to achieve the promised peace and prosperity.

Coinciding with the announcement of the Lok Sabha elections, the Akal Takht acting Jathedar issued a set of directives to the Shiromani Akali Dal headed by Badal to keep Panthic interests uppermost while fighting the polls. The Panthic principles on which the Shiromani Akali Dal was formed were not to be sacrificed at any cost. Regarding the choice of the candidates, the statement said the preference should be given to the baptized Sikhs and those who believed in and preached the principles of Sikhism.

With the poll campaign picking up, the Akali Dal attack on the Congress continued to sharpen, holding the party responsible for violence while laying thrust on Punjabiat and the Hindu-Sikh unity. The signal given out was that it was only through the emergence of a strong regional power of the Punjabis that the interests and aspirations of Punjab and its rights could be articulated and protected. The effort was to project the Akali Dal as the party which would play its historical role in the form of dynamic regional force in the political arena of the country. No more Panthic slogans. The party was on the offensive against the Congress and its vicious and deadly politics on the secular agenda of Punjabiat.

The Shiromani Akali Dal suffered a minor split on March 30 with former AISSF chief Manjit Singh reviving his Akali Dal (Manjit). Manjit Singh was eyeing the share in the Lok Sabha tickets but Badal refused to accommodate.

The Shiromani Akali Dal, in its election manifesto and the policy programme released at Talwandi Sabo at its Baisakhi conference in April, pledged to fight for more autonomy to the states in the context of the Anandpur Sahib Resolution, scrapping of all previous accords and agreements on river waters and filling up the Punjab portion of the Satluj Yamuna Link Canal, transfer of Chandigarh and other left out Punjabi speaking areas to Punjab, free power for tubewells for irrigation and pensions to all above 65 years of age. The party resolved to seek support of the other like minded parties for getting more powers to the states. The party promised to set up a commission headed by a Supreme Court judge to go into the genesis of militancy related violence and the role of the Congress. The party adopted, with some modifications, the draft policy and programme released earlier in February.

At a separate conference organized under the banner of Sant Samaj, the United Akali Dal, the Sikh Students Federation and the Bharati Kisan Union (Lakhowal) promised to keep alive the glorious Sikh traditions after coming into power. During militancy, this Kisan Union had been supporting the cause of the militancy for sometime.

The year 1996 saw the revival of the moderate Akali politics in full form. In the Lok Sabha elections, even the leaders like Simranjit Singh Mann shunned the radical ideology in favour of the socio-economic issues. The Shiromani Akali Dal – BSP combination won 11 out of 13 Lok Sabha seats. This was the first reflection of the accumulated anger of the people against the Congress. The elections set the trend for the 1997 Assembly elections. The BJP had extended tactical support to the Akalis in four seats while putting up its own candidates in some other seats. Ironically, it was the Congress which had been claiming credit for restoring peace in the state after years of turmoil. The peace card did not work for the Congress in the election. The rout of the Congress was virtually total in the rural areas. What dictated the choice of the voters were the police excesses, non-governance and rampant corruption. The seeds for the future Akali Dal –BJP alliance were sown with the Akali Dal extending unconditional support to the BJP to form government at the Centre led by Atal Behari Vajpayee. The long period of isolation of the Akali Dal at the national level had ended. The working committee of the Shiromani Akali Dal formalized the unconditional support to the BJP at the Centre at its June 2 meeting at Amritsar.

In reaction to the extension of unconditional support to the BJP by Badal to form the government at the national level, a new Akali Dal was floated by one section lacking mass base. Prof. Darshan Singh, former Akal Takht Jathedar, announced the formation of Shiromani Akali Dal (Panthic) headed by Sant Ajit Singh on May 27 at Amritsar. He said Badal had ceased to be the representative of the Sikhs due to the shift from Panth to Punjabiat. Painting BJP as anti-Sikh, he termed the unconditional support to the BJP as blunder. This new outfit had the backing of the Panthic Council of the Sant Samaj. The working committee of this faction included Gurtej Singh, Harbant Singh Kahlon, Harcharan Singh Rode, Atinderpal Singh, Rajdev Singh, Talib Singh Sandhu, Gurkirpal Singh, Manjit Singh Tarn Tarani, Sarabjit Singh Jammu, Harinder Singh Kahlon, Bhagwan Singh, Kanwar Singh Dhami, Jasvir Kaur, Dhian Singh Mand, Shamsher Singh Sammewali, Balbir Singh, Gurdip Singh, Jagjit Singh, Sukhinder Singh, Inderjit Singh, Hari Singh, Jaswant Singh, Inder Singh Khaira, Sarup Singh and Virsa Singh. The political goal of the new Akali Dal was the Anandpur Sahib resolution of 1973.

The Shiromani Akali Dal parted company with the Bahujan Samaj Party following that party's decision to go in for alliance with the Congress in Uttar Pradesh. The decision was taken at the Political Affairs Committee meeting of the party held at Anandpur Sahib on July 4. The committee also praised the role of Tohra saying the Sikh community would always be proud of him who not only maintained the sanctity of religious places during the critical juncture but also frustrated the conspiracies against the statutory body. The reference obviously was to the period when militants had "disbanded" this body. The party appealed to the people to frustrate the attempts of the Congress to take over the management of the Sikh shrines indirectly and vote for the Shiromani Akali Dal in the general election to the SGPC. The resolution said the Congress and the Communist Party had always conspired to weaken the Akali Dal. The Congress, during the 1955, 1965 and the 1979 elections had set up the so called Sadh Sangat Board, Desh Bhagat Board and the Dal Khalsa to control the management of shrines and the party was trying the same tactics again.

The BJP, at a meeting of its office bearers and other prominent leaders at Ludhiana on July 12, reciprocated the decision taken by the Akali Dal on alliance in the next Assembly elections. The underlying idea was the Hindu-Sikh unity. It was decided to organize joint rallies with the alliance partner.

The Akali Dal (Manjit) merged with the Akali Dal (Panthic) on July 12 to challenge Shiromani Akali Dal in the elections to the general house of the SGPC. Panthic faction spokesman Gurtej Singh favoured contesting the SGPC elections on non-party basis and proposed the setting up of a Panthic Board consisting of eminent Sikhs to select the candidates.

Atal Behari Vajpayee, George Fernandes, Maneka Gandhi and Madan Lal Khurana were the senior leaders from Delhi who attended the shaheedi conference at Longowal on August 20 on the death anniversary of Harchand Singh Longowal. It was Tohra who strongly defended the alliance with the BJP at the conference saying it was the Congress which had been exploiting religion for vested interests. This author had commented that it was to be seen as to how would the SGPC chief fit into the Khaki shorts of the Sangh Parivar. Tohra had just laughed away the comment saying, "Our skin is too thick".

Senior Shiromani Akali Dal leader Kuldip Singh Wadala raised the banner of revolt against Badal and resigned from all party posts on August 31. He was opposed to the alliance with the BJP and the projection of Tohra as the next president of the SGPC after the general house elections. He favoured incorporating constructive aspects of the militant movement into party's policy and programme.

The Akali Dal (Badal) was seen to be heading towards crisis as Dhindsa also resigned from the office of the Secretary General of the party on September 9 protesting against denial of tickets to his supporters in Sangrur district in the forthcoming elections to the general house of the SGPC. At the same time, Wadala questioned the authority of Badal in allotting party tickets without taking the party leadership into confidence.

NOTES

1. The Indian Express, January 28, 1994.
2. The Indian Express, April 18, 1994.
3. The Indian Express, May 1, 1994.
4. The Indian Express, May 5, 1994.
5. The Indian Express, May 22, 1994.
6. The Indian Express, May 30, 1994.
7. The Indian Express, Juk9, 1994.
8. The Tribune, September 25, 1995.

18

Back to Power Politics

The one Akali leader who had remained virtually totally marginalized during militancy was Parkash Singh Badal and now he was leading in the race to grab power heading the team which had already shed its Panthic credentials and consciously opted for the agenda of Punjabiat thereby triggering the transformation of the Shiromani Akali Dal which had all along played the historical role of articulating the Sikh concerns. He had entered the fast forward mode, the scenario which could not be visualized a year ago. He was exhibiting his great survival instinct. That thousands had died in the state could just be forgotten as a bad dream. The militant Sikh struggle for sovereignty had never been the agenda of the Shiromani Akali Dal and hence the issues involved could be conveniently ignored, though at times the party had supported the radicals. But then so was to be the case regarding the issues concerning Punjab and the Sikhs which had been dear to the Akali Dal all these years. Now the sole agenda was to capture power. Of course, the ultimate demand for sovereignty raised by the radicals was not in isolation from the concerns taken up by the moderate Akali Dal both before and after Independence of the country. The next trial of strength after the Lok Sabha elections, this one within the Sikhs matrix, was to be the general elections to the Shiromani Gurdwara Parbandhak Committee.

The SGPC, elected by the Sikh voters, both men and women, through adult franchise under the Sikh Gurdwara Act, 1925, perhaps has no parallel in the world. Though it is entrusted with the responsibility of managing the notified historical Sikh shrines in Punjab, Haryana, Himachal Pradesh and the Union territory of Chandigarh, it has been playing a much wider dynamic role in the religio-political affairs of this community, articulating the collective Sikh consciousness, initially the basic character of this body which has been diluted over the years.

The Sikh women got the voting right under the 1925 legislation much ahead of their counter-parts in many of the advanced democracies in the West. Ever since its inception, the SGPC has been an Akali affair, despite the best efforts, though indirect, by the other political parties, mainly the Congress after the partition of the country, to control this mini-Parliament of the Sikhs. The prolonged spell of militancy had delayed the elections to the general house of this body last held in 1979. The general house has a term of five years but continues till the next elections.

The general house elections of the SGPC in October, 1996 reflected the changing trends both in the Sikh religio-political affairs as well as the state polity. The Lok Sabha elections had set the trend for the future political scenario in the state and the SGPC elections further consolidated this trend which was predominantly not only in favour of the Shiromani Akali Dal in general but also Badal. Significantly, this trend was palpable among a section of the Hindus also during the campaigning though non-Sikhs are not entitled to vote in these elections. It was perhaps for the first time that the leaders of the Hindu fundamentalist Bharatiya Janata Party at the local level campaigned in support of the Akali candidates in the SGPC elections. Of course, it was just a moral support but the signals were very meaningful. This has to be seen in the context of the efforts by the militants and the hardliners whose actions were targeted at bringing about vertical split in the Punjabi society.

The trends about the emerging permutations and combinations after the revival of moderate politics were available from the poll campaign by the veteran Akali leader Gurcharan Singh Tohra who, many a times accompanied by the local BJP leaders, could be seen ruthlessly attacking the radicals and laying emphasis on cementing the Hindu-Sikh ties. There is no earlier record of the BJP leaders at the local level campaigning for the mainstream Akali Dal candidates in the Gurdwara elections and it marked a new trend. The election was seen as an opportunity for the moderate Akalis to totally reject the radical ideology which the party had come to support. And launching the frontal attack on the now completely marginalized militants was Tohra, who, at one stage in his life, had been accused of hobnobbing with them and also being soft towards Sant Jarnail Singh Bhindranwale and providing him the much needed legitimacy during the initial stage.

He was perhaps competing with Badal by projecting himself more secular leader than his rival in the Akali Dal. However, the problem with him was that he had confined himself mainly to the SGPC domain, not entering the state legislative politics, though he had been a Member of Parliament, both Lok Sabha and Rajya Sabha, for long time. Moreover, in the moderate Akali stream, he was considered to be a hardliner. Perhaps it was his long association with the SGPC which has to hammer religio-political concerns of the community that got him this image, though in practice, he was more secular than many moderate Akali leaders and also closer to the people at the grassroots.

It was time for the star campaigner in the SGPC elections not only to reject the radicals but also hit them hard. "It is time for the Sikhs to give a burial to the radical ideology and cement the Hindu-Sikh ties, reject the radicals once and for all and chart out for themselves a course of action which would serve the community well", was the refrain of Tohra during the campaign.[1] He was setting the new agenda, not only for Akali Dal but also Punjab.

He himself was contesting the general house elections for the fourth time. His campaign style was different from other leaders. He would hand over the money donated by the people during the day to the candidate from the constituency concerned he would campaign for. He recalled during the campaign while sharing his earlier moments with this author that at the time of his first election, he was given Rs. 1400 by the party and he returned part of the amount after the election. He campaigned on a bicycle in that election. He was complimented by party Secretary Ajmer Singh for this unprecedented gesture. He lorded over this mini-Parliament of the Sikhs for the record more than a quarter of a century and his personal life remained unblemished. And he was the person who dictated the political agenda of the Sikhs for years. All his life, he lived in his moderate house in his native Tohra village. He never removed the large size photograph of Sant Bhindranwale from his drawing room. Here was a leader who would very rarely use the official car to which the president of the SGPC is entitled to. And he would not burden this body managing the Sikh shrines with his telephone bills or petrol for his private car which he would use for official purposes. He used to be referred to from the stages as "Panth da roshan dimag (enlightened brain of the Panth)".

For years together, his residence in Tohra village was without a telephone. Among his contemporaries, he was a class apart. He did not use the spring board of the SGPC for his larger political interests, unlike Parkash Singh Badal who had also ventured into the Akali politics through the SGPC and was elected to the its executive committee in 1955 at its October 16 meeting. The two stalwarts can be compared yet another level and that is their respective native villages. In Tohra village, the sarpanch elected to the post used to be his nominee. In Badal village, during the period under comparison, the sarpanch used to be the candidates from the opposite camp. The vertical division in Badal village used to be clearly discernible. Tohra had helped at least one member from almost every family from his village to get a job, in either public or private sector. He was also instrumental in the construction of a mosque for the microscopic Muslim community in his village. Tohra also had the distinction of being perhaps the only Akali stalwart who had close association with people from the academics with whom he would interact for hours.

There is yet another interesting comparison between the two leaders at the level of the people. During the 1996 Lok Sabha campaign, the youngsters in Badal village had formed Naujawan Sabha and set up camps on the two sides of the road passing through the village. They would stop the cars carrying press stickers and request the media persons to see the condition in the village of the former chief minister. Appalling is a mild word to describe the situation prevailing then. It explained why the family had all these years failed to have sarpanch of its choice. Even the government hospital, then 25-bedded, was without electricity connection and the only room which was being used by the doctor to treat patients had the power line from the nearby house. On the other hand, Tohra village was a model of development in that area.

But then none among his contemporary politicians in the region could match Badal in the long race and the capacity to wait for the opportune moment, a leader who would not spare his opponent.

During his election campaign, even Simranjit Singh Mann, the leader who all these years had been identified with the radical ideology, re-invented himself and promised better educational facilities and a new bank to provide cheaper loan to the Sikhs during the poll campaign. No more the talk of Sikh homeland. On his agenda were the English medium schools in every tehsil and a professional college at the district headquarter. "Our children do not qualify even to become clerks while those of the ranks of the Bharatiya Janata Party grab top posts", he would say. He gave the slogan of 'Tohra Hatao-Panth Bachao'(Remove Tohra-Save Panth).[2]

The Shiromani Akali Dal in its election manifesto for the SGPC polls released at Amritsar on October 3, promised enactment of All India Gurdwara legislation besides amendments to the Sikh Gurdwara Act, 1925 in the short run. The manifesto suggested setting up of the gurdwara service commission and the gurdwara building and art and cultural commission. It was also proposed to constitute the Sikh education commission and the dalit welfare commission. It was also proposed to celebrate the forthcoming tercentenary of the birth of the Khalsa, while mooting a World Sikh University. Many of the promises were later conveniently forgotten. This manifesto was once again a clean break with the immediate past. The party was making a new beginning at every level.

The Shiromani Akali Dal made a clean sweep in these elections held on October 13 after a gap of 17 years on the intervention of the Punjab and Haryana High Court which had been petitioned by Tohra. Out of 170, the Shiromani Akali Dal captured 155 seats. Opposing the SAD were Akali Dal (Amritsar) and the Akali Dal (Panthic) supported by the Bahujan Samaj Party and the Sant Samaj. The results reflected almost total consolidation of the Lok Sabha trend in favour of the Shiromani Akali Dal which had been subjected to direct onslaught during militancy. This election was further consolidation of Badal's leadership. "The landslide victory of Akali Dal led by Parkash Singh Badal in the election to the general house of the Shiromani Gurdwara Parbandhak Committee is the manifestation of reinforcement of liberal democratic politics and the traditional Sikh ethos. The result could well set the trend for the elections to the state Assembly, which are due in February next".[3] The Shiromani Akali Dal had re-emerged virtually from the ashes as this consolidation was not just in favour of this oldest regional party in the country but also against radical thought. The very leaders whose credibility had come to be questioned years ago had against become relevant again.

The SGPC released the much awaited White Paper on Operation Bluestar on the eve of the SGPC poll on October 10 alleging the army operation was pre-planned and the onslaught against the Sikhs was launched by then Prime Minister Indira Gandhi to teach the Sikhs a lesson for opposing the Emergency. This white paper was counter to the official white paper released by the government years earlier immediately after Operation Bluestar. It was a belated attempt to counter the government white paper.

Differences arose among the factions which had joined hands to oppose the mainstream Akali Dal after humiliating defeat in these elections with Akali Dal (Panthic) President Sant Ajit Singh leveling a wild allegation that Mann had connived with Tohra.

On the other hand, the human rights wing of the Shiromani Akali Dal dissociated itself from the party on November 1 alleging the party leaders were indifferent to the disappearance of human rights wing General Secretary Jaswant Singh Khalra. Its chairman Jaspal Singh Dhillon also opposed party's alliance with the BJP dubbing it as anti-minority outfit.

Meanwhile, Akal Takht Jathedar designate Ranjit Singh was released from Tihar jail on October 12 on parole. He had been convicted on the charge of assassinating Nirankari Chief Gurbachan Singh. Jasvir Singh Rode, Sawinder Singh, Jaswant Singh and Kashmir Singh, who had been appointed Jathedars of Akal Takht, Takht Keshgarh Sahib, Takht Damdama Sahib and Head Granthi of Akal Takht respectively by the militants, resigned paving the way for the installation of Ranjit Singh. The resignations were just symbolic as they had already been sacked by the SGPC.

With the focus now being on the Assembly elections, Badal, on Diwali day, suggested an all party front to defeat the Congress. In an hour long interview, he described the Congress as a "gang of corrupt people who had commercialized politics". He also promised probe into corruption in the then Congress regime. At the same time, he allayed the apprehensions being expressed in the political circles about the likely interference by the members of his family in the administration after the party was voted to power, saying, he had been the chief minister twice earlier and there had never been such a complaint.[4]

Badal promised an era of peace and development after coming into power. One of the priorities listed was uniting the Punjabis who had been the victim of divide and rule policy of the Congress. "Peace in Punjab is very dear to us. We will make all endeavors to ensure peace and harmony that will last. The unity of all Punjabis could be the only true and dependable basis of lasting peace and there could be no social and political stability without Punjabi unity", he said while launching Operation Deliverance on November 15 as the final phase of the mass movement started by his party way back in 1993.

Atal Behari Vajpayee virtually kick started the Akali Dal – BJP campaign for the Assembly elections from Ludhiana on December 1 by participating in a massive display of unity of Punjabis. The resolution passed at the rally promised clean, efficient, responsive and transparent dispensation and political system. The resolution stressed the need to have a fresh look at the over centralized polity with a view to evolve new positive equations of the Centre-State relationship in tune with the present day needs and circumstances. It was a marked shift from the demand for autonomy.

The political resolution stated: "Punjab has, during the last one decade or so, passed through a long tragedy and trauma, during which the Sikhs suffered victimization from many sides, particularly due to Machiavellian and perfidious policies of the government. The Congress has always tried to create an atmosphere of hatred among the communities, in pursuance of its divide and rule strategy. But this spirit of Punjabiat has ever remained powerful. There have been onslaughts on the Sikh shrines; the sanctity of the gurdwaras has been defiled and the Sikh self-dignity has been sought to be undermined. But under the leadership of the Shiromani Akali Dal, the Punjabis have not allowed the Congress policies and strategies to succeed at all in the state. The Shiromani Akali Dal is the protector of the Sikh dignity in Punjab and in other parts of the country. In fact, the Sikh dignity is an inseparable constituent of the Punjabi dignity.

"On this occasion, the Shiromani Akali Dal, in unison with the BJP and its other allies, reiterates its commitment to the Panth, Punjab, Punjabi and Punjabiat.

"The first challenge is that of having a fresh look at the over centralized polity with a view to evolve new positive equations of the Centre-State relations in tune with the present day needs; strengthening of the states would imply and lead to the strengthening of the country as a whole. There is need for giving right orientation and momentum to the developmental process by giving more powers to the states. Another challenge is to re-link economic development with social justice so that the benefits of economic development percolate down to the people at the grass-roots level".

Further, the party said, "Our top priority is to ensure in the country, and in particular in Punjab, a clean, efficient, responsive and transparent dispensation and political system, oriented towards the interests and aspirations of the people. This could be possible only if the Congress policies followed during the last 50 years of divide and rule are done away with, paving the way for fraternal harmony and real abiding peace". The party promised free power and canal water to the farmers and abolition of octroi, thus appeasing both the rural as well as the urban sectors. Despite anti-Congress wave in the state, Akali Dal was not taking any chances and thus resorting to politics of populism.

The political affairs committee of the Akali Dal formally decided to have alliance with the Bharatiya Janata Party in the forthcoming Assembly elections on the basis of a common minimum programme at its meeting on December 7 at Chandigarh. This alliance was projected as invincible in the years to come with the Shiromani Akali Dal representing the Sikhs and BJP the Hindus. However, this myth was shattered within less than three years in the Lok Sabha elections in 1999 when the alliance, going against the trend at the national level, faced humiliating defeat in the state. Of course, this alliance had provided the much needed respectability to the Sikhs at the national level by restoring their dignity. This was very important aspect of the relationship in the context that virtually the entire community had been dubbed as anti-national by the Congress and had been at the receiving end all the years during militancy. This was the single biggest contribution of the alliance with the BJP.

In the competitive politics of pandering, Congress Chief Minister

Rajinder Kaur Bhattal promised almost everything under the sun to the people in the state, beginning with free power for tubewells to the farmers holding less than seven acres of land, at a rally at Ludhiana on December 22. However, the announcement of elections on December 30 held back the implementation of her 51-point action plan. She had been brought in by the Congress leadership close to the elections as a damage control exercise to replace Harcharan Singh Brar. Congress gave a call to the countrymen in general and the Punjabis in particular to confront the communal and divisive forces represented by the Shiromani Akali Dal and the Bharatiya Janata Party. The party demanded transfer of Chandigarh and left out Punjabi speaking areas to Punjab and apportionment of the river waters on the riparian principle. Interestingly, in an attempt to woo Sikh voters, the party appealed to the United Nations to celebrate Khalsa tercentenary falling in 1999 as "Year of the Humanity". The show had been organized to counter Akali Dal which had earlier put up a massive performance at Ludhiana.

Tohra was re-elected as the President of the SGPC for the 23rd time on December 20.

Continuing with its anti-Congressism at the Jor Mela conference at Fatehgarh Sahib on December 26, 1996, the Shiromani Akali Dal, without mentioning the Anandpur Sahib Resolution, reiterated that Centre should have only defence, finance, foreign affairs and communications and the constitution should be re-written accordingly. The party also demanded scrapping of Article 356 of the Constitution. The main thrust again was on Punjabis and Punjabiat with a promise of peace and prosperity and a clean administration.

Meanwhile, Ranjit Singh was installed as the 29th Jathedar of Akal Takht on December 31.

Amarinder Quits Akali Dal

As the Akali Dal entered into poll alliance with the Bharatiya Janata Party, the Congress opted for tacit understood with the Communist Party of India over 10 seats to contest the Assembly elections as the Congress-Bahujan Samaj Party talks broke down over seat sharing. Out of a total of 117 seats, the Akali Dal allotted 25 seats to the BJP. The Akali Dal –BJP combine at its Maghi conference at Muktsar on January 13, 1997 promised to get the long denied economic, political and religious justice to the state. BJP President L. K. Advani was there to demonstrate support to the Akali Dal.

Amarinder Singh, who was denied the party ticket for the Assembly elections, quit the Akali Dal along with his supporters on January 18, alleging dictatorship by Badal and Tohra. He said he had no intention of joining the Congress. However, he later returned to the Congress to become Chief Minister in 2002. Amarinder Singh and 34 of his supporters were expelled from the Akali Dal on January 27.

The Akali Dal-BJP alliance, in its common minimum programme, targeted the Congress for pursuing divisive politics and promised to maintain peace at all costs. The alliance announced that after coming into power, it would set up a judicial commission to expose the Congress hand behind 'terrorism' in the state. The promise of providing free power and canal water were also there. On the river waters dispute, the alliance called for resolution in accordance with the riparian principle. The alliance MLAs were to declare their assets within 90 days which was never done.

The Shiromani Akali Dal, in its manifesto, while referring to the Anandpur Sahib Resolution, said, "True federalism as contained in the Anandpur Sahib Resolution alone can broaden the bonds of unity and integrity of the great Indian nation". The party stressed on genuine autonomy within the federal framework. It rejected all accords and awards on river waters and demanded apportionment on riparian principles.

On the other hand, the Congress attacked the Anandpur Sahib Resolution with the usual refrain of its being secessionist. The party blamed the inner contradictions in the Akali politics and the Sikh-Nirankari confrontation in 1978 as the root cause of militancy. The Congress manifesto also talked of immediate transfer of Chandigarh and left out Punjabi speaking areas to Punjab and resolution of river water dispute on riparian principles.

Akali Government Era

The February 7 elections restored the competitive and vibrant democracy in the state after a gap of about 19 years. The Barnala regime in-between could not be termed as an era of competitive and vibrant democracy. The results of the Assembly elections held in February, 1997 were predictable. It was a clean sweep for the Akali Dal –BJP alliance and a record victory by capturing 93 seats out of 117. The Akali Dal had bagged 74 seats, besides one Independent who could not be given the party symbol in time. The Congress trailed with just 14 seats. The people had reposed their total and complete faith again in Shiromani Akali Dal and its President Parkash Singh Badal who had emerged as a symbol of the Punjabi unity. He and his associates, at one time, had been completely marginalized by the radical politics. The trend was in continuation of the process which had earlier started with the Lok Sabha elections in 1996 followed by the SGPC general house elections the same year. Badal himself contested both from Lambi and Qila Raipur. He later resigned from Qila Raipur. Bahujan Samaj Party entered into seat adjustment with Akali Dal (Amritsar) and these parties got one seat each.

Badal, as Chief Minister, also opted for retaining the office of the party President, which, along with other factor, resulted in the parting of ways with SGPC chief and his long time associate Gurcharan Singh Tohra. From day one of the Akali Dal coming into power, Tohra had some reservations about the style of functioning of Badal. While Badal was taking oath as the Chief Minister in Punjab Cricket Association stadium at Mohali, Tohra was commenting on the likely style of Badal's governance in private conversation with this author at the same venue and he did not prove wrong as the events unfolded. He was the opinion that the state needed some bold and innovative steps for governance as the bureaucracy had wrecked the system during long period of President's rule which was not expected from Badal going by his past style of functioning.

The alliance government spelled out its political agenda in the first session of the newly elected Assembly in the Governor's Address which called for immediate and comprehensive initiative from the Centre for a just and satisfactory solution to the long pending demands and grievances of the people in the state. The government demanded immediate transfer of Chandigarh and left-out Punjabi speaking areas to Punjab, settlement of the river waters dispute on riparian principles, punishment to the guilty of November 1984 carnage and judicious solution to all the remaining problems faced by the people. These were projected as the demands of all Punjabis. Punjab, Punjabi and the Punjabiat were the main components of the political agenda. However, no concrete steps were ever taken during the five year regime of the government to settle these long pending issues. The Akali Dal was the partner in the National Democratic Alliance government at the Centre headed by A. B. Vajpayee but preferred to ignore these issues.

The Akali Dal, at its Hola Mohalla conference at Anandpur Sahib on March 24, revived the demand for the review of Centre-State relations to provide for a truly federal structure on the pattern of the Anandpur Sahib Resolution. The logic advanced was that it would not be possible to fulfill the poll promises without more powers to the states. The ruling Akali Dal already had an excuse to backtrack from its promises.

An important event in the religious domain was restoring Maryada at the newly built Akal Takht on April 13. All these years, the Akal Takht had been under construction after demolition of the government repaired structure. Family members of Sant Jarnail Singh Bhindranwale, Satwant Singh and Harjinder Singh Jinda were honoured at Akal Takht at that function where Finance Minister Capt. Kanwaljit Singh represented the state government. The SGPC later distanced itself from the honouring of the family members of the militant leaders saying Tohra had presented siropa (robe of honour) only to Damdami Taksal chief Thakar Singh and that it was Thakar Singh who had honoured the next of kin of the militants. At the same time, the SGPC press release maintained that those who attacked the Darbar Sahib complex were the enemies of the Sikhs and those who had sacrificed their life for protecting the shrine were the martyrs. It said, "It is for the Sikh community to decide as to who is the martyr" and the Sikhs did not need any certificate from any political leader in this regard.

This affair witnessed Badal making yet another paradigm shift. He criticized the event saying that the people of Punjab had given a forceful mandate for peace and prosperity and assured peace would not be allowed to be disturbed at any cost. "We have taken upon ourselves the responsibility of preserving peace and amity", he said adding forces out to disturb communal harmony would be dealt with a firm hand. Earlier, senior BJP leaders Atal Behari Vajpayee and Sushma Swaraj had conveyed their displeasure to Badal and Tohra over the incident. Badal clarified that the presence of Tohra at the ceremony was incidental.

However, Tohra did not agree with the views of the Chief Minister who said the next day that it was an internal affair of the Sikhs. At the same time, he made it clear that he had presented siropa only to Thakar Singh who had in turn honoured the families of the militant leaders. Quoting history and Sikh tradition, he said any ruler or invader who had attacked Darbar Sahib or any other sacred shrine was an enemy of the Sikh Panth and any Sikh who had laid down his or her life while avenging the attack was their shaheed (martyr)".[5] In his own style, he had justified the honouring of the families of the militants. These very people had earlier been honoured and Khalistan resolutions passed in the presence of Badal but now he had opted to take a different stand when in power.

Akal Takht Jathedar Bhai Ranjit Singh was of the view that such functions would not disturb peace. He clarified the relatives of the martyrs were honoured by him on behalf of the Taksal and not the SGPC. He allayed the apprehensions that the honouring of the relatives would disturb peace. "I will be responsible if this incident leads to any form of violence", he asserted.[6]

The Akali Dal retained the Qila Raipur Assembly seat in the bye-election held in May end. The seat had been vacated by Badal who had opted for Lambi, the Badal family fiefdom.

This time when the Akalis were in power in the state, the anniversary of Operation Bluestar on June 6 was observed at Akal Takht in a different way. No speeches were made. No kin of the militants was honoured. Bhai Ranjit Singh paid homage to the martyrs by placing a siropa on historical weapons kept at Akal Takht. Tohra was present. Badal had attended this function earlier only once in 1986.

Badal was re-elected President of the party at its delegate session at Amritsar on June 8. His name was proposed by Tohra, though in principle, he was opposed to the idea of the office of the party president and the chief minister being entrusted to one person. The delegate session resolved to work for the federal set up with autonomy to the states. The party, in its political resolution, stuck to the demand for the transfer of Chandigarh to Punjab and punishment to the guilty of November, 1984 carnage.

The Akali Dal government backtracked from the poll promise of setting up a judicial commission to go into genesis of militant violence in the state with Badal, on August 8, advancing the logic that nothing much would come out of it and it would only lead to mud slinging. "We should look to the future", he said. At the same time, he maintained that the Parliament should pass a resolution condemning Operation Bluestar. "All should apologize for that action", he added. He said the need of the hour was Punjabi unity which other parties earlier had been trying to vitiate for narrow political interests. "We are totally focused on Punjabi unity, peace and development and these are totally un-negotiable articles of faith with us", he asserted. He was speaking at a meet-the-press programme at the Chandigarh Press Club.[7] This decision of the Akali Dal government should be seen in the context of the allegations of aiding and abetting militancy the party had been leveling against the Congress even before Operation Bluestar. Here was an opportunity to prove the charge. Such an inquiry would also have exposed the entire state operations. However, the priorities had now changed. Badal had decided to bury the bitter and brutal past.

Badal announced the new party working committee on August 23. The office bearers included Jagdev Singh Talwandi, Surjan Singh Thekedar, Ranjit Singh Brahmpura and Gurdev Singh Badal (all Senior Vice-presidents), Kabul Singh, Amarjit Singh Bhatia and Sujan Singh (Vice-presidents), Sukhdev Singh Dhindsa (Secretary General), Balwinder Singh Bhunder, Capt. Kanwaljit Singh and Prem Singh Chandumajra (General Secretaries) and Kirpal Singh Badungar (Secretary). The members of the executive committee included Gurcharan Singh Tohra, Surjit Singh Barnala, Major Singh Uboke, Amrik Singh Aliwal, Ravi Inder Singh, Sewa Singh Sekhwan, Tota Singh, Prem

Singh Lalpura, Natha Singh Dalam, Manjit Singh Calcutta, Mohinder Singh Brar, Baldev Singh Khiala, Hari Singh Zira, Sarup Singh, Col. Jasmer Singh Bala, Narinder Singh, Harnirpal Singh, Sarwan Singh Phillaur, Inderjit Singh Zira, Sampuran Singh Cheema, Kirpal Singh Libra, Charanjit Singh Atwal, Ajaib Singh Mukhmailpur, Bibi Jagir Kaur, Parkash Chand Garg, Virsa Singh Valtoha, Adaish Partap Singh, Upinderjit Kaur, Jasdev Singh Sandhu, Chhajju Ram, Ujagar Singh Rangretta, Mal Singh Ghuman, Avtar Singh Makkar, Mohinder Singh Nawan Shahar, Sewa Singh and Raghujit Singh.

President K. R. Narayan on November 8, granted remission of the remaining sentence of Bhai Ranjit Singh who had earlier come out on parole. A petition to this effect had earlier been submitted by the SGPC which was pursued by both Badal and Tohra. Tohra was re-elected President of the SGPC on November 28.

From Anti-centre to Pro-centre

The Akali Dal, while in power, made another paradigm shift in its policy, from being anti-Centre all these years to being pro-Centre. With the Congress in power at the Centre for a long spell, the Akalis used to thrive on anti-Centrism and discrimination to Punjab. Under that situation, anti-Centrism and anti-Congressism used to be synonymous for the Akali Dal. Of course, the Akalis were part of the Janata government at the Centre which came into power in 1977 after Emergency. However, the pro-Centrism of the Akalis was not too pronounced at that time. It was for the first time that the Akali Dal started talking of playing a major role at the Centre. It was Prime Minister I. K. Gujral, who was in office only for a few months, who partly influenced this thinking, apart from the partnership with the BJP. This shift from total confrontation to total cooperation was complete when Atal Behari Vajpayee took over as the Prime Minister of the National Democratic Alliance government in Delhi.

Continuing its anti-Congress crusade, the ruling Akali Dal, at its Jor Mela conference at Fatehgarh Sahib on December 26, gave a call to annihilate the Congress from all over the country in the ensuing Lok Sabha elections.

The SAD-BJP alliance swept the Lok Sabha elections held in February, 1998 by decimating the Congress in all the 13 seats in the state. However, this massive mandate was to be frittered away within a year. Congress President Sonia Gandhi, during her election campaign in Chandigarh, came close to apologizing for Operation Bluestar when she referred to the "June 6, 1984 events" and said she understood the hurt to the Sikh psyche but in the same breath, also said that her family was also "hurt". On the anti-Sikh carnage following assassination of her mother-in-law Indira Gandhi, she said, "As a widow and as a mother, I empathize with the victims. This should have never happened. My husband also felt that way".[8]

In its election manifesto, the Shiromani Akali Dal opposed the scrapping of Article 370 of the constitution which provides for special status to Jammu and Kashmir. The party reiterated its commitment to the complete restructuring of the constitution for more powers to the states. It called for scrapping of Article 356 which empowers the Centre to dismiss the state governments and making prior consent of the chief minister concerned necessary for the appointment of the Governor. The manifesto made it clear that the party always had complete faith in peace, amity and universal brotherhood, love and understanding between the two communities and prosperity for all. The party lambasted the Congress for pushing the country into fratricidal bloodshed through engineered riots and state sponsored terrorism.

Prem Singh Lalpura, MLA, who won from Tarn Taran in the Lok Sabha elections, opted for the Assembly seat. He was later expelled from the party.

In a significant development, Amarinder Singh, the Congress candidate from Patiala in the Lok Sabha elections, in the second week of April, lodged a complaint with the Akal Takht against Tohra for seeking the support of the Nirankaris for Akali Dal candidate Prem Singh Chandumajra. The complaint was finally dismissed by Bhai Ranjit Singh as Tohra pleaded not guilty. However, it had later come to be known that Tohra did go to the Nirankari gathering, though not intentionally. He had accompanied Chandumajra who had arranged the election meeting. He realized within no time that he was at a wrong place and left the hall immediately. It all happened within a few seconds. He made up his mind to go to apologize at Akal Takht but somehow, that never happened. He carried the burden of this guilt of violating the Akal Takht directive of 1978 against the Nirankaris till the end.

The Akali Dal, at its Baisakhi conference at Talwandi Sabo in April, 1998 demanded immediate transfer of Chandigarh and other Punjabi speaking areas, besides adjudication of the river water dispute. The party also demanded stringent punishment for the guilty of November, 1984 carnage. The party talked of true federal structure, scrapping of Article 356 and appointment of Governor with the consent of the chief minister concerned. Interestingly, at a separate conference, the Congress also made similar noises on the territorial and the river waters dispute.

Riding the anti-Congress wave, the Akali Dal retained both Tarn Taran Parliamentary seat and the Sham Chaurasi Assembly seat in the bye-elections held in early June.

BJP Under Attack

Though the Akali Dal was on winning spree, the sailing at some other levels was not smooth. This was both within the party and also in relations to the alliance partner. And raising the question mark on the attitude of the BJP was Tohra. The relations between the Akali Dal and the BJP seemed to be on the rocks when he took the alliance partner to task, especially the national leadership of the BJP, on the issue of long pending demands of the state saying the BJP led government at the Centre had not been safeguarding the interests of the Akali Dal. His outburst followed the meeting he and Badal had with Prime Minister Atal Behari Vajpayee. He had also one-to-one meeting with the Prime Minister. The issues he listed which had hurt the sentiments of the Punjabis included the move to transfer the Punjabi dominated Udham Singh Nagar in Uttar Pradesh to the proposed hill state of Uttaranchal and shelving of important projects like the proposed refinery in Bathinda district and the Chandigarh-Morinda rail link. In his perception, there was little difference between the Congress and the BJP governments in Delhi so far as the Akali Dal was concerned.[9]

Taking extreme position for the first time about relationship with the BJP, Tohra again equated the party with the Congress a few weeks later, saying "The Akali Dal- BJP coalition is functioning well in Punjab but I am not satisfied with the attitude of the BJP high command" especially in relations to the demands concerning the state. He added, "BJP is no different from the Congress. The BJP should do some introspection. We fully understand that the BJP has the limitation of not being in a majority. But then it is a question of the attitude. The river waters dispute should be referred to the Supreme Court or the tribunal and resolved on the basis of riparian principles as applicable elsewhere. The recommendations of the Eradi Tribunal are not acceptable as riparian law was ignored by this tribunal. Then the BJP leaders say the Akalis never demanded Chandigarh. Where is the question of demanding Chandigarh? It belongs to Punjab and it should be transferred immediately. Even on the issue of Udham Singh Nagar, the attitude of the BJP high command was not sympathetic. How can I say that I am satisfied with the BJP at the centre when there is no positive response even on the issues which are not inter-state"?[10]

His outburst followed several meetings he and Badal held with Vajpayee, Deputy Prime Minister L. K. Advani and others on the issues concerning Punjab. The SGPC chief had also taken up the issue of exemption to Sikh women two wheeler drivers from wearing helmets which had been made compulsory. He was disgusted that the BJP ruled government in which the Akali Dal was a partner had not accepted even this demand which directly concerned the Sikh religion. Wearing a cap is a taboo for the Sikhs and helmet is considered to be one form of the cap. The law was later amended for all women. It was Tohra who used to do most of the talking at such meetings and Badal used to be a good listener. It was this state of affairs which had contributed to his outburst against the BJP which was not sudden. For weeks, he used to talk about this attitude of the BJP in private. Moreover, it was not for the first time that he had fired the salvo at the BJP as he had lambasted Badal for playing into the hands of the Sangh Parivar years ago also before the advent of militancy.

It was not just the political domain where the situation was getting hot. Crisis also characterized the religious domain of the Sikhs. This was the time when differences cropped up among the members of the clergy with Takht Keshgarh Sahib Jathedar Prof. Manjit Singh taking the decision against attending any meeting at Akal Takht to protest against the humiliating behaviour of Bhai Ranjit Singh. In retaliation, Bhai Ranjit Singh, in an unprecedented move, banned the participation of Prof. Manjit Singh and Takht Damdama Sahib Jathedar Giani Kewal Singh in the meetings until Prof. Manjit Singh submitted the accounts of the World Sikh Council and Giani Kewal Singh explained the reason for boycotting the meetings of the clergy. Tohra commented, "Family quarrels should not be taken to streets". Giani Kewal Singh challenged the authority of the Akal Takht Jathedar in banning them from the meetings. Badal also took the position that the rift among the members of the clergy was a family affair which would be resolved keeping in view the interests of the Panth.[11] That was not to be.

Interestingly, though Badal himself had earlier backtracked, it was BJP state party chief Daya Singh Sodhi who raked up the issue of setting up of a judicial commission to probe the genesis of 'terrorism' to expose the Congress. Alleging that several Congress leaders had been aiding and abetting terrorism, he stressed a probe was necessary.[12] Badal did not react.

Tohra was elected President of the SGPC for the record 25th term at its general house meeting on October 23. The general house adopted 24 resolutions. The SGPC demanded legal sanction for Takht Damdama Sahib as fifth Takht of the Sikhs, return of the historical documents and photograph taken away by the army during Operation Bluestar from the Sikh reference library in the Darbar Sahib complex, judicial inquiry into the November 1984 carnage, second language status for Punjabi in the neighbouring states, permission to carry 9-inch sword on international flights and handing over control of the Panjab University at Chandigarh to Punjab. Another resolution talked of separate personal law for the Sikhs and double citizenship for non-resident Indians. The general house also demanded exemption to the Sikh women from wearing helmets while riding two wheelers. The demand for separate personal law flowed from exclusive identity assertion.

Akali Dal Lands in Crisis

It was being apprehended for sometime. The Akali Dal finally landed into crisis with Tohra dropping the bomb shell which divided the party vertically. It was frontal attack from Tohra which Badal dreaded. In their love hate relationship suffering from trust deficit, Badal had not been ruling out some trouble from within the party, especially from the SGPC chief. His apprehension was influenced by his earlier experience as the Chief Minister when Tohra had led the revolt against him within the party. It was this apprehension which defined his association with the BJP despite repeated attacks on him on this issue.

This time, Tohra fired the salvo on December 10 in Jalandhar while talking to a news agency reporter at the residence of Bharpur Singh Balbir, a journalist and former associate of Harchand Singh Longowal. As per the interview put across by the wire service, he was of the opinion that Badal should quit as the party President to devote full time to governance. This was a few days after the defeat of the Akali Dal in the Adampur Assembly bye-election. He said it was imperative for a party representing a minority to have an independent president, especially when the party was in power. His logic was that a party representing a minority has to agitate for its demands which was not possible when the same person held the office of the chief minister as well as that of party president. Moreover, the party had been loosing ground because of inability of Badal to devote sufficient time to the organizational matters. The organisational leaders felt ignored by the ministers.

Late in the night in Delhi, Badal discussed the situation with his son Sukhbir Singh and arrived at the conclusion that as the fight had come into the open, it should be taken to the logical conclusion and the 'irritant' must be removed. Badal and his son decided to hit back. Frontal attack was launched against Tohra the very next day.

Talking to this author the same night, Tohra said that what the agency had released was off the record conversation at the residence of Balbir. Even before the Adampur bye-election, Tohra used to express the view in private that Badal should shed the organizational responsibility as the Akali Dal represented the Sikhs and a political party which claims to represent a powerful minority has to fight for its rights. This should be best left to the party president.

Both Badal and Tohra were to be together at a marriage reception near Ludhiana the next day and the SGPC chief thought that he would clarify the matter personally. Both of them were at the reception for about two hours. However, Badal did not even look towards Tohra. It was end of the matter and Tohra also decided against issuing any clarification. The fight had come out into the open.

And it was Tohra who, a few months earlier, had suggested to Badal to hand over the reigns of the government to his son Sukhbir Singh. Tohra himself narrated this incident to this author sometime before the Assembly elections in 2002 at the time when the unity parleys were on with Badal on the assurance that it would be kept a closely guarded secret as he had not shared that moment with any body till then. Badal just squirmed in his chair when it was cross checked with him.

Tohra Proposes Sukhbir as CM

The two leaders enjoyed very interesting relationship. Both of them would share their inner feelings with each other and often weep, literally, in each other's company. Here was one such moment. This was the time when Badal had been suffering from some disease for which he was to go to USA for treatment. Badal seemed to be very disturbed that day when Tohra visited him at the official residence in the morning to inquire about his health. It was October 23, 1998 and they were alone in the room. Suddenly, Badal broke down while talking and started weeping. Tohra tried to console him. Badal proposed let Tohra take over the reigns of the state as he was not in good health. At that emotional moment, Tohra proposed that Sukhbir should be entrusted with the responsibility of the Chief Minister. Badal did not agree saying his son was not yet mature enough to take up this responsibility. Tohra offered to personally supervise and help Sukhbir consolidate his position. The meeting lasted about half an hour.

Ironically, later when they parted company, Tohra used to charge Badal with promoting the interest of his son at the cost of the party and Badal would hit back dubbing him a Congress agent who nurtured the ambition of becoming the chief minister. That was their political compulsion as the reality was different. Even at the time when Tohra's relationship with Badal family was very bitter, Sukhbir would touch his feet whenever they met in the central hall in Parliament. This was one little known very humane aspect of their relationship.

On the day when Sukhbir was blessed with a son, it was Tohra who congratulated him late in the night on telephone. Badal rang up Tohra the very next morning within a few hours to thank him for the congratulatory message. The conversation remained confined to the family affairs. That was the time when the relations between Tohra and Badal were very bitter. Tohra was one towering Sikh leader who always cherished humanitarian aspect of relationships. Tohra's son, the only child, had died within days of the birth and somewhere in his heart he had that feeling for Sukhbir. He had an adopted daughter. This feeling got expression yet at a social get together at the newly built house of this author also. As he dropped in after the religious function was over, the kids were dancing in the adjacent room with music at high pitch. He volunteered to join the kids. And he danced with them. That was perhaps rarest of the rare moment in his life.

Five Tohra associates in the cabinet – Maheshinder Singh Grewal, Manjit Singh Calcutta, son-in-law Harmel Singh, Surjit Singh Kohli and Inderjit Singh Zira- submitted their resignations on December 14. Contacted by Badal, they refused to reconsider their decision. They had the apprehension that with the factional fight getting intensified, they would be sacked from the cabinet. In their identical resignation letters, they described as highly objectionable and unfortunate the character assassination and humiliating charges leveled by some ministers against Tohra and deplored the failure of the Chief Minister to check the tirade.

The disciplinary action committee of the Akali Dal issued a show cause notice to Tohra on December 17 for violating the party discipline. As the factional fight flared up, Vajpayee intervened to pacify the situation. However, Badal was not in favour of the intervention from Vajpayee in the internal affairs of the Akali Dal.[13] Both Badal and Tohra shared the stage at Fatehgarh Sahib Jor Mela conference in December, exchanged siropas but gave no indication of the differences having been resolved. Badal did not respond to the unity tune of Tohra and his associates.

The Akal Takht interceded on December 31 and directed Badal against taking any action against the SGPC chief till April 15 in view of the Khalsa tercentenary celebrations in April. The Hukamnama said, "To celebrate the Khalsa tercentenary year unitedly and interpret the feelings of the Sikh sangat, the high priests direct the Akali Dal high command not to take any action against each other till April 15". The Hukamnama also prohibited the disciplinary action committee from proceeding further on the reply filed by Tohra. Significantly, Takht Keshgarh Sahib Jathedar Prof. Manjit Singh and Takht Damdama Sahib Jathedar Giani Kewal Singh did not attend the meeting of the high priests. Prof. Manjit Singh later said the interference in political affairs was not in the interest of the Panth. He, along with Giani Kewal Singh, was of the opinion that the religious leaders should first resolve their own differences rather than meddling in political affairs like Akali unity. He perhaps forgot that before the Assembly elections, he had himself been interfering in the Akali affairs to unite various factions. Bhai Ranjit

Singh justified the intervention and joined issues with the two jathedars arguing Akal Takht was the supreme temporal seat of the Sikhs representing synergy of religion and politics and as such, the institution was fully authorized to take such a step. He blamed Prof Manjit Singh for shifting his stand frequently. He also commented that both Tohra and Badal were not fighting for any Panthic agenda but only self interest.

It is the intervention by Akal Takht which is dreaded by the Akali Dal Chief Minister. Badal had faced this situation even during his earlier tenure as the Chief Minister beginning 1977 when Tohra and then Akali Dal President Jagdev Singh Talwandi had sought the arbitration of the supreme temporal seat while submitting their resignations from their respective offices on September 27, 1979. They said in their resignation letter, "We have tried all this time to save the Panth from the bitter attacks from anti-Panthic forces and maintain unity. However, Badal, who believes in the theory of 'Hindu Sikh Unity and Divide the Panth' is trying to divide the Akali Dal and the Panth to cling to power. Therefore we demand resignation of this leader trying to divide the Panth, damage the Sikhs by diluting their faith in the religion, making Punjab bilingual, making Sikhs slaves of the Hindus for all times to come, and indulging in corruption at every level, promoting nepotism and fratricidal factionalism".[14] This was the severest ever indictment of an Akali Dal Chief Minister by the Presidents of the Akali Dal and the SGPC. The two leaders had also leveled serious allegations of corruption against Badal.

For the smooth sailing of the Akali Dal government, a sort of balance has to be maintained between the office of the Chief Minister, the Akal Takht Jathedar, the SGPC President and the Akali Dal chief. The alternative is to have dummies to head the religio-temporal institutions as was the situation witnessed later. In this case, Badal opted for confrontation both with the SGPC chief and the Akal Takht Jathedar as he was confident about his supremacy in the legislative domain. It was also precisely for this reason that apprehending such problems, he had kept the office of the party president with him.

Reacting sharply to the directive, 10 of the 15 members of the SGPC executive committee owing allegiance to Badal, in an unprecedented move, questioned the Hukamnama and appealed for its withdrawal. They included Kewal Singh, Balbir Singh Pannu, Raghujit Singh, Hardalbir Singh, Bhagwant Singh, Satnam Singh, Suba Singh, Mal Singh Ghuman, Gurpal Singh and Joga Singh who passed a resolution to this effect which described the Hukamnama as a one sided intervention by Bhai Ranjit Singh. These members took notice of the exclusion of Prof. Manjit Singh and Giani Kewal Singh from the meeting and said the one sided decision was against the established Panthic traditions. Bhai Ranjit Singh refused to oblige them while issuing a warning that the critics of the Hukamnama would be dealt with severely. He offered to quit if so desired by the SGPC.

At the time of the allotment of tickets during elections to the general house of the SGPC in 1996, Tohra had completely left it to Badal who happened to be the party president. It was for this reason that the general house was dominated by the Badal supporters. Every time the two leaders united, Tohra never insisted on his share and the unity would be unconditional on his part. Perhaps such magnanimity was part of his nature.

In yet another related move, the state government sacked the chairman and two members of the Sikh Gurdwara Judicial Commission. Commission chairman Kashmir Singh was a Tohra supporter. The tenure of the commission is co-terminus with the term of the general house of the SGPC but it had not been reconstituted after the general house election in 1996, though the SGPC had made recommendation to this effect to the state government in 1997. Later, the Badal government fully used the new commission in this fight against Tohra. The disputes relating to the SGPC are referred to this commission for adjudication.

Badal, for the first time, had stepped into the religious domain, the space hitherto occupied by Tohra. It is a different matter that at the beginning of his political career, he was nominated to the executive committee of the SGPC. He took command of the Khalsa tercentenary celebrations with a subservient role given to the SGPC and Akal Takht. Tohra attended the meeting to discuss the preparations for the celebrations.

Badal assumed the command of the celebrations formally at a meeting of the Akali Dal MPs, MLAs, members of the SGPC, party working committee and the district jathedars at Anandpur Sahib on January 7 which was also attended by Tohra . He was authorized to chalk out the programme and constitute various committees. It was perhaps for the first time that the religio-political powers in the Akali Dal had been vested in one person. All these years, Badal had been identified with the development agenda having pro-farmer image. Badal's hegemony on the Sikh religio-political matrix was complete which had its negative aspects also. Henceforth, he himself was to be responsible for all that went wrong. Earlier, Tohra used to act as his much needed shock absorber.

Within two days of the Anandpur Sahib meeting, Tohra supporters were on the offensive and questioned the disbanding of the Gurdwara Commission. The memorandum addressed to Badal was purported to have been signed by 92 SGPC members. However, most of the signatures had been faked by the Tohra supporters. This memorandum was another provocation to the Badal men to launch all out offensive against Tohra. The reaction to this claim of strength was quick as the Badal faction paraded 112 members at Jalandhar on January 10. These members included 47 members whose names had appeared on the memorandum submitted to Badal earlier on the Gurdwara Commission issue.

The situation in the Akali Dal before the formal split was reflected at the Maghi conference of the party at Muktsar on January 14 which was boycotted by Tohra and his supporters. Surjit Singh Barnala fully backed Badal at this conference.

A new dimension was added to the religio-political crisis in the Akali Dal as 131 SGPC members made a submission to Bhai Ranjit Singh to withdraw the Hukamnama. The withdrawal of Hukamnama is a debatable issue as according to one section of the Sikh community, it can neither be amended not withdrawn. However, that depends upon the situation, as the later events proved. A confrontation was also developing between the party and the Akal Takht Jathedar. Bhai Ranjit Singh refused to oblige the Badal camp.

Tohra and his supporters boycotted the meeting convened by Badal at Chandigarh on January 18 to chalk out the detailed programme for the Khalsa tercentenary celebrations. They had earlier boycotted the Maghi conclave at Muktsar. Sukhdev Singh Bhaur, a close associate of Tohra, was suspended from the Akali Dal on January 21, 1999.

The crisis was further precipitated as the Akal Takht Jathedar, on January 25, summoned Prof. Manjit Singh, Badal supporter Daily Ajit proprietor Barjinder Singh Hamdard and a correspondent of the paper Major Singh to appear on February 11. They were summoned in connection with the publication of extracts from a controversial book 'Vanity Incarnate' which had been banned by the state government. The Sikh clergy also directed the group of 131 SGPC members to testify before February 11 as to whether they had themselves signed the appeal to withdraw the Hukamnama. Prof. Manjit Singh was summoned for sharing stage with two ex-communicated Sikhs Preet Singh Sandhu and Harkirat Singh. These US based Sikh leaders were ex-communicated for violating the Hukamnama on Langar which prohibited tables and chairs in the langar hall of the gurdwaras, a practice which had started in the West. It was for the third time in the history of Akal Takht that the Jathedar of another Takht had been summoned. Bhai Ranjit Singh had earlier banned Prof. Manjit Singh and Giani Kewal Singh from attending the meetings of the clergy at Akal Takht.

In another related development, the Akal Takht Jathedar served a two-day notice on February 2 on Badal to adopt the radical agenda of the recent Sikh struggle. This development set Akal Takht in direct confrontation with the Badal government. Adopting this agenda which was based on the "Sikhs are a separate nation" doctrine meant taking radical stance. The decision to serve this notice on Badal was taken at a conclave of Sikh organizations and sects at Akal Takht. Bhai Ranjit Singh warned of violence at Khalsa tercentenary celebrations at Anandpur Sahib in case Badal did not submit to Akal Takht. It was also decided to organize a function parallel to that of Badal at Anandpur Sahib on April 14. The leaders were of the view that the Panthic agenda should find reflection in the tercentenary celebrations. Bhai Ranjit Singh made it clear in case Badal failed to give such a commitment, the Khalsa tercentenary would be celebrated under the aegis of Akal Takht. The Akali leadership was equated with stagnant water which emanated foul smell. Tohra did not attend the meeting but sat with hundreds of devotees in front of Akal Takht. Later, Bhai Ranjit Singh clarified in the face of mounting onslaught that he was not a supporter of Khalistan. His emphasis was on preserving the separate and exclusive identity of the Sikhs within India.[15]

Going by the atmosphere in the Darbar Sahib complex that day with hundreds of devotees waiting for the outcome of the meeting, it seemed that the days of the Badal government were numbered. At least such was the feeling one had while witnessing the proceedings of the meeting and the mood of the people gathered in front of this supreme temporal seat for prayer and politics. However, the Badal government survived the crisis. The meeting at Akal Takht was a harsh indictment of the Badal government which was attacked for not adopting the 'Sikhs are a nation' doctrine.

Earlier, in another unprecedented move, the Akal Takht Jathedar inserted a full page advertisement in the newspapers carrying his letter written to Badal on February 9 putting across his side of the story in which he clarified that he was not in favour of Khalistan but stood for the distinct identity of the Khalsa Panth. He wrote to Badal: "You have destroyed the spirit of sacrifice of Akali Dal and made it your personal property and that of your yes-men. After ascending to power, the importance of religious institutions has become meaningless for you. He who till now was denouncing the entry of police in the Golden Temple complex, is himself sending police inside this sacred place to grab Harmandir Sahib and the Akal Takht... you have mastered the art of using religious institutions to your advantage. When not in power, you raise a hue and cry over the danger to the Panth and religion. But after getting power, you try to subjugate religious leaders with the authority of the power you have acquired. Only psychopathic Jathedars are deemed as great and for you, everything is regarded as saleable because you are surrounded by an army of sycophants and saleable persons".

In a swift and dramatic move for which Badal later came under attack for denigrating the supreme Sikh institutions, the executive committee of the SGPC at a meeting at Amritsar on February 10 suspended Bhai Ranjit Singh and appointed Giani Puran Singh in his place after the earlier choice in the morning, Giani Mohan Singh, Head Granthi of Darbar Sahib, declined the offer. It was the day of chaos. The ten members of the SGPC loyal to Badal held a meeting in the morning to appoint Giani Mohan Singh. The meeting of the executive was held on the directive of the Sikh Gurdwara Judicial Commission. The executive met again in the evening in circuit house to appoint Giani Puran Singh who took over on February 15. It was the second meeting about which questions were raised as the Gurdwara Commission had issued directions to hold only the first meeting. The resolution passed at the meeting of the executive said that due to unnecessary confrontation between the three Jathedars, the sentiments of the Sikhs were hurt and a serious threat was being posed to the unity and harmony of the Panth. The resolution also made a mention of the plot purchased by Bhai Ranjit Singh at Mohali under a confusing identity. The resolution stated: "The executive committee reached the conclusion that to maintain Panthic maryada and to prevent any harm to the Sikh tercentenary celebrations, the Jathedar should resign... We have decided to suspend Bhai Ranjit Singh and a 30-day notice has been served on him".

The executive also endorsed the appeal made by 131 members earlier to withdraw the Hukamnama issued on December 31. It was said that by turning down the request, Bhai Ranjit Singh had posed a threat to the very existence of the SGPC. The meeting also authorized Badal to make arrangements for the tercentenary celebrations. Bhai Ranjit Singh questioned his suspension. Tohra announced the next day that he would boycott all government functions in protest and mobilize the masses against the "unprincipled" Badal government.

Badal, at a rally at Rajpura on February 12, rejected the Panthic agenda directive and asserted his party was committed to the Moga Declaration. In a pointed attack, he alleged Tohra had joined hands with the Congress to topple his government. On the other hand, Tohra, on February 13, gave a call to the people to purge Badal to save Akali Dal and other Panthic organizations. For the first time since inception of the crisis, he charged Badal with amassing wealth through corruption.

Badal said in an interview that Tohra nurtured the political ambition of becoming the chief minister. He saw no wrong in cherishing such an ambition but felt the party should not be sabotaged in that process.[16] The SGPC members loyal to Badal at a meeting on March 12 authorized him to announce Tohra's successor. The meeting was attended by 136 out of 170 members.

Tohra finally submitted his resignation on March 15 from the SGPC presidency, a day before the requisitioned meeting of the general house of the SGPC was to take up the no-confidence motion against him. The resignation came within six hours of the executive committee meeting held at a historical gurdwara at Jind in Haryana under tight security which was boycotted by 10 members loyal to Badal. He blamed the Chief Minister for denigrating the high Sikh institutions and said he was prepared even to leave the country in case the dignity of Akal Takht was restored by bringing back Bhai Ranjit Singh. Tohra had good relations with then Haryana Chief Minister Bansi Lal and that was the reason for holding the meeting there.

Jagir Kaur, a dalit, who headed the cash rich Dera of Sant Prem Singh Muralewale at Begowal in Kapurthala district, was elected as the first woman president of the SGPC at the general house meeting on March 16. She was a first time member of the SGPC general house who was also a minister in the Badal cabinet. The domination of Badal in both the political as well as religious domain was now absolute. In an attempt to consolidate his hold over the SGPC members loyal to him, Badal made a subtle move. For the first time in the history of the SGPC, discretionary grant of Rs. 50,000 each was allowed to the members. For the SGPC members and office bearers, the concept of Sewa (selfless service) was over. The SGPC was heading towards an era where the President would opt for luxury cars purchased from the offerings of the devotees. Not that this body was earlier free from corruption. However, till then, it was confined to the lower levels. That culture was to change. This is the cost the Sikhs as a community were to pay under the new dispensation. Tohra would rarely use the official car. He would not bill this organization even for the petrol expenses of the car he used. That culture of selfless service ended with him. After desecration, now was the era of denigration of Sikh institutions and that too on the altar of power politics.

The Khalsa Tercentenary

Prime Minister Vajpayee presided over the Khalsa tercentenary celebrations at a mega show on April 8 at Anandpur Sahib. The event was unprecedented with lakhs of people from all over the globe converging to this birth place of the Khalsa during the week long celebrations. It was for the first time in the history of this most nascent religion of the world that the centenary of revolutionary baptism of the Sikhs transforming them into Khalsa (the pure) by the 10th Lord, Guru Gobind Singh, had been celebrated on such a mega scale. Due to historical reasons, the earlier two centenaries could not be observed. The Khalsa had been created as a religio-political entity but ironically, the events associated with the tercentenary lacked political content. Although it was the 300th anniversary of the event relating to this religion (not of the religion) which had far-reaching religio-political ramifications due to its revolutionary content, it ended up mainly as an emotional extravaganza. It was time for the community to do the introspection and set the agenda for the future. However, the leadership had once again failed the community. There was no indication from the mega event that for more than a decade a few years earlier, a section of this community had launched the struggle to re-occupy its own geo-political space. This was not the case with the ruling Badal faction alone. Even the suggestion to the supporters of Tohra to raise the slogan of "Raj Karega Khalsa (The Khalsa shall rule)" even for five minutes at 11.00 AM all over the city on the Baisakhi day did not find favour on the argument that it might dub the Akali faction as radical. And "Raj Karega Khalsa" is part of the daily Sikh prayer.

Tohra alleged violation of Sikh Maryada at the main function attended by the Prime Minister. This function to mark the Khalsa tercentenary was organized without the presence of Guru Granth Sahib. Even Takht Keshgarh Sahib Jathedar Prof. Manjit Singh was absent from the main stage.

The polarization in the Akali matrix was complete during the tercentenary celebrations. The Tohra camp attacked Badal for hijacking the celebrations and violating the maryada. Amidst mounting criticism, Badal made an effort to justify the actions of the state government. He said in a statement on March 11 in the run up to the celebrations, "Those trying to paint the great Khalsa event as a sarkari (government) show are violating the sanctity of the occasion and guilty of trying to insult the proud Khalsa heritage. In their desperation, they have even started talking about violence and blood-shed during the celebrations... they have forgotten that the SAD has played a leading role as a Panthic organization over the past 80 years. The government headed by it in Punjab is not an ordinary government but it is a true representative of the Punjabis and the Panth. As such, it is not only its right but its sacred duty to take part in the historic event of the Khalsa symbolizing the universal humanistic message of the great Gurus". None questioned the right of the Akali Dal government to organize the show. Questions had been raised about the way it had been done.

More than 20 lakh people visited Anandpur Sahib during the celebrations. However, the Akali Dal faced humiliating defeat in the Lok Sabha elections a few months later the same year. It turned out to the biggest non-political event in the history of the Khalsa born as political entity.

Earlier in a letter written to Tohra on March 8, about two dozen members of the SGPC lambasted him saying, "The most disturbing aspect of the problem is that there is a frighteningly ominous shadow both in your words as well as deeds. You have been trying to terrorize the devout masses by openly issuing threats of violence and bloodshed during these celebrations if you are now allowed to have your way. The question now is not of allowing you to have a few more days as President. The real issue that concerns us is one of saving the Khalsa celebrations from the dangerous impact of your deadly intentions. The Panth cannot take any chances by allowing you an opportunity to put your ominous designs into practice at this historic hour".

One of the resolutions adopted by the Tohra faction during the celebrations at Anandpur Sahib on April 14 stated: "The Akal Takht Jathedar and the jathedars of other Takhts neither come under the purview of the Gurdwara Act nor the service rules apply to them. Therefore, this congregation accepts the supremacy of the status of Akal Takht and his (Jathedar's) independent functioning".

Earlier on February 20, 1999, the Dharam Parchar Committee of the SGPC had passed a very significant resolution taking out the Takhts from the jurisdiction of the Sikh Gurdwara Act, 1925, arguing the jurisdiction of the SGPC constituted under that act was limited to Punjab, Haryana, Himachal Pradesh and the Union Territory of Chandigarh. However, the same was not the case with the Takhts whose writ runs large all over the globe wherever the members of the community are spread. "Akal Takht cannot be bound within the confines of the Sikh Gurdwara Act because there is no reference to Sarbat Khalsa, Gurmata and the Hukamnama in the Act", the resolution said. It further said, "The Dharam Parchar Committee is of the considered opinion that the Jathedar of Akal Takht can neither be suspended, nor his explanation sought. This right vests only with the Sarbat Khalsa".[17] The minutes of this resolution were approved at the next meeting when Jagir Kaur had taken over as President. Her objection was overruled as she was not part of the Dharam Parchar committee when this resolution was adopted. The minutes are approved at the next meeting. The Sikh Gurdwara legislation can be amended only by the Parliament as it is an inter-state body corporate. Years earlier, the SGPC, under Tohra's presidency, had ended the practice of giving salary to the high pretests which was converted into honorarium to remove the impression of their being employees.

Another resolution adopted by the Tohra faction on April 14 charged Badal and his associates with violation of the principles of Akal Takht. Yet another resolution referred to the 1984 events and demanded that the Parliament should pay tribute to the martyrs of Operation Bluestar and apologize to the Sikh community. The Tohra faction mainly targeted Badal at the tercentenary celebrations and failed to give any concrete alternative programme to the Sikhs.

Ranjit Singh Sacked

Bhai Ranjit Singh, the Akal Takht Jathedar under suspension, was finally sacked by the SGPC on April 28 and replaced by acting Jathedar Giani Puran Singh. Rejecting the decision of the SGPC executive to remove him, Bhai Ranjit Singh directed Badal and his coterie to appear at Akal Takht on or before May 20 or face the consequences. He rejected the decision to replace him saying it was the Akal Takht which was supreme and not the SGPC. However, this rejection was an exercise in futility. The executive adopted a resolution opposing the setting up of the Pakistan Sikh Gurdwara Parbandhak Committee. It was decided that as a mark of protest, the SGPC would not send Jathas of Sikh pilgrims to Pakistan in June on the occasion of martyrdom day of Guru Arjan Dev. The blunder in opposing the PGPC was realized much later.

The religio-political crisis in the Akali Dal reached its climax with the expulsion of Tohra from the party for six years on May 14. The decision was taken unanimously by the political affairs committee of the oarty. He was charged with anti-party activities and hobnobbing with the Congress. The party adopted a resolution at a public meeting organized at Fatehgarh Sahib on May 16 appealing to the Akal Takht to reopen the case relating to Tohra's alleged interaction with the Nirankaris at Patiala during the 1998 Lok Sabha elections. However, Giani Puran Singh rejected the demand saying the decision taken at the supreme temporal seat could not be reviewed.

In a move to confront Badal, Tohra started organizing Akali Dal Bachao (Save Akali Dal) committees at the district level culminating in the setting up of the Sarv Hind (All India) Shiromani Akali Dal at Alamgir in Ludhiana district on May 30 in an effort to add third dimension to the otherwise bipolar Punjab polity. The turn out at the public meeting was beyond the expectation of the organizers. The political resolution passed at the congregation stated: "The Shiromani Akali Dal (In this case, the Sarv Hind Shiromani Akali Dal) is the true representative of the Sikh Panth, having its main base in Punjab, and it symbolizes the entire Sikh community. Shiromani Akali Dal upholds the right of the Sikh minority community to maintain its distinct character and spares no efforts to secure their interests. The party is legitimately proud of its role in the fight for the freedom of the country. We are firm in our resolve to perform these complimentary roles. We re-assert out commitment to pursue our traditional goals........the Shiromani Akali Dal believes in the unity, integrity and the security of India, simultaneously being alert against all attempts to suppress human rights and fundamental freedoms by the misuse of the power of the state. The vibrant character and pro-active role of the Shiromani Akali Dal has been misinterpreted and misconstrued in the past by ruling cliques with the ulterior motive of defaming the Sikhs in a most shame faced and diabolical manner and method. This august assembly of the Shiromani Akali Dal declares in the clearest terms that we shall not permit anybody to erode the distinct identity of the Sikhs".

The 'Panthic Convention' also released a charge sheet against Badal. The charges included confronting Akal Takht, government interference in the religious affairs of the Sikhs and denigrations of the Sikh institutions, self projection at the Khalsa tercentenary, playing fraud on the Guru and the Panth, backtracking from the poll promise and misuse of official position. However, the new Akali Dal outfit miserably failed to add the third dimension to the Punjab polity, except that it succeeded in damaging the prospects of the Shiromani Akali Dal in the subsequent Lok Sabha and the Assembly elections. The party confined itself only to Badal bashing, without outlining any positive programme.

The Badal government, in a move to prevent anti-Badal Akali factions from observing anniversary of Operation Bluestar on June 6 at Akal Takht, rounded up Akali Dal (Amritsar) President Simranjit Singh Mann and its General Secretary Ram Singh. The SGPC, separately, made it clear that no group would be allowed to make political speeches inside the shrine. The SGPC decided to organize only prayer to pay tributes to the martyrs. Badal said the government would not allow anybody to take law into his hands while denying having attended the anniversary in the past.

Badal, on June 6, 1999 presided over a party meeting at Chandigarh which was attended by 27 out of 30 district presidents. The meeting was the show of strength by him which adopted resolutions praising Badal for leading the Punjabis and the Panth and making tercentenary celebrations a success. Another resolution condemned the breakaway Akali leaders who were attacked for damaging the party and the Sikhs. The third resolution appealed to the people of the country to give a befitting defeat to the Congress in the forthcoming Lok Sabha elections.

The Akali Dal expelled Prem Singh Chandumajra and Surjan Singh Thekedar on June 19 and decided to seek explanation from a group of MLAs including Manjit Singh Calcutta, Mahesh Inder Singh Grewal, Harmel Singh, Inderjit Singh Zira, Surjit Singh Kohli, Bikramjit Singh Khalsa, Hira Singh Gabria, Gurdev Singh Sidhu, Jagtar Singh Rajla and Daljit Kaur for supporting Tohra. The expulsion of Thekedar and Chandumajra was just a formality as they had already deserted the Badal faction. The decision to this effect was taken at a meeting of the political affairs committee. The resolution adopted at the meeting lambasted Tohra for playing into the hands of the Congress.

The impact of the religio-political crisis in the Akali matrix was reflected in the Lok Sabha elections held in September, 1999 in which the Congress bagged eight seats, the Akali Dal retained only two, with one seat each going to the BJP, Akali Dal (Amritsar) and the CPI. The split in the Akali votes went in favour of the Congress which had contested the elections in alliance with the CPI. Badal received a personal set back with the ignominious defeat of his son Sukhbir Singh from Faridkot. Sukhbir lost the elections despite massive development works undertaken in that constituency by way of the eradication of the water logging problem which had turned the area virtually into a hell. The development agenda was just not enough to get him elected from the constituency having heavy concentration of dalit voters as the people wanted to teach a lesson to the Badal family for arrogant behaviour. Sukhbir's mother Surinder Kaur who was in-charge of campaigning in the Malout segment, had been conveyed about a week before the election about the likely defeat of her son. On the day the election results were announced, the official residence of the Chief Minister was totally deserted, with not a soul there except some staff.

However, Badal continued to dominate in the religio-political domain as evident from the subsequent re-election of Jagir Kaur as the SGPC chief. At the same time, there was no doubt that he was under tremendous pressure from within as could be made out from the cabinet expansion, the exercise he carried out on December 31. As against five vacancies caused by the resignation of Tohra associates, he inducted 15 ministers at the time when the committee on fiscal reforms had proposed downsizing of the government to check the growing expenditure. Now there was no check on the members of the ruling party and this was the price Badal had to pay to keep his flock together. The party conveniently forgot the massive mandate the people of Punjab had given in 1997. Corruption increased manifolds in the government and the SGPC after this split.

In the Lok Sabha elections, the ruling Akali Dal sought mandate for political stability, economic prosperity, social harmony and on the issue of persons of foreign origin in political life of the country. The party manifesto pleaded for the setting up of a genuine federal structure and an end to the politics of confrontation between the Centre and the states. The party favoured cooperative federalism, stressing that was the only way to preserve the rich cultural, linguistic, religious and social diversity. The party also promised eradication of corruption. The Lok Sabha poll was seen as a referendum between the great son of India (Atal Behari Vajpayee) and a person of foreign origin (Sonia Gandhi). Ironically, this was the major issue hammered by Badal in his election speeches, not the one concerning the state or the Sikhs. The manifesto pledged the party to continue to work for the fulfillment of the just and long pending demands including the settlement of river waters dispute on the riparian principle and transfer of Chandigarh and left-out Punjabi speaking areas to Punjab. The manifesto claimed the restoration of Punjabi unity as among the major achievements. The Vajpayee card did not work in this state.

Ranjit Singh campaigned in the Lok Sabha elections with a sharp attack on Badal while sparing the Congress. He made the alleged denigration of Akal Takht by Badal as the major election issue. For him, the fight was between the Panth and Badal. The Tohra faction, in its election manifesto, referred to the backtracking by the Shiromani Akali Dal government from the poll promises and the alleged denigration of the Sikh institutions, etc. It stated: "Mr. Badal succeeded in his designs for the politicization of religion, officialization of the holy Akal Takht, commercialization of politics and Congressization of the Akali Dal, and thereby usurping political and religious prowess of the Sikhs. Thus has ended the internal democracy in the party. He has paved the way for the return of the Congress party to power". The last sentence proved to be predictive as the Congress returned to power in the 2002 Assembly elections. However, there could have been other reasons also and not the only ones mentioned in the assessment of the situation by the Tohra faction.

Badal, in a statement issued on October 7, while accepting the verdict of the people "with total humility and dignified democratic grace", promised sincere introspection and immediate remedial steps. "We would take it as a case of people spurring the Shiromani Akali Dal to strive harder to meet their sky high expectations from our government", he added. He ridiculed the demand made by the Congress of his resignation as an act of hasty political opportunism and said the Congress and the Left in the state had hardly any reason to feel proud of the fact that they had won a few extra seats with the open support of

Gurcharan Singh Tohra and his followers, who realizing their immediate extinction from the political map of Punjab, openly exhorted their supporters to vote for the Congress and the Left candidates. He said Tohra and his coterie had been totally wiped out from not only the political map of Punjab but also from the minds of the Sikh masses. Tohra owed an explanation to the people of Punjab for helping the Congress which was responsible for Operation Bluestar, Delhi riots and atrocities committed against the Punjabis. The Chief Minister also sought fresh mandate from the Akali Dal Legislature Party while holding a veiled threat for the dissolution of the Assembly. Tohra, however, in a statement the same day, held the politics unleashed by Badal and his "non-Akali" advisers responsible for the situation while demanding his resignation.

Coming under pressure, Badal also sought mandate from the legislature party which expressed full faith in the "solid, clear and farsighted leadership" being provided by him to the party and the state. He sought this fresh mandate from the MLAs in the wake of the signature drive launched against him by Ravi Inder Singh with the support of the Sarv Hind Shiromani Akali Dal.[18] The resolution stated: "The meeting condemns the unprincipled campaign of deliberate misinformation started by some unscrupulous and opportunistic elements against the Punjab government and the Chief Minister, Mr. Parkash Singh Badal, and cautions the Punjabis against the activities of these opportunistic elements. This campaign is aimed only at weakening the SAD. The Congress Party, which is the enemy number one of Punjab and the country, is now in league with certain elements that stand alienated from the Panth and is hatching conspiracies with a view to vitiate the hard won atmosphere of peace, amity, prosperity and stability in the state. The sole objective of the Congress conspiracies is to set peace and Punjabi unity on fire to push the state back into a dark era. This meeting reiterates the resolve of the Shiromani Akali Dal under the able leadership of Mr. Badal to expose and defeat these conspiracies. Mr. Badal today symbolizes the setting up of the federal structure and a new socio-economic system in the country and truly spearheads a people's movement against forces of communal divide. Over the past decade and a half, he has waged a fearless and relentless battle to salvage the honour and glory of the Panth and Punjab and has steered the people successfully out of a zone of darkness in which the Congress conspiracies had pushed Punjab. The vilification campaign launched against him and his colleagues is targeted at disrupting peace, stability and democratic process in Punjab. Mr. Badal's singular contribution to heighten the glory of the Panth during the tercentenary celebrations of the birth of the Khalsa remains a matter of abiding pride for the SAD and for every Punjabi. He forcefully represents Punjab, Punjabi and Punjabiat and has led the state into an era of Punjabi unity by freeing it from the venom injected into the system by the Congress."

The political affairs committee of the Akali Dal, which met at Chandigarh earlier on October 11, too had reposed faith in Badal's leadership following similar exercise undertaken by the district jathedars two days earlier. The resolution passed at the meeting lambasted Tohra saying the election mandate was also against him and other opportunistic elements that were in league with the Congress. It said, "Jathedar Tohra and his coterie have helped the Congress to give a blow to the pride of Punjab by extending full help to the Congress Party directly and indirectly".

Badal also sought mandate from the party at a meeting of the office bearers, district presidents and the members of the SGPC at a meeting on November 26. The meeting authorized Badal to take any action against the dissidents.

On the other hand, the working committee and the district presidents of the Sarv Hind Shiromani Akali Dal, at a meeting at Ludhiana on October 23, said the replacement of Badal was imperative to fulfill the purpose for which the Akali Dal was set up. The betrayal by him had undermined the Akali struggle for safeguarding Panthic thought, Panthic interests and Panthic directions. The Lok Sabha polls verdict was not against the Akali Dal but against the violation of Sikh tenets and traditions, challenge to the supremacy of Akal Takht and for splitting the party. The resolution said it was also a vote against the failure of the Badal government, rampant corruption and the financial crisis.

In yet another blow to the anti-Badal faction in the Akali matrix, Jagir Kaur was re-elected President of the SGPC at its general house meeting on November 10 defeating Surjit Singh Cheema put up by the SHSAD by a margin of 77 votes in the direct contest.

The resolutions passed at that general house meeting demanded an end to the quota system in the army recruitment, restoration of reservation of seats for donors in the charitable medical institutions run by the SGPC, legal status to Takht Damdama Sahib through an act of Parliament, increase in the number of Sikh judges in the high court and the Supreme Court, etc. The general house also demanded handing back the control of the Panjab University in Chandigarh to Punjab and declaring all the cities built by the Sikh Gurus as holy. The legal status to Takht Damdama Sahib meant recognition in accordance with the Sikh Gurdwara Act. While the SGPC had been raising this demand, a section within the community was of the opinion that Akal Takht should be taken out of the purview of the Sikh Gurdwara Act on the logic that the seat of Sikh sovereignty cannot be compromised by making it subservient to a legislation enacted by the state.

The Working Committee of the Shiromani Akali Dal on December 15 authorized the party President to take any step to confront the challenges to the party and his leadership from within and outside. The issue of more powers to the states through a federal set up was now again on the agenda of the Akali Dal. It was part of the strategy to meet the challenge, if any, from the somewhat tough stand by the Tohra faction on such issues. The meeting called for restructuring of the constitution to provide for the true federal structure. The working committee also authorized the political affairs committee to take emergency decisions.

It was decided to sack Ravi Inder Singh, a member of the Political Affairs Committee of the Akali Dal, from the party for anti-party activities for six years. The working committee also reiterated the demand for the setting up of a judicial commission to probe the November, 1984 carnage.

Continuing with its anti-Badal campaign, the SHSAD, at its meeting on December 22, resolved to seek inquiry by the Central Bureau Investigation or the high court judge into the corruption in the Badal government. It was decided to meet the President and the Prime Minister for this purpose. The party accused Badal of backtracking on the issues concerning Punjab for his narrow vested interests. The party expressed the determination to formulate the strategy for getting more powers to the states in association with other like-minded parties.

NOTES

1. The Indian Express, October 10, 1996.
2. The Indian Express, October 8, 1996.
3. Jagtar Singh, The Indian Express, October 15, 1996.
4. Jagtar Singh, The Indian Express, November 12, 1996.
5. The Tribune, April 21, 1997.
6. The Indian Express, April 22, 1997.
7. The Indian Express, August 9, 1997.
8. The Hindu, January 26, 1998.
9. The Indian Express, June 18, 1998.
10. Jagtar Singh, The Indian Express, September 7, 1998.
11. The Tribune, August 29, 1998.
12. The Indian Express, September 19, 1998.
13. The Indian Express, December 18, 1998.

14. Quoted from the original letter.
15. The Indian Express, February 16, 1999.
16. The Indian Express, February 28, 1999.
17. Quoted from the original resolution.
18. The Indian Express, November 1, 1999.

19

Sikh Agenda and Akali Dal

As the Akali Dal had been created as a Sikh party which continued to articulate ambitions and aspirations of the community till the eighties, the era of the government headed by this party beginning 1997 after the militant movement had been crushed is significant so far as the Sikh agenda is concerned. The government headed by Parkash Singh Badal distanced itself from almost every issue taken up during the period of militancy. This era defines the politics of the leaders at the helm of affairs and that politics was only the power politics. This is the era when the Akali Dal stopped having even pretensions of being a party representing the concerns of the Sikhs, virtually no different from the Congress. Though the party had adopted the agenda of Punjabiat at its convention at its 75th anniversary convention at Moga earlier, it had for some time continued to have the pretensions of the party protecting the Sikh interests.

The religio-political matrix of the Shiromani Akali Dal continued to be turbulent with unprecedented developments at the time when Chief Minister Parkash Singh Badal dominated the religious domain of the Sikhs also in his capacity as the party President and had emerged as the most powerful leader who could appoint and remove all those occupying the high religio-political offices at will. All the Sikh institutions were at his command. Being the most powerful leader was perhaps also his weakest point. The religious affairs proved to be the slippery ground for him as he was not conversant with the deeper nuances of the politics of the religious institutions. Earlier, under the garb of reforms, the militants had damaged these institutions. Now the politics of religion had become subservient to Badal's vested political interests. This was especially so after he parted company with Shiromani Gurdwara Parbandhak Committee President Gurcharan Singh Tohra, the longest serving president of this body. Although the two leaders again joined hands after the Akali Dal lost to the Congress in the elections, Tohra died with a feeling of having been betrayed by Badal. At crucial moments, Badal's actions betrayed ignorance of the long term repercussions of the controversies which erupted during that period. But then these actions could also be part of his strategy and tactics to remain at the centre stage. The turbulence in the religio-political matrix was not due to ideological reasons but part of the power struggle, ambition to rule but at the very personal level and not part of the collective Sikh consciousness.

At the time when Shiromani Akali Dal had become uni-polar after Tohra's exit, here was the first test for Badal. The religio-political leadership of the Sikhs came to be embroiled in controversy on the issue of the implementation of the first ever Sikh almanac known as the Nanakshahi calendar prepared by Canada based Pal Singh Purewal. At the political level, this calendar was the re-assertion of the exclusive and independent Sikh identity, the issue which, for a long time, had been dear to the SGPC and the Akali Dal. The almanac had been cleared for implementation by the general house of the SGPC during Tohra's presidency with effect from 1999 but was withheld later. However, then Akal Takht Jathedar Bhai Ranjit Singh favoured consensus to be evolved on it before its implementation as it was considered to be a very sensitive issue. The calendar also aimed at rectifying some distortions in the religious affairs attributed mainly to the influence of deras and the so called sants who were opposed to its implementation. The calendar had fixed the dates for the important Sikh events.

The calendar was finally given a green signal for implementation at the meeting chaired by SGPC President Jagir Kaur on June 30, 1999. Bhai Ranjit Singh had set up a committee with representatives from Sant Samaj, the SGPC and the World Sikh Council, to suggest changes, if any. This committee was later dissolved and the decision taken to implement it. The decision was to land Jagir Kaur in a deep crisis as a section of the community, mainly the sants, the self styled religious leaders who were part of the Sant Samaj, opposed it.

As the decision triggered controversy, the high Sikh clergy, on December 23, appointed a 7-member committee to go into the implementation of the contentious calendar. The decision to appoint the committee was taken after a closed door meeting the members of the clergy had with Jagir Kaur, the Sant Samaj and some Sikh organizations. The committee rejected this calendar on January 6, 2000. The very next day, three members of the panel resigned in protest, alleging the decision to reject the calendar was contrived. They included Purewal, Ajit Singh and Rai Jasbir Singh. All these three members favoured implementation of the calendar. Akal Takht Jathedar Giani Puran Singh rejected their resignations.

Senior BJP leader and Local Bodies Minister Balramji Dass Tandon reacted to the calendar saying it would divide the Punjabi society in particular and the nation in general. In private, even Badal was not happy with the decision to implement it as this development had the potential to rock the alliance with the BJP as evident from Tandon's reaction and Badal could not afford it. The dates fixed for the Sikh events in this calendar differed from the calendar being followed in the country. Ironically, it was Badal who himself released the same calendar later in 2003 when out of power. The Punjab government, after some initial hesitation, adopted this calendar for fixing holidays for some of the Sikh religious events.

Some gurpurabs (events associated with the Sikh Gurus) were celebrated by the SGPC in accordance with the Nanakshahi calendar. However, Giani Puran Singh refused to lead the procession on January 5, 2000 on the eve of this Gurpurab at Amritsar associated with Guru Gobind Singh the date for which had been fixed under the Nanakshahi calendar. Defying the SGPC, he participated in the parallel Gurpurab celebrations organized by some Sikh organizations according to the earlier prevalent calendar on January 14. The Gurpurab celebrations on January 5 were in accordance with the Nanakshahi calendar. The procession on January 14 was taken out by the Sant Samaj. The 7-member committee was recast by dropping Sant Mangal Singh. The new 11-member committee was to submit its report by March 15.

Jagir Kaur Ex-communicated

As the crisis in the religious domain continued to deepen on the issue of the Nanakshahi calendar, Giani Puran Singh, on January 23, 2000 unilaterally restrained the 11-member committee from functioning. This panel had been set up by five high priests, the Dharam Parchar Committee and the SGPC executive at a joint meeting on January 11. Earlier on January 21, committee convener Dr. Kharak Singh had also involved four more persons. Giani Puran Singh also removed four members nominated by Dr. Kharak Singh who included Dr. Bachan Singh Bachan, who had been restrained from working as the SGPC Secretary by the Sikh Gurdwara Judicial Commission, SGPC member Kiranjot Kaur, Dr. Paramjit Singh Goraya and Dr. Darshan Singh. The SGPC questioned the decision to dissolve the panel.

The hard-line taken by Giani Puran Singh against the Nanakshahi calendar which hammered the exclusive and separate Sikh identity can best be understood from the six-page pamphlet distributed by the

Punjab unit of the Rashtriya Swayamsewak Sangh detailing Khalsa tercentenary celebrations. On page two of this pamphlet, it is mentioned that it was Giani Puran Singh who had received the RSS organized Khalsa Sirjana March at Darbar Sahib. In his speech on the occasion, Giani Puran Singh had traced the lineage of the Sikh Gurus to Lav and Lush, the two sons of Hindu god Lord Rama. This statement of his had raised a lot of hue and cry in the Sikh circles at that time. The Nanakshahi calendar is the assertion of the exclusive Sikh identity and this perspective is not palatable to the Sangh Parivar. Again, it was Thakar Singh, acting Chief of Damdami Taksal, who received the march at its headquarters at Mehta Chowk. The RSS later opened channels with the Taksal which was also opposed to the implementation of the calendar. The religious code of conduct (Maryada) practiced by this seminary differs with the one approved by the SGPC after lengthy deliberations and followed in the Darbar Sahib complex.

In an unprecedented move, Jagir Kaur was excommunicated by Giani Puran Singh from the Sikh Panth on January 25, 2000. He issued the controversial Hukamnama (directive) from Guna, a small town in Madhya Pradesh while on way to Takht Hazoor Sahib at Nanded in Maharashtra. There was another reason for this hasty action on the part of Giani Puran Singh. It was a newspaper report anticipating his sack appearing the same day which was the reason for the extreme provocation. Giani Puran Singh had pre-empted any move of the SGPC to remove him. Jagir Kaur had summoned a meeting of the executive committee on January 27 and the actions of Giani Puran Singh were to come under scrutiny at that meeting. On the surface of it, the extreme action was taken against the first woman president of the SGPC for "repeatedly violating the directives of the Akal Takht". The Hukamnama was faxed to the newspaper offices from Guna.

Giani Puran Singh also summoned all the executive committee members of the SGPC to appear at Akal Takht on February 2 while canceling its January 27 meeting. He said in the Hukamnama, "I have taken this step in accordance with the Sikh traditions. I could have taken this step on my own but a meeting of the five Amritdhari Sikhs was held here and this decision was taken". He did not explain the hurry in taking such a sensitive decision. Such decisions are supposed to be taken by the five sanctified high priests.

In a counter move, the other high priests including Giani Kewal Singh, Jathedar of Takht Damdama Sahib, Giani Mohan Singh, Head Granthi of Darbar Sahib, Giani Bhagwan Singh, Head Granthi of Akal Takht, Giani Gurbachan Singh and Giani Charan Singh of Darbar Sahib, rejected the Hukamnama issued from Guna on the logic that it was not in consonance with the Sikh traditions. It was argued that on such a sensitive issue, the meeting should have been held at Akal Takht and the action initiated only after taking explanation from the person concerned.

In this case, Jagir Kaur was not given the opportunity to explain her side. She questioned the Hukamnama issued by Giani Puran Singh arguing it was just a statement. The political affairs committee of the Akali Dal which took stock of the situation adopted an ambivalent attitude towards the Hukamnama. Though the party adopted this attitude, Badal was worried over the developments. He was of the opinion that Jagir Kaur should not have opened Pandora's Box by implementing the Nanakshahi calendar.

Reacting to the unprecedented development, Tohra said as the procedure for the appointment of Giani Puran Singh was questionable, so were his actions and moreover, what could one expect from a person who himself had been appointed in violation of the established norms. At the same time, he maintained the Hukamnama could not be violated and Jagir Kaur should apologize at Akal Takht and for that she must first resign from the presidency of the SGPC.[1] He did not find anything technically wrong in the actions of the Akal Takht Jathedar.

The SGPC chief, in an attempt to pave the way for resolving the religio-political crisis, made it clear she would present herself at Akal Takht as and when summoned. She maintained she had not received any written directive from Akal Takht on the issue. "My entire life is dedicated to Akal Takht. It is the duty of every Sikh to be committed to the Rehat Maryada, ideas and traditions of Akal Takht. I am always prepared to present myself at Akal Takht as and when directed or summoned", she said in a statement.[2] An emotionally upset SGPC chief did not know as to what crime she had committed which invited such harsh punishment. Badal had a close door meeting with the ex-communicated SGPC chief at Phagwara.

Giani Puran Singh, on February 2, restrained Jagir Kaur from functioning as the SGPC chief till her re-admission into the Sikh Panth which further deepened the crisis. The Hukamnama issued from Akal Takht also directed nine out of 15 members of the SGPC executive to undergo religious punishment for implementing the Nanakshahi calendar. These members included Hardalbir Singh Shah, Raghujit Singh Virk, Joga Singh, Bhagwant Singh, Suba Singh, Pritam Singh Bhatia, Gurbax Singh Purain and Harbans Singh Manjhpur. However, Prof. Manjit Singh and Giani Kewal Singh, Jathedars of Takht Keshgarh Sahib and Damdama Sahib respectively, Giani Mohan Singh and Giani Bhagwan Singh did not attend the meeting convened by Giani Puran Singh. Jagir Kaur turned recluse for several days.

Coming out of her self-imposed 'ekantwas'(hibernation), a defiant Jagir Kaur, while indirectly challenging the action against her, not only offered obeisance at Darbar Sahib and Akal Takht but also chaired a meeting in her capacity as the SGPC chief. Giani Bhagwan Singh offered prayer at Akal Takht on her behalf for her success in the ongoing Panthic crisis. This was a direct challenge to the authority of the Akal Takht Jathedar.

Giani Puran Singh was under attack from several Sikh organizations on this issue. A one day convention organized by the Institute of Sikh Studies at Chandigarh on February 13 demanded removal of Giani Puran Singh and ridiculed the way he gathered five Sikhs to proclaim the edict from Guna. The resolution passed at the convention also warned of growing interference in the Sikh affairs by the BJP and questioned the continuation of Badal as the party chief since he was heading the 'Punjabi' Party and not the Akali Dal, the party which used to articulate the Sikh aspirations. The RSS was alleged to be the hidden force behind the action against Jagir Kaur.

She wrote to the Akal Takht Jathedar on March 2 expressing her desire to appear at the Sikh temporal seat provided the sanctified five high priests summoned her. She had been persuaded for about 8 hours into writing this letter by a well wisher. The controversial Hukamnama ex-communicating the SGPC chief virtually stood rejected in practice as she attended the delegate session of the Akali Dal on March 3. The next day, Giani Puran Singh warned the Sikh leaders against sharing stage with the ex-communicated SGPC chief. He said her presence at the delegate session had lowered the dignity and Maryada of Akal Takht.

The Jathedar summoned Jagir Kaur on March 11 to present herself the next day to seek an apology for violating the directive with regard to Nanakshahi calendar. In the one page letter addressed to her, Giani Puran Singh said, "The Nanakshahi calendar was not accepted by a majority of the Sikh sangat. Akal Takht had received a number of complaints in this regard. The five high priests had constituted a sub-committee to look into the calendar. It was directed by Akal Takht not to implement the Nanakshahi calendar till the committee submitted its report. However, in gross violation of Akal Takht directive, you celebrated the birth anniversary of Guru Gobind Singh on January 5 instead of January 14. Hence you were ex-communicated from the Sikh Panth. You can appear before Akal Takht at 11.00 AM for seeking unconditional apology".

Yet in an yet another unprecedented move in the Sikh history, Giani Puran Singh, on March 12, ex-communicated three high priests including Prof. Manjit Singh, Jathedar Takht Keshgarh Sahib, Giani Kewal Singh,

Jathedar, Takht Damdama Sahib and Giani Bhagwan Singh, Head Granthi, Akal Takht, and two SGPC members Pritam Singh Bhatia and Jaswinder Singh on the charge of being in league with Jagir Kaur and restrained them from functioning. Earlier, they had staged a walk out from a meeting convened at Akal Takht to award religious punishment to Jagir Kaur. She made a dramatic appearance in the Darbar Sahib complex after keeping Giani Puran Singh waiting for more than an hour on the appointed day. She bulldozed her way to Akal Takht and returned after paying obeisance.

Directive to Badal to Replace Jagir Kaur

Going a step further, the Akal Takht Jathedar, on March 13, directed Badal to replace president of the SGPC and Jathedars of Takht Keshgarh Sahib and Takht Damdama Sahib and Head Granthi of Akal Takht. The directive was issued to pre-empt any move of the SGPC executive to sack him at the March 16 meeting. She had announced her decision to chair the meeting. However, it was not within the purview of Badal to take action on this directive as the SGPC is a statutory body with a prescribed procedure for the election of the President.

In yet another unprecedented move, the March 12 directive issued by Giani Puran Singh was rejected by another set of five high priests, excluding Giani Puran Singh, on March 14. The meeting, presided over by Giani Gurbachan Singh, acting Head Granthi of Darbar Sahib, was attended by Bhai Mann Singh, Head Granthi of Takht Damdama Sahib, Bhai Sukhwinder Singh, Head Granthi of Takht Keshgarh Sahib, Giani Nirmaljit Singh, Head Granthi of Gurdwara Chheherta Sahib and Giani Joginder Singh, Granthi of Darbar Sahib. They said in a statement that Giani Puran Singh had denigrated Maryada of the takhts by having his letter faxed from a public call office in Guna. They justified the action of Jagir Kaur in not presenting herself before Giani Puran Singh at Akal Takht.

Jagdev Singh Talwandi, chairman of the disciplinary action committee of the Akali Dal, held a closed door meeting with Giani Puran Singh on March 15 in the presence of Baba Kashmira Singh and Baba Mangal Singh. Jagir Kaur, in turn, postponed the scheduled SGPC executive committee meeting.

The representatives of various Sikh organizations, including the Dal Khalsa, Akali Dal (Amritsar), Damdami Taksal, Akal Federation and the Khalsa Action Committee, sought removal of Giani Puran Singh. The resolution passed at the meeting described the Hukamnama issued from Guna as gross violation of maryada. Giani Puran Singh was accused of being in league with the Rashtriya Swayamsewak Sangh.

Another resolution lambasted the SGPC for appointing incapable persons to such high offices. The conclave asked all the controversial high priests to quit in the larger interests of the Sikh Panth.

The Shiromani Akali Dal formally intervened to sort out the religio-political crisis with the political affairs committee of the party at a meeting on March 19 directing Jagir Kaur to present herself at Akal Takht.

Baba Kashmira Singh, who supported Giani Puran Singh, called on the ex-communicated SGPC chief at her residence at Chandigarh in the evening of March 18 to resolve the crisis. The meeting lasted less than an hour. She wrote another letter to the Akal Takht Jathedar saying she was prepared to present herself at the Takht provided that all the five priests sanctified by Panthic traditions were present.

The SGPC executive moved swiftly on March 28 and finally sacked Giani Puran Singh from the office of the Akal Takht Jathedar and suspended him from his original post as Granthi of Darbar Sahib. He was ordered to report at Muktsar during his suspension. The meeting, chaired by Jagir Kaur, was attended by seven members including Gurpal Singh, Satnam Singh Bhairupa, Suba Singh, Joga Singh Phaguana, Joginder Singh Panjrath and Pritam Singh Bhatia. Giani Joginder Singh Vedanti was appointed the new Jathedar. Earlier during the day, Giani Puran Singh had ex-communicated four SGPC members - Raghujit Singh Virk, Satnam Singh Bhairupa, Gurpal Singh and Pritam Singh Bhatia. The SGPC acted at the time when Badal was contemplating some steps to defuse the religio-political crisis. The apprehension was that Giani Puran Singh might also suspend Badal from the Panth. Badal had got a letter written that day in the morning which Jagir Kaur was to be asked to sign and send to Akal Takht to resolve the crisis.

The excommunication of Jagir Kaur and the three high priests was revoked by the high priests at a meeting on March 29 which was attended by Jathedar Vedanti, Giani Mohan Singh, Head Granthi, Darbar Sahib, Giani Gurbachan Singh and Giani Charan Singh, both granthis of Darbar Sahib and Giani Rawel Singh, Granthi of Akal Takht. This meeting rejected all the Hukamnamas, declarations and directives issued by Giani Puran Singh between January 25 and March 28. The high priests described the Hukamnamas issued by Giani Puran Singh as declarations which were product of narrow mindedness and caused colossal damage to the Sikh Panth. The high priests apologized to the Sikh Panth for the agony caused by the arbitrary decisions taken by Giani Puran Singh.

The Tohra supporters protested against Jagir Kaur presiding over the budget session of the SGPC on March 30. The general house urged the Centre to take up the demand for disbanding the Pakistan Sikh

Gurdwara Parbandhak Committee with Pakistan. Another resolution demanded transfer of Chandigarh and other left-out Punjabi speaking areas to Punjab, adjudication of river waters dispute on riparian principle and punishment to the guilty of November 1984 carnage. The general house also called upon the Centre to hand over control of the Panjab University at Chandigarh to Punjab. Another demand related to according second language status to Punjabi in the neighbouring states. The general house endorsed the action taken against Giani Puran Singh.

Jagir Kaur spoke her mind for the first time since the developments leading to her ex-communication in an interview. She said, "No individual has the right to ex-communicate any person from the Panth. What has been bestowed upon by the Guru cannot be taken away by any individual. One can never get punishment from the house of God. There can be no room for dictatorship in the Panth which has democratic traditions...I was not worried about myself. I only wanted the procedure to be followed. Finally, the truth has emerged victorious. The Guru himself created the situation in which Giani Puran Singh committed one mistake after another even as there was no move to sack him".[3] The crisis in the religious domain was over.

Earlier at its Maghi convention at Muktsar on January 14, 2000 the party put up a massive show. The senior BJP leadership was present to lend support to Badal. And back in Chandigarh, Ravi Inder Singh managed to mobilize more than 30 MLAs against the Chief Minister that day. The senior journalists from Chandigarh who had gone to Muktsar to cover the convention were conveyed about the likely revolt against Badal's leadership. The rebels decided to meet again as the total was one short of the magic figure. The information leaked out and damage control exercise was undertaken immediately. The crisis had been averted.

The Akali Dal, on January 16, expelled four Tohra loyalists – Mahesh Inder Singh Grewal, Inderjit Singh Zira, Harmel Singh and Daljit Kaur- from the party. The party took this step to counter the dissident activity. The expelled leaders reacted saying it was an attempt by Badal to cover up his misdeeds, nepotism and corruption which had reached all time high.

Badal was re-elected President of the party on March 3 at the delegate session at Amritsar. The delegate session reiterated the demand for autonomy and federal structure for faster development. Another resolution demanded adjudication of the river waters dispute on riparian principles. Through yet another resolution, the party accused the Congress of complicating just demands of the state. The delegate session also demanded transfer of Chandigarh and other left out Punjabi speaking areas. It also urged the Centre to take initiative to punish the guilty of November 1984 carnage. The party rejected the formation of the Pakistan Gurdwara Parbandhak Committee headed by General Javed Nasir, a former director general of the Inter-Services Intelligence. It was decided to review the policy programme for which Badal was authorized to constitute a 5-member committee. Though Akali Dal was partner in power at the Centre, the Badal government did not take up with the National Democratic Alliance government the long pending inter-state issues for resolution. The resolutions relating to these issues were an exercise in futility and at the most, a formality. These were the very issues on which the Akali Dal had launched the agitation in 1982.

The Shiromani Akali Dal, at its Baisakhi convention at Anandpur Sahib on April 13, through a resolution warned the people against the moves of the anti-Panthic forces, which, in league with the Congress, were trying to weaken the party, the SGPC and the state government. The hint about Tohra was too obvious in the resolution. The Baisakhi convention is normally organized by the party at Takht Damdama Sahib, Talwandi Sabo.

Shadow of the Sangh Parivar

All this time during the Akali Dal rule, the RSS was expanding its activities in Punjab describing the Sikhs as militant wing of the Hindus. The Indian Express was the first to expose the invasion of the saffron brigade in Khaki in Punjab on February 20, 2000.[4] The Sikh organizations including the Dal Khalsa and the Akali Dal (Amritsar) decided to confront this penetration by the Hindu fundamentalist organization and systematic distortion of Sikh history. The RSS had brought out huge literature on the Sikh history for distribution in the state giving its own interpretation. The RSS had covered hundreds of villages by then, especially in the border districts. Interestingly, the first hint about the activities of the RSS in the Punjab countryside came from the Amritsar based veteran Communist leader Satya Pal Dang who had come across some pamphlets having been distributed in the Tarn Taran area and not the Sikh leaders.

The three day conclave of the Rashtriya Sikh Sangat, the Sikh front of the RSS, beginning April 28 in Chandigarh was the provocation for some radical and other Sikh organizations to stage protest on April 29 and demand ban on the activities of the Sangh Parivar outfits in Punjab. These organizations staged dharna near the venue of the conclave. These organizations stressed that "Sikhs are a separate nation and any attempt to change this status in word or deed will be contested and resisted" and warned saying, "The present peace in Punjab hangs on a precipice as no attempt has been made by the state or the centre to solve any language, border, water or political issues pending for years. The Badal-BJP government will be squarely responsible for all consequences if the RSS sponsored anti-Sikh network is not curtailed and stopped".

It was Kanwarpal Singh of Dal Khalsa who was instrumental in organizing this protest and other organizations which participated included the Akali Dal (Amritsar), Human Rights and Democratic Forum, Sikh Missionary College, Gurmat Prasar Sewa Society, Khalsa Conference, Youth Akali Dal, Guru Gobind Singh Sewa Society, Guru Granth Sahib Sewa Society, Sukhmani Sewa Society, Young Khalsa Dal, Shaheed Baba Deep Singh Akhara, The Sikh Network, Gurmat Chetna Taalmel Committee, the coordination committee of Chandigarh gurdwaras and the coordination committee of Mohali gurdwaras. Ironically, none of the senior Akali leaders, neither from the Badal nor the Tohra factions, at that time, questioned the designs of the RSS. It was the Sangh parivar which cashed upon the alliance of the BJP with the Akali Dal to expand its activities in the remote rural areas of the border state.

Earlier, the Institute of Sikh Studies, in a resolution on April 7 while appealing to the Punjab Chief Minister to "put an end to this vicious propaganda of the RSS so that it may not lead to 1978 situation with the Nirankaris", said, "The recent agenda of the RSS in the name of propagating the ideas and ideals of Guru Gobind Singh through their shakhas especially in the Punjab countryside is a subtle attempt to assimilate the Sikhs into the Hindu fold. Their covert moves to destroy the Sikh identity, distort Sikh history and manipulate the Sikh institutions to suit their designs of assimilation must be resisted tooth and nail. It is unfortunate that Badal Akali Dal is playing a second fiddle to the BJP which has always opposed the vital issues of Punjab river waters, inclusion of Chandigarh and Punjabi speaking areas in Punjab and more autonomy for the state".

Of course, a congregation of various Sikh organizations at Akal Takht on May 14 reiterated that the Sikhs were a separate nation and directed the Akali Dal to make efforts for incorporating this in the constitution of the country. A resolution passed in this context asked Badal to form a committee of Sikh intellectuals and legal experts to prepare a draft paper on this subject. In a statement issued under the seal of Akal Takht, Jathedar Vedanti cautioned the Sikhs against the activities of certain anti-Panthic forces which were trying to create confusion about the Sikh identity. The Jathedar also imposed a ban on statements on the controversial Dasam Granth. The writings in this book are ascribed to Guru Gobind Singh by a section of the Sikhs and it is installed at Takht Patna Sahib and Takht Hazoor Sahib. The RSS and some Sikh organizations have been propagating it as the writings of the 10th Sikh Guru. Some of the writings in this book are considered to be highly controversial.

While on the one hand, the re-assertion of exclusive Sikh identity was an answer to the process of hegemonisation initiated by the RSS which treats the Sikhs to be part of the greater Hindu family, it also posed a threat to Badal's agenda of Punjabiat. "The evolution of the Sikh identity as exclusive and autonomous is part of this historical process even as parallel tendencies have at various times challenged this assertion. Now there is one difference. It is perhaps for the first time that the Akal Takht, the supreme temporal seat of the Sikhs, has stepped in to institutionalize this exclusive identity".[5]

However, the priorities of the Akali Dal at that time were different which had nothing to do with covert attack on Sikhism by such organizations. Identity assertion had for years been the agenda of the Akali Dal which, during militancy, had come to be identified with the radicals. The concerns of the Akali Dal during that period would have to be seen in this context as the party did not want to be associated even remotely with any such cause having tinge of radical politics. The Akali Dal was more concerned with its own assertion in the Akali domain. Confronted by the increasing dissidence, the Shiromani Akali Dal filed two petitions with the Assembly Speaker demanding disqualification of 11 MLAs, all supporters of Tohra. Besides Ravi Inder Singh, they included Manjit Singh Calcutta, Inderjit Singh Zira, Maheshinder Singh Grewal, Surjit Singh Kohli, Harmel Singh, Hira Singh Gabria, Jagtar Singh Rajla, Bikramjit Singh Khalsa, Gurdev Singh Sidhu and Daljit Kaur.

Meanwhile, Badal faction of Akalis got a shot in the arm as the party captured the Delhi Sikh Gurdwara Management Committee in the annual election of the executive committee held on May 12, 2000.

Of course, though the concerns were different, the ruling Akali Dal was at one level indirectly trying to revive the Panthic agenda as evident at the Operation Bluestar anniversary function at Akal Takht on June 6 which was attended by Jagir Kaur, Giani Mohan Singh, Head Granthi, Darbar Sahib, Giani Kewal Singh, Jathedar, Takht Damdama Sahib, Giani Bhagwan Singh, Head Granthi, Akal Takht, Simranjit Singh Mann, Satnam Singh and Kanwarpal Singh from Dal Khalsa and others. It was the statement of Jathedar Vedanti which indicated the mood in the ruling Akali Dal to revive the Panthic agenda in the run up to the next Assembly elections. Significantly, Jathedar Vedanti justified the revenge taken by the Sikhs for the sacrilege of the Darbar Sahib complex in 1984. In a 3-page statement, he said, "When tyrants and foreign invaders came to know about this they never missed a chance to demolish this source of strength of the Sikhs. Nadir Shah, Ahmed Shah, Zakaria Khan, Massa Rangar and Indira Gandhi had worked on such ill-designed policies and had to pay the price for that". He said the names of those who attained martyrdom while defending Akal Takht and Darbar Sahib from the invaders would be remembered for all times to come by the Sikhs. He made a fervent appeal to the splintered Akalis to come to a single platform to pursue the Sikh cause. The attempt to revive the Panthic agenda could also be seen in the context of the competitive politics as the Akali faction headed by Tohra was laying greater emphasis on the Panthic issues.

The Shiromani Akali Dal finally expelled nine dissident MLAs from the party on June 13. They included Ravi Inder Singh, Manjit Singh Calcutta, Surjit Singh Kohli, Gurdev Singh Sidhu, Bikramjit Singh Khalsa, Hira Singh Gabria, Jagtar Singh Rajla, Ranjit Singh Chhajjalwaddi and Baldev Singh Khiala. Actions had earlier been taken against Mahesh Inder Singh Grewal, Harmel Singh, Inderjit Singh Zira and Daljit Kaur. The decision was taken at a meeting of the political affairs committee.

The SHSAD spelled out its agenda in a series of resolutions passed at its convention at Gurdwara Amb Sahib, Mohali, on July 21. The party appealed to the legislators and the like minded parties to adopt a resolution on state autonomy in the Assembly on the pattern of Anandpur Sahib Resolution. The party referred to the 1968 Batala resolution and the 1973 and 1978 versions of the Anandpur Sahib resolution and demanded the constitution should be reviewed for this purpose. The party also took up the issue of enactment of the All India Gurdwara legislation. The party dwelt on the long pending demands which had been swept under the carpet by the ruling Akali Dal and committed itself to get the same accepted. These included territorial and river water issues. The party also demanded release of the detained Sikh youth and highlighted socio-economic demands of various sections of the people in the state.

These two Akali parties submitted memoranda to the national commission constituted to review working of the constitution in July. While the SAD talked of federal structure on the basis of 1978 version of the Anandpur Sahib Resolution, the SHSAD laid stress on its 1973 version. The SAD also demanded amendment in Article 25 of the constitution which clubs Sikhs with the Hindus. The SHSAD called for abolition of Articles 355 and 356 which empower the Centre to dismiss the state governments.

Despite Centre's refusal to keep Udham Singh Nagar out of the newly created state of Uttaranchal as demanded by the Akalis, the political affairs committee of the Akali Dal at its meeting on August 6 at Chandigarh decided against pulling out of the Vajpayee government. The demand of the Akali Dal to keep this district out of the new state had virtually strained the relations between the two alliance partners at one stage. Udham Singh Nagar had large number of Sikh settlers and the Akali Dal had been articulating their demand for a long time. However, it was too well known that Badal would not confront the BJP as the priority now was his own political survival.

The Akal Takht Jathedar once again adopted the pro-active role while calling upon the Sikh leadership on August 14 to work for the release of the Sikhs lodged in jails for years without trial. Tohra reacted saying the statement was vague as it was not clear how the Panth could act in this case. It was for the Chief Minister to take up the issue with the Centre. Two days later, the Jathedar again took up the issue of exclusive and autonomous Sikh identity saying there was no reason why the Sikhs should not have their separate personal law. In his first ever interview to the media, the Jathedar said he had twice written to the ruling Akali Dal to take up the issue of exclusive Sikh identity with the constitutional review panel set up by the Centre.[6]

Akalis Ditch Anandpur Sahib Resolution

All these years, the Akalis had been swearing by the Anandpur Sahib Resolution. Ironically, the resolution came up for discussion in the Assembly as private member's resolution on September 8, 2000 but was allowed to be talked out, not adopted. Badal was conspicuous by his absence during the crucial debate. Moved by Ajit Inder Singh Mofer from the Akali Dal (Amritsar), who later joined the Congress, the resolution stated: "This House strongly recommends to the state government that the policy programme drafted by the Shiromani Akali Dal at Sri Anandpur Sahib in 1973 with a view to establishing a true federal polity in India, which was later adopted by the Shiromani Akali Dal at its conference held at Ludhiana in 1978, be presented to the constitution review panel constituted by the Government of India". This further exposed the Shiromani Akali Dal. This was the resolution around which the Sikh struggle had revolved till Operation Bluestar with both Sant Jarnail Singh Bhindranwale and Harchand Singh Longowal demanding its acceptance. Now when in power, the Shiromani Akali Dal refused to adopt it in the Assembly.

The Sunam Assembly bye-election witnessed Tohra distancing himself from the 1973 version of the Anandpur Sahib resolution in favour of the watered down 1978 version. The election result from this seat was the re-assertion of the bipolarity of the Punjab polity. However, Tohra continued to be hopeful of providing third dimension even after the Sunam election result. He was of the view that the coming together of the SHSAD, Akali Dal (Amritsar), Communist Party of India (Marxist) and the Bahujan Samaj Party could provide the much needed third alternative. The CPI(M) had supported the SHSAD candidate in Sunam. He said the long pending issues on which the Akali Dal-BJP combine had backtracked after coming into power should be taken up.[7]

Badal announced the new working committee of the party on November 5 which included Parkash Singh Majitha (Patron), Jagdev Singh Talwandi, Ranjit Singh Brahmpura and Gurdev Singh Badal (all senior vice-presidents), Amarjit Singh Bhatia and Sujan Singh (Vice-Presidents), Sukhdev Singh Dhindsa (Secretary General), Balwinder Singh Bhunder, Capt. Kanwaljit Singh and Baldev Singh Mann (General Secretaries), Prof Kirpal Singh Badungar (Secretary) and Bibi Jagir Kaur, Charanjit Singh Atwal, Sewa Singh Sekhwan, Tota Singh, Nirmal Singh Kahlon, Adesh Partap Singh Kairon, Sarwan Singh Phillaur, Ujagar Singh Rangretta, Natha Singh Dalam, Raja Narinder Singh, Charanji Lal Garg, Charanjit Singh Walia, Amrik Singh Aliwal, Ajaib Singh Mukhmailpur, Sampuran Singh Cheema, Hari Singh Zira, Raghujit Singh, Onkar Singh Thapar and Avtar Singh Makkar (Members).

In another development, Talwandi replaced Jagir Kaur as the president of the SGPC at the general house meeting on November 30. Jagir Kaur, who faced murder charge relating to her daughter Harpreet Kaur, had not been given even a hint that she was being replaced. Badal had not given any indication to Talwandi also about the new assignment. Tohra had called on Talwandi in the morning that day. It was this meeting which was stated to have influenced Badal'c choice.

Within days of the election of Talwandi, Giani Puran Singh was appointed Head Granthi of Darbar Sahib on December 9. However, in an unprecedented move, he opted against participating in the meetings of the clergy. Jathedar Vedanti clarified on December 22 that the presence of the Darbar Sahib Head Granthi in the meetings of the clergy was obligatory. The SGPC executive, a day earlier, had endorsed the decision of Giani Puran Singh to stay away from the meetings.

The SHSAD at its December 2 convention to revive the Panthic agenda, called upon the people to remain alert against anti-Panthic, anti-Punjab and anti-national communal forces which posed a big danger to the democratic polity of the country. Indirectly hitting out at BJP and its allies, the resolution said the communal and anti-minority forces posed a big danger to the principles of secularism and religious independence. It stated that earlier, in an attempt to please the majority, the Congress adopted policies of social, religious and economic discrimination towards minorities and now organizations like the RSS had adopted the policy of hegemonisation and assimilation. The history and culture of the Sikhs was now being distorted to portray them as part of the Hindus and the independent Sikh identity was under threat. The convention called upon all democratic forces to present issue based unity to the people to cobble up the third front and provide alternative to the Congress as well as the BJP misrule both in Punjab and at the national level. The convention also demanded Badal's resignation.

The ruling Akali Dal hit back at its Jor Mela conference on December 26 at Fatehgarh Sahib alleging the Congress and some forces colluding with that party were trying to mislead the people. The attack was directed against Tohra faction. People in Nawanshahar and Sunam Assembly bye-elections had rejected these forces which had tried to harm Punjab in league with the Congress. The convention lauded the services of Badal to Punjab.

Assembly Condemns Bluestar, 1984 Carnage

Badal government received flak from the clergy when Jathedar Vedanti and Prof. Manjit Singh, on January 13, 2001 accused the ruling coalition and the police of being directly responsible for the wide spread drug menace in the state. There was no reaction either from the ruling party or the state government.

The SHSAD decided not to oppose Sukhbir Singh Badal in the Rajya Sabha poll held on February 22, 2001 who was elected unopposed. This was a personal decision of Tohra and shared with the party only at the last stage. Unaware of the thinking of Tohra on this issue, some party leaders had tried to put up a candidate during his absence for a few days when he had gone to Mumbai. Though putting up a candidate to oppose Sukhbir would not have affected the outcome of the election, it was a well meaning gesture on the part of the Akali stalwart. The decision not to oppose Sukhbir was in a way a positive signal conveyed to Badal as at an informal level, efforts were on to bring the two Akali stalwarts closer again. Despite the bitterness at the political, the contact at the social level had continued. Sukhbir was declared elected in the absence of any other candidate.

In the Majitha Assembly bye-election held in February, the Panthic issues were again on the agenda of the Shiromani Akali Dal with the party recalling Operation Bluestar and the associated events. The Congress was targeted for tarnishing the image of the Sikhs. The ruling Akali Dal retained the seat.

As the Shiromani Akali Dal entered the election mode, effort was on to exploit contentious emotive issues like transfer of Chandigarh and adjudication of river water dispute on riparian principles as was clear from the Governor's Address to the Assembly on the opening day of the budget session in March 2001 which is considered to be the agenda of the ruling party.

The Punjab Assembly, on March 15, 2001, for the first time during the past 17 years, adopted a resolution condemning the November 1984 carnage. The non-official resolution was moved by Akali Dal MLA Sukhvinder Singh Aulakh and Jagdish Sawhney from the BJP. Badal again stayed away from the House. The resolution stated: "The House unanimously resolves to condemn the senseless killings of Punjabis, especially Sikhs, in Delhi and other parts of the country in the 1984 massacre engineered by politically motivated people with the intention of deriving political mileage. This House welcomes the constitution of the Nanavati Commission and strongly recommends to the government to take immediate steps to approach the central government and the state governments concerned to bring the killers, who have so far escaped the clutches of law, to book and ensure the severest possible punishment to them so that the communal (sic) fabric of the country is maintained". The Congress members were not present in the House due to their suspension.

Carrying forward this approach of going back to the Panthic agenda, Operation Bluestar was also condemned in the Assembly on March 22. However, Badal was again conspicuous by his absence from the House during the debate on this non-official resolution. The amendment moved by Manjit Singh Calcutta holding the Congress government at the Centre responsible for the army action was not adopted. All these years, the Akali Dal had been attacking the Congress for this biggest trauma the Sikhs underwent in independent India. Badal's absence from the House that day was also meaningful. The resolution, moved by Gurdip Singh Bhullar from the Shiromani Akali Dal, condemned the senseless action wherein innocent devotees were killed in the precincts of the Darbar Sahib complex. The House recommended to the state government to convey the feelings to the Centre. Laxmi Kanta Chawla from the Bharatiya Janata Party staged a walk out objecting to the procedure of moving the resolution. Apart from the other compulsions, what made the ruling party to initiate this resolution was the threat from Tohra loyalists to move this resolution and resign from the House in the eventuality of the Speaker rejecting it.

The SGPC, at its meeting of the general house on March 30, sought Vatican status for Amritsar. Welcoming the condemnation of Operation

Bluestar in the state Assembly, the general house demanded that such a resolution should also be passed in the Parliament. Another resolution condemned the alleged atrocities on the Sikhs in various parts of the country. These resolutions were in accordance with the donning of the Panthic role again by the Akali Dal once again with an eye on the next Assembly elections.

After remaining ex-communicated from the Sikh Panth for 17 years, Nihang chief Santa Singh was re-admitted on April 4 after undergoing the religious punishment. He had been excommunicated for undertaking repair of Akal Takht damaged during Operation Bluestar on government's behalf.

As the issue of Sant Jarnail Singh Bhindranwale being dead or alive continued to be raked up, the 15-member committee of various Sikh organizations, on May 8 at a meeting at Amritsar, declared him a martyr. The committee said the non-acceptance of the reality by the Damdami Taksal was a conspiracy of the government to nullify the issues for which the Sant stood. The members of the committee included Narain Singh, Dilbagh Singh Gill, President, Sikh League International, Ajit Singh Bains, Chairman, Punjab Human Rights Organisation, Surinderpal Singh of Sikh Students Federation, Jaspal Singh Dhillon of Human Rights and Democracy Forum, Kanwarpal Singh (Dal Khalsa), Surinder Singh Ghariala, Kulbir Singh Kaura (World Sikh Council), Paramjit Kaur Khalra, Amrik Singh Muktsar, Kirpal Singh Randhawa, Mohinder Singh Grewal and Gurtej Singh. The death of Sant Bhindranwale had been confirmed by Apar Singh Bajwa who was Deputy Superintendent of Police (City), Amritsar, during Operation Bluestar. He had seen the body and was present at the time of cremation along with Amritsar Deputy Commissioner Ramesh Inder Singh, the Superintendent of Police (CID) Pandit Harjit Singh and several army officers. According to him, the Army allowed him to cover the body of the Sant with a sheet and cremation was done as per the Sikh rites.[8]

The Akal Takht Jathedar, on June 5, directed Talwandi to constitute a fact finding committee to go into the controversy. The coordination committee rejected the proposal of Jathedar Vedanti of setting up of a probe panel on Sant Bhindranwale controversy. Talwandi tried to set at rest the controversy on June 25 saying the Sant was declared martyr at the World Sikh Convention held in 1995 when his family was honoured along with the relatives of other martyrs.

In a tactical move to woo the Hindu votes in the forthcoming Assembly elections, the Akali Dal allotted the vacant Rajya Sabha seat to BJP on May 30. The seat had been vacated by Rajmohinder Singh of the Akali Dal after his election from Majitha to the Assembly in the bye-election. However, the Hindu base of the BJP had already shifted towards the Congress.

The Akal Takht Jathedar, while addressing the congregation on the anniversary of Operation Bluestar on June 6, regretted that the successive governments had failed to pass resolution in Parliament to apologize for the army action and heal the wounded Sikh psyche. He gave a call to the Sikh political and religious organizations to get united to face the challenges before the Panth. He said it was a matter of grave concern that no organization seemed to have unambiguous Panthic agenda.

The Akali groups opposed to the Shiromani Akali Dal, on August 5, announced the setting up of the Panthic Morcha to contest the Assembly elections with Sarabjot Singh Bedi, chairman of Sant Samaj, as its convener. The constituents included factions like the SHSAD and the Akali Dal (Amritsar) and individuals like Ravi Inder Singh. The new conglomerate rejected the Moga Declaration. The Morcha demanded the dismissal of the Badal government in a memorandum submitted to Governor J. F. R. Jacob on October 17.

The Political Affairs Committee of the Shiromani Akali Dal, as usual, at its meeting at Chandigarh on August 8, authorized Badal to select candidates for the ensuing Assembly elections. Badal also got the authorization to negotiate with the other like-minded parties and take action against those violating the party discipline. He also held a meeting with the district presidents.

Badal, whose hip bone was fractured in the run up to the elections, started addressing workers meetings district wise at his residence after some recovery. He moved out from Chandigarh for poll campaign on January 3, 2002. The elections were announced earlier on December 26. The Akali Dal entered the poll arena as if the battle had already been lost. The assessment of the intelligence agencies was also conveyed to Badal much before the elections according to which, the Congress had the chance of winning about 62 seats. Badal was advised to change some of the candidates but he preferred to ignore the recommendation. The Akali Dal lost all the seats from which change of candidates had been suggested.

The Shiromani Akali Dal, which had become uni-polar after the exit of Gurcharan Singh Tohra, lost the elections held on February 13. Out of the total 117 seats, the Congress won 62 seats, SAD 41 seats, BJP 3 seats, independents nine and two seats went to the CPI, including Malout, the election for which was held in April. Some of the independents who made it to the Assembly were Akali rebels. Of course, the Akali Dal managed to retain its base in the rural areas. It was the Hindu-Dalit combination which swung the fortunes of the Congress.

The Hindu base of the BJP had shifted in the elections towards the Congress. Apart from the anti-incumbency, it was split in the Akali Dal which made way for the exit of the party from the seat of power. The return of the Congress to power signaled the change in Punjab at another level in the context of its anti-Sikh image.

Days before the elections, Tohra had finally decided against joining hands with Badal saying he would prefer a level playing field, meaning he would like to see Badal's ouster from power. He had made up his mind marking the end of unity talks which had been on for more than a year between the two leaders through various channels. He had been in a dilemma for some time. He opted for this line after about an hour of discussion on the subject with this author in Chandigarh. About the likely pressure from Prime Minister Atal Behari Vajpayee after the decision was made public, he was categoric that none could now influence him to change his mind. He said several intermediaries had brought all sorts of proposals on behalf of Badal. However, he said Badal had not shifted his stand even once from the parameters which had been outlined by one of the intermediaries at the start of the unity parleys. Badal had made it clear that he would not appear at Akal Takht but was prepared to restore presidency of SGPC to Tohra and accommodate his associates in the allotment of tickets in the Assembly elections. He had been accused of violating Akal Takht edict by the Tohra faction. Earlier in the first week of November also, Tohra was of the firm opinion that there could be no unity with Badal but later had softened his stand. Badal had been accused of violating the Akal Takht edict on unity for which Tohra wanted him to appear at Akal Takht for atonement.

Within minutes of Tohra driving out of the local SGGS College after this interaction, this author received a call from Manjit Singh Calcutta saying 98 per cent of the spade work had been done and the unity initiative just needed the final push. However, by that time, all was over and Tohra had not taken even his close associates in the party into confidence while taking that final decision. Only he could have taken such a decision as he had no personal stakes. Manjit Singh just refused to believe that the unity efforts had met the dead end.

One of the channels between the two leaders had opened in May, 2000 and to be more precise, on May 5. Here is Tohra's first reaction to the proposal, "My domain is mainly religious. Badal and his men denigrated Akal Takht. The restoration of dignity of the institution is my only condition. I do not seek any office". The unity initiative had started on a note of trust deficit. In Tohra's perception, the dignity of Akal Takht could be restored in this case only with Badal presenting himself at the supreme temporal seat to atone for defiance.

This time, the fight between the two had been too bitter. Badal had accommodated people in the space vacated by Tohra associates and in any give and take, some heads were likely to roll which was the main concern. Badal's general leading the fight in the field initially was Finance Minister Capt. Kanwaljit Singh and it was after a long time that he realized that he was being used. Tohra had maintained very cordial relations with Kanwaljit's father Dara Singh and during his last days, he had requested the SGPC chief to take care of his son. Tohra conveyed his feelings for Kanwaljit to a common link and it only then that Capt. Kanwaljit Singh sobered down. His problem was that he wanted to occupy the space vacated by Tohra in the Akali Dal so far as the Patiala politics was concerned. It was not without reason that Capt. Kanwaljit Singh was Tohra's choice for the Lok Sabha election from Patiala in 2004 after the unity in place of Prem Singh Chandumajra.

Both the leaders kept on shifting their stands. Badal, at one stage, seemed to be inclined to issue a soft statement to select journalists in favour of unity while Tohra wanted Badal to relinquish the office of the party president also. As the anti-Badal forces joined hands to form Panthic Morcha, Tohra dilly dallied for some time to give time to Badal to firm up his mind. Once the Morcha was formalized, Tohra again toughened his stand. At one stage, a meeting between the two leaders was arranged but it never materialized. Tohra was not conveyed the message by the person who was entrusted with this job. Badal waited for him in Delhi.

At one stage, Badal made it clear that he would offer more than the status quo ante which meant more tickets to Tohra associates. However, Tohra persisted with the demand that Badal should appear at Akal Takht and he himself was willing to accompany the Chief Minister. Badal did not like the idea. This was the time when Badal was bedridden due to hip bone fracture. When it was pointed that the issue involved was wider as it concerned the future of his son Sukhbir also, he quipped, "I had my inning". He seemed to have resigned to the situation.

Himachal Pradesh BJP leader Prem Kumar Dhumal also tried to intervene and the signals were positive. Persuaded by him, Badal had agreed to visit Tohra at his native village. The move did not take off as some advisers did not favour unity and these advisers included a senior journalist. It was very interesting situation. Tohra was in a dilemma as he got the signal about likely visit by Badal. Nothing had been settled and his problem was that he would not have said no to Badal had he been bold enough to call upon Tohra at his native village. Badal's problem was the situation in case Tohra refused to respond positively to the gesture. The two leaders had met once when Badal was admitted to a Delhi hospital. Both of them shed tears and the matter just ended there as there was to reference to the political issues.

Haryana Chief Minister Om Parkash Chautala who was close to Badal at the family level also intervened during the last days of December, 2001 after the announcement of elections. He invited Tohra to a breakfast meeting. He offered more seats to Tohra on Badal's behalf. However, Tohra did not budge from the pre-condition of the re-instatement of Ranjit Singh as the Akal Takht Jathedar saying the issue was not the apportionment of seats in the forthcoming elections or the presidency of the SGPC.

Tohra, who had taken tough stand again on the re-instatement of Ranjit Singh as the Akal Takht Jathedar, tried to assure Badal that it would end up as a positive step. However, Badal did not take any risk going by the unpredictable style of functioning of Ranjit Singh despite assurance by Tohra. It was after such deliberations that Tohra decided to meet Badal again only at a level playing field. The Shiromani Akali Dal lost some seats due to the candidates of the Sarv Hind Shiromani Akali Dal of Tohra in the field. The united Akalis might have checked the return of the Congress in Punjab. But the moot point is to what purpose. The ruling Akali Dal had failed to adopt resolution even on its own policy programme that was the Anandpur Sahib resolution in the Assembly. By the time the Shiromani Akali Dal went out of office, the party had ceased to articulate the Sikh aspirations marking the completion of the process of its transformation from the Panthic outfit to Punjabi party and then to just another political party in the state. And Gurcharan Singh Tohra was the last of the stalwarts from the genre of the traditional Akalis who talked in the Panthic idiom.

Both the leaders finally joined hands again in 2003 and the formal announcement to this effect was made at Patiala on June 13. The way for unity was cleared after Badal appeared at Akal Takht on June 5 in the case relating to the violation of December 31 Hukamnama issued when Ranjit Singh was the Akal Takht Jathedar. However, it was just a formality. This was the condition put up by Tohra at the start of the unity talks before the Assembly elections. A few weeks before the chapter of their discard was to close, Badal in a subtle way conveyed that the contribution of Tohra to the Panth was unprecedented but it was ironic that he had to dub him as the Congress agent out of political compulsion. He had given out his mind. The same day, the message was conveyed to Tohra whose response was positive. Rest is part of the history.

And it was Tohra who resurrected Badal when he was arrested and lodged in Patiala jail in the corruption case along with his son. It would not be out of context to bring on record interaction with Tohra outside Patiala jail during that period. It was his routine those days to reach the jail in the morning along with his supporters and camp there throughout the day. It was one such day and he had finished his address to the hundreds of people gathered there which was in defence of Badals and targeted at Chief Minister Capt. Amarinder Singh. All along, ever since his first charge sheet submitted to Akal Takht in 1979, he had been lambasting Badal for corruption, both on the record and off the record. The SGPC chief was not maintaining good health those days. He was persuaded to take some rest in his car and it was during that interaction that this author questioned his defence of Badal on the corruption issue. He took more than ten minutes to explain his position and he was convincing. For him, the corruption case against Badal aimed at finishing the Akali Dal which had been articulating the Sikh concerns and this was his major worry. He went back to history and gave the example of Sardar Sham Singh Attari who came out of his self imposed hibernation during the crisis the Sikh Panth faced. Tohra had taken upon himself the mantle of Sardar Sham Singh Attari. For him, it was not a case just against Badal but its ramifications were very serious as here was another effort to finish the Akali Dal.

However, by the time he died on March 31, 2004 after a few months, he was a person totally dejected and disillusioned with Badal, feeling betrayed and humiliated. He poured out his heat at more than an hour long meeting, the last with him, on March 11 at the residence of Dr. Balkar Singh at Patiala. He had not put up any pre-conditions for unity as per his nature. However, Badal had been dilly dallying on the issue of accommodating his associates in the organizational structure of the party. "I just cannot go on fighting. I have neither the will nor the capacity to fight. You convey my feelings to Badal. He should accord due respect to my associates," these were his last words.

He confronted Badal several times in his political life despite being aware of his limitation as he lacked matching resources. But then he had opted for a clean political life though he cherished higher political ambition. Every time he would continue to hope for unity. It was towards the later years that it dawned on him that he should not have confined himself to the SGPC domain and ventured into state legislative politics. Akali politics in Punjab might have been different had he taken a plunge in the legislative politics of the state at the earlier stage or opted out of active politics and the SGPC to work for the welfare of the Panth at the later stage. However, it was too late. His death marked the closure of a chapter on Sikh politics. By that time, the basic character of the Shiromani Akali Dal whose political course he had dictated at crucial moments had undergone a transformation from a Panthic outfit to an ordinary political party and going by its practice when in power, no different from the Congress.

Though the concept of Punjabiat had originated with him, he had always been convinced that the Panthic character of the Akali Dal should not be diluted as the Sikhs must have a political outfit which articulates the issues concerning their community. Sant Jarnail Singh Bhindranwale had come to the centre stage riding the Sikh issues and the phenomenon of political violence had been introduced in the Punjab polity later.

Historically, this region has been subjected to turbulences and never looked back. The political violence which rocked Punjab in the eighties but failed to take the shape of a cohesive movement is considered now to be a close chapter. The cost paid by the people has been too high. Of course, there is little change in the socio-economic reality as compared to the period when the ambition to rule among a section of the Sikhs along with some other factors radicalized the situation. However, there is one very significant change. The Akalis no more raise the slogan of discrimination against the Sikhs or articulate other concerns of the community. The assimilation in the national mainstream is now complete.

NOTES

1. The Indian Express, February 2, 2000.
2. The Indian Express, February 1, 2000.
3. The Indian Express, April 2, 2000.
4. Jagtar Singh, The Indian Express, February 20, 2000.
5. Jagtar Singh, The Indian Express, May 16, 2000.
6. Jagtar Singh, The Indian Express, August 17, 2000.
7. The Indian Express, November 4, 2000.
8. The Tribune, May 20, 2001.

20

Ambition to Rule

The Sikh ambition to rule is rooted in the very origin of this most nascent religion in the world with separate, autonomous and exclusive identity, which is also political along with being a religious entity. This ambition has been reflected from time to time in the recent history in the demand for autonomy at one level and at the extreme, to Khalistan, the sovereign Sikh state. The repeated assertion of exclusive identity during this period is also related to the apprehension of being hegemonised by the majority community in the country. This apprehension becomes all the stronger when the fundamentalist organizations like the Rashtriya Swayamsewak Sangh describe the Sikhs as part of the Hindu mainstream. At the political level, there has also been the feeling of being discriminated against, perceived or otherwise, especially since the partition of the country. Moreover, political power is considered to be an instrument to propagate and protect religion (Raj bina nahin dharma chale hai). The misadventure that was the recent struggle for homeland was thus not without its roots in the collective Sikh psyche.

For the community which at one time held sway in this region (Khalsa Raj), the ambition to rule has its own logic. This psyche was one of the factors which contributed to the first ever militant struggle in free India launched by a section of this community for getting this ambition fulfilled. The Sikhs are settled virtually not only in all parts of the country but the community is also globalized like the Jews who finally got their homeland. Though the Delhi Sikh Gurdwara Management Committee at one stage supported the demand for Khalistan, the Sikhs settled in other parts of India were not participants in this struggle. Of course, the demand for Khalistan came to be supported from a sections of the Sikhs settled abroad. There is one common factor and that is maintaining exclusive identity. However, maintaining exclusive and independent identity is a separate issue which is related to the very existence of this religio-political entity but this issue does not necessarily leads to the demand for a sovereign Sikh state.

The Shiromani Akali Dal, whose creation was rooted in the gurdwara liberation struggle, metamorphosed into a body which came to articulate the Sikh concerns, ambitions and aspirations and as such, it was not just an ordinary political party. This very character defines the very first two objectives of the Shiromani Akali Dal as enshrined in the party constitution. The party continued to maintain that character till its transformation in the nineties when a conscious shift was made from the Panthic agenda. However, these two objectives continued to be part of the party constitution. Despite representing the community whose ambition to rule is part of its psyche, the mainstream Akali Dal has never opposed the Indian state per se. It was this mainstream Akali Dal which got marginalized during the militant struggle for the sovereign Sikh state. The Anandpur Sahib Resolution which advocates greater autonomy, the implementation of which was one of the demands of the Akali Dal, is not secessionist in character. The demand for Khalistan used to be voiced by some splinter groups and came to be raised forcefully for the first time only after Operation Bluestar. The demand pointed to the hurt Sikh psyche in the post Bluestar period though other designs were also at play, including the role played by the Indian and international agencies. But then the ambition to rule in the Sikh psyche can invariably be exploited by the vested interests.

"The essence of the Sikh identity lies in the dual character of Sikhism which is not only an other-worldly path of soul salvation, but also a this worldly ideology with socio-political concerns; correspondingly, the Sikhs are not only a religious group but also a political people".[1]

In a way, this character of the Sikh corporate got institutionalized for the first time with the founding of Akal Takht (Throne of Almighty) in front of Darbar Sahib, but at a certain angle, by the Sixth Guru, Guru Hargobind. It was set up as a sovereign institution symbolizing temporal power in the sovereign Indian state. It is this institution where the Sikhs used to take collective decision at one stage in history. This democratic tradition of this institution got stifled later. The transition from the religious group to the political people was complete on the Baisakhi of 1699 at Anandpur Sahib with the creation of the Khalsa Panth by the 10th Lord, Guru Gobind Singh. The creation of the Khalsa Panth was the reinforcement of the separate Sikh identity, marking the completion of the progression which started with Guru Nanak founding the new religion, different from Hinduism and Islam.

The political consolidation of this community started with Baba

Gurbaksh Singh popularly known as Banda Singh Bahadur who was handed over the command by Guru Gobind Singh. It was in 1810 that Banda Bahadur proclaimed political sovereignty after conquering some areas of Punjab, thus laying the foundation of the Sikh rule. The seal of the state ruled by him read, "Sikhe zad bar har du alam tegh-i-Nanak Sahib ast" which meant that the Sikh people stake their claim to the political and spiritual sovereignty.

However, it was the reign of Maharaja Ranjit Singh which saw the ascendancy and consolidation of the Sikh power, the Sikh Raj. In the Indian sub-continent, this Sikh ruled state was the last to be annexed by the British ten years after the death of Maharaja Ranjit Singh which marked the end of the Sikh Rule in 1849. The region in which this religion proliferated came to be known as the "country of the Sikhs".[2] It was a different matter that the Sikhs constituted the third ethnic group in the region after the Muslins and the Hindus and their rule did not last long. Punjab's wars with the British India government were described as and continue to be portrayed as the Anglo-Sikh wars. This concept of the Sikh Raj left a distinct mark on the collective consciousness of the Sikhs. The Sikhs constituted the third political group in all the parleys with the British in the pre-partition period. The Akali Dal continued to hammer this standpoint in the post-partition period. This ambition to rule came to be reflected in the succeeding developments from time to time and has been dictating the political dynamics of Punjab. In this context, the politics of Punjab is predominantly the Sikh politics.

The partition of India in 1947 divided Punjab with Muslim dominated large areas becoming part of Pakistan. Punjab on the Indian side was trifurcated again in 1966 and for the first time in the history, a province was created in the region in which the Sikhs were in majority. The political dynamics of this state is dictated by the Sikh politics. The Hindu politics in this region has always been by and large the reaction to the Sikh politics. Due to this ethnic composition, the politics in the state has become highly polarized. However, this communalization is issue based and gets manifested only from time to time. This division is reflected yet at another level. Here is just one instance. The Hindu leaders make it a point that a dignitary going to pay obeisance at Darbar Sahib should also visit Durgiana Mandir though this shrine has no such historical significance. The region witnessed communal tension earlier in the sixties on the language issue as the majority of the Punjabi Hindus opted for Hindi as the mother tongue during the census, the distortion which was rectified years later after considerable damage had been done to the common heritage of Punjabiat. The Punjabi Suba movement had also divided the state along communal lines with the Hindu majority pressing the demand for Maha Punjab (Greater Punjab).The river waters dispute with the neighbouring non-riparian states also had similar over tones, with one section in Punjab advocating that river waters be treated as national asset.

The Sikh politics virtually remained dormant for a long time after the annexation of Punjab by the British and the first sign of the revival of activity was the reformist Singh Sabha movement starting in 1873 from Amritsar followed by the formation of the Chief Khalsa Diwan. Despite being pro-government, the Chief Khalsa Diwan voiced the Sikh concerns by asserting the Sikh identity. "A strong plea by the Chief Khalsa Diwan was made to Lord Dufferin, the Viceroy of India, in 1888 for recognition of Sikhs as a separate community"[3]. The Singh Sabha movement was launched to counter the growing influence of the Arya Samaj, a Hindu reformist movement which was considered to be an attack on the Sikh religion. The Arya Samaj movement questioned the distinct identity of the Sikhs. However, the activities of the Chief Khalsa Diwan were confined mainly to the upper sections of the Sikh society.

The gurdwara liberation movement which finally led to the formation of the Shiromani Gurdwara Parbandhak Committee was the rallying point for the Sikhs in the early twentieth century. Hundreds of Sikhs went to jail as part of this one of the most peaceful agitations launched to liberate the Sikh shrines from the corrupt and degenerate priests who had started resorting to anti-Sikh practices. It was this agitation which finally restored the control of the Darbar Sahib complex and other historical shrines to the Sikh community represented by the SGPC. The setting up of the 175-member Shiromani Gurdwara Parbandhak Committee on November 15, 1920 to manage the shrines marked the watershed in the Sikh religio-political affairs under the British rule. The collective consciousness of the Sikhs came to be reflected through this body. The SGPC had been set up following the invitation sent from Akal Takht to the Panthic organizations with the initiative taken by Kartar Singh Jhabbar. The committee met on December 12 to elect Sunder Singh Majithia, Harbans Singh Attari and Sunder Singh Ramgarhia as the President, Vice-President and the Secretary respectively.

The first proposal to set up a managing committee for Darbar Sahib was mooted on October 14, 1920 at a meeting the Sikh leaders had with the Amritsar Deputy Commissioner after the community had taken over the control of the holiest of the holy shrine. The invitation was conveyed by Sunder Singh Ramgarhia, Sarabrah of Darbar Sahib. As none of these Sikh leaders present could speak English, a message was sent to Khalsa College to depute some teachers. Dharam Singh, Basant Singh, Teja

Singh Bhuchhar, Teja Singh Chuharkana and Kartar Singh Jhabbar along with four teachers from the Khalsa College including Kashmira Singh and Bawa Harkishan Singh met the Deputy Commissioner. He offered to formally hand over the control of Darbar Sahib to a committee constituted by the community. After consultation with the Sikh leaders waiting for them outside DC's residence, it was decided to constitute a nine member committee. The committee was handed over the control in writing by the Deputy Commissioner. The next step was the formation of the SGPC.

The Akali Dal came into existence as a volunteer force and political wing of the SGPC on December 14, 1920 with Sarmukh Singh Jhabal as its President to liberate other shrines of the community and its formation was announced from Akal Takht. The Sikh political aspirations came to be articulated through the SGPC which donned the role of Parliament of the Sikhs, with the Akali Dal, constituted by it, being subservient to it. It was after years that the roles got reversed. The gurdwara liberation movement brought the Sikhs into direct confrontation with the government. The SGPC set up in 1920 was registered as a society on April 30, 1921 at Amritsar. The first political action of this body was the call for the boycott of Prince of Wales then visiting India.[4] The SGPC became a statutory body with the enactment of the Sikh Gurdwara Act, 1925.

As the government in Delhi moved towards proportional representation in the legislature on communal basis, the Shiromani Akali Dal, at its meeting on January 29, 1928 at Amritsar, resolved that the "the communal elections are not in the interest of the country but as the Congress and the Muslim League have accepted this award, the Sikhs should be given one third seats with the one third share in administration. The Sikhs would not accept the governance by one majority. The interests of the Sikhs in Sindh and the Frontier should be protected".[5] After the Hindus and the Muslims, the Sikhs were the third largest ethnic group in the region and here was the assertion for political rights.

The SGPC focused on the Sikh identity in a different way when its general house at its meeting on August 30, 1930 registered its protest against the non-inclusion of the colour symbolizing the Khalsa in the Congress tri-colour and called upon the Sikhs against organizing any activity under the Congress flag. It was decided on behalf of the Akali Dal that all activities should be undertaken only under the Panthic flag.[6] In the Congress tri-colour, saffron, white and green represented the Hindus, the minorities in general and the Muslims respectively.

However, the first major assertion in the political domain by this body entrusted with the responsibility of managing the shrines was witnessed in 1932 when its general house at a meeting on March 1 made it clear through a resolution that it would not accept any state structure in which the rights of the Sikhs were not fully protected. The resolution adopted by the SGPC expressed the apprehensions of danger to the Sikh shrines in a state structure dominated by the majority of one community coming to power through majority vote.[7] It was this resolution which had sown the seeds for the creation of the Sikh majority state. The political goal of the Anandpur Sahib resolution could also be traced to this resolution. This resolution was in accordance with the resolution earlier adopted by Akali Dal on January 29, 1928 at its conference at Amritsar demanding equal share in the state power under proportional representation.[8]

With the political aspirations of Muslims getting articulated mainly through the Muslim League, the SGPC and the Akali Dal went on a collision course with that party. In the process, Akali Dal joined hands with the Congress. The Akali Dal, at its meeting at Amritsar on October 27, 1937, directed the party MLAs to join the Congress to confront the communal elements and strengthen the nationalist forces. The party also called upon its members to join the Congress as part of this policy. The provocation for this resolution was the decision of the ruling Unionist Party members to join the Muslim League, which, the resolution said, had exposed the communal tendencies of that party.[9] It may be mentioned here that Akali Dal once again join hands with Congress in 1957 when its candidates contested on the Congress ticket.

What had influenced the party in exercising this choice was the Congress declaration at its Lahore session in 1929 which had assured the Sikhs that no resolution in any future constitution would be acceptable to the Congress that did not give them the full satisfaction. The Akali leaders trusted the Congress but only to be betrayed years later.

Again, the working committee of the Akali Dal, at its May 15, 1938 meeting, urged the Congress and Mahatma Gandhi to keep its promise made earlier that the Congress would not enter into any agreement with the Muslim League which was not acceptable to the Sikhs.[10] These resolutions aimed at protecting the Sikh interests.

Azad Punjab

The Akali Dal, for the first time, demanded re-organization of Punjab at its All India Akali conference at Vahila Kalan (District Lyallpur, now in Pakistan) on July 24, 1942. This would have to be seen in the context of the political situation in this sub-continent. This resolution in a way articulated the Sikh aspirations as the main concern that was emphasized was that the balance in the re-organized state to be known as Azad Punjab should be in the hands of the Sikhs. The party working committee resolution on June 7, 1943 specified the districts compromising this region which included Ambala, Jalandhar and Lahore divisions and Lyallpur, Montgomery and parts of Multan districts from Multan division.[11]

The demand for the Sikh home land was made by the Akali Dal at the All Parties Sikh Conference at Amritsar on August 20, 1944. A sub-committee was constituted headed by Master Tara Singh on the Sikh state demand.[12]

However, the concept of a sovereign state of Khalistan was first articulated by Dr. V. S Bhatti of Ludhiana in 1940 to counter the March 23, 1940 Lahore resolution of the All India Muslim League on Pakistan. Dr. Bhatti proposed Khalistan as a buffer between India and Pakistan.[13] The districts which were to be part of the proposed buffer state of Khalistan included Ludhiana, Jalandhar, Ambala, Ferozepur, Amritsar, Lahore, Lyallpur, Gujranwala, Sheikhupura, Montgomery, Hissar, Rohtak and Karnal, the princely states of Nabha, Patiala, Jind, Faridkot, Kalsia and Malerkotla and the Shimla group of states supervised by the Deputy Commissioner of Shimla. The head of the proposed state of Khalistan was to be the Maharaja of Patiala. The approach to the sea to this landlocked state was to be provided through a corridor via Sind, Bahawalpur and Rajputana.

There is an important aspect of the demand for Khalistan conceptualized at that time as it appealed more to the non-Akali Sikhs including those in the Congress to confront the demand for Pakistan. "It particularly appealed to Baba Gurdit Singh of Kamagata Maru fame".[14] He had founded the Independent Congress Party in Punjab in 1937. He organized two conventions on this issue in 1940. The second convention was attended by about 120 Sikh delegates from various Sikh organizations. The territories to be included in Khalistan were discussed in the second convention. Jammu was to be included in Khalistan as it was part of the Khalsa Raj under Maharaja Ranjit Singh and so was North-West Frontier Province upto Jamraud. The logic was that this was the territory between Satluj and Chenab rivers which had been annexed by the British. It was proposed to set up Guru Raj Darbar Khalsa Board for the purpose consisting of 21 members with power to add ten or more members.

However, the demand did not find favour with the senior leaders of neither the Akali Dal nor the Congress. Akali Dal President Master Tara Singh, who was also a member of the Punjab Provincial Congress and the All India Congress Committee, opposed the concept of Khalistan mooted by Dr. Bhatti. Earlier, yet another conference was organized at Jagraon on May 24, 1940 by the Sikhs of Malwa which demanded Khalistan in case Pakistan was to be created. The Akali Dal advocated the demand for Azad Punjab which continued to be on its agenda till May, 1944.

Master Tara Singh had his own concept of Sikh rule which he unfolded in his presidential address at a conference at Bhawanigarh, then in Patiala state, on October 12, 1940, saying, "If you want to live as dependent upon the foreign or native qaum, it would be suicidal. We want Swaraj, a Swaraj in which the Sikhs should not be slaves...I demand independence. I do not want slavery of the British, the Muslims, the Hindus, the Germans or the Russians".[15] This articulation is considered to be the demand for Azad Punjab. However, finally, the Sikhs decided to be part of India.

The Sikh representatives including Master Tara Singh, Giani Kartar Singh, Sampuran Singh Lyallpuri, Surjit Singh Majithia, Bhai Jodh Singh, Swarn Singh, Ujjal Singh and Ishar Singh Majhail submitted a memorandum to the Sapru Committee in 1944 in favour of a Sikh state while opposing Pakistan. The memorandum demanded that "in case Pakistan was created, the Sikhs would insist on the creation of a Sikh state which would include a substantial majority of Sikh population and their important shrines, historic gurdwaras and places with provision for transfer and exchange of population and property".[16] At the Shimla Conference of 1945, Master Tara Singh agreed to the creation of Pakistan subject to the condition that Mohammed Ali Jinnah would agree to a separate state for the Sikhs.

However, what was all the more significant was the resolution adopted by the SGPC as it is a statutory body. The general house of this mini-Parliament of the Sikhs pressed the demand for sovereign Sikh state on the basis of exclusive and autonomous identity at its meeting on March 9, 1946. The resolution said: "The Sikhs are a separate nation. The Sikh state is imperative for the protection of Sikh religious places, culture, Sikh traditions, dignity and freedom and their progress. This house appeals to the Sikhs to make all possible efforts for its achievement." This resolution, moved by its Vice-President Basant Singh Kukarpind was adopted unanimously.[17]

Within days of the SGPC adopting this resolution, the Shiromani Akali Dal ratified this demand on March 22, 1946. The resolution adopted by the Akali Dal states: "Whereas the Sikhs being attached to the Punjab by intimate bonds of holy shrines, property, language, tradition and history claim it as their homeland and holy land which the British took as a 'trust' from the Sikh ruler during his minority and whereas the entity of the Sikhs is being threatened by the Muslims on account of the persistent demand of Pakistan and on the other hand of the danger of absorption by the Hindus, the executive committee of the Akali Dal demands the preservation and protection of religious, cultural, economic and political rights of the Sikh population and their important sacred shrines and historical gurdwars with provision for the transfer and exchange of population and property".[18] This was a few days before the visit of the Cabinet Mission to solicit views of the political parties. The Cabinet Mission had given three choices to the Sikh representatives on the transfer of power, including that of an autonomous Sikh state.

Three Sikh leaders, Master Tara Singh, Giani Kartar Singh and Harnam Singh raised the demand for the Sikh state with the Cabinet Mission, though individually. Master Tara Singh proposed that in case India was to be divided, Sikhs should be conceded an independent Sikh state. The Sikhs were in majority only in two Tehsils, Moga in Ferozepur district and Tarn Taran in Amritsar district. Harnam Singh seconded Master Tara Singh while suggesting transfer of population and property. Giani Kartar Singh proposed that the Sikhs should have a province of their own in undivided India.

Sir Stafford Cripps was deputed by the British government to India in 1942. Among others, he also met Sikh leaders. Sardar Dasaundha Singh and Capt Naunihal Singh Mann, representing the Khalsa League formed by the then Maharaja of Patiala, at a meeting with him, favoured carving out special area for the Sikhs where there could be plebiscite to decide as to whether they should join the first or the second union in the event of there being two unions.[19] The Akalis also reiterated the same demand. Punjab Governor Sir B Glancy, in September, 1944, informed Viceroy Lord Wavell that various proposals were made to him to establish some kind of Sikh state.[20]

Later Punjab Governor Sir Evan Jenkins wrote to Lord Wavell, "Master Tara Singh, on his return from Delhi at a meeting with him, demanded either Khalistan with transfer of population or a new state stretching from Jamuna to the Chenab in which the Sikhs would not be oppressed" .Giani Kartar Singh met Sir Jenkins on July 10, 1947 with the proposal that the Sikh state would be a buffer between India and Pakistan.[21]

Before the partition of India, Swaran Singh, who later rose to be the foreign minister, pleaded for Sikh homeland saying since Mohammad Ali Jinnah insisted on a sovereign Pakistan, Sikhs had no alternative but to demand a homeland of their own. "For the Sikhs, it is a matter of life and death", he said while making this demand to Sir Jenkins, who in turn conveyed it to Lord Mountbatten in a secret report dated May 3, 1947.[22]

At another level, Communist Party of India leader Dr. Gangadhar Adhikari wrote a booklet in 1946 advocating the Sikh state with the right to self determination for the community. He proposed that Hindi speaking Ambala division should be kept out. Right to self determination was one of the demands voiced by the radicals during militancy. Further, it stated: "Except the Hindi speaking areas of Ambala division, the Sikh dominated areas in central Punjab should have the right to have its own constituent Assembly which should decide as to join Pakistan or Hindustan federation".[23] A few months before the partition of the country in 1947, Jinnah offered to the Sikhs through Master Tara Singh and also the Maharaja of Patiala a sovereign Sikh state comprising areas lying in the west of Panipat and east of river Ravi on the understanding that the proposed state would confederate with Pakistan. Master Tara Singh rejected the offer.

The Sikh leaders had decided to throw their lot with India. The Congress Working Committee in its meting on August 10, 1946 offered an olive branch to the Sikhs saying, "The Working Committee assures the Sikhs that that the Congress will give them all possible support in removing their legitimate grievances and in securing adequate safeguards for the protection of their just interest in the Punjab".[24] That was not to be.

It was in the context of the assurances extended by the Congress to the Sikhs that the Sikh and the Hindu members of the Punjab Assembly met at New Delhi in July, 1947 and resolved: "In the divided Indian Punjab, special constitutional measures are imperative to meet just aspirations and rights of the Sikhs".[25] This perhaps was the only time that the vocal Punjabi Hindus supported the Sikh cause during that period.

As the Sikhs felt betrayed and cheated, the post-partition period witnessed increasing emphasis on the theme of exclusive and separate identity. Master Tara Singh started emphasizing the point that the Sikh culture was different from that of the Hindus. He demanded right to self-determination in the religious, social, political and other affairs.[26] He reiterated this demand on October 10, 1949, saying, "The Sikh culture is separate from that of Hindus. The Sikh culture is Gurmukhi culture with Gurmukhi as their language and this is conceded by the Hindus. Their history and traditions and their heroes are also different and so is their social regime. In this context, there is no reason as to why should they not stake claim to the right to self-determination".[27] The demand was again raised by the Shiromani Akali Dal (Master Tara Singh) at its

Ludhiana conference in May, 1965 through a resolution moved by Justice (Retd) Gurnam Singh and seconded by Giani Bhupinder Singh which stated, "This conference resolves there is no alternative to the demand for self determination for the Sikhs self preservation within the Indian Republic".[28]

The decision taken by the Akali Dal to work jointly with the Congress in 1937 was reversed by the former at its working committee meeting on July 20, 1950 when the party directed its legislators to come out of the Congress. This was in protest against the post-partition policies of the Congress government. Ironically, a few years later, the Akali Dal again repeated the mistake of joining hands with the Congress with the Akali leaders contesting the 1957 election on the Congress ticket.

The first Akali government formed in Pepsu (Patiala and East Punjab States Union), the region comprising Patiala and other princely states which was later merged with Punjab, was dismissed by the Centre in 1953. This action of the Congress government at the Centre reinforced the perception of discrimination. That was the first elected government which achieved the distinction of having been dismissed by the Centre in free India.

Meanwhile, the State Reorganization Commission headed by Justice Fazal Ali set up by the Centre in December, 1953, in its report in 1955, rejected the Akali Dal demand for the re-organization of Punjab on linguistic basis. The Akali Dal had raised this demand following re-organization of other states on this criterion. This further provoked the Akalis who made the demand for Punjabi Suba one-point agenda of the party. The government responded by putting a ban even on the slogan of Punjabi Suba which resulted in the first Punjabi Suba agitation in 1955. That the demand was perceived as bordering Sikh state was evident earlier in 1954 from the statement then chief minister Bhim Sain Sachar had issued after a meeting with Master Tara Singh on January 21 in Chandigarh. He said Master Tara Singh demanded a Sikh state and not Punjabi Suba.[29]

The Morcha, launched on May 10, 1955 from Amritsar with Master Tara Singh leading the first group of satyagrahis, was withdrawn on July 12 after the government withdrew the ban on Punjabi Suba slogan. The Akali Dal had raised four slogans as part of the Punjabi Suba agitation namely 'Azad Bharat Zindabad', 'Hindu Sikh Ekta Zindabad', Punjabi Suba Zindabad' and 'Haryana Prant Zindabad'.[30] The state government had imposed Section 144 all over the state prohibiting assembly of five or more persons. It was decided that the party would not violate Section 144 and groups of four volunteers each would court arrest daily against the ban on Punjabi Suba Zindabad slogan. It may be mentioned that parts of present Haryana were merged in Punjab in 1857 though this region had no religious or cultural contiguity with this state.

The Pradesh Congress Committee welcomed decision of the government to withdraw ban on raising the Punjab Suba Zindabad slogan with 13 members voting in favour and four against it. Significantly, those who opposed the withdrawal of ban included Chaudhary Devi Lal and Prof. Sher Singh, both from the region which is now Haryana.[31] It is pertinent to note that the Akali Dal government headed by Parkash Singh Badal which came to power in 1997 installed statute of Chaudhary Devi Lal on the Punjab-Haryana border.

The Punjabi Suba agitation assumed importance from another aspect. Those who went to jail as part of this morcha included Head Granthi of Darbar Sahib Giani Bhupinder Singh, Akal Takht Jathedar Giani Achhar Singh, Darbar Sahib Manager Gurdial Singh, SGPC acting Secretary Giani Teja Singh and Secretary Prof. Harbhajn Singh. In the history of Darbar Sahib, Giani Bhupinder Singh was the second Head Granthi to have been arrested after the first Head Granthi Bhai Mani Singh who attained martyrdom. Others who participated in the morcha included then SGPC executive committee member Parkash Singh Badal, Baba Hira Singh Bhattal and his wife Bibi Harnam Kaur (along with three daughters including Rajinder Kaur and less than a month old youngest son). Baba Hira Singh was the father of Rajinder Kaur Bhattal born in 1946 in Lahore jail who became the Punjab Chief Minister in 1996 heading a Congress ministry. More than 12000 persons went to jail which also included all the 15 Akali MLAs of the Punjab Assembly, 8 members of the Pepsu Assembly, 2 MPs, 3 members of the Legislative Council and 111 members of the SGPC.

The SGPC, at its general body meeting on October 16, 1955, while rejecting the report of the States Reorganisation Commission, supported the demand for Punjabi Suba.

The stand taken by the Communist Party of India on Punjabi Suba as evident from the debate in March, 1956, in the state Assembly on the Re-organisation Act is very significant where Harkishan Singh Surjeet said, "Punjab is not being re-organized on linguistic basis despite the commitment of the All India Congress Committee to reorganize the states on linguistic basis".[32]

The Akali Dal reiterated the demand for Punjabi Suba at its Amritsar convention on October 12, 1958 and took out a march in Delhi on March 15, 1959. At its Hola Mohalla conference at Anandpur Sahib in 1960, the Akali Dal reversed the 1957 decision and directed the legislators and MPs to come out of the Congress.

The party, on May 23, 1960, gave a call for another protest march in Delhi on June 12. This was the beginning of the second Punjabi Suba agitation. It was during this movement that senior Akali leaders undertook fast unto death as form of peaceful struggle. However, these fasts were abandoned which eroded the credibility of the traditional Akali leadership. This was the period of prolonged confrontation with the government. The state was finally re-organized in November 1, 1966.

The reorganization of the state coincided with the introduction of high yielding varieties of crops which paved the way for green revolution and prosperity in Punjab. This prosperity in a section of the Punjabi society further raised the political ambitions. The leadership of Akali Dal, the second oldest political party in the country founded in 1920 articulating the Sikh sentiments, passed into the hands of the land owning classes during this period.

Akali Dal President Sant Fateh Singh, in 1963, also favoured transfer of Punjabi speaking Sri Ganganagar district of Rajasthan to Punjabi Suba. Articulating the demand for the Punjabi speaking state, he argued, "We are not concerned with the population percentage of any community in the Punjabi speaking state.... we want a Punjabi Suba purely on linguistic basis and we are not concerned whether Sikhs are in a majority or minority in that state.... We want that Punjabi speaking area be demarcated in a uni-lingual Punjabi Suba... Hindus, Sikhs, Muslims and Harijans would enjoy the same status and there would be no question of any kind of discrimination".[33] Earlier, the party made its stand clear on this issue at its 14th All India Akali Conference held at Ludhiana in 1963.

Sikhstan

As the Centre accepted the demand for re-organization of the state on linguistic basis and the re-organized state of Punjab came into being on November 1, 1966 while keeping out the capital city of Chandigarh, the Akali Dal moved on to the demand for Sikhstan which was to be an autonomous state within India. Here was a very significant shift, especially in the context of the deep polarization years later on the issue of Anandpur Sahib Resolution on which the party never contested elections. However, the Assembly and Lok Sabha elections in Punjab in 1967 were contested by the Shiromani Akali Dal on Sikhstan issue. The political resolution to this effect was adopted by the Shiromani Akali Dal at its working committee meeting on July 20, 1966 at Delhi and ratified at its 17th All India conference at Ludhiana on December 11 the same year. The resolution states: "Having come to the inescapable conclusion that a section of the political Hindus, having key powers in the political India, have a firm plan of degrading and liquidating Sikhs from the mainstream of free India, and it is for this purpose that the new boundaries of the Punjab have been determined by the government of India so as to eventually relegate and contain Sikhs in a narrow, undeveloped and suppressed reserved area, on the pattern of Jewish ghettos in medieval Europe, and reserved area of apartheid in certain modern states. Now therefore, the Sikhs resolve and proclaim their determination to resist, through all legitimate means, all such attempts to devalue and liquidate the Sikhs people in a free India and consequently demand that following steps be taken forthwith, by the rulers of India, to assure and enable the Sikhs to live as respectable and equal citizens of Union of India".

The party demanded Sikhstan be created as an autonomous region within India by transferring areas to Punjab deliberately kept out of the state at the time of re-organization. These areas included Dalhousie which earlier was part of Gurdaspur district, Ambala district including Chandigarh, Pinjore, Kalka and Ambala Sadar, entire Una tehsil which was earlier part of Hoshiarpur district, area of Nalagarh called Desh, Sirsa tehsil, sub-tehsils of Tohana and Guhla and Ratia block of Hisar district, Shahbad block of Karnal district and also the contiguous portions of Ganganagar district of Rajasthan. The party demanded all the contiguous Sikh areas should form one administrative unit which was to be Sikhstan, the Sikh Homeland. The party demanded this region a special autonomous constitutional status on the analogy of Jammu and Kashmir as was envisaged in the Constitution Act of India.

The party called for suitable political and constitutional measures to be adopted, in relations to other states of the union of India, such as, provision of deterrent punishments for those found guilty of discrimination and prejudicial acts against Sikhs residing in these states, including statutory reserved appointments of adequate number of Sikhs as judges, legislators, policemen and executive officials.

The manifesto referred to the 'commitment and promise' made before partition of the country by the 'Hindu leaders' of the Indian national Congress to carve out a special autonomous region for the Sikhs and said it was because of these commitments that the Sikhs had rejected the offer of a sovereign state between India and Pakistan which was to include the territory between river Jhelum in the North and river Ghaggar in the South. However, the leaders of the 'Hindu Congress' backtracked after Independence.

The controversy on the Anandpur Sahib Resolution, the opposition to which was the main plank on which Congress went to polls in 1984 after Operation Bluestar, tantamount to exploiting an issue on which the Akali Dal had already contested the Lok Sabha and Assembly elections in 1967 without much notice having been taken at the national level. This Sikhstan resolution was the precursor to the Anandpur Sahib Resolution. There is not much qualitative difference between the Sikhstan resolution and the Anandpur Sahib Resolution adopted in 1973. Given this background, it was a deliberate and calculated design to misdirect the political discourse by the Congress. And the election symbol of Akali Dal in the 1967 elections was the open hand which years later was allotted by the Election Commission to Congress.

There is yet another very interesting reference in the 1967 manifesto while advocating Sikhstan and it is in the context of strengthening defence forces with reference to neighbouring Pakistan. The Akali Dal manifesto talked of natural and historical boundaries of the country and stated that the areas which had been left out during partition in 1947 should be recaptured.[34] Punjab had been the victim of partition with major territories becoming part of Pakistan, including Nankana Sahib, the birthplace of Guru Nanak Dev, the founder of the Sikh faith.

While claiming to be the political outfit representing the Sikhs, the Akali Dal offered to join hand with any political party which had patriotic and democratic credentials while recalling unparallel contributions made by the Sikhs towards freedom struggle. The party also demanded adequate representation to the Sikhs in the government services in other states and end to the discrimination against them. The Akali Dal blamed the 'Hindu Congress' for discrimination against the Sikhs to "push them out" of the mainstream.

Though demanding autonomous Sikhstan, at no point of time during this period the party ever exhibited secessionist tendencies. Rather in the manifesto for the 1969 mid term Assembly elections, the thrust of the party was on "complete unity of the Punjabis". It was in a separate note on the manifesto that the party President Sant Fateh Singh talked of more powers to the states and that too "to maintain unity of the country". There was no reference to the demand for Sikhstan in the 1969 manifesto.

The period from 1967 to 1969 is marked by yet another shift in the stand of the Akali Dal which is known as the Batala resolution. The demand for Sikhstan finds no mention in the political resolution the party adopted at the Batala conference in 1968 which mainly talked of autonomy.

Party President Sant Fateh Singh in his presidential address on September 28 at Batala mainly talked of autonomy and more powers to the states saying, "It is clear from what has been happening since 1967 elections that the Centre is determined to dilute the powers of the states.

After the misuse of powers by the Centre in West Bengal, Bihar, Uttar Pradesh, Haryana and Punjab, the situation calls for necessary amendments in the constitution. The dangerous game being played to dismiss the state governments has endangered both the constitution and democracy. This disease must be taken care of immediately. The remedy is to make the states autonomous by giving more powers. The powers of the governors should be curtailed. The governors should be elected and not nominated by the Centre".

The party passed a resolution stressing the demand for autonomy at this conference known as the Batala Resolution. This resolution stated: "This conference of the Shiromani Akali Dal is of the considered opinion that the country has witnessed vital changes in the political sphere during the last 20 years....it is imperative that under the changing situation, the centre-state relations should be given a fresh look.... The constitution of the country should be reviewed to revise the centre-state relations... Shiromani Akali Dal demands that the country should have a real federal structure with greater autonomy to the states. The Shiromani Akali Dal feels that the interference by the Centre in the internal matters of the states and the hurdles being created in the functioning of the state governments are a threat to the unity and integrity of the country". The party also appealed to the states to raise their voice against such tendencies of the Centre. At the time this resolution was adopted, Punjab was under President's rule which had been imposed on August 13, 1968.

There are striking parallels between the Sikhstan resolution and the Anandpur Sahib resolution of 1973 and the Batala resolution and the diluted Anandpur Sahib Resolution of 1978.

The Akali Dal talked of structural changes in the constitution in the 1971 Lok Sabha elections manifesto also with the aim of bringing about economic justice and establishing egalitarian society and stressed the need for a federal set up for the entire country.

Provincial autonomy was again the main issue the party took up in the 1972 Assembly elections and the slogan given in the manifesto was "Greater provincial autonomy with minimum central authority". The party extended the logic that this devolution of powers in favour of the states would strengthen them. The party talked of discrimination against the Sikhs and betrayal by the Congress by way of backtracking on the promises made during the pre-partition period. The Akali demand during this period remained confined to autonomy within the parameters of the Indian constitution. There was no reference to the demand for Sikhstan in the manifestos for the 1971 Lok Sabha and the 1972 Assembly elections.

It is in this background that the Khalistan slogan was raised for the first time by former Punjab finance minister Dr. Jagjit Singh Chohan in London in September, 1971. While the demand for Sikhstan had been raised by the Shiromani Akali Dal through a resolution, the demand for Khalistan was just a slogan. He placed an advertisement in the New York Times on October 13, 1971 proclaiming an Independent Sikh state. He had also visited Pakistan during that period.

Although the Anandpur Sahib Resolution of 1973 used to be talked about in political circles, this resolution came under focus mainly when Sant Jarnail Singh Bhindranwale brought it on his agenda after its implementation had been demanded by the Akali Dal. It is the 1973 version that is perceived to be the forceful assertion of the political ambitions of the Sikhs as there was no ambiguity and the main emphasis was on Sikh concerns. Interestingly, no mention of this resolution was made by the Akali Dal in the manifesto on which the party contested the Lok Sabha and the Assembly elections in 1977 and 1980.

The political goal of the Anandpur Sahib Resolution, 1973, states: "The political goal of the Panth, without doubt, is enshrined in the commandments of the Tenth Lord, in the pages of the Sikh history and in the very heart of the Khalsa Panth, the ultimate objective of which is the pre-eminence of the Khalsa. The fundamental policy of the Shiromani Akali Dal is to seek the realization of this birth right of the Khalsa through creation of congenial environment and a political set up". According to this resolution, Centre's interference was to be restricted to defence, foreign relations, currency and general communications. This resolution also called for the Indian constitution to be recast on real federal principles, with equal representation at the Centre to all the states.

The party demanded that "all Punjabi speaking areas deliberately kept out of Punjab, such as Dalhousie in Gurdaspur district; Chandigarh, Pinjore-Kalka and Ambala Saddar etc in Ambala district; the entire Una tehsil of Hoshiarpur district; the Desh area of Nalagarh; Shahabad and Guhla blocks of Karnal district; Tohna sub-tehsil, Ratia block and Sirsa tehsil of Hissar district and six tehsils of Ganganagar district in Rajasthan be merged with Punjab to constitute the single administrative unit where the interests of the Sikhs and Sikhism are specifically protected". Significantly, these areas happened to be Hindu dominated and Sant Longowal at the time of the launch of the Dharamyudh morcha said while pressing for its implementation that in case the Centre conceded this demand, the Akalis would never come into power with a dominant role in Punjab on their own. This demand was in accordance with the 1966 party resolution.

What is all the more significant is that though the original version was diluted in 1978, the political aim of the Akali Dal enshrined in its constitution in 1974 continues broadly to be the one as defined in the 1973 version of the Anandpur Sahib resolution. This political aim conceptualized is as follows: "To reinforce the exclusive identity and strive for the creation of geo-political environment in which national sentiments and aspirations of the Sikh Panth are fully manifested". This objective had been cleared by the party working committee on September 2, 1974.

It was rather a watered down version of the 1973 resolution which was adopted at the 2-day general house meeting of the party in 1978 at Ludhiana beginning October 28 when the Akali Dal government was in power. The sense of political deprivation was not there at that time. It states: "The Shiromani Akali Dal realizes that India is a federal and republican geographical entity of different languages, religions and cultures. To safeguard the fundamental rights of the religious and linguistic minorities, to fulfill the demands of the democratic traditions and to pave the way for economic progress, it has become imperative that the Indian constitutional infrastructure should be given a real federal shape by redefining the Centre and State relations and rights on the lines of aforesaid principles and objectives".

Further: " The Shiromani Akali Dal emphatically urges upon the Janata government to take cognizance of the different linguistic and cultural sections, religious minorities as also the voice of millions of people and recast the constitutional structure of the country on real and meaningful federal principles to obviate the possibility of any danger to the national unity and the integrity of the country and further, to enable the states to play a useful role for the progress and prosperity of the Indian people in their respective areas by the meaningful exercise of their powers".

There is no reference to the aspirations of the Sikhs in this resolution. Even the word Sikh is not found in the political resolution of the 1978 version. It was the 1973 version the implementation of which used to be stressed upon by Sant Bhindranwale whose refrain would be that it was not his demand but that of the Akali Dal and his job was to see that the Akalis did not betray the resolution. It was this version which carried the clause that any person not convicted by the court should be allowed to possess small arms upto carbines without any licence, the only obligation being the registration. Sant Bhindranwale used to quote this clause while giving a call to the Sikhs to get armed.

However, it was the speech of then Shiromani Gurdwara Parbandhak Committee chief Gurcharan Singh Tohra while moving the political resolution at the Ludhiana conference which was all the more significant. He based his logic for autonomous states on the basis of the post-independence experience and the Emergency era. Excerpts from the speech: "The very fact that we still talk of the need of emotional unity and are still worried about centrifugal tendencies shows that despite our strong Centre, we are far away from the goal of national cohesion. The truth of the matter is that centrifugal tendencies are there mainly as a reaction to the centralizing trends of our polity aimed at uniformity in the name of unity and conformity, in the name of cohesion. If we really desire national integration, then what is required is a basic change in approach to the problem under reference. We will have to discard the political stereotype that a monolithic Centre, fortified by unitary constitution, capable of enforcing uniformity and conformity, is the only guarantee for national integration and territorial integrity of our country. India is a country characterized by religious, cultural, ethnic and linguistic diversity. This diversity is reflected in the variety of nations, nationalities and minorities living in India, making it a multi-national society at the empirical level. In such a situation, national integration is realizable only in and through a pluralistic society which alone can ensure unity in diversity, as against the unitarian society that aims at uniformity and conformity. So far, the majoritarian approach has been like this: Conform or be reduced to a sub-national level. Far from seeking Indianization of the Hindu tradition, what has been attempted at is Hinduaziation of the Indian tradition. The centrifugal tendencies in fact arise as a reaction against such an approach.

"If we really seek a genuine national integration, conditions must be created wherein our nations, minorities and nationalities would get woven into the national fabric while keeping intact their identity and essence. The requisite conditions can be created only in the form of a pluralistic society which by its very nature demands a federal framework. It is only in such a federalized set up that the Sikh community (which is a nation, sui generic, as well as a national minority) and other nations, nationalities and minorities including our tribal groups can hope to keep their identity intact and inviolate. A unitary polity leads to a unitary society with little scope for the flowering of religious, cultural and ethnic variety....It would be worthwhile to understand the class character of the plea for a monolithic Centre. As the historical experience of the developing countries shows, monopoly capitalism, far from being opposed to state capitalism, in fact, derives sustenance and strength from the latter, as state capital requires a concentration of power at the apex, so the logic of circumstances makes monopoly capitalism seek a strong monolithic Centre for its own vested interest. Whether public sector of economy gravitates towards state capitalism or leads to socialism depends to a very large extent on the way political power is organized. From this angle federalization of polity and decentralization of power is essential for public sector developing along democratic non-capitalist lines".[35] More important than the resolution was Tohra's thesis on federal structure.

Under pressure from the Janata Party led government at the Centre in which the Akali Dal was a partner, Chief Minister Parkash Singh Badal in 1979 cancelled the conference of the like-minded chief ministers on autonomy issue.

The Badal government was dismissed in June, 1980, by the Indira Gandhi led Congress government at the Centre at the time when it still had more than two years to go. This was perceived as yet another act of discrimination by the Congress against the Sikhs. This put the Akali Dal once again on the path of confrontation with the Congress government. Earlier, the Akali Dal had consistently opposed the imposition of the draconian Emergency. Out of power, the party again started talking of Sikh ambitions and aspirations. The concerns, compulsions and interests of the Akali leadership are different when in power and out of power. If the Akali leadership has time and again been accused of adopting opportunistic policies, the charge is not without substance.

The general house of the Shiromani Akali Dal at its two day meeting starting from August 19, 1980 at Amritsar resolved: "The Shiromani Akali Dal has come to the conclusion that in view of the present political situation in the country, the only way out is decentralization to give more powers to the states. It is for this reason that the Shiromani Akali Dal has consistently been saying that the constitution of the country should be rewritten to make it truly federal so that the powers are decentralized by way of providing more fiscal and political powers to the states. For the creation of such an autonomous state, the Shiromani Akali Dal firmly demands that in the context of the historic Anandpur Sahib Resolution, the constitution should be rewritten to provide real federal structure and create a geo-political environment in which the Sikh aspirations find full reflection and the states become more prosperous".[36] The issue of Sikh aspirations provided the competing ground to the Akali factions in the subsequent period. This resolution is again very significant as the party again talked of geo-political environment of the Sikhs which was the main theme of the 1973 version of the Anandpur Sahib resolution which the party had diluted in 1978.

In the 1977 manifesto of the Shiromani Akali Dal for the Lok Sabha and Assembly elections, no reference had been made to the Anandpur

Sahib resolution or the Sikh aspirations. The manifesto reads: "Shiromani Akali Dal is a political party pledged to the establishment of society based on economic, political, social and cultural justice. It is therefore, committed to a secular, democratic and socialistic society of Guru Gobind Singh's conception. Shiromani Akali Dal, unlike many other parties in the country, has its own traditions and history spread over six decades. Shiromani Akali Dal always stood in the front rank in the struggle for freedom of conscience and liberation of the country. Its role in promoting national reconstruction and territorial integrity of the country is commendable."

Of course, the main aim outlined was imparting a real federal structure to the Indian constitution with greater autonomy for the federating states, but without any reference to the Anandpur Sahib Resolution. The manifesto stated that while reappraising the constitution, the authority of the President of India to dismiss state governments should be withdrawn and a permanent autonomous commission appointed at the Centre and the state level to supervise protection of the rights of the national, social, religious, cultural and linguistic minorities. An autonomous commission should also be appointed with equal representation from the concerned states for settling inter-state disputes. The emphasis was on economic development. Of course, the manifesto also referred to the territorial and river waters disputes. On the territorial dispute, it favoured transfer of Chandigarh and other Punjabi speaking areas but did not specify these areas. The party demanded annulment of "arbitrary" division of Ravi- Beas waters.

Again in the manifesto for the 1980 Lok Sabha polls, the Akali Dal omitted reference to the Anandpur Sahib Resolution on which the party was to launch Dharamyudh morcha two years later. The major card the party played was the achievements of its government in the state since 1977. The party reiterated its commitment to national reconstruction and territorial solidarity of the country while stressing that the Akali Dal would continue its struggle for imparting a real federal structure to the constitution with greater autonomy. The mention to the territorial and water disputes was again there. There was no reflection of any communal tinge in the manifestos of 1977 and 1980. The 1980 manifesto focused mainly on the economic issues while stressing the demand for reappraisal of the constitution to give it a real federal structure with greater autonomy for the states and taking away the powers of the President to dismiss a state government.

It is in this context that the August, 1980 resolution of the Akali Dal assumes all the more importance as the struggle launched by Sant Bhindranwale revolved around this issue.

This was the time when the radical tinge in the Akali matrix had already been activated. The Dal Khalsa had been set up on August 6, 1978 at Chandigarh whose aim was the setting up of a sovereign Sikh state. It was the Akali Dal government which was in power at that time which had been repeatedly coming under attack from a section of the Sikh society for soft-pedaling the Nirankari issue. The All India Sikh Students Federation had also become active by this time.

In the competitive Akali politics, the Akali Dal (Talwandi) at its 2-day World Sikh Convention beginning August 19, 1980 at Anandpur Sahib, resolved to prepare itself for launching agitation on its own version of the Anandpur Sahib Resolution which defines the political objective in these words: "An autonomous region in the North of India should be set up forthwith wherein the Sikhs' interests are constitutionally recognized as of primary and special importance .... The Sikh autonomous region may be conceded and declared as entitled to frame its own constitution on basis of having all powers to and for itself except foreign relations, defence and communications".

In the Panthic politics, the splinter groups normally take the extreme position. Again at its World Sikh Convention organized at Anandpur Sahib on April 13, 1982, this splinter group demanded "autonomous Des Punjab" on the basis of the 1973 version of the Anandpur Sahib Resolution. The Sikh leaders abroad were also queering the pitch for the Sikh state by that time, though not necessarily theocratic. US based Sikh leader Ganga Singh Dhillon, who headed the Nankana Sahib Foundation, in his speech distributed at this convention of the Talwandi faction, defined this autonomous Des Punjab in the following words: "The legitimate boundaries of Des Punjab should be brought into one unit, given complete autonomy under constitutional protection and recognition as a distinct national entity within the Indian union, as is presently accorded to Kashmir... acceptance of the reality of Sikh nationhood... Punjabi speaking Des Punjab does not mean partition. There can be many nationalities within a country's boundaries and there is nothing in this definition that threatens the unity of India... the unity and dignity of the Khalsa Panth and the unity and dignity of India are intertwined". The party also demanded separate personal law for the Sikhs. It was the Congress which was ruling both at the Centre and in Punjab at that time.

Earlier at the 54th 3-day All India Sikh Education Conference organized by the Chief Khalsa Diwan at Chandigarh in 1981 starting March 13, Dhillon, in his presidential address, had talked about the ambition of the Sikhs to be independent. This otherwise non-political conference adopted five resolutions including the setting up of an

International Sikh Secretariat for the economic, educational, cultural, political and religious activities relating to the Sikh nation. The fourth resolution looked innocuous but had its political overtones. It states: "To strive for getting rights to preserve this great heritage bestowed upon the Sikhs by Guru Gobind Singh and work for the betterment of our future independently at the religious, cultural and economic level". The Chief Khalsa Diwan later disassociated itself from these resolutions at a meeting on April 16.

Dhillon, at an informal interaction with the media persons in Chandigarh, had distributed his photograph with Pakistan President General Zia ul Haq which was not carried by any newspaper at that time. However, the same photograph later used to be published by the newspapers to prove his nexus with Pakistan. He had personal relationship with General Zia and was a frequent visitor to Pakistan. Yet another leader who had been raising the demand for Khalistan for several years was Dr. Chohan.

However, Dr. Chohan had already announced the setting up of his National Council of Khalistan from the Darbar Sahib complex on June 16, 1980 through his deputy Balbir Singh Sandhu. The Khalistan envisaged by him was to include Punjabi speaking areas from Haryana, Himachal Pradesh and Rajasthan also. All communities and sections of society were to have equal religious rights under this dispensation. Moreover, there was to be no economic exploitation of anybody or section of the society.

With Sant Bhindranwale emerging on the scene, the issue of exclusive and sovereign Sikh identity came to be continuously underscored. The basis of his assertions was the Anandpur Sahib Resolution. His main slogan was discrimination over the years against the Sikhs by the rulers in Delhi. This issue had repeatedly been raised by the Akali Dal. However, now the atmosphere was getting tense. Violence had already been introduced in the political system in Punjab by that time with the killing of Nirankari chief Gurbachan Singh in April, 1980 to avenge the killing of 13 Sikhs by the Nirankaris in 1978.

Ironically, it was the Akali Dal which came under attack for adopting radical politics though the party had never talked of a separate Sikh state. For years the Akali Dal only confined itself to the demand for autonomy, of course with variations, from Sikhstan to Anandpur Sahib Resolution of 1973 and then its 1978 version and again to the Sikh aspirations. Still, the party remained on the defensive on this issue at the national level. At this very stage itself, Akali Dal President Harchand Singh Longowal had made explicit distinction from the demand for Khalistan in November, 1981 saying his party was only for greater autonomy on the basis of Anandpur Sahib Resolution.[37]

One of the reasons advanced by Indira Gandhi for the army attack on the Darbar Sahib complex in June, 1984 was the apprehension of the proclamation of the Khalistan government by the radicals holed up there. Longowal had repeatedly said the demand for the Sikh state was being encouraged by the ruling Congress as part of its larger designs. The National Council of Khalistan had been proclaimed way back in 1980 and that too, from the Darbar Sahib complex. The Dal Khalsa had raised the slogan of Khalistan much earlier.

The issue of Khalistan cropped up in the Punjab Vidhan Sabha as earlier as on March 25, 1982 when the non-official resolution moved by Communist Party of India group leader Raj Kumar came up for discussion. The resolution condemned the protagonists of Khalistan. However, Speaker Brij Bhushan Mehra, after about 45 minutes of debate, called off the discussion on the resolution. The ruling came after the House discussed whether this resolution should be taken up or not. Chief Minister Darbara Singh was in favour of discussion while his party colleagues opposed it. Sant Ram Singla from the Congress opposed it arguing the issue involved the sovereignty and integrity of the country and constitutionally, could not be discussed in any state legislature. Similar views were expressed by Birdevinder Singh while Gopal Krishan Chatrath (Congress) argued the House could not go back once the resolution had been moved. Ravi Inder Singh (Shiromani Akali Dal) opposed the discussion while Chand Singh Chopra (CPI-M) was for it. Surjit Singh Barnala (Shiromani Akali Dal) pointed out the constitution did not permit discussion in which secessionist ideas could be openly supported. Baldev Singh Mann (Shiromani Akali Dal) said in case the state government wanted the state to be on fire, his party was prepared for it. Yash (Cong) said once the resolution had been moved, the members had a right to speak. He said the Akalis were running from the debate. However, the discussion was disallowed on the technical plea that Babu Singh did not have the authority to move the resolution listed in the name of Raj Kumar, who himself was not present in the House.

No major democratic political outfit or Sant Bhindranwale raised this demand for Khalistan till Operation Bluestar. The army action had delivered the biggest ever shock to the Sikhs in free India for whom the situation had now changed. The Akalis had ceased to be of much relevance as the subsequent events proved. The attack on the Darbar Sahib complex concerned the entire Sikh Diaspora and not any particular section within the Sikh society. It had now become a Sikh issue.

The first major political event after the assassination of Indira Gandhi and the genocide of the Sikhs in planned reaction during the post-Bluestar period was the signing of the Rajiv-Longowal Accord which paved the way for the Assembly elections in the state. The manifesto of the Shiromani Akali Dal for the 1985 Assembly elections mainly talked of taking all possible measures for restoring peace and normalcy in the state.

Defining political philosophy of the Akali Dal, the manifesto stated that "the party is pledged to the establishment of society based on economic, political, social and cultural justice. It is therefore, committed to the society of Guru Gobind Singh's concept. The Akali Dal, unlike many other parties in the country, has its own traditions and history spread over more than six decades. Its record in promoting national reconstruction and territorial solidarity of the country is second to none". The party demanded more powers to the states on the pattern of Anandpur Sahib Resolution which had already been referred to the Sarkaria Commission as per the terms of the Rajiv-Longowal accord. The manifesto hailed the Punjab accord as a success achieved by the Akali Dal and aimed at "affording justice to Punjab and safeguarding the vital interests of the people of the state in political, economic, social and cultural matters". However, these issues were no more relevant in the post-Bluestar scenario and neither was the Rajiv-Longowal accord. The Akali Dal had failed to comprehend this ground reality.

Ever since the start of the militant movement, the demand for Khalistan, for the first time, was formally and forcefully raised by the radicals on April 29, 1986. This is attributed mainly to Operation Bluestar on the surface. However, it was only at the level of a slogan in the absence of any concrete strategy to transform it into a reality. Taking up this issue was the Panthic Committee, constituted as the umbrella organization of the militant outfits engaged in the armed struggle for the attainment of the Sikh state. To get this demand wider support, this announcement was got endorsed at the Sarbat Khalsa organized by the militant organizations at Akal Takht on January 26, 1987, which justified it saying it was necessary "in view of the situation created by the union government".

Here goes the proclamation: "The five member Panthic Committee constituted by the Sarbat Khalsa convened by the Damdami Taksal, today hereby declares the formation of Khalistan. This declaration of the Khalistan is made before the Khalsa Panth as well as the Sikh community so that all of us may, in accordance with our individual capacity, contribute to its cause mentally and financially. Today the five member Panthic Committee calls upon the entire Sikh nation to be ready for all types of sufferings and scarifies. The wish of the Khalsa is to achieve the declared objective by the Guru's ace, love and affection. We are not interested in creating any upheaval or in shedding undue blood and we expect the same from others too. We express our firm faith in resolving all the issues cordially and through a dialogue with the Hindu majority and Government of India. We hope that the Government of India will not be blinded by an anti-Sikh attitude underlying Brahminism and will face the reality by giving recognition to the formation of Khalistan".

Various militant outfits continued to raise this slogan for Khalistan. The slogan did not get support from any section of the Shiromani Akali Dal leadership initially. Neither was there any long term strategy chalked out by the radicals to create mass support for this slogan to convert it into at least a demand. This proved to be the single biggest weakness of the militant movement which lacked an effective political front. It was too late when moves were initiated towards that direction. It was proposed to re-organize the Akali Dal for this purpose. The leaders who were approached on behalf of the militant organizations on this issue included Parkash Singh Badal and Sukhdev Singh Dhindsa towards the end of the decade.

This political goal of Khalistan, however, was again diluted when then Akal Takht acting Jathedar Prof. Darshan Singh, as part of the unity move, "reorganized" the Akali Dal and specified its political goal in February, 1987, which stated: "It is firm belief of the Shiromani Akali Dal that the Khalsa Panth created by the 10th Lord, Guru Gobind Singh, is a separate and independent (adri ate swatanter qaum) nation whose political goal is based on the principle of the pre-eminence of the Khalsa (Khalse de bol-bale). Hence the main aim of the Shiromani Akali Dal is to maintain this separate identity of the Panth and create a geo-political environment in which the aspirations of the Sikh nation are manifested". Prof. Darshan Singh made it clear that the political goal was neither secessionist nor against the national interests. This was in contravention to the demand for a sovereign Sikh state raised by the radical Sikh organizations. He was in touch with the Centre at that time.

The moderate Akali stream was completely marginalized in the November, 1989 elections to the Lok Sabha in which most of the candidates supported by the radicals were elected. Some of these candidates had earlier been raising the slogan of Khalistan. However, they contested the elections under the Indian constitution. The agenda of these candidates in the Lok Sabha poll was not the demand for Khalistan.

This demand was reiterated by the All India Sikh Students Federation after the Lok Sabha elections in December when its General Secretary Harminder Singh Sandhu, after his release from jail, said the government should negotiate with the militants on the Sikh state.

In the wider perspective, the issue of Sikh identity was taken up at other levels and in different context also, though not of political power. "It is only in recent years that Sikhism has become fully self-conscious about its identity in all its dimensions, both individual and collective. This identity consciousness is a positive phenomenon and must not be confused with religious sectarianism, social exclusivism or political separatism: exclusivism in all its forms is alien to the spirit of Sikh liberalism and universalism. Having been always a small minority – even when the Sikhs had acquired political power in the 18th century and established a sovereign state – they have remained concerned about assimilative dangers to their identity, to their very being as a distinctive group. The growth of self-consciousness on the part of contemporary Sikhism and Sikh society in recent years has made the Sikhs all the more aware of the existential concerns of their being a distinctive ethno-religious and ethno-political group".[38]

The changing emphasis was again evident in the manifesto of the Mann faction of the Akali Dal for the aborted June, 1991 elections which earlier on the Baisakhi of 1990 had demanded the right to self-determination. It is only in the last paragraph of the manifesto that there is reference to the word sovereignty. It said, "Gurbani, the word of the Guru, shall be its (Shiromani Akali Dal) guiding light to rejuvenate the spirit of the Khalsa, to regain sovereignty, which is a sui-generis characteristic of the Khalsa". The manifesto took note of the Sikhs as a global community saying, "The Shiromani Akali Dal recognizes its kinship with and responsibility towards the Sikh Diaspora in India and abroad. It would encourage exchanges and interface with them to increase cross-fertilization of ideas, concepts and schemes. Policies of the Sikh nation will take into account the fears and aspirations of the Sikh fraternity scattered by time and tide all over India and other countries of the world".

Significantly, the demand for a sovereign Sikh state was articulated by none other than Tohra, Badal and Mann in the memorandum submitted to the United Nations on April 22, 1992 on behalf of the Shiromani Akali Dal and the SGPC. It reads: "Demilitarisation and decolonization of the Punjab is crucial and indispensable to enable the Sikh people to enjoy full freedom to exercise their economic, social and cultural rights. Like all free people of the world, the Sikh nation, in accordance with the UN Declaration on the granting of independence to colonial countries and people seeks an independent and sovereign state to break the shackles of apartheid, slavery, colonialism and retrograde political system and structure". This memorandum was never followed up with any mass democratic action by these leaders or the Sikh organizations.

However, it was on May 1, 1994 that while adopting the Amritsar Declaration at Akal Takht on May 1, 1994 that the Akali Dal threatened to launch peaceful struggle for a sovereign Sikh state. The resolution states: "The Akali Dal, being a champion of Punjabi culture based on Guru Granth Sahib, reiterates its commitment for waging a struggle within democratic norms for the creation of such a separate region for the Sikhs where they can enjoy a glow of freedom. The Congress had made solemn promises before the partition of the country for the creation of such a region which were never implemented. At the turn of history, when on the one hand, there was unrest in the South-East Asian countries; the European nations were making efforts for restructuring themselves in a changed political scenario. In such a situation, the liberation from political exploitation would be a beacon of light for other cultural entities. The Akali leaders feel that India is a subcontinent consisting of various nations and cultures, each one with distinct heritage. This sub-continent needs restructuring of its polity into a confederation of various cultures, so that each one could make effective development. If the government of India failed to restructure the Indian polity, the Akali Dal would be left with no other alternative but to wage struggle for a sovereign Sikh state". The Akali Dal reverted to its normal agenda later. The radical tinge was no more discernible in the Sikh political matrix.

Yet another paradigm shift was discernible when the Shiromani Akali Dal announced a new policy and programme after unity between Badal and Tohra on April 14, 1995. This policy programme formed the basis of the political line adopted by the party at its 75th anniversary programme at Moga. Significantly, this shift came at the time when militancy had virtually been brought under check after more than a decade of turbulence. This era marked the revival of the traditional Akali politics with the marginalized leaders like Badal and Tohra again occupying the central space. This policy and programme changed the very character of the Akali Dal in the coming years. It is a different matter that the seeds of Punjabiat can also be traced to the 1969 manifesto of the Akali Dal for the mid term Assembly elections.

This policy programme states: "Stressing that the fundamental character of the Indian civilization is its pluralistic nature, reflected in the composite quality and structure of Indian society enriched by diversity of languages, cultures and religions – and that this is the bedrock of national unity of the country, the Shiromani Akali Dal views with concern the homogenizing challenges to this characteristic of our society – the challenges threatening not only the integrity of India but also the minorities as well. This contradiction between the rising

Unitarian trends and forces and the pluralistic tendencies is becoming acute and critical day by day, disorienting the national polity consequently. For overcoming this situation, it is essential to federalize the national polity – this being the categoric imperative of pluralism of Indian society. This would ensure the minorities in a plural dispensation.

"The Preamble to the constitution should be amended so as to incorporate the expression federal to characterize the Republic of India as such, essential for highlighting and preserving the plural character of Indian society.

"The relations between the Union and the states be redrawn on federal lines. The centre should keep with itself, in the Union List, defence, foreign affairs, communication and currency".

This policy programme was for all Punjabis. The spirit of Punjabiat got further consolidated about a year later at the 75th anniversary conference of the party organized at Moga on February 25, 1996. During the post-militancy period beginning with the Moga conference, the Shiromani Akali Dal underwent a major transformation. The political philosophy which emanated from that conference later came to be known as the Moga Declaration, though no formal resolution to that effect was adopted. The Party talked of Punjab, Punjabi and Punjabiat. In the keynote address, the emphasis was on more powers to the states and internal autonomy. The party expressed its firm resolve to maintain peace.

In the manifesto for the 1996 Lok Sabha poll, the selling card of the Shiromani Akali Dal was peace and progress. The effort was to take remedial steps for the society which had been fractured by violence from both the sides. The party favoured the setting up of a commission comprising judges of the Supreme Court to go into the role of the Congress in encouraging and inciting terrorism and divisive politics. The reference to the Anandpur Sahib Resolution was there but in a different context. It stated: "The Akali Dal would seek the cooperation of the individuals and parties with the right thinking for the reconstruction of India as a truly secular, democratic and federal entity as that precisely is the approach of the Anandpur Sahib resolution". The main thrust was on socio-economic issues concerning various sections of society. It was in this manifesto that the party promised free power and water for the agriculture sector which was implemented after the party came into power in the February 1997 Assembly poll.

The transformation of the Akali Dal was complete as evident from the manifesto for the 1997 Assembly elections in which the thrust was once again on completely identifying the party with the Indian State. "The glorious saga of sacrifices made by the party for the Sikh Panth,

Punjab and India cannot be matched by any other political party. It played a leading role in the freedom movement and was in the vanguard of resistance struggle against infamous Emergency of Mrs. Indira Gandhi and the Congress party, till it was revoked. These struggles and sacrifices comprise significant chapters of our history. The long and valiant endeavours for the rights of the Sikhs, the Punjab and the Punjabi culture are a saga of sacrifices in which lakhs of people went to jails and hundreds lost their lives. No other political party can claim to have suffered as much championing the cause of Punjab, freedom, democracy and human rights".

This manifesto also talked of Anandpur Sahib Resolution saying "The Shiromani Akali Dal promises that true federalism as contained in the Anandpur Sahib Resolution can alone broaden the unity and integrity of the great Indian nation". Again it amounted to fully identifying with the Indian state. There was no reference to the federal structure or the Anandpur Sahib Resolution in the common minimum programme released by the alliance partners, the SAD and the Bharatiya Janata Party. The slogan in the common minimum programme was: "Peace with honour; prosperity for all; and, welfare of the entire people".

This thrust continued in the 1998 Lok Sabha elections as well as the party declared total commitment to the welfare of the country and its people. It said, "To ensure welfare and prosperity for all and to pave the way for all round development in the country, the Shiromani Akali Dal rededicates itself to working with like minded parties for the creation of a new social and economic order in the country". The shift from anti-centrism which was synonymous with anti-Congressism was complete with the Akali Dal declaring " The era of confrontation has been effectively ended and replaced with a forward looking thrust on working together for the over-all good of the state and the nation". Further, the party declared: "The Shiromani Akali Dal will carry the fragrance of this social revolution to the rest of the country, working hand in hand with its allies for a prosperous future of the people of the country. Our goal now, as always, is: Peace, amity and prosperity for all". It has to be read in the context of an earlier paragraph which states: "the greatest achievement by far of the past 11 months or so has been the giving final burial to the politics of divisiveness and fratricidal bloodshed indulged in by the Congress party". This manifesto is the further reinforcement that the Shiromani Akali Dal had been anti-centre, but never anti-state.

In the September1999 Lok Sabha poll, the party sought mandate on political stability, economic prosperity and social harmony and made the foreign origin of Congress president Sonia Gandhi a major issue which essentially was the BJP agenda. The party also pleaded for a genuinely federal structure with more fiscal and constitutional powers to the states. The manifesto said, "The era of unseemly confrontation between the centre and the states, perpetuated by the successive Congress governments, must be ended conclusively in favour of cooperative federalism".

The Shiromani Akali Dal, in July, 2000, submitted a memorandum to the National Commission set up to review the functioning of the constitution. The memorandum, in the context of 1978 version of the Anandpur Sahib Resolution, stressed the need for autonomous states with the Centre retaining only federal functions in respect of defence, external affairs, currency and general administration. The party called for incorporating the expression federal in the Preamble of the Constitution.

The Sarv Hind Shiromani Akali Dal went a step ahead in this race. While demanding autonomy, the party proposed that the quantum of autonomy should be decided keeping in view the peculiar situation of a particular state. The memorandum divided the states in three categories, those with dominant Hindi speaking population, with dominant Hindu population but not Hindi speaking and non-Hindi speaking with dominant non-Hindu population. The state should be able to effectively protect, preserve and flourish its distinct identity. The role of the centre should be confined to defence, foreign affairs, currency and general communication. The party also proposed amendment to Clause 25 II (B) of the constitution to ensure distinct identity of the Sikhs.

In this background, it was not unusual for the 2002 manifesto for the Assembly polls to focus on the development programmes, rather than the political thrust. Of course, the reference was there to the restructuring of centre-state relations to provide for true federal structure and the issues like the territorial and river waters. The transformation of the party was complete by this poll. The distinction between the Shiromani Akali Dal representing a minority community which is in majority in Punjab having the ambition to rule, and any other political party, just vanished. It was in the second part of the manifesto that the party talked of federal structure based on cooperative federalism. The exclusive and distinct identity of the Sikhs ceased to be an issue for the mainstream Akali Dal.

However, the Akali Dal again tried to harp on its Panthic character while claiming to be the champion of Punjabiat in its manifesto for the Lok Sabha elections in 2004. The party maintained that it would continue to strive to maintain the exclusive and separate religious and cultural identity of the Sikhs within the country and abroad and protect their rights.

And as per the manifesto of this party for the 2007 Assembly elections, the setting up of the true federal structure is the only way to strengthen national unity. The Akali Dal succeeded only in marginally improving upon its performance as compared to 2002 elections. This time, the Hindu vote bank shifted away from the Congress in favour of the Bharatiya Janata Party. It is the BJP which enabled the Akali Dal to come into power. This election once again established that although not in majority, the deciding role is with the Hindus, though the political discourse is defined by the Sikhs. The aspirations of the Sikhs and Sikhstan had ceased to be the issues with the Shiromani Akali Dal much earlier. The basic character of the Shiromani Akali Dal of representing the collective Sikh consciousness has got eroded over the years. The assimilation of the Sikhs in the political process is now complete, of course barring one miniscule section of the community. But then, the political violence in Punjab is cyclical.

NOTES

1. Ahluwalia, Jasbir Singh: Sovereignty of the Sikh Doctrine, Bahri Publications, New Delhi, 1983, p. 152.
2. Cunningham, JD: History of the Sikhs, Stavic Publications PvtLtd, Amritsar, 2000, p. 1.
3. Wallace,Paul and Chopra, Surinder: Political Dynamics of Punjab, GNDU, Amritsar, 1981, p. 8.
4. Nirankari, Mann Singh, Panthic Matte, 2002, p. 2.
5. Ibid, p. 50.
6. SGPC Da Panjah Sala Itihas, Sikh Itihas Research Board, SGPC, Amritsar, 1982, p. 78.
7. Ibid, p. 89.
8. Nirankari, Mann Singh, Panthic Matte, 2002, p. 50.
9. Ibid, p. 67.
10. Ibid, p. 75.
11. Ibid, p. 107.
12. Ibid, p. 111.
13. Bal Riar, Sukhmani: The Politics of the Sikhs, Unistar, 2006, p. 53.
14. Ibid, p. 56.
15. Presidential Address, Kalgidhar Press, Lahore, Published by General Secretary, Shiromani Malwa Riyasti Akali Dal, Bhawanigarh.
16. Bal Riar, Sukhmani: The Politics of the Sikhs, Unistar, 2006, p. 64.
17. SGPC Da Panjah Sala Itihas, Sikh Itihas Research Board, SGPC, Amritsar, 1982, pp. 230-1.
18. The Tribune, March 23, 1946 Quoted by Bal Riar p. 95.
19. Transfer of Powers, Vol I, p. 580.
20. Transfer of Powers Vol V, p. 43.

21. Transfer of Poeers, Vol XII, p. 74.
22. Transfer of Powers, Vol II, P. 25.
23. Adhikari, Gangadhar: Azad Hindustan Vich Azad Deshbhoomi, 1946 Translated by Avtar Singh Malhotra, Progressive Publishers, Lahore.
24. Bal Riar, Sukhmani: The Politics of the Sikhs, Unistar, 2006, p. 122.
25. Quoted from the Shiromani Akali Dal manifesto for 1972 Assembly elections.
26. The Tribune, February 26, 1948.
27. Sarhadi, Ajit Singh: Punjabi Sube Di Gatha, Lokgeet Parkashan, Sirhind, 1992, p. 196.
28. Ibid, p. 420.
29. Zakhmi, Karam Singh: Punjabi Sube Morche Di Twarikh, SGPC, Amritsar, p. 18.
30. Ibid, p. 26.
31. Ibid, p. 97.
32. Sarhadi, Ajit Singh: Punjabi Sube Di Gatha, Lokgeet Parkashan, Sirhind, 1992, p. 242.
33. Sant Fateh Singh: Our stand on Punjabi Suba, October 14, 1963, Published by Akali Dal.
34. Quoted from the original manifesto.
35. Federal Polity: The Speech of Gurcharan Singh Tohra, Publiched by Secretary, Shiromani Akali Dal, Amritsar.
36. Quoted from the original resolution.
37. The Indian Express, November 4, 1981.
38. Ahluwalia, Jasbir Singh, The Indian Express, January 13, 1990.

Annexure I

Unreported Statement of Badal, Barnala Issued on June 11, 1984

This is a voice of anguish of the Sikh people who today stand mortally wounded, for the repository of their faith to uphold the principles of justice, equality and dignity of man and love of God, stands destroyed by the might of the Indian army. After nearly two centuries of Abdali's invasion, Sri Akal Takht Sahib stands blasted. The Golden Temple complex of drenched with the blood of Sikh martyrs. Delhi once again has embarked upon a pogrom of systematic and well planned genocide of the Sikh people. The whole of Punjab is under the jack boots of the Indian army and no one can get on the road or even drive a bicycle in the whole state. Punjab is a prison house. Sikh nation is in chains.

Today Sikhs all over the world are in deep anguish and mourning. Under the command of the President and the Prime Minister the fascist and chauvinist forces of Hindu communalism have been unleashed to stamp out religious, cultural and racial minorities. The army was marshaled to destroy and desecrate the holiest of the holy Sikh shrine Sri Hamrandir Sahib and Sri Akal Takht Sahib so as to break the will of the Sikhs and reduce them to perpetual slavery. All human liberties-personal, civil, religious and political were denied and Punjab was sealed from every conscientious witness. The fury with which the operation was launched has put to shame any thing that happened to the people of East Pakistan in 1971 and Tamils in Sri Lanka.

Thousands of Sikhs have been butchered. All gurdwaras in Punjab and Chandigarh have been desecrated and looted and thousands of Sikhs have been taken into army custody. There is no independent press coverage and all newspapers of Punjab and Chandigargh have been sealed. Judging in this background the glorious fight put up by Sant Jarnail Singh Bhindranwale and other Sikhs to defy the might of the Indian army when the attack was launched at the Golden temple complex and tread the most glorious path shown by Sri Guru Arjan

Devji in June, 1606 which testifies the undaunting will of the Sikhs to make supreme sacrifice in the cause of religion human dignity, freedom of conscience and equality of man. This blatant and ruthless action of government is an act o vengeance as well because it were the Sikhs alone who had launched from the Golden temple an agitation against Emergency in 1975. who could ever think of resisting Hindu fascism which stark the land today under the shattered mask of Congress secularism like German's Nazism.

As a proud and valiant people who have suffered and sacrificed in the Indian national cause, they are looking up to the dormant conscience of democratic forces in India to raise their voice and assert against the unholy designs of Mrs. Gandhi and her party to alienate the mind and soul of Sikhs.

The government has virtually declared a war of the Sikhs. In this critical hour of their destiny the Sikhs declare their resolute determination to fight to the last man.

Shiromani Alkali Dal calls upon the Sikhs all over the world to observe June 17, 1984 as Ardas Divas (Prayer Day) . on that day bhog of Sru Guru Granth Sahib be performed and prayers should be held for the martyrs who laid down their lives while defending Sri Harmandir Sahib and Sri Akal Takht Sahib. All Sikh men and women would wear black turbans and chunis on that day. Every Sikh should sleep on the floor on the 17th night. By that day Sikhs should return every medal or award received from government of India as has already been done by some respectable Sikhs. The President, Sikh ministers, MPs, MLAs, Sikhs holding nominative or elective positions in corporations, boards etc should resign and show unity of mind and spirit with the martyrs and prepare themselves for the ensuing struggle.

Badal and Barnala Statement, June 11, 1984

This is a voice of anguish of the Sikh people who today stand mortally wounded, for the repository of their faith to uphold the principles of justice, equality and dignity of man and love of God, stands destroyed by the might of Indian Army. After nearly two centuries of Abdali's invasion, Sri Akal Takhat Sahib stands blasted. The Golden Temple cimplex is drenched with the blood of Sikh martyrs. Delhi once again has embarked upon a pogrom of systematic and well planned genocide of the Sikh people. The whole of Punjab is under the jack-boots of the Indian Army and no one can get on the road or even drive a bicycle in the whole State. Punjab is a prison house. Sikh nation is in chains.

Today Sikhs all over the world are in deep anguish and mourning. Under the command of the President and the Prime Minister the facist and chauvnist forces of Hindu communalism have been unleashed to stamp out religious, cultural and racial minorities. The army was marshalled to destroy and desecrate the holiest of the Holy Sikh shrine Sri Harmander Sahib and Sri Akal Takhat Sahib so as to break the will of the Sikhs and reduce them to perpetual slave ry. All human liberties - personal, civil, religious and political were denied and Punjab was sealed from every conscientious witness. The fury with which the operation was launched has put to shame any thing that happened to the people of East Pakistan in 1971 and Tamils in Sri Lanka.

Thousands of Sikhs have been butchered. All Gurdwaras in Punjab and Chandigarh have been desecrated and looted and thousands of Sikhs have been taken into army custody. There is no independent press coverage and all newspapers of Punjab and Chandigarh have been sealed. Judging in this background the glorious fight put up by Sant Jarnail Singh Bhindrawale and other Sikhs to defy the might of the Indian army when the attack was launched at the Golden Temple complex and tread the most glorious path shown by Sri Guru Arjan Dev ji in June, 1606 which testifies to the undying will of the Sikhs to make supreme sacrifice in the cause of religion human dignity, freedom of conscience and equality of man. This blatant and ruthless action of government is an act of vengenance as well because it were the Sikhs alone who had launched from the Golden Temple an agitation against Emergency in 1975. Who would ever think of resisting Hindu fasicism which starks the land today under the shattered mask of Congress secularism like German's Nazism.

As a proud and valiant people who have suffered and sacrificed in the Indian National cause, they are looking up to the dormant conscience of democratic forces in India to raise their voice and assert against the unholy designs of Mrs. Gandhi and her party to alienate the mind and soul of Sikhs.

The Government has virtually declared war on the Sikhs. In this critical hour of their destiny the Sikhs declare their resolute determi-

ੴ ਵਾਹਿਗੁਰੂ ਜੀ ਕੀ ਫਤਹ॥

ਦਫਤਰ: ਸ਼੍ਰੋਮਣੀ ਅਕਾਲੀ ਦੱਲ, ਸ੍ਰੀ ਅੰਮ੍ਰਿਤਸਰ।

ਸ੍ਰੀ ਅੰਮ੍ਰਿਤਸਰ: ਅਗਸਤ 20, 1980: ਸ਼੍ਰੋਮਣੀ ਅਕਾਲੀ ਦੱਲ ਦਾ ਅੱਜ ਦਾ ਇਹ ਸਮਾਗਮ ਭਾਈ ਫੌਜਾ ਸਿੰਘ ਤੇ ਉਨ੍ਹਾਂ ਦੇ ਨਾਮ ਰਸੀਏ ਸਾਥੀ 12 ਸਿੰਘਾਂ ਦੇ ਵੈਸਾਖੀ 1978 ਵਿਚ ਨਰਕਧਾਰੀਆਂ ਹੱਥੋਂ ਸ਼ਹੀਦ ਹੋ ਜਾਣ ਉਪਰੰਤ ਕਾਨ੍ਹਪੁਰ ਅਤੇ ਦਿੱਲੀ ਵਿਖੇ ਸ਼ਹੀਦ ਹੋਣ ਵਾਲੇ ਸਿੰਘਾਂ ਦੀ ਸ਼ਹਾਦਤ ਨੂੰ ਸਿੱਖ ਇਤਿਹਾਸ ਦਾ ਸੁਨਹਿਰੀ ਕਾਂਡ ਸਮਝਦਾ ਹੈ ਕਿਉਂਕਿ ਇਨ੍ਹਾਂ ਸਿੱਖ ਸ਼ਹੀਦਾਂ ਨੇ ਸਿੱਖੀ ਅਰਦਾਸ, ਸ਼ਬ-ਗੁਰੂ ਦੇ ਸਤਿਕਾਰ ਅਤੇ ਸਿੱਖ ਧਰਮ ਦੇ ਮੁਢਲੇ ਸਿਧਾਂਤਾਂ ਲਈ ਸ਼ਹੀਦੀਆਂ ਪ੍ਰਾਪਤ ਕੀਤੀਆਂ ਹਨ ਜਿਨ੍ਹਾਂ ਤੇ ਸਦਾ ਸਿੱਖ ਕੌਮ ਮਾਣ ਅਤੇ ਗੌਰਵ ਕਰਦੀ ਰਹੇਗੀ ਉਪਰੰਤ ਕਿਸੇ ਸੂਰਬੀਰ ਬਹਾਦਰ ਵਲੋਂ ਨਰਕਧਾਰੀ ਨੂੰ ਖਤਮ ਕਰਨ ਦਾ ਜੋ ਮਹਾਨ ਕਾਰਨਾਮਾ ਕੀਤਾ ਗਿਆ ਹੈ ਉਸ ਤੇ ਜਿਤਨਾ ਭੀ ਮਾਣ ਕੀਤਾ ਜਾਵੇ ਘਟ ਹੈ। ਇਸ ਸੰਬੰਧ ਵਿਚ ਇਹ ਸਮਾਗਮ ਸਰਬ ਸੰਮਤੀ ਨਾਲ ਇਹ ਭੀ ਪਰਵਾਨ ਕਰਦਾ ਹੈ ਕਿ ਨਰਕਧਾਰੀ ਦੇ ਕਤਲ ਦੇ ਸੰਬੰਧ ਵਿਚ ਫੜੇ ਗਏ ਨਿਰਦੋਸ਼ ਸਿੱਖਾਂ ਨਾਲ ਸਾਰੇ ਸਿੱਖ ਜਗਤ ਨੂੰ ਪੂਰਨ ਹਮਦਰਦੀ ਹੈ ਸਾਰੀ ਸਿੱਖ ਕੌਮ ਉਨ੍ਹਾਂ ਦੇ ਨਾਲ ਹੈ। ਇਹ ਅਜਲਾਸ ਦਿੱਲੀ ਗੁ: ਪ੍ਰ: ਕਮੇਟੀ ਅਤੇ ਹੋਰ ਸਿੱਖ ਸੰਸਥਾਵਾਂ ਅਤੇ ਵਿਅਕਤੀਆਂ ਦੀ ਸ਼ਲਾਘਾ ਕਰਦਾ ਹੈ ਜੋ ਉਨ੍ਹਾਂ ਦੇ ਪਰਵਾਰਾਂ ਦੀ ਸਹਾਇਤਾ ਅਤੇ ਮੁਕਦਮਿਆਂ ਦੀ ਪੈਰਵੀ ਲਈ ਉਦਮ ਕਰ ਰਹੇ ਹਨ। ਇਹ ਸਮਾਗਮ ਸੀ.ਬੀ.ਆਈ. ਵਲੋਂ ਕਈ ਸਿੰਘਾਂ ਨੂੰ ਅਕਾਰਣ ਤੰਗ ਕਰਨ ਅਤੇ ਸੰਤ ਜਰਨੈਲ ਸਿੰਘ ਜੀ (ਭਿੰਡਰਾਂ ਵਾਲਿਆਂ) ਨੂੰ ਜਾਣ ਬੁਝਕੇ ਝੂਠ ਦਾ ਸਹਾਰਾ ਲੈ ਕੇਸ ਵਿਚ ਫਸਾਉਣ ਦੀ ਭੀ ਪੁਰਜ਼ੋਰ ਨਖੇਦੀ ਕਰਦਾ ਹੈ ਅਤੇ ਕੇਂਦਰੀ ਸਰਕਾਰ ਤੋਂ ਮੰਗ ਕਰਦਾ ਹੈ ਕਿ ਨਰਕਧਾਰੀਆਂ ਦੀਆਂ ਪੁਸਤਕਾਂ "ਅਵਤਾਰ ਬਾਣੀ" ਅਤੇ "ਯੁਗ-ਪੁਰਸ਼" ਪੁਰ ਪਾਬੰਦੀ ਲਾਈ ਜਾਵੇ ਅਤੇ ਉਨ੍ਹਾਂ ਦੀਆਂ ਧਰਮ ਵਿਰੋਧੀ ਕਾਰਵਾਈਆਂ ਖਤਮ ਕਰਵਾਏ।

—o—

(ਭਾਨ ਸਿੰਘ)

ਸਕੱਤਰ ਜਨਰਲ,

ਸ਼੍ਰੋਮਣੀ ਅਕਾਲੀ ਦੱਲ, ਸ੍ਰੀ ਅੰਮ੍ਰਿਤਸਰ।